NCERT CHEMISTRY

REVISION WORK BOOK

Most Effective Revision & Concept Zipper for

JEE, NEET & CUET

Vol. 2 CLASS XII

Authors
Pooja Yadav
Harsh Kumar

arihant
SUCCESS AND NOTHING LESS

Super 6

ADVANTAGES OF REVISION WORK BOOKS

1. Learn with fun while practicing with Self Assessment.
2. Different question types are helpful in increasing the learning and understanding about **Core Concepts** and **Conceptual Applications**.
3. Figure based small methodical questions will also help in increasing **Figure Visualisation**.
4. Innovative style of practice in Work book manner helps in breaking the **monotonicity** of subject.
5. Complete sync with NCERT along with **Competition Connect** and **Competition Edge Up** helps in building the foundation for the preparation of competitions like JEE, NEET and CUET.
6. Questions with one word or maximum one sentence long answers are very helpful in **Faster Revision** and **Confidence Boost Up**.

arihant
SUCCESS AND NOTHING LESS

ARIHANT PUBLICATIONS (INDIA) LIMITED

Administrative & Production Offices

Regd. Office
'Ramchhaya' 4577/15, Agarwal Road, Darya Ganj, New Delhi -110002
Tele: 011- 47630600, 43518550

Head Office
Kalindi, TP Nagar, Meerut (UP) - 250002
Tel: 0121-7156203, 7156204

Sales & Support Offices
Agra, Ahmedabad, Bengaluru, Bareilly, Chennai, Delhi, Guwahati, Hyderabad, Jaipur, Jhansi, Kolkata, Lucknow, Nagpur & Pune.

PRICE ₹310.00

PO No : TXT-XX-XXXXXXX-X-XX

Published by Arihant Publications (India) Ltd.

For further information about the books published by Arihant, log on to www.arihantbooks.com or e-mail at info@arihantbooks.com

Follow us on

FAB 4 Features

NCERT Tracker
Every topic is tagged with NCERT page numbers for better syncing with NCERT.

TOPIC 1

Introduction and Types of Solution

NCERT Pg 1-2

1. The utility or importance of mixtures in our life depends upon their one unique property. Name this property ______________ .

2. Name the metal which is common in brass, german silver and bronze mixtures.

____

52. If pure substances have *A*—*A* and *B*—*B* type of interactions, then binary solutions have following type of interactions.

(i) ______________ (ii) ______________ (iii) ______________

Important Concept Tagging
Every question which is based on the important concept from JEE/NEET/CUET point of view is marked with *.

***53.** Consider the following compounds/ species.

(i) *n*-hexane + *n*-heptane (ii) Bromoethane and chloroethane
(iii) Benzene and toluene (iv) Ethanol and acetone
(v) Phenol and aniline (vi) Chloroform and acetone
(vii) Carbon disulphide and acetone

The number of compounds/species which show negative deviation from Raoult's law is

(a) 2 ☐ (b) 3 ☐ (c) 5 ☐ (d) 7 ☐

COMPETITION CONNECT

Competition Connect
Supplement containing related portions of old NCERT which are present in NEET/JEE/CUET syllabus but removed from latest NCERT.

TOPIC 7

Group 15 Elements : The Nitrogen Family

NCERT Pg 165-168

84. Write the name of any two metalloids belonging to group 15 elements.

____

85. Nitrogen in the earth crust occurs as Chile saltpetre and Indian saltpetre.

True ☐ False ☐

86. Choose the elements from the given pairs which are present

I. in bones as well as in living cells.
II. in proteins of plants and animals.

(a) As and Sb ☐ (b) P and N ☐ (c) N and Bi ☐ (d) Sb and N ☐

COMPETITION EDGE UP

1. *The molarity (M) of an aqueous solution containing 5.85 g of NaCl in 500 mL water is (Given: Molar mass Na: 23 and Cl: 35.5 g mol^{-1})* **[NCERT (New) Pg. 4, JEE Main, 2024]**

(a) 4 ☐ (b) 0.2 ☐
(c) 2 ☐ (d) 20 ☐

2. *The quantity which changes with temperature is* **[NCERT (New) Pg. 5, JEE Main, 2024]**

(a) molality ☐ (b) mole fraction ☐
(c) mass percentage ☐ (d) molarity ☐

3. *A solution of two miscible liquids showing negative deviation from Raoult's law will have* **[NCERT (New) Pg. 13, JEE Main 2024]**

7. *The Henry's law constant (K_H) values of three gases (A, B, C) in water are 145.2×10^{-5} and 35 K bar, respectively. The solubility of these gases in water follow the order* **[NCERT (New) Pg. 7, NEET 2024]**

(a) $B > A > C$ ☐ (b) $B > C > A$ ☐
(c) $A > C > B$ ☐ (d) $A > B > C$ ☐

8. *The plot of osmotic pressure π vs concentration ($mol\ L^{-1}$) for a solution gives a straight line with slope 25.73 L bar mol^{-1}. The temperature at which the osmotic pressure measurement is done is (Use : $R = 0.083$ L bar $mol^{-1}K^{-1}$)* **[NCERT (New) Pg. 21, NEET 2024]**

Competition Edge Up
Selected PYQs is Sync with NCERT Chapter.

CONTENTS

Chapter 01

Solutions

Scan and take Chapter Test

TOPIC 1

Introduction & Types of Solution

NCERT Pg 1-2

1. The utility or importance of mixtures in our life depends upon their one unique property. Name this property ________________.

2. Name the metal which is common in brass, german silver and bronze mixtures.

____

3. Match the appropriate fluoride concentration with its effect on our body.

Column I (Effect)		Column II (Fluoride conc.)
A. Teeth mottling	1.	1 ppm
B. Poisonous	2.	1.5 ppm
C. Tooth decay prevention	3.	Higher than 1.5 ppm

A. ________________ B. ________________ C. ________________

4. The common compound used in rat poison is

(a) NaCl ☐ (b) NaBr ☐

(c) NaF ☐ (d) All are correct ☐

5. "Intravenous injections are always dissolved in pure water before injecting".

True ☐ False ☐

6. Solutions are ________________ (homogeneous/heterogeneous) mixture of two or more than two components.

7. A homogeneous mixture has *A* and *B* in uniform manner throughout the mixture. Write *A* and *B* to complete the sentence.

A = ________________________ *B* = ________________________

Concepts of all questions bearing * are important for JEE/NEET/CUET.

8. Name the components of solution which

(i) determines the physical state of solution ______

(ii) usually present in largest quantity ______

(iii) can be of more than 1 type present in a solution ______

9. Write one example for each of the following solutions.

(i) One with solid solute and solid solvent ______.

(ii) One having liquid solute and solid solvent ______.

10. Amongst the following, the total number of species which is not an example of solid-solid solutions is

Copper dissolved in gold, ethanol dissolved in water, camphor in nitrogen gas, mixture of O_2 and N_2 gases, solution of hydrogen in palladium.

(a) 1 ☐ (b) 5 ☐ (c) 3 ☐ (d) 4 ☐

TOPIC 2

Expressing Concentration of Solutions

NCERT Pg 2-5

11. 'X' and 'Y' are the two possible ways in which the information of composition of a solution can be expressed. Here, X and Y are

X= ______ Y= ______

12. A solution having relatively very large quantity of ______ is called concentrated.

13. Consider the following statements,

I. 10% glucose in water by mass means 10 g of glucose in 100 g water.

II. Mass percentage is commonly used method in industrial chemical applications.

Here, correct statement(s) is/are

(a) Only I ☐ (b) Only II ☐

(c) Both I and II ☐ (d) None of these ☐

14. Write the correct concentration expression method in front of the hint.

Hint	Concentration expression method
(i) A method when solute present in trace quantity.	______
(ii) Method which is used commercially in medicine and pharmacy industry.	______
(iii) Method useful in relating some physical properties of solution like vapour pressure.	______

15. (i) Match the appropriate examples with their respective concentration expression methods.

Column I (Example description)		Column II (Conc. expression method)
A. 3.62 unit sodium hypochlorite in water.	1.	V/V
B. 35% solution of ethylene glycol.	2.	ppm
C. Sea water (1 L) with 6×10^{-3} g dissolved oxygen.	3.	Mass per cent

A. ____________ B. ____________ C. ____________

(ii) Write the commercial name of A and B given in the above example description.

A = ____________ B = ____________

16. Write outcomes for the following description.

In a binary mixture, if number of moles of A and B are n_A and n_B respectively, then

(i) mole fraction of $A(\chi_A)$ = ____________

(ii) mole fraction of $B(\chi_B)$ = ____________

(iii) $\chi_A + \chi_B$ = ____________

17. Sum of mole fraction of all the components of a solution is always ____________.

18. Mole fraction of ethylene glycol ($C_2H_6O_2$) in a solution containing 20% of $C_2H_6O_2$ by mass is

(a) 0.932 ☐ (b) 0.068 ☐

(c) 9.38 ☐ (d) 0.278 ☐

19. Choose the correct values of molarity from the given two values with respect to the given concentration.

Concentration	Molarity
(i) 0.25 mol of NaOH dissolved in 1 L	2.5 or 0.25
(ii) 5 g NaOH present in 450 mL solution	0.287 or 0.278

(i) ____________ (ii) ____________

20. 1 m KCl solution means 74.5 g of KCl dissolved in 1 kg of water.

True ☐ False ☐

***21.** Molality of solution having 2.5 g of ethanoic acid in 75 g of benzene is

(a) 0.565 mol/kg ☐ (b) 0.256 mol/kg ☐

(c) 0.556 mol/kg ☐ (d) 5.66 mol/kg ☐

22. If 22 g of benzene is dissolved in 122 g of carbon tetrachloride, mass percentage of benzene and CCl_4 is ____________ and ____________ respectively.

***23.** Fill the correct values of molarity in accordance with given concentration.

Concentration	Molarity
(i) 30 g of $Co(NO_3)_2.6H_2O$ in 4.3 L of solution	________
(ii) 30 mL of 0.5 M H_2SO_4 diluted to 500 mL	________

24. The mass of urea (NH_2CONH_2) required in making 2.5 kg of 0.25 molal aqueous solution will be

(a) 37 g ☐ (b) 73 g ☐
(c) 370 g ☐ (d) 1 g ☐

***25.** The density of 20% (mass/mass) aqueous KI is 1.202 g mL^{-1}. Then, the value of

(i) molality is ________
(ii) molarity is ________
(iii) mole fraction of KI is ________

26. Amongst the following, the total number of species not dependent on temperature is

molarity, molality, mole fraction, mass %, ppm

(a) 1 ☐ (b) 2 ☐ (c) 3 ☐ (d) 4 ☐

TOPIC 3 Solubility

NCERT Pg 5-9

27. Maximum amount of a solid solute that can be dissolved in a specified amount of a given solvent depends upon certain factors.

Enlist those factors.

(i) ________
(ii) Temperature
(iii) ________
(iv) ________

28. Which of the following pair is incorrect?

Solute	Solvent
(a) Sodium chloride	— Water
(b) Naphthalene	— Benzene
(c) Anthracene	— Water

29. A solute dissolves in a solvent when they have similar ________.

30. Name the process given in following description.

(i) The process in which solute particle separates out in form of solid state is ____________

(ii) The state at which number of solute particles going into the solution becomes equal to the number of the solute particles separating out is ____________

31. At equilibrium, the rate of dissolution of a solid solute in a volatile liquid solvent is

(a) less than rate of crystallisation ☐

(b) greater than rate of crystallisation ☐

(c) equal to rate of crystallisation ☐

(d) zero ☐

32. 100 g of A is dissolved in water to form a solution B. Further addition of small amount of A in B remains as a solid on the bottom of solution B. Thus, solution B is ____________. (saturated / unsaturated)

33. If dissolution process is exothermic, then solubility A with rise in temperature, while if process is endothermic, then solubility B with rise in temperature.

(a) A-increases, B-decreases ☐ (b) A-decreases, B-increases ☐

(c) Both A and B increases. ☐ (d) Both A and B decreases. ☐

34. Consider the following statements regarding the solubility of solid in liquid.

I. It is significantly affected by temperature change.

II. It is significantly affected by pressure change.

III. In a nearly saturated solution, the dissolution process is endothermic.

Mark (✓) and (×) under correct and incorrect with respect to given statement.

	Correct	Incorrect
I.	________	________
II.	________	________
III.	________	________

35. Consider the given figures (a) and (b) and answer the following.

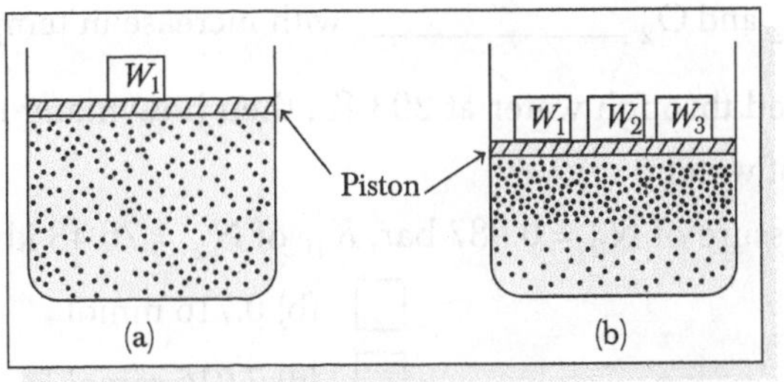

For solution of gases in a solvent

(i) Solubility of gas in which solution will be more (a) or (b) ? ____________

(ii) What will be the effect of pressure on solubility of gas? ____________

(iii) This activity explains which law of solubility of gas in liquid? ____________

36. According to Henry's law, $p = K_H \cdot \chi$. So, the graph between partial pressure of HCl gas (p) *versus* mole fraction of HCl in its solution in cyclohexane (χ) will be

(a) 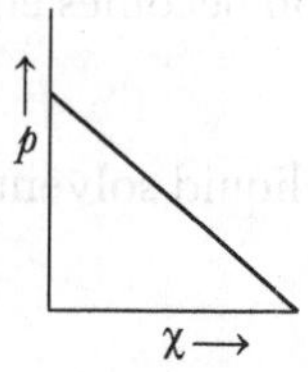

(b) 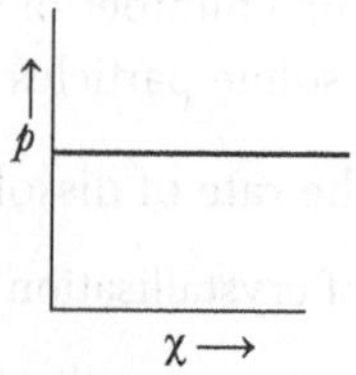

(c) 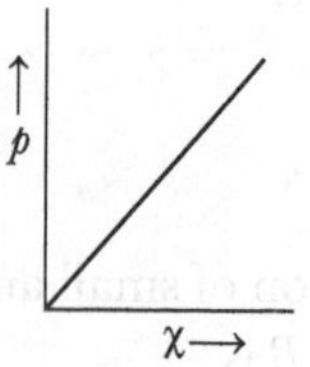

(d) 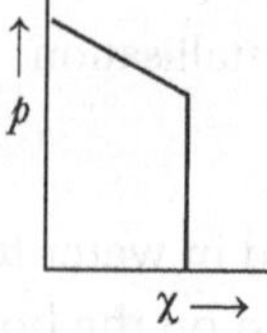

37. Gas A is more soluble in water than gas B at the same temperature. Which gas has higher value of K_H?

____

***38.** The value of the Henry's law constant for helium (He), hydrogen (H_2) and oxygen (O_2) gas are respectively 144.97 k bar, 69.16 k bar and 34.86 k bar at 293 K.
The increasing order of their solubility is _______________.

39. The values of Henry's law constant of O_2 and N_2 at two different temperatures is given below.

Gas	Temperature (K)	K_H (k bar)
N_2	293	76.48
N_2	303	88.84
O_2	293	34.86
O_2	303	46.82

Answer the following questions based on the above data.

(i) Solubility of N_2 is _______________ (less/more) than solubility of O_2 at 293 K.

(ii) Solubility of N_2 and O_2 _______________ with increase in temperature.

40. If N_2 gas is bubbled through water at 293 K, then how many millimoles of N_2 gas would dissolve in 1 litre of water ?
(Given, partial pressure of $N_2 = 0.987$ bar, K_H of $N_2 = 76.48$ kbar)

(a) 0.29 mmol
(b) 0.716 mmol
(c) 0.07 mmol
(d) 7.016 mmol

***41.** Which of the following applications is not based on Henry's law ?

(a) The solubility of CO_2 in soft drinks and soda water.
(b) The scuba divers suffer from bends which involves the blocking of capillaries.
(c) Altitude sickness
(d) Blood cells shrink when suspended in saline water

42. The low concentration of oxygen in the blood and tissue of people living at high altitude is due to __________ (high/low) atmospheric pressure.

43. What will be the value of Henry's law constant of H_2S, if the solubility of H_2S in water at STP is 0.195 m ?

(a) 822 bar ☐ (b) 228 bar ☐

(c) 282 bar ☐ (d) 302 bar ☐

44. The quantity of CO_2 in 500 mL of soda water, when packed under 2.5 atm CO_2 pressure at 298 K is .... (Given, K_H of $CO_2 = 1.67 \times 10^8$ Pa)

(a) 1.848 g ☐ (b) 0.848 g ☐

(c) 18.48 g ☐ (d) 84.8 g ☐

TOPIC 4

Vapour Pressure of Liquid Solutions

NCERT Pg 9-13

45. Identify the law which is stated as
"For any solution, the partial vapour pressure of each volatile component in the solution is directly proportional to its mole fraction".

(a) Henry's law ☐ (b) Raoult's law ☐

(c) Dalton's law ☐ (d) Gay-Lussac's law ☐

46. For an ideal solution, the plot of vapour pressure and mole fraction at constant temperature is given below.

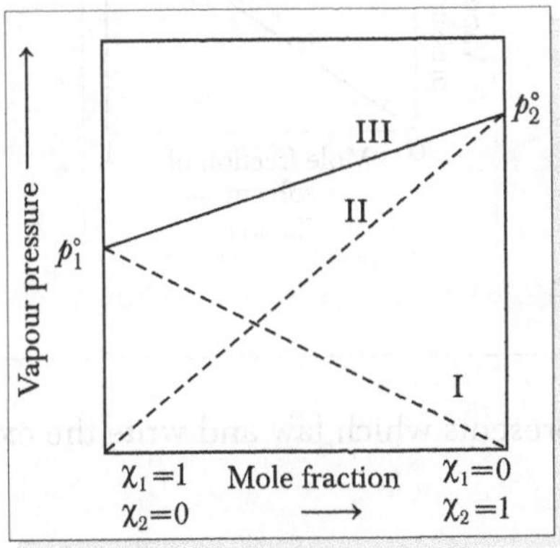

(i) Write the representation of given lines.

I. __________ II. __________ III. __________

(ii) Minimum value of p_{total} = __________

(iii) Maximum value of p_{total} = __________

(iv) p_{total} varies __________ with the mole fraction of component 2.

47. Match the following columns.

Column I (Laws)	Column II (Expressions)
A. Raoult's law	1. $p = K_H \chi$
B. Henry's law	2. $p_{Total} = p_1 + p_2$
C. Dalton's law	3. $p = \chi_1 p_1^\circ + \chi_2 p_2^\circ$

A. ______ B. ______ C. ______

48. A solution is prepared by mixing 25.5 g of $CHCl_3$ and 40 g of CH_2Cl_2.

(Given, $p^\circ_{CH_2Cl_2} = 415$ mm Hg and $p^\circ_{CHCl_3} = 200$ mm Hg)

What will be value of

(i) (a) mole fraction of $CHCl_3$ in gaseous phase is ______

(b) mole fraction of CH_2Cl_2 in gaseous phase is ______

(ii) Vapour pressure of solution is ______

49. A student added non-volatile solute to a solvent to give a solution. He measured the vapour pressure of pure solvent and the vapour pressure of solution containing solute. He noticed that

(i) the vapour pressure of solution is more than vapour pressure of solvent.

(ii) the vapour pressure of solution is less than vapour pressure of pure solvent.

The reason for change in vapour pressure of solution is ______.

50. Consider the given diagram and answer the following.

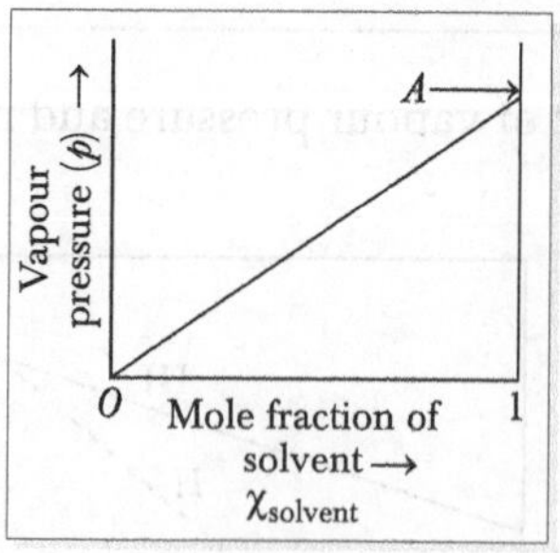

(i) 'A' point signifies ______.

(ii) The given diagram represents which law and write the expression for it ______.

TOPIC 5

Ideal and Non-ideal Solutions

NCERT Pg 13-15

51. Which of the given value(s) is/are equal to zero for an ideal solution?

(a) ΔH_{mix} ☐ (b) ΔV_{mix} ☐

(c) Both (a) and (b) ☐ (d) None of these ☐

52. If pure substances have *A—A* and *B—B* type of interactions, then binary solutions have following type of interactions.

(i) ____________ (ii) ____________ (iii) ____________

***53.** Consider the following compounds/ species.

(i) *n*-hexane + *n*-heptane
(ii) Bromoethane and chloroethane
(iii) Benzene and toluene
(iv) Ethanol and acetone
(v) Phenol and aniline
(vi) Chloroform and acetone
(vii) Carbon disulphide and acetone

The number of compounds/species which show negative deviation from Raoult's law is

(a) 2 ☐ (b) 3 ☐

(c) 5 ☐ (d) 7 ☐

***54.** Separate the examples of solutions which exhibit near to ideal solution, positive deviation and negative deviation from Raoult's law.

(i) Ethanol and acetone ____________

(ii) Chloroform and acetone ____________

(iii) Phenol and aniline ____________

(iv) Benzene and toluene ____________

55. The graphical representation of vapour pressure of two component systems as a function of composition is given alongside. By graphic inspection, name the type of deviation shown by this system from Raoult's law.

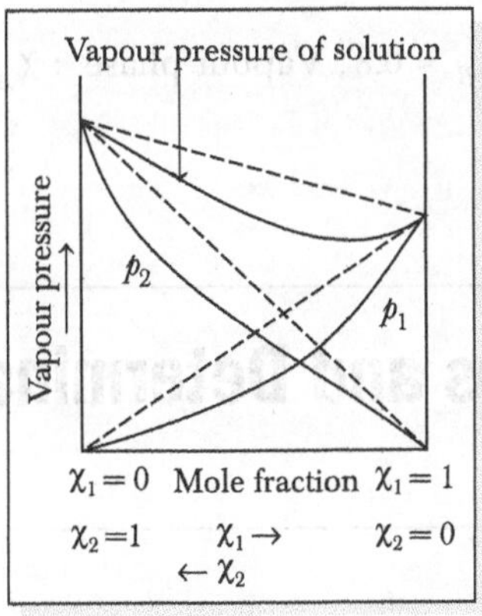

***56.** In non-ideal solution, what type of deviation shows the formation of maximum boiling azeotropes?

____

***57.** Match the following columns.

Column I (Example/Relations)		Column II (Terms)
A.	$CCl_4 + CHCl_3$	1. Raoult's law
B.	$C_6H_6 + H_2O$	2. Nearly ideal solution
C.	$p_A \propto \chi_A$	3. Negative deviation
D.	$p_A \approx p_A^{\circ} \chi_A$	4. Positive deviation

A. ________ B. ________ C. ________ D. ________

58. Nitric acid and water is an example of maximum boiling azeotrope, which has ________ % nitric acid and ________ % water by mass with a boiling point of 393.5 K.

59. Vapour pressure of pure liquids *A* and *B* are 450 and 700 mm of Hg respectively at 350 K. What will be composition of liquid mixture if total vapour pressure is 600 mm Hg and also identify the composition of vapour phase ?

(a) Liquid phase : $\chi_A = 0.4, \chi_B = 0.6$; Vapour phase : $\chi_A = 0.3, \chi_B = 0.7$ ☐

(b) Liquid phase : $\chi_A = 0.3, \chi_B = 0.7$; Vapour phase : $\chi_A = 0.3, \chi_B = 0.7$ ☐

(c) Liquid phase : $\chi_A = 0.4, \chi_B = 0.6$; Vapour phase : $\chi_A = 0.4, \chi_B = 0.6$ ☐

(d) Liquid phase : $\chi_A = 0.2, \chi_B = 0.8$; Vapour phase : $\chi_A = 0.8, \chi_B = 0.2$ ☐

TOPIC 6

Colligative Properties and Determination of Molar Mass

NCERT Pg 15-23

60. Colligative properties

(a) depend only on concentration of solute and independent of solute and solvents identity. ☐

(b) depend only on identity of solute and concentration of solute and independent of solvent identity. ☐

(c) depend only on identity of solvent and the concentration of solute and independent of solute's identity. ☐

(d) depend on concentration and identity of both solute and solvent. ☐

61. The vapour pressure of pure benzene at a certain temperature is 0.850 bar. A non-volatile, non-electrolyte solid weighing 0.5 g when added to 39.0 g of benzene (molar mass 78 g mol^{-1}), vapour pressure of the solution then is 0.845 bar. Identify the value of molar mass of solid substance.

(a) 170 g mol^{-1} ☐ (b) 701 g mol^{-1} ☐

(c) 70 g mol^{-1} ☐ (d) 100 g mol^{-1} ☐

62. Consider the following phase diagram.

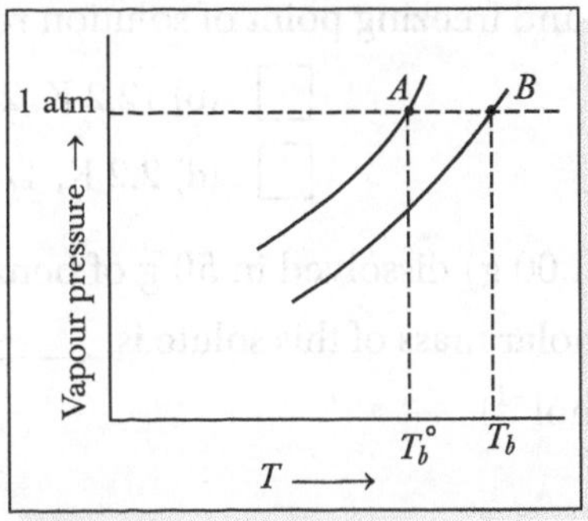

In the above phase diagram, normal boiling point of solution is represented by

(a) Point *A* ☐ (b) Point *B* ☐

(c) Both *A* and *B* points ☐ (d) None of these ☐

63. Write the other names of boiling point elevation constant (K_b) and also mention its units.

____

***64.** At which temperature will water boil, when 18 g of glucose ($C_6H_{12}O_6$) is dissolved in 1 kg of water (K_b for water = 0.52 K kg mol^{-1}) ? Given external pressure is 1.013 bar.

(a) 320 K ☐ (b) 730 K ☐ (c) 373.2 K ☐ (d) 0 K ☐

***65.** What will be the molar mass of 1.80 g non-volatile solute which is dissolved in 90 g of benzene when boiling point is raised from 353.23 K to 354.11 K ?
(K_b for benzene = 2.53 K kg mol^{-1})

(a) 85 g mol^{-1} ☐ (b) 58 g mol^{-1} ☐

(c) 78 g mol^{-1} ☐ (d) 87 g mol^{-1} ☐

66. Identify *A*, *B* and *C* from the given diagram showing ΔT_f, depression of the freezing point of a solvent in a solution.

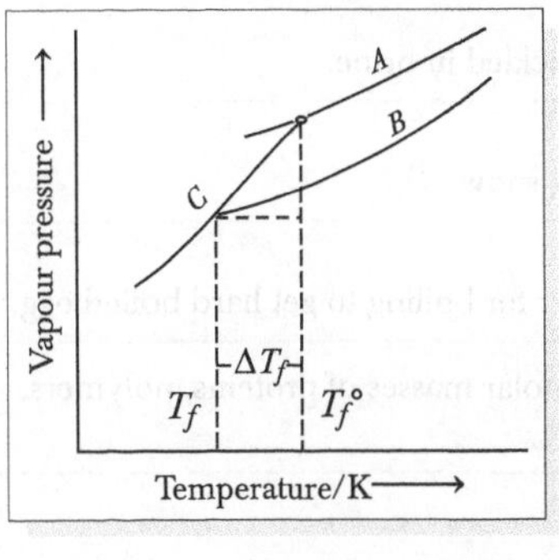

A = ____________ *B* = ____________ *C* = ____________

***67.** X and Y are two compounds, molecular mass of X is more than Y. If both compounds are taken in same quantity and their K_f values are also same, then depression in freezing point (ΔT_f) of two compounds are such that

(a) ΔT_f of $X > \Delta T_f$ of Y ☐ (b) ΔT_f of $X < \Delta T_f$ of Y ☐

(c) ΔT_f of $X = \Delta T_f$ of Y ☐ (d) ΔT_f of $X \geq \Delta T_f$ of Y ☐

68. When 45 g of ethylene glycol ($C_2H_6O_2$) is mixed with 600 g of water, then what will be the freezing point depression and freezing point of solution respectively ?

(a) 5.00 K, 268.15 K ☐ (b) 12.2 K, 210.95 K ☐

(c) 2.2 K, 270.95 K ☐ (d) 2.2 K, 473 K ☐

69. A non-electrolyte solute (1.00 g) dissolved in 50 g of benzene lowered the freezing point of benzene by 0.40 K. The molar mass of this solute is ______________________.

(Given, $K_f = 5.12$ K kg mol^{-1})

70. The flow of solvent from __________ solution to __________ solution across a semipermeable membrane is due to osmosis.

71. In which of the following cases blood cells will shrink ?

(a) When placed in water containing more than 0.9% (mass/ volume) NaCl solution. ☐

(b) When placed in water containing less than 0.9% (mass /volume) NaCl solution. ☐

(c) When placed in water containing 0.9% (mass/volume) NaCl solution. ☐

(d) When placed in distilled water. ☐

72. 200 cm^3 of aqueous solution of protein contains 1.26 g of protein, then the molar mass of protein is ______________.

(Given, osmotic pressure of the solution $\pi = 2.57 \times 10^{-3}$ bar at 300 K.)

(a) 68.000 g mol^{-1} ☐ (b) 61.012 kg mol^{-1} ☐

(c) 61.022 g mol^{-1} ☐ (d) Both (b) and (c) ☐

73. Name the colligative property involved for the following events/examples.

Events/Example	Colligative property
(i) Raw mango shrivel when pickled in brine.	__________
(ii) Sprinkling of salt in clearing snow.	__________
(iii) Little NaCl is added to water for boiling to get hard boiled egg.	__________
(iv) Widely used to determine molar masses of proteins, polymers, macromolecules etc.	__________

74. State whether True or False.

(i) Higher intake of salt results in puffiness or swelling called edema.

True ☐ False ☐

(ii) A bacterium on salted meat loses water, shrivels and dies through osmosis process.

True ☐ False ☐

75. Complete the following statements.

(i) Semipermeable membrane used in reverse osmosis is made up of ______________.

(ii) The phenomenon which is helpful in desalination of sea water is ______________.

***76.** Consider the following diagram,

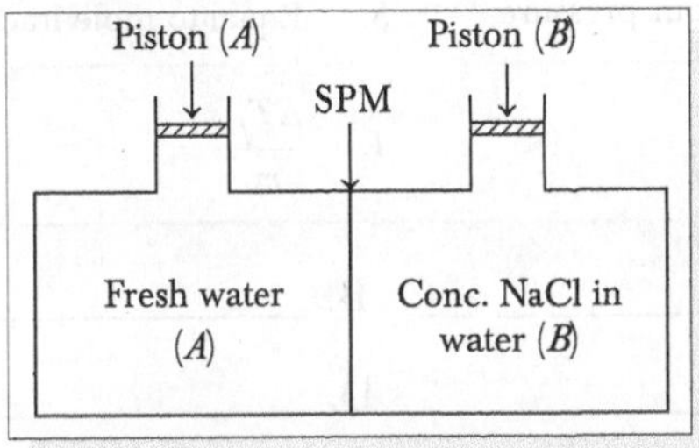

In the above set up, if pressure, greater than osmotic pressure is applied on piston *B*, then water will move from __________ to __________.

77. 50 g of urea (NH_2CONH_2) is dissolved in 850 g of water. Vapour pressure of pure water is 23.8 mm of Hg, then write the values of

(i) Vapour pressure of solution ______________

(ii) Relative lowering of vapour pressure ______________

78. The amount of sucrose (approx.) required to be added into 500 g of water so, that it boils at 100°C is ______________. (Given : Boiling point of water is 99.63°C)

(a) 121 g ☐ (b) 1.21 g ☐

(c) 111 g ☐ (d) 151 g ☐

79. Find out the mass of ascorbic acid ($C_6H_8O_6$) to be dissolved in 75 g of acetic acid to lower its melting point by 1.5°C. (K_f = 3.9 K kg mol^{-1})

(a) 5.08 g ☐ (b) 6 g ☐

(c) 8 g ☐ (d) 50.8 g ☐

80. Amongst the following the total number of species (in decinormal) that have van't Hoff factor equals to 5 is

$Al_2(SO_4)_3$, $BaCl_2$, $NaCl$, $CaCl_2$, $MgSO_4$

(a) 1 ☐ (b) 2 ☐

(c) 3 ☐ (d) 4 ☐

***81.** 1.0 g of polymer (molar mass = 185000) dissolved in 450 mL of water at 37°C. The osmotic pressure of solution is

(a) 31 Pa ☐ (b) 13 Pa ☐

(c) 48 Pa ☐ (d) 52 Pa ☐

82. Match the following columns.

Column I (Terms)		Column II (Expressions)
A. Ebullioscopic constant (K_b)	1.	$\pi = CRT$
B. Cryoscopic constant (K_f)	2.	$\frac{\Delta T_b \times w_A \times M_B}{1000 \times w_B}$
C. Lowering of vapour pressure	3.	Equal to mole fraction of solute
D. Osmotic pressure	4.	$\frac{\Delta T_f}{m}$

A. ____________________ B. ____________________

C. ____________________ D. ____________________

TOPIC 7

Abnormal Molar Masses

NCERT Pg 23-26

83. Dimerisation of ethanoic acid is due to ___*A*___ bonding which results in the ___*B*___ of calculated molar mass. The molar mass that is lower or higher than normal value is called ___*C*___.

A = ____________ *B* = ____________ *C* = ____________.

84. Complete the following expression.

van't Hoff factor (i) = ____________________.

85. Amongst the following, the total number of species not having van't Hoff factor 2 is ______.

$NaCl, KCl, MgSO_4, K_2SO_4, CaCl_2$

(a) 1 ☐ (b) 2 ☐

(c) 3 ☐ (d) 4 ☐

***86.** The values of van't Hoff factors for KCl, NaCl and K_2SO_4 respectively are **[NCERT Exemplar]**

(a) 2, 2 and 2 ☐ (b) 2, 2 and 3 ☐

(c) 1, 1 and 2 ☐ (d) 1, 1 and 1 ☐

***87.** 2 g of benzoic acid (C_6H_5COOH) dissolved in 25 g of benzene shows a depression in freezing point equal to 1.62 K. Molal depression constant for benzene is 4.9 K kg mol^{-1}. The percentage of association of acid is ____________.

(a) 92% ☐ (b) 69% ☐ (c) 99% ☐ (d) 70% ☐

***88.** 0.6 mL of CH_3COOH with density 1.06 g mL^{-1} is dissolved in 1 litre of water. Depression in freezing point is observed to be 0.0205°C. The van't Hoff factor and dissociation constant of acid are

(a) $i = 2.01, K_a = 2.86 \times 10^{-5}$ ☐ (b) $i = 1.041, K_a = 1.86 \times 10^{-5}$ ☐

(c) $i = 1.041, K_a = 10^{-5}$ ☐ (d) $i = 4.86, K_a = 1.86 \times 10^{-5}$ ☐

Assertion-Reason Questions

Given below are two statements, one is labelled as Assertion (A) and other is labelled as Reason (R). Select the most appropriate answer from the options given below.

(a) Both A and R are true and R is correct the explanation of A.
(b) Both A and R are true but R is not the correct explanation of A.
(c) A is true but R is false.
(d) A is false but R is true.

1. Assertion (A) A solution is a homogeneous mixure of two or more chemically non-reacting substances.

Reason (R) Solutions can be made between any two states of matter.

(a) ☐ (b) ☐ (c) ☐ (d) ☐

2. Assertion (A) A solution of hydrogen gas in palladium is a binary solution.

Reason (R) This solution contains 2 components i.e., hydrogen gas as a solute and palladium as a solvent.

(a) ☐ (b) ☐ (c) ☐ (d) ☐

3. Assertion (A) The solubility of a gas in a liquid increases with increase in pressure.

Reason (R) Solubility of a gas in liquid is directly proportional to pressure of the gas.

(a) ☐ (b) ☐ (c) ☐ (d) ☐

4. Assertion (A) When gas molecules are dissolved in liquid phase, the process is exothermic.

Reason (R) Dissolution of gas in liquid is similar to condensation as the gas molecules are present in liquid phase.

(a) ☐ (b) ☐ (c) ☐ (d) ☐

5. Assertion (A) If one component of a solution obeys Raoult's law over a certain range of composition, the other component will obey Henry's law in that range.

Reason (R) Raoult's law is a special case of Henry's law.

(a) ☐ (b) ☐ (c) ☐ (d) ☐

6. **Assertion** (A) Molarity of a solution changes with temperature.
Reason (R) Molarity is a colligative property.

(a) ☐ (b) ☐ (c) ☐ (d) ☐

7. **Assertion** (A) In maximum boiling azeotrope, the boiling point of azeotrope is higher than either of its pure components.
Reason (R) Boiling point of a liquid is the temperature at which its vapour pressure becomes equal to the external pressure.

(a) ☐ (b) ☐ (c) ☐ (d) ☐

8. **Assertion** (A) When methanol is added to water, boiling point of water decreases.
Reason (R) When a volatile solute is added to a volatile solvent elevation in boiling point is observed.

(a) ☐ (b) ☐ (c) ☐ (d) ☐

9. **Assertion** (A) When NaCl is added to water a depression is freezing point is observed.
Reason (R) The lowering of vapour pressure of a solution causes depression in the freezing point.

(a) ☐ (b) ☐ (c) ☐ (d) ☐

10. **Assertion** (A) Solutions having the same osmotic pressure are called isotonic solutions.
Reason (R) Ca^{2+} and K^+ ions are responsible for maintaining proper osmotic pressure balance in the cells of organism.

(a) ☐ (b) ☐ (c) ☐ (d) ☐

Case-Based Questions

1. An ideal solution may be defined as the solution which obeys Raoult's law exactly over the entire range of concentration. The solution for which vapour pressure is either higher or lower than that predicted by Raoult's law are called non-ideal solutions.

Non-ideal solutions can show either positive or negative deviations from Raoult's law depending on whether the A—B interactions in solution are stronger or weaker than A—A and B—B interactions.

(i) Which of the following solutions is/are ideal solution(s)?

I. Bromoethane and iodoethane II. Acetone and chloroform
III. Benzene and acetone IV. *n*-heptane and *n*-hexane

(a) Only I ☐ (b) I and II ☐
(c) II and III ☐ (d) I and IV ☐

(ii) For which of the following solutions ΔH_{mix} and ΔV_{mix} is negative.

(a) Acetone and aniline ☐ (b) Ethanol and cyclohexane ☐
(c) Acetone and CS_2 ☐ (d) Benzene and toluene ☐

(iii) Which of the following is incorrect for positive deviations?

(a) $A—B$ interactions in solution are weaker than $A—A$ and $B—B$ interactions. ☐

(b) $p_A < p_A^{\circ} \chi_A$ and $p_B < p_B^{\circ} \chi_B$ ☐

(c) Carbon tetrachloride and chloroform mixture is an example of positive deviations. ☐

(d) All of the above ☐

(iv) For water and nitric acid mixture which of the given graph is correct.

(a)
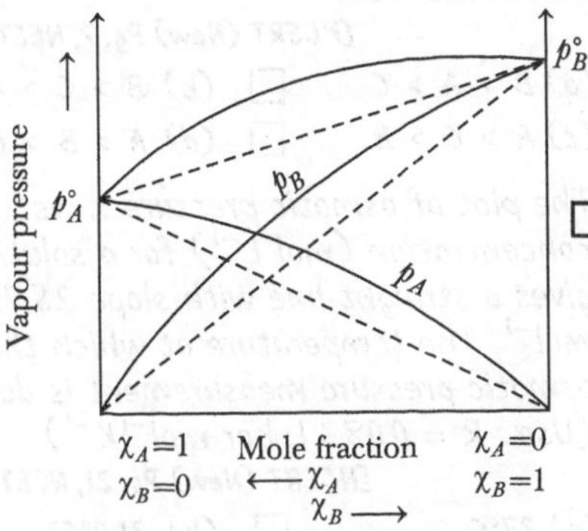

☐

(b)
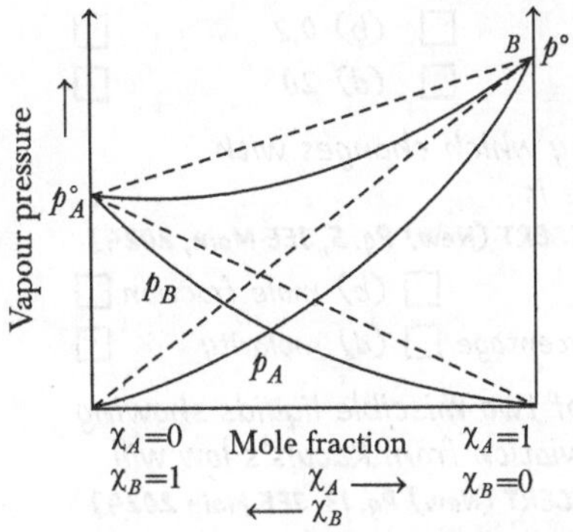

☐

(c)
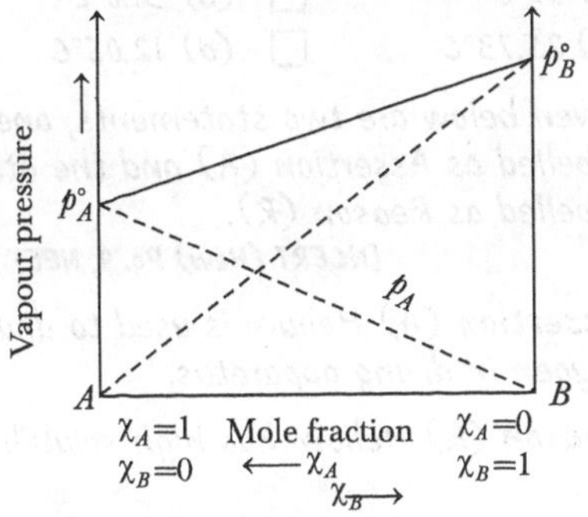

☐

(d) Both (a) and (b) ☐

2. The properties of the solutions which depend only on the number of solute particles but not on the nature of the solute are called colligative properties. Relative lowering in vapour pressure is also an example of colligative properties.
For an experiment, sugar solution is prepared for which lowering in vapour pressure was found to be 0.061 mm of Hg (vapour pressure of water at 20°C is 17.5 mm of Hg).

(i) Relative lowering of vapour pressure for the given solution is

(a) 0.00348 ☐ (b) 0.0061 ☐
(c) 0.122 ☐ (d) 1.75 ☐

(ii) The vapour pressure (mm of Hg) of solution will be

(a) 17.5 ☐ (b) 0.61 ☐
(c) 17.439 ☐ (d) 0.00348 ☐

(iii) Mole fraction of sugar in the solution is

(a) 0.00348 ☐ (b) 0.9965 ☐
(c) 0.061 ☐ (d) 1.75 ☐

(iv) If weight of sugar taken in 5 g in 108 g of water than molar mass of sugar is

(a) 358 ☐ (b) 120 ☐
(c) 240 ☐ (d) 400 ☐

COMPETITION EDGE UP

1. The molarity (M) of an aqueous solution containing 5.85 g of NaCl in 500 mL water is
(Given: Molar mass Na: 23 and Cl: 35.5 g mol^{-1}) **[NCERT (New) Pg. 4, JEE Main, 2024]**
(a) 4 ☐ (b) 0.2 ☐
(c) 2 ☐ (d) 20 ☐

2. The quantity which changes with temperature is
[NCERT (New) Pg. 5, JEE Main, 2024]
(a) molality ☐ (b) mole fraction ☐
(c) mass percentage ☐ (d) molarity ☐

3. A solution of two miscible liquids showing negative deviation from Raoult's law will have **[NCERT (New) Pg. 13, JEE Main 2024]**
(a) increased vapour pressure, increased boiling point ☐
(b) decreased vapour pressure, increased boiling point ☐
(c) increased vapour pressure, decreased boiling point ☐
(d) decreased vapour pressure, decreased boiling point ☐

4. Identify the mixture that shows positive deviations from Raoult's law.
[NCERT (New) Pg. 14, JEE Main, 2024]
(a) $(CH_3)_2CO + CS_2$ ☐
(b) $CHCl_3 + C_6H_6$ ☐
(c) $(CH_3)_2CO + C_6H_5NH_2$ ☐
(d) $CHCl_3 + (CH_3)_2CO$ ☐

5. We have three aqueous solutions of NaCl labelled as 'A', 'B' and 'C' with concentration 0.1 M, 0.01 M and 0.001 M, respectively. The value of van't Hoff factor (i) for these solutions will be in the order
[NCERT (New) Pg. 24, JEE Main, 2024]
(a) $i_A = i_B = i_C$ ☐ (b) $i_A > i_B > i_C$ ☐
(c) $i_A < i_C < i_B$ ☐ (d) $i_A < i_B < i_C$ ☐

6. A solution containing 10 g of an electrolyte AB_2 in 100 g of water boils at 100.52°C. The degree of ionisation of the electrolyte (α) is .... $\times 10^{-1}$. (Nearest integer)
[Given : Molar mass of AB_2 = 200 g mol^{-1}, K_b (Molal boiling point elevation constant of water) = 0.52 K kg mol^{-1}, boiling point of water = 100°C, AB_2 ionises as $AB_2 \longrightarrow A^{2+} + 2B^-$].
[NCERT (New) Pg. 24, JEE Main 2024]

7. The Henry's law constant (K_H) values of three gases (A, B, C) in water are 145.2×10^{-5} and 35 K bar, respectively. The solubility of these gases in water follow the order
[NCERT (New) Pg. 7, NEET 2024]
(a) B > A > C ☐ (b) B > C > A ☐
(c) A > C > B ☐ (d) A > B > C ☐

8. The plot of osmotic pressure π vs concentration (mol L^{-1}) for a solution gives a straight line with slope 25.73 L bar mol^{-1}. The temperature at which the osmotic pressure measurement is done is (Use : R = 0.083 L bar $mol^{-1} K^{-1}$)
[NCERT (New) Pg. 21, NEET 2024]
(a) 37°C ☐ (b) 31.0°C ☐
(c) 25.73°C ☐ (d) 12.05°C ☐

9. Given below are two statements, one is labelled as Assertion (A) and the other is labelled as Reason (R).
[NCERT (New) Pg. 9, NEET 2023]
Assertion (A) Helium is used to dilute oxygen in diving apparatus.
Reason (R) Helium has high solubility in O_2.
(a) Both A and R are true and R is the correct explanation of A. ☐
(b) Both A and R are true but R is not the correct explanation of A. ☐
(c) A is true but R is false. ☐
(d) R is true but A is false. ☐

10. In one molal solution that contains 0.5 mole of a solute, there is
[NCERT (New) Pg. 5, NEET 2022]
(a) 500 g of solvent ☐
(b) 100 mL of solvent ☐
(c) 1000 g of solvent ☐
(d) 500 mL of solvent ☐

11. Which one is not correct mathematical equation for Dalton's law of partial pressure?
Here, p = total pressure of gaseous mixture.
[NCERT (New) Pg. 10, NEET 2022]
(a) $p = n_1\frac{RT}{V} + n_2\frac{RT}{V} + n_3\frac{RT}{V}$ ☐
(b) $p_i = \chi_i p$, where p_i = partial pressure of ith gas χ_i = mole fraction of ith gas in gaseous mixture. ☐

(c) $p_i = \chi_i p_i^\circ$, where χ_i = mole fraction of ith gas in gaseous mixture, p_i° = pressure of ith gas in pure state. ☐

(d) $p = p_1 + p_2 + p_3$ ☐

12. The following solutions were prepared by dissolving 10 g of glucose ($C_6H_{12}O_6$) in 250 mL of water (p_1), 10 g of urea (CH_4N_2O) in 250 mL of water (p_2) and 10 g of sucrose ($C_{12}H_{22}O_{11}$) in 250 mL of water (p_3). The right option for the decreasing order of osmotic pressure of these solutions is

[NCERT (New) Pg. 21, NEET 2021]

(a) $p_2 > p_1 > p_3$ ☐
(b) $p_1 > p_2 > p_3$ ☐
(c) $p_2 > p_3 > p_1$ ☐
(d) $p_3 > p_1 > p_2$ ☐

13. A mixture of N_2 and Ar gases in a cylinder contains 7 g of N_2 and 8 g of Ar. If the total pressure of the mixture of the gases in the cylinder is 27 bar, the partial pressure of N_2 is

[Use : Atomic masses (in g mol^{-1}) : N = 14, Ar = 40]

[NCERT (New) Pg. 11, NEET (Sep.) 2020]

(a) 12 bar ☐ (b) 15 bar ☐
(c) 18 bar ☐ (d) 9 bar ☐

14. The mixture which shows positive deviation from Raoult's law is

[NCERT (New) Pg. 14, NEET (Sep.) 2020]

(a) benzene + toluene ☐
(b) acetone + chloroform ☐
(c) chlorothane + bromoethane ☐
(d) ethanol + acetone ☐

15. Isotonic solutions have same

[NCERT (New) Pg. 22, NEET (Oct.) 2020]

(a) vapour pressure ☐
(b) freezing temperature ☐
(c) osmotic pressure ☐
(d) boiling temperature ☐

Chapter 02

Electrochemistry

Scan and take Chapter Test

TOPIC 1

Introduction & Electrochemical Cell

NCERT Pg 31-32

1. Which of the following statement correctly depicts the relation between electrical energy and chemical reactions ?

(a) All non-spontaneous chemical reactions produce electrical energy. ☐

(b) All spontaneous chemical reactions use electrical energy. ☐

(c) All chemical reactions produce electrical energy. ☐

(d) Only spontaneous chemical reactions produce electrical energy. ☐

2. Transmission of sensory signals through cells to brain and communication between the cells are known to have electrochemical origin.

True ☐ False ☐

3. Which of the following convert chemical energy into electrical energy?

(a) Battery ☐ (b) Cell ☐ (c) Fuel cell ☐ (d) All of these ☐

4. Consider the given diagram of Daniell cell and answer the following.

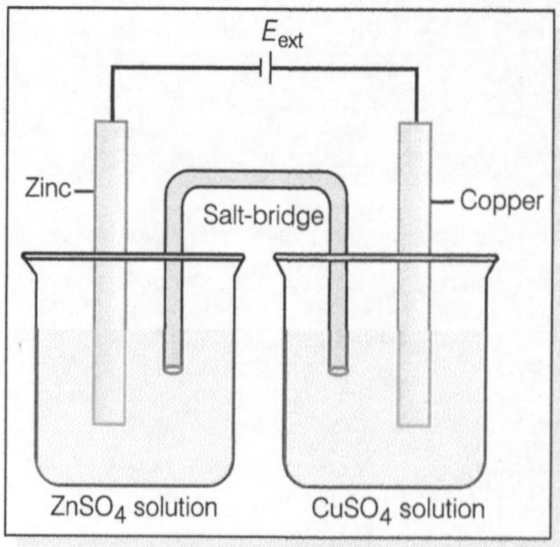

(i) Daniell cell converts __________ energy to __________ energy.

(ii) In the cell shown above current flow from

Zinc to copper electrode. ☐ Copper to zinc electrode. ☐

*Concepts of all questions bearing * are important for JEE/NEET/CUET.*

(iii) Electrons flow from
Zinc to copper electrode. ☐ Copper to zinc electrode. ☐

***5.** What happens in Daniell cell when
(i) $E_{ext} < 1.1\text{V}$ ____________
(ii) $E_{ext} = 1.1\text{V}$ ____________
(iii) $E_{ext} > 1.1\text{V}$ ____________

TOPIC 2

Galvanic Cells

NCERT Pg 33-36

6. In galvanic cell, Gibbs energy of non-spontaneous redox reaction is converted into useful electrical work.

True ☐ False ☐

7. Give the two half-cells reactions that occur in a Daniell cell containing Zn and Cu electrodes.

(i) ____________ (ii) ____________

8. The difference between the electrode potential of two electrodes when no current is drawn through the cell is called

(a) cell potential ☐ (b) cell emf ☐
(c) potential difference ☐ (d) cell voltage ☐

9. In standard electrode potential the concentration of all species in a half-cell is

(a) less than unity ☐ (b) more than unity ☐
(c) equal to unity ☐ (d) zero ☐

10. Fill in the blanks by choosing appropriate word(s) from given keywords.

emf of cell, electrolytic cell, $E^{\circ}_{cathode}$, dry cell, volts, E°_{anode}, cell potential, zero.

(i) Potential difference between two electrodes of galvanic cell is called ________ .
It is measured in ________ .

(ii) In a cell when no current is drawn, cell potential is called ____________ .

(iii) E°_{cell} = ____________ − ____________

11. Consider following cell reaction,

$$Cu(s) + 2Ag^{+}(aq) \longrightarrow Cu^{2+}(aq) + 2Ag(s)$$

Write the reactions occurs at

(i) cathode ____________ (ii) anode ____________

12. Read the following statement and mark (✓) and (×) in the given spaces under correct and incorrect.

I. The potential of an individual half-cell cannot be measured.

II. The standard hydrogen electrode consists of platinum coated electrode dipped in acidic solution and hydrogen gas is bubbled through it.

III. $E^{\circ}_{cell} = E^{\circ}_{left} - E^{\circ}_{right}$

	Correct	**Incorrect**
I.	______	______
II.	______	______
III.	______	______

13. Consider the reaction,

$$Zn(s) + 2Ag^{+}(aq) \longrightarrow Zn^{2+}(aq) + 2Ag(s)$$

The correct cell representation of the following cell is

(a) $Zn(s)|Zn^{2+}(aq)||Ag^{+}(aq)|Ag(s)$ ☐ (b) $Zn(s) + Ag^{+}(aq)||Zn^{2+}(aq) + 2Ag(s)$ ☐

(c) $Zn^{2+}|Zn||Ag|Ag^{+}$ ☐ (d) $Zn^{2+}(aq) + Zn(s)||Ag(s) + Ag^{+}(aq)$ ☐

14. Provide the required information for the standard hydrogen electrode.

(i) Pressure of H_2 gas ______________________.

(ii) Concentration of H^{+} ions ______________________.

15. Consider the following cell representations,

I. $Pt(s)|H_2(g, 1\text{ bar})|H^{+}(aq, 1\text{ M})||Cu^{2+}(aq, 1\text{ M})|Cu$; emf of cell = 0.34 V

II. $Pt(s)|H_2(g, 1\text{ bar})|H^{+}(aq, 1\text{ M})||Zn^{2+}(aq, 1\text{ M})|Zn$; emf of cell = – 0.76 V

Select the correct answer given in the brackets.

(i) Element which will be easily reduced than H^{+} ions__________ (Cu^{2+}/Zn^{2+}).

(ii) H^{+} ions cannot oxidise __________ (Cu/Zn).

(iii) Insoluble in HCl __________ (Cu/Zn).

***16.** The standard electrode potential ($E^{\ominus}$) values of Al^{3+}/Al, Fe^{3+}/Fe^{2+}, Ca^{2+}/Ca and Cr^{3+}/Cr are – 1.66 V, 0.77V, – 2.87 V and – 0.74 V, respectively. The correct decreasing order of reducing power of the metal is

(a) Fe > Cr > Al > Ca ☐ (b) Ca > Al > Cr > Fe ☐

(c) Ca > Al > Fe > Cr ☐ (d) Al > Ca > Fe > Cr ☐

17. Consider the following species.

(i) Pb (ii) Zn (iii) Cr (iv) Li

(v) H_2O_2 (vi) Cu (vii) Ag

The number of species which are stronger reducing agent than the H^{+}/H_2 couple is

(a) 3 ☐ (b) 4 ☐ (c) 5 ☐ (d) 7 ☐

18. The standard cell potential for the following galvanic cell, $Cr|Cr^{3+}||Cd^{2+}|Cd$ is ________.

[Given : $E^\circ_{Cr^{3+}|Cr} = -0.74$ V and $E^\circ_{Cd^{2+}|Cd} = -0.40$ V]

19. Match the item of Column I with Column II on basis of data given below.

$E^\circ_{F_2/F^-} = 2.87$ V, $E^\circ_{Li^+/Li^-} = -3.5$ V, $E^\circ_{Au^{3+}/Au} = 1.4$ V, $E^\circ_{Br_2/Br^-} = 1.09$ V

	Column I (Metals/Ions)	Column II (Properties)
A.	F_2	1. Metal is strongest reducing agent
B.	Li^+	2. Metal ion which is weakest oxidising agent
C.	Au	3. Non-metal (best oxidising agent)
D.	Li	4. Unreactive metal

A. ________ B. ________

C. ________ D. ________

20. Choose the correct species with respect to given statement.

Li, Au^{3+}, F^-, Br^-, Mg

(i) Metal ion which is an oxidising agent ________.

(ii) Anion that can be oxidised by Au^{3+} ________.

21. Electrochemical cells are extensively used for determining.

(i) ________

(ii) ________

(iii) ________

22. A negative E° means that the redox couple is a weaker reducing agent than the H^+/H_2 couple.

True ☐ False ☐

23. Standard electrode potential of Mg^{2+}/Mg can be determined by

(a) setting up cell of $Mg/MgSO_4$ (1 M) as one electrode and standard hydrogen electrode Pt, H as second. ☐

(b) $Mg | Mg^{2+}$ (1M) || H^+(1M)| H_2 (1 atm), Pt ☐

(c) $E^\circ_{cell} = E^\circ_{H^+/\frac{1}{2}H_2} - E^\circ_{Mg^{2+}/Mg}$; $E^\circ_{Mg^{2+}/Mg} = -E^\circ_{cell}$ ☐

(d) All of the above ☐

24. Which of the following substance can oxidise Fe^{2+} ions?

(a) Cl_2, Br_2, Zn ☐ (b) Mg^{2+}, Al^{3+}, Cl_2 ☐

(c) $Cl_2, Cr_2O_7^{2-}, Br_2$ ☐ (d) Zn, Al^{3+}, Br_2 ☐

TOPIC 3

Nernst Equation

NCERT Pg 36-40

25. Consider the following,

$$E_{cell} = E^{\circ}_{cell} - \frac{RT}{2F} \ln \frac{[Zn^{2+}]}{[Cu^{2+}]}$$

To increase E_{cell} of the given Nernst equation,

(i) concentration of Zn^{2+} ion ______________.

(ii) concentration of Cu^{2+} ion ______________.

26. Write the Nernst equation of the following cells :

(i) $Mg(s) \mid Mg^{2+}(0.001\,M) \mid\mid Zn^{2+}(0.0001\,M) \mid Zn(s)$

____

(ii) $Pb(s) \mid Pb^{2+}(0.001\,M) \mid\mid H^{+}(1\,M) \mid H_2(g)\,(1\text{ bar})\,Pt(s)$

____

27. Consider the following reaction,

$$Mg(s) + 2Ag^{+}(0.0001\,M) \longrightarrow Mg^{2+}(0.130\,M) + 2Ag(s)$$

(i) Write its cell representation ______________.

(ii) If E°_{cell} is 3.17 V, then the value of E_{cell} is ______________.

***28.** $2Al\,(s) + 3\,Cd^{2+}(0.1\,M) \longrightarrow 3\,Cd\,(s) + 2Al^{3+}(0.01\,M)$

(i) Represent the cell in which the above reaction takes place.

____

(ii) The value of E° for the cell is 1.260 V. What is the value of E_{cell} ?

____

29. At equilibrium, in Daniell cell, concentration of Zn^{2+} and Cu^{2+} ______________ (remains same/changes proportionally) and voltmeter gives ______________ (zero/unity) reading.

30. Write an equation which represents a relationship between equilibrium constant of reaction and standard potential of cell.

____

31. For the given reaction,

$$Cu\,(s) + 2Ag^{+}\,(aq) \longrightarrow Cu^{2+}\,(aq) + 2Ag(s)\,;\; E^{\circ}_{cell} = 0.46\text{ V}$$

Equilibrium constant (K_C) will be

(a) 15.6×10^{15} ☐ (b) 39.2×10^{15} ☐ (c) 3.92×10^{15} ☐ (d) 9.32×10^{15} ☐

32. E_{cell} is an intensive parameter but $\Delta_r G$ is an extensive thermodynamic property.

True ☐ False ☐

33. The standard Gibb's energy for given reaction is

$$Zn(s) + Cu^{2+}(aq) \longrightarrow Zn^{2+}(aq) + Cu(s) \qquad [\text{Given, } E^{\circ}_{cell} = 1.1\text{ V}]$$

(a) – 200.27 kJ/mol ☐ (b) – 112.27 kJ/mol ☐
(c) 212.27 kJ/mol ☐ (d) – 212.27 kJ/mol ☐

34. The potential of hydrogen electrode in a solution of pH = 10 will be ________________.

***35.** For the given reaction,

$$Ni(s) + 2Ag^{+}(0.002M) \longrightarrow Ni^{2+}(0.160M) + 2Ag(s)\ ;\ (E^{\circ}_{cell} = 1.05\text{ V})$$

emf of the cell is

(a) 1.05 V ☐ (b) 0.491 V ☐ (c) 0.914 V ☐ (d) 9.14 V ☐

36. For the cell reaction,

$$2Fe^{3+}(aq) + 2I^{-}(aq) \longrightarrow 2Fe^{2+}(aq)$$

$E^{\ominus}_{cell} = 0.12\text{ V}$ at 298 K. The standard Gibbs energy $(\Delta_r G^{\ominus})$ of the cell reaction is …… .
[Given that Faraday constant, $F = 96500\text{ C mol}^{-1}$]

(a) –23.16 kJ mol^{-1} ☐ (b) 46.32 kJ mol^{-1} ☐
(c) 23.16 kJ mol^{-1} ☐ (d) – 46.32 kJ mol^{-1} ☐

37. If the standard electrode potential for a cell is 4V at 300 K, the equilibrium constant (K) for the reaction,

$$Zn(s) + Cu^{2+}(aq) \rightleftharpoons Zn^{2+}(aq) + Cu(s)$$

at 300 K is approximately ($R = 8\text{ JK}^{-1}\text{mol}^{-1}, F = 96000\text{ C mol}^{-1}$)

(a) e^{-160} ☐ (b) e^{160} ☐ (c) e^{-80} ☐ (d) e^{320} ☐

38. The species undergoing disproportionation if the change in oxidation state of bromine corresponding to different emf values are given below is

$$BrO_4^- \xrightarrow{1.82\text{ V}} BrO_3^- \xrightarrow{1.5\text{ V}} HBrO \xrightarrow{1.595\text{ V}} Br_2 \xrightarrow{1.0652\text{ V}} Br^-$$

(a) Br_2 ☐ (b) BrO_4^- ☐ (c) BrO_3^- ☐ (d) HBrO ☐

TOPIC 4

Conductance of Electrolytic Solutions

NCERT Pg 41-50

39. Amongst the following, the total number of species which are conductors are

Graphite, Glass, Silicon, Ceramics, Alloys

(a) 2 ☐ (b) 3 ☐ (c) 4 ☐ (d) 5 ☐

40. Match the following columns.

Column I (Properties)	Column II (Respective formulas)
A. Resistance	1. $\kappa\frac{A}{l}$
B. Conductance	2. $\frac{1}{\rho}$
C. Conductivity	3. $\rho\frac{l}{A}$

A. ____________ B. ____________ C. ____________

41. Consider the following statements and mark (✓) and (✗) in the given below spaces under correct and incorrect.

I. On increasing length of wire to double, resistance of wire will be halved.

II. On decreasing area of cross-section, resistance increases.

III. The magnitude of conductivity depends on the nature of the material.

	Correct	Incorrect
I.	______	______
II.	______	______
III.	______	______

42. Complete the following table.

Terms	Units
(i) ____________	Ω (ohm)
(ii) ____________	Ω m
Conductivity	(iii) ____________

43. Arrange the following elements in increasing order of conductivity.

Silver, Sodium, Graphite, Iron

____

***44.** Out of 0.01 M KCl and 0.01 M HAc, which shows more conductivity?

____

***45.** Classify the following materials into insulators and semiconductors.

Glass, Silicon, CuO, Teflon, Germanium

____

46. Materials are classified into conductors, insulators and semiconductors on the basis of ____________.

47. Now-a-days, number of ceramic materials and mixed oxides also show superconductivity at temperature below 100 K.

True ☐ False ☐

48. Electronic conductance depends on

(a) nature and structure of metal ☐
(b) number of valence electrons per atom ☐
(c) temperature ☐
(d) All of the above ☐

49. Enlist the factors on which conductivity of ionic solution depends.

(i) ____________ (ii) ____________
(iii) ____________ (iv) ____________
(v) ____________

50. On increasing temperature, conductivity of metallic wire ___*A*___, while conductivity of electrolytic solution ___*B*___ (Fill *A* and *B* by using word increase or decrease).

$A=$ ____________ $B=$ ____________

51. While measuring the unknown resistance of an ionic solution by Wheatstone bridge, which of the following problems are faced?

I. Passing DC changes the composition of solution.
II. Solution cannot be connected to the bridge.
III. The length of metallic conductor changes.

(a) I and II ☐ (b) II and III ☐
(c) Only I ☐ (d) All of these ☐

52. As 'l' (distance between electrodes) and 'A' (area of cross-section) measurement is not convenient and unreliable, a new quantity is introduced, called ____________, represented by G^*.

$G^* =$ ____________
(Formula)

53. Consider the following statements and mark (✓) and (✗) in the given spaces under correct and incorrect.

I. The cell constant of cell depends upon the nature of electrodes.
II. The cell constant does not change with change in electrolyte.
III. The change in temperature affects the value of cell constant.

	Correct	**Incorrect**
I.	______	______
II.	______	______
III.	______	______

54. Match the following columns.

Column I (Electrical properties)	Column II (SI unit)
A. Specific conductance	1. S
B. Conductance	2. $S\ m^{-1}$
C. Equivalent conductance	3. m^{-1}
D. Cell constant	4. $S\ m^2\ g\ eq^{-1}$

A. ______ B. ______
C. ______ D. ______

55. When a concentrated solution of an electrolyte is diluted, then

(a) its specific conductance increases
(b) its equivalent conductance decreases
(c) its specific conductivity decreases and equivalent conductance increases
(d) its specific and equivalent conductance increases

56. Consider the given statement and answer the following.
Resistance of a conductivity cell filled with 0.1 mol L^{-1} KCl solution is 100 Ω. The conductivity of 0.1 mol L^{-1} KCl solution is 1.29 S/m. If the resistance of the same cell when filled with 0.02 mol L^{-1} KCl solution is 520 Ω, then the value of

(i) conductivity ______ (ii) molar conductivity ______

57. The electrical resistance of a column of 0.05 mol L^{-1} NaOH solution of diameter 1 cm and length 50 cm is 5.55×10^3 ohm. Write down the value of its

(i) resistivity ______
(ii) conductivity ______
(iii) molar conductivity ______

***58.** Conductivity (κ) ___*A*___ with decrease in concentration and molar conductivity increases with ___*B*___ in concentration because total volume of solution containing one mole of electrolyte also ___*C*___.

Select the correct option with respect to *A*, *B* and *C*.

(a) *A*-decreases, *B*-decrease, *C*-increases
(b) *A*-increases, *B*-increase, *C*-decreases
(c) *A*-increases, *B*-decrease, *C*-decreases
(d) *A*-decreases, *B*-decrease, *C*-decreases

***59.** The given graph represents equation, $\Lambda_m = \Lambda^\circ_m - AC^{1/2}$.

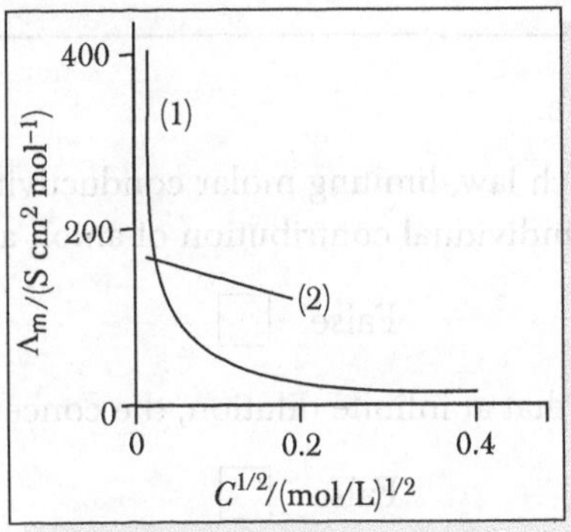

(i) Graph for weak electrolyte is (1) or (2) ____________________.

(ii) When concentration approaches zero for (1) electrolyte, molar conductivity is known as

____.

(iii) In the plot if slope equals to "$-A$", then the value of constant A for a given solvent and temperature depends on ____________________.

60. From given compounds, choose those compounds which have same value of constant 'A' in the given equation, $\Lambda_m = \Lambda^\circ_m - AC^{1/2}$

$NaCl$, $CaCl_2$, $MgSO_4$, CaF_2, $MgCl_2$

____

***61.** Molar conductivity of KCl solution at different concentration at 298 K are as follows

C/mol L^{-1}	Λ_m/S cm^2 mol^{-1}
0.000198	148.61
0.000309	147.29
0.000521	147.81
0.000989	147.09

(i) Related to the given data which of the following plot between Λ_m and $C^{1/2}$ is correct?

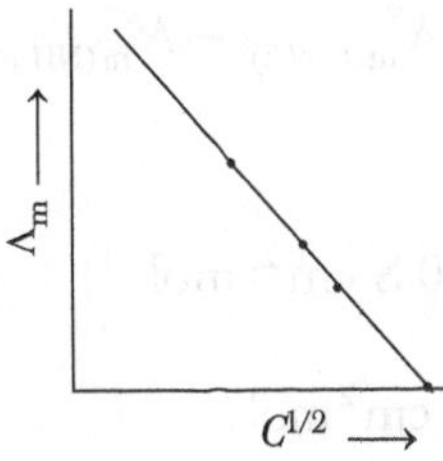

☐

(b)

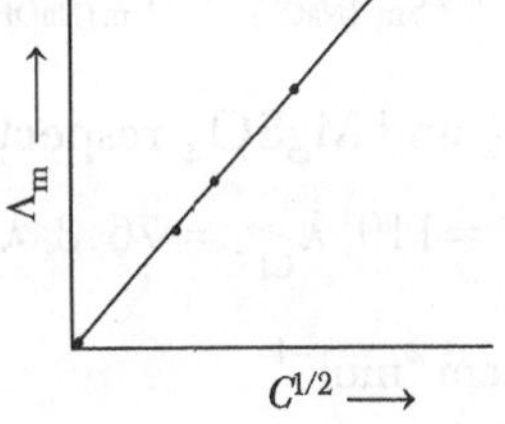

☐

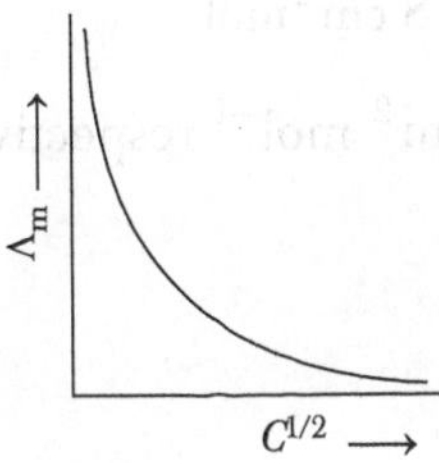

☐

(d)

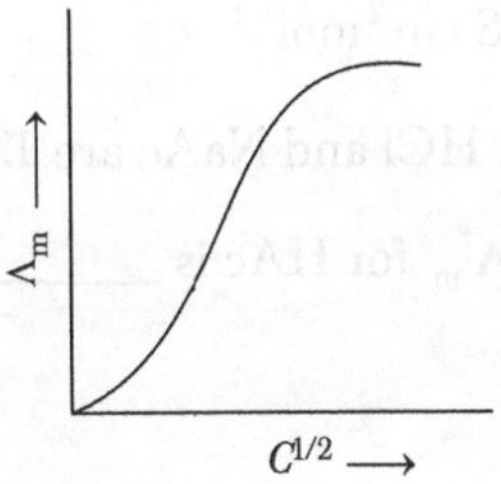

☐

(ii) Also find value of Λ°_m and A for KCl.

____

62. State whether True or False.

(i) According to Kohlrausch law, limiting molar conductivity of an electrolyte can be represented as sum of individual contribution of anion and cation of electrolyte.

True ☐ False ☐

(ii) Kohlrausch law shows that at infinite dilution, the concentration of ions increases.

True ☐ False ☐

63. Choose the correct one from the following pairs of ions which is having high limiting molar conductivity in water at 298 K.

(i) H^+ and OH^- ______________

(ii) Ca^{2+} and CH_3COO^- ______________

(iii) K^+ and Br^- ______________

64. For weak electrolyte, Λ°_m cannot be calculated by extrapolation of Λ°_m *vs* $C^{1/2}$ graph. Which of the following reason is correct?

(a) Λ°_m increases steeply on dilution especially near lower concentration. ☐

(b) Weak electrolyte ionise completely in solution. ☐

(c) Λ_m for weak electrolyte does not vary linearly with dilution. ☐

(d) Λ°_m of weak electrolyte is very low at lower concentration. ☐

65. Enlist any two applications of Kohlrausch law.

(i) ______________ (ii) ______________

66. $\Lambda^{\circ}_{m(NH_4OH)}$ is equal to ______________. **[NCERT Exemplar]**

(a) $\Lambda^{\circ}_{m\,(NH_4OH)} + \Lambda^{\circ}_{m\,(NH_4Cl)} - \Lambda^{\circ}_{m\,(HCl)}$ ☐ (b) $\Lambda^{\circ}_{m\,(NH_4Cl)} + \Lambda^{\circ}_{m\,(NaOH)} - \Lambda^{\circ}_{m\,(NaCl)}$ ☐

(c) $\Lambda^{\circ}_{m\,(NH_4Cl)} + \Lambda^{\circ}_{m\,(NaCl)} - \Lambda^{\circ}_{m\,(NaOH)}$ ☐ (d) $\Lambda^{\circ}_{m\,(NaOH)} + \Lambda^{\circ}_{m\,(NaCl)} - \Lambda^{\circ}_{m\,(NH_4Cl)}$ ☐

***67.** Λ°_m for $CaCl_2$ and $MgSO_4$ respectively are

(Given, $\lambda^{\circ}_{Ca^{2+}} = 119$, $\lambda^{\circ}_{Cl^-} = 76.3$, $\lambda^{\circ}_{Mg^{2+}} = 106$, $\lambda^{\circ}_{SO_4^{2-}} = 160$ S cm^2 mol^{-1})

(a) 287, 266 S cm^{2}mol^{-1} ☐ (b) 271.6, 266 S cm^{2}mol^{-1} ☐

(c) 271.6, 286 S cm^{2}mol^{-1} ☐ (d) 270.3, 278.6 S cm^{2}mol^{-1} ☐

68. Λ°_m for NaCl, HCl and NaAc are 126.4, 425.9 and 91.0 S cm^2 mol^{-1} respectively. The value of Λ°_m for HAc is ______________.

69. The conductivity of 0.001028 mol L^{-1} acetic acid is 4.95×10^{-5} S cm^{-1} and $\Lambda^{\circ}_{m\,(CH_3COOH)}$ is 390.5 S cm^2 mol^{-1}. Its dissociation constant would be

(a) 48.15 mol L^{-1} ☐ (b) 1.78×10^{-5} mol L^{-1} ☐

(c) 1.23×10^{-2} mol L^{-1} ☐ (d) 1.78×10^{-5} mol L^{-1} ☐

70. Conductivity of a solution decreases with dilution because

(a) number of ions increases when solution is diluted ☐

(b) number of ions decreases in a unit volume when solution is diluted ☐

(c) number of ions neither increases nor decreases on dilution ☐

(d) None of the above ☐

71. Λ°_{m} value of water can be determined by $\Lambda^{\circ}_{m}(H_2O)$ = ________________.

***72.** Degree of dissociation and dissociation constant of 0.025 mol L^{-1} methanoic acid are ________.
(Given, $\Lambda_m = 46.1$ S cm^2 mol^{-1}, $\lambda^{\circ}_{(H^+)} = 349.6$ S cm^2 mol^{-1}, $\lambda^{\circ}_{(HCOO^-)} = 54.6$ S cm^2 mol^{-1})

	Degree of dissociation	Dissociation constant	
(a)	0.114	3.67×10^{-4} mol L^{-1}	☐
(b)	1.14	3.67×10^{-4} mol L^{-1}	☐
(c)	1.14	3.67×10^{-5} mol L^{-1}	☐
(d)	0.114	6.37×10^{-4} mol L^{-1}	☐

73. Some limiting molar conductivities are given below.

$$\Lambda^{\circ}_{m\,(H_2SO_4)} = p \text{ S cm}^2\text{mol}^{-1}$$
$$\Lambda^{\circ}_{m\,(K_2SO_4)} = q \text{ S cm}^2\text{mol}^{-1}$$
$$\Lambda^{\circ}_{m\,(CH_3COOK)} = r \text{ S cm}^2\text{mol}^{-1}$$

Λ°_{m} (in S $cm^2 mol^{-1}$) for CH_3COOH will be

(a) $p - q + 2r$ ☐ (b) $p + q - r$ ☐ (c) $p - q + r$ ☐ (d) $\frac{(p - q)}{2} + r$ ☐

TOPIC 5

Electrolytic Cells and Electrolysis

NCERT Pg 51-54

74. If a DC voltage is applied between two copper strips dipped in $CuSO_4(aq)$ solution, then the reaction takes place at

(i) anode ________________ (ii) cathode ________________.

75. Write any two metals that are extracted electrolytically.

(i) ________________ (ii) ________________

76. According to Faraday's law, the amount of chemical reaction which occurs at any electrode is directly proportional to quantity of electricity passed through solution.

True ☐ False ☐

77. Faraday's laws of electrolysis are related to ______________ (molecular mass/equivalent mass) of electrolyte.

78. Faraday's laws of electrolysis fails when

(a) temperature is increased ☐ (b) inert electrodes are used ☐

(c) a mixture of electrolytes is used ☐ (d) none of these cases ☐

79. Choose the incorrect pair from the following.

(a) Equivalent weight – $\frac{\text{Atomic mass of metal}}{\text{No. of electrons}}$ ☐

(b) 1 Faraday – 96500 C mol^{-1} ☐

(c) Quantity of electricity – $\frac{\text{Current}}{\text{Time}}$ ☐

(d) Unit of Q – Coloumb ☐

80. The quantity of charge required to reduce

(i) 1 mole of Al^{3+} to Al = ______________.

(ii) 1 mole of Cu^{2+} to Cu = ______________.

81. A solution of $CuSO_4$ is electrolysed for 10 min with a current of 1.5 A. The mass of copper deposited at the cathode is

(a) 2.938 g ☐ (b) 0.2938 g ☐ (c) 0.92 g ☐ (d) 63 g ☐

82. The products of electrolysis depends on

(i) ______________ (ii) ______________.

***83.** If the electrode in electrolysis is inert, then it does not participate in chemical reaction.

True ☐ False ☐

84. On electrolysis of sulphuric acid, the following reactions are possible at anode.

Reaction A: $2H_2O(l) \longrightarrow O_2(g) + 4H^+(aq) + 4e^-$; $E^\circ_{cell} = +1.23$ V

Reaction B: $2SO_4^{2-}(aq) \longrightarrow S_2O_8^{2-}(aq) + 2e^-$; $E^\circ_{cell} = 1.96$ V

Which reaction is preferred in

(i) dilute sulphuric acid? ______________ (ii) concentrated sulphuric acid? ______________

85. Predict the products of electrolysis in each of the following

(i) An aqueous solution of $AgNO_3$ with silver electrodes.

____

(ii) An aqueous solution of $AgNO_3$ with platinum electrodes.

____

86. How many number of electrons flow through a metallic wire, if a current of 0.5 ampere flows through it for 2 hours ?

(a) 6.022×10^{23} ☐ (b) 3.011×10^{23} ☐ (c) 2.25×10^{22} ☐ (d) 4.50×10^{22} ☐

87. For the following reaction,

$$Cr_2O_7^{2-} + 14H^+ + 6e^- \longrightarrow 2Cr^{3+} + 7H_2O$$

To reduce 1 mole of $Cr_2O_7^{2-}$, the quantity of electricity required is

(a) 96487 C ☐ (b) 578922 C ☐ (c) 182974 C ☐ (d) 32487 C ☐

88. The electricity required in Coulomb for oxidation of 1 mole of FeO to Fe_2O_3 is ________.

TOPIC 6

Batteries

NCERT Pg 54-56

***89.** Battery is a device which consist of one or more electrochemical cells that are capable of converting into ____________ energy to ____________ energy.

90. Primary battery (leclanche cell) can be revised again by recharging it.

True ☐ False ☐

91. Write any two uses of leclanche cell.

(i) ____________ (ii) ____________

92. Which of the following statement regarding dry cell is incorrect?

(a) Dry cell is a compact form of leclanche cell. ☐

(b) Outer zinc container acts as anode. ☐

(c) Cathode is graphite rod surrounded by mixture of carbon and manganese (IV) oxide. ☐

(d) Electrolyte used is a paste of calcium chloride. ☐

93. Answer the following with respect to leclanche cell.

(i) Reaction at anode ____________

(ii) Reaction at cathode ____________

(iii) Formula of electrolyte used ____________

(iv) Change in oxidation state at cathode ____________

94. Consider the following statements and choose the correct option.

I. In mercury cell, mercury amalgam acts as anode and a paste of HgO and carbon as cathode.

II. Electrolyte paste of NH_4Cl and $ZnCl_2$ in mercury cell.

(a) Both I and II are correct. ☐ (b) Only I is correct ☐

(c) Only II is correct. ☐ (d) Both I and II are incorrect. ☐

95. Consider the following diagram and do as directed.

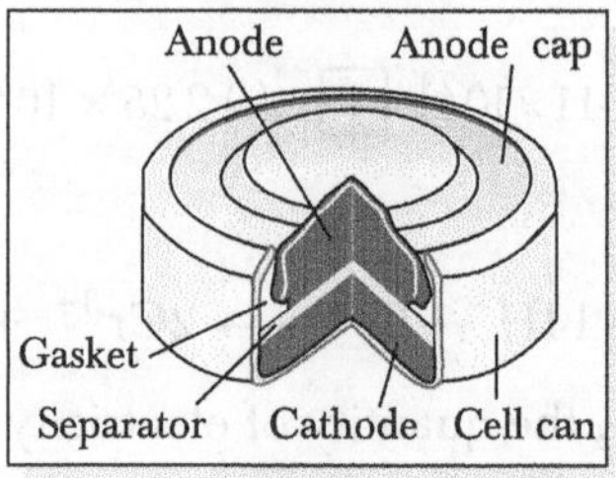

(i) Name of cell ____________________

(ii) Reaction occurs at anode ____________________

(iii) Reaction occurs at cathode ____________________

(iv) Oxidising and reducing agent ____________________

96. Cell potential of leclanche cell is __________, while cell potential of mercury cell is ________.

97. Which of the following statement is not true about lead storage cell ?

(a) Electrolyte used is an aqueous solution of sulphuric acid. ☐

(b) Anode is made up of lead. ☐

(c) Cathode is made up of lead (IV) oxide. ☐

(d) It is a primary cell. ☐

98. When lead storage battery is charged, products formed at anode and cathode are __________ and __________ respectively.

99. Amongst the following, the total number of species formed during charging the lead storage battery is

$Pb, PbO_2, H_2SO_4, PbSO_4, H_2O$

(a) 3 ☐ (b) 2 ☐ (c) 4 ☐ (d) 5

100. For the given reaction, answer the following in one word.

$$Pb(s) + PbO_2(s) + 2H_2SO_4(aq) \longrightarrow 2PbSO_4(s) + 2H_2O(l)$$

(i) Reaction represents a ______________ battery.

(ii) Electrolyte used in this battery is ______________ .

101. While charging the lead storage battery,

(a) $PbSO_4$ on anode is reduced to Pb ☐ (b) $PbSO_4$ on cathode is reduced to Pb ☐

(c) $PbSO_4$ on cathode is oxidised to PbO ☐ (d) $PbSO_4$ on anode is oxidised to PbO_2 ☐

102. Nickel-cadmium cell has longer life as well as cheaper than lead storage cell.

True ☐ False ☐

103. Identify '*a*' and '*b*' in the following nickel-cadmium cell reaction.

$$Cd(s) + a \longrightarrow b + Ni(OH)_2 + H_2O$$

$a =$ ______________________ $b =$ ______________________

104. Amongst the following, the total number of species formed at cathode of mercury cell is

MnO(OH), ZnO, Hg, OH^-, H_2O

(a) 2 ☐ (b) 3 ☐ (c) 4 ☐ (d) 5 ☐

105. Match the following columns.

Column I (Name of cell)	Column II (Uses)
A. Mercury cell	1. Automobiles and inverters
B. Lead storage battery	2. Transistor
C. Dry cell	3. Hearing aids

A. ______________ B. ______________ C. ______________

TOPIC 7 Fuel Cells

NCERT Pg 56-57

106. Consider the following statements.

I. Thermal plants produce electricity and also they do not cause pollution.

II. Galvanic cell which convert energy of combustion of fuel like H_2, CH_4 into electrical energy are called fuel cell.

Here, correct statement(s) is/are

(a) Only I ☐ (b) Only II ☐

(c) Both I and II ☐ (d) None of these ☐

107. Name two materials other than hydrogen that can be used as fuel in fuel cells.

(i) ______________________ (ii) ______________________

108. Based on the given diagram, answer the following.

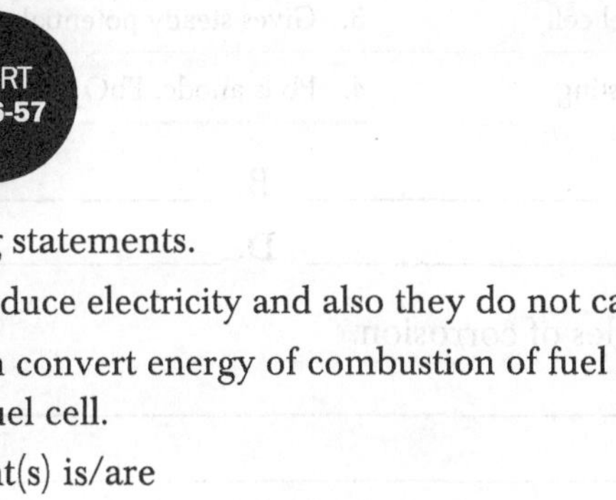

(i) Name of the cell ______________________.

(ii) In Apollo space program, this cell is used for

(a) ______________ (b) ______________

(iii) Two catalysts which can be used in this cell for increasing rate of electrode reaction are

(a) ______________ (b) ______________

(iv) Reaction involved in this cell ______________________.

TOPIC 8

Corrosion

NCERT Pg 57

109. Match the following columns. **[NCERT Exemplar]**

Column I	Column II
A. Lead storage battery	1. Maximum efficiency
B. Mercury cell	2. Prevented by galvanisation
C. Fuel cell	3. Gives steady potential
D. Rusting	4. Pb is anode, PbO_2 is cathode

A. ______________ B. ______________

C. ______________ D. ______________

110. Enlist any three examples of corrosion.

(i) ______________________.

(ii) ______________________.

(iii) ______________________.

111. Consider the following statements.

I. In corrosion, a metal is oxidised by loss of electrons to oxygen and form oxides.

II. In the process of rusting in iron overall reaction is

$$2Fe(s) + O_2(g) + 4H^+(aq) \longrightarrow 2Fe^{+2}(aq) + 2H_2O(l);\ E^\circ_{cell} = 1.67\ V$$

Which of the following statement(s) is/are incorrect?

(a) Both I and II ☐ (b) Only I ☐ (c) Only II ☐ (d) Neither I nor II ☐

112. The prevention of corrosion cannot be done by

(a) covering surface with chemical like bisphenol. ☐

(b) by providing sacrificial electrode of another metal like Mg, Zn etc. ☐

(c) to cover the surface by other metals like Sn, Zn etc. ☐

(d) by cover metal surface by very reactive metals like K, Na, etc. ☐

Assertion-Reason Questions

Given below are two statements, one is labelled as Assertion (A) and other is labelled as Reason (R). Select the most appropriate answer from the options given below.
(a) Both A and R are true and R is the correct explanation of A.
(b) Both A and R are true but R is not the correct explanation of A.
(c) A is true but R is false.
(d) A is false but R is true.

1. **Assertion** (A) In an electrochemical cell, anode and cathode are negative and positive electrodes respectively.
Reason (R) At cathode, oxidation takes place and at anode, reduction takes place.
(a) ☐ (b) ☐ (c) ☐ (d) ☐

2. **Assertion** (A) In nitric acid, Cu oxidised by nitrate ion and not by hydrogen ion.
Reason (R) Positive value of standard electrode potential indicates that hydrogen ion cannot oxidise Cu.
(a) ☐ (b) ☐ (c) ☐ (d) ☐

3. **Assertion** (A) $CuSO_4$ solution cannot safely be kept in a Zn vessel usually.
Reason (R) The position of zinc is lower than Cu in electrochemical series.
(a) ☐ (b) ☐ (c) ☐ (d) ☐

4. **Assertion** (A) We cannot store $CuSO_4$ solution in zinc pot.
Reason (R) E°_{cell} of $Zn|Zn^{2+} || Cu^{2+}|Cu$ is positive (i.e. 1.10 V), therefore zinc displaces copper.
(a) ☐ (b) ☐ (c) ☐ (d) ☐

5. **Assertion** (A) Galvanised iron does not rust.
Reason (R) Zinc has a more negative electrode potential than iron.
(a) ☐ (b) ☐ (c) ☐ (d) ☐

6. **Assertion** (A) λ_m for weak electrolytes increases sharply on dilution.
Reason (R) Degree of dissociation (α) of a weak electrolytes increases with dilution since $\alpha = \sqrt{\frac{K\alpha}{C}}$, so number of ions in solution increases.
(a) ☐ (b) ☐ (c) ☐ (d) ☐

7. **Assertion** (A) Electrolysis of NaCl solution gives chlorine gas at the anode.
Reason (R) The process has higher value of electrode potential and hence is the expected anode product.
(a) ☐ (b) ☐ (c) ☐ (d) ☐

8. **Assertion** (A) Conductivity of all electrolytes decreases on dilution.
Reason (R) On dilution number of ions per unit volume decreases.
(a) ☐ (b) ☐ (c) ☐ (d) ☐

9. **Assertion** (A) In electrolysis, the quantity of electricity needed for depositing 1 mole of silver is different from that required for 1 mole of copper.
Reason (R) The molecular weights of silver and copper are different.
(a) ☐ (b) ☐ (c) ☐ (d) ☐

10. **Assertion** (A) Secondary cells are those cells which can be recharged after use.
Reason (R) The products are electrolysed back to initial reactants during recharge of the cell.
(a) ☐ (b) ☐ (c) ☐ (d) ☐

Case-Based Questions

1. Standard electrode potentials are used for various processes.
It is used to measure relative strength of various oxidants and reductants.
It is used to calculate standard cell potential.
It is used to predict possible reactions.
A set of half reactions (in acidic medium) along with their standard reduction potential, $E°$ (in volt) values are given below :

$$I_2 + 2e^- \longrightarrow 2I^-; E° = 0.54 \text{ V}$$

$$Cl_2 + 2e^- \longrightarrow 2Cl^-; E° = 1.36 \text{ V}$$

$$Mn^{3+} + e^- \longrightarrow Mn^{2+}; E° = 1.50 \text{ V}$$

$$Fe^{3+} + e^- \longrightarrow Fe^{2+}; E° = 0.77 \text{ V}$$

$$O_2 + 4H^+ + 4e^- \longrightarrow 2H_2O; E° = 1.23 \text{ V}$$

(i) Which of the following statements is correct?
(a) Cl^- is oxidised by O_2 ☐ (b) Fe^{2+} is oxidised by iodine. ☐
(c) I^- is oxidised by chlorine ☐ (d) Mn^{2+} is oxidised by chlorine. ☐

(ii) The strongest reducing agent in the aqueous solution is
(a) I^- ☐ (b) Cl^- ☐ (c) Mn^{2+} ☐ (d) Fe^{2+} ☐

(iii) The emf of the following reaction is

$$I_2 + KCl \rightleftharpoons KI + Cl_2$$

(a) –0.82 V ☐ (b) +0.82 V ☐ (c) –0.73 V ☐ (d) +0.73 V ☐

(iv) Which of the following statements is correct for the following reaction?

$$Fe^{3+} + Mn^{2+} \longrightarrow Fe^{2+} + Mn^{3+}$$

(a) The emf of the cell is positive. ☐ (b) Fe^{3+} oxidises Mn^{2+}. ☐
(c) The reaction does not occur. ☐ (d) All are correct. ☐

2. The electrochemical cell shown below is concentration cell. $M|M^{2+}$ (saturated solution of a sparingly soluble salt, MX_2) $||M^{2+}$ (0.001 mol dm^{-3})$|M$

The emf of the cell depends on the difference in concentrations of M^{2+} ions at the two electrodes. The emf of the cell at 298 K is 0.059 V.

(i) The solubility product (K_{sp} mol^{3}dm^{-9}) of MX_2 at 298 K based on the information available for the given concentration cell is

$$\left(\text{Take } \frac{2.303 \times R \times 298}{F} = 0.059\right)$$

(a) 2×10^{-15} ☐ (b) 4×10^{-15} ☐

(c) 3×10^{-12} ☐ (d) 1×10^{-12} ☐

(ii) The value of ΔG (in kJ mol^{-1}) for the given cell is (Take 1F $= 96500$ C mol^{-1})

(a) 3.7 ☐ (b) -3.7 ☐

(c) 10.5 ☐ (d) -11.4 ☐

(iii) The equilibrium constant for the following reaction is

$$Fe^{2+} + Ce^{4+} \rightleftharpoons Ce^{3+} + Fe^{3+}$$

(Given, $E^\circ_{Ce^{4+}/Ce^{3+}} = 1.44$ V and $E^\circ_{Fe^{3+}/Fe^{2+}} = 0.68$ V)

(a) 7.6×10^{12} ☐ (b) 6.5×10^{10} ☐

(c) 5.2×10^{9} ☐ (d) 3.4×10^{12} ☐

(iv) To calculate the emf of the cell, which of the following options is correct.

(a) emf $= E_{\text{cathode}} - E_{\text{anode}}$ ☐ (b) emf $= E_{\text{anode}} - E_{\text{cathode}}$ ☐

(c) emf $= E_{\text{anode}} + E_{\text{cathode}}$ ☐ (d) None of these ☐

COMPETITION EDGE UP

1. How can an electrochemical cell be converted into an electrolytic cell?
[NCERT (New) Pg. 32, JEE Main 2024]

(a) Reversing the flow of ions in salt bridge. ☐

(b) Exchanging the electrodes at anode and cathode. ☐

(c) Applying an external opposite potential greater than E°_{cell}. ☐

(d) Applying an external opposite potential lower than E°_{cell}. ☐

2. For the electrochemical cell

$$M\,|\,M^{2+}\,||\,X\,|\,X^{2-}$$

If, $E^\circ_{(M^{2+}/M)} = 0.46$ V

and $E^\circ_{(X/X^{2-})} = 0.34$ V.

Which of the following is correct?
[NCERT (New) Pg. 33, JEE Main 2024]

(a) $E_{cell} = 0.80$ V ☐

(b) $E_{cell} = -0.80$ V ☐

(c) $M + X \rightarrow M^{2+} + X^{2-}$ is a spontaneous reaction. ☐

(d) $M^{2+} + X^{2-} \longrightarrow M + X$ is a spontaneous reaction. ☐

3. Identify the factor from the following that does not affect electrolytic of a solution.
[NCERT (New) Pg. 42, JEE Main 2024]

(a) The nature of the electrode used. ☐

(b) Concentration of the electrolyte ☐

(c) The nature of the electrolyte added ☐

(d) The natural of solvent used. ☐

4. The molar conductivity for electrolytes A and B are plotted against $C^{1/2}$ as shown below. Electrolytes A and B respectively are **[NCERT (New) Pg. 47, JEE Main 2024]**

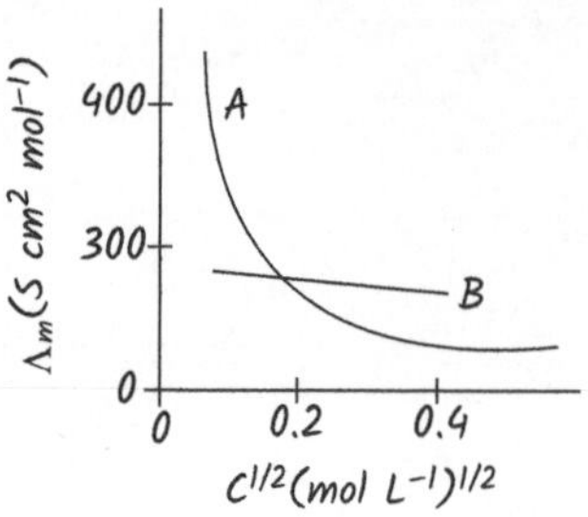

	A	B	
(a)	Weak electrolyte	Strong electrolyte	☐
(b)	Weak electrolyte	Weak electrolyte	☐
(c)	Strong electrolyte	Weak electrolyte	☐
(d)	Strong electrolyte	Strong electrolyte	☐

5. The quantity of silver deposited when one coulomb charge is passed through $AgNO_3$ solution. **[NCERT (New) Pg. 51, JEE Main 2024]**

(a) 1 electrochemical equivalent of silver ☐

(b) 1 chemical equivalent of silver ☐

(c) 1 g of silver ☐

(d) 0.1 g atom of silver ☐

6. Molar ionic conductivities of divalent cation and anion are 57 S cm^2 mol^{-1} and 73 S cm^2 mol^{-1} respectively. The molar conductivity of solution of an electrolyte with the above cation and anion will be
[NCERT (New) Pg. 45, JEE Main 2024]

(a) 130 S cm^2 mol^{-1} ☐

(b) 187 S cm^2 mol^{-1} ☐

(c) 260 S cm^2 mol^{-1} ☐

(d) 65 S cm^2 mol^{-1} ☐

7. For a strong electrolyte, a plot of molar conductivity against (concentration)$^{1/2}$ is a straight line, with a negative slope, the correct unit for the slope is
[NCERT (New) Pg. 47, JEE Main 2024]

(a) S cm^{2}mol$^{\frac{-3}{2}}$L$^{\frac{-1}{2}}$ ☐

(b) S cm^{2}mol^{-1}L$^{\frac{1}{2}}$ ☐

(c) S cm^{2}mol$^{\frac{-3}{2}}$L$^{\frac{1}{2}}$ ☐

(d) S cm^{2}mol$^{\frac{-3}{2}}$L ☐

8. Match List I with List II.
[NCERT (New) Pg. 52, NEET 2024]

List I (Conversion)		List II (Number of Faraday required)
A. 1 mole of H_2O to O_2	I.	3F
B. 1 mole of MnO_4^- to Mn^{2+}	II.	2F
C. 1.5 mole of Ca from molten $CaCl_2$	III.	1F
D. 1 mole of FeO to Fe_2O_3	IV.	5F

Choose the correct answer from the options given below:
(a) A-II, B-IV, C-I, D-III ☐
(b) A-III, B-IV, C-I, D-II ☐
(c) A-II, B-III, C-I, D-IV ☐
(d) A-III, B-IV, C-II, D-I ☐

9. Mass in grams of copper deposited by passing 9.6487 A current through a voltmeter containing copper sulphate solution for 100 seconds is (Given : Molar mass of Cu : 63 mol^{-1}, 1 F = 96487 C)
[NCERT (New) Pg. 52, NEET 2024]

(a) 3.15 g ☐ (b) 0.315 g ☐
(c) 31.5 g ☐ (d) 0.0315 ☐

10. The conductivity of centimolar solution of KCl at 25°C is 0.0210 $ohm^{-1}\ cm^{-1}$ and the resistance of the cell containing the solution at 25°C is 60 ohm. The value of cell constant is
[NCERT (New) Pg. 52, NEET 2023]

(a) 3.28 cm^{-1} ☐ (b) 1.26 cm^{-1} ☐
(c) 3.34 cm^{-1} ☐ (d) 1.34 cm^{-1} ☐

11. Given below are half-cell reactions

$$MnO_4^- + 8H^+ + 5e^- \longrightarrow Mn^{2+} + 4H_2O,$$
$$E^\circ_{Mn^{2+}/MnO_4^-} = -1.510\ V$$
$$\frac{1}{2}O_2 + 2H^+ + 2e^- \longrightarrow H_2O,$$
$$E^\circ_{O_2/H_2O} = +1.223\ V$$

Will the permanganate ion, MnO_4^- liberate O_2 from water in the presence of an acid?
[NCERT (New) Pg. 38, NEET 2022]

(a) No, because E°_{cell} = – 0.287 V ☐
(b) Yes, because E°_{cell} = + 2.733 V ☐
(c) No, because E°_{cell} = – 2.733 V ☐
(d) Yes, because E°_{cell} = + 0.287 V ☐

12. Find the emf of the cell in which the following reaction takes place at 298 K

$$Ni(s) + 2Ag^+(0.001\ M) \longrightarrow Ni^{2+}(0.001\ M) + 2Ag(s)$$

(Given that, E°_{cell} = 1.05 V,
$\frac{2.303\ RT}{F} = 0.059$ at 298 K)
[NCERT (New) Pg. 39, NEET 2022]

(a) 1.385 V ☐
(b) 0.9615 V ☐
(c) 1.05 V ☐
(d) 1.0385 V ☐

13. The molar conductivity of 0.007 M acetic acid is 20 S $cm^2\ mol^{-1}$. What is the dissociation constant of acetic acid ? Choose the correct option.
[$\lambda^\circ_{H^+}$ = 350 S $cm^2\ mol^{-1}$,
$\lambda^\circ_{CH_3COO^-}$ = 50 S $cm^2\ mol^{-1}$]
[NCERT (New) Pg. 45, NEET 2021]

(a) $1.75 \times 10^{-4}\ mol^{-1}\ L^{-1}$ ☐
(b) $2.50 \times 10^{-4}\ mol^{-1}\ L^{-1}$ ☐
(c) $1.75 \times 10^{-5}\ mol^{-1}\ L^{-1}$ ☐
(d) $2.50 \times 10^{5}\ mol^{-1}\ L^{-1}$ ☐

14. The molar conductance of NaCl, HCl and CH_3COONa at infinite dilution are 126.45, 426.16 and 91.0 S $cm^2\ mol^{-1}$ respectively. The molar conductance of CH_3COOH at infinite dilution is choose the right option for your answer.
[NCERT (New) Pg. 49, NEET 2021]

(a) 201.28 S $cm^2\ mol^{-1}$ ☐
(b) 390.71 S $cm^2\ mol^{-1}$ ☐
(c) 698.28 S $cm^2\ mol^{-1}$ ☐
(d) 540.48 S $cm^2\ mol^{-1}$ ☐

15. In a typical fuel cell, the reactants (R) and product (P) are
[NCERT (New) Pg. 56, NEET (Oct.) 2020]

(a) R = $H_2(g)$, $O_2(g)$; P = $H_2O_2(l)$ ☐
(b) R = $H_2(g)$, $O_2(g)$; P = $H_2O(l)$ ☐
(c) R = $H_2(g)$, $O_2(g)$, $Cl_2(g)$; P = $HClO_4(aq)$ ☐
(d) R = $H_2(g)$, $N_2(g)$; P = $NH_3(aq)$ ☐

16. Identify the reaction from following having top position in EMF series (Standard reduction potential) according to their electrode potential at 298 K.
[NCERT (New) Pg. 37, NEET (Oct.) 2020]

(a) $Mg^{2+} + 2e^- \longrightarrow Mg(s)$ ☐
(b) $Fe^{2+} + 2e^- \longrightarrow Fe(s)$ ☐
(c) $Au^{3+} + 3e^- \longrightarrow Au(s)$ ☐
(d) $K^+ + 1e^- \longrightarrow K(s)$ ☐

Chapter 03

Chemical Kinetics

Scan and take Chapter Test

TOPIC 1

Introduction & Rate of a Chemical Reaction

NCERT Pg 61-66

1. For any chemical reaction, chemistry to find out

(a) $\Delta G < 0$

(b) starting and terminating points of the reaction

(c) reaction speed

(d) All of the above

2. Chemical kinetics deals with the study of __________ and their __________.

3. Complete the following analogy.

Feasibility of reaction : A : : Rate of the reaction : B

A = __________ B = __________

4. Among the following, which process occurs instantaneously?

(a) Inversion of cane sugar.

(b) Rusting of iron.

(c) Hydrolysis of starch.

(d) Precipitation of silver chloride by mixing $AgNO_3$ and NaCl.

5. For a reaction,

$$R \rightarrow P$$

Rate of reaction can be expressed as

(i) __________ (ii) __________

6. Rate or speed of a chemical reaction tells us about which property.

____

7. The average rate and instantaneous rate of a reaction are equal when both of them have a time interval of zero.

True ☐ False ☐

Concepts of all questions bearing * are important for JEE/NEET/CUET.

8. For a reaction, $A \longrightarrow B$, the concentration of both reactants and products varies exponentially with time. Regarding this which of the following graph is correct ?

(a)
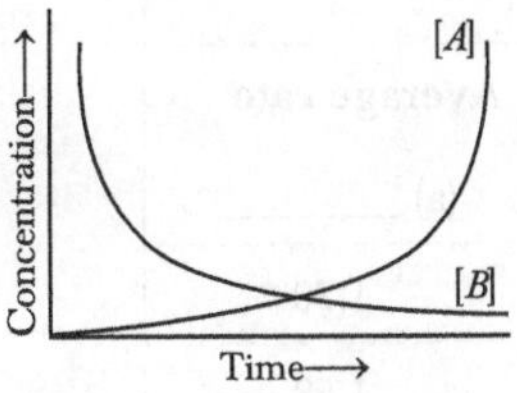

☐

(b)
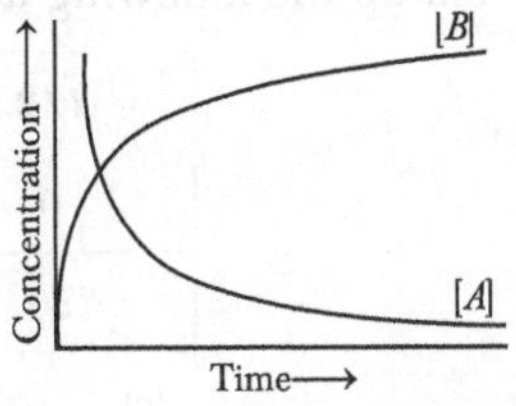

☐

(c)
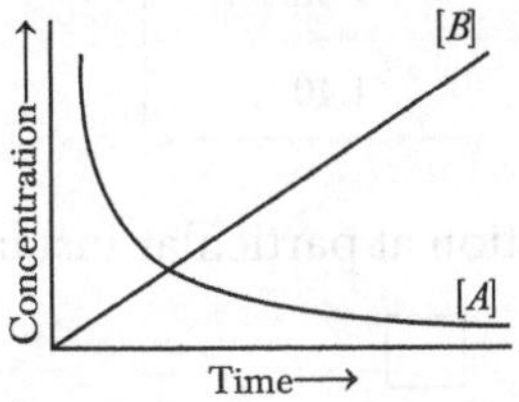

☐

(d)
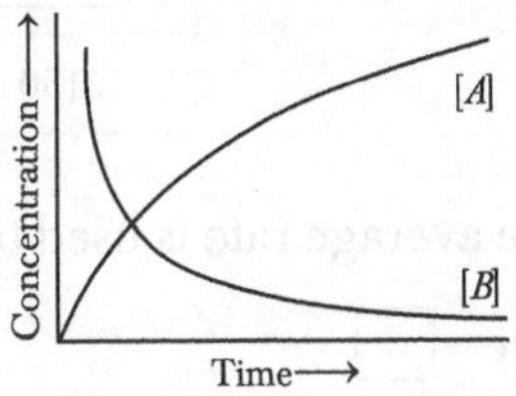

☐

9. Consider the following graphs and write what does slope *A* and *B* represents ?

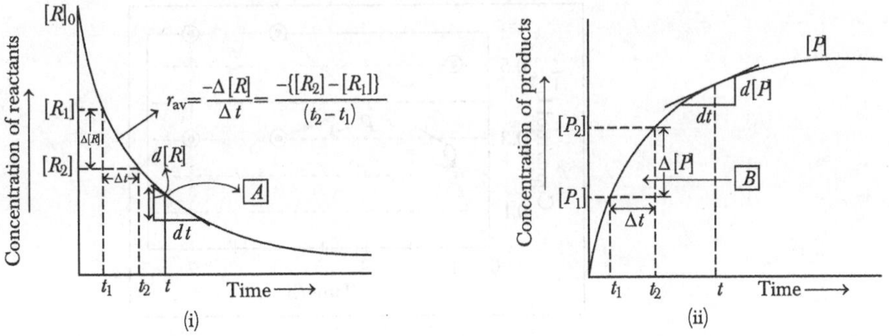

A. ______________________ *B.* ______________________

10. Units of rate equation will be atm s^{-1}, if the concentration of gases is expressed in terms of their partial pressure.

True ☐ False ☐

11. Consider the given table with appropriate data for the following reaction and its respective graph.

$$C_4H_9Cl + H_2O \longrightarrow C_4H_9OH + HCl$$

t/s	0	50	100	150	200	300	400	700	800
$[C_4H_9Cl]$/mol L^{-1}	0.100	0.0905	0.0820	0.0741	0.0671	0.0549	0.0439	0.0210	0.017

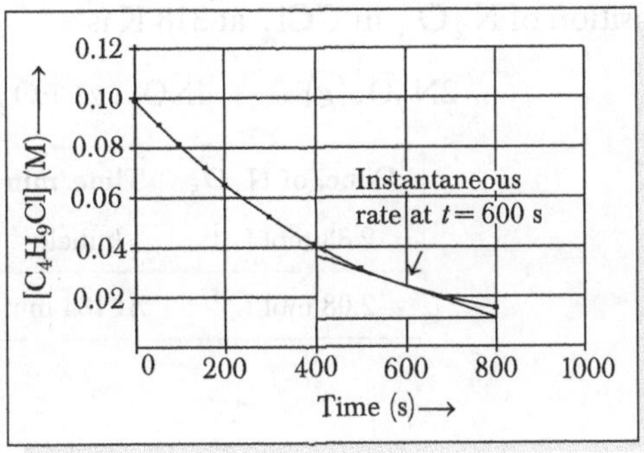

Answer the following

(i) Instantaneous rate of reaction at 600 s will be ________.

(ii) Fill up the following table.

$t/2$	$[C_4H_9Cl]/mol\ L^{-1}$	Average rate
0	0.100	(a) ________
50	(b) ________	1.70
(c) ________	0.0820	1.58
150	(d) ________	1.40

12. The average rate is used to predict the rate of reaction at particular instant.

True ☐ False ☐

13. The progress of the reaction, $P \rightarrow nQ$ with time is represented in the graph shown below.

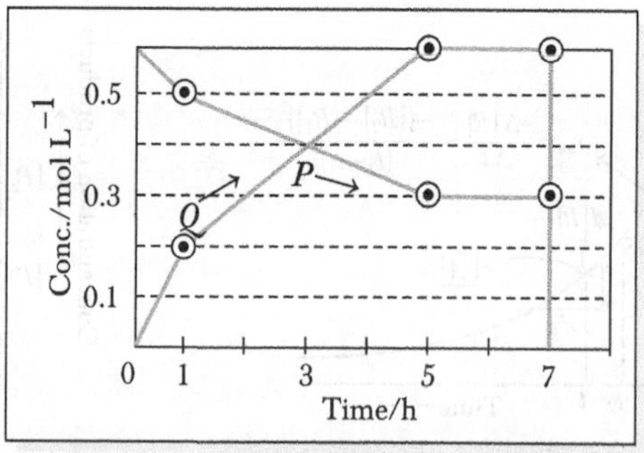

The initial rate of conversion of P will be

(a) $0.2\ mol\ L^{-1}h^{-1}$ ☐ (b) $0.4\ mol\ L^{-1}h^{-1}$ ☐

(c) $0.8\ mol\ L^{-1}h^{-1}$ ☐ (d) $0.1\ mol\ L^{-1}h^{-1}$ ☐

14. Which of the following expressions is correct for the rate of reaction given below?

$$5Br^-(aq) + BrO_3^-(aq) + 6H^+(aq) \longrightarrow 3Br_2(aq) + 3H_2O(l)$$ **[NCERT Exemplar]**

(a) $\frac{\Delta[Br^-]}{\Delta t} = 5\frac{[\Delta H^+]}{\Delta t}$ ☐ (b) $\frac{\Delta[Br^-]}{\Delta t} = \frac{6}{5}\frac{[\Delta H^+]}{\Delta t}$ ☐

(c) $\frac{\Delta[Br^-]}{\Delta t} = \frac{5}{6}\frac{[\Delta H^+]}{\Delta t}$ ☐ (d) $\frac{\Delta[Br^-]}{\Delta t} = 6\frac{[\Delta H^+]}{\Delta t}$ ☐

15. The decomposition of N_2O_5 in CCl_4 at 318 K is

$$2N_2O_5(g) \longrightarrow 4NO_2(g) + O_2(g)$$

Conc. of N_2O_5	Time/min
$2.33\ mol\ L^{-1}$	Initially
$2.08\ mol\ L^{-1}$	At 184 min

The average rate of this reaction and rate of production of NO_2 respectively are

Average rate of reaction	Rate of production of NO_2	
(a) 0.40×10^{-10} mol L^{-1}/h	3.87×10^{-2} mol $L^{-1}min^{-1}$	☐
(b) 4.07×10^{-2} mol L^{-1}/h	2.72×10^{-3} mol $L^{-1}min^{-1}$	☐
(c) 4.07 mol L^{-1}/h	27.2×10^{-5} mol $L^{-1}min^{-1}$	☐
(d) 3.87 mol L^{-1}/h	4.72×10^{-3} mol $L^{-1}min^{-1}$	☐

16. For the reaction, $R \longrightarrow P$

Concentration of reactant changes from 0.03 M to 0.02 M in 25 min. Its average rate of reaction will be

(a) 6.67×10^{-6} Ms^{-1} ☐ (b) 7.02×10^{-6} Ms^{-1} ☐

(c) 4×10^{-4} Ms^{-1} ☐ (d) 8.41×10^{-5} Ms^{-1} ☐

17. In a reaction, $2A \longrightarrow$ products, concentration of A decreases from 0.5 mol L^{-1} to 0.4 mol L^{-1} in 10 min. The average rate will be 5×10^{-3} M min^{-1}.

True ☐ False ☐

***18.** For the reaction,

$$2N_2O_5(g) \longrightarrow 4NO_2(g) + O_2(g)$$

The rate of formation of $NO_2(g)$ is 2.8×10^{-3} Ms^{-1}. The rate of disappearance of N_2O_5 is __________ Ms^{-1}.

(a) 1.4×10^{-3} ☐ (b) 1.6×10^{-5} ☐ (c) 2.5×10^{-3} ☐ (d) 4.7×10^{-7} ☐

TOPIC 2

Factors Influencing Rate of a Reaction

NCERT Pg 66-71

19. Name the factors on which rate of reaction depends.

____

20. For a reaction,

$$aA + bB \longrightarrow cC + dD; \text{ Rate} \propto [A]^x [B]^y$$

Exponents x and y are always equal to the stoichiometric coefficients a and b.

True ☐ False ☐

***21.** Consider the following reaction,

$$2NO(g) + O_2(g) \longrightarrow 2NO_2(g); \text{ Rate} = k[NO]^2 [O_2]$$

Fill in the blanks.

Concentration of NO	Concentration of O_2	Rate
Doubled	Constant	(i) ______
Constant	(ii) ______	Doubled

22. Rate law cannot be determined from balanced chemical equation if

I. reverse reaction is involved.

II. it is an elementary reaction.

III. it is a sequence of elementary reactions.

IV. any of the reactants is in excess.

Choose the correct statement(s) using given codes.

(a) I, II and III ☐ (b) II, III and IV ☐

(c) I, III and IV ☐ (d) Only II ☐

23. Which one of the following statements for the order of a reaction is incorrect? **[NCERT Exemplar]**

(a) Order is not influenced by stoichiometric coefficient of the reactants. ☐

(b) Order of reaction is sum of power to the concentration terms of reactants to express the rate of reaction. ☐

(c) Order of reaction is always whole number. ☐

(d) Order can only be determined experimentally. ☐

24. Arrange the following rate expression in increasing pattern for their order of reactions.

$$\text{Rate} = k[A]^{1/2}[B]^{3/2},\ \text{Rate} = k[A]^{1}[B]^{0},\ \text{Rate} = k[A]^{3/2}[B]^{-1}$$

I. II. III.

---

25. Complete the following table.

Reaction order	Unit of rate constant (k)
(i) ______	s^{-1}
Zero	(ii) ______
(iii) ______	$mol^{-1} L\ s^{-1}$

***26.** Identify the order of reaction from given rate constants.

(i) $k = 2.3 \times 10^{-5}\ L\ mol^{-1} s^{-1}$ (ii) $k = 3 \times 10^{-4} mol\ L^{-1} s^{-1}$

	Order of reaction (i)	Order of reaction (ii)	
(a)	1	0	☐
(b)	0	1	☐
(c)	2	0	☐
(d)	1	2	☐

27. Separate unimolecular, bimolecular and trimolecular reactions from the following.

(i) Decomposition of ammonium nitrate ________________

(ii) Decomposition of hydrogen iodide ________________

(iii) $2NO + O_2 \longrightarrow 2NO_2$ ________________

(iv) $2H_2O_2 \xrightarrow[\text{Alkaline}]{I^-} 2H_2O + O_2$ ________________

28. Consider the following statements.

I. In a complex reaction, molecularity of slowest step is same as the order of overall reaction.

II. Molecularity is not applicable for elementary reaction.

III. Fastest step in a reaction control rate of overall reaction and as rate determining step.

Mark (✓) and (✗) under correct and incorrect with respect to given statements.

	Correct	Incorrect
I.	______	______
II.	______	______
III.	______	______

TOPIC 3

Integrated Rate Equations

NCERT Pg 71-78

29. Consider the following statements,

I. For rate law, $r = k[A]^{1/2}[B]^2$, order of reaction is 2.5.

II. Order of a reaction can't be zero or in fraction.

Choose the incorrect statement(s).

(a) Both I and II ☐ (b) Only I ☐ (c) Only II ☐ (d) None of these ☐

30. Write the order of reaction in which rate of reaction is equal to rate constant.

____

31. Consider the following statements.

I. A zero order reaction means rate of reaction is independent of concentration of reactant.

II. Sum of power of concentration of reactants and products in rate law expression is called order of chemical reaction.

Which of the following statement(s) is correct?

(a) Only I ☐ (b) Only II ☐ (c) Both I and II ☐ (d) Neither I nor II ☐

32. At high pressure the following reaction is zero order.

$$2NH_3(g) \xrightarrow[\text{Pt (catalyst)}]{1130\ K} N_2(g) + 3H_2(g)$$

Which of the following option is incorrect for this reaction?

(a) Rate of reaction becomes equal to rate constant. ☐

(b) Rate of reaction depends on concentration of ammonia. ☐

(c) Rate of decomposition of ammonia will remain constant until ammonia disappears completely. ☐

(d) Further increase in pressure will change the rate of reaction. ☐

33. Thermal decomposition of HI on gold surface is an example of ______________.

***34.** Which of the following graph is correct for a zero order reaction?

(a) 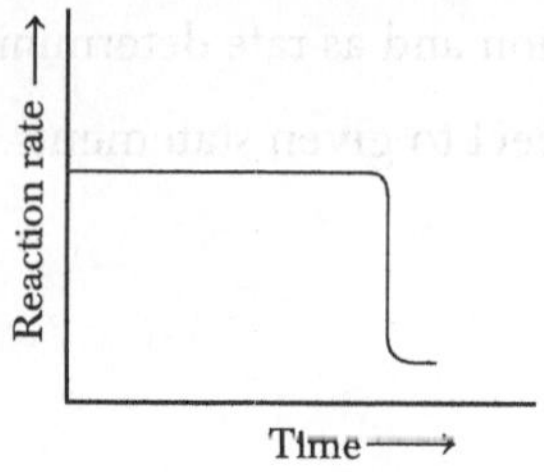

☐

(b) 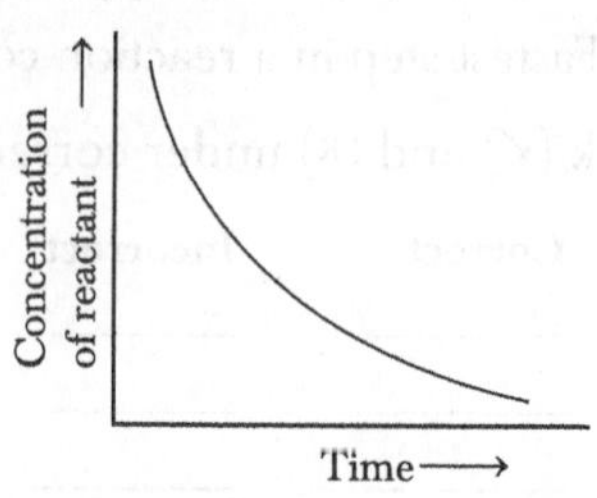

☐

(c) 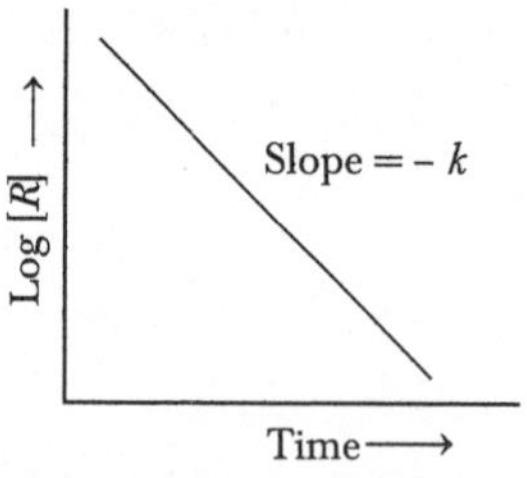

☐

(d) Both (b) and (c) ☐

35. Write the order of reaction whose rate is proportional to the first power of concentration of reactant.

____

36. Hydrogenation of ethene is an example of __________ (zero/first) order reaction.

37. Amongst the following, the total number of species undergoing unimolecular decomposition reaction.

$NH_4, NO_2, HI, N\bar{O}, \bar{O}_3, N_2O_5$

(a) 2 ☐ (b) 3 ☐ (c) 4 ☐ (d) 5 ☐

38. Consider the following statements.

I. Rate of a first order reaction depends upon the concentration of reactant.

II. Radioactive decay of unstable nuclei takes place by zero order kinetics.

Which of the above statement(s) is/are correct?

(a) Only I ☐ (b) Only II ☐

(c) Both I and II ☐ (d) Neither I nor II ☐

39. Amongst the following, the total number of species undergoing first order reaction on decomposition.

$NH_3, N_2O_5, N_2O, H_2O_2, NO_2$

(a) 2 ☐ (b) 3 ☐ (c) 4 ☐ (d) 5 ☐

40. Which of the following reaction does not follows first order kinetics?

I. Decomposition of N_2O_5 II. Decomposition of N_2O

III. Decay of radium IV. Reverse Haber process

(a) I and II ☐ (b) II and IV ☐

(c) Only IV ☐ (d) I, II and III ☐

41. Amongst the following, the total number of species which on undergoing photochemical reaction are an example of pseudo first order reaction.

Cane sugar, Acetyl chloride, Ethyl acetate, Sodium acetate, Triglycerides

(a) 2 ☐ (b) 3 ☐ (c) 4 ☐ (d) 5 ☐

42. Mechanism of a hypothetical reaction, $P_2 + Q_2 \longrightarrow 2PQ$ is given below.

$$P_2 \rightleftharpoons P + P \text{ (fast)}$$
$$P + Q_2 \longrightarrow PQ + Q \text{ (slow)}$$
$$P + Q \longrightarrow PQ \text{ (fast)}$$

The overall order of the reaction will be

(a) 1 ☐ (b) 2 ☐

(c) 0 ☐ (d) pseudo order reaction ☐

***43.** The initial concentration of N_2O_5 in the first order reaction,

$$N_2O_5(g) \longrightarrow 2NO_2(g) + \frac{1}{2}O_2(g) \text{ was } 1.24 \times 10^{-2} \text{ mol L}^{-1} \text{ at 318 K.}$$

The concentration of N_2O_5 after 60 min was 0.20×10^{-2} mol L^{-1}. The rate constant of the reaction at 318 K will be

(a) 3.04 min^{-1} ☐ (b) 0.0304 mol s^{-1} ☐

(c) 0.0304 min^{-1} ☐ (d) Both (b) and (c) ☐

44. The following data were obtained during the first order thermal decomposition of $N_2O_5(g)$ at constant volume.

$$2N_2O_5(g) \longrightarrow 2N_2O_4(g) + O_2(g)$$

Time/s	Total pressure/(atm)
0	0.5
100	0.512

The correct rate constant for given information is

(a) $9.48 \times 10^{-4}\ s^{-1}$ ☐ (b) $49.8 \times 10^{-10}\ s^{-1}$ ☐

(c) $4.98 \times 10^{-4}\ s^{-1}$ ☐ (d) None of these ☐

45. Which of the following pair is incorrectly matched?

(a) Zero order reaction – $t_{1/2} \propto [R]_0$ ☐

(b) First order reaction – $t_{1/2}$ is independent of $[R]_0$ ☐

(c) First order reaction – $t_{1/2} \propto 1/[R]_0$ ☐

(d) None of the above ☐

46. Half-life of first order reaction having $k = 5.5 \times 10^{-14}\ s^{-1}$ will be ____________.

47. For the decomposition of azoisopropane into hexane and nitrogen at 543 K, the following data is obtained.

$$(CH_3)_2CH\ N{=}NCH(CH_3)_2 \longrightarrow N_2 + C_6H_{14}$$

Experiment	Time(s)	Total pressure (mm Hg)
I.	0	35.0
II.	360	54.0

The value of rate constant at 360 s is

(a) $2.17 \times 10^{-3}\ s^{-1}$ ☐ (b) $3.25 \times 10^{-3}\ s^{-1}$ ☐

(c) $3.25 \times 10^{-3}\ min^{-1}$ ☐ (d) $1.98 \times 10^{-3}\ s^{-1}$ ☐

48. For first order reaction, time required for completion of 99.9% will be

(a) 5 times of half-life of reaction ☐ (b) 10 times of half-life of reaction ☐

(c) 2.5 times of half-life of reaction ☐ (d) None of these ☐

49. Complete the following table.

Order of reaction	Integrated rate law	Half-life	Unit of k
1	(i) ____________	$\ln 2/k$	(ii) ____________
(iii) ____________	$kt = [R]_0 - [R]$	(iv) ____________	$mol\ L^{-1}s^{-1}$

***50.** Consider a first order gas phase decomposition reaction given below,

$$A(g) \longrightarrow B(g) + C(g)$$

The initial pressure of the system before decomposition of A was p_i. After lapse of time 't' total pressure of the system increased by x units and became 'p_t'. The rate constant (k) for the reaction is given as **[NCERT Exemplar]**

(a) $k = \dfrac{2.303}{t} \log \dfrac{p_i}{p_i - x}$ ☐ (b) $k = \dfrac{2.303}{t} \log \dfrac{p_i}{2p_i - p_t}$ ☐

(c) $k = \dfrac{2.303}{t} \log \dfrac{p_i}{2p_i + p_t}$ ☐ (d) $k = \dfrac{2.303}{t} \log \dfrac{p_i}{p_i + x}$ ☐

51. Reactions whose molecularity is one but order is more than one are known as pseudo first order reactions.

True ☐ False ☐

52. Acid hydrolysis of ester in aqueous solution is an example of __________ reaction.

53. Consider the following reaction,

$$C_{12}H_{22}O_{11} + H_2O \xrightarrow{H^+} C_6H_{12}O_6 + C_6H_{12}O_6$$

(i) Write the rate law__________________.

(ii) Predict the order of the reaction__________________.

***54.** Hydrolysis of methyl acetate in aqueous solution has been studied by titrating the liberated acetic acid against sodium hydroxide.

Time/min	0	30	60	90
Concentration of ester (mol L^{-1})	0.8500	0.8004	0.7538	0.7096

During this reaction, concentration of water remains 55 mol L^{-1}. Rate of this reaction is expressed as rate = k' $[CH_3COOCH_3]$ $[H_2O]$, then value of k' is

(a) 3.64×10^{-5} mol L^{-1} ☐
(b) 6.34×10^{-5} mol^{-1} L min^{-1} ☐
(c) 3.64×10^{-5} mol^{-1} L min^{-1} ☐
(d) 6.34 mol^{-1} L min^{-1} ☐

55. For a first order reaction ($k = 1.15 \times 10^{-3}$ s^{-1}), time required to reduce 5 g of reactant to 3 g will be

(a) 450 minute ☐
(b) 540 second ☐
(c) 444 second ☐
(d) 444 minute ☐

56. Time required to decompose SO_2Cl_2 to half of its initial amount is 60 min. If the decomposition is a first order reaction, the rate constant of the reaction is __________.

TOPIC 4

Temperature Dependence of the Rate of a Reaction

NCERT Pg 78-82

57. Most of the reactions are retarded with increase in temperature.

True ☐ False ☐

58. The correct increasing order of the time taken for half of the decomposition of N_2O_5 at the temperature 50°C, 0°C and 25°C will be

(a) 50°C < 0°C < 25°C ☐
(b) 50°C < 25°C < 0°C ☐
(c) 0°C < 25°C < 50°C ☐
(d) 0°C < 50°C < 25°C ☐

59. In a mixture of $KMnO_4$ and $H_2C_2O_4$, potassium permanganate gets decolourised slower at a higher temperature.

True ☐ False ☐

60. In the Arrhenius equation, $k = Ae^{-E_a/RT}$

(i) Pre-exponential factor is ______________________.

(ii) Factor $e^{-E_a/RT}$ corresponds to ______________________.

61. Consider the following graph.

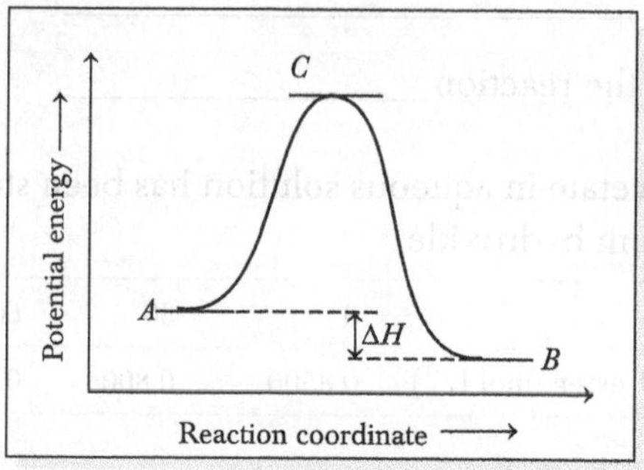

(i) Point which represents energy of reactant ______________.

(ii) Point which represents activated complex is ______________.

62. In general energy is ______________ (released/absorbed) when activated complex decomposes to form product.

63. On which factor final enthalpy of the reaction depends?

____

***64.** Consider the figure and mark the correct option.

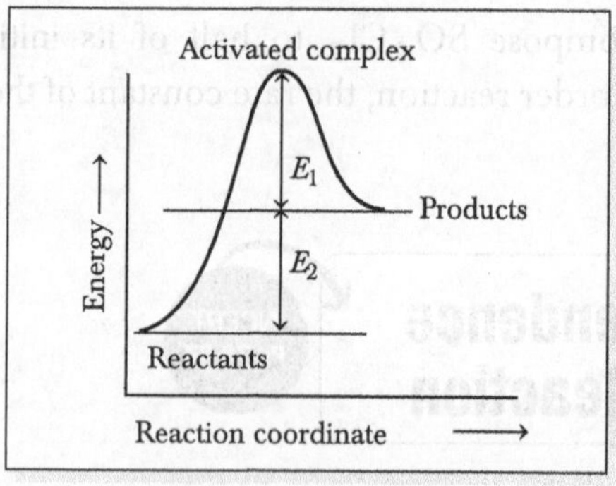

(a) Activation energy of forward reaction is $E_1 + E_2$ and product is less stable than reactant. ☐

(b) Activation energy of forward reaction is $E_1 + E_2$ and product is more stable than reactant. ☐

(c) Activation energy of both forward and backward reaction is $E_1 + E_2$ and reactant is more stable than product. ☐

(d) Activation energy of backward reaction is E_1 and product is more stable than reactant. ☐

65. All the molecules in the reacting species do not have same kinetic energy.

True ☐ False ☐

***66.** In the following graph, what does *A* represents?

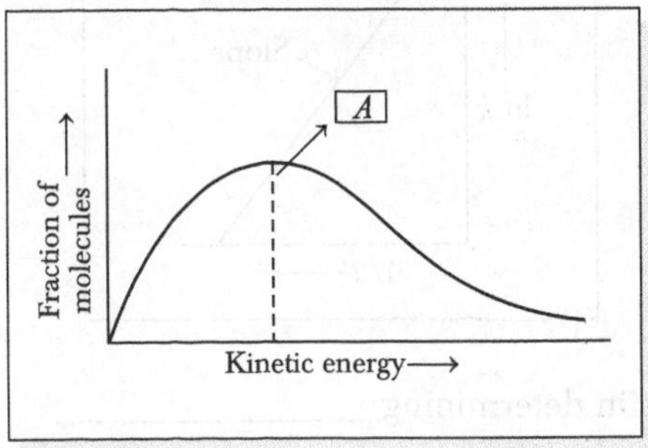

A = ______________________________

67. According to Maxwell Boltzmann distribution of energy, fraction of molecules with most probable kinetic energy ______ (increases/decreases) at high temperature.

68. Consider the following graph.

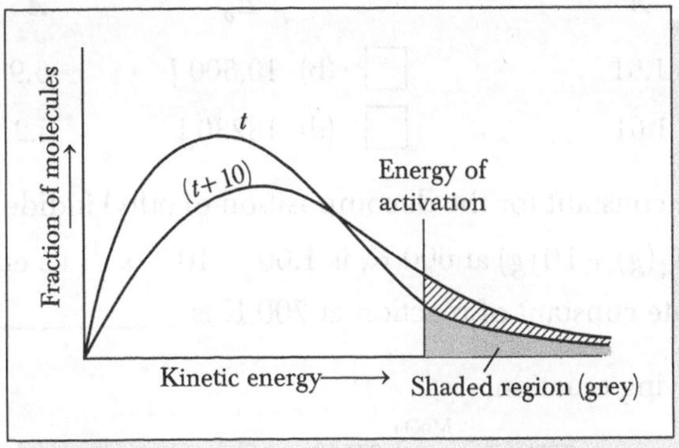

(i) Shaded region (grey) represents

(a) fraction of molecules reacting at $t+10$. ☐ (b) fraction of molecules reacting at t. ☐

(ii) On increasing temperature, the area under the curve ______ and curve shifts to ______ side.

69. Consider the following statements.

I. Increasing the temperature of substance, increases the fraction of molecules with energies greater than E_a.

II. On increasing temperature by 10°C, rate of reaction gets halved.

Here, incorrect statement(s) is/are

(a) Only I ☐ (b) Only II ☐

(c) Both I and II ☐ (d) Neither I nor II ☐

70. Answer the following questions with respect to the given graph.

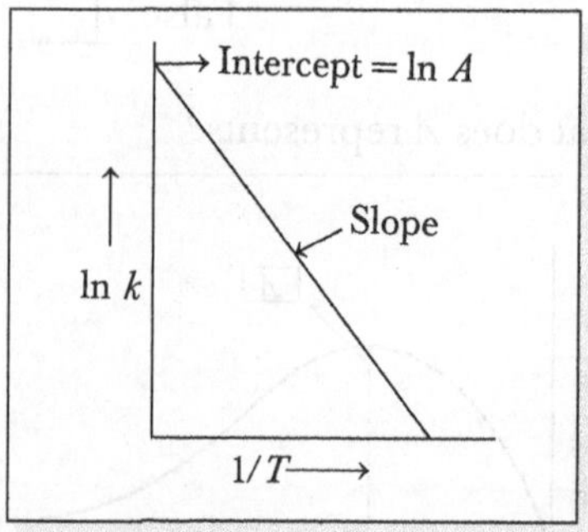

(i) Slope of graph helps in determining ______________ .

(ii) Write the equation for the graph when k_1 and k_2 are the values of rate constants at temperature T_1 and T_2.

***71.** The rate constants of a reaction at 500 K and 700 K are $0.02\ s^{-1}$ and $0.07\ s^{-1}$ respectively. The values of E_a and A respectively are

	E_a	A			E_a	A	
(a)	20900 J	1.61	☐	(b)	10,500 J	5.9	☐
(c)	18230.8 J	1.61	☐	(d)	18230 J	6.2	☐

72. The first order rate constant for the decomposition of ethyl iodide by the reaction, $C_2H_5I(g) \longrightarrow C_2H_4(g) + HI(g)$ at 600 K, is $1.60 \times 10^{-5}\ s^{-1}$, its energy of activation is 209 kJ/mol. The rate constant of reaction at 700 K is ______________.

73. Consider the following reaction,

$$2KClO_3 \xrightarrow{MnO_2} 2KCl + 3O_2$$

Here, the effect of MnO_2 on the rate of reaction is ______________.

74. Name the substance which reduces the rate of a reaction.

75. Catalyst form permanent bonds with reactants which results in making an intermediate complex to yield product.

True ☐ False ☐

76. Consider the following curve,

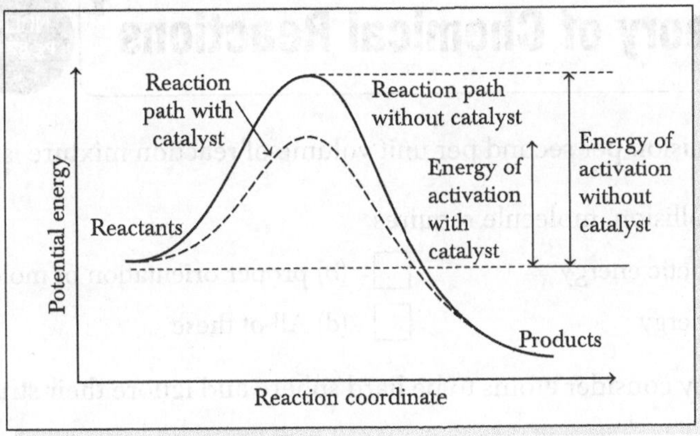

On the basis of the above curve, identify the incorrect statement.

(a) Catalyst provides an alternative pathway. ☐

(b) It increases the activation energy between reactants and products. ☐

(c) It lowers the potential energy barrier. ☐

(d) It reduces the activation energy between reactants and products. ☐

77. Select the one factor which is affected by the catalyst.

ΔH, ΔS, ΔG, E_a

____

78. Which of the following is not correct about the catalyst?

(a) It catalyses the forward and backward reaction to same extent. ☐

(b) It alters ΔG of the reaction. ☐

(c) It does not change equilibrium constant of a reaction. ☐

(d) It provides on alternate mechanism by reducing activation energy between reactants and products. ☐

79. Consider the following statements regarding catalyst.

I. In the presence of a catalyst, heat is evolved during reaction.

II. Catalyst can catalyse non-spontaneous reaction very fast and effectively.

Which of the following statement(s) is/are correct for a catalyst?

(a) Both I and II ☐ (b) Only I ☐

(c) Only II ☐ (d) None of these ☐

TOPIC 5

Collision Theory of Chemical Reactions

NCERT Pg 82-83

80. Number of collision per second per unit volume of reaction mixture is known as ________.

81. For effective collision, molecule requires

(a) sufficient kinetic energy ☐ (b) proper orientation of molecules ☐

(c) activation energy ☐ (d) All of these ☐

82. Collision theory consider atoms to be hard sphere and ignore their structure.

True ☐ False ☐

83. Consider the following,

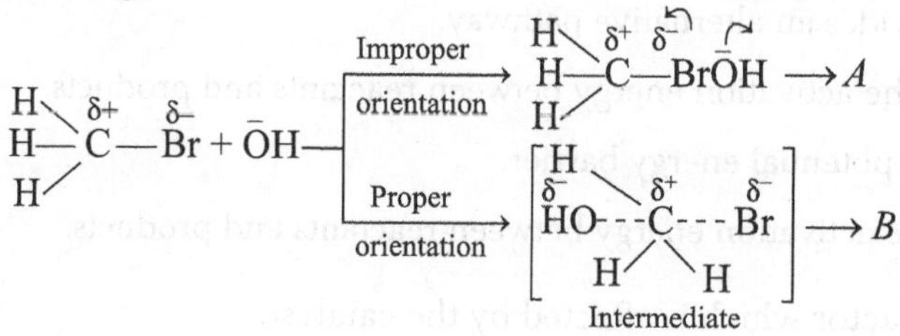

What will come in place of *A* and *B* in the above reaction ?

	A	*B*	
(a)	No products	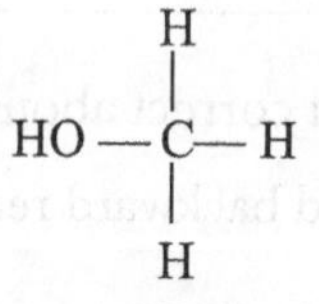	☐
(b)	No products	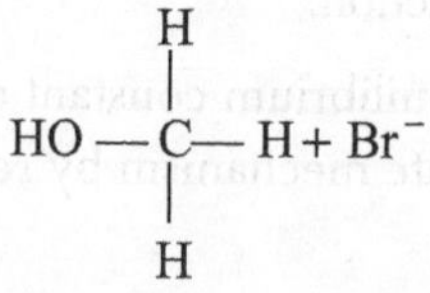	☐
(c)	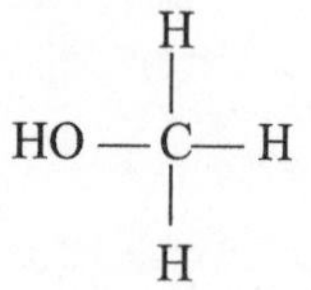	No products	☐
(d)	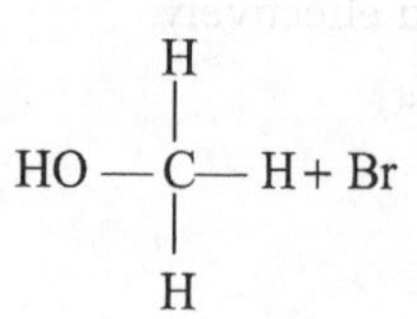	No products	☐

84. The effect of temperature on rate constant can be

(a) rate constant decreases with increase in temperature. ☐

(b) rate constant increases and nearly double with increase in temperature by 10K. ☐

(c) rate constant does not depends on temperature. ☐

(d) All of the above ☐

***85.** The rate of chemical reaction doubles for an increase of 10 K in absolute temperature from 298 K. Its E_a will be

(a) 52.9 kJ mol^{-1} ☐ (b) 52897 kJ mol^{-1} ☐

(c) 50.2 kJ mol^{-1} ☐ (d) 528.97 kJ mol^{-1} ☐

86. For reaction,

$$2HI(g) \longrightarrow H_2 + I_2(g)\ (E_a = 209.5\ \text{kJ mol}^{-1})\ (T = 581\ \text{K})$$

The fraction of molecules of reactants having energy equal to or greater than activation energy is ________________.

87. A first order reaction is 50% completed in 40 minutes at 300 K and in 20 minutes at 320 K. The activation energy of the reaction is

(a) 30.03 kJ mol^{-1} ☐ (b) 27.66 kJ mol^{-1} ☐

(c) 55.23 kJ mol^{-1} ☐ (d) 25.78 kJ mol^{-1} ☐

Assertion-Reason Questions

Given below are two statements, one is labelled as Assertion (A) and other is labelled as Reason (R). Select the most appropriate answer from the options given below.

(a) Both A and R are true and R is correct the explanation of A.
(b) Both A and R are true but R is not the correct explanation of A.
(c) A is true but R is false.
(d) A is false but R is true.

1. Assertion (A) Rate can also be expressed as rate of change in partial pressure of the reactant or the product.

Reason (R) For a gaseous reaction at constant temperature, concentration is directly proportional to the partial pressure of the species.

(a) ☐ (b) ☐ (c) ☐ (d) ☐

2. Assertion (A) Order and molecularity are same for all chemical reactions.

Reason (R) Order is determined experimentally and molecularity is the sum of the stoichiometric coefficient of rate determining elementary step.

(a) ☐ (b) ☐ (c) ☐ (d) ☐

3. Assertion (A) Molecularity greater than 3 is not observed.

Reason (R) The overall molecularity of a complex reaction is molecularity of the slowest step.

(a) ☐ (b) ☐ (c) ☐ (d) ☐

4. **Assertion** (A) Order of reaction can be zero or fractional.

Reason (R) We cannot determine order from balanced chemical equation.

(a) ☐ (b) ☐ (c) ☐ (d) ☐

5. **Assertion** (A) For a first order reacttion, $t_{1/2}$ is independent of rate constant.

Reason (R) For a first order reaction, $t_{1/2} \propto [R]_0$

(a) ☐ (b) ☐ (c) ☐ (d) ☐

6. **Assertion** (A) Rate of reaction doubles when concentration of reactant is doubled if it is a first order reaction.

Reason (R) For first order kinetics,

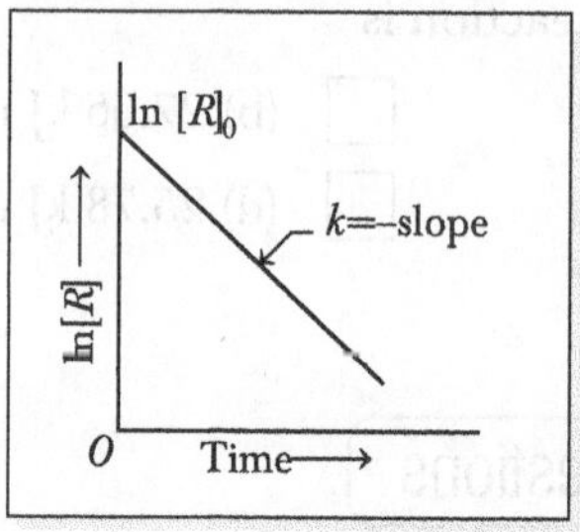

(a) ☐ (b) ☐ (c) ☐ (d) ☐

7. **Assertion** (A) The rate of a reaction sometimes does not depend on concentration.

Reason (R) Lower the activation energy, faster is the reaction.

(a) ☐ (b) ☐ (c) ☐ (d) ☐

8. **Assertion** (A) Rate constants determined from Arrhenius equation are fairly accurate for simple as well as complex molecules.

Reason (R) Reactant molecules undergo chemical change irrespective of their orientation during collision.

(a) ☐ (b) ☐ (c) ☐ (d) ☐

9. **Assertion** (A) The enthalpy of reaction remains constant in the presence of a catalyst.

Reason (R) A catalyst participating in the reaction, forms different activated complex and lowers down the activation energy but the difference in energy of reactant and product remains the same.

(a) ☐ (b) ☐ (c) ☐ (d) ☐

10. **Assertion** (A) All collision of reactant molecules lead to product formation.

Reason (R) Only those collisions in which molecules have correct orientation and sufficient kinetic energy lead to compound formation.

(a) ☐ (b) ☐ (c) ☐ (d) ☐

Case-Based Questions

1. For the reaction,

$$2NO(g) + Cl_2(g) \longrightarrow 2NOCl(g),$$

the following data were collected. All the measurements were taken at 263 K.

Experiment No.	Initial [NO] (M)	Initial $[Cl_2]$ (M)	Initial rate of disapp. of Cl_2 (M/min)
1.	0.15	0.15	0.60
2.	0.15	0.30	1.20
3.	0.30	0.15	2.40
4.	0.25	0.25	?

(i) The molecularity of the reaction is

(a) 1 ☐ (b) 2 ☐ (c) 3 ☐ (d) 4 ☐

(ii) The overall order of the reaction is

(a) 2 ☐ (b) 0 ☐ (c) 1 ☐ (d) 3 ☐

(iii) The value of rate constant is

(a) 150.32 M^{-2} min^{-1} ☐ (b) 200.08 M^{-1} min^{-1} ☐

(c) 177.77 M^{-2} min^{-1} ☐ (d) 155.75 M^{-1} min^{-1} ☐

(iv) The initial rate of disappearance of Cl_2 in experiment 4 is

(a) 1.75 M min^{-1} ☐ (b) 3.23 M min^{-1} ☐

(c) 2.25 M min^{-1} ☐ (d) 2.77 M min^{-1} ☐

2. A reaction is said to be the first order if the rate of the reaction depends upon one concentration term only. For a first order reaction of the type, $A \rightarrow$ Products, the rate of the reaction is given as : rate $= k[A]$. The differential rate law is given as $\frac{d[A]}{dt} = -k[A]$. The integrated rate law is : $\frac{\ln[A]}{[A]_0} = -kt$, where $[A]$ is the concentration of reactant left at time t and $[A]_0$ is the initial concentration of the reactant, k is the rate constant.

(i) The unit of rate constant for a first order reaction is

(a) s^{-1} ☐ (b) mol L^{-1} s^{-1} ☐ (c) L mol^{-1} s^{-1} ☐ (d) L^2 mol^{-2} s^{-1} ☐

(ii) Half-life period of a first order reaction is 10 min. Starting with initial concentration 12 M, the rate after 20 min is

(a) 0.693×3 M min^{-1} ☐ (b) 0.693×4 M min^{-1} ☐

(c) 0.0693 M min^{-1} ☐ (d) 0.0693×3 M min^{-1} ☐

(iii) 50% of a first order reaction is complete in 23 minutes. Calculate the time required to complete 90% of the reaction.

(a) 70.4 min ☐ (b) 76.4 min ☐ (c) 38.7 min ☐ (d) 35.2 min ☐

(iv) The half-life period of a 1st order reaction is 60 minutes. What percentage will be left over after 240 minutes?

(a) 6.25% ☐ (b) 4.25% ☐ (c) 5% ☐ (d) 6% ☐

COMPETITION EDGE UP

1. Given below are two statements:
[NCERT (New) Pg. 65, JEE Main 2024]

Statement I The rate law for the reaction $A + B \longrightarrow C$ is rate $(r) = k\,[A]^2\,[B]$. When the concentration of both A and B is doubled, the reaction rate is increased "x" times.

Statement II

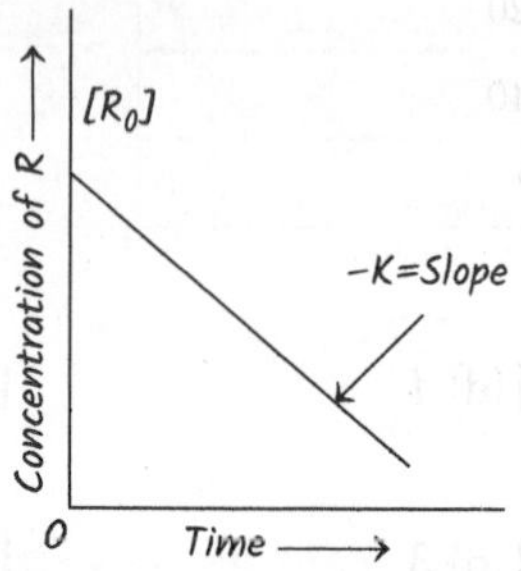

The figure is showing "the variation in concentration against time plot" for a "y" order reaction.

The value of $x + y$ is ....

2. NO_2 required for a reaction is produced by decomposition of N_2O_5 in CCl_4 as by equation,

$$2N_2O_5(g) \longrightarrow 4NO_2(g) + O_2(g)$$

The initial concentration of N_2O_5 is 3 mol L^{-1} and it is 2.75 mol L^{-1} after 30 minutes.

The rate of formation of NO_2 is $x \times 10^{-3}$ mol L^{-1} min^{-1}, value of x is ....
(Nearest integer)
[NCERT (New) Pg. 72, JEE Main 2024]

3. Integrated rate law equation for a first order gas phase reaction is given by (where p_i is initial pressure and p_t is total pressure at time t)
[NCERT (New) Pg. 75, JEE Main 2024]

(a) $k = \dfrac{2.303}{t} \times \dfrac{p_i}{(2p_i - p_t)}$ ☐

(b) $k = \dfrac{2.303}{t} \times \log \dfrac{p_i}{(2p_i - p_t)}$ ☐

(c) $k = \dfrac{2.303}{t} \times \log \dfrac{2p_i}{(2p_i - p_t)}$ ☐

(d) $k = \dfrac{2.303}{t} \times \log \dfrac{(2p_i - p_t)}{p_i}$ ☐

4. Time required for 99.9% completion of a first order reaction is .... times the time required for completion of 90% reaction. (Nearest integer)
[NCERT (New) Pg. 73, JEE Main 2024]

5. $r = k[A]$ for a reaction, 50% of A is decomposed in 120 minutes. The time taken for 90% decomposition of A is .... minutes. **[NCERT (New) Pg. 73, JEE Main 2024]**

6. The rate of first order reaction is 0.04 mol $L^{-1}s^{-1}$ at 10 minutes and 0.03 mol $L^{-1}s^{-1}$ at 20 minutes after initiation. Half-life of the reaction is .... minutes. (Given, $\log 2 = 0.3010$, $\log 3 = 0.4771$)
[NCERT (New) Pg. 76, JEE Main 2024]

7. For a certain reaction, the rate $= k\,[A]^2\,[B]$, when the initial concentration of A is tripled keeping concentration of B constant, the initial rate would **[NCERT (New) Pg. 65, JEE Main 2024]**

(a) increase by a factor of six ☐
(b) increase by a factor of nine ☐
(c) increase by a factor of three ☐
(d) decrease by a factor of nine ☐

8. Activation energy of any chemical reaction can be calculated if one knows the value of
[NCERT (New) Pg. 80, NEET 2024]

(a) rate constant at standard temperature ☐
(b) probability of collision ☐
(c) orientation of reactant molecules during collision ☐
(d) rate constant at two different temperatures ☐

9. Which plot of ln k vs 1 / T is consistent with Arrhenius equation?
[NCERT (New) Pg. 80, NEET 2024]

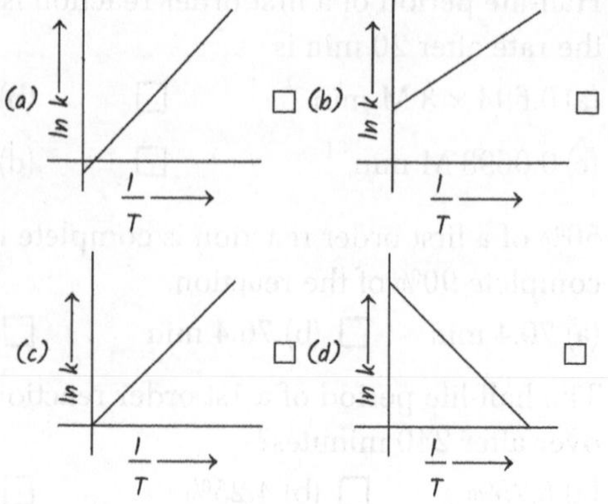

10. *The rate of a reaction quadruples when temperature changes from 27°C to 57°C. Calculate the energy of activation.*

[Given, R = 8.314 J $K^{-1} mol^{-1}$, log4 = 0.6021] **[NCERT (New) Pg. 81, NEET 2024]**

(a) 38.04 kJ/mol ☐ (b) 380.4 kJ/mol ☐
(c) 3.80 kJ/mol ☐ (d) 3804 kJ/mol ☐

11. *For a first order reaction A → products, initial concentration of A is 0.1 M, which becomes 0.001 M after 5 minutes. Rate constant for the reaction in min^{-1} is*
[NCERT (New) Pg. 73, NEET 2022]

(a) 0.9212 ☐ (b) 0.4606 ☐
(c) 0.2303 ☐ (d) 1.3818 ☐

12. *For a reaction, A → B, enthalpy of reaction is – 4.2 kJ mol^{-1} and enthalpy of activation is 9.6 kJ mol^{-1}. The correct potential energy profile for the reaction is shown in option.*
[NCERT (New) Pg. 79, NEET 2021]

(a)
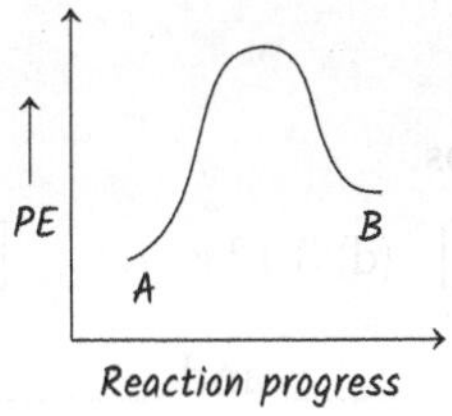

☐

(b)
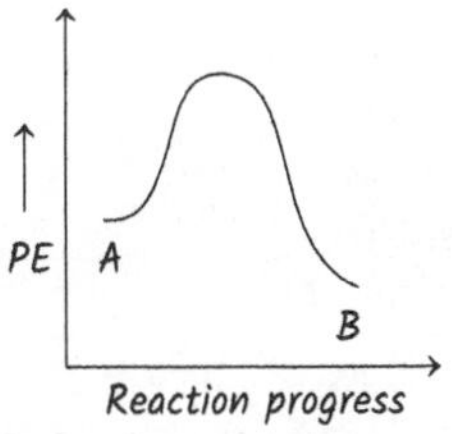

☐

(c)
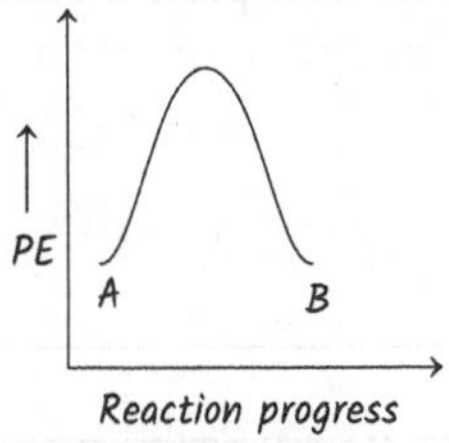

☐

(d)
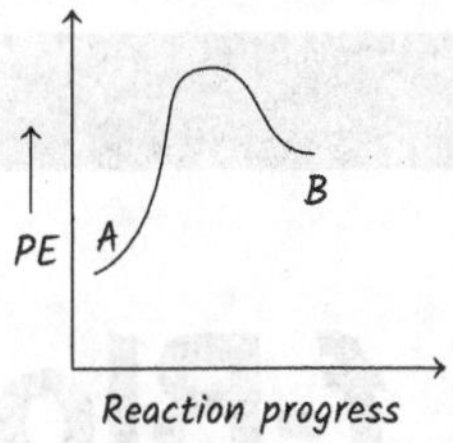

☐

13. *The slope of Arrhenius plot $\left(\ln k \text{ vs } \frac{1}{T}\right)$ of first order reaction is – 5×10^3 K. The value of E_a of the reaction is*
[Given, R = 8.314 $JK^{-1} mol^{-1}$]
[NCERT (New) Pg. 81, NEET 2021]

(a) 41.5 kJ mol^{-1} ☐
(b) 83.0 kJ mol^{-1} ☐
(c) 166 kJ mol^{-1} ☐
(d) – 83 kJ mol^{-1} ☐

14. *An increase in the concentration of the reactants of a reaction leads to change in*
[NCERT (New) Pg. 82, 83, NEET 2020]

(a) heat of reaction ☐
(b) threshold energy ☐
(c) collision frequency ☐
(d) activation energy ☐

15. *The rate constant for a first order reaction is 4.606×10^{-3} s^{-1}. The time required to reduce 2.0 g of the reactant to 0.2 g is*
[NCERT (New) Pg. 73, NEET (Sep.) 2020]

(a) 200 s ☐ (b) 500 s ☐
(c) 1000 s ☐ (d) 100 s ☐

16. *The half-life for a zero order reaction having 0.02 M initial concentration of reactant is 100 s. The rate constant (in mol L^{-1} s^{-1}) for the reaction is*
[NCERT (New) Pg. 76, NEET (Oct.) 2020]

(a) 1.0×10^{-4} ☐
(b) 2.0×10^{-4} ☐
(c) 2.0×10^{-3} ☐
(d) 1.0×10^{-2} ☐

Chapter 04

d- and *f*-Block Elements

Scan and take Chapter Test

TOPIC 1

Introduction, Position and Electronic Configurations of *d*-Block Elements in the Periodic Table

NCERT Pg 89-91

1. The *d*-block of the periodic table contains the elements of the groups

(a) 4-12 ☐ (b) 4-13 ☐ (c) 3-12 ☐ (d) 3-13 ☐

2. The elements present in $4f$ and $5f$-series are known as ____________ and ____________ respectively.

3. State whether True or False.

(i) Zinc, cadmium and mercury are not regarded as transition metals.

True ☐ False ☐

(ii) According to IUPAC, transition metals are those metals which have complete *d*-subshell.

True ☐ False ☐

4. Give the name of transition metals

(i) which are used in making jewellery. ____________

(ii) which are industrially important. ____________

***5.** The electronic configuration of Cu(II) is $3d^9$, whereas that of Cu(I) is $3d^{10}$. Which of the following statement is correct?

(a) Cu(II) is more stable. ☐ (b) Cu(I) is more stable. ☐

(c) Stability of Cu(II) and Cu(I) are same. ☐ (d) None of these ☐

6. In case of chromium, electron jumps from ____________ ($4s$ to $3d$/ $3d$ to $4s$) to attain half-filled set and the energy gap between $3d$ and $4s$ orbitals is ____________ (large/small).

Concepts of all questions bearing * are important for JEE/NEET/CUET.

***7.** Generalised electronic configuration of Zn, Cd and Hg is represented by

(i) $(n-1)d^{1-10}\ ns^{1-2}$ ☐ (ii) $(n-1)d^{10}\ ns^{2}$ ☐

8. Enlist any four characteristics exhibited by transition elements due to their partially filled *d*-orbitals.

(i) ____________ (ii) ____________

(iii) ____________ (iv) ____________

9. Amongst the following, the total number of species not having 7 electrons in outermost *d*-orbital.

Cu, Ru, Rh, Ir, Pt

(a) 1 ☐ (b) 2 ☐ (c) 3 ☐ (d) 5 ☐

10. Write electronic configuration of silver in

(i) Ground state ____________

(ii) +2 oxidation state ____________

TOPIC 2

General Properties of the Transition Elements (*d*-Block)

NCERT Pg 92-104

11. Select the physical properties exhibited by transition elements from the following.

Malleability, Low tensile strength, Insulators, High thermal conductivity, Lustre.

____

12. Categorise the transition elements (Cr, Ni, Cu, Zn, Tc, Mo) under different lattice structures.

ccp, bcc, hcp

____

13. On the basis of the given figure, answer the following questions.

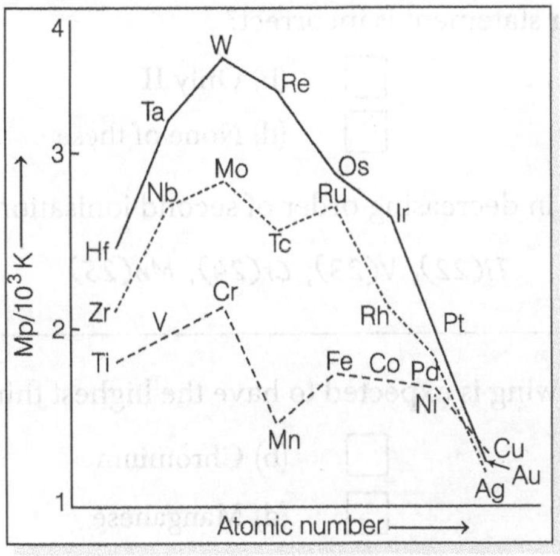

(i) Why manganese has lower melting point than chromium?

____

(ii) Why do transition metals of 3*d*-series have lower melting point as compared to 4*d*-series?

____

(iii) In the third transition series, identify and name the metal with the highest melting point.

____

14. Select the incorrect pair from the following about transition elements.

(a) Melting and boiling point – High ☐
(b) Enthalpy of atomisation – High ☐
(c) Volatility – High ☐
(d) Interatomic interaction – Strong ☐

15. The transition element having least enthalpy of atomisation is

(a) Zn ☐ (b) V ☐ (c) Fe ☐ (d) Cu ☐

16. Transition elements exhibit higher enthalpies of atomisation because of

(a) large number of paired electrons ☐
(b) large number of unpaired electrons ☐
(c) high melting point ☐
(d) None of the above ☐

17. Which of the following elements have positive electrode potential (M^{2+}/M) ?

(a) Fe ☐ (b) Cu ☐ (c) Co ☐ (d) Ni ☐

18. Name the phenomenon which is responsible for almost similar size of Zr and Hf.

____

19. Consider the following statements.

I. First ionisation enthalpy (IE_1) of Cr is less than that of Zn.

II. Second ionisation enthalpy (IE_2) of Zn is lower than that of Cr.

Which of the following statement is incorrect?

(a) Only I ☐ (b) Only II ☐
(c) Both I and II ☐ (d) None of these ☐

***20.** Arrange the following in decreasing order of second ionisation enthalpy.

Ti(22), V(23), Cr(24), Mn(25)

____

***21.** Which one of the following is expected to have the highest third ionisation enthalpy?

(a) Vanadium ☐ (b) Chromium ☐
(c) Iron ☐ (d) Manganese ☐

22. Which of the following factor is not responsible for different ionisation enthalpy values of transition elements?

(a) Force of attraction between electron and nucleus ☐

(b) Force of repulsion between electrons ☐

(c) Exchange energies ☐

(d) None of the above ☐

23. Tick the correct one.

Which one of the following has highest ionisation enthalpy ?

(a) (i) I.E. of Mn^{2+} ☐ (ii) I.E. of Cr^{+} ☐

(b) (i) I.E. of Co^{2+} ☐ (ii) I.E. of Fe^{2+} ☐

***24.** Name an element from first series of transition element which exhibit all oxidation states from + 2 to + 7.

____

25. Electronic configuration of transition element X in + 3 oxidation state is $[Ar]3d^5$. What is its atomic number?

(a) 25 ☐ (b) 26 ☐ (c) 27 ☐ (d) 24 ☐

____

26. Cr(VI) in the form of dichromate in acidic medium is a strong oxidising agent, whereas Mo(VI) in MoO_3 and W(VI) in WO_3 are not because

I. Cr(VI) is more stable than Mo (VI) and W(VI).

II. Mo(VI) and W(VI) are more stable than Cr(VI).

III. Higher oxidation states of heavier members of group 6 of transition series are more stable.

IV. Lower oxidation states of heavier members of group 6 of transition series are more stable.

Mark (✓) and (×) under correct and incorrect with respect to given reason.

	Correct	Incorrect
I.	______	______
II.	______	______
III.	______	______
IV.	______	______

27. In *p*-block and *d*-block elements, the lower oxidation states are favoured by heavier members.

True ☐ False ☐

***28.** Which of the following transition elements does not exhibit variable oxidation state?

(a) Mn ☐ (b) Fe ☐ (c) Sc ☐ (d) V ☐

29. The incorrect statement(s) about Cr^{2+} and Mn^{3+} is/are

(a) Cr^{2+} is a reducing agent. ☐

(b) Mn^{3+} is an oxidising agent. ☐

(c) both Cr^{2+} and Mn^{3+} exhibit d^4 electronic configuration. ☐

(d) when Cr^{2+} is used as reducing agent, the chromium ion attains d^5 electronic configuration. ☐

***30.** Choose the correct option regarding copper.

(i) E°_{value} (Negative/Positive) ______________________.

(ii) Hydration energy (Low/High) ______________________.

(iii) Atomisation energy (High/Low) ______________________.

31. Write formula of halide when the following metals exhibit highest oxidation number.

(i) Ti ______________ (ii) V ______________ (iii) Cr ______________

32. Which of the following element can form MF_3 type compound?

(a) Co ☐ (b) Cu ☐ (c) Ni ☐ (d) Zn ☐

***33.** Complete the following statements related to first row transition elements.

(i) The value of $E^{\circ}_{M^{2+}/M}$ is positive for __________ (Cu/Zn).

(ii) The highest negative $\Delta_{\text{hyd}} H^{\circ}$ value is shown by __________ (Mn/Ni).

34. Highest oxidation state of manganese in fluorides is + 4 (MnF_4) but its highest oxidation state in oxides is + 7 (Mn_2O_7) because

(a) fluorine is more electronegative than oxygen. ☐

(b) fluorine does not possess *d*-orbitals. ☐

(c) fluorine stabilises lower oxidation states. ☐

(d) in covalent compounds, fluorine can form single bond only while oxygen forms double bond. ☐

35. Arrange the following transition metal oxides in increasing oxidising power.

MnO_4^-, $Cr_2O_7^{2-}$, VO_2^+

____

***36.** Match the statements given in Column I with the oxidation states given in Column II.

Column I	Column II
A. Oxidation state of Mn in MnO_2	1. + 6
B. Most stable oxidation state of Mn.	2. + 4
C. Oxidation state of Cr in CrO_4^{2-}.	3. + 2

A. ______________ B. ______________ C. ______________

***37.** For the first row transition metals, the E°_{values} are

E°	V	Cr	Mn	Fe	Co	Ni	Cu
(M^{2+}/M)	− 1.18	− 0.91	− 1.18	− 0.44	− 0.28	− 0.25	+ 0.34

The irregularity in the E°_{values} is due to

(a) irregular variation of ionisation enthalpies ☐

(b) irregularity in sublimation enthalpies. ☐

(c) Both (a) and (b) ☐

(d) None of the above ☐

38. Match the Column I with Column II.

Column I (Substance)	Column II (Magnetic behaviour)
A. Paramagnetic	1. Attracted very strongly by magnetic applied field.
B. Diamagnetic	2. Weakly attracted by magnetic applied field.
C. Ferromagnetic	3. Repelled by magnetic applied field.

A. ____________ B.____________ C.____________

39. Out of Cr^{2+} and Fe^{2+}, ____________ is a better reducing agent with E°_{values} is equal to ____________.

40. Write two types of momentum which are associated with magnetic moment of unpaired electron.

(i) ____________ (ii) ____________

41. Complete the following regarding magnetic moment.

(i) It is determined by the number of ____________ and is calculated by using the ____________ formula.

(ii) Magnetic moment (μ) = ____________ .

***42.** Rank the following transition metal ions in increasing order of their magnetic moment.

Ti^{3+}, Mn^{2+}, Ti^{2+}, Sc^{3+}, Fe^{2+}, Co^{3+}

____

***43.** Spin only magnetic moment of $M^{2+}(aq)$ ion $(Z = 27)$ is

(a) 2.84 ☐ (b) 3.87 ☐ (c) 1.73 ☐ (d) 4.90 ☐

***44.** Select any two metallic ions which have almost same spin magnetic moment.

Co^{2+}, Mn^{2+}, Cr^{2+}, Cr^{3+}

____

***45.** Amongst the following, the total number of species having magnetic moment 3.87.

Ti^{3+}, V^{2+}, Co^{2+}, Cu^{2+}, Zn^{2+}

(a) 2 ☐ (b) 3 ☐ (c) 4 ☐ (d) 5 ☐

46. The frequency of light absorbed by transition metal ion is determined by the nature of ligand.

True ☐ False ☐

47. Fill the appropriate words in the following table containing transition metal ions and their colour in aqueous solution.

Metal ion	Colour
Sc^{3+}	(i) ________
(ii) ________	Yellow
(iii) ________	Purple
Cu^{2+}	(iv) ________
Mn^{2+}	(v) ________

48. Formula of two complex compounds formed by Fe are ____________ and ____________.

49. Which condition is not applicable for the complex formation by transition elements?

(a) Smaller size of transition metal ion. ☐

(b) Absence of vacant *d*-orbitals. ☐

(c) Availability of vacant *d*-orbitals. ☐

(d) High ionic charge density on metal ion. ☐

50. Which one of the following ions exhibits *d-d* transition and paramagnetism as well ?

(a) MnO_4^- ☐ (b) $Cr_2O_7^{2-}$ ☐

(c) CrO_4^{2-} ☐ (d) MnO_4^{2-} ☐

51. Consider the following as the reason for the catalytic properties of transition elements.

I. Variable oxidation states.

II. Vacant *d*-orbital

III. They combine with reactant molecules to form transition states and lower their activation energy.

IV. Due to inert pair effect.

Mark (✓) and (✗) under correct and incorrect with respect to given properties.

	Correct	Incorrect
I.	________	________
II.	________	________
III.	________	________
IV.	________	________

52. Match the catalysts given in Column I with the processes given in Column II.

Column I (Catalyst)	Column II (Process)
A. Nickel	1. Haber's process
B. V_2O_5	2. Hydrogenation of vegetable oil
C. Finely divided iron	3. Contact process

A. ____________ B. ____________ C. ____________

53. Interstitial compounds are formed when small atoms are trapped inside the crystal lattice of metals. Which of the following is not the characteristic property of interstitial compounds?

(a) They have high melting points in comparison to pure metals. ☐

(b) They are very hard. ☐

(c) They retain metallic conductivity. ☐

(d) They are chemically very reactive. ☐

54. Mention any two examples of non-stoichiometric interstitial compounds of transition elements.

(i) ____________ (ii) ____________

55. An alloy is ____________ (homogeneous/heterogeneous) solid solution. They are ____________ (soft/hard) and have high ____________ (melting point/boiling point).

56. Select the incorrect pair for alloys and their substituents.

(a) Bronze – Copper and Tin ☐ (b) Steel – C, Cr, Ni and Mo ☐

(c) Brass – Zinc and Tin ☐ (d) All are correct pair ☐

57. Which of the following transition elements is not used for production of variety of steels?

(a) Vanadium ☐ (b) Chromium ☐ (c) Manganese ☐ (d) Aluminium ☐

***58.** In the following reaction,

$$3\overset{x}{Mn}O_4^{2-} + 4H^+ \longrightarrow 2\overset{y}{Mn}O_4^- + \overset{z}{Mn}O_2 + 2H_2O$$

Write down the oxidation states of Mn represented as x, y and z.

$x =$ ____________ $y =$ ____________ $z =$ ____________

TOPIC 3

Some Important Compounds of Transition Elements

NCERT Pg 105-108

59. As the oxidation number of transition metal in oxides increases, ionic character also increases.

True ☐ False ☐

60. Extract amphoteric oxides from the following oxides.

Mn_2O_7, V_2O_5, CrO_3, CrO, Cr_2O_3, V_2O_4

____

***61.** Which of the following will not act as oxidising agent?

(a) CrO_3 ☐ (b) MoO_3 ☐ (c) CrO_4^{2-} ☐ (d) None of these ☐

62. When a chromite ore _A_ is fused with sodium carbonate in free excess of air and the product is dissolved in water, a yellow solution of compound _B_ is obtained. After treatment of _B_ with H_2SO_4, compound _C_ can be crystallised from solution. Identify *A*, *B* and *C*.

A = _______________ *B* = _______________ *C* = _______________

63. Write the products of the following the reaction,

$Na_2Cr_2O_7 + 2KCl \longrightarrow$ _______________ + _______________

64. Out of $K_2Cr_2O_7$ and $Na_2Cr_2O_7$, which one is

(i) used as an oxidising agent in organic chemistry? _______________

(ii) used as primary standard in volumetric analysis? _______________

65. When acidified $K_2Cr_2O_7$ solution is added to Sn^{2+} salts, then Sn^{2+} changes to

(a) Sn ☐ (b) Sn^{3+} ☐ (c) Sn^{4+} ☐ (d) Sn^{+} ☐

66. Acidified $K_2Cr_2O_7$ oxidises Fe(III) salts to Fe(II) salts.

True ☐ False ☐

67. Consider the following structure and answer the following.

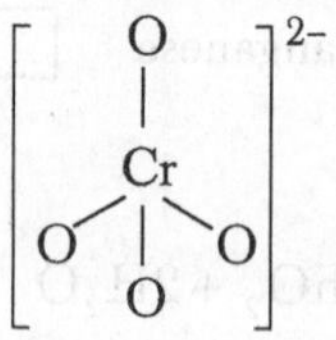

A

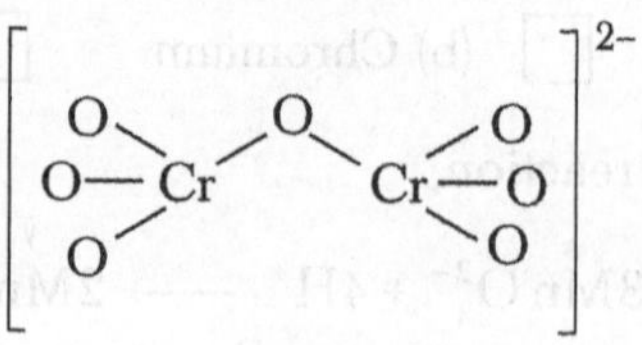

B

(i) Shape of *A* ion is _______________.

(ii) Bond anlge between Cr—O—Cr in *B* is _______________.

68. Consider the following compounds/species.

(i) $CuSO_4$ (ii) H_2O_2 (iii) Cl_2 (iv) O_3

(v) $FeCl_3$ (vi) HNO_3 (vii) $Na_2S_2O_3$

The number of compounds/species that can oxidise aqueous iodide to iodine is

(a) 2 ☐ (b) 5 ☐ (c) 6 ☐ (d) 7 ☐

69. An oxide of manganese X is fused with KOH in presence of an oxidising agent and dissolved in water, it gives a dark green solution of compound Y.

Then, $Y \xrightarrow[\text{Neutral/Acidic}]{\text{Disproportionate}} Z$ (Purple compound)

Identify X, Y and Z.

X = ________ Y = ________ Z = ________

70. Amongst the following, the total number of species oxidised by acidified potassium dichromate.

I^-, Sn^{2+}, Fe^{2+}, H_2S, Cu^{2+}

(a) 1 (b) 2 (c) 3 (d) 4

71. Consider the following statements.

I. Manganate and permanganate ions are tetrahedral.

II. Green manganate ion is diamagnetic, while purple permanganate ion is paramagnetic.

Here, correct statement(s) is/are

(a) Only I (b) Only II (c) Both I and II (d) None of these

72. $KMnO_4$ acts as an oxidising agent in acidic as well as in alkaline medium. Write products formed when

(i) alkaline $KMnO_4$ is treated with KI. ________

(ii) acidified $KMnO_4$ is treated with KI. ________

73. Which of the following reaction is disproportionation reaction?

(a) $3MnO_4^{2-} + 4H^+ \longrightarrow 2MnO_4^- + MnO_2 + 2H_2O$

(b) $2KMnO_4 \longrightarrow K_2MnO_4 + MnO_2 + O_2$

(c) $2MnO_4^- + 3Mn^{2+} + 2H_2O \longrightarrow 5MnO_2 + 4H^+$

(d) $Fe^{2+} + MnO_4^- + 8H^+ \longrightarrow Mn^{2+} + 4H_2O + 5Fe^{3+}$

74. Write a compound which is isostructural to $KMnO_4$.

____

75. How many moles of $KMnO_4$ are required to oxidise 5 moles of oxalic acid ?

(a) 3 (b) 10

(c) 5 (d) 2

76. Complete the following reactions.

(i) $5NO_2^- + 2MnO_4^- + 6H^+ \longrightarrow$ ________ + ________ + $3H_2O$

(ii) $8MnO_4^- + 3S_2O_3^{2-} + H_2O \longrightarrow$ ________ + ________ + $2OH^-$

77. The catalyst used to oxidise manganous salt to MnO_2 is $CuSO_4$.

True ☐ False ☐

78. HCl is not used in oxidation reactions of $KMnO_4$ in acidic medium because

(a) both HCl and $KMnO_4$ act as oxidising agents. ☐

(b) $KMnO_4$ oxidises HCl into Cl_2 as well. ☐

(c) $KMnO_4$ is a weaker oxidising agent than HCl. ☐

(d) $KMnO_4$ acts as reducing agent in the presence of HCl. ☐

79. The compound which is used for decolourisation of oil is ________ ($KMnO_4$/ $K_2Cr_2O_7$).

TOPIC 4

The Lanthanoids

NCERT Pg 108-111

80. Which lanthanoid does not occur naturally?

(a) Lanthanum ☐ (b) Plutonium ☐

(c) Cerium ☐ (d) Promethium ☐

81. The chemistry of actinoids is much more complicated due to

(i)________________ (ii)________________

82. The reason of lanthanoid contraction is

(a) increasing nuclear charge ☐

(b) decreasing nuclear charge ☐

(c) negligible screening effect of f-orbitals ☐

(d) decreasing screening effect ☐

83. Consider the following statements.

I. Common oxidation state for all lanthanoids is + 3.

II. Yb shows + 3 oxidation state which has f^{14} configuration.

The incorrect statement(s) is/are

(a) Only I ☐ (b) Only II ☐

(c) Both I and II are incorrect. ☐ (d) Both I and II are correct. ☐

***84.** The electronic configuration of bivalent europium and trivalent cerium are

(Atomic number of Xe = 54, Ce = 58 and Eu = 63)

(a) $[Xe]4f^7$ and $[Xe]4f^1$ ☐ (b) $[Xe]4f^7 6s^2$ and $[Xe]4f^2 6s^2$ ☐

(c) $[Xe]4f^2$ and $[Xe]4f^7$ ☐ (b) $[Xe]4f^4$ and $[Xe]4f^9$ ☐

85. State whether True or False.

(i) The formation of Ce(IV) is favoured by its noble gas configuration.

True ☐ False ☐

(ii) E°_{value} of Ce^{4+}/Ce^{3+} is + 1.74 V which suggest that it can reduce water.

True ☐ False ☐

86. Consider the following statement(s) regarding lanthanoids.

I. Ce(IV) is a good analytical reagent.

II. Eu^{2+} is a strong reducing agent.

III. Tb(IV) is a strong reducing agent.

Mark (✓) and (×) under correct and incorrect with respect to given statement.

	Correct	Incorrect
I.	______	______
II.	______	______
III.	______	______

87. Match the property given in Column I with the elements given in Column II.

Column I (Property)	Column II (Element)
A. Lanthanoid which shows + 4 oxidation state	1. Pm
B. Lanthanoid which can show + 2 oxidation state	2. Ce
C. Radioactive lanthanoid	3. Gd
D. Lanthanoid which has $4f^7$ electronic configuration in + 3 oxidation state.	4. Eu

A. ______ B. ______

C. ______ D. ______

***88.** Choose from the follownig pairs of lanthanoid ion

(a) La^{3+} and Ce^{4+} (b) La^{3+} and Lu^{3+} (c) Yb^{2+} and Lu^{4+} (d) Tm^{2+} and Eu^{3+}

which is/are

(i) Colourless ______ (ii) Paramagnetic ______

89. The first ionisation enthalpies of the lanthanoids are around ______ kJ mol^{-1} and second about ______ kJ mol^{-1}.

90. Fill the missing products in the given reaction.

(i) $Ln + X_2 \longrightarrow$ ______ (ii) $Ln + H_2O \longrightarrow$ ______ + ______ (iii) $Ln + O_2 \longrightarrow$ ______

91. The product obtained on heating lanthanoids (Ln) with nitrogen is

(a) LnN ☐ (b) LnN_3 ☐ (c) Ln_3N_2 ☐ (d) Ln_2N_3 ☐

92. Choose the correct word given in the brackets for the following statements.

(i) Mixed oxides of lanthanoids are employed in (Television screen/Petroleum cracking).

(ii) Magnesium based alloy are used in (Bullets/X-ray screen).

(iii) Lanthanoid oxides are used in (Lighter flint/Television screen).

____

93. Misch metal consists of a lanthanoid metal and iron with traces of S, C, Ca and Al.

True ☐ False ☐

TOPIC 5

The Actinoids

NCERT Pg 111-113

***94.** There are 15 elements in actinoid series. Which of the following does not belong to this series?

(a) U ☐ (b) Np ☐

(c) Tm ☐ (d) Fm ☐

95. General electronic configuration of actinoids is ______________________________.

96. Actinoid contraction is greater from element to element than lanthanoid contraction because

(a) 4f-orbitals have more poorer shielding effect than 5f-orbitals. ☐

(b) 5f-orbitals have more poorer shielding effect than 4f-orbitals. ☐

(c) shielding effect of 4f and 5f-orbital are same. ☐

(d) None of the above ☐

97. The main reason for more number of oxidation state of actinoids than the corresponding lanthanoids is

(a) more energy difference between 5f and 6d-orbitals than 4f and 5d-orbitals. ☐

(b) less energy difference between 5f and 6d-orbitals than 4f and 5d-orbitals. ☐

(c) large atomic size of actinoids. ☐

(d) more reactive nature of actinoids than lanthanoids. ☐

98. Which of the following actinoids have one electron in 6d-orbital?

Pu, Am, U, Pa, No, Np

____

99. Mention two actinoids which can show oxidation states upto + 7.

(i) ______________ (ii) ______________

100. State whether True or False.

(i) Paramagnetic nature of actinoids is due to unpaired electrons in $(n-2)f$- orbital.

True ☐ False ☐

(ii) The actinoids are highly reactive metals, especially when finally divided.

True ☐ False ☐

101. The actinoides that shows +7 oxidation states is

(a) U, Np ☐ (b) Pu, Am ☐

(c) Np, Pu ☐ (d) Am, Cm ☐

102.

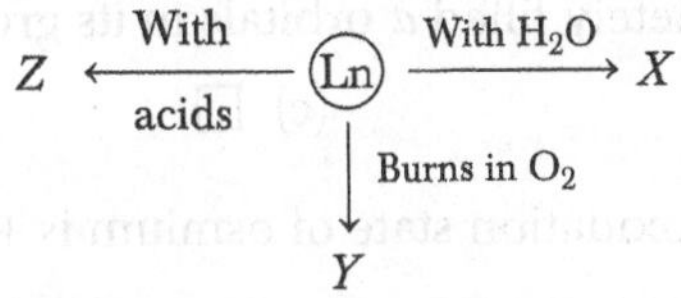

The *X*, *Y* and *Z* respectively are

(a) $Ln_2O_3, H_2, Ln(OH)_3 + 3H_2$ ☐ (b) $LnO_3 + H_2, Ln_2O_3, H_2$ ☐

(c) $H_2, Ln_2O_3, Ln(OH)_3 + H_2$ ☐ (d) $Ln(OH)_3 + H_2, Ln_2O_3, H_2$ ☐

TOPIC 6

Some Applications of *d*- and *f*-Block Elements

NCERT Pg 113-114

103. Match the compounds given in Column I with uses given in Column II.

Column I (Compound)		Column II (Use)	
A.	MnO_2	1.	Catalyse ethyne to ethanol
B.	$TiCl_4$	2.	Photography industry
C.	$PdCl_2$	3.	Zieglar-Natta catalyst
D.	AgBr	4.	Dry battery cell

A. ____________ B. ____________

C. ____________ D. ____________

104. State whether True or False.

(a) The photographic industry rely on the special light sensitive properties of AgBr.

True ☐ False ☐

(b) The term 'silver' UK coins are a Ag/Ni alloy.

True ☐ False ☐

Assertion-Reason Questions

Given below are two statements, one is labelled as Assertion (A) and other is labelled as Reason (R). Select the most appropriate answer from the options given below.

(a) Both A and R are true and R is the correct explanation of A.
(b) Both A and R are true but R is not the correct explanation of A.
(c) A is true but R is false.
(d) A is false but R is true.

1. **Assertion** (A) Scandium is a transition element but zinc is not.
Reason (R) Zinc has completely filled *d*-orbitals in its ground state.
(a) ☐ (b) ☐ (c) ☐ (d) ☐

2. **Assertion** (A) The highest oxidation state of osmium is + 8.
Reason (R) Osmium is a 5*d*-block element.
(a) ☐ (b) ☐ (c) ☐ (d) ☐

3. **Assertion** (A) Fluorine has the ability to stabilise the highest oxidation state.
Reason (R) High lattice energy or high bond enthalpy in terms of higher covalent compounds are responsible for stable fluorides of higher oxidation state.
(a) ☐ (b) ☐ (c) ☐ (d) ☐

4. **Assertion** (A) Mn and Zn have more negative E°_{value} than expected from general trend.
Reason (R) Stability of half-filled *d*-subshell in Mn^{2+} and completely filled *d*-subshell in zinc are related to their E°_{values}.
(a) ☐ (b) ☐ (c) ☐ (d) ☐

5. **Assertion** (A) Iron (III) catalyses the reaction between iodide and persulphate ions.
Reason (R) Transition metals act as catalyst.
(a) ☐ (b) ☐ (c) ☐ (d) ☐

6. **Assertion** (A) Solution of Na_2CrO_4 in water is intensely coloured.
Reason (R) Oxidation state of Cr in Na_2CrO_4 is + 6.
(a) ☐ (b) ☐ (c) ☐ (d) ☐

7. **Assertion** (A) MnO is basic whereas Mn_2O_7 is acidic.
Reason (R) Higher the oxidation state of a transition metal in its oxide, greater is the acidic character.
(a) ☐ (b) ☐ (c) ☐ (d) ☐

8. **Assertion** (A) In the reaction between potassium permanganate and potassium iodide, permanganate ions acts as oxidising agent.
Reason (R) Oxidation state of manganese changes from + 2 to + 7 during reaction.
(a) ☐ (b) ☐ (c) ☐ (d) ☐

9. **Assertion** (A) Zirconium (Zr) and Hafnium (Hf) have almost same radius.

Reason (R) The radii of members of third transition series are similar to members of second series due to lanthanoid contraction.

(a) ☐ (b) ☐ (c) ☐ (d) ☐

10. **Assertion** (A) Actinoids form relatively less stable complexes as compared to lanthanoids.

Reason (R) Actinoids can utilise their $5f$ orbitals along with $6d$-orbitals in bonding but lanthanoids do not use their $4f$-orbital for bonding.

(a) ☐ (b) ☐ (c) ☐ (d) ☐

Case-Based Questions

1. The unique behaviour of Cu having a positive $E°$ value accounts for its inability to liberate H_2 from acids. Only oxidising acids (nitric and hot conc. sulphuric acid) react with Cu, the acids being reduced. The stability of the half-filled subshell in Mn^{2+} and the completely filled configuration in Zn^{2+} are related to their $E^{\circ}_{(M^{3+}/M^{2+})}$ values. The low value for Sc reflects the stability of Sc^{3+} which has a noble gas configuration. The comparatively high value for Mn shows that $Mn^{2+}(d^5)$ is particularly stable, whereas a comparatively low value for Fe shows the extra stability of $Fe^{3+}(d^5)$. The comparatively low value for V is related to the stability of V^{2+} (half-filled t_{2g} level).

(i) Standard reduction electrode potential of Zn^{2+}/Zn is – 0.76 V. This means

(a) ZnO cannot be reduced to Zn by H_2 under standard conditions. ☐
(b) Zn cannot liberate H_2 with concentrated acids. ☐
(c) Zn generally the anode in an electrochemical cell. ☐
(d) Zn generally the cathode in an electrochemical cell. ☐

(ii) $E°$ values for the couples Cr^{3+}/Cr^{2+} and Mn^{3+}/Mn^{2+} are –0.41 and +1.51 volt respectively. These values suggest that

(a) Cr^{2+} acts as a reducing agent whereas Mn^{3+} ☐
(b) Cr^{2+} is more stable than Cr^{3+} state ☐
(c) Mn^{2+} is more stable than Mn^{2+} ☐
(d) Cr^{2+} acts as an oxidising agent whereas Mn^{3+} acts as a reducing agent ☐

(iii) The reduction potential values of *M*, *N* and *O* are + 2.46, – 1.13 and – 3.13 V, respectively. Which of the following order is correct regarding their reducing property?

(a) $O > N > M$ ☐ (b) $O > M > N$ ☐
(c) $M > N > O$ ☐ (d) $M > O > N$ ☐

(iv) The stability of $Cu^{2+}(aq)$ rather than $Cu^{+}(aq)$ is due to

(a) more negative $\Delta_{hyd}H°$ of $Cu^{2+}(aq)$ ☐
(b) less negative $\Delta_{hyd}H°$ of $Cu^{2+}(aq)$ ☐
(c) more positive $\Delta_{hyd}H°$ of $Cu^{2+}(aq)$ ☐
(d) less positive $\Delta_{hyd}H°$ of $Cu^{2+}(aq)$ ☐

2. The f-block elements are those in which the differentiating electron enters the $(n-2)f$ orbital. There are two series of f-block elements corresponding to filling of $4f$ and $5f$-orbitals. The series of $4f$-orbitals is called lanthanoides. Lanthanoides show different oxidation states depending upon stability of f^0, f^7 and f^{14} configuration, through the most common oxidation states is +3. There is a regular decrease in size of lanthanoides ions with increase in atomic number which is known as lanthanide contraction.

*(i) The atomic numbers of three lanthanoide elements X, Y and Z are 65, 68 and 70, respectively, their Ln^{3+} electronic configuration is

(a) $4f^8, 4f^{11}, 4f^{13}$ ☐ (b) $4f^{11}, 4f^8, 4f^{13}$ ☐
(c) $4f^0, 4f^2, 4f^{11}$ ☐ (d) $4f^3, 4f^7, 4f^9$ ☐

(ii) Lanthanoide contraction is observed in

(a) Gd ☐ (b) At ☐ (c) Xe ☐ (d) Te ☐

*(iii) Which of the following is not the configuration of lanthanoid?

(a) [Xe] $4f^{10} 6s^2$ ☐ (b) Xe] $4f^1 5d^1 6s^2$ ☐
(c) [Xe] $4d^{14} 5^{10} 6s^2$ ☐ (d) [Xe] $4f^7 5d^1 6s^2$ ☐

(iv) Name a member of the lanthanoid series which is well known to exhibit +4 oxidation state.

(a) Cerium (Z = 58) ☐ (b) Europium (Z = 63) ☐
(c) Lanthanum (Z = 57) ☐ (d) Gadolinium (Z = 64) ☐

COMPETITION EDGE UP

1. *The metal that shows highest and maximum number of oxidation state is* **[NCERT (New) Pg. 96, JEE Main 2024]**

(a) Ti ☐ (b) Fe ☐
(c) Co ☐ (d) Mn ☐

2. *The electronic configuration of einsteinium is (Given atomic number of einsteinium = 99)* **[NCERT (New) Pg. 96, JEE Main 2024]**

(a) $[Rn]5f^{12}6d^0 7s^2$ ☐
(b) $[Rn]5f^{11}6d^0 7s^2$ ☐
(c) $[Rn]5f^{13}6d^0 7s^2$ ☐
(d) $[Rn]5f^{10}6d^0 7s^2$ ☐

3. *The number of element from the following that do not belong to lanthanoids is* **[NCERT (New) Pg. 110, JEE Main 2024]**

Eu, Cm, Dr, Tb, Yb and Lu

(a) 5 ☐ (b) 4 ☐ (c) 3 ☐ (d) 1 ☐

4. *The electronic configuration for neodymium is [Atomic number of neodymium 60]* **[NCERT (New) Pg. 110, JEE Main 2024]**

(a) $[Xe]5f^7 7s^2$ ☐ (b) $[Xe]4f^4 6s^2$ ☐
(c) $[Xe]4f^1 6s^1 6s^2$ ☐ (d) $[Xe]4f^6 6s^2$ ☐

5. *'Spin only' magnetic moment is same for which of the following ions?* **[NCERT (New) Pg. 102, NEET 2024]**

A. Ti^{3+} B. Cr^{2+} C. Mn^{2+}
D. Fe^{2+} E. Sc^{3+}

Choose the most appropriate answer from the options given below.

(a) B and D only ☐ (b) A and E only ☐
(c) B and C only ☐ (d) A and D only ☐

6. *The E° value for the Mn^{3+}/Mn^{2+} couple is more positive than that of Cr^{3+}/Cr^{2+} or Fe^{3+}/Fe^{2+} due to change of* **[NCERT (New) Pg. 101, NEET 2024]**

(a) d^5 to d^4 configuration ☐
(b) d^5 to d^2 configuration ☐
(c) d^4 to d^5 configuration ☐
(d) d^3 to d^5 configuration ☐

7. *The pair of lanthanoid ions which are diamagnetic is* **[NCERT (New) Pg. 110, NEET 2024]**

(a) Ce^{4+} and Yb^{2+} ☐
(b) Ce^{3+} and Eu^{2+} ☐
(c) Gd^{3+} and Eu^{3+} ☐
(d) Pm^{3+} and Sm^{3+} ☐

8. The stability of Cu^{2+} is more than Cu^{+} salts in aqueous solution due to **[NCERT (New) Pg. 100, NEET 2023]**

(a) enthalpy of atomisation ☐
(b) hydration energy ☐
(c) second ionisation enthalpy ☐
(d) first ionisation enthalpy ☐

9. The electronic configuration of Pt (atomic number=78) is **[NCERT (New) Pg. 91 NEET 2022]**

(a) $[Kr]4f^{14}5d^{9}6s^{1}$ ☐
(b) $[Kr]4f^{14}5d^{10}$ ☐
(c) $[Xe]4f^{14}5d^{10}$. ☐
(d) $[Xe]4f^{14}5d^{8}6s^{2}$. ☐

10. Gadolinium has a low value of third ionisation enthalpy because of **[NCERT (New) Pg. 110, NEET 2022]**

(a) high exchange enthalpy ☐
(b) high electronegativity ☐
(c) high basic character ☐
(d) small size ☐

11. The incorrect statement among the following is **[NCERT (New) Pg. 112, NEET 2021]**

(a) actinoid contraction is greater for element to element than lanthanoid contraction. ☐
(b) most of the trivalent lanthanoid ions are colourless in the solid state. ☐
(c) lanthanoids are good conductors of heat and electricity. ☐
(d) actinoids are highly reactive metals, especially when finely divided. ☐

12. Zr (Z = 40) and Hf (Z = 72) have similar atomic and ionic radii because of **[NCERT (New) Pg. 109, NEET 2021]**

(a) belonging to same group ☐
(b) diagonal relationship ☐
(c) lanthanoid contraction ☐
(d) having similar chemical properties ☐

13. Match the followings aspects with the respective metal.

Aspects	Metal
A. The metal which reveals a maximum number of oxidation states.	I. Scandium
B. The metal although placed in 3d block is considered not as a transition element.	II. Copper
C. The metal which does not exhibit variable oxidation states.	III. Manganese
D. The metal which in +I oxidation state in aqueous solution undergoes disproportionation.	IV. Zinc

Select the correct option. **[NCERT (New) Pg. 97, NEET (Oct.) 2020]**

	A	B	C	D	
(a)	I	IV	II	III	☐
(b)	III	IV	I	II	☐
(c)	III	I	IV	II	☐
(d)	II	IV	I	III	☐

14. The calculated spin only magnetic moment of Cr^{2+} ion is **[NCERT (New) Pg. 102, NEET (Sep.) 2020]**

(a) 4.90 BM ☐ (b) 5.92 BM ☐
(c) 2.84 BM ☐ (d) 3.87 BM ☐

15. Identify the incorrect statement. **[NCERT (New) Pg. 97, NEET (Oct.) 2020]**

(a) The transition metals and their compounds are known for their catalytic activity due to their ability to adopt multiple oxidation states and to form complexes. ☐
(b) Interstitial compounds are those that are formed when small atoms like H, C or N are trapped inside the crystal lattices of metals. ☐
(c) The oxidation states of chromium in CrO_4^{2-} and $Cr_2O_7^{2-}$ are not the same. ☐
(d) $Cr^{2+}(d^4)$ is a stronger reducing agent than $Fe^{2+}(d^6)$ in water. ☐

Chapter 05

Coordination Compounds

Scan and take Chapter Test

TOPIC 1

Introduction & Werner's Theory of Coordination Compounds

NCERT Pg 118-120

1. Compounds in which metal atoms are bound to a number of anions or neutral molecules are called

(a) Coordination compound ☐ (b) Complex compound ☐

(c) Both (a) and (b) ☐ (d) None of these ☐

2. Mention those coordination compounds of the following elements which have biological significance.

(i) Magnesium ____________ (ii) Cobalt ____________

3. Haemoglobin and chlorophyll are the coordination compounds of nickel and iron respectively.

True ☐ False ☐

4. Enlist any three applications of coordination compounds in chemical processes.

(i) ____________

(ii) ____________

(iii) ____________

5. The primary valency of the following binary compounds is

(i) $CrCl_3$ ____________

(ii) $CoCl_2$ ____________

(iii) $PdCl_2$ ____________

Concepts of all questions bearing * are important for JEE/NEET/CUET.

6. Complete the following table regarding the formulation of cobalt (III) chloride-ammonia complexes.

Colour	Formula	Solution conductivity corresponds to
Yellow	(i) ________	1 : 3 electrolyte
(ii) ________	$[CoCl_2(NH_3)_4]^+Cl^-$	(iii) ________
Purple	(iv) ________	1 : 2 electrolyte

7. Two compounds having identical empirical formula but different properties. Such compounds are termed as homoleptic compounds.

True ☐ False ☐

8. The primary valencies are ________ (non-ionisable/ ionisable) and are satisfied by ________ (positive/negative) ions.

9. Consider the following statements.

I. The secondary valency is equal to the coordination number and is fixed for a metal.

II. The ions or groups bound by the secondary linkages to metal have characteristic spatial arrangement with respect to different coordination number.

Which of the above statement(s) is/are correct ?

(a) Only I ☐ (b) Only II ☐

(c) Both I and II ☐ (d) Neither I nor II ☐

10. Consider the following formula and answer the following.

$$\underbrace{[CoCl_2(NH_3)_4]^+}_{A}\ \underset{B}{\underset{\downarrow}{Cl^-}}$$

(i) *A* is referred as ________.

(ii) *B* is referred as ________.

***11.** Amongst the following, the total number of species not having octahedral geometry is

$[Co(NH_3)_6]^{3+}$, $[Ni(CO)_4]$, $[CoCl(NH_3)_5]^{2+}$, $[PtCl_4]^{2-}$, $[CoCl_2(NH_3)_4]^+$

(a) 2 ☐ (b) 4 ☐

(c) 5 ☐ (d) 6 ☐

12. On the basis of the following observations made with aqueous solutions, assign secondary valencies to metals in the following compounds.

	Formula	Moles of AgCl ppt. per mole of compounds with excess $AgNO_3$	Secondary valencies
(i)	$PdCl_2 \cdot 4NH_3$	2	________
(ii)	$NiCl_2 \cdot 6H_2O$	2	________
(iii)	$PtCl_4 \cdot 2HCl$	0	________
(iv)	$CoCl_3 \cdot 4NH_3$	1	________
(v)	$PtCl_2 \cdot 2NH_3$	0	________

13. Which of the following pair contains complex salt and double salt respectively ?

(a) $[Cu(NH_3)_4]SO_4$, $FeSO_4 \cdot 7H_2O$ ☐ (b) $[Cu(NH_3)_4]SO_4$, $KCl \cdot MgCl_2 \cdot 6H_2O$ ☐

(c) $FeSO_4 \cdot K_4[Fe(CN)_6]$, $[Ni(CO)_4]$ ☐ (d) $MgSO_4 \cdot 7H_2O$, $CuSO_4$ ☐

14. Consider the following statements.

I. Double salt and complexes are formed by combination of two or more stable compounds in stoichiometric ratio.

II. Complex ions like $[Fe(CN)_6]^{4-}$ dissociate into simple ions like Fe^{2+} and CN^- ions when dissolved in water.

Here, correct statement(s) is/are

(a) Only I ☐ (b) Only II ☐

(c) Both I and II ☐ (d) Neither I nor II ☐

15. Select the odd one from the following compounds.

(a) $FeSO_4 \cdot (NH_4)_2SO_4 \cdot 6H_2O$ ☐ (b) $KAl(SO_4)_2 \cdot 12H_2O$ ☐

(c) $CoCl_3 \cdot 3NH_3$ ☐ (d) $(NH_4)_2Fe(SO_4)_2 \cdot 6H_2O$ ☐

TOPIC 2

Definitions of Some Important Terms Pertaining to Coordination Compounds

NCERT Pg 121-122

16. Ni^{2+} and Fe^{3+} in $[NiCl_2(H_2O)_4]$ and $[Fe(CN)_6]^{3-}$, respectively are referred to as ________. (Lewis acids/Lewis bases).

17. Write an example of each of the following.

(i) Ligand as simple ions ________

(ii) Ligand as small molecules ________

(iii) Ligand as larger molecules ________

(iv) Ligand as macromolecules ________

18. Match the following Column I with Column II.

Column I (Types of ligands)	Column II (Example of ligands)
A Tetradentate	1. $N(CH_2CH_2NH_2)_3$
B. Unidentate	2. Ethane-1, 2-diamine
C. Didentate	3. H_2O
D. Hexadentate	4. Ethylenediaminetetraacetate ion

A. ______________________ B. ______________________

C. ______________________ D. ______________________

19. Complete the following analogy.
A ligand that is attached to central metal ion by two or more donor atoms simultaneously : *A* : : A ligand which has two different donor atoms and either of them participates in the complex : *B*

(a) *A* : Polydentate ligand, *B* : Didentate ligand

(b) *A* : Didentate ligand, *B* : Ambidentate ligand

(c) *A* : Ambidentate ligand, *B* : Chelate ligand

(d) *A* : Chelate ligand, *B* : Ambidentate ligand

***20.** The correct structure of EDTA is represented by

(a) 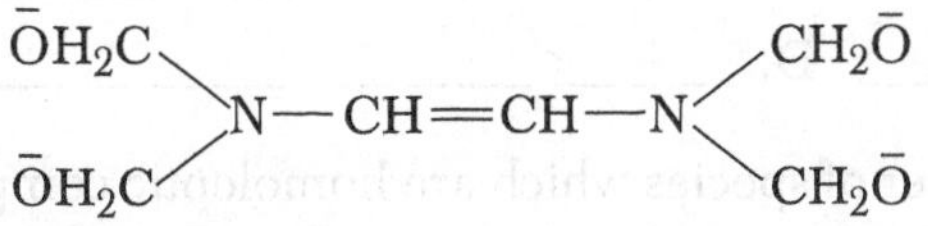

(b) 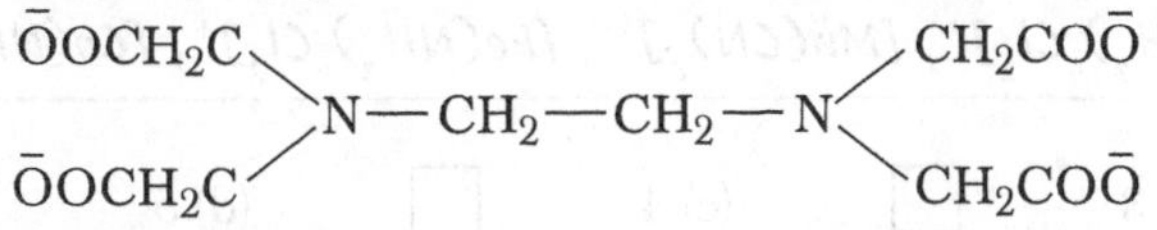

(c) 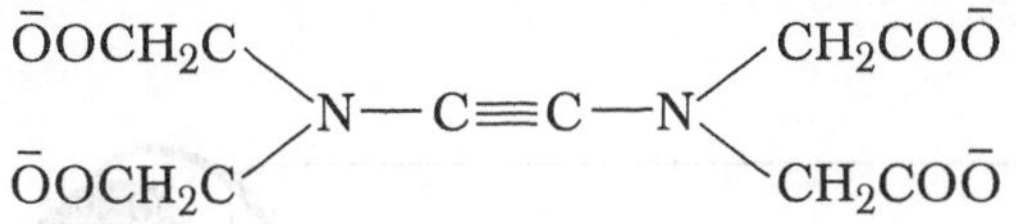

(d) 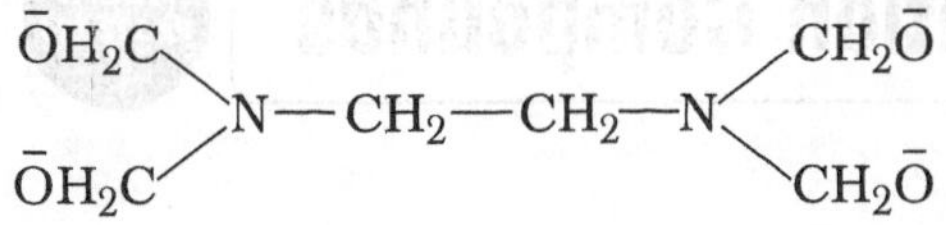

21. Write the name of the ligands shown below.

(i) 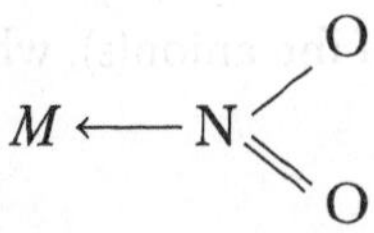 ______________ (ii) $M \longleftarrow O–N{=}O$ ______________

22. Which of the following statements is not correct for coordination number ?

(a) It is the number of ligand donor atoms to which metal is directly bonded. ☐

(b) It is determined only by the number of π-bonds formed by ligand with the central atom. ☐

(c) Coordination number of Fe and Co in $[Fe(C_2O_4)_3]^{3-}$ and $[Co(en)_3]^{3+}$ is 6. ☐

(d) Coordination number of Pt in $[PtCl_6]^{2-}$ is 6. ☐

23. Complete the table given below of coordination compounds and their shapes.

Compounds	Shapes
$[Co(NH_3)_6]^{3+}$	(i) ________
$[PtCl_4]^{2-}$	(ii) ________
(iii) ________	Tetrahedral

24. Match the following columns.

Column I (Complex species)	Column II (Oxidation state)
A. $[Cu(CN)_4]^{3-}$	1. +2
B. $[Co(NH_3)_4(H_2O)Cl]SO_4$	2. +3
C. $[Co_2(CO)_8]$	3. +1
D. $K_2[Zn(OH)_4]$	4. 0

A. ____________ B. ____________

C. ____________ D. ____________

***25.** Amongst the following, the total number of species which are homoleptic complexes.

$[Cr(NH_3)_6]^{3+}$, $[Co(NH_3)_4Cl_2]^+$, $[Mn(CN)_6]^{4-}$, $[Fe(NH_3)_4Cl_2]^+$, $[Co(NH_3)_6]^{3+}$

(a) 2 ☐ (b) 3 ☐ (c) 4 ☐ (d) 5 ☐

TOPIC 3

Nomenclature of Coordination Compounds

NCERT Pg 122-124

26. Consider the following statements.

I. While writing the formula, if more than one ligands are present then the placement of a ligand in the list depends upon its charge.

II. The charge of the cation(s) should be balanced by the charge of the anion(s), while writing the formula.

Which of the following statement(s) is/are correct ?

(a) Only I ☐ (b) Only II ☐

(c) Both I and II ☐ (d) Neither I nor II ☐

27. In $[Cr(NH_3)_3(H_2O)_3]Cl_3$ complex,

(i) number of neutral ligands are ______.

(ii) the oxidation number of chromium is ______.

28. Write the formulae for the following coordination compounds.

(i) Tetraammineaquachloridocobalt (III) chloride ______

(ii) Potassium tetrahydroxidozincate (II) ______

(iii) Potassium trioxalatoaluminate (III) ______

(iv) Dichlorido*bis*-(ethane-1, 2-diamine) cobalt (III) ion ______

***29.** Write the IUPAC names of the following coordination compounds.

(i) $[Pt(NH_3)_2Cl(NO_2)]$ ______ (ii) $K_3[Cr(C_2O_4)_3]$ ______

(iii) $[CoCl_2(en)_2]Cl$ ______ (iv) $[Co(NH_3)_5(CO_3)]Cl$ ______

***30.** Select the incorrect pair of coordination compound and corresponding formula.

(a) Tetraamminediaquacobalt(III) chloride – $[Co(H_2O)_2(NH_3)_4]Cl_3$

(b) Potassiumtetracyanonickelate(II) – $K_3[Ni(CN)_4]$

(c) *Tris* (ethane-1, 2-diamine) chromium(III) chloride – $[Cr(en)_3]Cl_3$

(d) Amminebromidochloridonitrito-N-platinate (II) ion – $[Pt(NH_3)BrCl(NO_2)]^-$

31. Complete the following table.

Formula	IUPAC name	Oxidation state
$[PtCl_2(en)_2](NO_3)_2$	Dichlorido*bis*-(ethane-1, 2-diamine) platinum (IV) nitrate	(i) ______
(ii) ______	Iron (III) hexacyanidoferrate (II)	+ 2
$[Co(NH_3)_6]Cl_3$	(iii) ______	+ 3
$[Co(NH_3)_5Cl]Cl_2$	(iv) ______	+ 3

***32.** Match the IUPAC name given in Column II with the formula given in Column I.

Column I (Formula)	Column II (IUPAC name)
A. $K_3[Fe(CN)_6]$	1. Potassiumtrioxalatoferrate (III)
B. $K_3[Fe(C_2O_4)_3]$	2. Potassiumtetrachloridopalladate (II)
C. $K_2[PdCl_4]$	3. Diamminechlorido (methylamine) platinum (II) chloride
D. $[Pt(NH_3)_2Cl(NH_2CH_3)]Cl$	4. Potassium hexacyanoferrate (III)

A. ______ B. ______

C. ______ D. ______

TOPIC 4

Isomerism in Coordination Compounds

NCERT Pg 125-128

33. Identify *A, B, C* and *D*.

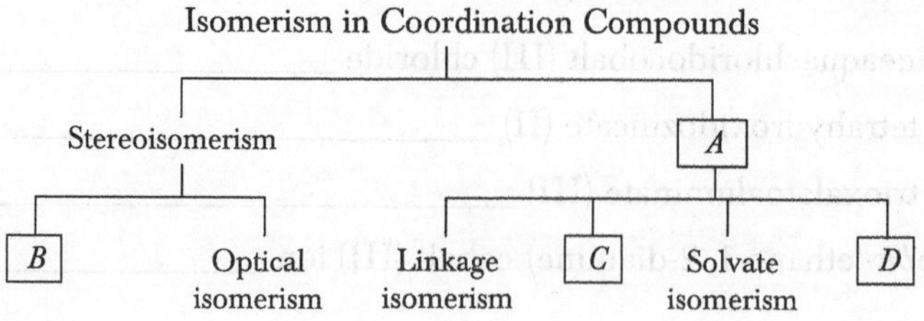

A = ______________ *B* = ______________

C = ______________ *D* = ______________

34. Stereoisomers have same ____*X*____ but different ____*Y*____. Write '*X*' and '*Y*'.

X = ______________ *Y* = ______________

35. Select the complex ion which shows geometrical isomerism.

(a) $[Cr(H_2O)_3Cl]^+$ ☐ (b) $[Pt(NH_3)_2Cl_2]$ ☐

(c) $[Co(CN)_5(NC)]^{3-}$ ☐ (d) $[Co(NH_3)_6]^{3+}$ ☐

36. Geometrical isomerism arises in ______ (homoleptic/heteroleptic) complexes due to ______ (different/same) possible geometric arrangements of the ligands.

37. Select the *cis*-isomers from the following. (More than one option can also be correct)

(a) 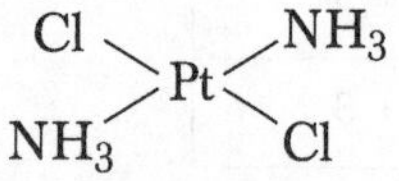 ☐ (b) 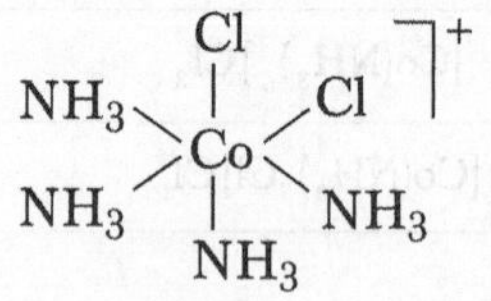 ☐

(c) 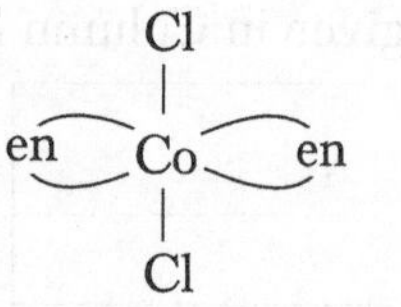 ☐ (d) 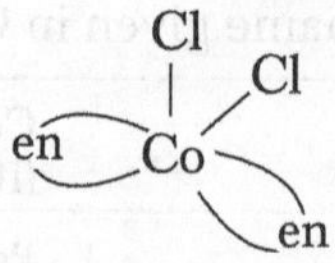 ☐

38. Amongst the following, the total number of species have shown *cis-trans* isomerism.

$[Co(NH_2—CH_2—CH_2—NH_2)_2Cl]^+$, $[CrCl_2(C_2O_4)_2]^{3-}$, $Fe(H_2O)_4(OH)_2^+$, $[Co(NH_3)_4(H_2O)(Cl)]^{2+}$, $[Fe(NH_3)_2(CN)_4]^-$

(a) 1 ☐ (b) 2 ☐ (c) 4 ☐ (d) 5 ☐

39. Which of the following complex will exhibit *facial* and *meridional* isomerism ?

(a) $[Co(NH_3)Cl_3]$ ☐ (b) $[Co(NH_3)Cl_2]Cl$ ☐

(c) $[Co(en)_3]Cl_3$ ☐ (d) $K_3[Co(CN)_4Cl_2]$ ☐

40. Geometrical isomerism is not possible in tetrahedral complexes having two different types of unidentate ligand.

True ☐ False ☐

41. Consider the following statements.

I. $[MA_2B_2]$ type tetrahedral complexes will show geometrical isomerism.

II. Optical isomerism is common in octahedral complexes involving dentate ligands.

Here, incorrect statement(s) is/are

(a) Only I ☐ (b) Only II ☐ (c) Both I and II ☐ (d) None of these ☐

42. Identify the optically active compounds from the following.

(a) *trans*-$[Co(en)_2Cl_2]^+$ ☐ (b) $[Co(en)_3]^{3+}$ ☐

(c) $[Cr(NH_3)_5Cl]$ ☐ (d) Both (a) and (b) ☐

43. Draw structures of geometrical isomers of $[Fe(NH_3)_2(CN)_4]^-$

(i)____________________. (ii) ____________________.

44. Out of the following two coordination entities tick the correct one, which is chiral (optically active) ?

(a) *cis*-$[CrCl_2(ox)_2]^{3-}$ ☐ (b) *trans*-$[CrCl_2(ox)_2]^{3-}$ ☐

45. Palladium complexes of the type $[Pd(C_6H_5)_2(SCN)_2]$ and $[Pd(C_6H_5)_2(NCS)_2]$ are

(a) Coordination isomers ☐ (b) Linkage isomers ☐

(c) Ionisation isomers ☐ (d) Geometrical isomers ☐

46. Complex $[Co(NH_3)_5(NO_2)]Cl_2$ is obtained in two form, i.e. red form and yellow form. Mention the atom through which the ligand is bound to the central metal atom.

(i) Red ____________________ (ii) Yellow ____________________

47. $[Co(NH_3)_6][Cr(CN)_6]$ and $[Cr(NH_3)_6][Co(CN)_6]$ exhibit

(a) Linkage isomerism ☐ (b) Solvate isomerism ☐

(c) Coordination isomerism ☐ (d) Ionisation isomerism ☐

48. Write the coordination isomer of $[Cu(NH_3)_4][PtCl_4]$.

____

49. Give an example of type of isomerism in which ligand displaces counter ion and *vice-versa*.

____

50. Solvate isomerism is also known as hydrate isomerism for any solvent.

True ☐ False ☐

51. The kind of isomerism exists between $[Cr(H_2O)_6]Cl_2$ (violet) and $[Cr(H_2O)_5Cl]Cl_2 \cdot H_2O$ (greyish green) is

(a) Linkage isomerism ☐ (b) Solvate isomerism ☐

(c) Ionisation isomerism ☐ (d) Coordination isomerism ☐

52. Tick the correct type of isomerism shown by following complexes.

(i) $K[Cr(H_2O)_2(C_2O_4)_2]$ — Geometrical ☐ Optical ☐ Both ☐

(ii) $[Co(en)_3]Cl_3$ — Geometrical ☐ Optical ☐ Both ☐

(iii) $[Pt(NH_3)(H_2O)Cl_2]$ — Geometrical ☐ Optical ☐ Both ☐

TOPIC 5

Bonding in Coordination Compounds

NCERT Pg 128-135

53. $[Co(NH_3)_5Cl]SO_4$ reacts with Ba^{2+} to produce white precipitate of $BaSO_4$, while $[Co(NH_3)_5SO_4]Cl$ does not react.

True ☐ False ☐

54. Complete the following table of coordination compound with its coordination number, hybridisation and shape.

Coordination number	Hybridisation	Shape of compound
6	sp^3d^2	(i) ________
(ii) ________	sp^3	Tetrahedral
4	(iii) ________	Square planar

55. Consider the following statements.

I. $[Co(NH_3)_6]^{3+}$ is called low spin complex, while $[CoF_6]^{3-}$ is called high spin complex.

II. Coordination compounds with coordination number 5 exhibit octahedral geometry.

Which of the following statement(s) is/are correct?

(a) Only I ☐ (b) Only II ☐

(c) Both I and II ☐ (d) None of these ☐

56. Arrange the following ions in increasing order of magnetic moment.

Ti^{2+}, Sc^{3+}, Ti^{3+}, V^{2+}

____

***57.** Which of the following pair of ions does not possess same number of unpaired electrons ?

(a) Cr^{2+}, Mn^{3+} ☐ (b) Mn^{2+}, Fe^{3+} ☐

(c) Fe^{2+}, Co^{3+} ☐ (d) Mn^{3+}, Fe^{2+} ☐

***58.** Amongst the following, the total number of species which have sp^3d^2 hybridisation.

$[MnCl_6]^{3-}$, $[FeF_6]^{3-}$, $[Mn(CN)_6]^{3-}$, $[CoF_6]^{3-}$, $[BrF_2]^-$

(a) 2 ☐ (b) 3 ☐ (c) 4 ☐ (d) 5 ☐

59. Which is diamagnetic among the following inner orbital octahedral complex ions ?

(a) $[Mn(CN)_6]^{3-}$ ☐ (b) $[Fe(CN)_6]^{3-}$ ☐

(c) $[Fe(CN)_6]^{4-}$ ☐ (d) All of these ☐

60. $[Mn(CN)_6]^{3-}$ has magnetic moment of two unpaired electrons, while $[MnCl_6]^{3-}$ has magnetic moment of 3 unpaired electrons.

True ☐ False ☐

61. Mention the number of unpaired electrons in following compound.

(i) $[CoF_6]^{3-}$ ______ (ii) $[FeF_6]^{3-}$ ______

***62.** Which of the following information is incorrect about $[MnBr_4]^{2-}$ complex ?

(a) Tetrahedral shape ☐

(b) Paramagnetic ☐

(c) Possess magnetic moment = 5.9 BM ☐

(d) sp^3d^2-hybridisation ☐

63. Consider the following statements regarding valence bond theory.

I. It does not give quantitative interpretation of magnetic data.

II. It explains the colour exhibited by coordination compounds.

III. It helps in distinguishing weak and strong ligands.

IV. It does not give quantitative interpretation of kinetic stability of coordination compounds.

Mark (✓) and (×) under correct and incorrect with respect to given statements.

	Correct	Incorrect
I.	______	______
II.	______	______
III.	______	______
IV.	______	______

64. In a coordination entity, the electronic configuration of the central metal ion is $t_{2g}^3 e_g^1$.

(i) Is the coordination compound a high spin or low spin complex?

______

(ii) Draw the crystal field splitting diagram for the above complex.

______

65. The degenerate orbitals of $[Cr(H_2O)_6]^{3+}$ are

(a) d_{yz} and d_{z^2} ☐ (b) d_{z^2} and d_{xz} ☐

(c) $d_{x^2-y^2}$ and d_{xy} ☐ (d) d_{xz} and d_{yz} ☐

66. The energy of two e_g orbitals will increase by (3/5) Δ_o and three t_{2g} will increase by (2/5) Δ_o, when splitting of *d*-orbitals occur in octahedral crystal field.

True ☐ False ☐

***67.** Arrange the following ligands in increasing order of field strength.

Cl^-, SCN^-, $C_2O_4^{2-}$, en, $[EDTA]^{4-}$, F^-

____

68. Complete the following statement with appropriate words.

Ligands for which $\Delta_o < P$ are known as ____________ (weak/strong) field ligands and form ____________ (low/high) spin complexes.

69. The colour of coordination compounds depends on crystal field splitting. Arrange the following complexes in decreasing order of wavelength of light absorbed in visible region.

$[Co(NH_3)_6]^{3+}$, $[Co(CN)_6]^{3-}$, $[Cu(H_2O)_4]^{2+}$

____

70. Two complexes $[Cr(NH_3)_6]Cl_3$ (*A*) and $[Cr(H_2O)_6]Cl_3$ (*B*) are violet and yellow coloured, respectively. The incorrect statement regarding them is

(a) Δ_o value for (*B*) is less than that of (*A*). ☐

(b) Both absorb energies corresponding to their complementary colours. ☐

(c) Δ_o values of (*A*) and (*B*) are calculated from the energies of violet and yellow light, respectively. ☐

(d) Both are paramagnetic with three unpaired electrons. ☐

71. Complete the following table of coordination compounds with colour of light absorbed and colour of coordination entity.

Coordination compounds	Colour of light absorbed	Colour of coordination entity
$[Ti(H_2O)_6]^{3+}$	Blue green	(i) __________
$[CoCl(NH_3)_5]^{2+}$	(ii) __________	Violet
(iii) __________	Blue	Yellow orange

72. Colour of coordination compounds is due to *d-f* transition of the electrons.

True ☐ False ☐

73. On heating $[Ti(H_2O)_6]Cl_3$, violet colour changes to ________ (orange/colourless), while water turns the colour of anhydrous copper sulphate to ________ (white/blue).

74. Identify X, Y and Z for the following reaction when molar ratio of en (ethane-1, 2-diamine) and nickel are 1 : 1, 2 : 1 and 3 : 1 respectively.

$$\underset{\text{Green}}{[Ni(H_2O)_6]^{2+}(aq)} + \text{en}\,(aq) \longrightarrow \underset{\text{(Pale blue)}}{X(aq)} + 2H_2O$$

$$X(aq) + \text{en}\,(aq) \longrightarrow \underset{\text{(Blue/purple)}}{Y(aq)} + 2H_2O$$

$$Y(aq) + \text{en}\,(aq) \longrightarrow \underset{\text{(Violet)}}{Z(aq)} + 2H_2O$$

X = ________ Y = ________ Z = ________

75. Ruby is aluminium oxide (Al_2O_3) containing about 0.5 -1% Fe^{3+} ions.

True ☐ False ☐

76. Select the complex which is paramagnetic in nature due to the presence of weak field ligand.

$[Ni(CN)_4]^{2-}$, $[NiCl_4]^{2-}$, $[Ni(CO)_4]$

____

77. Out of $[Fe(H_2O)_4]^{3+}$ and $[Fe(CN)_4]^{3-}$, which one is strongly paramagnetic?

____

78. Which one of the following is an inner orbital complex as well as diamagnetic in behaviour ?

(a) $[Zn(NH_3)_6]^{2+}$ ☐ (b) $[Cr(NH_3)_6]^{3+}$ ☐

(c) $[Co(NH_3)_6]^{3+}$ ☐ (d) $[Ni(NH_3)_6]^{2+}$ ☐

79. Mention the number of unpaired electrons in square planar $[Pt(CN)_4]^{2-}$ ion.

____

80. Oxidation state of Mn in $[Mn(H_2O)_6]^{2+}$ and $[Mn(CN)_6]^{4-}$ is + 2.

Answer the following questions based on the above information.

(i) Which one is strong field ligand ? (H_2O / CN^-) ________

(ii) The compound which contains more unpaired electrons ? ($[Mn(H_2O)_6]^{2+}$ / $[Mn(CN)_6]^{4-}$)

____

TOPIC 6

Bonding in Metal Carbonyls

NCERT Pg 135-136

81. Select the incorrect pair.

(a) Tetracarbonylnickel (0) – Tetrahedral

(b) Pentacarbonyliron (0) – Tetrahedral

(c) Hexacarbonyl chromium (0) – Octahedral

(d) All are correct pair

82. Draw the structure of

(i) $Fe(CO)_5$ ____________ (ii) $[Mn_2(CO)_{10}]$ ____________

83. $[Co_2(CO)_8]$ displays

(a) no Co—Co bond, four terminal CO and four bridging CO.

(b) no Co—Co bond, six terminal CO and two bridging CO.

(c) one Co—Co bond, four terminal CO and four bridging CO.

(d) one Co—Co bond, six terminal CO and two bridging CO.

84. The donation of lone pair of electrons of carbonyl carbon into the vacant orbital of metal atom result in ________ bond.

(a) sigma (b) pi (c) delta (d) synergic

85. The M—C π bond is formed through

(a) donation of electrons from half-filled d-orbital of metal to empty π-orbital of CO.

(b) donation of electrons from filled d-orbitals of metal to empty π-orbital of CO.

(c) donation of electron pair from filled d-orbital of metal to empty π^* of CO.

(d) donation of electron pair of half-filled d-orbital to empty π^* of CO.

86. Which of the following does not have a metal-carbon bond?

(a) $Al(OEt)_3$ (b) EtBr

(c) $Ni(CO)_4$ (d) $K[Pt(C_2H_4)_3Cl_3]$

87. Choose the incorrect statement from the following.

(a) Deca carbonyl manganese (0) is made up of two square pyramidal $Mn(CO)_5$ units joined by a Mn—Mn bond.

(b) The metal-carbon bond in metal carbonyls possess only π character.

(c) The metal to liquid bonding creates a synergic effect.

(d) Tetracarbonyl nickel (0) is tetrahedral.

TOPIC 7

Importance and Applications of Coordination Compounds

NCERT Pg 136-137

88. The compound that inhibits the growth of tumors is

(a) *trans*-$[Pt(Cl)_2(NH_3)_2]$ ☐ (b) *cis*-$[Pd(Cl)_2(NH_3)_2]$ ☐

(c) *cis*-$[Pt(Cl)_2(NH_3)_2]$ ☐ (d) *trans*-$[Pd(Cl)_2(NH_3)_2]$ ☐

89. Hardness of water is estimated by simple titration with ________________.

90. Excess of copper and iron are removed by formation of coordination compounds with the help of chelating ligands X and Y respectively. Write X and Y.

X = ________________ Y = ________________

***91.** Enlist any two uses of EDTA.

(i) ________________ (ii) ________________

92. Impure nickel is converted to $[Ni(CO)_4]$ which is decomposed to yield pure nickel. This is an example of purification of metal with the help of coordination compounds.

True ☐ False ☐

93. Coordination compounds also finds its extensive application in

(i) ________________. (ii) ________________. (iii) ________________.

94. Consider the following statements.

I. By addition of zinc to $[Au(CN)_2^-]$ solution, gold can be separated in metallic form.

II. Articles cannot be electroplated with silver and gold from $[Ag(CN)_2]^-$ and $[Au(CN)_2]^-$ solution.

Here, incorrect statement(s) is/are

(a) Only I ☐ (b) Only II ☐

(c) Both I and II ☐ (d) None of the statement ☐

95. Match the coordination compounds given in Column I with central metal atoms given in Column II.

	Column I (Coordination compounds)		Column II (Central metal atoms)
A.	Chlorophyll	1.	Iron
B.	Blood pigment	2.	Rhodium
C.	Wilkinson catalyst	3.	Cobalt
D.	Vitamin B_{12}	4.	Magnesium

A. ________________ B. ________________

C. ________________ D. ________________

96. In black and white photography, a complex ion of Ag is involved. Its formula is ______.

Assertion-Reason Questions

Given below are two statements, one is labelled as Assertion (A) and other is labelled as Reason (R). Select the most appropriate answer from the options given below.

(a) Both A and R are true and R is the correct explanation of A.
(b) Both A and R are false but R is not the correct explanation of A.
(c) A is true but R is false.
(d) A is false but R is true.

1. **Assertion** (A) NO_2^- and SCN^- ions are ambidentate ligands.
Reason (R) NO_2^- and SCN^- can ligate through two different atoms.
(a) ☐ (b) ☐ (c) ☐ (d) ☐

2. **Assertion** (A) Chelate are less stable than ordinary coordination compounds.
Reason (R) Chelates can be formed by bidentate ligands.
(a) ☐ (b) ☐ (c) ☐ (d) ☐

3. **Assertion** (A) Toxic metal ions are removed by the chelating ligands.
Reason (R) Chelate complexes tend to be more stable.
(a) ☐ (b) ☐ (c) ☐ (d) ☐

4. **Assertion** (A) Linkage isomerism arises in coordination compounds containing ambidentate ligand.
Reason (R) Ambidentate ligand has two different donor atoms.
(a) ☐ (b) ☐ (c) ☐ (d) ☐

5. **Assertion** (A) Square planar complexes having two different types of unidentate ligands coordinated with central metal ion show geometrical isomerism.
Reason (R) Geometrical isomerism arises in homoleptic complexes due to different possible geometric arrangement of the ligands.
(a) ☐ (b) ☐ (c) ☐ (d) ☐

6. **Assertion** (A) Complexes of MX_6 and MX_5L type, where X and L are unidentate does not show geometrical isomerism.
Reason (R) Geometrical isomerism is not shown by complexes of coordination number 4.
(a) ☐ (b) ☐ (c) ☐ (d) ☐

7. **Assertion** (A) According to crystal field theory during complex formation, the d-orbitals split and form two sets of orbitals e_g and t_{2g}.
Reason (R) Small splitting of d-orbitals occurs only in case of strong field ligands.
(a) ☐ (b) ☐ (c) ☐ (d) ☐

8. **Assertion** (A) $[Fe(CN)_6]^{3-}$ ion shows magnetic moment corresponding to two unpaired electrons.
Reason (R) It is due to d^2sp^3 type hybridisation.
(a) ☐ (b) ☐ (c) ☐ (d) ☐

9. **Assertion** (A) Oxidation state of Fe in $Fe(CO)_5$ is zero.
Reason (R) Synergic bonding takes place in $Fe(CO)_5$.

(a) ☐ (b) ☐ (c) ☐ (d) ☐

10. **Assertion** (A) $[Ti(H_2O)_6]^{3+}$ is coloured while $[Sc(H_2O)_6]^{3+}$ is colourless.
Reason (R) *d-d* transition is not possible in $[Sc(H_2O)_6]^{3+}$.

(a) ☐ (b) ☐ (c) ☐ (d) ☐

Case-Based Questions

1. Coordination compounds are formulated and named according to the IUPAC system.

- In ionic complex, the cation is named first and then the anion.
- In the coordination entity, the ligands are named first and then the central metal ion.
- When more than one type of ligands are present, they are named in alphabetical order of preference without any consideration of charge.

(i) The IUPAC name of $[Ni(CO)_4]$ is

(a) tetracarbonylnickel (II) ☐ (b) tetracarbonylnickel (0) ☐
(c) tetracarbonylnickelate (II) ☐ (d) tetracarbonylnickelate (0) ☐

(ii) As per IUPAC nomenclature, the name of complex $[Co(H_2O)_4(NH_3)_2]Cl_3$ is

(a) tetraaquadiamminecobalt (II) chloride ☐ (b) tetraaquadiamminecobalt (III) chloride ☐
(c) diamminetetraaquacobalt (II) chloride ☐ (d) diamminetetraaquacobalt (III) chloride ☐

(iii) Which of the following represents correct formula of dichlorido*bis*-(ethane-1, 2-diammine) cobalt(III) ion?

(a) $[CoCl_2(en)]^{2+}$ ☐ (b) $[CoCl_2(en)_2]^{2+}$ ☐
(c) $[CoCl_2(en)]^{+}$ ☐ (d) $[CoCl_2(en)_2]^{+}$ ☐

(iv) Correct formula of pentaamminenitro-o-cobalt (III) sulphate is

(a) $[Co(NO_2)(NH_3)_5]SO_4$ ☐ (b) $[Co(ONO)(NH_3)_5]SO_4$ ☐
(c) $[Co(NO_2)(NH_3)_4](SO_4)_2$ ☐ (d) $[Co(ONO)(NH_3)_4(SO_4)_2]$ ☐

2. Iron forms many complexes in its +2 and +3 oxidation states such as $[Fe(H_2O)_6]^{2+}$ (*A*); $[Fe(CN)_6]^{4-}$ (*B*); $[Fe(H_2O)_6]^{3+}$ (*C*); $[Fe(CN)_6]^{3-}$ (*D*) etc. They exhibit different magnetic properties and undergo different hybridisation of iron.

(i) The complex having maximum magnetic moment is

(a) (*A*) ☐ (b) (*B*) ☐ (c) (*C*) ☐ (d) (*D*) ☐

(ii) Which of the following does not represent correct configuration of the *d*-orbitals in the given complexes?

(a) (*A*) $t_{2g}^4 e_g^2$ ☐ (b) (*B*) $t_{2g}^2 e_g^0$ ☐ (c) (*C*) $t_{2g}^4 e_g^1$ ☐ (d) (*D*) $t_{2g}^5 e_g^0$ ☐

(iii) The spin only magnetic moment of complexes (*A*), (*B*), (*C*) and (*D*) are respectively (in BM)

(a) $2\sqrt{6}, 0, \sqrt{35}, \sqrt{3}$ ☐ (b) $0, 2\sqrt{6}, \sqrt{35}, \sqrt{3}$ ☐
(c) $\sqrt{15}, 2\sqrt{6}, \sqrt{3}, 0$ ☐ (d) $\sqrt{3}, \sqrt{8}, 0, \sqrt{15}$ ☐

(iv) Which of the given complexes are outer orbital complexes?

(a) (*A*) and (*B*) ☐ (b) (*B*) and (*C*) ☐ (c) (*A*) and (*C*) ☐ (d) (*B*) and (*D*) ☐

COMPETITION EDGE UP

1. The correct IUPAC name of $[PtBr_2(PMe_3)_2]$ is

[NCERT (New) Pg. 124, JEE Main 2024]

(a) bis(trimethylphosphine)dibromoplatinum (II) ☐
(b) dibromobis(trimethylphosphine) platinum(II) ☐
(c) bis[bromo(trimethylphosphine)] platinum (II) ☐
(d) dibromodi(trimethylphosphine) platinum (II) ☐

2. The correct IUPAC name of K_2MnO_4 is

[NCERT (New) Pg. 124, JEE Main 2024]

(a) potassium tetraoxopermanganate (VI) ☐
(b) dipotassium tetraoxidomanganate (VII) ☐
(c) potassium tetraoxidomanganate (VI) ☐
(d) potassium tetraoxidomanganese (VI) ☐

3. The coordination environment of Ca^{2+} ion in its complex with $EDTA^{4-}$ is

[NCERT (New) Pg. 129, JEE Main 2024]

(a) tetrahedral ☐
(b) trigonal prismatic ☐
(c) square planar ☐
(d) octahedral ☐

4. Match List-I with List-II.

	List-I		List-II
A.	$K_2[Ni(CN)_4]$	I.	sp^3
B.	$[Ni(CO)_4]$	II.	sp^3d^2
C.	$[Co(NH_3)_6]Cl_3$	III.	dsp^2
D.	$Na_3[CoF_6]$	IV.	d^2sp^3

Choose the correct answer from the options given below:

[NCERT (New) Pg. 129, JEE Main 2024]

(a) A-III, B-I, C-II, D-IV ☐
(b) A-III, B-I, C-IV, D-II ☐
(c) A-I, B-III, C-II, D-IV ☐
(d) A-III, B-II, C-IV, D-I ☐

5. If an iron (III) complex with the formula $[Fe(NH_3)_x(CN)_y]^-$ has no electron in its e_g orbital, then the value of $x + y$ is

[NCERT (New) Pg. 132, JEE Main 2024]

(a) 5 ☐ (b) 3 ☐
(c) 4 ☐ (d) 6 ☐

6. The correct sequence of ligands in the order of decreasing field strength is

[NCERT (New) Pg. 132, JEE Main 2024]

(a) $NCS^- > EDTA^{4-} > CN^- > CO$ ☐
(b) $CO > H_2O > F^- > S^{2-}$ ☐
(c) $^-OH > F^- > NH_3 > CN^-$ ☐
(d) $S^{2-} > ^-OH > EDTA^{4-} > CO$ ☐

7. $[Co(NH_3)_6]^{3+}$ and $[CoF_6]^{3-}$ are respectively known as **[NCERT (New) Pg. 132, JEE Main 2024]**

(a) spin paired complex, spin free complex ☐
(b) inner orbital complex, spin paired complex ☐
(c) outer orbital complex, inner orbital complex ☐
(d) spin free complex, spin paired complex ☐

8. Given below are two statements :

[NCERT (New) Pg. 123, NEET 2024]

Statement I $[Co(NH_3)_6]^{3+}$ is a homoleptic complex whereas $[Co(NH_3)_4Cl_2]^+$ is a heteroleptic complex.

Statement II Complex $[Co(NH_3)_6]^{3+}$ has only one kind of ligands but $[Co(NH_3)_4Cl_2]^+$ has more than one kind of ligands.

In the light of the above statements, choose the correct answer from the options given below.

(a) Both Statement I and Statement II are true. ☐
(b) Both Statement I and Statement II are false. ☐
(c) Statement I is true but Statement II is false. ☐
(d) Statement I is false but Statement II is true. ☐

9. Homoleptic complex from the following complexes is **[NCERT (New) Pg. 122, NEET 2023]**

(a) diamminechloridonitrito-N-platinum (II) ☐
(b) pentaamminecarbonatocobalt (III)chloride ☐
(c) triamminetriaquachromium (III) chloride ☐
(d) potassium trioxalatoaluminate (III) ☐

10. The IUPAC name of the complex $[Ag(H_2O)_2][Ag(CN)_2]$ is

[NCERT (New) Pg. 124, NEET 2022]

(a) diaquasilver (II) dicyanidoargentate (II) ☐
(b) dicyanidosilver (I) diaquaargentate (I) ☐
(c) diaquasilver (I) dicyanidoargentate (I) ☐
(d) dicyanidosilver (II) diaquaargentate (II) ☐

11. *Ethylene diaminetetraacetate (EDTA) ion is* **[NCERT (New) Pg. 124, NEET 2021]**

(a) hexadentate ligand with four O and two N donor atoms ☐
(b) unidentate ligand ☐
(c) bidentate ligand with two N donor atoms ☐
(d) tridentate ligand with three N donor atoms ☐

12. *Match List-I with List-II.* **[NCERT (New) Pg. 131, NEET 2021]**

List-I	List-II
A. $[Fe(CN)_6]^{3-}$	1. 5.92 BM
B. $[Fe(H_2O)_6]^{3+}$	2. 0 BM
C. $[Fe(CN)_6]^{4-}$	3. 4.90 BM
D. $[Fe(H_2O)_6]^{2+}$	4. 1.73 BM

Choose the correct answer from the options given below.

	A	B	C	D			A	B	C	D	
(a)	4	2	1	3	☐	(b)	2	4	3	1	☐
(c)	1	3	4	2	☐	(d)	4	1	2	3	☐

13. *Which of the following is the correct order of increasing field strength of ligands to form coordination compounds?* **[NCERT (New) Pg. 132, NEET (Sep.) 2020]**

(a) $SCN^- < F^- < CN^- < C_2O_4^{2-}$ ☐
(b) $F^- < SCN^- < C_2O_4^{2-} < CN^-$ ☐
(c) $CN^- < C_2O_4^{2-} < SCN^- < F^-$ ☐
(d) $SCN^- < F^- < C_2O_4^{2-} < CN^-$ ☐

14. *The calculated spin only magnetic moment of Cr^{2+} ion is* **[NCERT (New) Pg. 122 NEET 2020]**

(a) 4.90 BM ☐ (b) 5.92 BM ☐
(c) 2.84 BM ☐ (d) 3.87 BM ☐

15. *Match the coordination number and type of hybridisation with distribution of hybrid orbitals in space based on valence bond theory.*

Coordination number and type of hybridisation	Distribution of hybrid orbitals in space
A. 4, sp^3	I. trigonal bipyramidal
B. 4, dsp^2	II. octahedral
C. 5, sp^3d	III. tetrahedral
D. 6, d^2sp^3	IV. square planar

Select the correct option. **[NCERT (New) Pg. 124, NEET (Oct.) 2020]**

	A	B	C	D	
(a)	II	III	IV	I	☐
(b)	III	IV	I	II	☐
(c)	IV	I	II	III	☐
(d)	III	I	IV	II	☐

Chapter 06

Haloalkanes and Haloarenes

Scan and take Chapter Test

TOPIC 1

Introduction & Classification

NCERT Pg 159-161

1. Hybridisation of carbon atom to which halogen atom is attached in haloalkane and haloarenes are ____________ and ____________ respectively.

2. Antibiotic which is very effective for treatment of typhoid fever is

(a) paracetamol ☐ (b) chloramphenicol ☐

(c) amoxicillin ☐ (d) Both (b) and (c) ☐

3. Deficiency of which hormone causes a disease called goiter.

____

4. Match the following Column I with Column II.

Column I (Compounds)		Column II (Uses)	
A.	Chloroquine	1.	Blood substitutes in surgery
B.	Halothane	2.	Treatment of malaria
C.	Fluorinated compounds	3.	Used as anaesthetic

A. ____________ B. ____________ C. ____________

5. Select the odd one regarding the classification of haloalkanes.

Dihaloalkane, Secondary haloalkane, Monohaloalkane, Trihaloalkane.

____

6. The general formula for haloalkane is ____________.

7. Haloalkanes are classified as primary, secondary or tertiary according to nature of ____________ (carbon/hydrogen) to which halogen is attached.

Concepts of all questions bearing * are important for JEE/NEET/CUET.

***8.** The given compound is

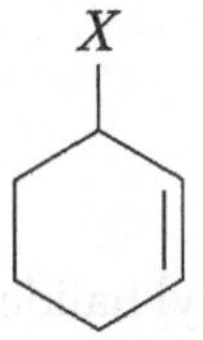

(a) allylic halide ☐ (b) vinylic halide ☐

(c) benzylic halide ☐ (d) All of these ☐

***9.** Draw the structure of 1° benzylic halide.

____

***10.** Vinylic halides are the compounds in which halogen atom is bonded to sp^3-hybridised carbon atom attached to carbon-carbon double bond.

True ☐ False ☐

***11.** Out of 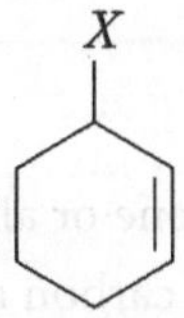 and 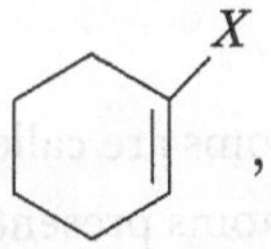, which one is vinylic halide ?

____

***12.** Halides in which $C(sp^2)$—X bond is present in ________ (allyl halide/aryl halide).

13. Out of the following compounds, how many are aryl halides?

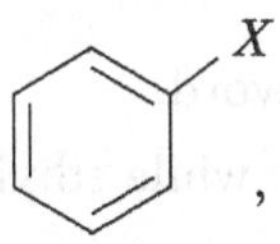, 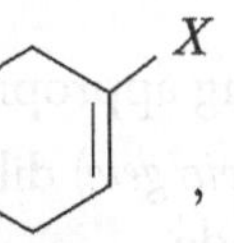, 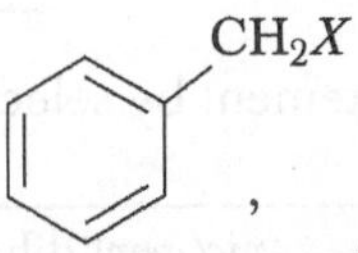, 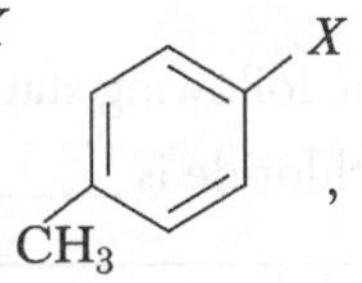

(a) One ☐ (b) Two ☐ (c) Three ☐ (d) Four ☐

14. Amongst the following, the total number of species given in its correct IUPAC name

(i) $(CH_3)_3CCH_2Br$
1-bromo-2,2-dimethylpropane

(ii) 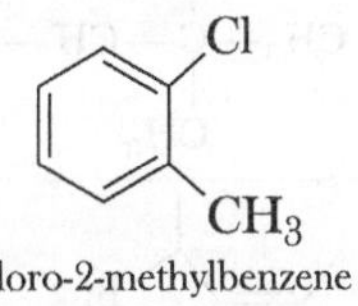
1-chloro-2-methylbenzene

(iii) $CHCl_3$
Trichloromethane

(iv) $CH_2=CHCH_2Br$
3-bromopropene

(v) 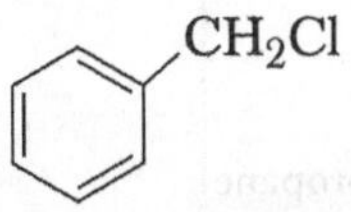
Chlorophenylmethane

(a) 1 ☐ (b) 3 ☐ (c) 4 ☐ (d) 5 ☐

TOPIC 2

Nomenclature

NCERT Pg 161-163

***15.** Complete the following table of alkyl/aryl halide with their common and IUPAC name.

Compound	Common name	IUPAC name
$H_3C-\underset{}{\overset{CH_3}{\overset{\vert}{C}H}}-CH_2-Cl$	*Iso*-butyl chloride	(i) ________
(ii) ________	*m*-dibromobenzene	1, 3-dibromobenzene
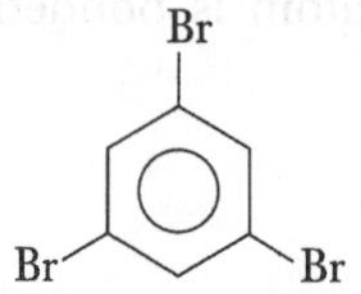	(iii) ________	1, 3, 5-tribromobenzene

16. Consider the following statements.

I. Dihaloalkanes having same type of halogen atoms are called alkylidene or alkylene dihalides.

II. Dihalogen compounds having both halogen atoms present on same carbon atom are called *vic*-dihalide.

Here, incorrect statement(s) is/are

(a) Only I ☐ (b) Only II ☐

(c) Both statements I and II ☐ (d) None of these ☐

17. Complete the following statement by selecting appropriate word.

Ethylidene chloride is ____________ (*vic/gem*) dihalide while ethylene dichloride is an example of ____________ (*vic/gem*) dihalide.

***18.** Match the following structures given in Column I with the names in Column II.

Column I (Structure)	Column II (Names)
A. $CH_3-\overset{CH_3}{\underset{CH_3}{\overset{\vert}{\underset{\vert}{C}}}}-CH_2-Br$	(i) 2-chlorotoluene
B. 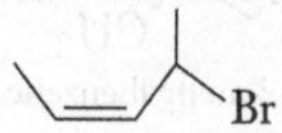	(ii) Chlorophenyl methane
C. 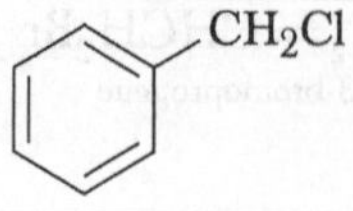	(iii) 2-bromo-3-pentene
D. 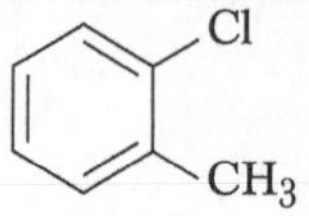	(iv) 1-bromo-2, 2-dimethylpropane

A. ____________ B. ____________

C. ____________ D. ____________

19. Select secondary bromides from the given compounds.

$(CH_3)_2CHBr$, $(CH_3)_3CCH_2Br$, $(CH_3)_2CBrCH_2CH_3$, $CH_3CH(Br)CH_2CH_3$

____

20. Select the incorrect pair of structures and their respective IUPAC names for the following.

(a) 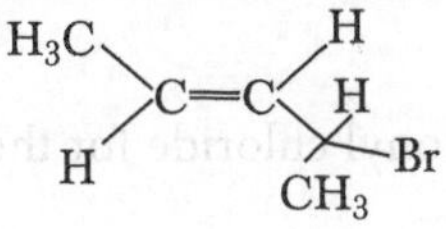 (4-bromopent-2-ene) ☐

(b) 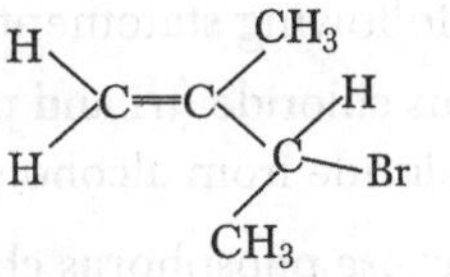 (3-bromo-2-methylbut-1-ene) ☐

(c) 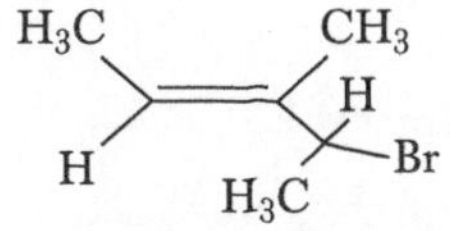 (4-bromopropane) ☐

(d) 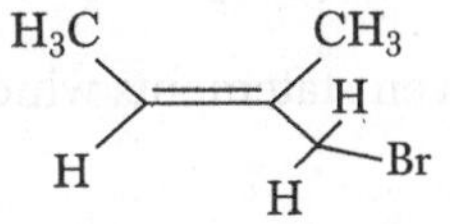 (1-bromo-2-methylbut-2-ene) ☐

21. Give the IUPAC name of the following structures.

(i) 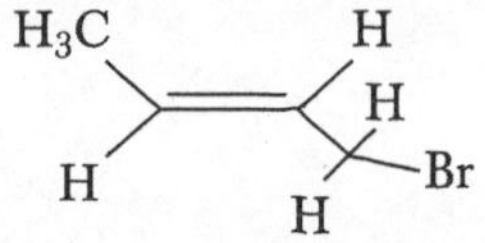 ______________________

(ii) 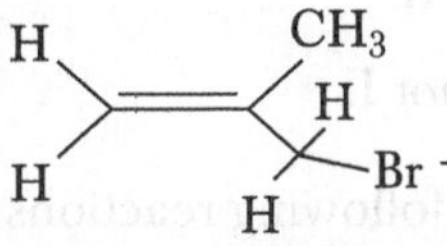 ______________________

22. The IUPAC name of 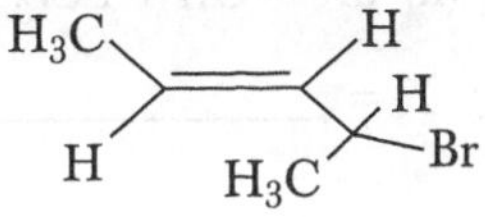 is 4-bromopent-2-ene

True ☐ False ☐

23. Give the structure of 1-bromo-4-*sec*-butyl-2-methylbenzene.

____

TOPIC 3

Nature of C—X bond

NCERT Pg 163-164

24. Carbon-halogen bond of alkyl halide is polarised because

(a) halogen atom is less electronegative ☐

(b) halogen atom is more electronegative than carbon atom ☐

(c) carbon bears negative charge while halogen bears positive charge ☐

(d) None of the above ☐

25. Arrange the following compounds in increasing order of C—X bond enthalpy,

CH_3—Cl, CH_3—I, CH_3—Br, CH_3—F

____

TOPIC 4

Methods of Preparations of Haloalkanes

NCERT Pg 164-166

26. Alkyl halides are best produced from __________ (alkanes/alcohols).

27. Consider the following statements.

I. Phosphorus chloride (tri and penta) are preferred over thionyl chloride for the preparation of alkyl chloride from alcohols.

II. It is so because phosphorus chloride gives pure alkyl halides.

Among the given statements which is/are correct ?

(a) Only I ☐

(b) Only II ☐

(c) Both I and II ☐

(d) Neither I nor II ☐

28. Consider the following reactions and identify X and Y.

(i) $R\text{—OH} + \text{HCl} \xrightarrow{X} R\text{—Cl} + H_2O$ (ii) $3R\text{—OH} + PCl_3 \longrightarrow 3R\text{—Cl} + Y$

X = __________ Y = __________

29. Complete the following reactions.

(i) $R\text{—OH} + SOCl_2 \longrightarrow$ ______ + ______ + HCl

(ii) $R\text{—OH} + \text{NaBr} + H_2SO_4 \longrightarrow$ ______ + ______ + H_2O

30. Name the acid in the presence of which R—I can be obtained by heating alcohol with KI in a good yield (95% approx.).

____

31. Which of the following statement is not correct for phenol?

(a) Aryl halide cannot be prepared by replacement of hydroxyl group of phenol with halogen atom. ☐

(b) Phenols react with halogen acids violently to produce aryl halide. ☐

(c) C—O bond of phenol is difficult to break to form aryl halide. ☐

(d) All of the above ☐

32. Tick the correct one.

For the given reaction,

$$CH_3CH_2CH_2CH_3 \longrightarrow CH_3CH_2CH_2CH_2Cl + CH_3CH_2\underset{\displaystyle |}{\overset{\displaystyle Cl}{C}}HCH_3$$

Reagent is used– $(\text{NaCl} + H_2SO_4)$ ☐ or $(Cl_2/\text{UV light})$. ☐

33. Which of the following monochloro structural isomers expected to be formed on free radical monochlorination of $(CH_3)_2CHCH_2CH_3$?

I. $(CH_3)_2CH\,CH_2CH_2Cl$

II. $(CH_3)_2CH\,CH\,(Cl)\,CH_3$

III. $(CH_3)_2C(Cl)\,CH_2CH_3$

IV. $CH_3CH\,(CH_2Cl)\,CH_2CH_3$

(a) I and II ☐

(b) II and III ☐

(c) II and IV ☐

(d) All of the above ☐

34. In Finkelstein reaction, NaCl or NaBr formed, is precipitated which facilitates forward reaction according to Le-Chatelier principle.

True ☐ False ☐

***35.** Which of the following is a halogen exchange reaction?

(a) $R—X + NaI \longrightarrow RI + NaX \; [X = Cl, Br]$ ☐

(b) $>C=C< + HX \longrightarrow >\underset{H}{C}-\underset{X}{C}<$ ☐

(c) $R—OH + HX \xrightarrow{ZnCl_2} R—X + H_2O$ ☐

(d) 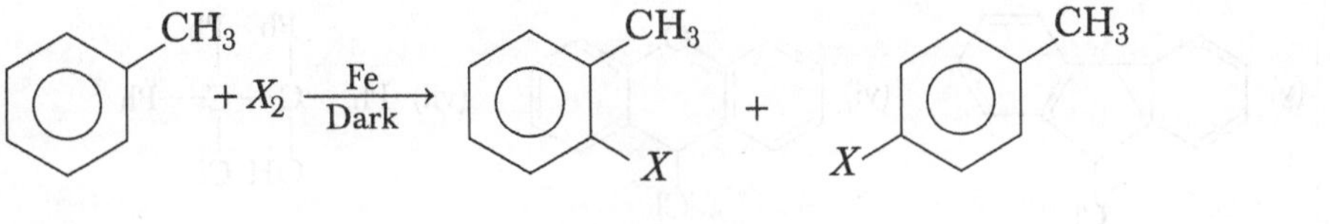 ☐

TOPIC 5
Preparation of Haloarenes

NCERT Pg 166-167

36. Identify the given reaction and choose the correct option.

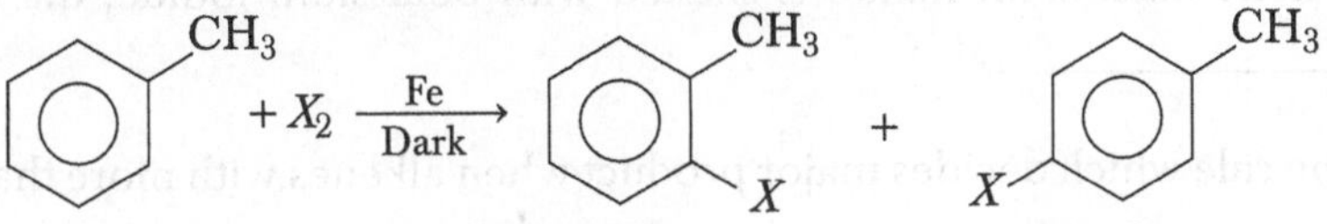

o-halotoluene *p*-halotoluene

(a) Electrophilic elimination reaction ☐

(b) Electrophilic substitution reaction ☐

(c) Free radical addition reaction ☐

(d) Nucleophilic substitution reaction ☐

37. *Ortho* and *para*-halotoluene can be easily separated due to large difference in their ________ (solubility/melting point).

38. Tick the correct one.

In the reaction of toluene with iodine, HIO_4/HNO_3 acts as

Oxidising agent ☐ Reducing agent ☐

***39.** Identify compound Y in the reaction given below.

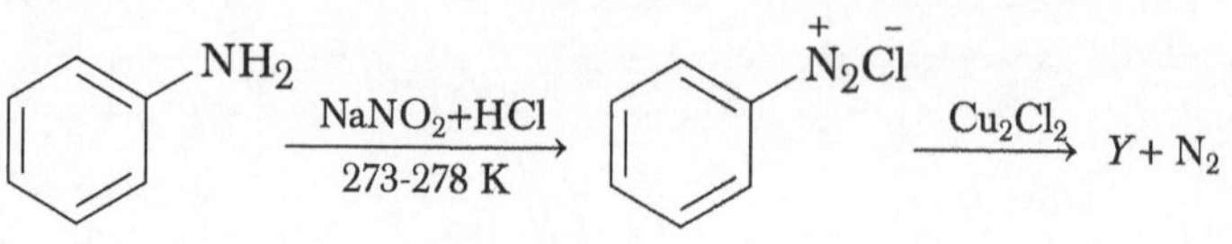

(a) 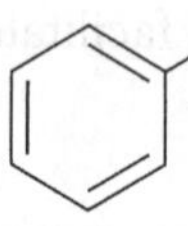 ☐ (b)  ☐ (c) 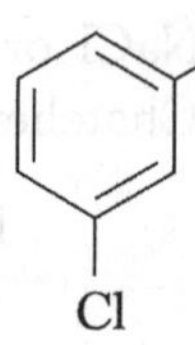 ☐ (d)  ☐

40. Consider the following compounds/ species.

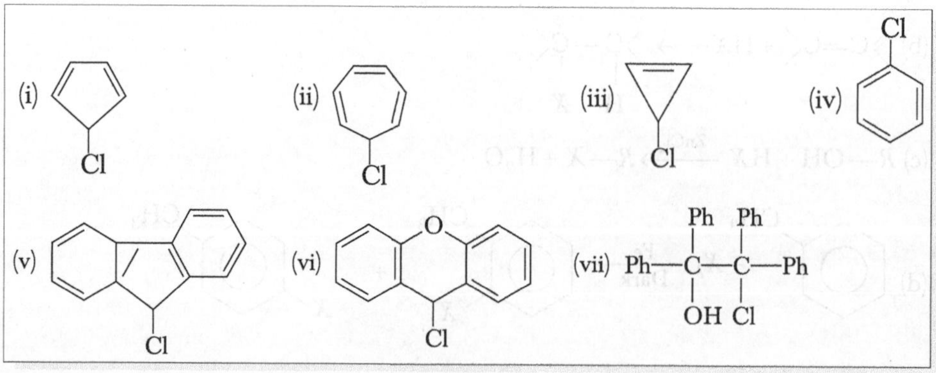

The number of compounds/species which will give white precipitate with aqueous $AgNO_3$.

(a) 2 ☐ (b) 5 ☐

(c) 6 ☐ (d) 7 ☐

41. When benzene diazonium halide is shaked with potassium iodide, the product(s) formed is/are ________.

42. Mention the rule which decides major product when alkenes with more than 2C-atoms reacts with HX.

____

43. A student observed that addition of bromine in CCl_4 to a compound X results in discharge of reddish brown colour of bromine.

(i) Compound X is–Ethane ☐ Ethene ☐

(ii) Reddish brown colour disappears due to formation of colourless compound ________.

(iii) Bromine test is a qualitative test to detect the presence of ______ (saturated/unsaturated) compounds.

44. Write the products for the following reactions.

(i) 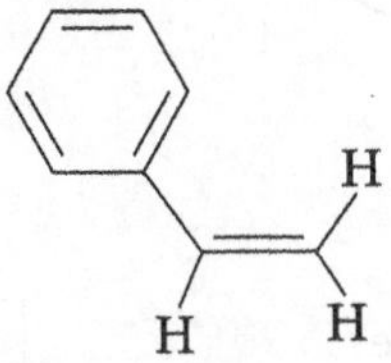 + HBr ⟶ ____________

(ii) 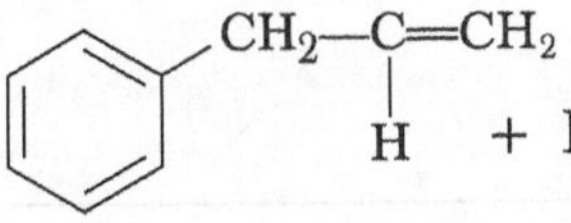 + HBr $\xrightarrow{\text{Peroxide}}$ ____________

***45.** Complete the following sentence by choosing appropriate words from brackets.

Alkyl fluorides are synthesised by heating an alkyl chloride/bromide in presence of ________ and ________ (CaF_2, CoF_2, Hg_2F_2, NaF).

46. Sulphuric acid is used during the reaction of alcohols with KI because it behaves as reducing agent.

True ☐ False ☐

47. Match isomers of C_5H_{12} given in Column I with the product formed given in Column II.

Column I (Isomers of C_2H_{12})	Column II (Product of photochemical chlorination)
A. Neopentane	1. Four isomeric monochloride
B. 2-methylbutane	2. Three isomeric monochloride
C. *n*-pentane	3. A single monochloride

A. ____________ B. ____________ C. ____________

48. Complete the following reaction,

(i) 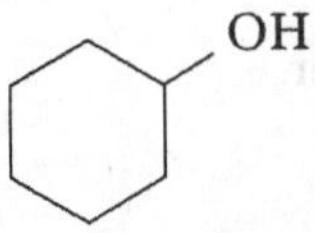 + $SOCl_2$ ⟶

(ii) 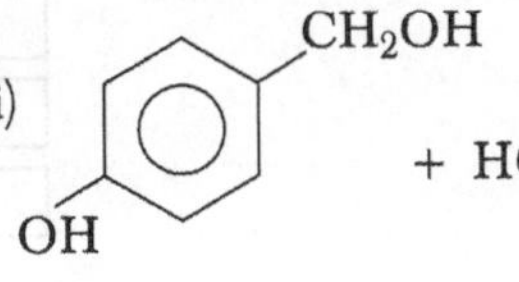 + HCl ⟶

49. Identify '*A*' in the following reaction.

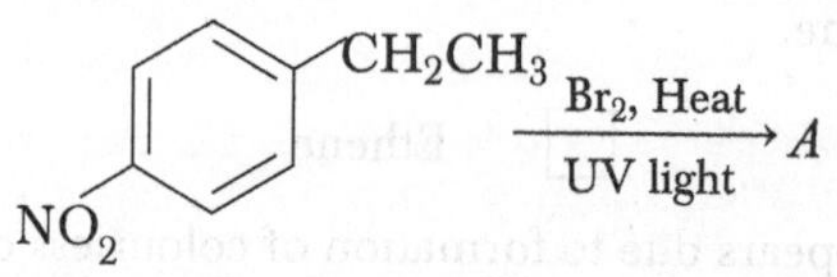

(a) 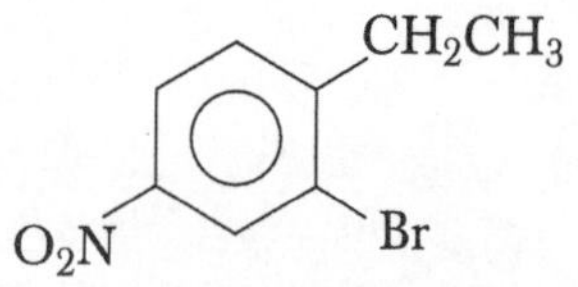 ☐

(b) 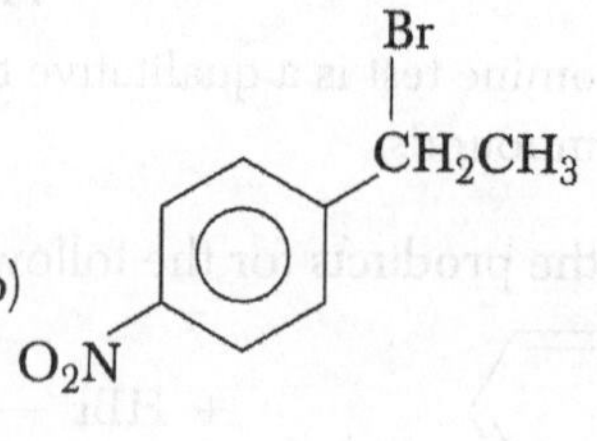 ☐

(c) 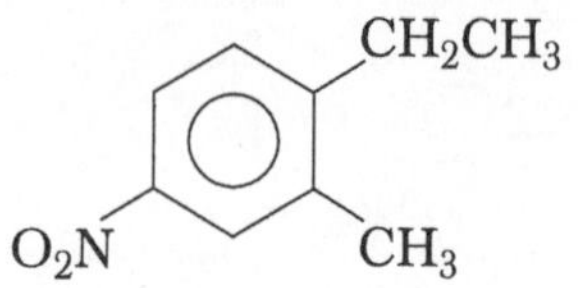 ☐

(d) All of these ☐

50. Name of the product(s) formed when,

(i) 1-methylcyclohexene reacts with HI ____________

(ii) cyclohexene reacts with Br_2 ____________

TOPIC 6

Physical Properties

NCERT Pg 167-169

51. Select the correct option given in bracket regarding the physical properties of pure haloalkanes.

(i) Appearance when pure (colourless/white/yellow) ____________

(ii) Odour (unpleasent/sweet/pungent) ____________

52. Choose the haloalkane which is not a gas at room temperature.

Methyl chloride, Hexyl chloride, Ethyl bromide, Chlorofluoromethane, Methyl bromide.

____

53. The boiling points of alkyl halide are higher than those of corresponding alkanes because of ____________ (H-bonding/dipole-dipole interaction).

54. For a given alkyl group, the boiling points of alkyl halide follow the order.

(a) $RI > RBr > RCl > RF$ ☐

(b) $RCl > RBr > RI > RF$ ☐

(c) $RI > RCl > RBr > RF$ ☐

(d) $RF > RBr > RI > RCl$ ☐

55. Which of the following statement(s) is/are best suited for the given figure?

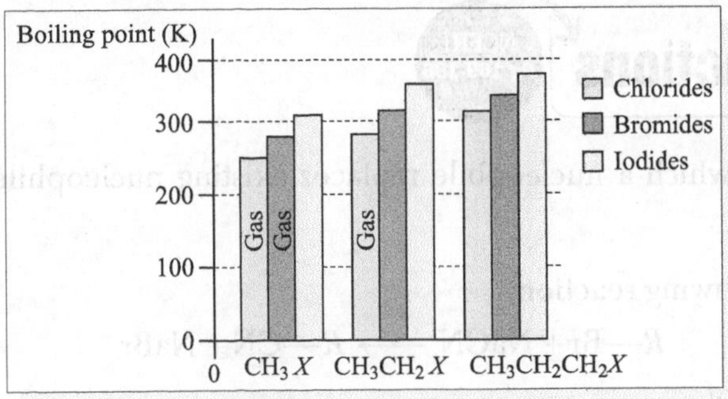

(a) The attraction gets stronger as molecules get bigger in size.

(b) The boiling point of alkyl halide is in order of *R*I > *R*Br > *R*Cl > *R*F.

(c) Magnitude of van der Waals' forces increases as mass of halogen atom increases.

(d) All of the above

56. Which of the following isomer has the highest melting point?

(a) 1, 2-dicholorbenzene

(b) 1, 3 -dichlorobenzene

(c) 1, 4-dichlorobenzene

(d) All isomers have same melting points

57. Organise the following haloalkanes in increasing order of density.

$n\text{-}C_3H_7Br$, $CHCl_3$, $n\text{-}C_3H_7Cl$

58. Which of the following statements are incorrect regarding haloalkanes?

I. Haloalkanes are very slightly soluble in water.

II. Solubility of haloalkanes in organic solvent is low.

III. Boiling point of isomeric haloalkanes increases with increase in branching.

IV. Density increases with increase in number of carbon atoms, halogen atoms in haloalkanes.

(a) I and II (b) II and III

(c) III and IV (d) II and IV

59. Arrange the given compounds in order of increasing boiling points.

(i) Bromomethane, bromoform, chloromethane, dibromomethane

(ii) 1-chloropropane, Isopropyl chloride, 1-chlorobutane.

TOPIC 7

Chemical Reactions

NCERT Pg 169-186

60. The reaction in which a nucleophile replaces existing nucleophile in a molecule is called ______________.

61. Consider the following reaction,

$$R\text{—Br} + \text{NaCN} \longrightarrow R\text{—CN} + \text{NaBr}$$

It is an example of

(a) elimination reaction ☐ (b) nucleophilic substitution ☐

(c) electrophilic substitution ☐ (d) oxidation-reduction ☐

62. Pick the odd one out in context of ambident nucleophiles.

CN^-, OH^-, NO_2^-

____

63. Which of the following is a correct statement for C_2H_5Br?

(a) It reacts with metallic Na to give ethane. ☐

(b) It gives nitroethane on heating with aqueous solution of $AgNO_2$. ☐

(c) It gives C_2H_5OH on boiling with alcoholic potash. ☐

(d) It forms diethylthioether on heating with alcoholic KSH. ☐

***64.** Answer the following questions in one word.

(i) Order of S_N2 reactions ______________________

(ii) Factor on which rate of reaction depends in S_N2 reaction ______________

***65.** Consider the following,

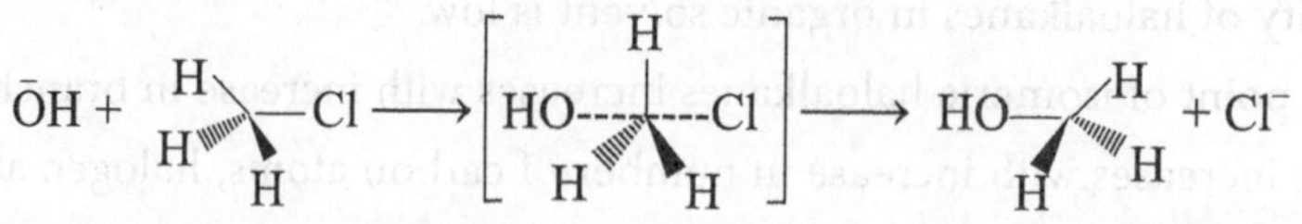

Select the incorrect statement for the S_N2 mechanism in given figure.

(a) As reaction progress, bond between carbon atom and nucleophile is formed with weakening of carbon atom and the leaving group bond. ☐

(b) There is the inversion of configuration. ☐

(c) The transition state is unstable and cannot be isolated. ☐

(d) Carbon atom is bonded to four atoms during the transition state. ☐

66. Consider the following,

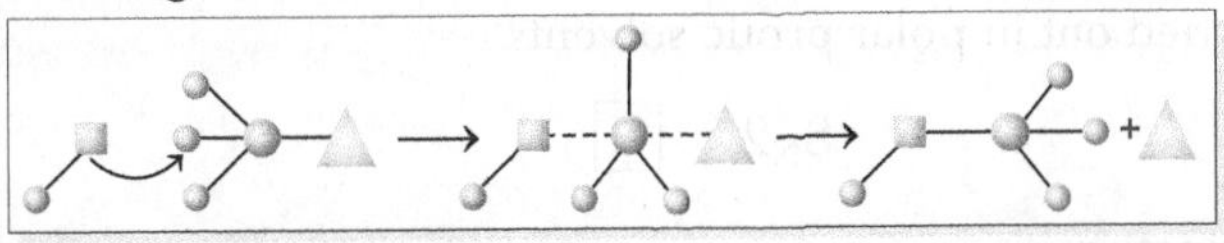

Square dot represents the incoming hydroxide ion, while triangle dot represents the outgoing halide ion.

I. It is second order kinetics.

II. Its rate depends upon the concentration of only one reactant.

III. This reaction occur in single step and no intermediate is formed.

Mark (✓) and (×) under correct and incorrect with respect to given statements.

	Correct	Incorrect
I.	______	______
II.	______	______
III.	______	______

67. The order of reactivity for S_N2 reaction is

Primary halide > Tertiary halide > Secondary halide.

True ☐ False ☐

***68.** For S_N2 reactions, order of reactivity for the following compounds is given as

Isopropyl halide, Ethyl halide, tert-butyl halide, Methyl halide

____

69. In which case the approach of nucleophile is easy in S_N2 reaction as shown in figure?

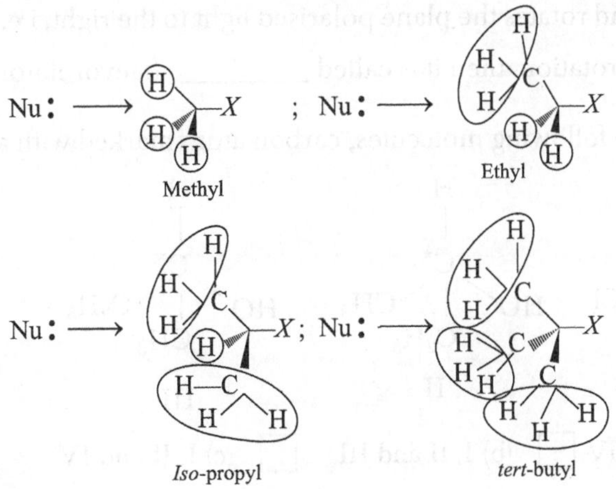

(a) Methyl ☐ (b) Ethyl ☐ (c) *Iso*-propyl ☐ (d) *tert*-butyl ☐

70. For the following reactions,

$$\underset{(A)}{(CH_3)_3CBr} + \underset{(B)}{^{-}OH} \longrightarrow \underset{(C)}{(CH_3)_3COH} + \underset{(D)}{Br^-}$$

Rate of reaction depends on the concentration of ______________.

71. Tick the correct one from the following.

(i) Reaction carried out in polar protic solvents

S_N1 ☐ S_N2 ☐

(ii) First order kinetics

S_N1 ☐ S_N2 ☐

***72.** Which of the following alkyl halides will undergoes S_N1 reaction most readily?

(a) $(CH_3)_3C—F$ ☐ (b) $(CH_3)_3C—I$ ☐

(c) $(CH_3)_3C—Cl$ ☐ (d) $(CH_3)_3C—Br$ ☐

73. In the following pairs of halogen compounds which would undergoes S_N2 reaction faster?

(i) 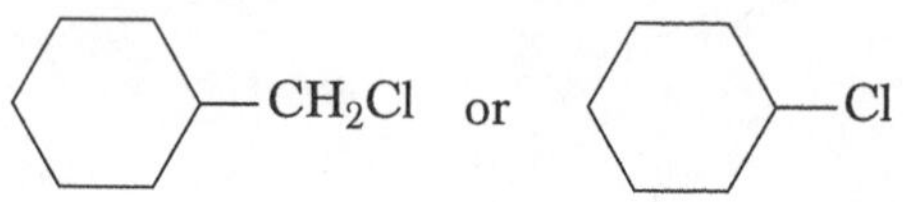 ____________

(ii) 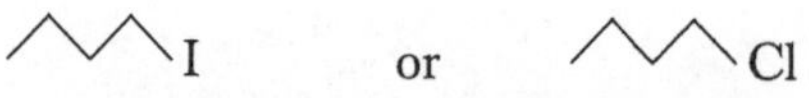 ____________

74. Which of the following order of reactivity are incorrect with respect to S_N1 and S_N2?

I. $CH_3CH_2CH_2CH_2Br < (CH_3)_2CHCH_2Br < CH_3CH_2CH(Br)CH_3 < (CH_3)_3CBr$ (S_N1)

II. $CH_3CH_2CH_2CH_2Br < (CH_3)_2CH\,CH_2Br < CH_3CH_2CH(Br)CH_3 < (CH_3)_3C\,Br$ (S_N2)

III. $C_6H_5C(CH_3)(C_6H_5)Br < C_6H_5CH(C_6H_5)Br < C_6H_5CH(CH_3)\,Br < C_6H_5CH_2Br$ (S_N1)

IV. $C_6H_5C(CH_3)(C_6H_5)\,Br < C_6H_5CH\,(C_6H_5)Br < C_6H_5CH(CH_3)Br < C_6H_5CH_2Br$ (S_N2)

(a) I and II ☐ (b) II and III ☐ (c) III and IV ☐ (d) I and IV ☐

75. If the compound rotates the plane polarised light to the right, i.e. ____________ (clockwise/anticlockwise) rotation, then it is called ________ (laevorotatory/dextrorotatory).

76. In which of the following molecules, carbon atom marked with asterisk (*) is asymmetric?

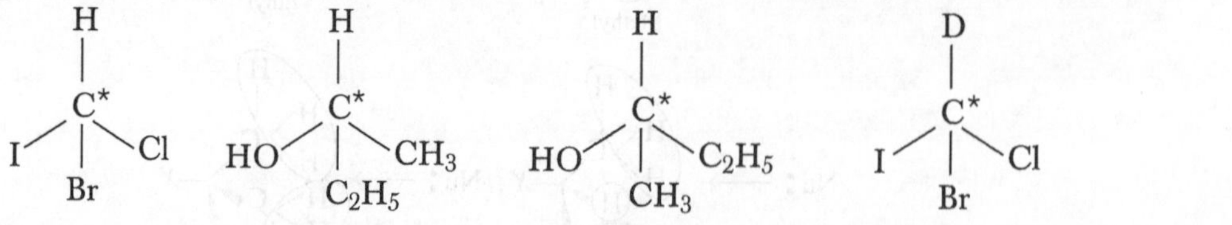

I II III IV

(a) I, II, III and IV ☐ (b) I, II and III ☐ (c) I, II and IV ☐ (d) I, III and IV ☐

77. Amongst the following, the total number of species not showing enantiomers is

Butan-2-ol, 2-hydroxypropanoic acid, 2-chlorobutane, 2-bromo-2-chlorobutane, Iso-propyl chloride

(a) 1 ☐ (b) 2 ☐ (c) 3 ☐ (d) 4 ☐

78. Amongst the following, the total number of species which are achiral molecules is

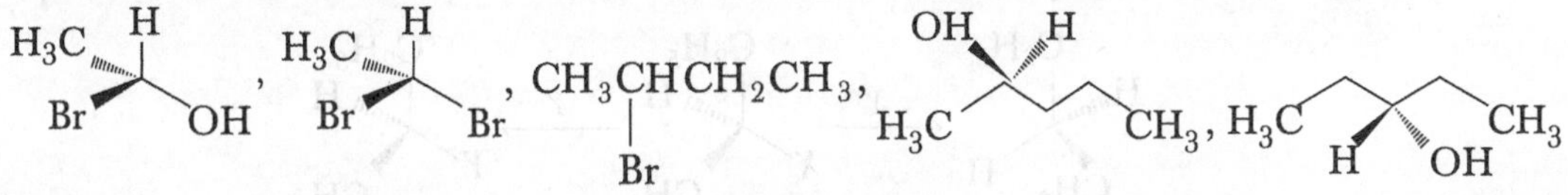

(a) 2 ☐ (b) 3 ☐ (c) 4 ☐ (d) 5 ☐

79. Consider the following figure of propan-2-ol and choose the correct option.

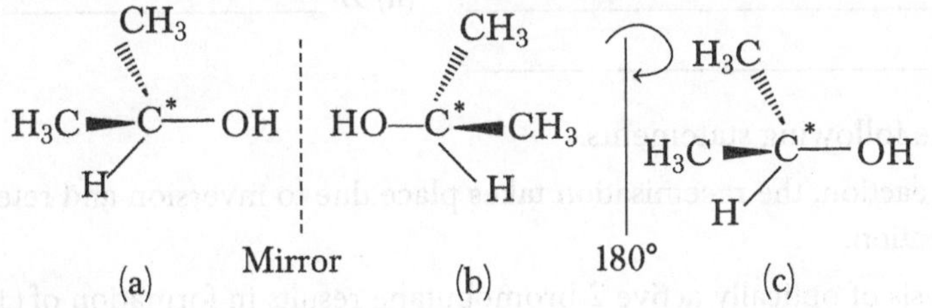

(i) Propan-2-ol is

(a) chiral molecule ☐ (b) achiral molecule ☐

(ii) Asterisk carbon in propan-2-ol is

(a) symmetric ☐ (b) asymmetric ☐

80. Consider the following structure of butan-2-ol with its mirror image and complete the given statements.

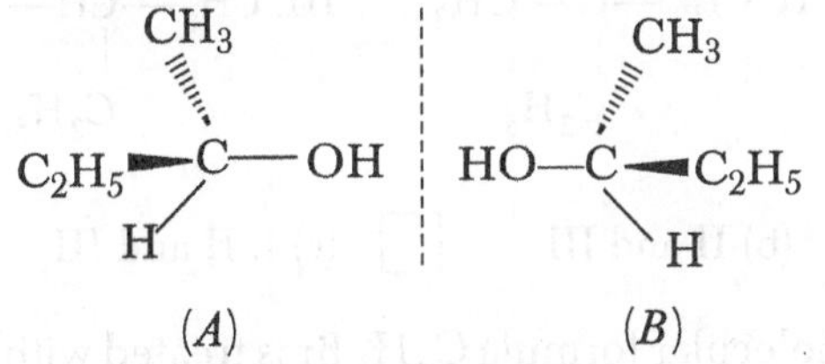

(i) *A* and *B* are ____________ of each other.

(ii) Equimolar mixture of *A* and *B* is known as ____________.

81. Enantiomers possess identical chemical properties but different physical properties.

Correct ☐ Incorrect ☐

82. Choose the chiral molecule(s) from each of the following pair of compounds.

(i) 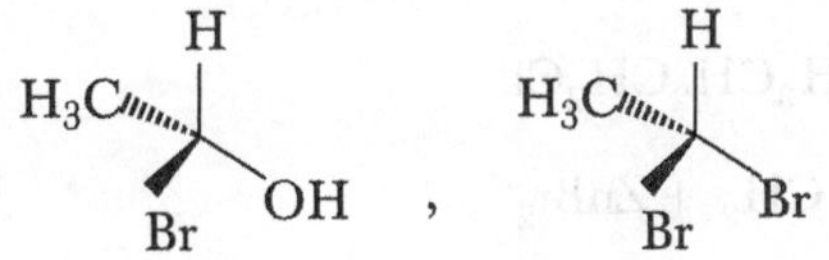 ____________

(ii) 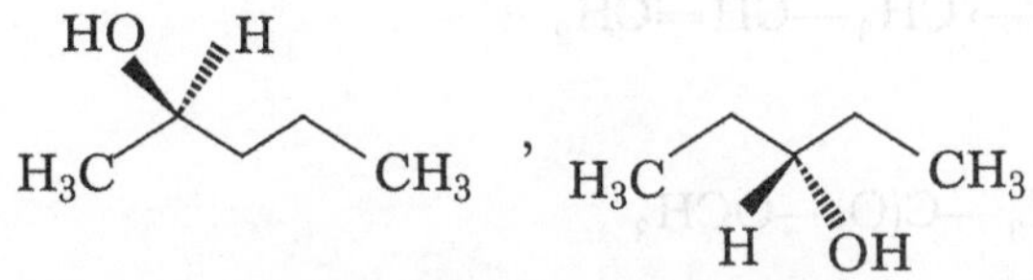 ____________

(iii) $CH_3CH(Br)CH_2CH_3$, $CH_3CH_2CH_2CH_2Br$ ____________

83. Mention the name of process which results in the formation of the following compound.

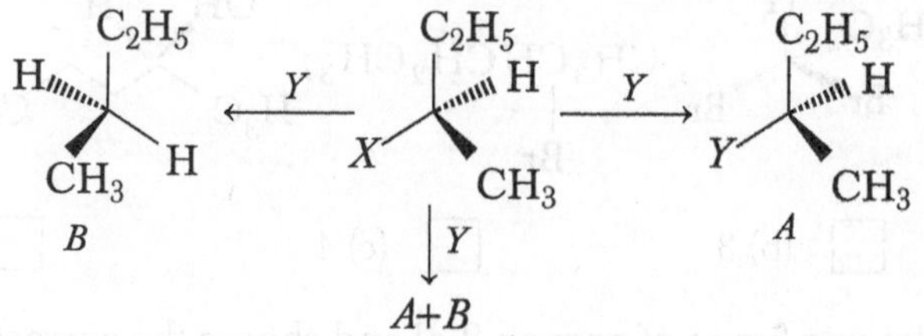

(i) A ____________________. (ii) B ____________________.

(iii) $A+B$ ____________________.

***84.** Consider the following statements.

I. In S_N1 reaction, the racemisation takes place due to inversion and retention of configuration.

II. Hydrolysis of optically active 2-bromobutane results in formation of (±)–butan-2-ol.

Here, correct statement(s) is/are

(a) Only I ☐ (b) Only II ☐ (c) Both I and II ☐ (d) None of these ☐

85. Which of the following compounds will give racemic mixture on nucleophilic substitution by OH^- ion?

I. $CH_3—CH(C_2H_5)—Br$ II. $CH_3—C(Br)(C_2H_5)—CH_3$ III. $CH_3—CH(C_2H_5)—CH_2Br$

(a) I and II ☐ (b) II and III ☐ (c) I, II and III ☐ (d) Only I ☐

86. Compound 'A' with molecular formula C_4H_9Br is treated with *aq.* KOH solution. The rate of reaction depends upon concentration of compound 'A' only. When another optically active isomer 'B' of this compound treated with *aq.* KOH solution, rate of reaction was found to dependent on concentration of compound and KOH both.
Write structure of 'A' and 'B'.

A = ____________________ B = ____________________

87. Which of the following reaction is an elimination reaction?

I. $CH_3—CH_2—CH_2—OH \xrightarrow{PCl_3} CH_3CH_2CH_2Cl$

II. $Br—CH_2—CH_2—Br \xrightarrow{Zn} CH_2=CH_2 + ZnBr_2$

III. $CH_3—CH(Cl)—CH_3 \xrightarrow{\text{Alc. KOH}} CH_3—CH=CH_2$

IV. $CH_3—COOH \xrightarrow{CH_3OH} CH_3—C(O)—OCH_3$

(a) I and II ☐ (b) II and III ☐

(c) II, III and VI ☐ (d) All of these ☐

88. The major product *Y* in the following reaction is

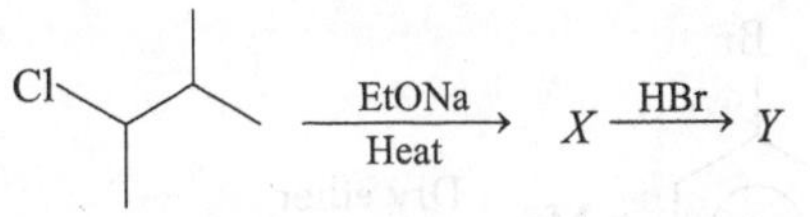

(a) 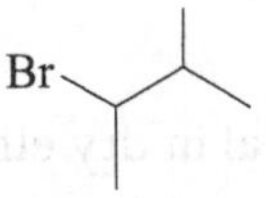

☐ (b) 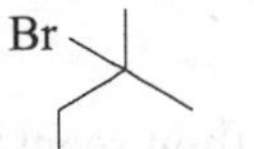

☐ (c) 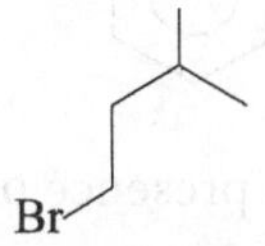

☐ (d) 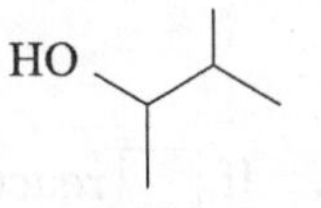

☐

89. Write the major product formed when 2-bromopentane reacts with nucleophile (OH^-).

____

90. Enlist three factors which determine whether a reaction will be S_N1, S_N2 or elimination.

(i) ____________ (ii) ____________ (iii) ____________

91. Write the name of the reactions figures (i) and (ii) represent.

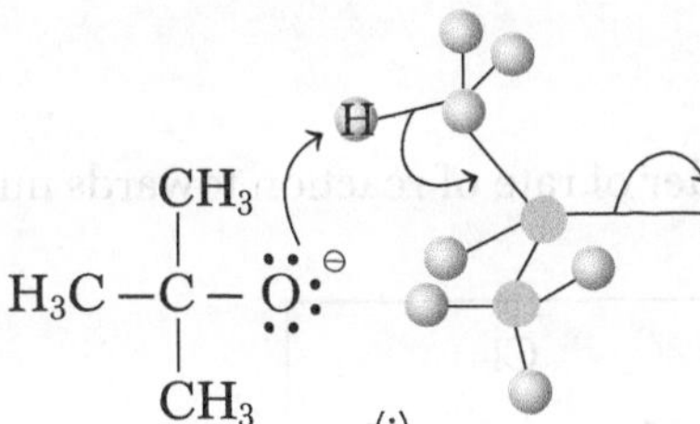

(i)

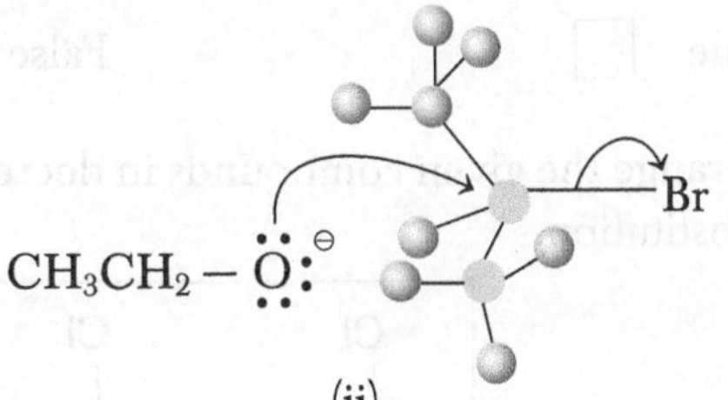

(ii)

(i) ____________ (ii) ____________

92. Among the following rules, the one which is applied in the given reaction is

$$CH_3CHBrCH_2CH_3 \xrightarrow{\text{Alc. KOH}}$$

I. $CH_3CH = CHCH_3$ (major product) II. $CH_2 = CHCH_2CH_3$ (minor product)

(a) Saytzeff's rule ☐

(b) Hofmann's rule ☐

(c) Markovnikov's rule ☐

(d) Kharasch effect ☐

93. Which of the following is correct regarding the route of a reaction?

(a) Primary alkyl halide will prefer S_N2 reaction. ☐

(b) Secondary alkyl halide will prefer S_N1/S_N2 or elimination depending upon strength of base/nucleophile. ☐

(c) Tertiary alkyl halide will prefer S_N1 or elimination depending upon stability of carbocation. ☐

(d) All of the above ☐

94. Complete the reaction given below.

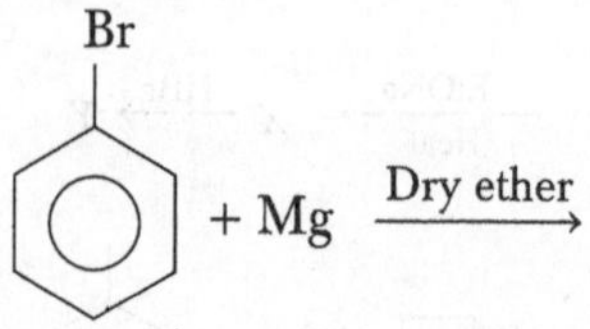

____

95. If  react with Cl_2 in presence of light and then react with Na metal in dry ether, final product is

(a) 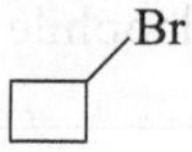

(b) 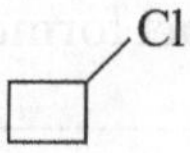

(c) 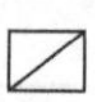

(d) 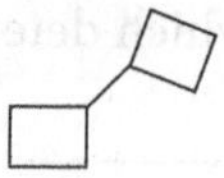

96. Haloarenes are more reactive towards nucleophilic addition reactions.

True ☐ False ☐

97. Arrange the given compounds in decreasing order of rate of reaction towards nucleophilic substitution.

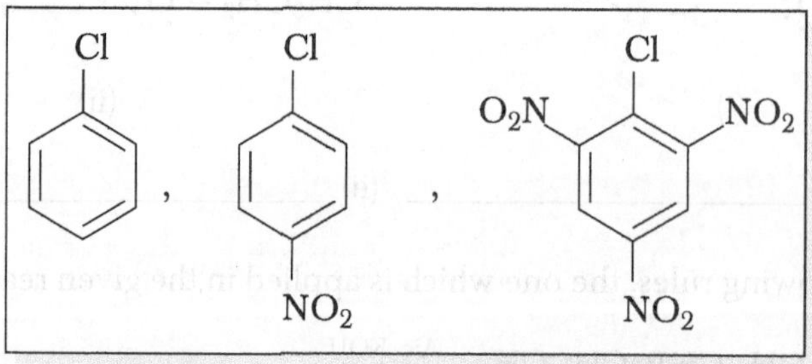

____

***98.** Complete the following reactions.

(i) 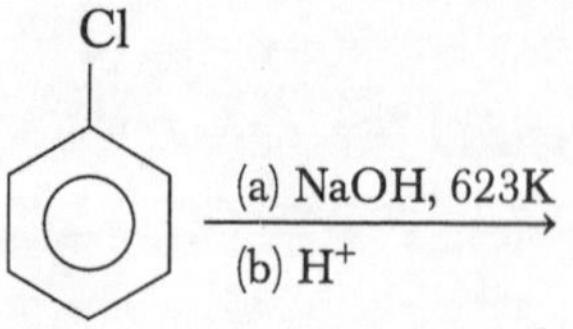

____

(ii) 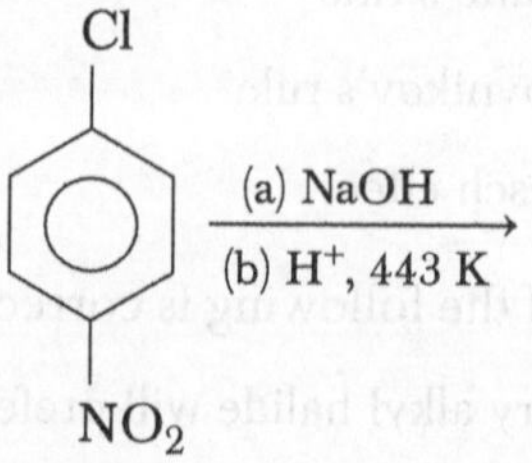

____

(iii) 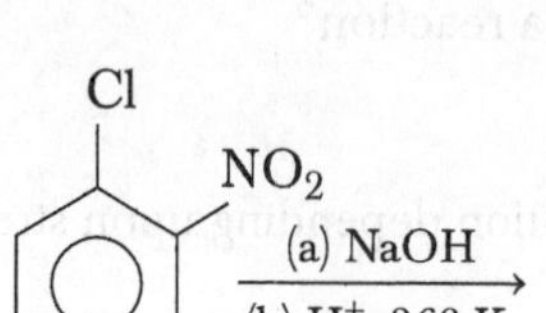

____

99. 2, 4, 6-trinitrochlorobenzene on treatment with warm water produces.

(a) Chlorobenzene 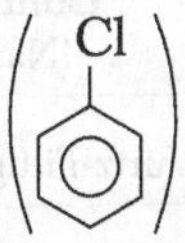 ☐ (b) Picric acid 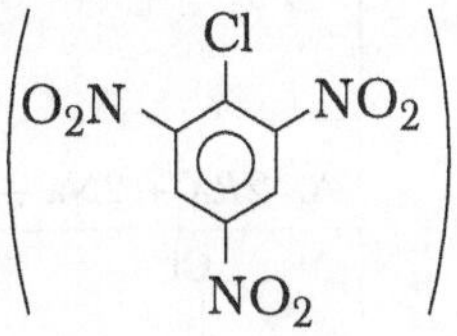 ☐

(c) Phenol 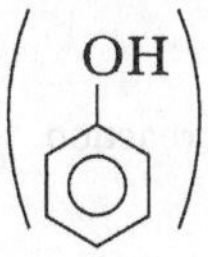 ☐ (d) No product form ☐

100. Pick the incorrect statement with respect to nucleophilic substitution reaction of haloarenes.

(a) Presence of nitro group at *ortho* or *para*- position increases reactivity of haloarenes. ☐

(b) Nitration of chlorobenzene leads to formation of *m*-nitrochlorobenzene. ☐

(c) —NO_2 group is a *m*-directing group. ☐

(d) Picric acid is formed when trinitrochlorobenzene treated with warm water. ☐

101. The compound C_7H_8 undergoes the following reactions,

$$C_7H_8 \xrightarrow{3Cl_2/\Delta} A \xrightarrow{Br_2/Fe} B \xrightarrow{Zn/HCl} C$$

The product '*C*' is

(a) 3-bromo-2, 4, 6-trichlorotoluene ☐ (b) *o*-bromotoluene ☐

(c) *m*-bromotoluene ☐ (d) *p*-bromotoluene ☐

102. Complete the analogy with respect to electrophilic substitution reaction of chlorobenzene.

Conc. H_2SO_4 : 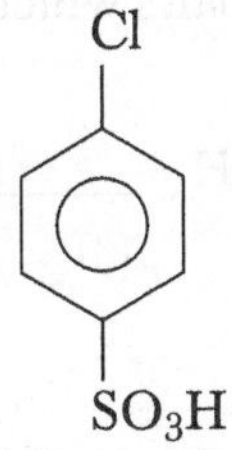 :: CH_3COCl + Anhydrous : *X*

(Reagent) (Major product) (Reagent) (Major product)

Identify *X*.

(a) 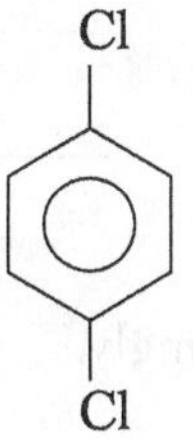 ☐ (b) 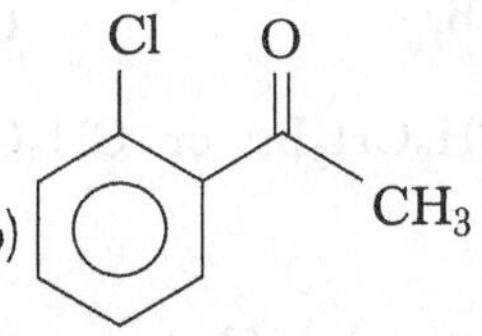 ☐

(c) 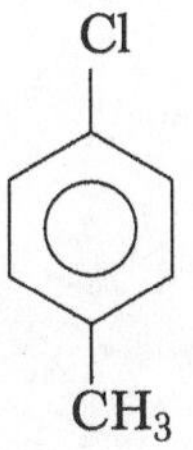 ☐ (d) 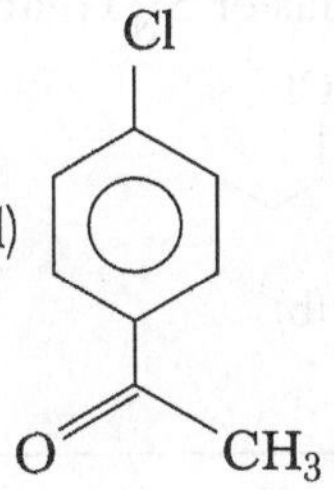 ☐

***103.** Match the following reactions in Column I with the names given in Column II.

Column I (Reactions)	Column II (Names)
A. $2RX + 2Na \longrightarrow RR + 2NaX$	1. Wurtz-Fittig reaction
B. 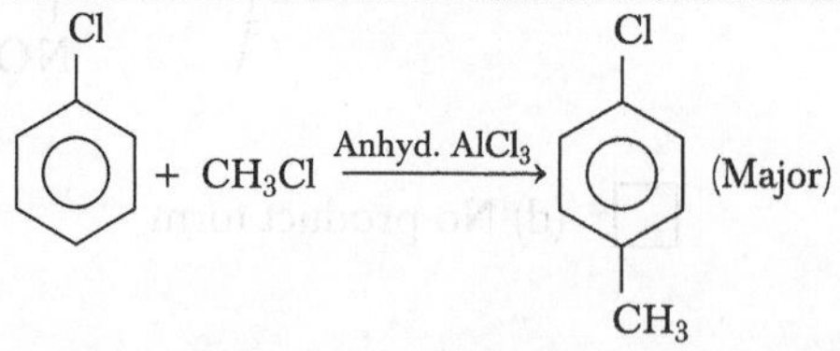	2. Nitration reaction
C. 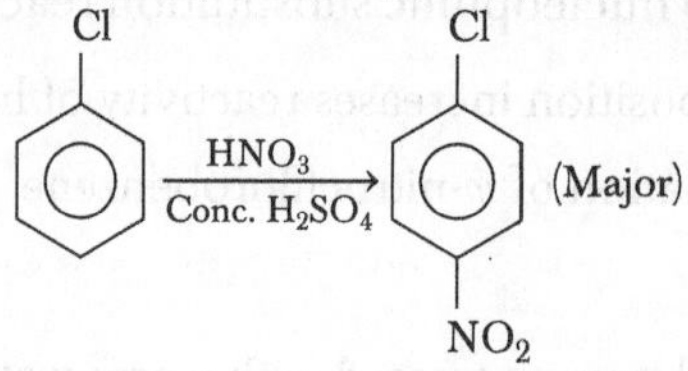	3. Wurtz reaction
D. 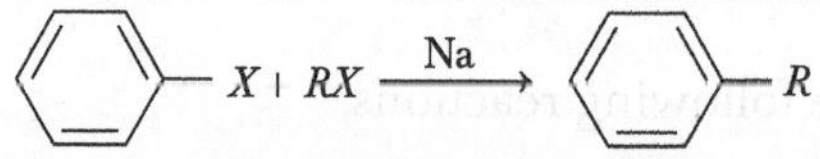	4. Friedel-Craft reaction

A. ____________________ B. ____________________

C. ____________________ D. ____________________

104. Write the Fittig reaction and name the product formed.

____

105. Extract those alkyl halide from following pairs which expect to react more rapidly by S_N2 mechanism.

(i) $CH_3CH_2CH_2CH_2Br$ or $CH_3CH_2CH(Br)CH_3$ ____________________

(ii) $CH_3CH_2CH(Br)CH_3$ or $CH_3—C(CH_3)_2—Br$ ____________________

(iii) $CH_3CH(CH_3)CH_2CH_2Br$ or $CH_3CH_2CH(CH_3)CH_2CH_2Br$ ____________________

106. In the following pairs of halogen compounds, choose the option accordingly.

(i) Which undergoes faster S_N1 reaction?

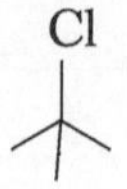

(a)

and

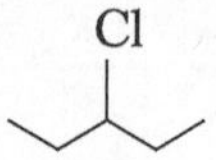

(b)

____

(ii) Which undergoes faster S_N1 reaction?

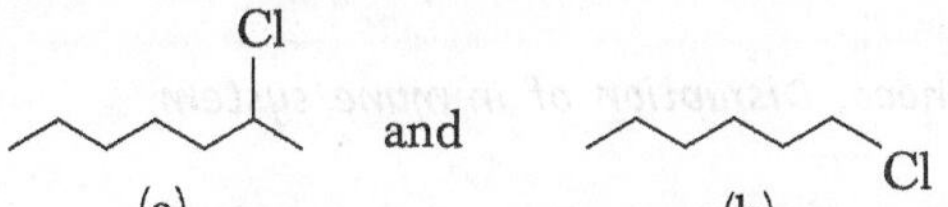

(a) and (b)

---

107. Identify, *A, B, C, D, E, R* and *R′* in the following.

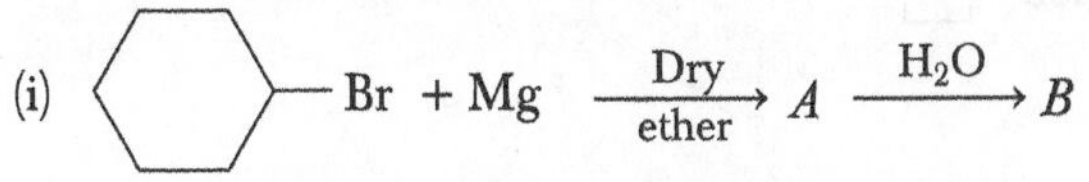

(ii) $R—Br + Mg \xrightarrow[\text{ether}]{\text{Dry}} C \xrightarrow{D_2O} CH_3\underset{\displaystyle D}{\underset{|}{C}}HCH_3$

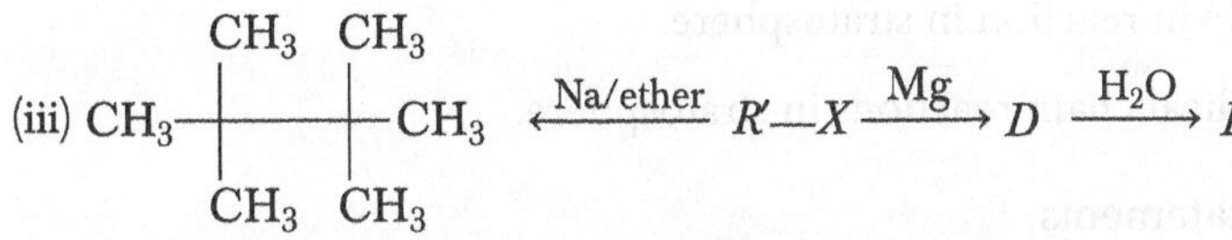

A = ______ *B* = ______ *C* = ______

D = ______ *E* = ______ *R* = ______

R′ = ______

TOPIC 8
Polyhalogen Compounds
NCERT Pg 187-188

108. The correct formula of methyl dichloride is ______ ($ClC \equiv CCl$ / CH_2Cl_2).

109. The IUPAC name of chloroform is ______.

110. Compound *X* is slowly oxidised by air in the presence of light to an extremely poisonous gas *Y*. Therefore, compound *X* is stored in closed dark coloured bottles. Identify *X* and *Y*.

X = ______ *Y* = ______

111. The antiseptic properties of iodoform is due to

(a) liberation of iodine ☐ (b) smell of iodoform ☐

(c) colour of iodoform ☐ (d) None of these ☐

112. The chloro compound which can be used as fire extinguisher is

(a) CH_3Cl ☐ (b) $CoCl_2$ ☐

(c) CCl_4 ☐ (d) $CHCl_3$ ☐

113. Exposure to lower levels of compound *X* in air can lead to slightly impaired hearing and vision. Identify compound *X*.

______

114. Pick the odd one out in context of the effect of depletion of ozone layer.

Skin cancer, Eye disease, Diarrhoea, Disruption of immune system.

____

115. Formula of freon-12 is $CHCl_3$.

True ☐ False ☐

116. Which among the following is true?

(a) Freon does not initiate radical chain reactions in stratosphere. ☐

(b) Iodoform initiate radical chain reaction in stratosphere. ☐

(c) Freon initiate radical chain reaction in stratosphere. ☐

(d) Chloroform initiate radical chain reactions in stratosphere. ☐

117. Consider the following statements.

I. Chloroform vapours depress the central nervous system.

II. Paul Muller in Switzerland discovered the effectiveness of DDT as fertilizers.

Which of the following statement(s) is/are incorrect.

(a) Only I ☐ (b) Only II ☐

(c) Both I and II ☐ (d) None of these ☐

118. Name the compound which is employed as a solvent for fats, alkaloids, iodine and other substances.

(a) Dichloromethane ☐ (b) Trichloromethane ☐

(c) Triiodomethane ☐ (d) Tetrachloromethane ☐

119. Match the following compounds given in Column I with the effects given in Column II.

Column I (Compounds)	Column II (Effects)
A. Dichloromethane	1. Causes liver cancer
B. Chloroform	2. Direct contact can burn cornea of eye
C. Freons	3. Depress nervous system
D. Carbon tetrachloride	4. Ozone layer depletion

A.______________ B.______________

C.______________ D.______________

120. Expand DDT and give it IUPAC and structure.

____

Assertion-Reason Questions

Given below are two statements, one is labelled as Assertion (A) and other is labelled as Reason (R). Select the most appropriate answer from the options given below.
(a) Both A and R are true and R is the correct explanation of A.
(b) Both A and R are true but R is not the correct explanation of A.
(c) A is true but R is false.
(d) A is false but R is true.

1. **Assertion** (A) $CH_2 = CH—CH_2 —X$ is an examples of allyl halides.

Reason (R) These are the compounds in which the halogen atom is bonded to an sp^2 hybridised carbon atom.

(a) ☐ (b) ☐ (c) ☐ (d) ☐

2. **Assertion** (A) Melting points of isomeric dihalobenzenes are nearly the same.

Reason (R) Isomeric dihalobenzenes have same molecular masses.

(a) ☐ (b) ☐ (c) ☐ (d) ☐

3. **Assertion** (A) CH_4 does not react with Cl_2 in dark.

Reason (R) In dark, there is no such energy for free radicals formation.

(a) ☐ (b) ☐ (c) ☐ (d) ☐

4. **Assertion** (A) Boiling point increases with increase in size and mass of halogen atom.

Reason (R) Due to decrease in van der Waals' force, boiling point increases with increase in mass of halogen atom.

(a) ☐ (b) ☐ (c) ☐ (d) ☐

5. **Assertion** (A) Aryl halides are highly reactive towards nucleophilic substitution reactions.

Reason (R) In case of haloarenes, halogen atom is attached to sp^2 hybridised carbon atom.

(a) ☐ (b) ☐ (c) ☐ (d) ☐

6. **Assertion** (A) KCN reacts with methyl chloride to give methyl cyanide only.

Reason (R) CN^- is an ambident nucleophile.

(a) ☐ (b) ☐ (c) ☐ (d) ☐

7. **Assertion** (A) In monohaloarenes, further electrophilic substitution occurs at *ortho* and *para* position.

Reason (R) Halogen atom is a ring deactivator.

(a) ☐ (b) ☐ (c) ☐ (d) ☐

8. **Assertion** (A) Hydrolysis of (–) – 2-bromooctane proceeds with inversion of configuration.

Reason (R) This reaction proceeds through the formation of carbocation.

(a) ☐ (b) ☐ (c) ☐ (d) ☐

9. **Assertion** (A) Haloarenes are less reactive than haloalkenes towards nucleophilic substitution reaction.

Reason (R) It is difficult to break a shorter bond (169 pm) in haloarenes than a longer C—Cl bond (177 pm) in haloalkenes.

(a) ☐ (b) ☐ (c) ☐ (d) ☐

10. **Assertion** (A) Aryl iodides can be prepared by reaction of arenes with iodine in the presence of an oxidising agent.

Reason (R) Oxidising agent oxidises I_2 into HI.

(a) ☐ (b) ☐ (c) ☐ (d) ☐

Case-Based Questions

1. Nucleophilic substitution reactions are of two types; substitution nucleophilic bimolecular (S_N2) and substitution nucleophilic unimolecular (S_N1) depending on molecules taking part in determining the rate of reaction.

Reactivity of alkyl halide towards S_N1 and S_N2 reaction depends on various factors such as steric hindrance, stability of intermediate or transition state and polarity of solvent. S_N2 reaction mechanism is favoured mostly by 1° alkyl halide then 2° and then 3°. This order is reversed in case of S_N1 reactions.

(i) Which of the following is most reactive towards nucleophilic substitution reaction?

(a) C_6H_5Cl ☐ (b) $CH_2{=}CHCl$ ☐
(c) $ClCH_2CH{=}CH_2$ ☐ (d) $CH_3CH{=}CHCl$ ☐

(ii) Isopropyl chloride undergoes hydrolysis by

(a) S_N1 ☐ (b) S_N2 ☐
(c) S_N1 and S_N2 ☐ (d) Neither S_N1 nor S_N2 ☐

(iii) The most reactive nucleophile among the following is

(a) CH_3O^- ☐ (b) $C_6H_5O^-$ ☐
(c) $(CH_3)_2CHO^-$ ☐ (d) $(CH_3)_3CO^-$ ☐

(iv) 3° alkyl halides are practically inert to substitution by S_N2 mechanism because of

(a) insolubility ☐ (b) instability ☐
(c) inductive effect ☐ (d) steric hindrance ☐

2. A chloro compound (*A*) on reduction with Zn-Cu and ethanol gives the hydrocarbon (*B*) with five carbon atoms. When (*A*) is dissolved in dry ether and treated with sodium metal, it gave 2, 2, 5, 5-tetramethylhexane. The treatment of (*A*) with alcoholic KCN gives compound (*C*).

(i) The compound (*A*) is

(a) 1-chloro-2, 2-dimethyl propane ☐
(b) 1-chloro-2, 2-dimethyl butane ☐
(c) 1-chloro-2-methyl butane ☐
(d) 2-chloro-2-methyl butane ☐

(ii) The reaction of (C) with Na, C_2H_5OH gives

(a) $(CH_3)_3CCH_2CONH_2$ ☐ (b) $(CH_3)_3CNH_2$ ☐
(c) $(CH_3)_3CCH_2CH_2NH_2$ ☐ (d) $(CH_3)_2CHCH_2NH_2$ ☐

(iii) The reaction of (A) with *aq.* KOH will preferably favour

(a) S_N1 ☐ (b) S_N2 ☐
(c) $E1$ ☐ (d) $E2$ ☐

(iv) Compound (B) is

(a) *n*-pentane ☐ (b) 2, 2-dimethyl propane ☐
(c) 2-methyl butane ☐ (d) None of these ☐

COMPETITION EDGE UP

1. *Total number of stereo isomers possible for the given structure.*
[NCERT (New) Pg. 176, JEE Main 2024]

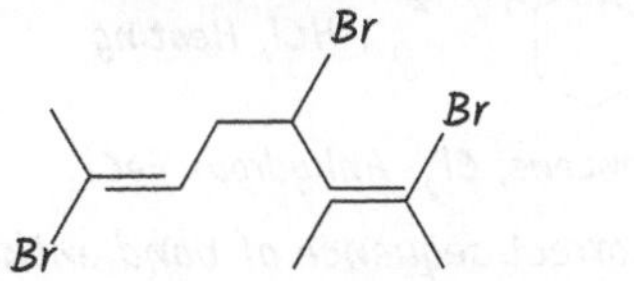

(a) 4 ☐ (b) 3 ☐
(c) 2 ☐ (d) 8 ☐

2. *Identify the major product in the following reaction.* **[NCERT (New) Pg. 182, JEE Main 2024]**

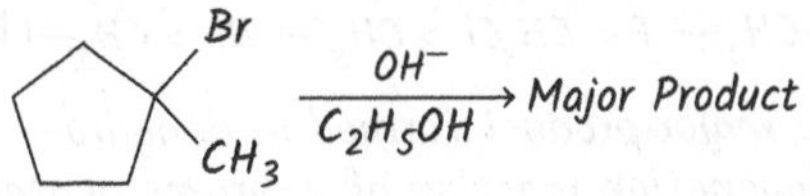

(a) 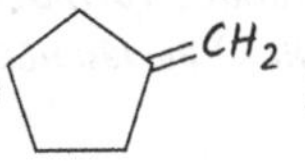 ☐ (b) 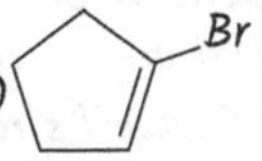 ☐

(c) 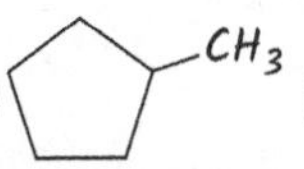 ☐ (d) 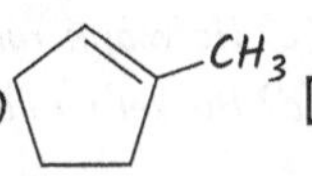 ☐

3. *Identify structure of 2, 3-dibromo-1-phenylpentane.*
[NCERT (New) Pg. 162, JEE Main 2024]

(a) 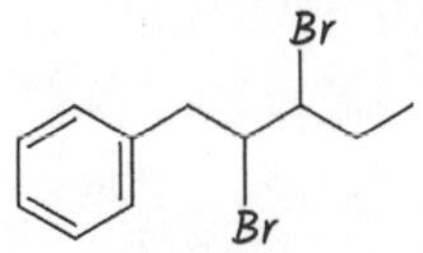 ☐

(b) 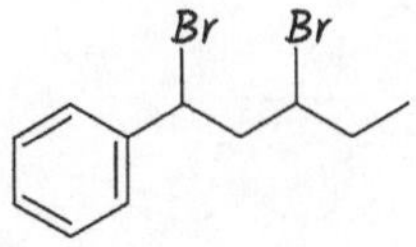 ☐

(c) 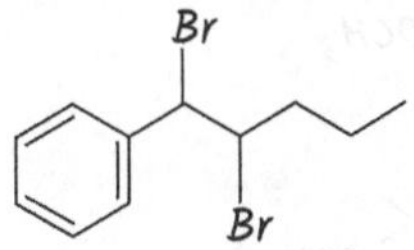 ☐

(d) 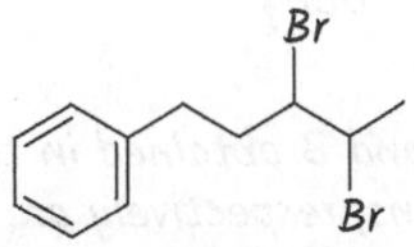 ☐

4. *Example of vinylic halide is*
[NCERT (New) Pg. 161, JEE Main 2024]

(a) 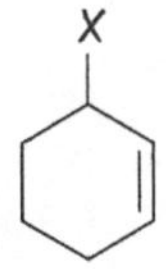 ☐ (b) 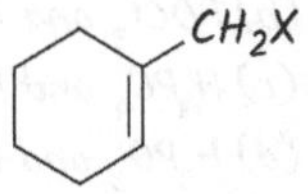 ☐

(c) 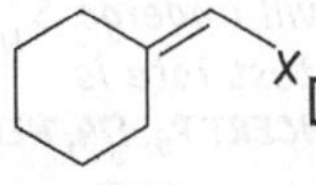 ☐ (d) 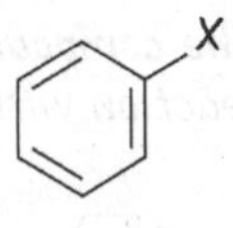 ☐

5. *Alkyl halide is converted into alkyl isocyanide by reaction with*
[NCERT (New) Pg. 165, JEE Main 2024]

(a) KCN ☐ (b) NaCN ☐
(c) NH_4CN ☐ (d) AgCN ☐

6. *Which among the following compounds will undergo fastest S_N2 reaction?*
[NCERT (New) Pg. 172, JEE Main 2024]

(a) 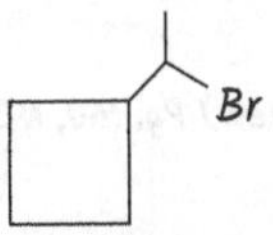 ☐ (b) 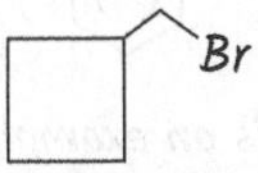 ☐

(c) 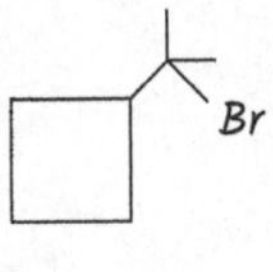 ☐ (d) 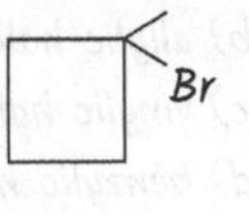 ☐

7. 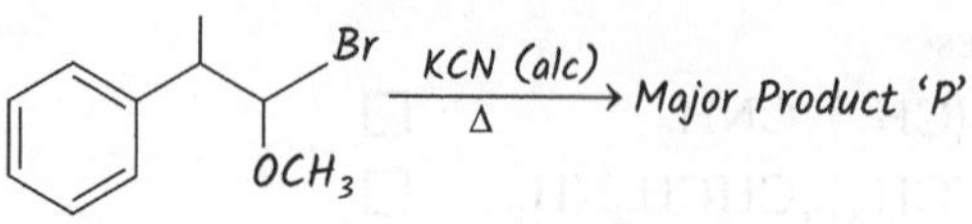

In the above reaction product 'P' is **[NCERT (New) Pg. 166, JEE Main 2024]**

(a) 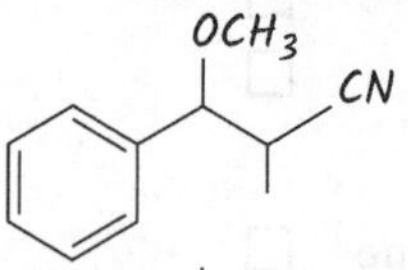

☐

(b) 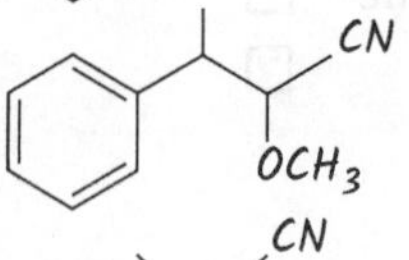

☐

(c) 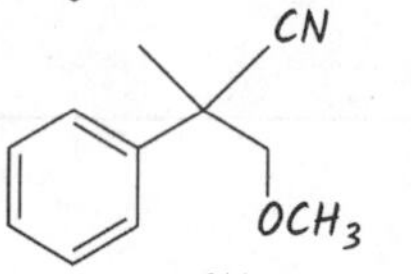

☐

(d) 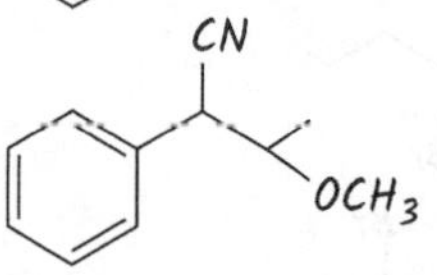

☐

8. The products A and B obtained in the following reactions, respectively are **[NCERT Pg. 164, NEET 2024]**

$3ROH + PCl_3 \longrightarrow 3RCl + A$

$ROH + PCl_5 \longrightarrow RCl + HCl + B$

(a) $POCl_3$ and H_3PO_3 ☐
(b) $POCl_3$ and H_3PO_4 ☐
(c) H_3PO_4 and $POCl_3$ ☐
(d) H_3PO_3 and $POCl_3$ ☐

9. The compound that will undergo S_N1 reaction with the fastest rate is **[NCERT Pg. 174, NEET 2024]**

(a) 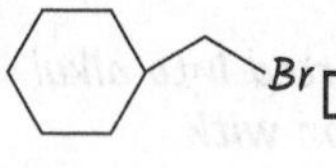

☐ (b) 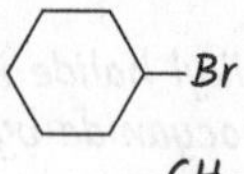

☐

(c) 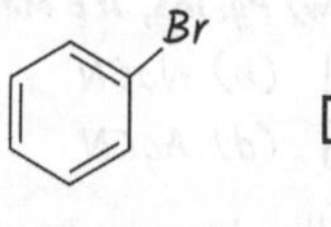

☐ (d) 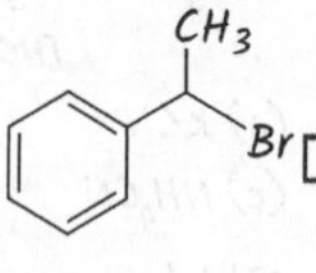

☐

10. The given compound,

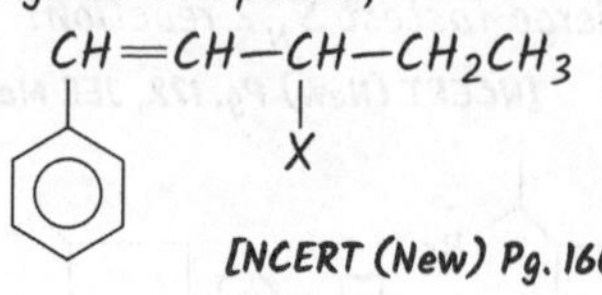

[NCERT (New) Pg. 160, NEET 2023]

is an example of
(a) aryl halide ☐
(b) allylic halide ☐
(c) vinylic halide ☐
(d) benzylic halide ☐

11. The incorrect statement regarding chirality is **[NCERT (New) Pg. 179, NEET 2022]**

(a) S_N1 reaction yields 1 : 1 mixture of both enantiomers. ☐
(b) the product obtained in S_N2 reaction of haloalkane having chirality at the reactive site shows inversion of configuration. ☐
(c) enantiomers are superimposable mirror image of each other. ☐
(d) a racemic mixture shows zero optical rotation. ☐

12. Which of the following sequence of reactions is suitable to synthesise chlorobenzene? **[NCERT (New) Pg. 166 NEET 2022]**

(a) Phenol, $NaNO_2$, HCl, CuCl ☐

(b) 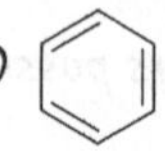 , HCl ☐

(c) 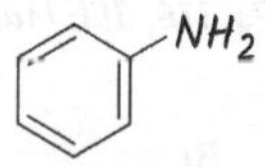

, HCl, Heating ☐

(d) Benzene, Cl_2, Anhydrous $FeCl_3$ ☐

13. The correct sequence of bond enthalpy of C—X bond is **[NCERT (New) Pg. 163, NEET 2021]**

(a) $CH_3—Cl > CH_3—F > CH_3—Br > CH_3—I$ ☐
(b) $CH_3—F < CH_3—Cl < CH_3—Br < CH_3—I$ ☐
(c) $CH_3—F > CH_3—Cl > CH_3—Br > CH_3—I$ ☐
(d) $CH_3 — F < CH_3Cl > CH_3 — Br > CH_3—I$ ☐

14. The major product formed in dehydrohalogenation reaction of 2-bromo pentane is pent-2-ene. This product formation is based on **[NCERT (New) Pg. 180 NEET 2021]**

(a) Saytzeff's rule ☐
(b) Hund's rule ☐
(c) Hofmann rule ☐
(d) Huckel's rule ☐

15. Which of the following will not undergo S_N1 reaction with OH^- ? **[NCERT (New) Pg. 173 & 174, NEET (Oct.) 2020]**

(a) $CH_2{=}CH—CH_2Cl$ ☐
(b) $(CH_3)_3CCl$ ☐

(c) 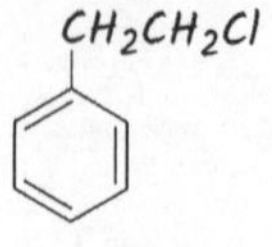

☐

(d) 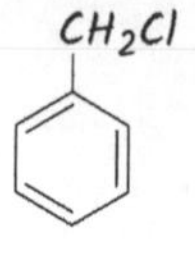

☐

Chapter 07

Alcohols, Phenols and Ethers

Scan and take Chapter Test

TOPIC 1

Introduction & Classification

NCERT Pg 194-195

1. Alcohols, phenols and ethers are basic compounds for the formation of __________, __________ and __________ respectively (detergents/fragrances/fibers/antiseptics) use most appropriate 3 words for both the fill ups.

2. Alcohols and phenols are formed when __________ atom is replaced by __________ group in an hydrocarbon, aliphatic and aromatic respectively.

(a) H-atom, —OH group ☐ (b) —OH, $-\overset{\overset{\displaystyle O}{||}}{C}-$ ☐

(c) —C atom, —Cl ☐ (d) —N-atom, —CH_2 group ☐

3. Name the alcohol which is an important component of ordinary spirit used for polishing wooden furniture.

____

4. The substitution of a hydrogen atom in a hydrocarbon by alkoxy or aryloxy group leads to formation of ether.

True ☐ False ☐

5. Consider the following statements.

I. An alcohol contains one or more (—OH) group directly attached to carbon atom(s) of an aliphatic system – (CH_3OH)

II. Phenol contains —OH group(s) attached to carbon atom(s) directly to the aromatic system. – ($C_6H_5CH_2OH$)

Concepts of all questions bearing * are important for JEE/NEET/CUET.

Which of the above statement(s) is/are correct?

(a) Only I ☐ (b) Only II ☐

(c) Both I and II ☐ (d) Neither I nor II ☐

6. The substitution of a hydrogen atom in a hydrocarbon by an __________ (alkoxy/hydroxyl) or __________ (aryloxy/carbonyl) group yields another class of compounds known as ethers.

7. Write formula for simplest ether.

____

8. Ethers can also be obtained by substituting hydrogen atom of hydroxyl group by —*R*/Ar group in

(a) alcohols ☐ (b) phenols ☐

(c) alcohols or phenols ☐ (d) hydrocarbon ☐

9. Give one example for each of the following.

(i) Trihydric alcohol __________

(ii) Monohydric alcohol

(iii) Dihydric alcohol__________

10. Consider the following statements.

I. Monohydric alcohols are classified on the basis of hybridisation of the carbon to which — OH group is attached.

II. Primary, secondary and tertiary monohydric alcohols can be depicted as

$$-CH_2-OH \quad >CH-OH \quad >C-OH$$

(1°) (2°) (3°)

Which of the above statement(s) is/are correct?

(a) Only I ☐ (b) Only II ☐

(c) Both I and II ☐ (d) Neither I nor II ☐

11. Identify the secondary alcohols from the following set

I. $CH_2CH_2CH(OH)CH_3$ II. $(C_2H_5)_3COH$

III. 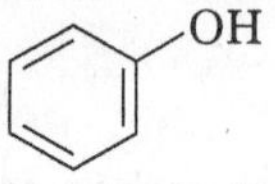

IV. 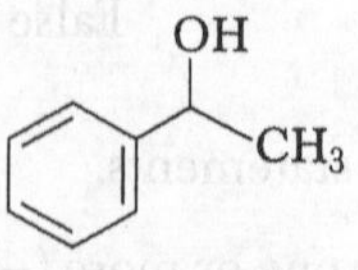

(a) I and IV ☐ (b) I and III ☐

(c) I and II ☐ (d) I, III and IV ☐

12. In allylic alcohols, the —OH group is attached to a __________ (sp^2/sp^3) hybridised carbon adjacent to C—C __________ (double/triple) bond.

13. Choose the odd one out with respect to allylic alcohols.

$CH_2{=}CH{-}CH_2{-}OH$, $(CH_3)_2CH{-}OH$, $CH_2{=}CH{-}C(CH_3)_2{-}OH$, $CH_2{=}CH{-}CH(CH_3){-}OH$

____

14. In benzylic alcohols, the —OH group is attached to sp^2-hybridised carbon atom of the aromatic ring.

True ☐ False ☐

15. Which of the following is not an example of benzylic alcohol?

(a) 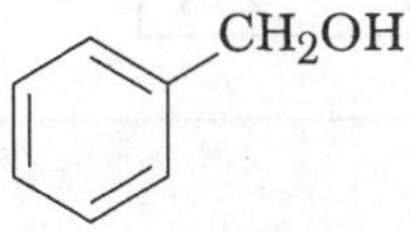 ☐

(b) 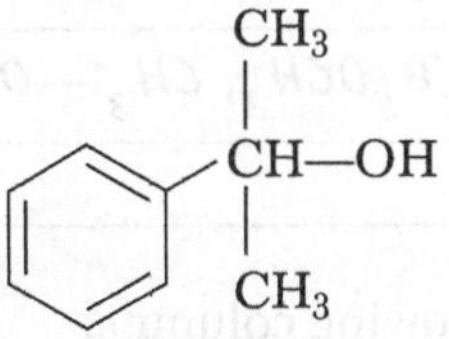 ☐

(c) 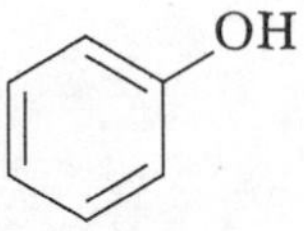 ☐

(d) 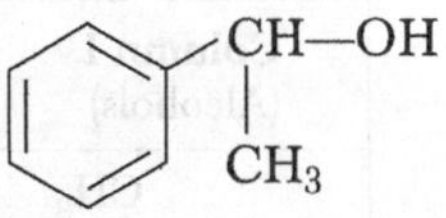 ☐

16. Allylic and benzylic alcohols can be primary, secondary or tertiary.

True ☐ False ☐

17. In vinylic alcohols, the —OH group is bonded to ______________ (C—C/C=C), i.e. to a ____________ (vinylic/allylic) or to an ________ (alkyl/aryl) carbon.

18. $CH_2{=}CH{-}OH$ is an example of vinylic alcohol.

True ☐ False ☐

19. Match the following Column I with Column II.

Column I (Compounds)	Column II (Names)
A. $CH_2{=}CH{-}OH$	1. Phenol
B. $C_6H_5{-}OH$	2. Vinylic alcohol
C. $CH_2{=}CH{-}CH_2OH$	3. Tertiary alcohol
D. $(CH_3)_3C{-}OH$	4. Allylic alcohol

A. ______________________ B. ______________________

C. ______________________ D. ______________________

20. Identify the incorrect match from the following.

(a) CH_3CH_2OH – C_{sp^3}—OH ☐

(b) 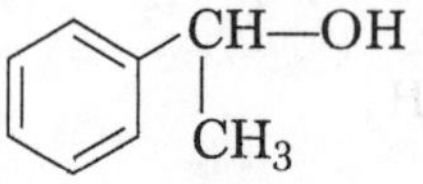 – C_{sp^3}—OH ☐

(c) 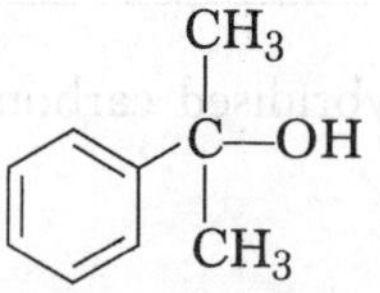 – C_{sp}—OH ☐

(d) $CH_2{=}CH{-}OH$ – C_{sp^2}—OH ☐

21. Pick the odd one out from the following with respect to mixed ethers.

$C_2H_5OCH_3$, $CH_3{-}O{-}C_6H_5$, $C_2H_5OC_6H_5$, $C_2H_5O{-}C_2H_5$

____

22. Match the following columns.

Column I (Alcohols)	Column II (Type of Alcohols)
A. $CH_3{-}C(CH_3)_2{-}OH$	1. Primary alcohol
B. $H_2C{=}CH{-}CH_2{-}OH$	2. Secondary alcohol
C. 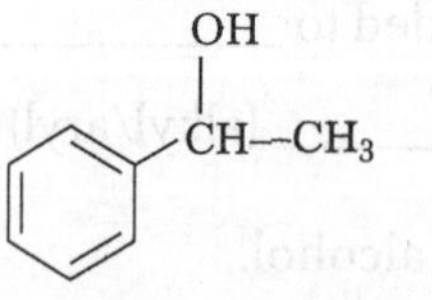	3. Tertiary alcohol

A. __________ B. __________ C. __________

23. Which of the following is not an example of allylic alcohols?

(a) $CH_2{=}CH{-}CH_2OH$ ☐

(b) 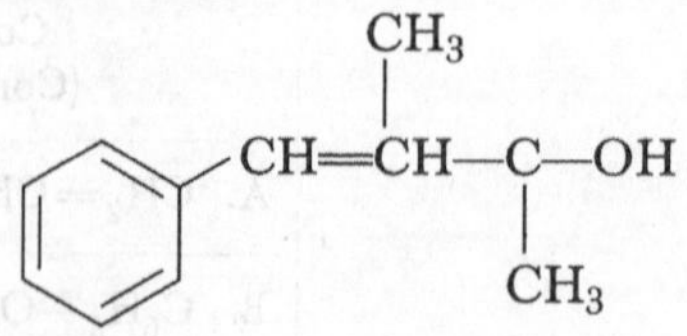 ☐

(c) 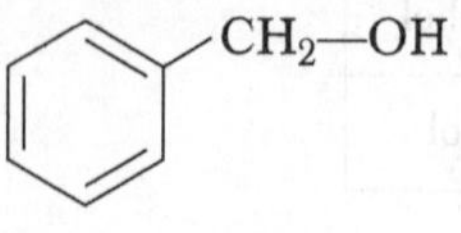 ☐

(d) 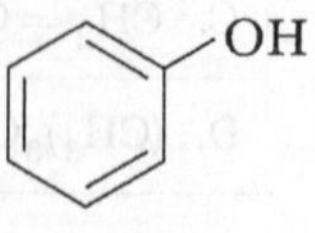 ☐

TOPIC 2

Nomenclature

NCERT Pg 195-198

24. The common name of an alcohol is derived from common name of ________ group and adding the word ____________ to it.

25. Write formula for first member of homologous series of alcohols.

____

26. Consider the following statements.

I. The IUPAC name of alcohol is derived from the name of alkane from which it is derived.

II. In IUPAC name of an alcohol "ne" of alkane is substituted by the suffix "ol".

Which of the above statement(s) is/are correct?

(a) Only I ☐ (b) Only II ☐

(c) Both I and III ☐ (d) Neither I nor II ☐

27. Tick the correct one.

While naming alcohol in IUPAC system, the longest carbon chain is numbered starting at the end.

Nearest to —OH group ☐ α- to hydroxyl group ☐

28. For naming polyhydric alcohols in IUPAC system, the 'e' of alkane is substituted by suffix 'ol'.

True ☐ False ☐

29. Write the IUPAC name of the following compounds.

(i) $HO—CH_2—CH_2—OH$ ______________

(ii) $CH_2(OH)—CH(OH)—CH_2(OH)$ ______________

30. Complete the following table.

Compound	Common name	IUPAC name
$CH_3CH_2CH_2OH$	(i) ________	(ii) ________
(iii) ________	*Iso*-propyl alcohol	(iv) ________
(v) ________	(vi) ________	Butan-2-ol

31. Name of few alcohols are given draw the structures of these alcohols.

(i) Ethan-1, 2-diol ____________________

(ii) Cyclohexanol ____________________

(iii) 2-methylcyclopentanol ____________________

32. Match the following columns.

	Column I (Compounds)	Column II (Names)
A.	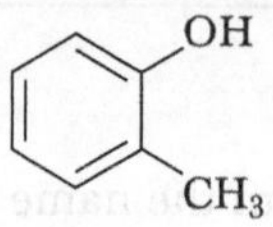	1. Phenol
B.	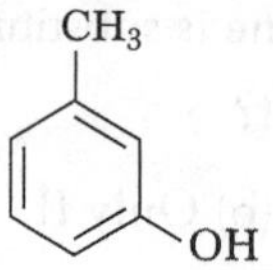	2. *o*-cresol
C.	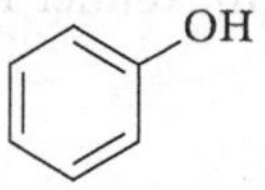	3. 4-methylphenol
D.	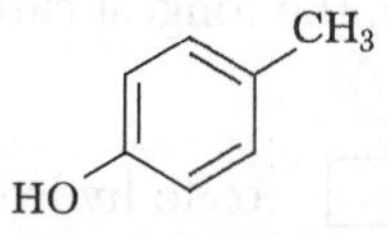	4. *m*-cresol

A. ____________________ B. ____________________

C. ____________________ D. ____________________

33. Choose the incorrect structure with respect to its respective common name.

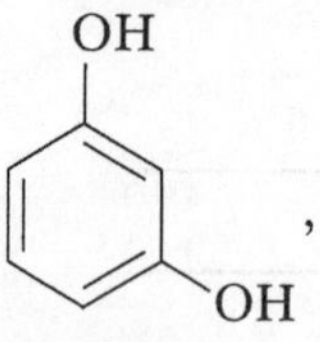
Hydroquinone ,

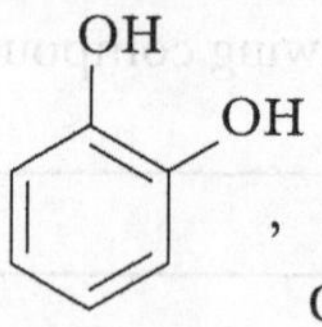
Catechol ,

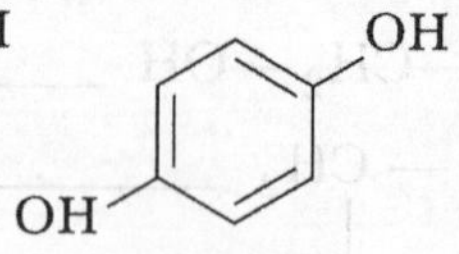
Quinol

____

34. While writing common names of ethers, the names of alkyl/aryl groups are written as separate words __________ and adding 'ether' at end.

(a) starting with name of alkyl group ☐

(b) starting with name of aryl group ☐

(c) in alphabetical order ☐

(d) starting with bulkier group ☐

35. Complete the following table.

Compound	Common name	IUPAC name
CH_3-O-CH_3	(i) ________	(ii) ________
(iii) ________	Methyl *n*-propylether	(iv) ________
(v) ________	(vi) ________	Ethoxybenzene

36. Match structures in Column I with their correct IUPAC names in Column II.

Column I (Structures)	Column II (IUPAC names)
A. $C_6H_5-O-CH_2-CH_2-\underset{\underset{CH_3}{\vert}}{CH}-CH_3$	1. 1, 2-dimethoxyethane
B. $CH_3-O-CH_2-CH_2-OCH_3$	2. Methoxybenzene or anisole
C. $C_6H_5OCH_3$	3. 3-methylbutoxybenzene

A. ________ B. ________ C. ________

37. Tick the correct structure of 2-ethoxy-1, 1-dimethylcyclohexane.

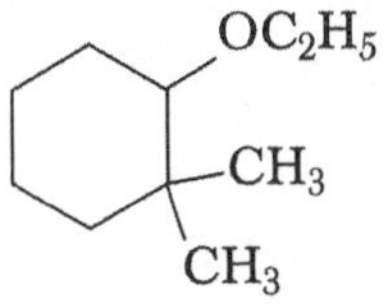

☐

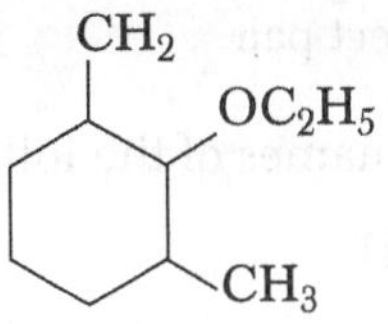

☐

38. The correct name for $C_2H_5OC_2H_5$ is

(a) diethyl ether ☐ (b) ethyl ether ☐

(c) ethyl diether ☐ (d) ethyl methyl ether ☐

39. According to IUPAC system, ethers are the hydrocarbon derivatives in which ________ their (oxygen/hydrogen) atom is replaced by an ________ (—OR/—OH)or ________ (—OAr/Alkanone)group.

40. In IUPAC nomenclature of ethers, the larger (*R*) group is chosen as the parent hydrocarbon.

True ☐ False ☐

41. Draw structures of the following compounds.

(i) 2, 6-dimethylphenol ________

(ii) 1-ethoxy-2-nitrocyclohexane ________

(iii) 4-chloro-2, 3-dimethylpentan-1-ol ________

42. The correct name of $CH_3—\underset{\displaystyle CH_3}{\underset{|}{CH}}—O—C_2H_5$ is

2-ethoxypropane ☐ Propyl ethyl ether ☐

43. Identify the incorrect pair(s) from the following.

(a) $CH_3—CH_2—\underset{\displaystyle CH_2Cl}{\underset{|}{CH}}—\overset{\displaystyle CH_3OH}{\overset{|}{CH}}—\underset{\displaystyle CH_3}{\underset{|}{CH}}—CH_3$ - 4-chloromethyl-2-*iso*-propylpentan-1-ol ☐

(b) 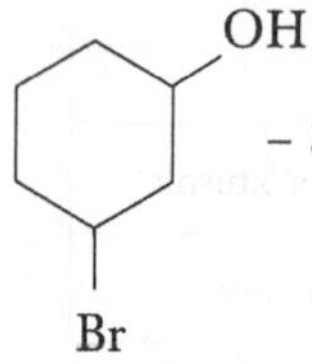 - 3-bromocyclohexanol ☐

(c) $CH_2=CH—\underset{\displaystyle OH}{\underset{|}{CH}}—CH_2—CH_2—CH_3$ - Hex-1-en-3-ol ☐

(d) All are correct pair ☐

44. Write IUPAC names of the following compound.

(i) $CH_3—\underset{\displaystyle C_2H_5}{\underset{|}{\overset{\displaystyle CH_3}{\overset{|}{C}}}}—\underset{\displaystyle OH}{\underset{|}{CH}}—CH_3$ ________________

(ii) $H_3C—\underset{\displaystyle CH_3}{\underset{|}{C}}=\underset{\displaystyle Br}{\underset{|}{C}}—CH_2—OH$ ________________

TOPIC 3

Structure of Functional Group

NCERT Pg 198-199

45. In alcohols, the oxygen of the —OH group is attached to ________ by ________ bond formed by overlap of sp^3-hybridised orbital of oxygen and ________ hybridised orbital of carbon

(a) carbon, π, sp^3 ☐
(b) carbon, σ, sp^2 ☐
(c) carbon, σ, sp^3 ☐
(d) hydrogen, σ, sp^2 ☐

46. Arrange the following in increasing order of bond angle between C—O—H and C—O—C.

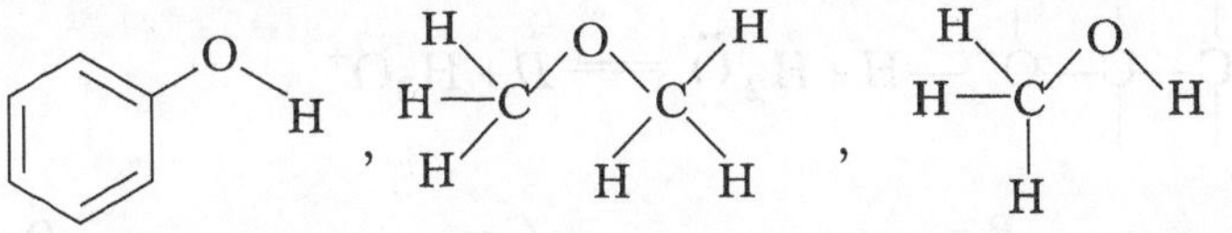

____

47. Consider the following statements.

I. The carbon-oxygen bond length in methanol is slightly less than that in phenol.

II. The reason for difference in C—O bond length in phenol and methanol is sp^2-hybridised carbon attached to oxygen in former.

Which of the above statement(s) is/are correct?

(a) Only I
(b) Only II
(c) Both I and II
(d) Neither I nor II

48. Oxygen present in ether contains

(a) two bond pairs and two lone pairs of electrons
(b) one bond pair and two lone pairs of electrons
(c) two bond pairs and one lone pair of electrons
(d) three bond pairs and one lone pair of electrons

49. (i) The bond angle in ethers is slightly ____________ (smaller/greater) than tetrahedral angle.

(ii) The C—O bond length of ethers and ____________ (alcohols/phenols) is same.

TOPIC 4

Alcohols and Phenols

NCERT Pg 199-213

50. Alkenes on reaction with water in acidic medium form ethers.

True ☐ False ☐

51. Name the rule that helps in predicting the product in reaction of unsymmetrical alkenes with water in presence of acid as a catalyst.

____

52. Predict the products of the following reaction.

$$CH_3—CH{=}CH_2 + H_2O \xrightleftharpoons{H^+} \text{\_\_\_\_\_\_\_\_}$$

53. Identify the missing species in the following mechanism.

***Step* I.** $H_2O + H^+ \longrightarrow A$

***Step* II.** $>C{=}C< + A \longrightarrow B + H_2O \longrightarrow C$

Step III. $-\overset{\overset{\displaystyle H}{|}}{\underset{|}{C}}-\overset{\overset{\displaystyle H}{|}}{\underset{|}{C}}-\overset{+}{O}-H + H_2\ddot{O} \rightleftharpoons D + H_3O^+$

$A =$ ____________ $B =$ ____________ $C =$ ____________ $D =$ ____________

***54.** Determine *X*, *Y* and *Z* in the following reaction.

$$CH_3{-}CH{=}CH_2 + (H{-}BH_2)_2 \longrightarrow X \xrightarrow{CH_3CH=CH_2} (CH_3{-}CH_2{-}CH_2)_2BH$$

$$\xrightarrow{CH_3CH=CH_2} Y \xrightarrow[H_2O]{H_2O/3H_2O_2,\ \bar{O}H} Z + B(OH)_3$$

$X =$ ____________ $Y =$ ____________ $Z =$ ____________

55. Consider the following statements.

I. During hydroboration-oxidation, boron gets attached to sp^2 carbon which is less substituted or carry greater number of hydrogens.

II. The alcohol formed as result of hydroboration-oxidation looks as if it is taken the pathway opposite to Markownikoff's rule.

Which of the above statement(s) is/are correct?

(a) Only I ☐ (b) Only II ☐

(c) Both I and II ☐ (d) Neither I nor II ☐

56. Write reagents required for the following conversion.

(i) $R{-}CHO + H_2 \longrightarrow RCH_2OH$ ____________

(ii) $R{-}\overset{\overset{\displaystyle O}{\|}}{C}{-}R' \longrightarrow R{-}\underset{\underset{\displaystyle OH}{|}}{CH}{-}R'$ ____________

57. Complete the following analogy with respect to the product formed.
Compound formed on treating ketones with lithium aluminium hydride : *A* :: Compound formed on reduction of aldehydes using sodium borohydride : *B*

(a) *A* : Primary alcohols
B : Secondary alcohols ☐

(b) *A* : Secondary alcohols
B : Primary alcohols ☐

(c) *A* : Primary alcohols
B : Tertiary alcohols ☐

(d) *A* : Tertiary alcohols
B : Primary alcohols ☐

58. Predict the product(s) of the following reaction.

(i) $R{-}COOH \xrightarrow[\text{(b) } H_2O]{\text{(a) } LiAlH_4}$ ____________

(ii) $R{-}COOH \xrightarrow[\text{(b) } H_2\text{, catalyst}]{\text{(a) } R'OH,\ H^+}$ ____________

***59.** Choose the incorrect reaction from the following.

(a) $\underset{\text{Propene}}{CH_3—CH=CH_2} + H_2O \xrightarrow{H^+} \underset{\text{Propan-1-ol}}{CH_3—CH_2—CH_2—OH}$

(b) $\underset{\text{Butanal}}{CH_3—CH_2—CH_2—CHO} \xrightarrow[Pd]{H_2} \underset{\text{Butan-1-ol}}{CH_3CH_2CH_2CH_2OH}$

(c) $\underset{\text{Propanone}}{CH_3—\overset{O}{\overset{\|}{C}}—CH_3} + \underset{\text{Methyl magnesium bromide}}{CH_3MgBr} \xrightarrow{H_2O} \underset{\text{2-methyl propan-2-ol}}{CH_3—\underset{CH_3}{\overset{CH_3}{\overset{|}{\underset{|}{C}}}}—OH}$

(d) All are correct reaction.

60. Phenols are also known as ______________ acid.

61. Monochlorination of toluene in sunlight followed by hydrolysis with *aq.* NaOH yields. **[NCERT Exemplar]**

(a) *o*-cresol
(b) *m*-cresol
(c) 2, 4-dihydroxy toluene
(d) benzyl alcohol

---

62. Complete the following reaction.

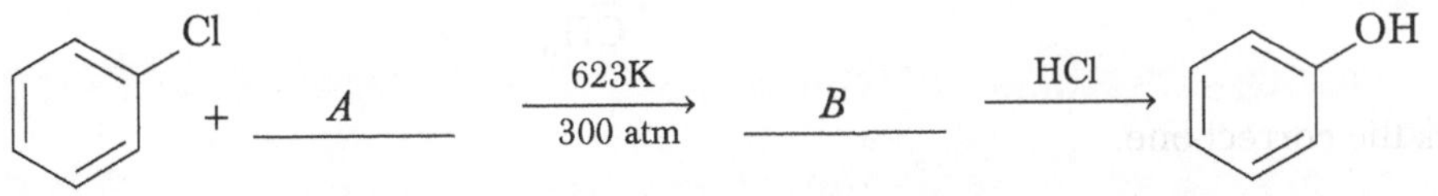

A = ______________ B = ______________

63. Benzene on reaction with oleum gives A. This A when further heated with molten sodium hydroxide followed by acidification of its product gives B . Identify A and B.

A = ______________ B = ______________

64. Determine the reagents required in following conversion.

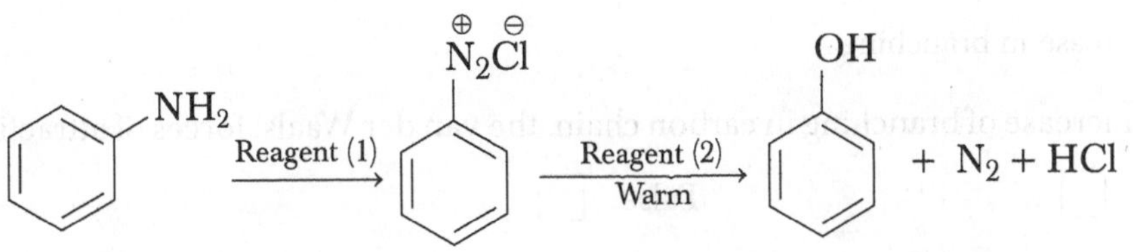

Reagent (1) and Reagent (2) are

(a) $NaNO_2$ + HCl, NaOH
(b) $NaNO_2$ + HCl, H_2O
(c) HNO_3, NaOH
(d) HNO_3, HCl

65. Consider the following reactions,

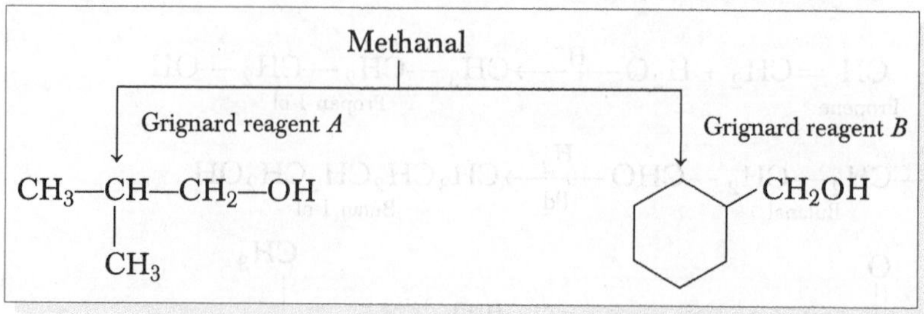

Write structures for Grignard reagent *A* and Grignard reagent *B*.

A = ____________________ *B* = ____________________

66. Predict the reactants for the following reactions.

(i) ____________ $\xrightarrow{H_2O/H^+}$ $CH_3—\underset{\substack{|\\OH}}{CH}—CH_3$

(ii) ____________ $\xrightarrow{NaBH_4}$ 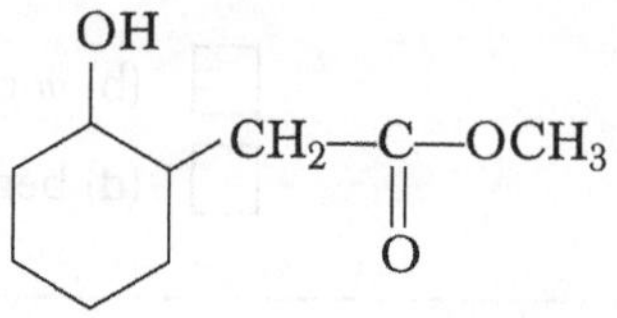

(iii) ____________ $\xrightarrow{NaBH_4}$ $CH_3—CH_2—\underset{\substack{|\\CH_3}}{CH}—CH_2OH$

67. Tick the correct one.

The properties of alcohols and phenols are chiefly due to

alkyl/aryl group ☐ hydroxyl group ☐

68. The boiling points of alcohols and phenols increases with

(a) decrease in number of carbon atoms ☐

(b) decrease in van der Waals' forces ☐

(c) increase in branching ☐

(d) decrease in branching ☐

69. With increase of branching in carbon chain, the van der Waals' forces of attraction increases.

True ☐ False ☐

70. Lower molecular mass alcohols are

(a) miscible in limited amount of water ☐

(b) miscible in excess of water ☐

(c) miscible in water in all proportions ☐

(d) immiscible in water ☐

71. Arrange the following in order of their decreasing boiling points.

(i) Pentan-1-ol, methanol, butan-2-ol, ethanol, butan-1-ol ____________

(ii) Pentan-1-ol, *n*-butane, pentanal, ethoxyethane ____________

***72.** Given are two reactions of alcohols

(i) $R\text{—}OH + \rangle C^{+}\text{—} \longrightarrow R\text{—}O\text{—}\overset{|}{\underset{|}{C}}\text{—} + H^{+}$

(ii) $R\text{—}CH_2\text{—}OH + H^{+} \longrightarrow R\text{—}CH_2\text{—}\overset{+}{O}H_2$

Answer the following questions with respect to above reactions.

(a) ____________ acts as nucleophile in reaction (i).

(b) ____________ acts as electrophile in reaction (ii).

73. Predict the product(s) of the following reactions.

(i) $6CH_3\text{—}\overset{\overset{CH_3}{|}}{\underset{\underset{CH_3}{|}}{C}}\text{—}OH + 2Al \longrightarrow$ ____________

(ii) 2 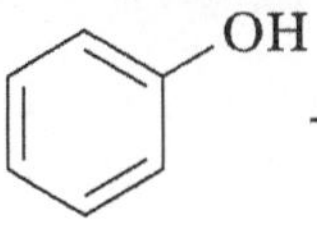 + 2Na $\longrightarrow$ ____________

74. Choose the appropriate reactant for the following conversion.

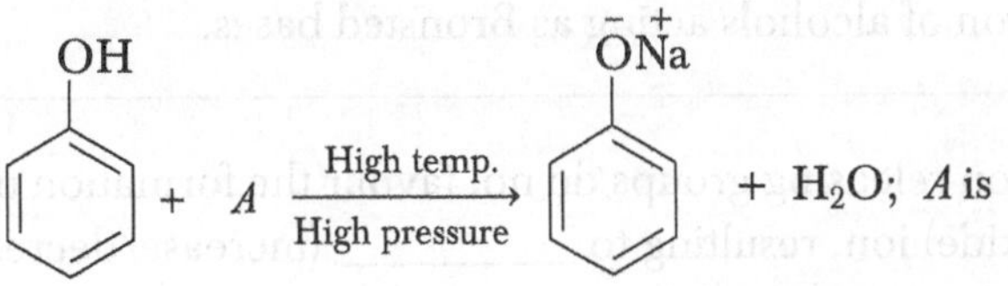

(a) $NaAlO_2$ ☐ (b) $NaHCO_3$ ☐

(c) NaOH ☐ (d) Na_2SO_4 ☐

75. Select the appropriate choice on the basis of following reaction and statement.

$$B: + H\text{—}\ddot{\underset{\cdot\cdot}{O}}\text{—}R \longrightarrow B\text{—}H + :\ddot{\underset{\cdot\cdot}{O}}R$$

Alcohols and phenols (based on above reaction) act as

Bronsted bases ☐ Bronsted acids ☐

76. An electron releasing group ____________ (increases/decreases) electron density on oxygen which ____________ (increase/decrease) the polarity of O—H bond.

***77.** Arrange the following alcohols in increasing order of their acidic strength.

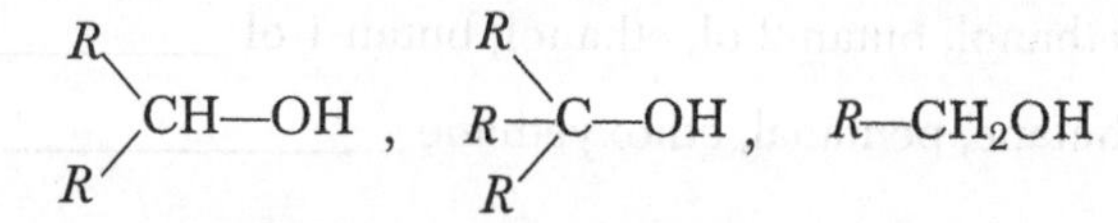

____

78. Aliphatic alcohols are stronger acids than water.

Yes ☐ No ☐

79. The given reaction of water with an alkoxide.

$$R—\bar{O} + H—O—H \longrightarrow R—O—H + \bar{O}H$$

Answer the following questions with respect to the above reaction.

(i) Acid in above reaction is ____________.

(ii) Base in above reaction is ____________.

(iii) ____________ is acting as conjugate acid.

(iv) ____________ is acting as conjugate base.

80. Alcohols can act as

(a) Bronsted acids only ☐

(b) Bronsted bases only ☐

(c) Both Bronsted acid and Bronsted base ☐

(d) Neither Bronsted acid nor-Bronsted base ☐

81. Mention the reason of alcohols acting as Bronsted bases.

____

82. In phenols electron releasing groups do not favour the formation of ____________ (epoxide/phenoxide) ion, resulting to __________ (increase/decrease) in acidic strength.

83. Which of the following is less acidic than phenol ?

Nitrophenol ☐ Cresol ☐

84. Arrange the following in order of increasing acidic strength.

Phenol, o-nitrophenol, m-nitrophenol, m-cresol, p-cresol, Ethanol

____

85. Which of the following is most acidic? **[NCERT Exemplar]**

(a) Benzyl alcohol ☐ (b) Cyclohexanol ☐

(c) Phenol ☐ (d) *m*-chlorophenol ☐

86. Complete the following table.

Reactant A	Reactant B	Reagent H^+	Product(s)
Ar—OH	(i) ________	H^+	$Ar-O-\overset{O}{\overset{\|}{C}}-R' + H_2O$
R—OH	$(R'CO)_2O$	(ii) ________	(iii) ________ + ________

87. Name the acetyl compound that possesses analgesic anti-inflammatory and antipyretic properties.

____

88. (i) Predict the product(s) for the following reaction. Also write their names.

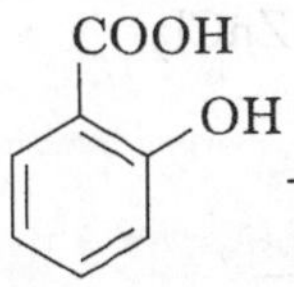 $+ (CH_3CO)_2O \xrightarrow{H^+}$ ________ + ________

(ii) The above reaction is an example of ________.

89. Which of the following reactions involves cleavage of (C—O) bond in alcohols?

(a) Reaction with metals ☐ (b) Reaction with base ☐

(c) Reaction with hydrogen halides ☐ (d) Esterification ☐

90. Alcohols react with hydrogen halides to form two products A and B. Write generalised reaction of alcohols with hydrogen halide and identify 'A' and 'B'.

A = ________ B = ________

91. Phenol does not undergo nucleophilic substitution reaction easily due to

(a) acidic nature of phenol ☐

(b) partial double bond character of C—OH bond ☐

(c) partial double bond character of C—C bond ☐

(d) instability of phenoxide ion ☐

***92.** Reaction of alcohols with Lucas reagent is a distinguishing test of alcohols.

Match the (type of alcohol) Column I with appropriate observation (shown by that alcohol) in Column II.

Column I (Reactions)	Column II (Observations)
A. Primary alcohol + Lucas reagent	1. Turbidity produced immediately
B. Secondary alcohol + Lucas reagent	2. No turbidity or delayed turbidity is produced at room temperature
C. Tertiary alcohol + Lucas reagent	3. Turbidity produced at slow rate

A. ________ B. ________ C. ________

93. ______________ (alkyl/aryl halides) are responsible for producing turbidity in solution on reaction of alcohols with Lucas reagent.

94. $CH_3—CH_2—OH \longrightarrow CH_3—CH_2—Cl$

Number of reagents from the following which can be used to carry out this transformation are:

PCl_5, PCl_3, $SOCl_4$, HCl, $ZnCl_2$, $NaCl$, Cl_2

(a) 3 ☐ (b) 4 ☐ (c) 5 ☐ (d) 6 ☐

95. Alcohols cannot undergo dehydration to form alkenes in presence of

(a) conc. H_3PO_4 ☐ (b) conc. H_2SO_4 ☐

(c) anhydrous zinc or alumina ☐ (d) conc. $HCl + ZnCl_2$ ☐

***96.** Predict the product(s) in the following reaction.

(i) $C_2H_5OH \xrightarrow[443\ K]{H_2SO_4}$ ______________

(ii) $CH_3—\underset{OH}{\underset{|}{CH}}—CH_3 \xrightarrow[440\ K]{85\%\ H_3PO_4}$ ______________

(iii) $CH_3—\underset{CH_3}{\underset{|}{\overset{CH_3}{\overset{|}{C}}}}—OH \xrightarrow[358\ K]{20\%\ H_3PO_4}$ ______________

97. Arrange the following in order of their increasing ease towards dehydration reaction in acidic medium.

Secondary alcohol, Primary alcohol, Tertiary alcohol

____

98. Identify the most stable carbocation from the following.

Primary carbocation, Secondary carbocation, Tertiary carbocation.

____

99. During dehydration of alcohols to alkenes by heating with conc. H_2SO_4, the initiation step is

(a) protonation of alcohol molecule ☐ (b) formation of carbocation ☐

(c) elimination of water ☐ (d) formation of an ester ☐

100. A reaction which involves removal of dihydrogen from an alcohol molecule is called ______________.

101. Choose the correct option for the given reaction, when acidified potassium dichromate is taken as the reagent.

$$RCH_2OH \xrightarrow{\text{Oxidation}} A \longrightarrow B$$

(a) $A = R—\overset{\overset{\displaystyle O}{\|}}{C}—OH$ $B = R—\overset{\overset{\displaystyle R}{|}}{C}=O$ ☐

(b) $A = R—CHO$ $B = RCOOH$ ☐

(c) $A = RCOR$ $B = RCOOH$ ☐

(d) $A = RCHO$ $B = RCOR$ ☐

***102.** The number of reagents from the following which can convert ethanol to aldehyde is

$KMnO_4 / H^+$, $K_2Cr_2O_7/H^+$, DIBAL-H, CrO_3, PCC, PDC, O_3

(a) 4 ☐ (b) 5 ☐ (c) 3 ☐ (d) 2 ☐

103. Tick the correct one.

The appropriate reagent for the following conversion,

$$R—CH_2OH \longrightarrow RCHO$$

Acidified $KMnO_4$ ☐ CrO_3 ☐

104. Write the reagents required for the following conversions.

	Conversions	Reagent required
(i)	$CH_3—CH=CH—CH_2OH \downarrow CH_3—CH=CH—CHO$	________
(ii)	$R—\underset{\underset{\displaystyle OH}{|}}{CH}—R' \longrightarrow R—\overset{\overset{\displaystyle O}{\|}}{C}—R'$	________
(iii)	$R—CH_2OH \xrightarrow{573\text{ K}} RCHO$	________

105. Which of the following reaction is incorrect?

I. $CH_3—\underset{\underset{\displaystyle OH}{|}}{CH}—CH_2—CH_3 \xrightarrow[573\text{ K}]{Cu} CH_3—\overset{\overset{\displaystyle O}{\|}}{C}—CH_2CH_3$

II. $CH_3—\underset{\underset{\displaystyle CH_3}{|}}{\overset{\overset{\displaystyle CH_3}{|}}{C}}—OH \xrightarrow[573\text{ K}]{Cu} CH_3—\overset{\overset{\displaystyle O}{\|}}{C}—CH_3$

(a) Only I ☐ (b) Only II ☐

(c) Both I and II ☐ (d) Neither I nor II ☐

106. A methanol poisoned patient is treated by giving intravenous infusions of diluted methanol.

True ☐ False ☐

107. Why phenol undergoes electrophilic substitution more easily than benzene?

____

108. Predict the product(s) for the following reaction.

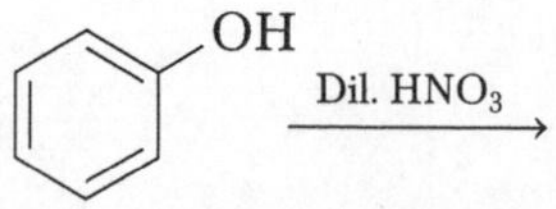

____

109. The *ortho* and *para* isomers of nitrophenol can be separated by ______________ (steam distillation/evaporation).

***110.** Tick the correct one.

Which shows intramolecular hydrogen bonding?

o-nitrophenol ☐ or *p*-nitrophenol ☐

111. *p*-nitrophenol is more volatile than *o*-nitrophenol and shows more association of molecules.

True ☐ False ☐

112. Choose the correct option with respect to the product formed in following reaction,

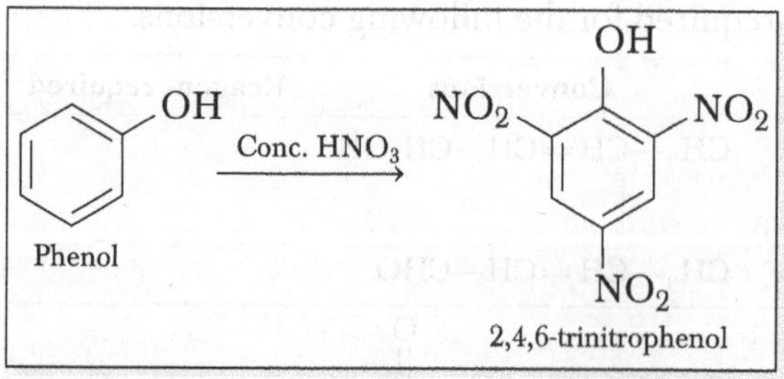

The product formed is known as ______________ and is a ______________

(a) picric acid, strong base ☐ (b) picric acid, strong acid ☐

(c) lucas acid, strong base ☐ (d) lucas acid, strong acid ☐

113. Phenols undergoes halogenation by two ways as shown below.

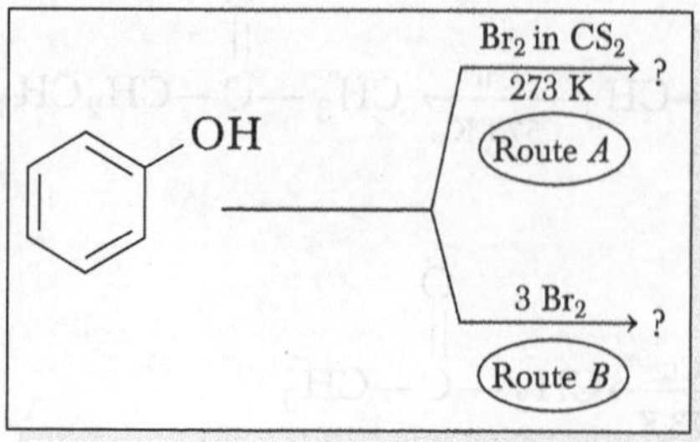

Identify the product(s) formed by Route *A* and Route *B*.

Route *A* = ______________ Route *B* = ______________

114. In halogenation of phenol, __________ (Lewis base/Lewis acid) is not required due to highly __________ (activating/deactivating) effect of __________ (—OH/—Ar) group.

***115.** Tick the correct one.

On dinitration of 3-methyl phenol, the major product obtained is

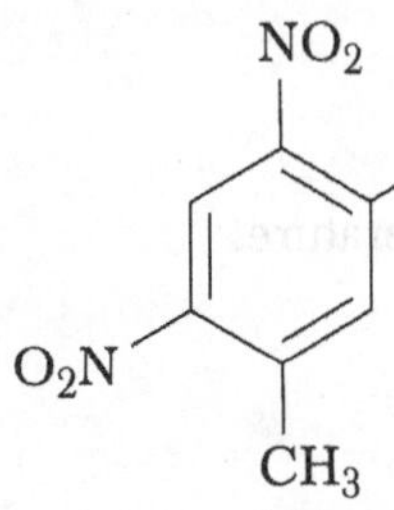

(A) ☐ Or

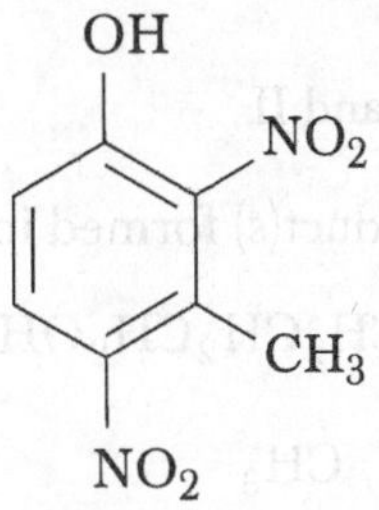

(B) ☐

116. Predict the product(s) formed by following reaction.

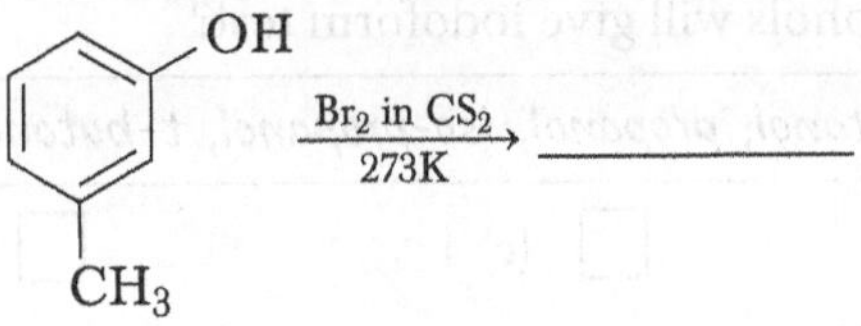

117. Phenyl methanoate on mononitration gives product X in major amount. Determine X.

X = __________

118. Complete the following reaction,

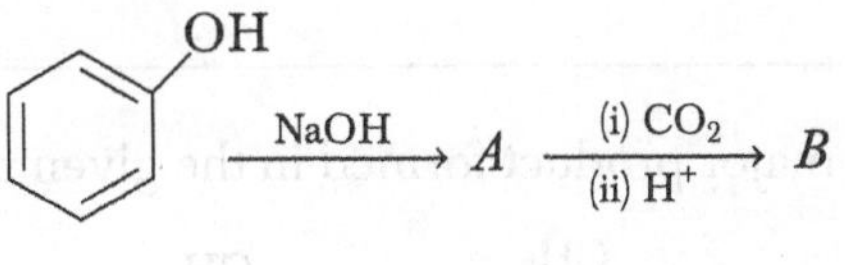

A = __________ B = __________

***119.** Identify the reagent required in the following reaction.

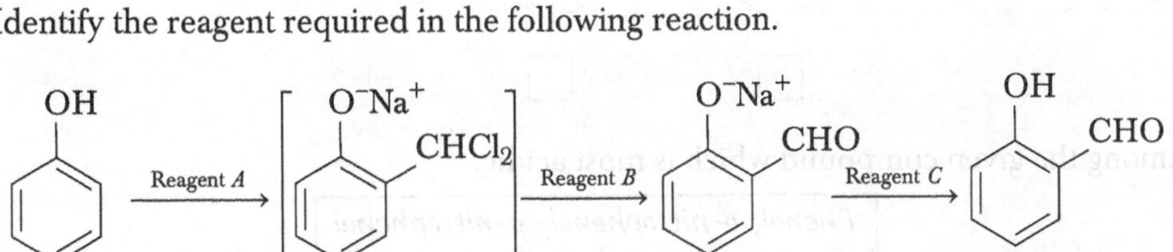

A = __________ B = __________ C = __________

***120.** Which of the following reaction is incorrect?

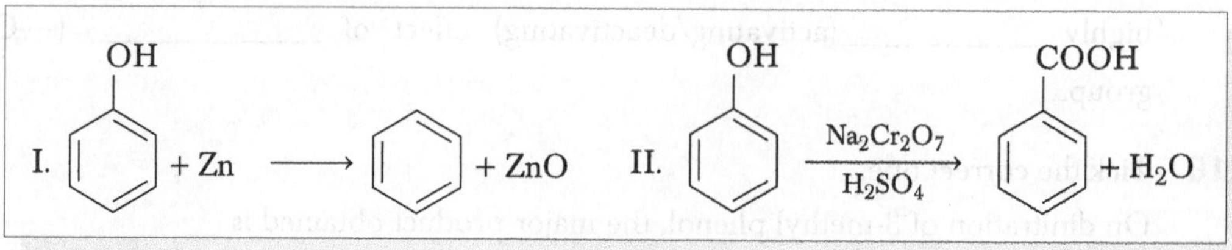

(a) Only I ☐ (b) Only II ☐

(c) Both I and II ☐ (d) Neither I nor II ☐

***121.** Write product(s) formed in the following reactions at room temperature.

(i) $CH_3CH_2CH_2CH_2OH + HCl \xrightarrow[ZnCl_2]{Anhyd.}$ ________________

(ii) $CH_3-\underset{OH}{\overset{CH_3}{\overset{|}{\underset{|}{C}}}}-C_2H_5 + HCl \xrightarrow[ZnCl_2]{Anhyd.}$ ________________

122. How many of the following alcohols will give iodoform test?

Methanol, Ethanol, iso-butanol, propanol, iso-propanol, t-butanol, phenol

(a) 1 ☐ (b) 2 ☐ (c) 4 ☐ (d) 3 ☐

123. How can you convert

(i) 2-methylbutan-2-ol to 2-bromo-2-methylbutane?

____

(ii) butan-1-ol to 1-chlorobutane?

____

***124.** Identify and tick on the major product formed in the given reaction.

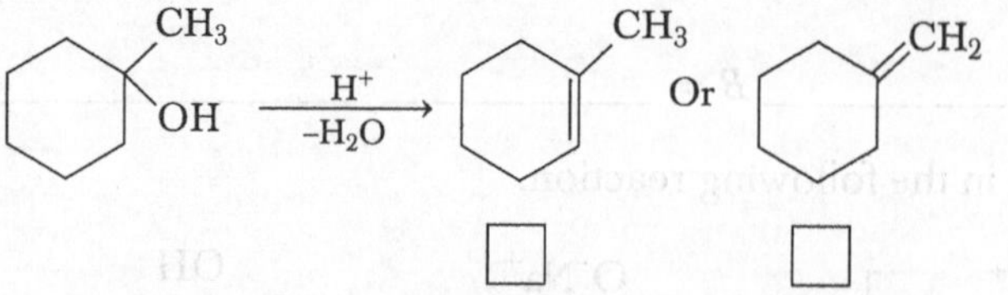

***125.** Among the given compound which is most acidic.

Phenol, o-nitrophenol, p-nitrophenol

____

126. Draw the reasonating structure of the following.

(i) Phenoxide ion ________________

(ii) *p*-nitrophenoxide ion ________________

TOPIC 5

Some Commercially Important Alcohols

NCERT Pg 214

127. ______________ is also known as 'wood spirit' and was produced by ______________ of wood.

128. The reagent required for the conversion given below is

$$CO + 2H_2 \xrightarrow[573\text{-}673\ K]{200\text{-}300\ atm} CH_3OH$$

(a) $ZnO - Cr_2O_3$ ☐ (b) Invertase ☐

(c) H_2SO_4 ☐ (d) H_2, Pd ☐

129. Complete the following reaction.

(i) $C_{12}H_{22}O_{11} + H_2O \xrightarrow{\text{Invertase}}$ ________ + ________

(ii) ____________ $\xrightarrow{\text{Zymase}}$ ________ $+ 2CO_2$

130. Alcohol '*A*' is obtained from sugar "molasses" by fermentation process in anaerobic conditions. It is a colourless liquid with boiling point of 351 K. '*A*' is made unfit for drinking commercially by mixing some amount of compound '*B*' (to give it a colour) and '*C*' (for foul smell).

Answer the following questions.

(i) Alcohol '*A*' is ______________

(ii) Compound '*B*' is ______________

(iii) Compound '*C*' is ______________

(iv) Process of adding '*B*' and '*C*' to '*A*' is called as ______________ of alcohol.

TOPIC 6

Ethers

NCERT Pg 215-221

131. Predict the products for the following reactions.

(i) $CH_3CH_2OH \xrightarrow[443\ K]{H_2SO_4}$ ______________

(ii) $CH_3CH_2OH \xrightarrow[413\ K]{H_2SO_4}$ ______________

132. Formation of ether by dehydration of alcohols in the presence of a protic acid is a/an

(a) S_N2 reaction ☐ (b) S_N1 reaction ☐

(c) E2 reaction ☐ (d) E1 reaction ☐

133. Consider the following statements.

I. Williamson's synthesis involves S_N1 attack of alkoxide ion on primary alkyl halide.

II. Williamson's synthesis can be represented as

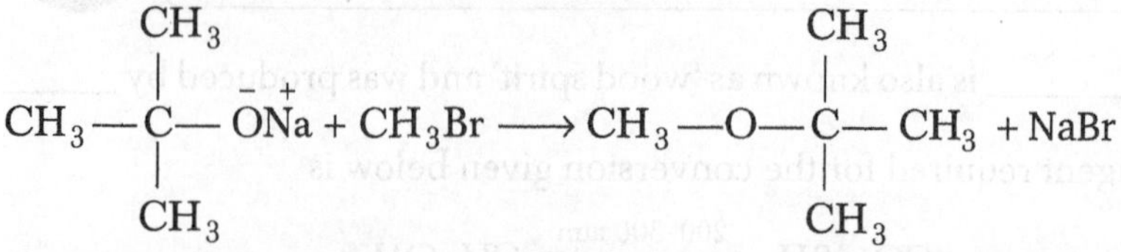

Which of the given statement(s) is/are correct?

(a) Only I ☐ (b) Only II ☐
(c) Both I and II ☐ (d) Neither I nor II ☐

---

134. The major product formed by the following reaction is

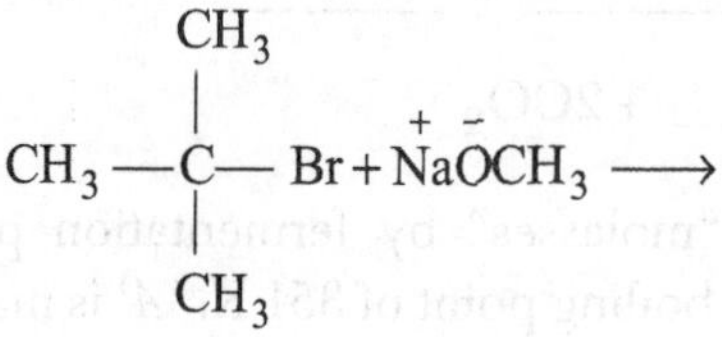

(i) 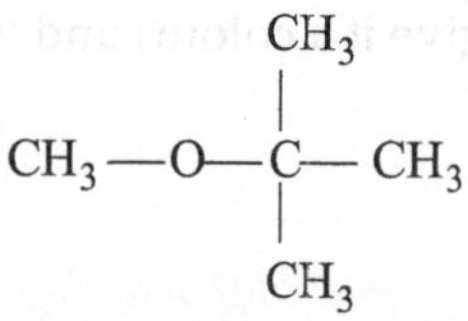 Or (ii) 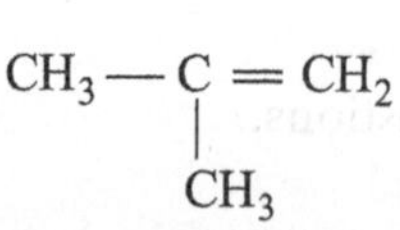

☐ ☐

135. Write Williamson's synthesis reaction for the preparation of *t*-butylethyl ether.

---

136. Complete the following reaction.

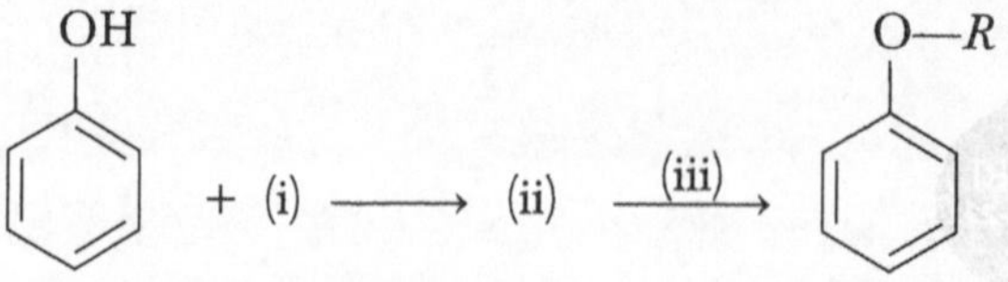

(i) ____________ (ii) ____________ (iii) ____________

137. Arrange the following in order of their decreasing boiling points.

n-pentane, ethoxyethane, butan-1-ol

---

138. Miscibility of ethers in water is due to

(a) net dipole moment ☐ (b) polar nature of C—O bond ☐
(c) hydrogen bonding ☐ (d) presence of —*R* group ☐

139. Hydrogen halides react with ethers and alcohol to give product(s) as

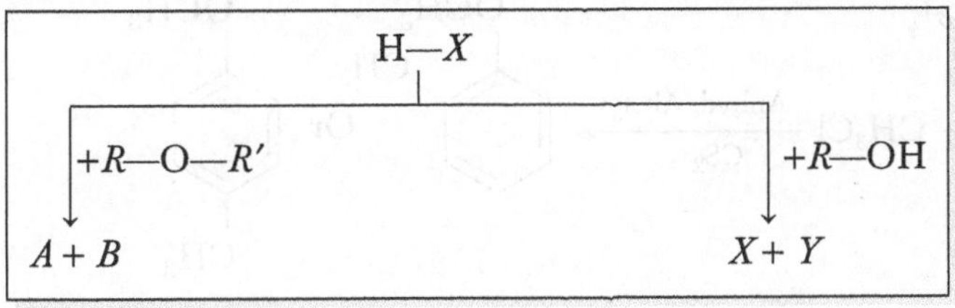

Identify the products formed.

A = ________ B = ________ X = ________ Y = ________

140. Arrange the following hydrogen halides on the basis of their increasing reactivity towards ethers:

HBr, HI, HCl

____

***141.** Analyse if the following reaction is forming the expected products or not.

$$CH_3-\underset{CH_3}{\overset{CH_3}{\underset{|}{\overset{|}{C}}}}-O-CH_3 + HI \longrightarrow CH_3-\underset{CH_3}{\overset{CH_3}{\underset{|}{\overset{|}{C}}}}-OH + CH_3I$$

Yes ☐ No ☐

142. (i) and (ii) given below contain the products formed by the reaction of an ether with HI. Identify the ether required for the products formed.

(i) $CH_3-CH_2-CH_2-OH + CH_3-CH_2-\underset{CH_3}{\overset{CH_3}{\underset{|}{\overset{|}{C}}}}-I$ ________

(ii) 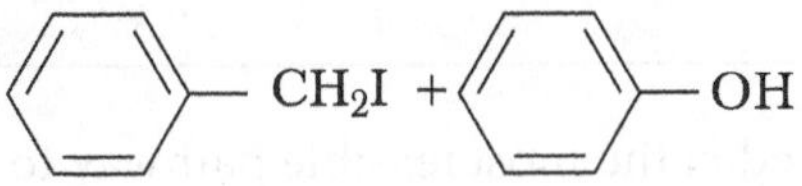

____

143. Pick the odd one out.

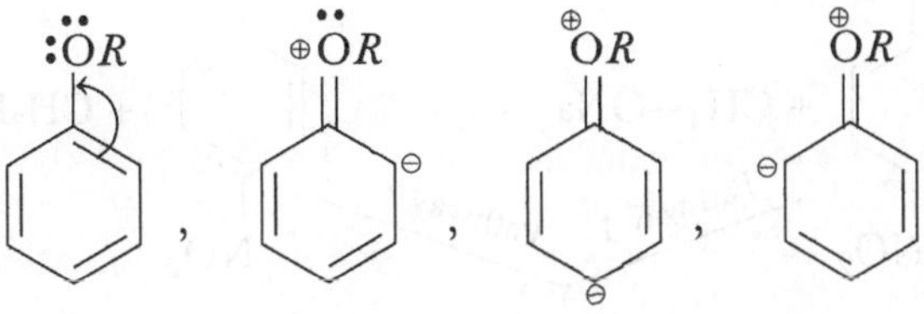

____

144. Determine X and Y in the following reaction.

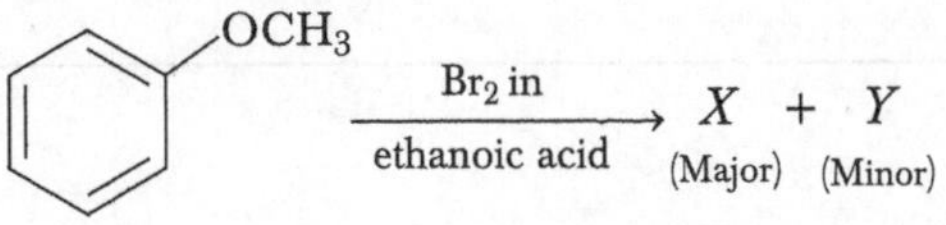

X = ________ Y = ________

***145.** Tick the major product formed in the following conversions.

(i) 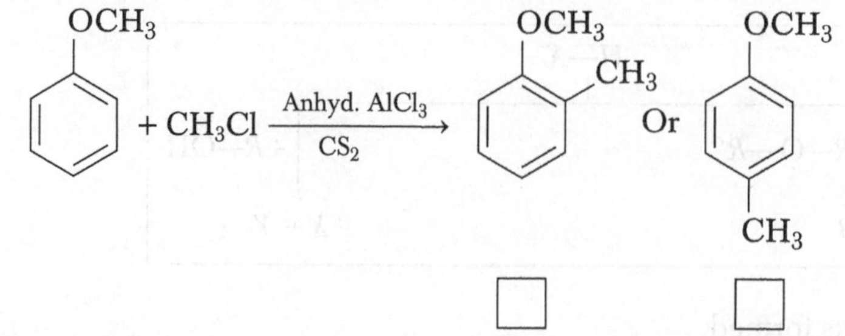

(ii) 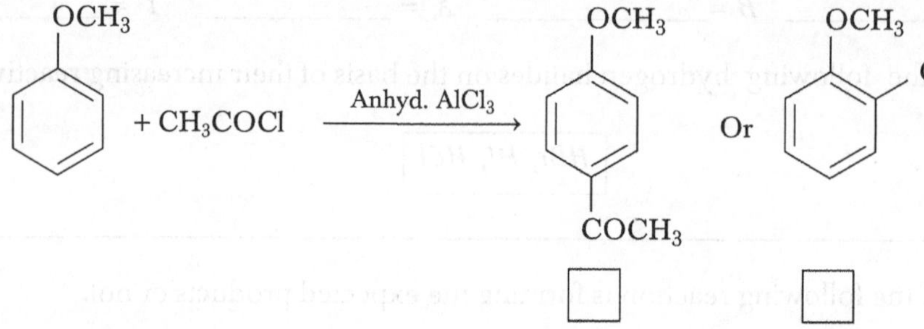

146. Complete the following reaction.

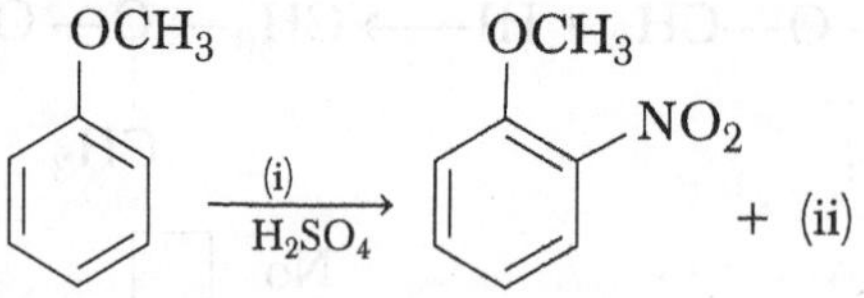

(i) ______ (ii) ______

147. Following reaction is an example of a name reaction.

$$CH_3CH_2—\underset{\displaystyle CH_3}{\underset{|}{CH}}—\underset{\displaystyle CH_3}{\underset{|}{CH}}—O^-Na^+ + CH_3CH_2Br \longrightarrow CH_3CH_2—\underset{\displaystyle CH_3}{\underset{|}{CH}}—\underset{\displaystyle CH_3}{\underset{|}{CH}}—OC_2H_5 + NaBr$$

Write the name of the reaction.

____

148. Consider the following and identify *X* and predict the most feasible pathway to form *X*.

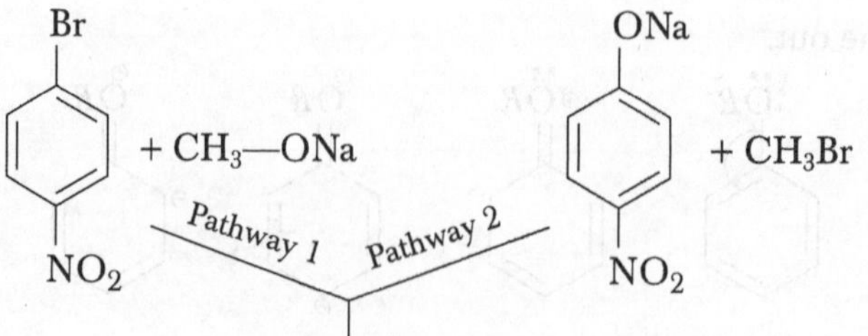

X = ______________________________

149. Match the following columns.

	Column I (Conversions)		Column II (Reagents)
A.	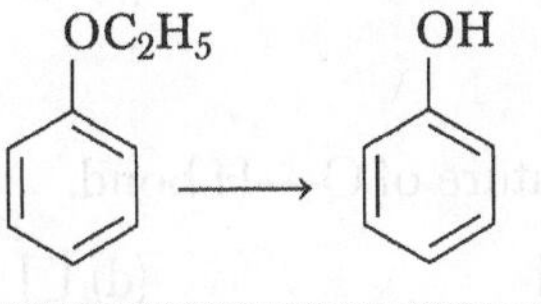	1.	HI
B.	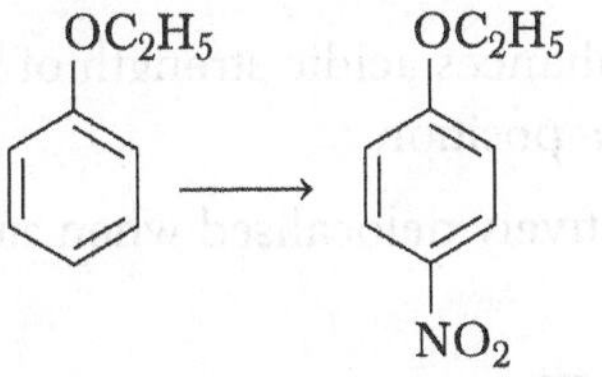	2.	HBr, 373 K
C.	$(CH_3)_3C-OC_2H_5 \longrightarrow CH_3-\underset{CH_3}{\overset{CH_3}{\underset{\vert}{\overset{\vert}{C}}}}-I$	3.	Conc. H_2SO_4 + Conc. HNO_3

A. ____________ B.____________ C. ____________

Assertion-Reason Questions

Given below are two statements, one is labelled as Assertion (A) and other is labelled as Reason (R). Select the correct answer from options given below.

(a) Both A and R are true and R is the correct explanation of A.
(b) Both A and R are true, but R is not the correct explanation of A.
(c) A is true, but R is false.
(d) A is false, but R is true.

1. **Assertion** (A) Ethers are classified as simple and mixed ethers.

Reason (R) If oxygen atom is attached to two alkyl or two aryl groups, it is simple ether. If oxygen atom is attached to an alkyl and aryl group, it is mixed ether.

(a) ☐ (b) ☐ (c) ☐ (d) ☐

2. **Assertion** (A) The bond angle in alcohols is slightly less than tetrahedral angle (109°28′).

Reason (R) Deviation in bond angle is due to repulsion between lone pairs of electrons present on oxygen.

(a) ☐ (b) ☐ (c) ☐ (d) ☐

3. **Assertion** (A) The boiling points of alcohols and phenols are higher than hydrocarbons and ethers of comparable molecular masses.

Reason (R) Ethers and hydrocarbons lack intermolecular hydrogen bonding.

(a) ☐ (b) ☐ (c) ☐ (d) ☐

4. **Assertion** (A) Anisole reacts with HI to form methyl iodide and phenol.
Reason (R) Iodide ion combines with larger group to form stable intermediate.
(a) ☐ (b) ☐ (c) ☐ (d) ☐

5. **Assertion** (A) Alcohols are acidic in nature.
Reason (R) Acidity of alcohols is due to polar nature of O—H bond.
(a) ☐ (b) ☐ (c) ☐ (d) ☐

6. **Assertion** (A) Electron withdrawing group enhances acidic strength of phenols more when present at *ortho* and *para*-positions than at *meta*- position.
Reason (R) The negative charge is more effectively delocalised when substituent (e^- withdrawing) is at *ortho* and *para*-position.
(a) ☐ (b) ☐ (c) ☐ (d) ☐

7. **Assertion** (A) Reimer-Tiemann reaction of phenol gives salicylic acid as the major product.
Reason (R) The intermediate species in the reaction is a carbene.
(a) ☐ (b) ☐ (c) ☐ (d) ☐

8. **Assertion** (A) Drinking denatured alcohol may cause blindness and even death.
Reason (R) Methanol is oxidised to methanal and then methanoic acid which is responsible for causing blindness and death.
(a) ☐ (b) ☐ (c) ☐ (d) ☐

9. **Assertion** (A) Ethers behave as bases in the presence of protic acids such as H_2SO_4.
Reason (R) Ethers have an oxygen atom having lone pairs of electrons.
(a) ☐ (b) ☐ (c) ☐ (d) ☐

10. **Assertion** (A) Boiling points of ethers are much lower than the boiling points of alcohols.
Reason (R) The C—O bonds in ethers are polar and thus they have a net dipole moment.
(a) ☐ (b) ☐ (c) ☐ (d) ☐

Case-Based Questions

1. Alcohols and phenols, distinguished by the presence of a hydroxyl (—OH) group, showcase intriguing reactivity trends. The oxygen's electronegativity polarises the O—H bond, making the hydrogen acidic. However, the acidity is influenced by the nature of the carbon to which —OH group attached. In alcohols, the acidity decreases as we move from primary to secondary to tertiary due to the electron-donating inductive effect of alkyl groups. Phenols, with the —OH bonded directly to an aromatic ring, exhibit enhanced acidity due to resonance stabilisation of the phenoxide ion. Ethers, lacking the —OH group, are relatively inert but can be cleaved by strong acids.

(i) Which of the following would most readily donate a proton (H^+)?
(a) $(CH_3)_3COH$ (*tert*-butyl alcohol) ☐ (b) $(CH_3)_2CHOH$ (*iso*-propyl alcohol) ☐
(c) C_6H_5OH (phenol) ☐ (d) CH_3CH_2OH (ethanol) ☐

(ii) Upon reaction with neutral $FeCl_3$, which compound would produce a violet colour?

(a) CH_3CH_2OH (ethanol) ☐ (b) CH_3OCH_3 (dimethyl ether) ☐

(c) C_6H_5OH (phenol) ☐ (d) CH_3COOH (acetic acid) ☐

(iii) Which of the following reagents would effectively cleave the C—O bond in $CH_3OCH_2CH_3$ (ethyl methyl ether)?

(a) Dilute NaOH ☐ (b) H_2O ☐

(c) Concentrated H_2SO_4 ☐ (d) Br_2 in CCl_4 ☐

(iv) Which compound would you expect to have the highest boiling point due to stronger intermolecular forces?

(a) $CH_3CH_2OCH_2CH_3$ (diethyl ether) ☐

(b) $CH_3CH_2CH_2CH_2OH$ (butan-1-ol) ☐

(c) $CH_3CH_2CH(OH)CH_3$ (butan-2-ol) ☐

(d) $(CH_3)_3COH$ (*tert*-butyl alcohol) ☐

2. Ethers, organic compounds with the general formula *R*—O—*R'*, where *R* and *R'* are alkyl or aryl groups, possess a unique chemical character. The oxygen atom, with its two lone pairs of electrons, imparts a bent molecular geometry and slight polarity to the molecule. However, unlike their alcohol counterparts, ethers lack the polar O—H bond responsible for hydrogen bonding. This absence significantly impacts their physical properties, leading to lower boiling points compared to alcohols of similar molecular weight. While relatively inert, ethers can undergo cleavage reactions with strong acids like hydroiodic acid (HI) or hydrobromic acid (HBr), yielding alkyl halides and alcohols. Additionally, ethers can form explosive peroxides upon prolonged exposure to air, posing a potential safety hazard.

(i) Which of the following properties is not characteristic of ethers?

(a) Relatively unreactive ☐

(b) Formation of hydrogen bonds ☐

(c) Lower boiling points than alcohols of similar molecular weight ☐

(d) Susceptibility to cleavage by strong acids ☐

(ii) The reaction of diethyl ether ($CH_3CH_2OCH_2CH_3$) with HI would primarily yield

(a) ethyl iodide (CH_3CH_2I) and ethanol (CH_3CH_2OH) ☐

(b) ethyl iodide (CH_3CH_2I) and water (H_2O) ☐

(c) ethanol (CH_3CH_2OH) and iodomethane (CH_3I) ☐

(d) ethyl iodide (CH_3CH_2I) and iodomethane (CH_3I) ☐

(iii) Which of the following ethers is most likely to form explosive peroxides upon prolonged exposure to air?

(a) Diphenyl ether ☐ (b) Tetrahydrofuran ☐

(c) Anisole ☐ (d) Diethyl ether ☐

(iv) Ethers are commonly used as solvents due to their

(a) high reactivity ☐

(b) ability to form hydrogen bonds with solutes ☐

(c) high polarity ☐

(d) relatively inert nature ☐

COMPETITION EDGE UP

1. *Identify the product A and product B in the following set of reactions.*
[NCERT (New) Pg. 199, JEE Main 2024]

$$CH_3-CH=CH_2 \begin{cases} \xrightarrow{H_2O,\ H^+} \text{Major product A} \\ \xrightarrow[H_2O,\ H_2O_2,\ \bar{O}H]{(BH_3)_2} \text{Major product B} \end{cases}$$

(a) A- $CH_3CH_2CH_3$, B-$CH_3CH_2CH_3$ ☐
(b) A- $CH_3-CH(OH)-CH_3$, B- $CH_3CH_2CH_2-OH$ ☐
(c) A- $CH_3CH_2CH_2-OH$, B- $CH_3CH(OH)-CH_3$ ☐
(d) A- $CH_3CH_2CH_2-OH$, B- $CH_3CH_2CH_2-OH$ ☐

2. $CH_3CH_2-OH \xrightarrow[\text{(iii) NaOH, CaO, }\Delta]{\text{(i) Jone's reagent, (ii) } KMnO_4} P$

Consider the above reaction sequence and identify the major product P.
[NCERT (New) Pg. 210, JEE Main 2024]

(a) Methoxymethane ☐
(b) Methanoic acid ☐
(c) Methane ☐
(d) Methanal ☐

3. *Given below are two statements : one is labelled as Assertion (A) and the other is labelled as Reason (R).*

Assertion (A) Alcohols react both as nucleophiles and electrophiles.
[NCERT (New) Pg. 204, JEE Main 2024]

Reason (R) Alcohols react with active metals such as sodium, potassium and aluminium to yield corresponding alkoxides and liberate hydrogen.

In the light of the above statements, choose the correct answer from the options given below.

(a) A is false but R is true. ☐
(b) A is true but R is false. ☐
(c) Both A and R are true but R is not the correct explanation of A. ☐
(d) Both A and R are true and R is the correct explanation of A. ☐

4. *Products A and B formed in the following set of reactions are*
[NCERT (New) Pg. 199, JEE Main 2024]

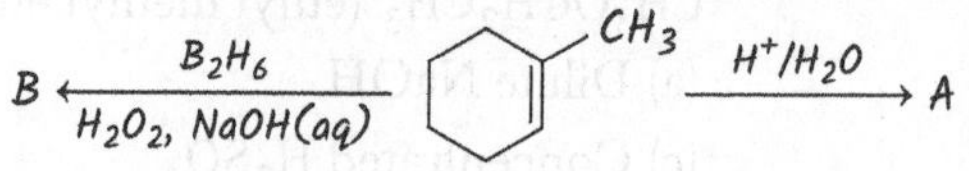

(a) A = 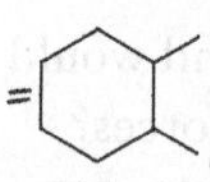 B = 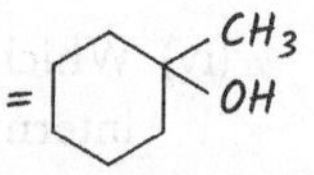

(b) A = 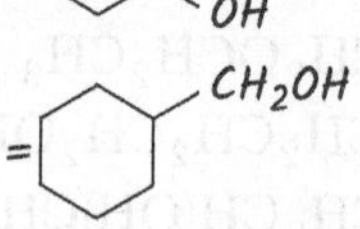 B = 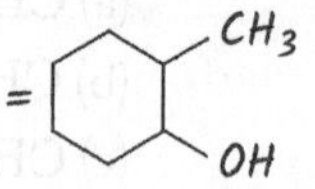

(c) A = 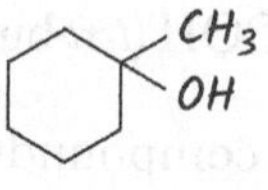 B = 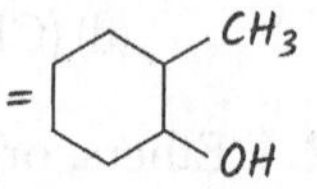

(d) A = 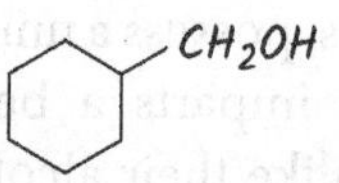 B = 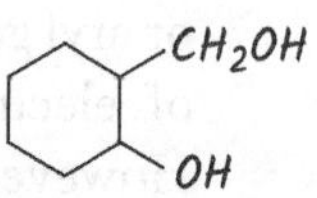

5. *Major product formed in the following reaction is a mixture of*
[NCERT (New) Pg. 217, JEE Main 2024]

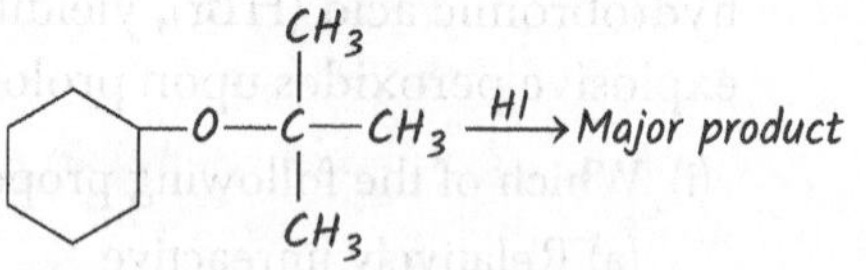

(a) 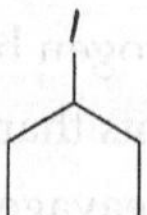 and $(CH_3)_3COH$ ☐

(b) 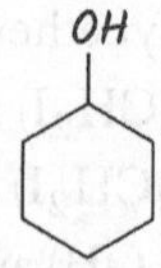 and $CH_3-C(CH_3)_2-I$ ☐

(c) 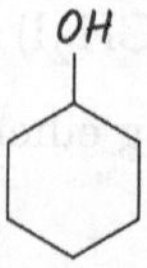 and $(CH_3)_3COH$ ☐

(d) 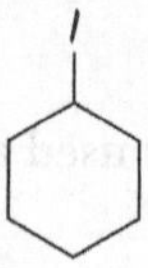 and $(CH_3)_3Cl$ ☐

6. *In Reimer-Tiemann reaction, phenol is converted into salicylaldehyde through an intermediate. The structure of intermediate is* **[NCERT (New) Pg. 213, JEE Main 2024]**

(a) 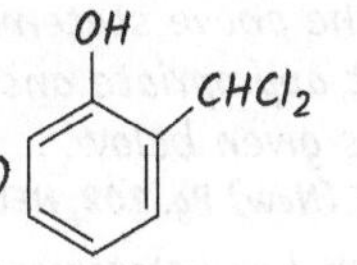 ☐ (b) 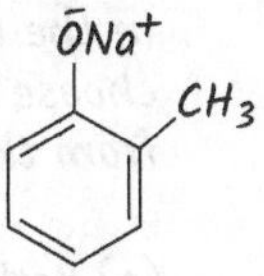 ☐

(c) 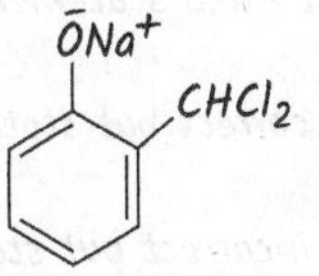 ☐ (d) 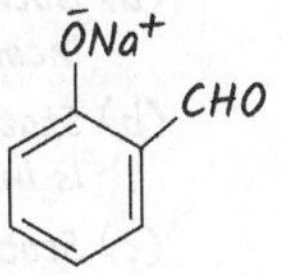 ☐

7. *The major product (P) in the following reaction is* **[NCERT (New) Pg. 217, JEE Main 2024]**

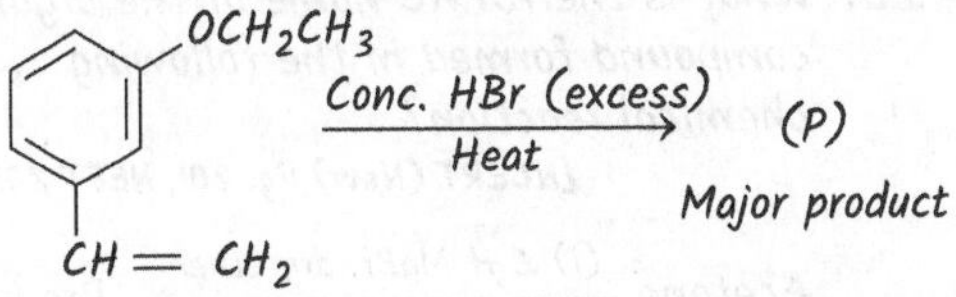

(a) 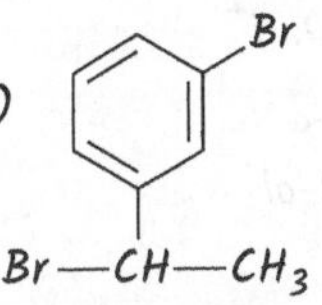 ☐ (b) 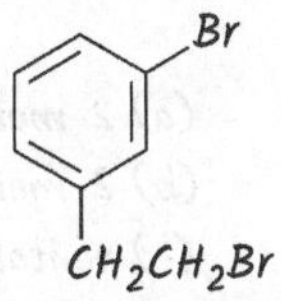 ☐

(c) 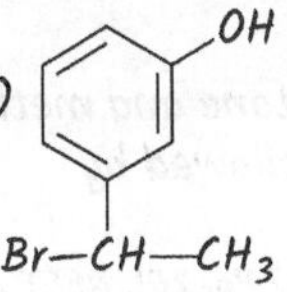 ☐ (d) 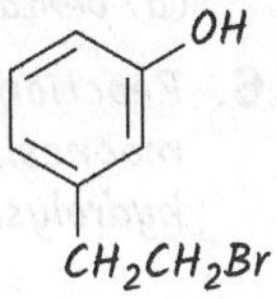 ☐

8. *Given below are two statements.* **[NCERT (New) Pg. 208-211, JEE Main 2024]**

Statement I *p-nitrophenol is more acidic than m-nitrophenol and o-nitrophenol.*

Statement II *Ethanol will give immediate turbidity with Lucas reagent.*

In the light of the above statements, choose the correct answer from the options given below

(a) Both Statement I and Statement II are true. ☐

(b) Both Statement I and Statement II are false. ☐

(c) Statement I is true but Statement II is false. ☐

(d) Statement I is false but Statement II is true. ☐

9. *Identify the major products A and B respectively in the following set of reactions.* **[NCERT (New) Pg. 208-207, JEE Main 2024]**

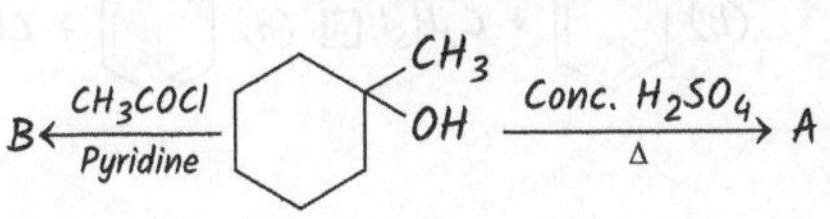

(a) A = 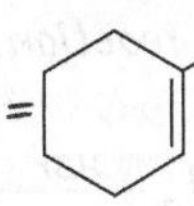 and B = 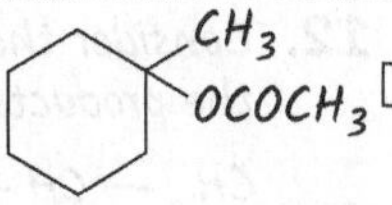 ☐

(b) A = 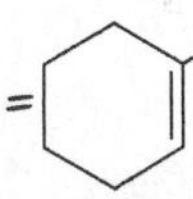 and B = 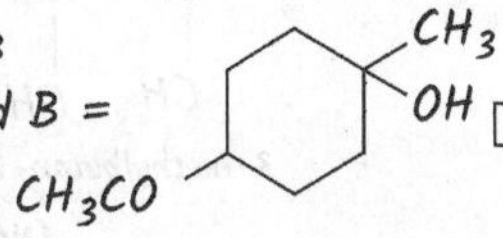 ☐

(c) A = 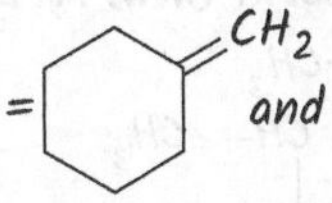 and B = 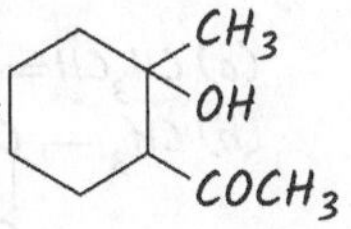 ☐

(d) A = 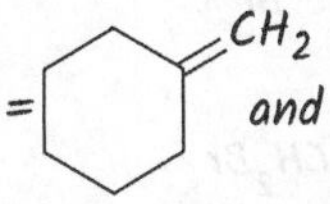 and B = 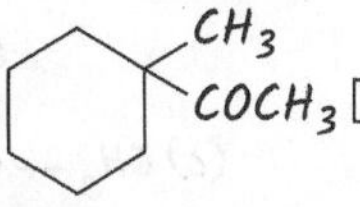 ☐

10. *Which one of the following alcohols reacts instantaneously with Lucas reagent?* **[NCERT (New) Pg. 208, NEET 2024]**

(a) $CH_3CH_2CH_2CH_2OH$ ☐

(b) $CH_3CH_2-CH(CH_3)-OH$ ☐

(c) $CH_3-CH(CH_3)-CH_2OH$ ☐

(d) $CH_3-C(CH_3)_2-OH$ ☐

11. *Major products A and B formed in the following reaction sequence are* **[NCERT (New) Pg. 209, NEET 2024]**

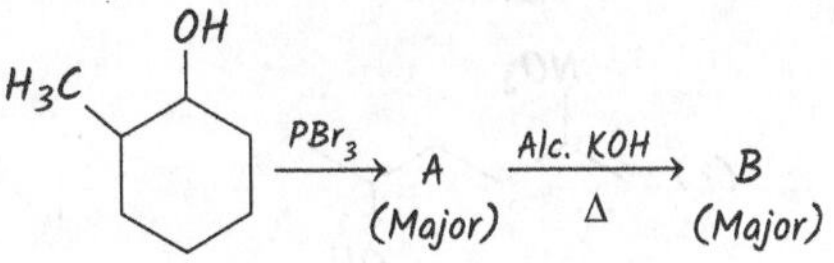

(a) A = 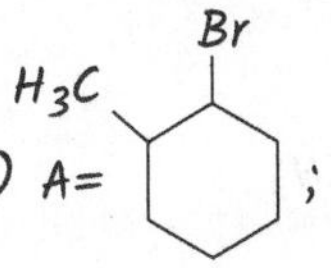 ; B = 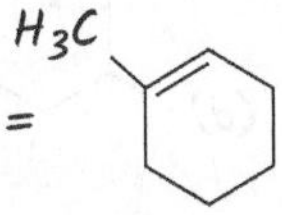 ☐

(b) A = 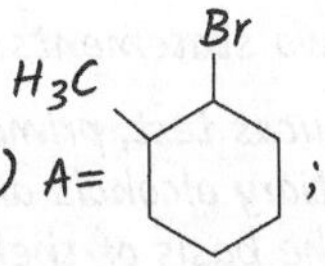 ; B = 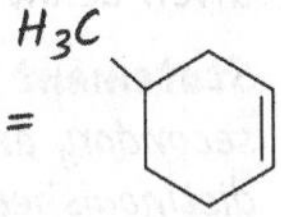 ☐

(c) A = 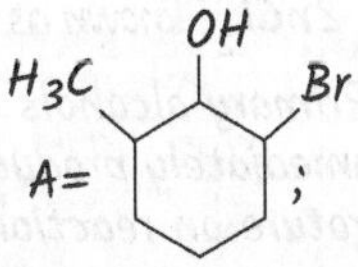 ; B = 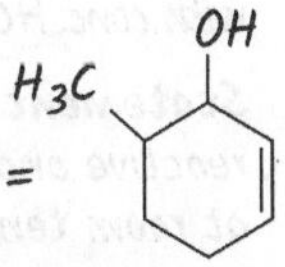 ☐

(d) A = 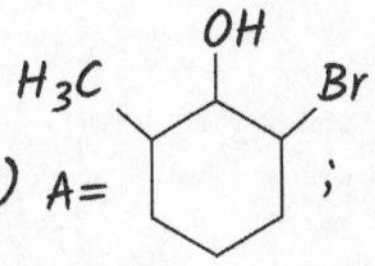 ; B = 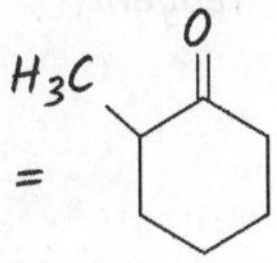 ☐

12. *Consider the following reaction and identify the product (P).*

$$CH_3-\underset{\underset{CH_3}{|}}{CH}-\underset{\underset{OH}{|}}{CH}-CH_3 \xrightarrow{HBr} \text{Product (P)}$$

3-methylbutan-2-ol

[NCERT (New) Pg. 208, NEET 2023]

(a) $CH_3CH{=}CH{-}CH_3$ ☐

(b) $CH_3-\underset{\underset{CH_3}{|}}{CH}-\underset{\underset{Br}{|}}{CH}-CH_3$ ☐

(c) $CH_3-\underset{\underset{CH_3}{|}}{\overset{\overset{CH_3}{|}}{C}}-CH_2Br$ ☐

(d) $CH_3-\underset{\underset{CH_3}{|}}{\overset{\overset{Br}{|}}{C}}-CH_2-CH_3$ ☐

13. *Which amongst the following will be most readily dehydrated under acidic conditions?*

[NCERT (New) Pg. 209, NEET 2023]

(a) 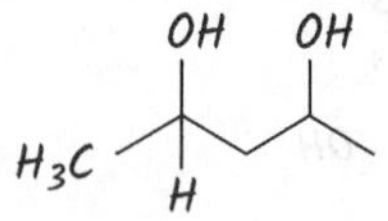 ☐

(b) 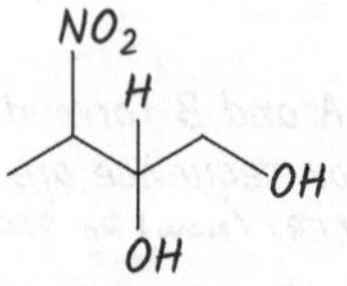 ☐

(c) 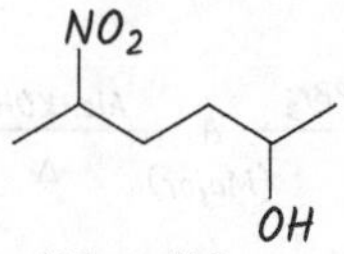 ☐

(d) 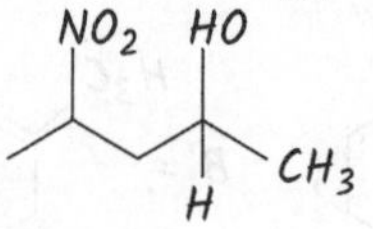 ☐

14. *Given below are two statements.*

Statement I *In Lucas test, primary, secondary and tertiary alcohols are distinguished on the basis of their reactivity with conc. HCl + $ZnCl_2$, known as Lucas reagent.*

Statement II *Primary alcohols are most reactive and immediately produce turbidity at room temperature on reaction with Lucas reagent.*

In the light of the above statements, choose the most appropriate answer from the options given below.

[NCERT (New) Pg. 208, NEET 2022]

(a) Both statement I and statement II are incorrect. ☐

(b) Statement I is correct but statement II is incorrect. ☐

(c) Statement I is incorrect but statement II is correct. ☐

(d) Both statement I and statement II are correct. ☐

15. *What is the IUPAC name of the organic compound formed in the following chemical reaction?*

[NCERT (New) Pg. 201, NEET 2021]

$$\text{Acetone} \xrightarrow[\text{(ii) } H_2O,\ H^+]{\text{(i) } C_2H_5MgBr,\text{ dry ether}} \text{Product}$$

(a) 2-methylbutan-2-o ☐

(b) 2-methylpropan-2-ol ☐

(c) pentan-2-ol ☐

(d) pentan-3-ol ☐

16. *Reaction between acetone and methyl magnesium chloride followed by hydrolysis will give*

[NCERT (New) Pg. 201, NEET 2020]

(a) iso-propyl alcohol ☐

(b) sec-butyl alcohol ☐

(c) tert-butyl alcohol ☐

(d) iso-butyl alcohol ☐

17. $CH_3CH_2CH{=}CH_2 \xrightarrow[H_2O,H_2O_2,OH^-]{B_2H_6} Z$

what is Z?

[NCERT (New) Pg. 200, NEET (Oct.) 2020]

(a) $CH_3CH_2CH_2CH_2OH$ ☐

(b) $CH_3CH_2\underset{\underset{OH}{|}}{C}HCH_3$ ☐

(c) $CH_3CH_2CH_2CHO$ ☐

(d) $CH_3CH_2CH_2CH_3$ ☐

18. *Anisole on cleavage with HI gives:*

[NCERT (New) Pg. 218, NEET (Sep.) 2020]

(a) 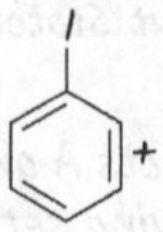 + CH_3OH ☐

(c) 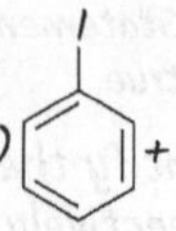 + C_2H_5OH ☐

(b) 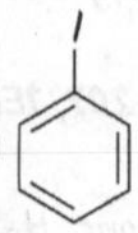 + C_2H_5I ☐

(d) 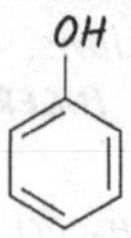 + CH_3I ☐

Chapter 08

Aldehydes, Ketones and Carboxylic Acids

Scan and take Chapter Test

TOPIC 1

Introduction, Nomenclature and Structure of Carbonyl Group

NCERT Pg 227-231

1. Organic compounds with carbonyl group contain carbon-oxygen __________ bond.
2. In aldehydes, the carbonyl group is bonded to two carbon atoms whereas in ketones, the carbonyl is bonded to a carbon and one or more hydrogen atoms.

   True ☐ False ☐

3. Match the following Column I with appropriate option in Column II.

Column I (Compounds)	Column II (Structures)
A. Carboxylic acid	1. 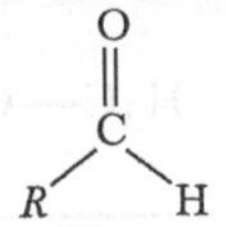
B. Acyl halide	2. 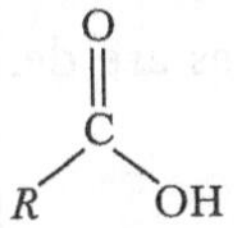
C. Aldehyde	3. 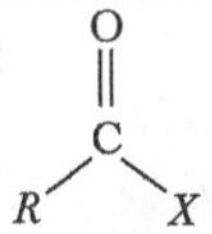 (X = Halogen)
D. Amide	4. 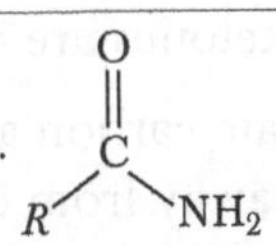

A.__________ B.__________ C. __________ D.__________

*Concepts of all questions bearing * are important for JEE/NEET/CUET.*

4. Pick the odd one out from the following compounds.

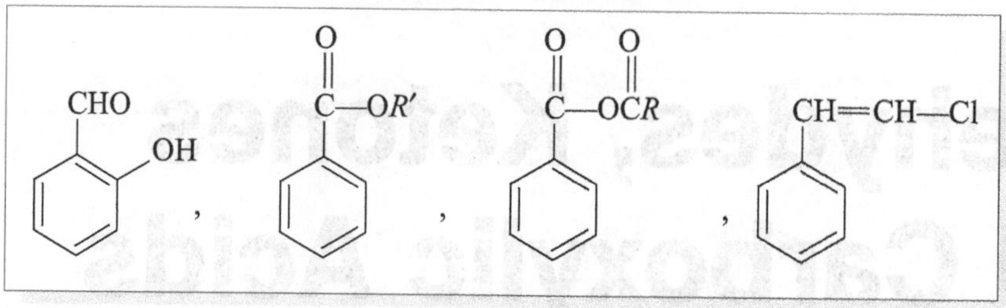

---

5. Vanillin which is used for adding flavour is obtained from ____________________.

6. Consider the following statements.

I. Meadow sweet is used for obtaining salicylaldehyde.

II. Cinnamaldehyde is obtained from cinnamon which has very pleasant fragrance.

Which of the above statement(s) is /are correct?

(a) Only I ☐ (b) Only II ☐

(c) Both I and II ☐ (d) Neither I nor II ☐

7. Name the ketone which is used as solvent to prepare materials like adhesives, paints, resins, perfumes, plastics, fabrics etc.

---

8. The common names of most aldehydes are derived from the common names of their corresponding ____________ (alcohols/carboxylic acids).

9. Write the common name of the following compound.

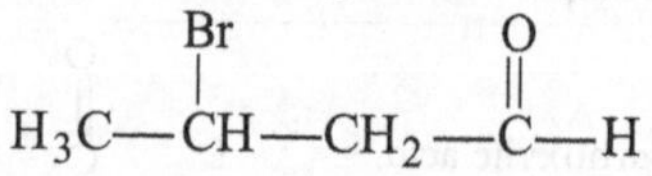

---

10. The common names of ketones are derived by naming ________ bonded to the carbonyl group.

(a) three alkyl groups ☐ (b) three aryl groups ☐

(c) two alkyl or aryl groups ☐ (d) two hydrogen atoms ☐

11. Complete the following analogy.

Locations of substituents on ketones are indicated by Greek letters *A*, *B* and so on.

A : Greek letter used to indicate carbon atoms next to carboxyl group :: *B* : Greek letter used to indicate two carbons away from carbonyl group.

(a) $A : \alpha\beta'$, $B : \beta\alpha'$ ☐ (b) $A : \alpha\alpha'$, $B : \beta\beta'$ ☐

(c) $A : \alpha'\beta$, $B : \alpha\beta'$ ☐ (d) $A : \beta\beta'$, $B : \alpha\alpha'$ ☐

12. Alkyl phenyl ketones are usually named by adding the name of ____________ (alkyl/acyl) group as prefix to the word phenone.

13. Write the structures of the following compounds whose common names are given below.

(i) Acetophenone ____________

(ii) Propiophenone ____________

(iii) Benzophenone ____________

14. The IUPAC names of open chain aliphatic aldehydes and ketones are derived from the names of their corresponding acids by replacing acid with –one and –al respectively.

True ☐ False ☐

15. The IUPAC names of aliphatic aldehydes is written by replacing –e of parent alkane by suffix is

(a) –one ☐ (b) –el ☐

(c) –al ☐ (d) –one ☐

16. While writing IUPAC names of cyclic ketones, ____________ is numbered one.

17. Complete the following analogy.

A : IUPAC name of simplest aromatic aldehyde carrying aldehyde group on benzene ring::
B : IUPAC name of aromatic aldehyde carrying aldehyde group on benzene ring and a nitro substituent at 4th position.

(a) *A* : Benzene carbaldehyde, *B* : 4-nitrobenzene carbaldehyde ☐

(b) *A* : Carbaldehyde, *B* : 4- nitrobenzene ☐

(c) *A* : Benzene aldehyde, *B* : 4-nitrobenzene ☐

(d) *A* : Aldobenzene, *B* : 4-nitroaldobenzene ☐

***18.** Complete the following table with suitable options.

Structure	Common name	IUPAC name
$(CH_3)_2CHCHO$	Isobutyraldehyde	(i) ____________
(ii) ____________	α-methoxypropionaldehyde	2-methoxy propanal
$CH_2{=}CHCHO$	(iii) ____________	Prop-2-enal
(iv) ____________	*m*-bromobenzaldehyde	3-bromobenzaldehyde

***19.** Amongst the following, the total number of species/compounds that are correctly given corresponding to its IUPAC name.

(i) $(CH_3)_2CHCHO$
2-methylpropanol

(ii) $(CH_3)_2C{=}CHCOCH_3$
4-methylpent-3-en-2-one

(iii)

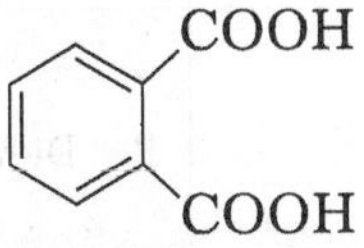

Benzene-1, 2-dicarboxylic acid

(iv) $HOOC(CH_2)_2COOH$
Butanedioic acid

(v) $HOOC(CH_2)_4COOH$
Hexanedioic acid

(a) 2 ☐ (b) 5 ☐

(c) 3 ☐ (d) 4 ☐

20. Write IUPAC names of the following ketones.

(i) $CH_3COCH_2CH_2CH_3$ ____________ (ii) 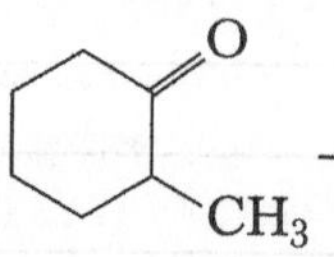 ____________

(iii) $(CH_3)_2C{=}CHCOCH_3$ ____________

21. The carbonyl carbon atom is

(a) *sp* - hybridised ☐ (b) sp^2 - hybridised ☐

(c) sp^3-hybridised ☐ (d) sp^3d-hybridised ☐

22. In structure of carbonyl group containing compounds, the carbonyl carbon and the three atoms attached to it lie on ____________ (same/different) plane and the ____________ (π-electron/σ-electron) cloud is above and below this plane.

23. Consider the following statements.

I. In structure of the carbonyl group, the bond angles are approximately 120°.

II. The expected structure of the carbonyl group is trigonal coplanar.

Which of the above statement(s) is/are correct ?

(a) Only I ☐ (b) Only II ☐ (c) Both I and II ☐ (d) Neither I nor II ☐

24. Complete the following analogy with respect to structure of carbonyl group.
Electrophilic centre in carbonyl group: *A* : : Nucleophilic centre in carbonyl group : *B*

(a) *A* : Carbonyl oxygen, *B* : Carbonyl carbon ☐

(b) *A* : Carbonyl carbon, *B* : Carbonyl oxygen ☐

(c) *A* : Hydrogen, *B* : Carbonyl oxygen ☐

(d) *A* : Carbonyl carbon, *B* : Hydrogen ☐

25. Match the following Column I with Column II.

Column I (Compounds)	Column II (Structures)
A. 3-hydroxybutanal	1. 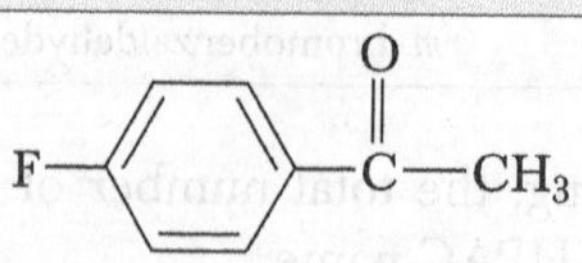
B. Di-*sec* - butyl ketone	2. 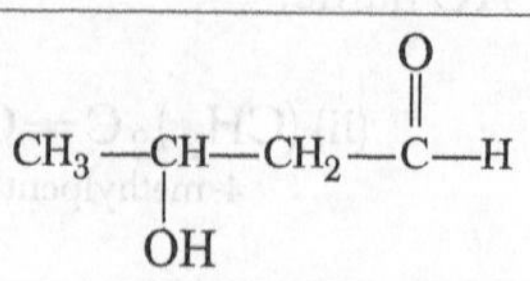
C. 4-fluoroacetophenone	3. 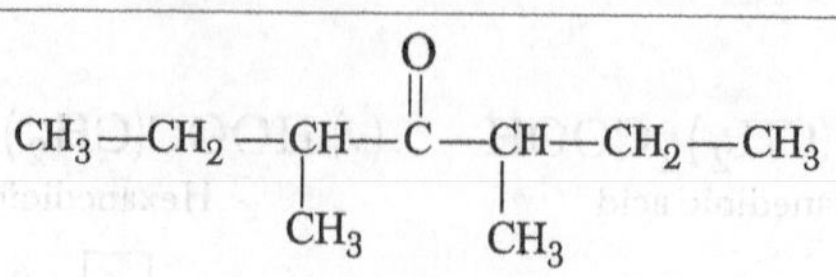

A. ____________ B. ____________ C. ____________

TOPIC 2

Preparation of Aldehydes and Ketones

NCERT Pg 231-234

26. Aldehydes and ketones cannot be prepared by which method ?

(a) By oxidation of alcohols
(b) By hydrogenation of alcohols
(c) Ozonolysis of alkenes
(d) Hydration of alkynes

27. Complete the analogy with respect to the method of preparation of carbonyl compounds.
Product formed by oxidation of primary alcohols : A :: Product formed by oxidation of secondary alcohols : B

(a) A : Aldehyde, B : Ketone
(b) A : Ketone, B : Aldehyde
(c) A : Aldehyde, B : Acid
(d) A : Acid, B : Ketone

28. (i) The ____________ (dehydrogenation/reduction) method is a suitable method for the preparation of aldehydes and ketones from volatile alcohols.

(ii) Na or Mg are used as metal catalysts in this method.

True   False

29. Addition of water to alkynes (higher than ethyne) in the presence of H_2SO_4 and $HgSO_4$ leads to formation of ____________ as the product.

30. Addition of water to ethyne gives acetaldehyde in the presence of

(a) H_2SO_4 and Hg_2SO_4
(b) H_2SO_4 and $HgSO_4$
(c) HCl and Hg_2SO_4
(d) HCl and Zn dust

31. Identify X, Y, A and B in the following reactions.

(i)

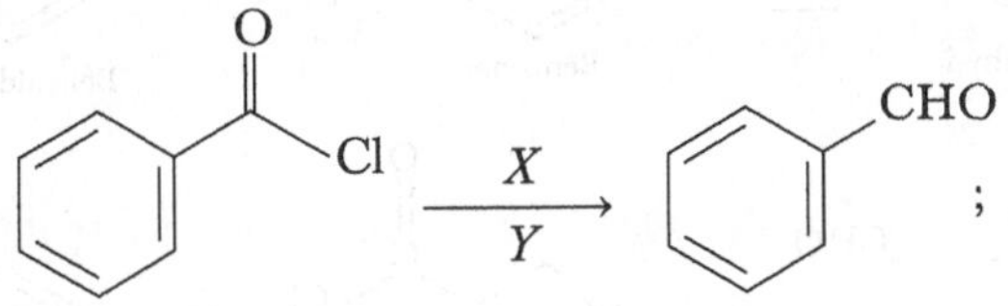

Benzoyl chloride   Benzaldehyde

; X= ____________ Y= ____________

(ii) $RCN + SnCl_2 + HCl \longrightarrow A \xrightarrow{H_3O^+} B$; A= ____________ B= ____________

32. The major product of the following reaction is

$$R—C \equiv N \xrightarrow[\text{(ii) } H_2O]{\text{(i) } AlH(i\text{-}Bu)_2} ?$$

(a) RCHO
(b) RCONH$_2$
(c) RCOOH
(d) RCH_2NH_2

***33.** Write the reagents *A* to *D* used for the following conversions.

(i) $CH_3(CH_2)_9-\overset{\overset{O}{\parallel}}{C}-OC_2H_5 \xrightarrow[B]{A} CH_3(CH_2)_9-\overset{\overset{O}{\parallel}}{C}-H$

(ii) 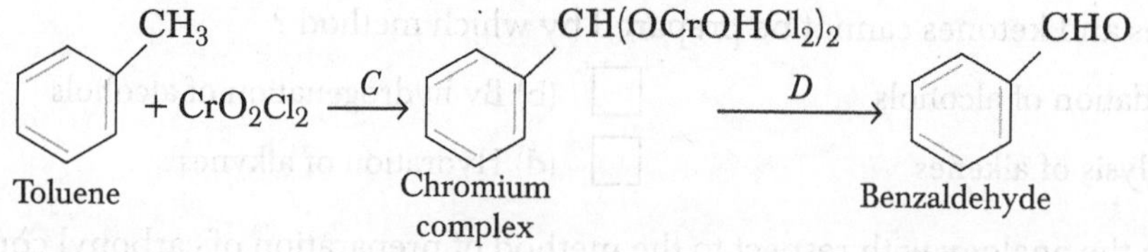

A = ______ *B* = ______ *C* = ______ *D* = ______

34. Toluene undergoes following reactions in given conditions to give products '*A*' and '*B*'.

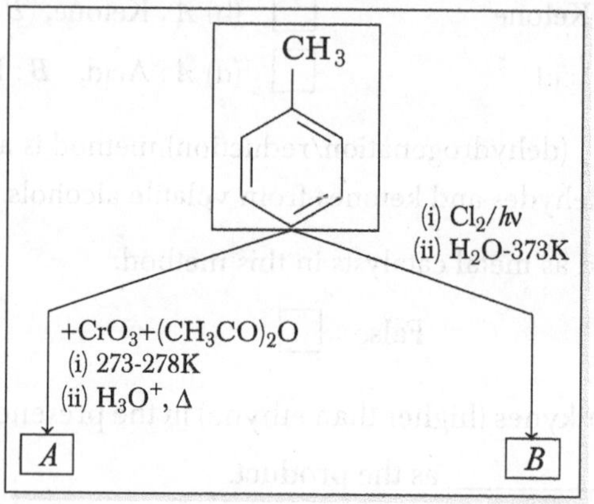

Determine the products '*A*' and '*B*'.

A = ______ *B* = ______

***35.** Gattermann-Koch reaction can be given as

(a) 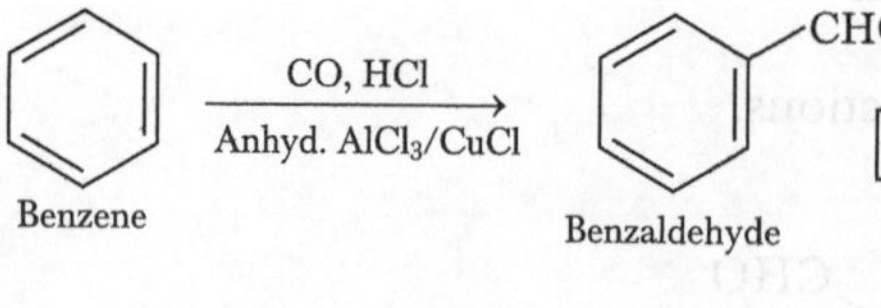

(b) 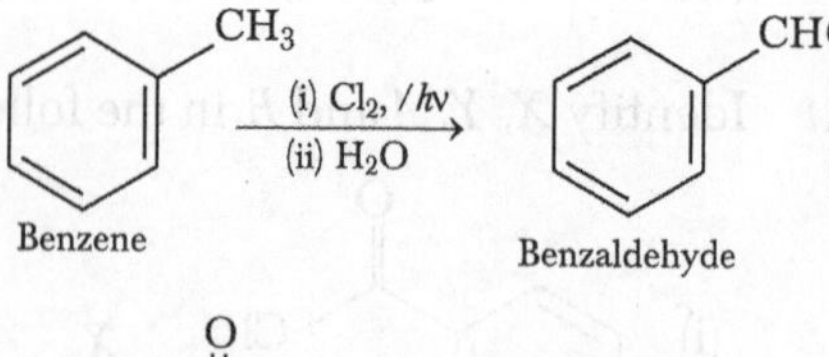

(c) 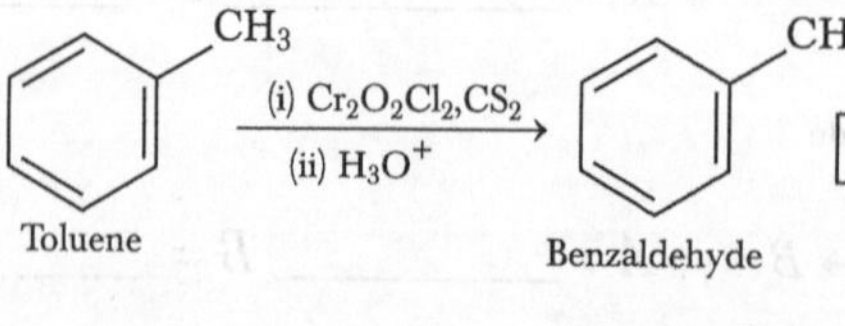

(d) 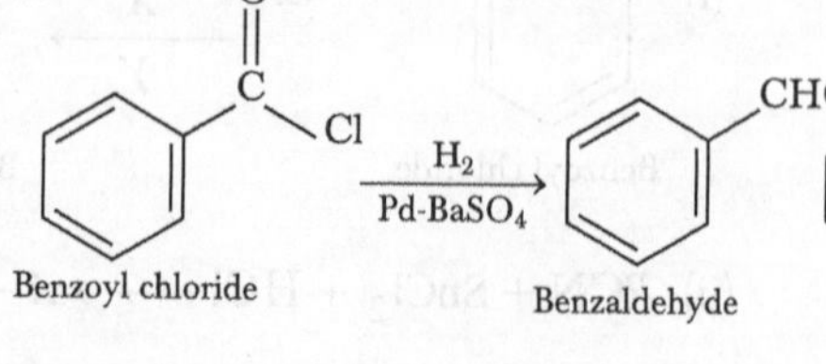

36. Write the structures of products for the following reactions.

(i) $CH_3-CH_2-C\equiv N + C_6H_5MgBr \xrightarrow[\text{(b) } H_3O^+]{\text{(a) Ether}}$ ______.

(ii)  $+ \text{Ar}-\overset{\overset{O}{\parallel}}{C}-\text{Cl} \xrightarrow{\text{Anhyd. AlCl}_3}$ ______.

37. Predict the correct intermediate and product in the following reaction.

$$H_3C-C\equiv CH \xrightarrow[HgSO_4]{H_2O,\, H_2SO_4} \underset{A}{\text{Intermediate}} \longrightarrow \underset{B}{\text{Product}}$$

(a) $A = H_3C-\underset{SO_4}{\underset{|}{C}}=CH_2$; $B = H_3C-\underset{O}{\underset{\|}{C}}-CH_3$ ☐

(b) $A = H_3C-\underset{OH}{\underset{|}{C}}=CH_2$; $B = H_3C-\underset{SO_4}{\underset{|}{C}}=CH_2$ ☐

(c) $A = H_3C-\underset{O}{\underset{\|}{C}}-CH_3$; $B = H_3C-C\equiv CH$ ☐

(d) $A = H_3C-\underset{OH}{\underset{|}{C}}=CH_2$; $B = H_3C-\underset{O}{\underset{\|}{C}}-CH_3$ ☐

38. Match the following Column I with Column II.

Column I (Conversion)	Column II (Reagent)
A. Hexan-l-ol to hexanal	1. PCC
B. Cyclohexanal to cyclohexanone	2. O_3/H_2O – Zn dust
C. Allyl alcohol to propenal	3. $C_5H_5\overset{+}{N}HCrO_3Cl^-$(PCC)
D. But-2-ene to ethanal	4. Anhyd. CrO_3

A. ____________________ B. ____________________

C. ____________________ D. ____________________

***39.** Recognise *X* and *Y* in the following reactions.

(i) 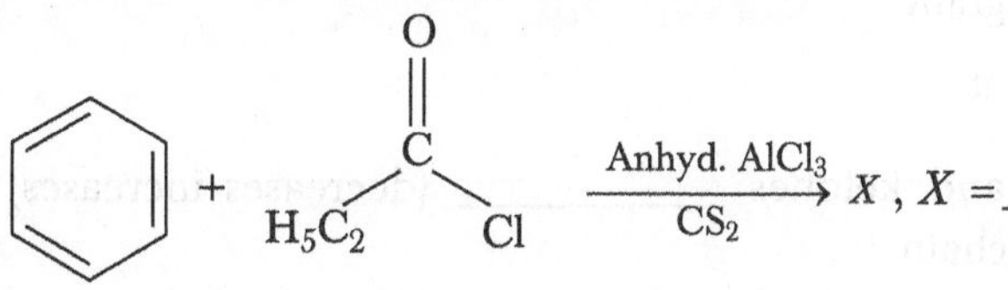

X, X = ____________________

(ii) $H_3C-C\equiv C-H \xrightarrow{Y} H_3C-\underset{}{\overset{O}{\overset{\|}{C}}}-CH_3$, Y = ____________________

TOPIC 3

Physical Properties

NCERT Pg 235

40. Consider the following statements.

I. Boiling points of aldehydes and ketones are lower than hydrocarbons and other compounds of comparable molecular masses.

II. There is a weak molecular association in aldehydes and ketones due to dipole-dipole interaction.

Which of the above statement(s) is/are correct?

(a) Only I ☐

(b) Only II ☐

(c) Both I and II ☐

(d) Neither I nor II ☐

41. The boiling points of aldehydes and ketones are lower than ________ (alcohols/ethers) of similar molecular masses due to absence of intermolecular hydrogen bonding.

42. Arrange the following in order of increasing boiling points.

(i) Methoxyethane, Propan-1-ol, *n*-butane, Propanal, Acetone ________________

(ii) $CH_3CH_2CH_2CH_2OH$, $H_5C_2—O—C_2H_5$, $CH_3CH_2CH_2CHO$, $CH_3CH_2CH_2CH_3$

____

43. Lower members of aldehydes and ketones cannot form hydrogen bond with water. Hence, these compounds are immiscible in water.

True ☐ False ☐

44. As size of the aldehyde molecule increases, the odour becomes

(a) more pungent and less fragrant ☐

(b) less pungent and more fragrant ☐

(c) more pungent and more fragrant ☐

(d) less pungent and less fragrant ☐

45. The stability of aldehydes and ketones ________ (decreases/increases) rapidly on increasing the length of alkyl chain.

46. Many naturally occurring aldehydes and ketones are used in the blending of perfumes and flavouring agents.

True ☐ False ☐

TOPIC 4

Chemical Reactions and Uses of Aldehydes and Ketones

NCERT Pg 236-244

47. During nucleophilic addition reactions in aldehydes and ketones, the hybridisation of carbonyl carbon changes from ____________ to ____________.

48. Consider the following statements.

I. Carbon atom of functional group in benzaldehyde is less electrophilic than propanal.

II. Benzaldehyde is very reactive as compared to propanal.

III. The polarity of the carbonyl group is reduced in benzaldehyde.

Mark (✓) and (×) under correct and incorrect with respect to the given statements.

	Correct	**Incorrect**
I.	________	________
II.	________	________
III.	________	________

49. Match the following Column I with Column II.

Column I (Reactants)	**Column II** (Products)
A. $>C{=}O + :\bar{C}N$	1. $>C(OSO_2Na)(OH)$
B. $>C{=}O + NaHSO_3$	2. $R{-}CH(OR')(OR') + H_2O$
C. $R{-}CHO \xrightarrow[HCl]{2R'OH}$	3. $>C(CN)(OH)$

A. ____________ B. ____________ C. ____________

50. Product formed when benzaldehyde is treated with 1 equivalent of CH_3MgBr will be

(a) 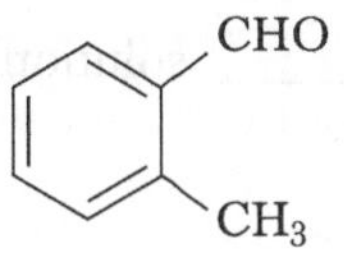 ☐

(b) 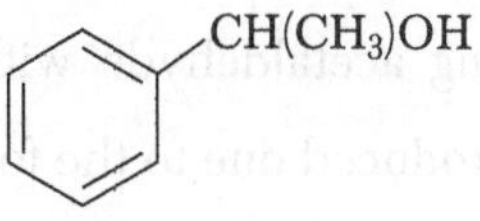 ☐

(c) 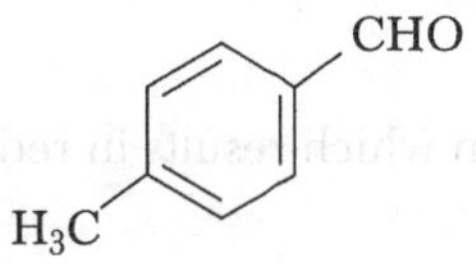 ☐

(d) 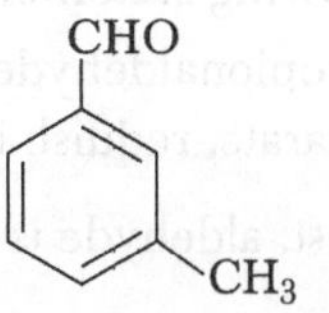 ☐

51. Identify the products of the following reactions:

(i) $\underset{R}{\overset{R}{>}}C=O + \begin{matrix} CH_2-OH \\ | \\ CH_2-OH \end{matrix} \underset{\text{Dil. HCl}}{\overset{\text{HCl gas}}{\rightleftharpoons}} ? + ?$ (ii) $\underset{R}{\overset{R}{>}}C=O + H_2N-R \longrightarrow ? + ?$

52. Complete the following table.

Reactant	Carbonyl derivative	Product name
$>C=O$ + (i)________	$>C=N-OH$	(ii)________
$\underset{R}{\overset{R}{>}}C=O + H_2N-\overset{H}{\overset{\vert}{N}}-C_6H_5$	(iii)________	(iv)________
$>C=O$ + (v)________	(vi)________	Semicarbazone

53. Name the reagent(s) which can be used for reducing ketones to secondary alcohols.

____

***54.** The correct structure of the product *A* formed in the reaction.

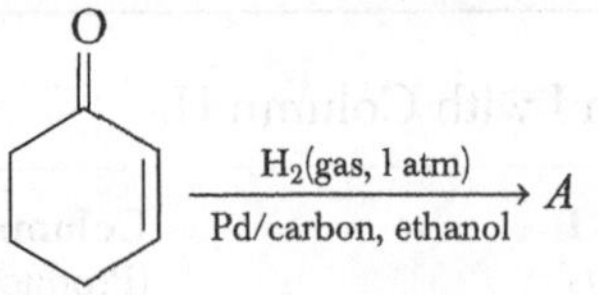

(a) 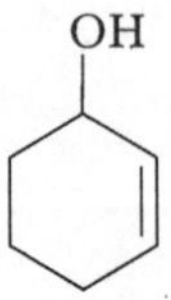 ☐ (b) 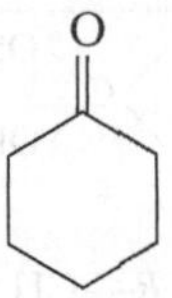 ☐ (c) 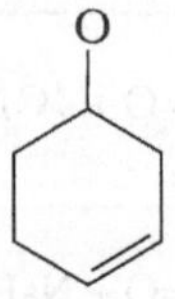 ☐ (d) 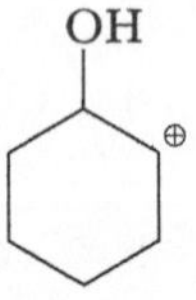 ☐

***55.** Write reactions for the following name reactions.

(i) Clemmensen reduction ____________ (ii) Wolff-Kishner reduction ____________

56. The reagent used to distinguish aldehydes from ketones is

(a) $[Cu(NO_3)_3]NH_3$ ☐ (b) $[Ag(NH_3)_2]NO_3$ ☐

(c) $Pb(NH_3)_2$ ☐ (d) $CuSO_4.NH_3$ ☐

57. On warming acetaldehyde with freshly prepared ____________ solution, a bright silver mirror is produced due to the formation of ____________.

58. Consider the following statements.

I. On heating propionaldehyde with mixture of aqueous copper sulphate and sodium potassium tartarate, reddish brown precipitate is obtained.

II. In Fehling's test, aldehyde is oxidised to carboxylate anion which results in red-brown precipitate.

Which of the above statement(s) is /are correct?

(a) Only I ☐ (b) Only II ☐ (c) Both I and II ☐ (d) Neither I nor II ☐

59. Name aldehydes which do not give positive Fehling test.

____

60. Give a test to distinguish between pentane-2-one and pentan-3-one.

____

61. Complete the following statement with suitable group.

Detection of __________ or __________ groups can be done by using iodoform reaction with sodium hypoiodite.

62. Consider the following compounds/species.

(i) CH_3CHO (ii) $CH_3CH(OH)CH_3$ (iii) $C_6H_5CH_2OH$
(iv) $C_2H_5COCH_3$ (v) CH_3COOH (vi) CH_3OH
(vii) CH_3COOCH_3

The number of compounds/ species which can undergo haloform reaction with I_2/NaOH.

(a) 2 ☐ (b) 3 ☐ (c) 5 ☐ (d) 7 ☐

***63.** Identify *A* and *B* in the following reactions.

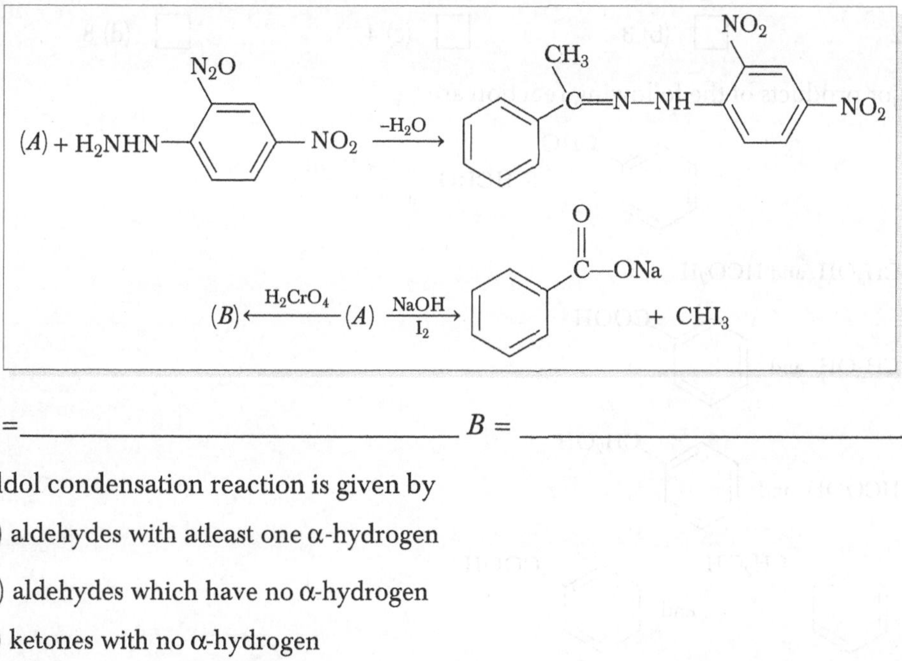

A = ____________________ *B* = ____________________

***64.** Aldol condensation reaction is given by

(a) aldehydes with atleast one α-hydrogen ☐

(b) aldehydes which have no α-hydrogen ☐

(c) ketones with no α-hydrogen ☐

(d) alcohols with α-hydrogen ☐

65. Identify the missing compounds in the given reaction.

$$CH_3CHO + CH_3CH_2CHO \xrightarrow[B]{A} C + CH_3{-}CH{=}\underset{}{\overset{CH_3}{\overset{|}{C}}}{-}CHO + D + E$$

A = ____________ *B* = ____________ *C* = ____________

D = ____________ *E* = ____________

66. Aldehydes which do not have ________ undergo Cannizzaro reaction, on heating with ________.

67. Consider the following compounds/ species.

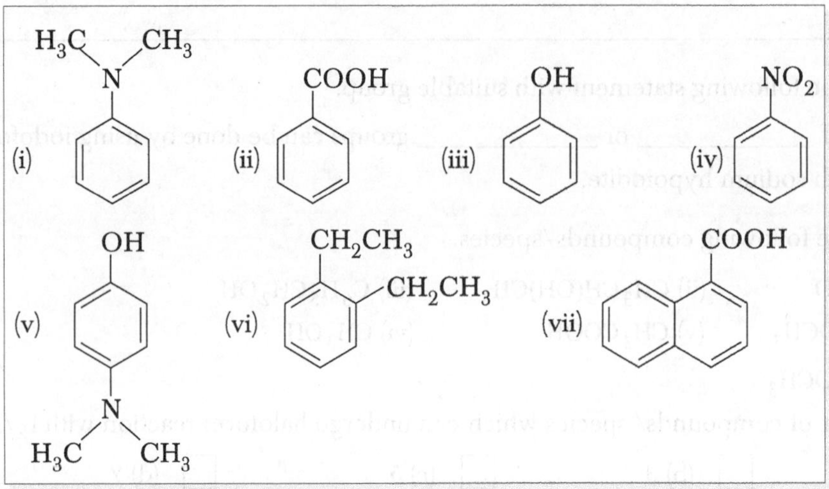

The number of compounds soluble in aqueous NaOH is

(a) 2 ☐ (b) 3 ☐ (c) 4 ☐ (d) 8 ☐

68. Major products of the following reaction are

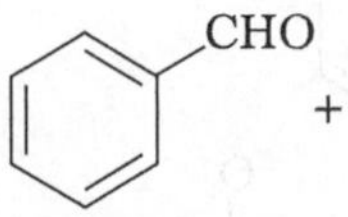

$+ \ HCHO \xrightarrow[\text{(ii) } H_3O^+]{\text{(i) 50\% NaOH}}$

(a) CH_3OH and HCO_2H ☐

(b) CH_3OH and 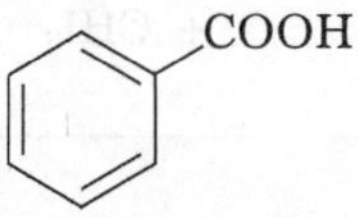 ☐

(c) HCOOH and 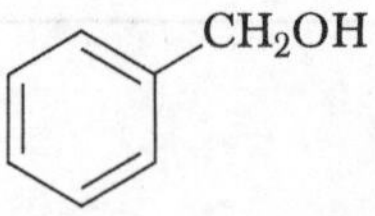 ☐

(d) 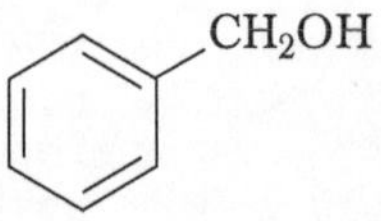 and 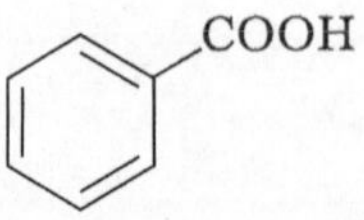 ☐

69. Predict the product(s) of the following reactions.

(i) 2 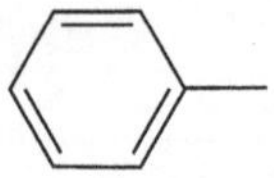 CHO + Conc. NaOH $\xrightarrow{\Delta}$ ________

(ii) 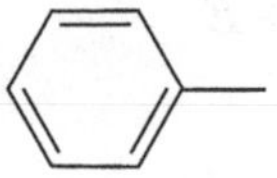 CHO $\xrightarrow[273\text{-}283K]{HNO_3/H_2SO_4}$ ________

70. Cannizzaro reaction is not given by ________. **[NCERT Exemplar]**

(a) 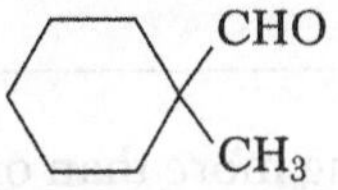 ☐ (b) 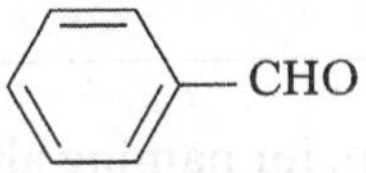 ☐

(c) HCHO ☐ (d) CH_3CHO ☐

***71.** Arrange the following compounds in decreasing order of their reactivity towards nucleophilic addition reaction.

Ethanal, Propanone, Propanal, Butanone

____

72. Complete the following table.

Reactants	Reagent	Product
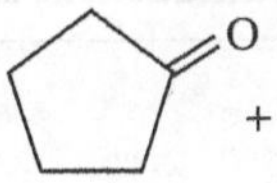 + (i)________	(ii)________	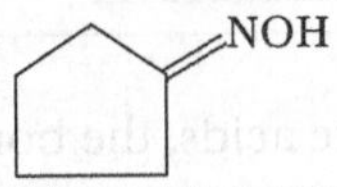
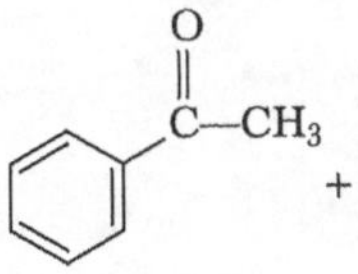 + $CH_3CH_2NH_2$	H^+	(iii)________ + (iv)________

73. Name the carbonyl compound which is used for preserving biological specimens.

____

TOPIC 5

Nomenclature and Structure of Carboxyl Group

NCERT Pg 244-245

74. The carboxyl group consists of

(a) carbonyl group and halide ☐

(b) carbonyl group and alkyl group ☐

(c) carbonyl group and aryl group ☐

(d) carbonyl group and hydroxyl group ☐

75. The common names of carboxylic acids end with suffix ________ and are derived from ________ names of their natural sources.

76. Pick the odd one out in context of their nomenclature.

Acetic acid, Butyric acid, Propanoic acid, Formic acid

____

77. Name the acid which was first obtained from red ants.

____

78. In IUPAC system, for naming aliphatic carboxylic acids containing more than one carboxyl group, the carboxylic carbon is numbered one.

True ☐ False ☐

79. Complete the blanks in the following table.

Structure	Common name	IUPAC name
(i) $(CH_3)_2CHOOH$	________	________
(ii) ________	Oxalic acid	________
(iii) ________	________	Propane-1,2,3- tricarboxylic acid

80. In carboxylic acids, the bonds of the carboxyl carbon are in

(a) one plane and separated by 109°28′ ☐

(b) one plane and separated by 120° ☐

(c) different plane and separated by 109°28′ ☐

(d) different plane and separated by 120° ☐

81. Out of the given choices, which one is more electrophilic?

Carboxylic carbon or Carbonyl carbon

____

TOPIC 6

Methods of Preparation of Carboxylic Acids and Physical Properties

NCERT Pg 245-249

82. Match the following Column I with Column II.

Column I (Reactions)	Column II (Respective reagents)
A. $RCH_2OH \longrightarrow RCOOH$	1. $KMnO_4$ - KOH, Δ, H_3O^+
B. $CH_3(CH_2)_3 CH_2OH \longrightarrow CH_3(CH_2)_8 COOH$	2. Acidic $KMnO_4$, H_3O^+
C. 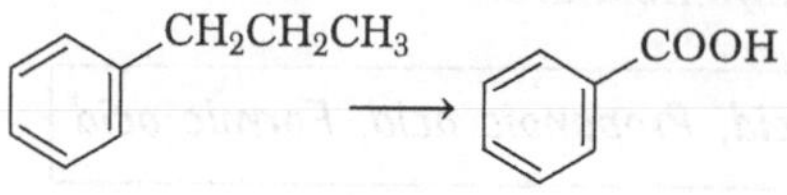	3. CrO_3 - H_2SO_4 (Jones reagent)

A. ________ B. ________ C. ________

83. Write reactions for the conversion of

(i) alkyl cyanide to carboxylic acid ____________________

(ii) benzamide to benzoic acid ____________________

84. Predict the product(s) of the following reactions.

(i) $R—Mg—X + CO_2 \xrightarrow[H_3O^+]{\text{Dry ether}} ?$ ____________________

(ii) $RCOCl \xrightarrow[(b)\ H_3O^+]{(a)\ \bar{O}H/H_2O} ?$ ____________________

(iii) $(C_6H_5CO)_2O \xrightarrow{H_2O} ?$ ____________________

85. Benzoic ethanoic anhydride on hydrolysis gives mixture of two products.

True ☐ False ☐

86. Determine *X*, *Y* and *Z* in following conversions:

(i) 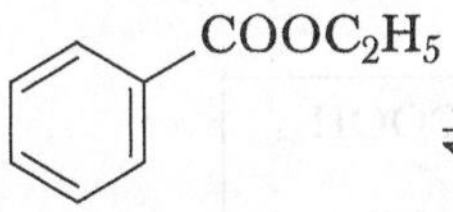 $\overset{H_3O^+}{\rightleftharpoons} X + Y$

(ii) $C_6H_5CH_2OH \xrightarrow[(b)KCN]{(a)HBr} Z \xrightarrow{\Delta/H_3O^+} C_6H_5CH_2COOH$

X = ____________ Y = ____________ Z = ____________

87. Consider the following statements.

I. Butan-1-ol can be converted into butanoic acid by using Jones reagent.

II. On heating cyclopentane with $KMnO_4$ - H_2SO_4, it forms adipic acid.

III. Tollen's reagent oxidises butanal to butanoic acid.

Mark (✓) and (×) under correct and incorrect with respect to the given statements.

	Correct	**Incorrect**
I.	______	______
II.	______	______
III.	______	______

***88.** Arrange the following in the increasing order of their property indicated.

(i) Ethanol, ethanoic acid, benzoic acid (Boiling point) ____________________

(ii) Benzoic acid, phenol, picric acid, salicylic acid (pK_a value) ____________________

TOPIC 7

Chemical Reactions & Uses of Carboxylic Acids

NCERT Pg 249-254

89. Unlike phenols, carboxylic acids react with __________ and __________ to evolve CO_2.

90. Consider the following statements.

I. Trifluoroacetic acid is the strongest carboxylic acid.

II. Larger the pK_a value, stronger is the acid.

Which of the above statement(s) is/are correct?

(a) Only I ☐ (b) Only II ☐

(c) Both I and II ☐ (d) Neither I nor II ☐

***91.** The correct order of strengths of the carboxylic acids.

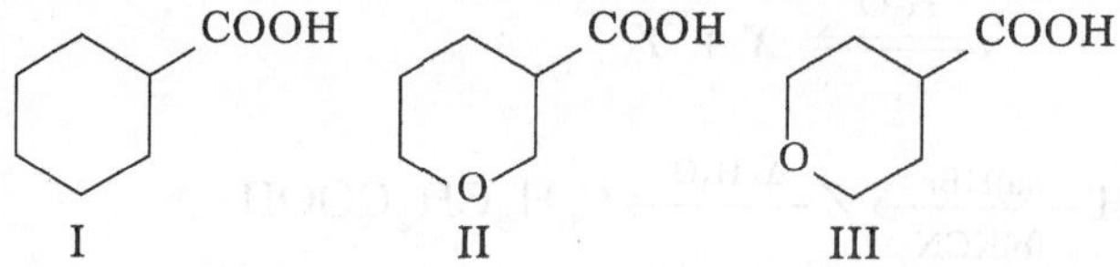

is

(a) I > II > III ☐ (b) II > III > I ☐

(c) III > II > I ☐ (d) II > I > III ☐

92. Arrange the following in order of decreasing acidity.

(i) Ethanol, Phenol, Mineral acid, Carboxylic acid __________

(ii) NC—CH_2COOH, HCOOH, $CHCl_2$COOH, C_6H_5COOH, $BrCH_2$COOH, C_2H_5COOH.

____

93. Direct attachment of phenyl or vinyl to carboxylic acid __________ the acidity of corresponding acid.

(a) increases ☐ (b) decreases ☐

(c) does not affect ☐ (d) can increase or decrease both ☐

94. The correct order of increasing acidic strength is

(a) phenol < ethanol < chloroacetic acid < acetic acid ☐

(b) ethanol < phenol < chloroacetic acid < acetic acid ☐

(c) ethanol < phenol < acetic acid < chloroacetic acid ☐

(d) chloroacetic acid < acetic acid < phenol < ethanol ☐

95. Predict the product(s) of the following reactions.

(i) $2CH_3—\overset{\overset{\Large O}{||}}{C}—OH \xrightarrow[P_2O_5,\ \Delta]{H^+,\ \Delta}$ ________________

(ii) $RCOOH + PCl_5 \longrightarrow$ ________________

(iii) $CH_3COOH + NH_3 \xrightarrow{\Delta}$ ________________

96. Determine *X* and *Y* in the following reaction,

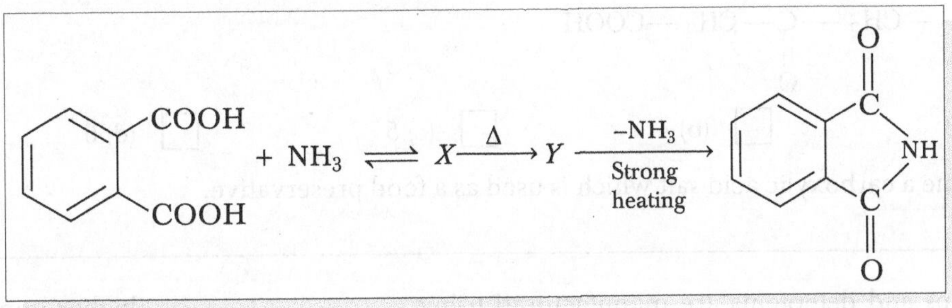

$X =$ ________________ $Y =$ ________________

97. Write the equation involved in Hell-Volhard Zelinsky reaction.

____

***98.** Match the following Column I with Column II.

Column I (Conversions)		**Column II** (Reagents)
A.	$RCOOH \longrightarrow RCH_2OH$	1. Br_2 / $FeBr_3$
B.	$RCOONa \longrightarrow R—H$	2. B_2H_6 / H_3O^+
C.	$R—CH_2—COOH \longrightarrow R—\underset{\underset{\Large X}{|}}{CH}—COOH$	3. NaOH and CaO, Δ
D.	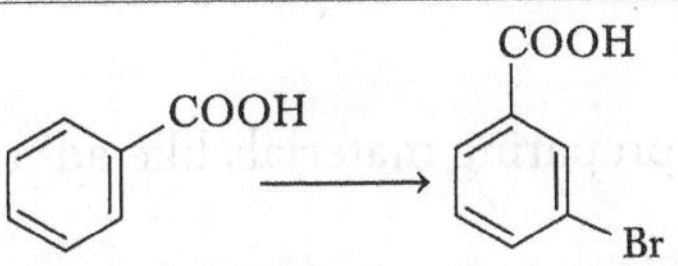	4. X_2/Red P, H_2O

A. ________________ B. ________________

C. ________________ D. ________________

99. CH_2FCOOH is stronger acid than $CH_2ClCOOH$.

True ☐ False ☐

100. Amongst the following, the total number of species that can rather easily be decarboxylated is

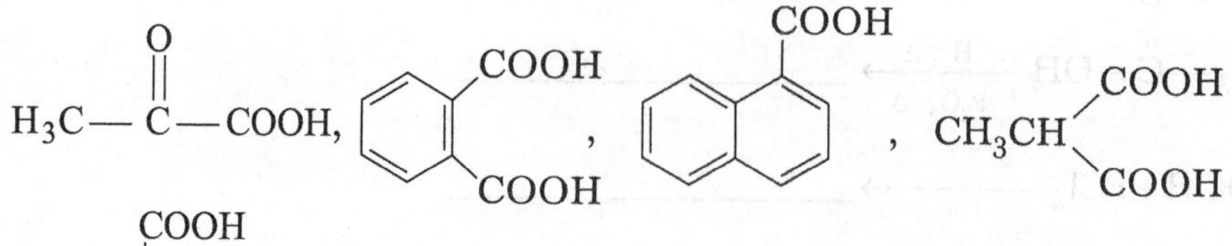

$H_3C-CH(COOH)-CH_2-COOH$, $CN-CH_2-CH(OH)-COOH$,

$NO_2-CH_2-C(=O)-CH_2-COOH$

(a) 3 ☐ (b) 4 ☐ (c) 5 ☐ (d) 6 ☐

101. Name a carboxylic acid salt which is used as a food preservative.

____

102. Soaps and detergents are manufactured using ______________ (higher mineral acids/ higher fatty acids.)

Assertion-Reason Questions

Given below are two statements, one is labelled as Assertion (A) and other is labelled as Reason (R). Select the appropriate answer from options given below.

(a) Both A and R are true and R is the correct explanation of A.
(b) Both A and R are true but R is not the correct explanation of A.
(c) A is true but R is false.
(d) A is false but R is true.

1. Assertion (A) Aldehydes and ketones are used in food products and pharmaceuticals to add flavours.

Reason (R) They are manufactured for preparing materials like adhesive, paints, resins, plastics etc.

(a) ☐ (b) ☐ (c) ☐ (d) ☐

2. Assertion (A) The carbon-oxygen double bond of carbonyl compounds is polar in nature.

Reason (R) The polarity of carbon-oxygen double bond of carbonyl compounds is due to higher electronegativity of carbon relative to oxygen.

(a) ☐ (b) ☐ (c) ☐ (d) ☐

3. Assertion (A) Ozonolysis of alkenes followed by reaction with Zn dust and water can give aldehydes and ketones or mixture of both.

Reason (R) Substitution pattern of the alkene is responsible for type of product formed.

(a) ☐ (b) ☐ (c) ☐ (d) ☐

4. **Assertion** (A) The boiling points of given compounds follow the order :
$CH_3CH_2CH_2CHO \approx CH_3CH_2CH_2CH_2CH_3 < CH_3CH_2CH_2CH_2OH \approx C_2H_5OC_2H_5$
Reason (R) Boiling point depends upon the nature of intermolecular forces.
(a) ☐ (b) ☐ (c) ☐ (d) ☐

5. **Assertion** (A) Ketones are more reactive than aldehydes in nucleophilic addition reactions.
Reason (R) Ketones are more sterically and electronically hindered than aldehydes.
(a) ☐ (b) ☐ (c) ☐ (d) ☐

6. **Assertion** (A) Acetaldehyde undergoes aldol condensation whereas, formaldehyde does not.
Reason (R) Aldol condensation requires presence of α-hydrogen in the carbonyl compound.
(a) ☐ (b) ☐ (c) ☐ (d) ☐

7. **Assertion** (A) α-hydrogen atom of carbonyl compounds is acidic in nature.
Reason (R) α-hydrogen is directly attached to carbon next to carbonyl carbon.
(a) ☐ (b) ☐ (c) ☐ (d) ☐

8. **Assertion** (A) Cannizzaro reaction is an example of disproportionation reaction.
Reason (R) One molecule undergoes self oxidation while another undergoes self reduction.
(a) ☐ (b) ☐ (c) ☐ (d) ☐

9. **Assertion** (A) 2, 2-dimethyl propanol undergoes Cannizzaro reaction with conc. NaOH.
Reason (R) Cannizzaro reaction is a disproportionation reaction.
(a) ☐ (b) ☐ (c) ☐ (d) ☐

10. **Assertion** (A) Higher carboxylic acids are insoluble in water.
Reason (R) As the chain length of hydrocarbon increases, hydrophilic interactions increases.
(a) ☐ (b) ☐ (c) ☐ (d) ☐

Case-Based Questions

1. A tertiary alcohol H upon acid catalysed dehydration gives a product *I*. Ozonolysis of *I* leads to compounds *J* and *K*. Compound *J* upon reaction with KOH gives benzyl alcohol and a compound *L* whereas *K* on reaction with KOH gives only *M*.

M = 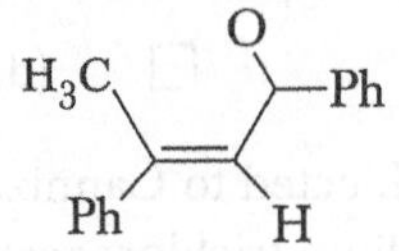

(i) Compound H is formed by the reaction of

(a) 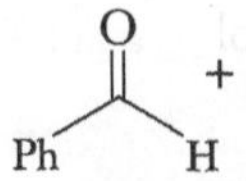 + PhMgBr ☐

(b) 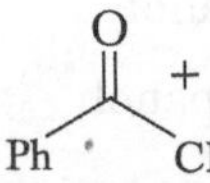 + $PhCH_2MgBr$ ☐

(c) 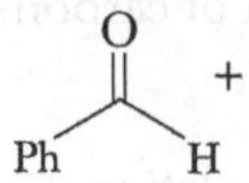 + $PhCH_2MgBr$ ☐

(d) 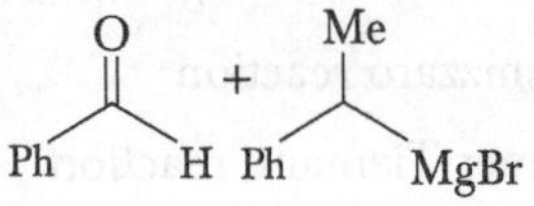 ☐

(ii) The structures of compounds *J*, *K*, *L* respectively, are

(a) $PhCOCH_3$, $PhCH_2COCH_3$ and $PhCH_2COO^-K^+$ ☐

(b) $PhCHO$, $PhCH_2CHO$ and $PhCOO^-K^+$ ☐

(c) $PhCOCH_3$, $PhCH_2CHO$ and $CH_3COO^-K^+$ ☐

(d) $PhCHO$, $PhCOCH_3$ and $PhCOO^-K^+$ ☐

(iii) The structure of compound *I* is

(a) 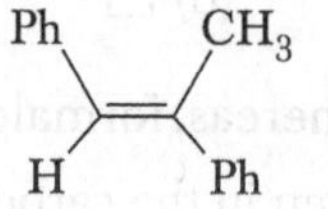 ☐ (b) 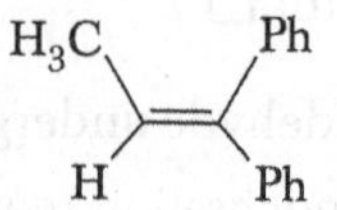 ☐

(c) 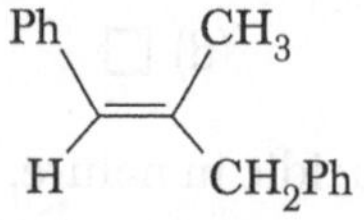 ☐ (d) 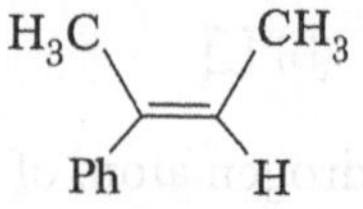 ☐

(iv) When (*J*) is treated with acetic anhydride in the presence of corresponding salt of an acid, the product obtained is

(a) cinnamic acid ☐ (b) crotonic acid ☐

(c) maleic acid ☐ (d) benzylic acid ☐

2. When an aldehyde with no α-hydrogen reacts with concentrated NaOH, half the aldehyde is converted to carboxylic acid salt and other half is converted to an alcohol. In other words, half of the reactant is oxidised and other half is reduced. The reaction is known as Cannizzaro reaction.

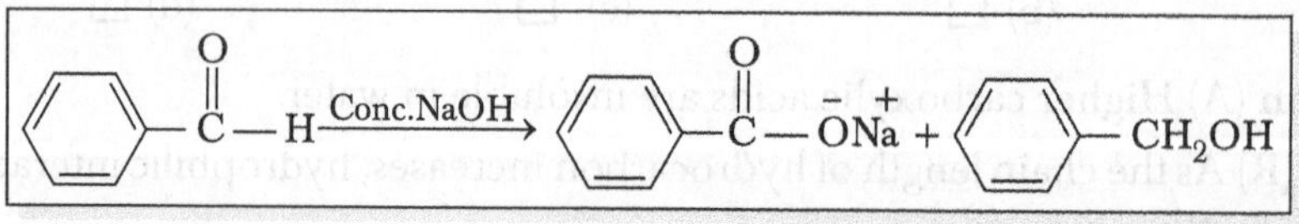

(i) A mixture of benzaldehyde and formaldehyde on heating with aqueous NaOH solution gives

(a) benzyl alcohol and sodium formate ☐ (b) sodium benzoate and methanol ☐

(c) sodium benzoate and sodium formate ☐ (d) benzyl alcohol and methanol ☐

(ii) Which of the following compounds will undergo Cannizzaro reaction?

(a) CH_3CHO ☐ (b) CH_3COCH_3 ☐

(c) C_6H_5CHO ☐ (d) $C_6H_5CH_2CHO$ ☐

(iii) Trichloroacetaldehyde is subjected to Cannizzaro's reaction by using NaOH. The mixture of the products contains sodium trichloroacetate ion and another compound. The other compound is

(a) 2, 2, 2-trichloroethanol ☐ (b) trichloromethanol ☐

(c) 2, 2, 2-trichloropropanol ☐ (d) chloroform ☐

(iv) Which of the following reaction will not result in the formation of carbon-carbon bond?

(a) Cannizzaro reaction ☐ (b) Wurtz reaction ☐

(c) Reimer-Tiemann reaction ☐ (d) Friedel Craft's acylation ☐

COMPETITION EDGE UP

1. *Identify major product "X" formed in the following reaction:*

[NCERT (New) Pg. 233, JEE Main 2024]

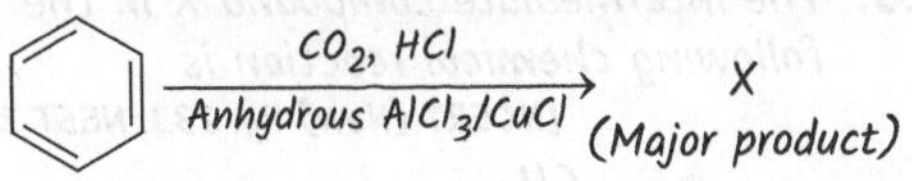

(a) 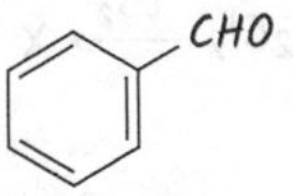 ☐

(b) 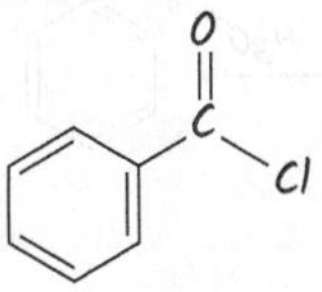 ☐

(c) 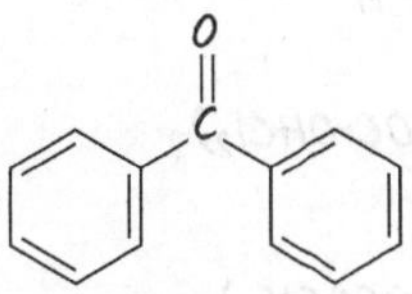 ☐

(d) 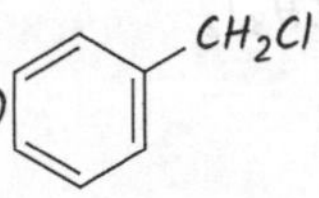 ☐

2. *Which among the following aldehydes is most reactive towards nucleophilic addition reactions?*

[NCERT (New) Pg. 236, JEE Main 2024]

(a) $C_2H_5-\overset{O}{\overset{||}{C}}-H$ ☐

(b) $H-\overset{O}{\overset{||}{C}}-H$ ☐

(c) $C_3H_7-\overset{O}{\overset{||}{C}}-H$ ☐

(d) $CH_3-\overset{O}{\overset{||}{C}}-H$ ☐

3. *Identify the name reaction.*

[NCERT (New) Pg. 233, JEE Main 2024]

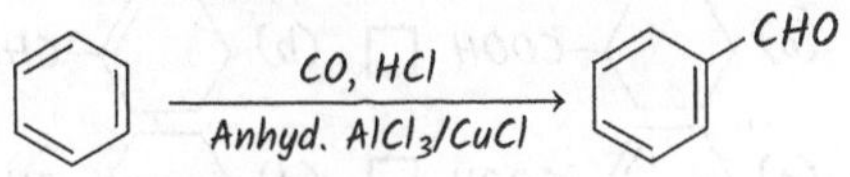

(a) Etard reaction ☐

(b) Gattermann-Koch reaction ☐

(c) Stephen reaction ☐

(d) Rosenmund reduction ☐

4. *Structure of 4-methylpent-2-enal is*

[NCERT (New) Pg. 230, JEE Main 2024]

(a) $CH_3-CH_2-\underset{CH_3}{\underset{|}{C}}=CH-\overset{O}{\overset{||}{C}}-H$ ☐

(b) $H_2C=\underset{H}{\underset{|}{C}}-\overset{CH_3}{\overset{|}{\underset{H}{\underset{|}{C}}}}-CH_2-\overset{O}{\overset{||}{C}}-H$ ☐

(c) $CH_3-\underset{CH_3}{\underset{|}{CH}}-CH=CH-\overset{O}{\overset{||}{C}}-H$ ☐

(d) $CH_3-CH_2-CH=\underset{CH_3}{\underset{|}{C}}-\overset{O}{\overset{||}{C}}-H$ ☐

5. *Given below are two statements.*

[NCERT (New) Pg. 241, JEE Main 2024]

Statement I *Acidity of α-hydrogens of aldehydes and ketones is responsible for aldol reaction.*

Statement II *Reaction between benzaldehyde and ethanal will not give cross-aldol product.*

In the light of the above statements, choose the most appropriate answer from the options given below:

(a) Both Statement I and Statement II are incorrect ☐

(b) Both Statement I and Statement II are correct ☐

(c) Statement I is incorrect but Statement II is correct ☐

(d) Statement I is correct but Statement II is incorrect ☐

6. *Identify the product in the following reaction.*

[NCERT (New) Pg. 246, JEE Main 2024]

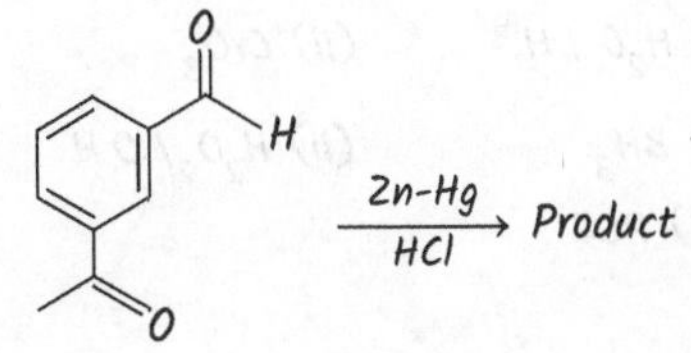

(a) 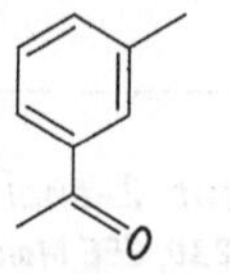 ☐ (b) 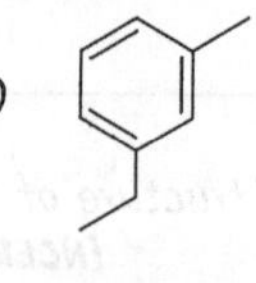 ☐

(c) 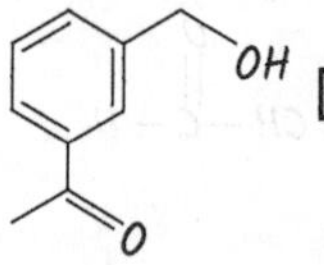 ☐ (d) 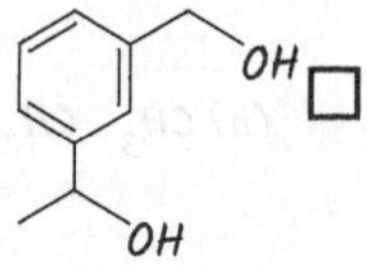 ☐

7. *The correct sequence of acidic strength of the following aliphatic acids in their decreasing order is*
[NCERT (New) Pg. 250, JEE Main 2024]

$CH_3CH_2COOH, CH_3COOH, CH_3CH_2CH_2COOH, HCOOH$

(a) $CH_3COOH > CH_3CH_2COOH > CH_3CH_2CH_2COOH > HCOOH$

(b) $HCOOH > CH_3COOH > CH_3CH_2COOH > CH_3CH_2CH_2COOH$

(c) $HCOOH > CH_3CH_2CH_2COOH > CH_3CH_2COOH > CH_3COOH$

(d) $CH_3CH_2CH_2COOH > CH_3CH_2COOH > CH_3COOH > HCOOH$

8. *Identify the product (P) in the following reaction :*
[NCERT (New) Pg. 253, JEE Main 2024]

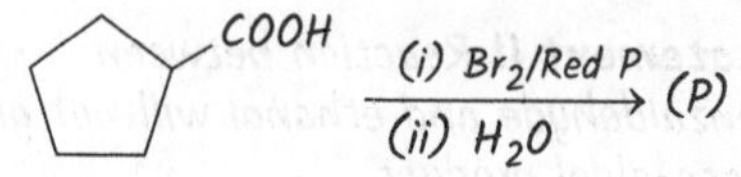

(a) 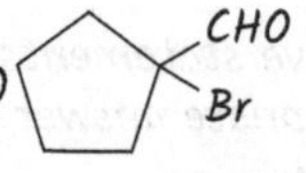 ☐ (b) 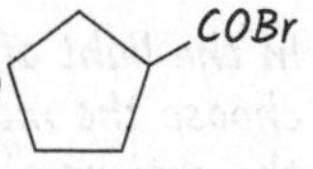 ☐

(c) 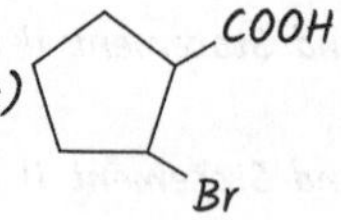 ☐ (d) 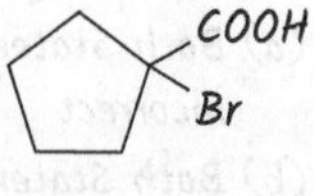 ☐

9. *Identify the correct reagents that would bring about the following transformation.*
[NCERT (New) Pg. 234, NEET 2024]

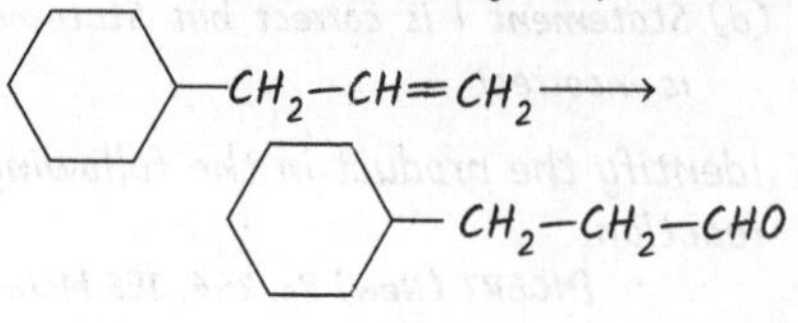

(a) (i) $H_2O / H^{\oplus}$ (ii) CrO_3 ☐

(b) (i) BH_3 (ii) $H_2O_2/\overset{\ominus}{O}H$ (iii) PCC ☐

(c) (i) BH_3 (ii) $H_2O_2/\overset{\ominus}{O}H$ (iii) Alk. $KMnO_4$ (iv) $H_3O^{\oplus}$ ☐

(d) (i) $H_2O / H^{\oplus}$ (ii) PCC ☐

10. *The intermediate compound X in the following chemical reaction is*
[NCERT (New) Pg. 233, NEET 2021]

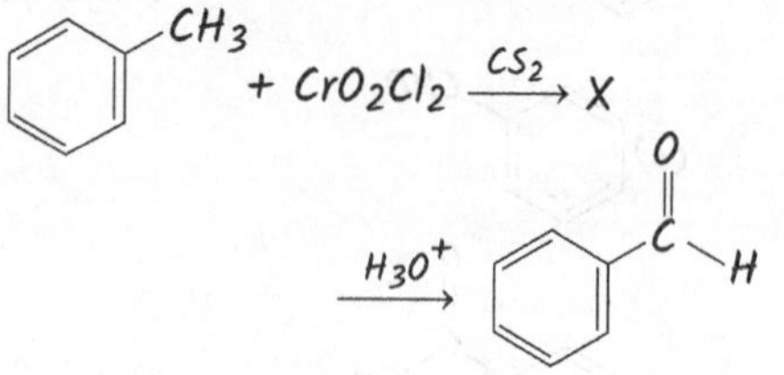

(a) 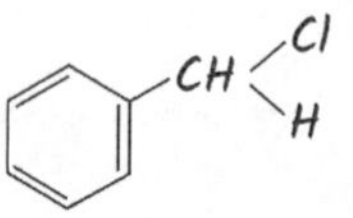 ☐

(b) 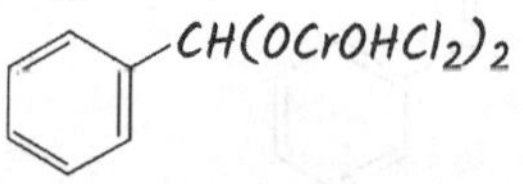 ☐

(c) 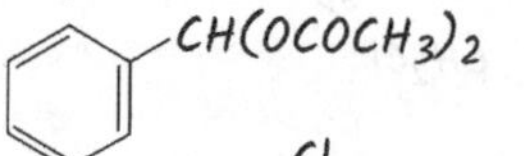 ☐

(d) 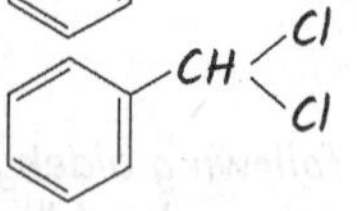 ☐

11. *Reaction between benzaldehyde and acetophenone in the presence of dilute NaOH is known as*
[NCERT (New) Pg. 242, NEET (Sept.) 2020]

(a) Cannizzaro's reaction ☐

(b) Cross Cannizzaro's reaction ☐

(c) Cross aldol condensation ☐

(d) Aldol condensation ☐

12. *Complete the following reaction.*

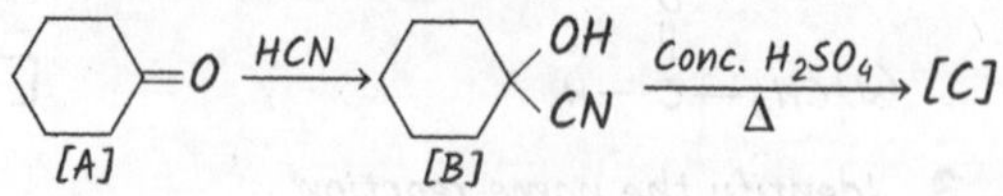

is .... **[NCERT (New) Pg. 237, NEET 2023]**

(a) 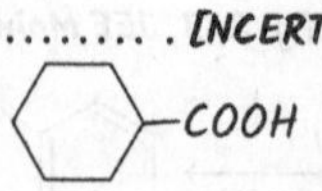 ☐ (b) 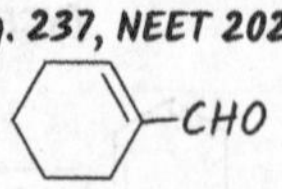 ☐

(c) 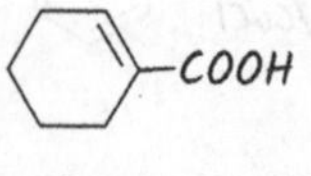 ☐ (d) 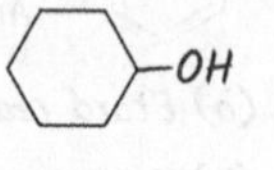 ☐

13. *Identify product (A) in the following reaction.* **[NCERT (New) Pg. 239, NEET 2023]**

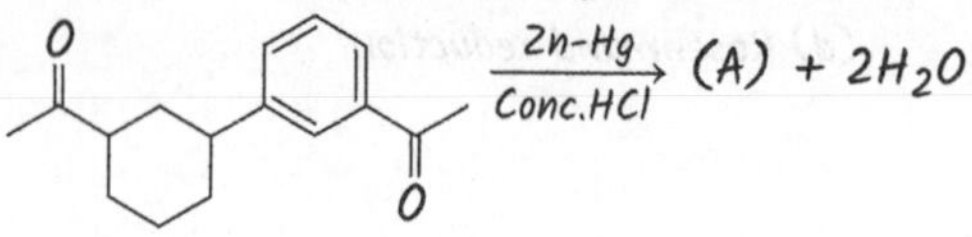

(a) 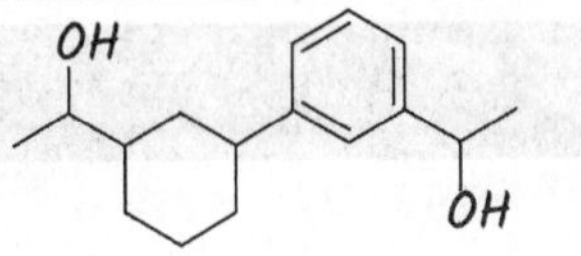

(b) 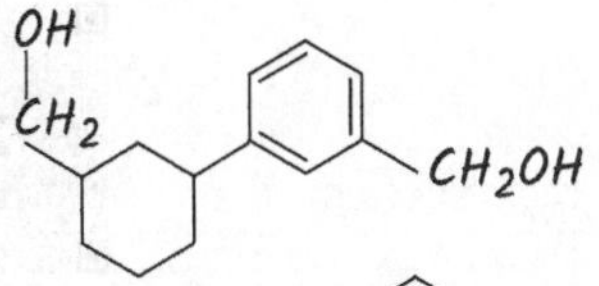

(c) 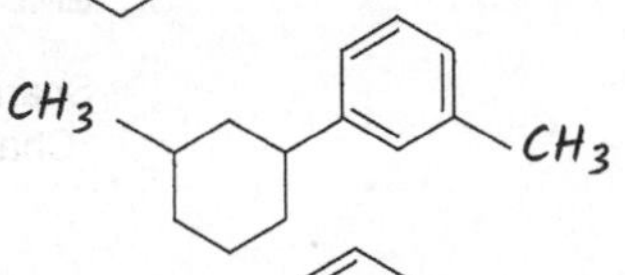

(d) 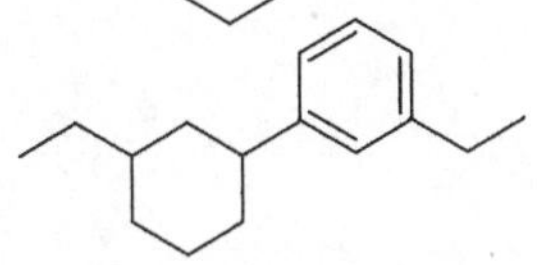

(c) 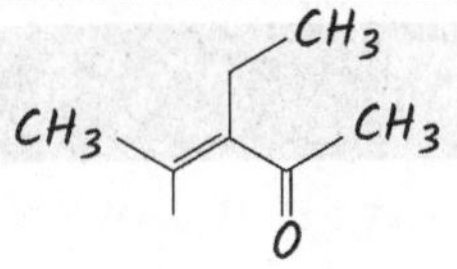

(d) 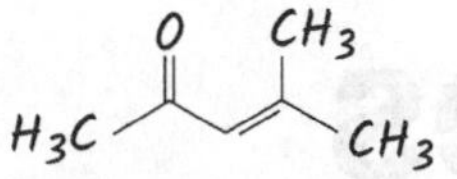

14. *Which one of the following is not formed when acetone reacts with 2-pentanone in the presence of dilute NaOH followed by heating?* **[NCERT (New) Pg. 241, NEET 2022]**

(a) 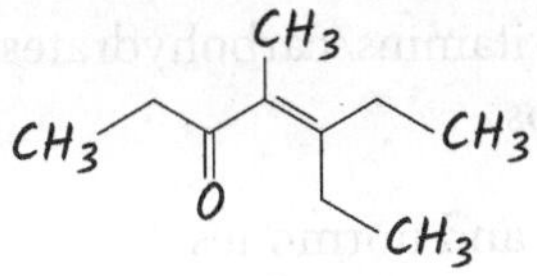

(b) 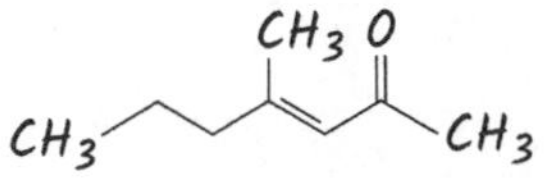

15. *Match List-I with List-II.*

List-I (Products formed)	List-II (Reaction of carbonyl compound with)
(A) Cyanohydrin	(i) NH_2OH
(B) Acetal	(ii) RNH_2
(C) Schiff's base	(iii) Alcohol
(D) Oxime	(iv) HCN

Choose the correct answer from the options given below **[NCERT (New) Pg. 236, NEET 2022]**

(a) (A) - (ii), (B) - (iii), (C) - (iv), (D) - (i)

(b) (A) - (i), (B) - (iii), (C) - (ii), (D) - (iv)

(c) (A) - (iv), (B) - (iii), (C) - (ii), (D) - (i)

(d) (A) - (iii), (B) - (iv), (C) - (ii), (D) - (i)

Chapter 09

Amines

Scan and take Chapter Test

TOPIC 1

Introduction

NCERT Pg 259

1. Amines are derived from ammonia molecule by replacing one or more hydrogen atoms with

(a) aryl group(s) only ☐ (b) alkyl group(s) only ☐

(c) aryl/alkyl group(s) ☐ (d) hydroxyl group ☐

2. In nature, amines are found in _______ and _______ (proteins/vitamins/carbohydrates/fats). Choose most appropriate 2 words and place them in fill ups.

3. Synthetic example of amine containing substances are alkaloids and hormones.

True ☐ False ☐

4. Consider the following statements.

I. Adrenaline and ephedrine are biologically active compounds containing amino group.

II. Both adrenaline and ephedrine are used to decrease/reduce the blood pressure.

Which of the above statement(s) is/are correct?

(a) Only I ☐ (b) Only II ☐

(c) Both I and II ☐ (d) Neither I nor II ☐

5. Match the following Column I with Column II.

Column I (Compound)	Column II (Uses)
A. Novocain	1. Antihistaminic drug
B. Benadryl	2. Surfactants
C. Quaternary ammonium salt	3 Preparation of dyes
D. Diazonium salt	4. Anaesthetic (dentistry)

A. ______________________ B. ______________________

C. ______________________ D. ______________________

Concepts of all questions bearing * are important for JEE/NEET/CUET.

TOPIC 2

Classification & Structure of Amines

NCERT Pg 259-260

6. Pick the odd one out from the following on the basis of type of amines.

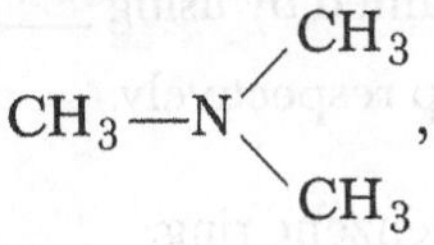, $CH_3—NH_2$, $C_6H_5—NH_2$, $CH_3—NH—CH_3$

____

7. The geometry of amines is ________ (pyramidal/square planar) and the nitrogen orbitals are ________ (sp^2/sp^3) hybridised.

8. Pick the odd one out on the basis of type of amine.

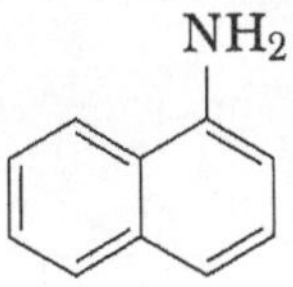, $(C_2H_5)_2NH$, 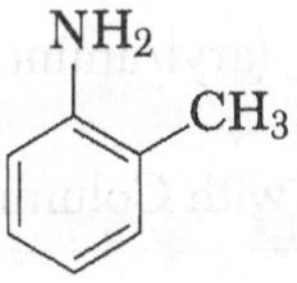, $(C_2H_5)_2CHNH_2$

____

9. Complete the following analogy.

One hydrogen of ammonia replaced by one tertiary alkyl group : A : : Two hydrogens of ammonia replaced by one alkyl and one aryl group : B

(a) A : Primary amine, B : Tertiary amine ☐

(b) A : Primary amine, B : Secondary amine ☐

(c) A : Secondary amine, B : Primary amine ☐

(d) A : Secondary amine, B : Tertiary amine ☐

10. Consider the following statements.

I. Secondary amines are derived by replacing two hydrogen atoms of primary amine.

II. The second alkyl/aryl group in secondary amines can be same or different with first one.

Which of the above statement(s) is/are correct?

(a) Only I ☐ (b) Only II ☐

(c) Both I and II ☐ (d) Neither I nor II ☐

11. Mixed amines contain

(a) two same alkyl groups ☐ (b) two same aryl groups ☐

(c) different alkyl or aryl groups ☐ (d) two nitrogen atoms ☐

TOPIC 3

Nomenclature

NCERT Pg 260-262

12. Name an aliphatic amine in common system containing one carbon atom.

____

13. In common system, secondary and tertiary amines are named by using ________ and ________ prefixes before the name of ________ group respectively.

14. In arylamines, —NH_2 group is directly attached to the benzene ring.

True ☐ False ☐

15. Give the common name of the most simplest aryl amine.

____

16. While naming aryl amines according to IUPAC system, suffix ____________ ('*e*'/'*a*') of arene is replaced by ____________ (aryl/amine).

17. Match the following Column I with Column II.

Column I (Structure)	Column II (Name)
A. 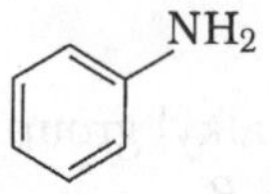	1. 4-bromoaniline
B. 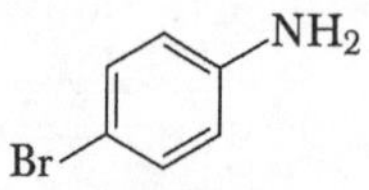	2. N, N-dimethyl aniline
C. 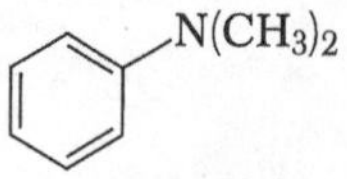	3. Benzenamine

A. ____________ B. ____________ C. ____________

18. Complete the following table.

Amine	Common Name	IUPAC Name
$CH_3CH_2CH_2NH_2$	(i) ____________	(ii) ____________
(iii) ____________	Isopropylamine	(iv) ____________
(v) ____________	(vi) ____________	N, N-diethyl-butan-1-amine
$NH_2—CH_2—CH=CH_2$	(vii) ____________	(viii) ____________

19. Classify the following amines as primary (1°), secondary (2°) and tertiary (3°) amines.

(i) $CH_3(CH_2)_3NH_2$ ____________

(ii) $(CH_3)_2CHCH_2NH_2$ ____________

(iii) $C_3H_7—N(CH_3)—H$ ____________

(iv) $CH_3—N(C_2H_5)—CH_3$ ____________

20. Write IUPAC name of the following amines.

(i) $C_2H_5—N(C_2H_5)—H$ ____________ (ii) $CH_3—CH(CH_3)—NH—CH_3$ ____________

TOPIC 4

Preparation of Amines

NCERT Pg 262-265

21. Alkyl or benzyl halide on reaction with ethanolic solution of ____________ (amine/ammonia) undergoes ____________ (electrophilic/nucleophilic) substitution reaction.

22. The process of cleavage of the C — *X* bond by ammonia molecule is called

(a) hydrolysis ☐ (b) ammonolysis ☐

(c) halogenation ☐ (d) Hofmann degradation ☐

____

23. During ammonolysis reaction, primary amine obtained in first step behaves as an electrophile and reacts further with alkyl halide to form secondary and tertiary amines.

True ☐ False ☐

***24.** Complete the following,

$$C_6H_5NO_2 \xrightarrow{Sn/HCl} A \xrightarrow{Br_2/H_2O} B \xrightarrow[273\text{-}278\ K]{NaNO_2/HCl} C \xrightarrow[\Delta]{HBF_4} D$$

A = ____________ B = ____________ C = ____________ D = ____________

25. Complete the missing elements in the following reaction.

$$RNH_2 \xrightarrow{RX} \text{(i)} \xrightarrow{\text{(ii)}} R_3N$$

(i) ____________ (ii) ____________

26. Write the product(s) of the following reaction.

$$R - \overset{+}{N}H_3X^- + NaOH \longrightarrow \_\_\_\_\_\_$$

27. The disadvantage of ammonolysis reaction is the formation of ________ of amines.

28. Arrange the alkyl halides in increasing order of their reactivity with amines.

RBr, RI, RCl

____

29. Predict the alkyl products of the following reactions.

(i) $C_2H_5Cl \xrightarrow[\text{(b) } 3C_2H_5Cl]{\text{(a) } NH_3}$ ______________

(ii) $C_6H_5CH_2Cl \xrightarrow[\text{(b) } 2CH_3Cl]{\text{(a) } NH_3}$ ______________

***30.** Identify the reagents required for the following conversions.

(i) $R - C{\equiv}N \xrightarrow{?} R - CH_2 - NH_2$ ______________

(ii) $R - \overset{\overset{\displaystyle O}{\|}}{C} - NH_2 \xrightarrow[\text{(b) ?}]{\text{(a) ?}} R - CH_2 - NH_2$ ______________

***31.** Determine *X*, *Y* and *Z* in the following reaction.

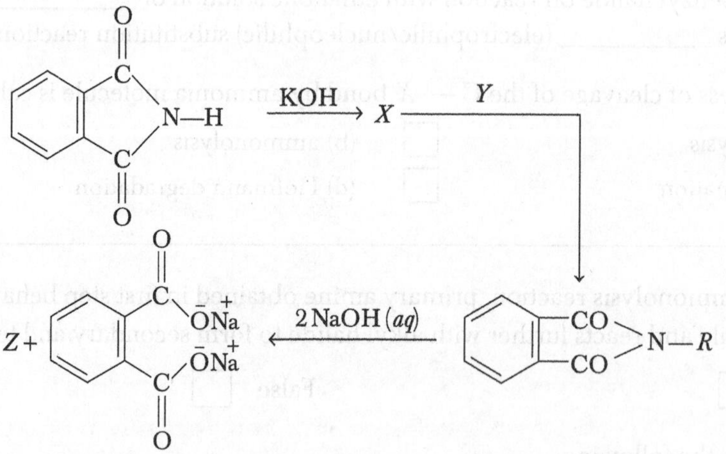

X = ______________ *Y* = ______________ *Z* = ______________

32. Which of the following can be prepared by Gabriel method from their corresponding halides or tosylates?

Allylamine, tert-butylamine, Diethylamine, Neopentylamine, o-nitroaniline, m-nitroaniline, Propylamine

(a) 5 ☐ (b) 4 ☐ (c) 2 ☐ (d) 3 ☐

33. Write the equation of Hofmann-bromamide degradation reaction.

____

34. Consider the following reactions.

(a) $R—C \equiv N \xrightarrow{LiAlH_4}$

(b) $R—\overset{O}{\overset{\|}{C}}—NH_2 \xrightarrow{LiAlH_4}$

(c) $R—\overset{O}{\overset{\|}{C}}—NH_2 \xrightarrow{Br_2 + OH^-}$

(d) $R—\overset{O}{\overset{\|}{C}}—CH_3 + H_3C—NO_2 \xrightarrow{NaOH}$

(e) 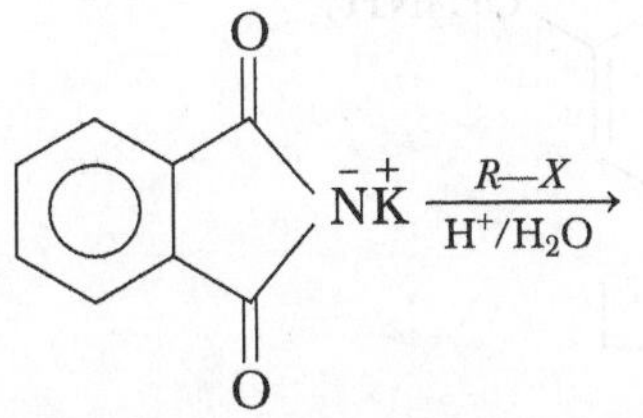

The number of reactions that will yield amines is

(a) 3 ☐ (b) 2 ☐ (c) 4 ☐ (d) 5 ☐

35. Convert the following.
Chloroethane to methanamine______________________________

36. The amine formed after Hofmann-bromamide degradation reaction contains

(a) one carbon less than parent amide ☐

(b) one carbon more than parent amide ☐

(c) same member of carbon as present in parent amide ☐

(d) two carbon less then parent amide ☐

37. Consider the following reactions.

$$\text{I. } CH_3—CH_2Cl \xrightarrow[NaCN]{Ethanolic} CH_3—CH_2—C \equiv N \xrightarrow{Oxidation} CH_3CH_2CH_2NH_2$$

$$\text{II. } C_6H_5—CH_2Cl \xrightarrow[NaCN]{Ethanolic} C_6H_5CH_2—C \equiv N \xrightarrow{H_2/Ni} C_6H_5—CH_2—CH_2—NH_2$$

Which of the above reaction(s) is/are correct?

(a) Only I ☐ (b) Only II ☐

(c) Both I and II ☐ (d) Neither I nor II ☐

38. Butanamide on treatment with bromine in ethanolic solution of sodium hydroxide gives amine '*A*'. Identify '*A*'.

A = ______________________________

***39.** How many of the following amines will give carbylamine test?

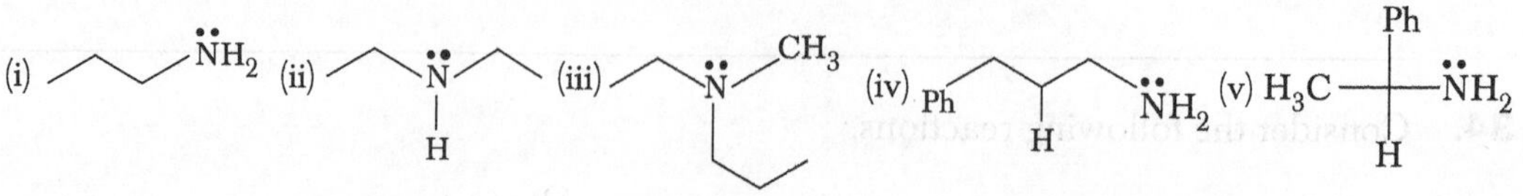

(a) 3 ☐ (b) 4 ☐ (c) 5 ☐ (d) 2 ☐

***40.** Is the following reaction correct?

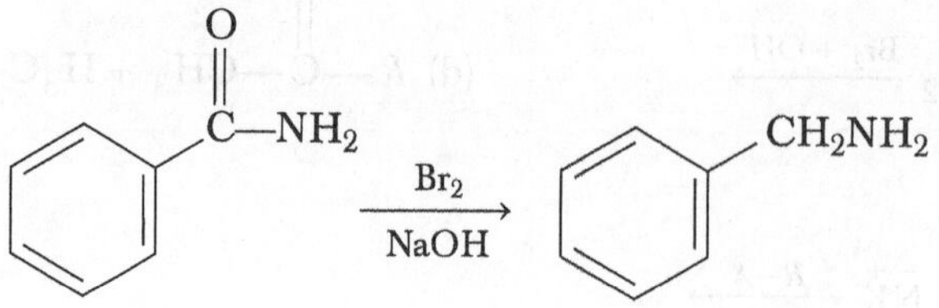

Yes ☐ No ☐

41. Match the following Column I with Column II.

Column I (Reactions)	Column II (Reagents)
A. 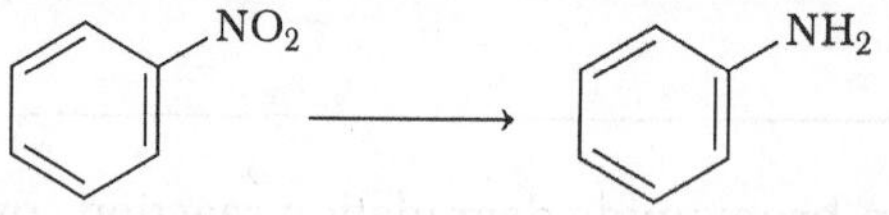	1. $2CH_3I, \Delta$
B. 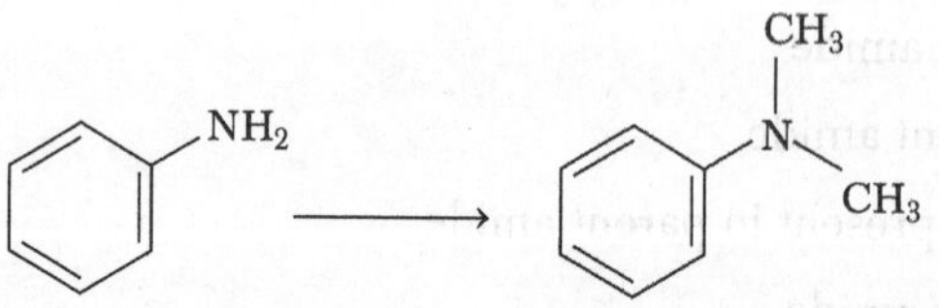	2. $LiAlH_4, H_3O^+$
C. $NC—(CH_2)_4—CN \longrightarrow H_2N—(CH_2)_6—NH_2$	3. Fe/HCl

A. ________ B. ________ C. ________

TOPIC 5

Physical Properties

NCERT Pg 265-266

42. Lower aliphatic amines have ____________ (fishy/fruity) odour.

43. Choose the incorrect pair of amine and its respective physical state.

Amines		Physical state
(a) Lower aliphatic amines	–	Gas
(b) Primary amine with 4 carbon atoms	–	Gas
(c) Higher amines	–	Solid
(d) All pairs are correct.		

44. Aniline and aryl amines are colourless and are stable towards atmospheric oxidation.

True ☐ False ☐

45. Lower aliphatic amines are

(a) soluble in water ☐ (b) insoluble in water ☐

(c) partially soluble in water ☐ (d) sparingly soluble in water ☐

46. Arrange the following compounds in an increasing order of their solubility in water.

$C_6H_5NH_2$, $(C_2H_5)_2NH$, $C_2H_5NH_2$

____

47. Which of the given relation is applicable for solubility with respect to molar mass of amines?

(a) Solubility $\propto$ molar mass of amines ☐

(b) Solubility $\propto$ 1/molar mass of amines ☐

(c) Solubility $\propto$ no. of carbon atoms ☐

(d) None of the above ☐

48. Higher amines are ____________ (soluble/insoluble) in water.

49. Consider the following statements.

I. Alcohols are less polar than amines.

II. Amines form weaker intermolecular hydrogen bonds than alcohols.

Which of the above statement(s) is/are correct?

(a) Only I ☐ (b) Only II ☐

(c) Both I and II ☐ (d) Neither I nor II ☐

50. Which one of the following amines will have more intermolecular association due to hydrogen bonding ?

Primary amines / Secondary amines

____

51. Tertiary amines show ____________ (extensive/moderate/no) intermolecular association due to the absence of hydrogen atom.

52. Arrange the following in increasing order of their boiling points.

Primary amines, Secondary amines, Tertiary amines

____

53. Which of the following will have highest boiling point?

$n\text{-}C_4H_9NH_2$, $n\text{-}C_4H_9OH$, $(C_2H_5)_2NH$, $C_2H_5N(CH_3)_2$

____

TOPIC 6

Chemical Reactions

NCERT Pg 266-274

54. Mention two reasons in the support of amines being reactive.

(i) ______ (ii) ______

55. Primary, secondary and tertiary amines show difference in reactivity due to difference in number of hydrogen atoms attached to their nitrogen atom.

True ☐ False ☐

56. Due to the presence of lone pair/unshared electron pair on amines, it behaves as

(a) electrophile ☐ (b) nucleophile ☐

(c) electrofuge ☐ (d) nucleofuge ☐

57. Amines are ______ (acidic/basic/neutral) in nature.

58. Write a reaction to show basic character of amine.

______

59. Identify *A*, *B* and *C* in the following reaction,

$$R-\overset{+}{N}H_3X^- + A \longrightarrow R\ddot{N}H_2 + B + C$$

$A =$ ______ $B =$ ______ $C =$ ______

60. Tick the correct one.

Salts of amines are insoluble in

Water ☐ Ether ☐

61. Amines have unshared pair of electrons on nitrogen atom which makes them to acts as

(a) Lewis bases ☐ (b) Lewis acids ☐

(c) Bronsted acid ☐ (d) Bronsted base ☐

______

62. Larger the value of K_b, ______ (higher/lower) will be the value of pK_b.

63. Which effect is responsible for making aliphatic amines much more stronger bases than ammonia?

______

64. Tick the correct one

Which one of the given compounds is a weaker base?

Aromatic amines ☐ Ammonia ☐

65. ______ of the aryl group affects the basicity of aromatic amines.

(a) Electron withdrawing nature ☐ (b) Electron donating nature ☐

(c) $+I$-effect ☐ (d) $+M$-effect ☐

66. Consider the following statements.

I. Acidic character of an amine depends upon ease of formation of cation by accepting proton from the acid.

II. More stable the cation is relative to amine, more acidic is amine.

Which of the above statement(s) is/are correct?

(a) Only I ☐ (b) Only II ☐

(c) Both I and II ☐ (d) Neither I nor II ☐

67. Complete the analogy with respect to substituted amines.

Group responsible for increasing basic strength : *A* : : group responsible for decreasing basic strength : *B*.

(a) *A* : Electron releasing, *B* : Electron withdrawing ☐

(b) *A* : Electron attracting, *B* : *m*-directing ☐

(c) *A* : Electron releasing, *B* : *p*-directing ☐

(d) *A* : Electron attracting, *B* : Electron releasing ☐

68. Alkyl amines are ________ (stronger/weaker) bases than ammonia.

69. Arrange the following amines in increasing order of their basicity in gaseous phase.

Primary amines, NH_3, Tertiary amines, Secondary amines.

____

***70.** Choose the most stable ion out of the following options.

(a) 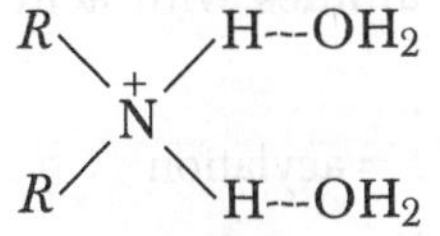 ☐ (b) 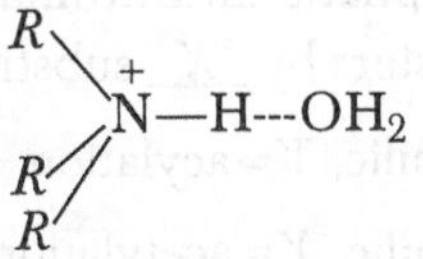 ☐

(c) 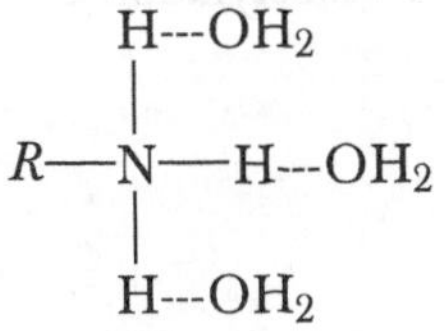 ☐ (c) None of these ☐

71. Alkyl group bulkier than —CH_3 on amines reduces steric hindrance to H-bonding.

True ☐ False ☐

72. Mention three factors responsible for deciding basic strength of alkyl amines in aqueous state.

(i) ________ (ii) ________ (iii) ________

***73.** Organise the following amines in increasing order of their basic strength in aqueous solution.

$(C_2H_5)_3N$, $(C_2H_5)_2NH$, NH_3, $C_2H_5NH_2$

____

74. Which of the following compound is least basic in aqueous medium?

(a) Primary amine ☐ (b) Tertiary amine ☐

(c) Ammonia ☐ (d) Secondary amine ☐

75. pK_b value of aniline is quite ____________ (high/low).

76. Choose the incorrect representation of resonance from the following.

(a) 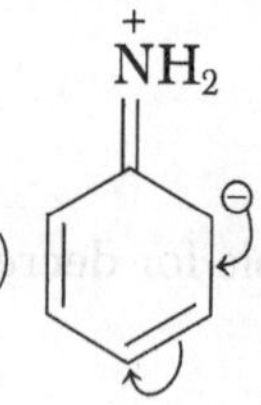 ☐ (b) 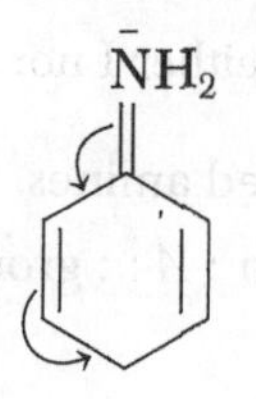 ☐ (c) 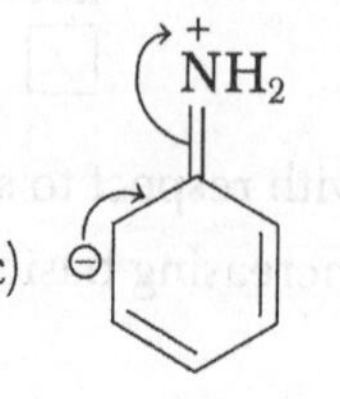 ☐ (d) All are correct ☐

***77.** Anilinium ion have two resonating structures.

True ☐ False ☐

78. Complete the analogy with respect to groups affecting basic strength of substituted aniline.

A : Increase basic strength when attached to aniline : : B : Decrease basic strength when attached to aniline.

(a) $A: -OCH_3, \quad B: -NO_2$ ☐ (b) $A: -NO_2, \quad B: -OCH_3$ ☐

(c) $A: -COOH, \quad B: -NO_2$ ☐ (d) $A: -X, \quad B: -SO_3H$ ☐

79. Reaction of aliphatic and aromatic primary and secondary amines with acid chloride or anhydride or esters by $\underline{X}$ substitution is called as $\underline{Y}$.

(a) X= electrophilic, Y= acylation ☐ (b) X= nucleophilic, Y= acylation ☐

(c) X= electrophilic, Y= acetylation ☐ (d) X= nucleophilic, Y= acetylation ☐

80. Predict the product(s) of the following reaction.

$$C_2H_5-\ddot{N}(H)-H + CH_3-\overset{O}{\overset{\|}{C}}-Cl \xrightarrow{\text{Base}} \underline{\hspace{6cm}}.$$

81. Complete the following reactions.

(i) $(C_2H_5)_2NH + \underline{\hspace{2cm}} \xrightarrow{\text{Base}} (C_2H_5)_2N-\overset{O}{\overset{\|}{C}}-CH_3 + HCl$

(ii) $\underline{\hspace{2cm}} + H_3C-\overset{O}{\overset{\|}{C}}-O-\overset{O}{\overset{\|}{C}}-CH_3 \xrightarrow{\text{Base}} C_6H_5-\underset{H}{\underset{|}{\ddot{N}}}-\underset{O}{\underset{\|}{C}}-CH_3 + \underline{\hspace{2cm}}.$

82. Amines react with benzoyl chloride as

$$CH_3-NH_2 + C_6H_5COCl \longrightarrow CH_3NHCOC_6H_5 + HCl$$

The name of this reaction is ____________________.

83. Give the equation representing carbylamine reaction.

____

84. Isocyanides or carbylamines are fruity smelling substances.

True ☐ False ☐

85. Which of the following amines do not show the carbylamine reaction?

(a) Primary amines only ☐ (b) Secondary amines only ☐

(c) Secondary and tertiary amines ☐ (d) Primary and secondary amines ☐

86. Primary aliphatic amines on reaction with nitrous acid liberates __________ gas which is used in estimation of __________ and __________.

87. Methylamine reacts with HNO_2 to form **[NCERT Exemplar]**

(a) $CH_3—O—N{=}O$ ☐ (b) $CH_3—O—CH_3$ ☐

(c) CH_3OH ☐ (d) CH_3CHO ☐

88. Identify the reagents from the following conversion.

$$R—NH_2 + HNO_2 \xrightarrow{(i)} [R—\overset{+}{N_2}\overset{-}{Cl}] \xrightarrow{(ii)} R—OH + N_2 + HCl$$

(i) __________ (ii) __________

***89.** Predict the product(s) for the following reaction.

$$C_6H_5—NH_2 \xrightarrow[273\ K-278\ K]{NaNO_2\ +\ 2HCl} \text{__________}$$

90. Write the name and the formula of Hinsberg's reagent.

____

91. Determine A and B in the following reaction.

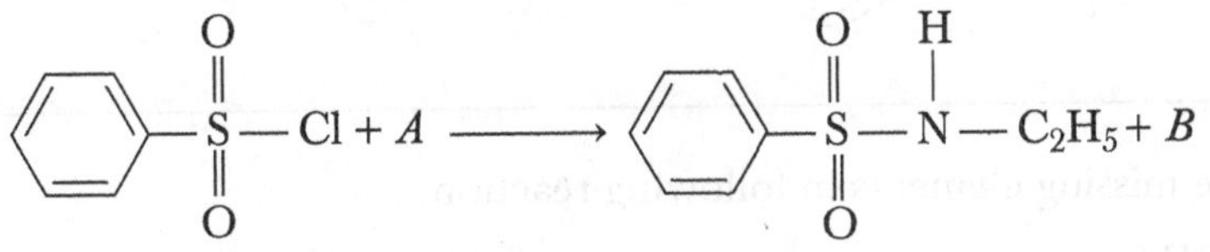

A = __________ B = __________

92. Consider the following statements.

I. Hydrogen attached to nitrogen in sulphonamide is strongly basic due to the presence of strong electron withdrawing sulphonyl group.

II. Sulphonamides are soluble in alkali.

Which of the above statement(s) is/are correct?

(a) Only I ☐ (b) Only II ☐ (c) Both I and II ☐ (d) Neither I non II ☐

93. Write structure of the product(s) formed on reaction of benzene sulphonyl chloride with N, N-diethylamine.

____

94. Tick the correct one.

N, N-diethylbenzene sulphonamide is __________ in alkali.

Soluble ☐ Insoluble ☐

95. Identify *A* and *B* in the given reactions.

	Column I (Reactions)	Column II (Reagents)
I.	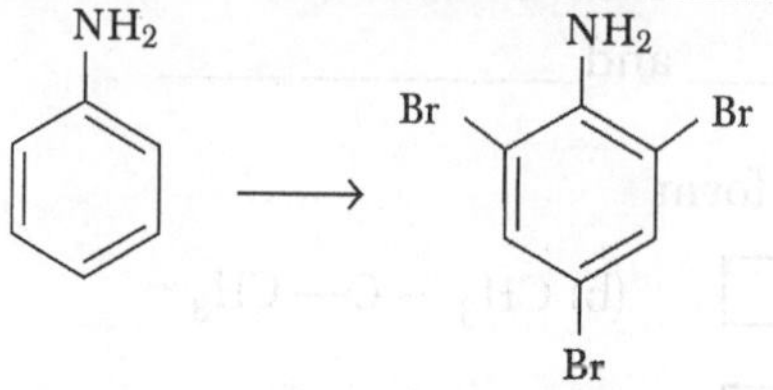	A. ________
II.	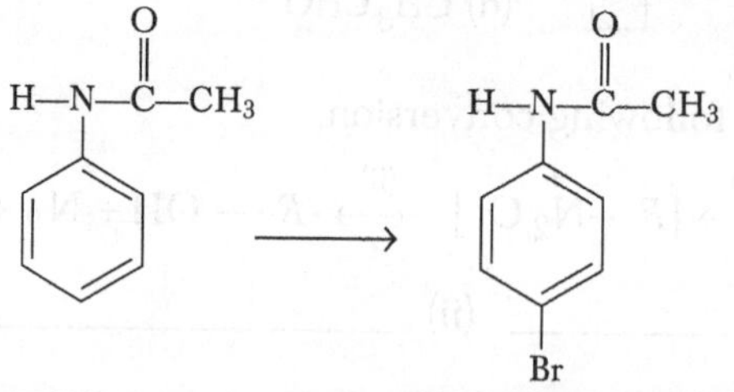	B. ________

96. Write reactions which involve the conversion of aniline to 4-bromoaniline.

____

***97.** Predict the product(s) for the following reaction

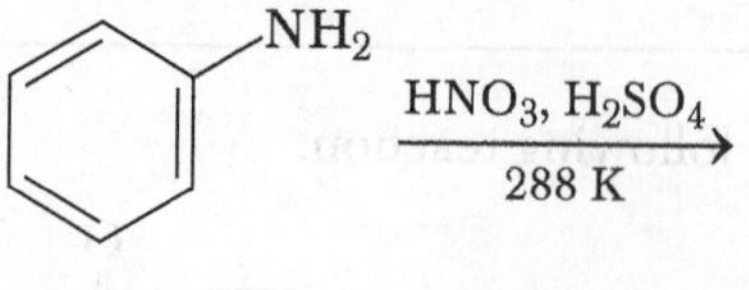

____

***98.** Identify the missing elements in following reaction.

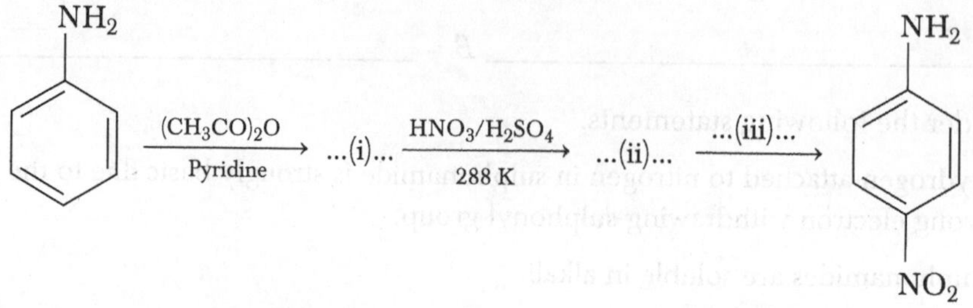

(i) ______________ (ii) ______________ (iii) ______________

99. Choose the correct product for the following reaction.

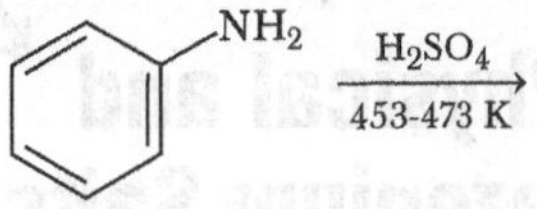

(a) 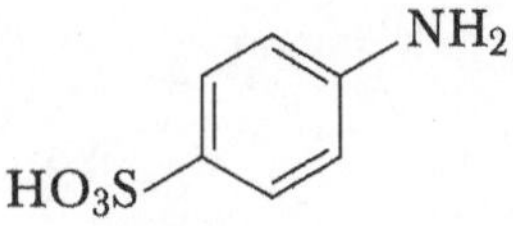 ☐ (b) 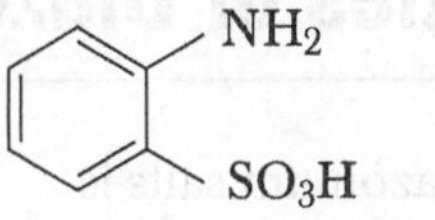 ☐

(c) 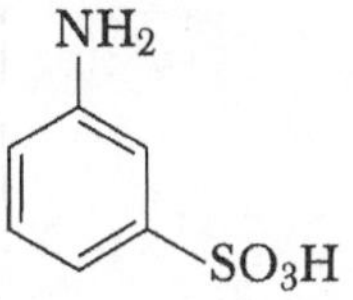 ☐ (d) 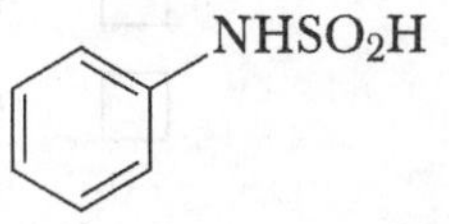 ☐

100. ____________ does not undergo Friedel-Crafts reaction (alkylation and acetylation) due to the formation of salt with aluminium chloride.

***101.** Arrange the following in decreasing order of basic strength.

CH_3NH_2, $(CH_3)_2NH$, $(CH_3)_3N$, $C_6H_5NH_2$, $C_6H_5CH_2NH_2$

____

102. Complete the following table.

Reactant *A*	Reactant *B*	Product
$CH_3CH_2CH_2NH_2$	(i) ____________	$CH_3CH_2CH_2\overset{+}{N}H_3\overset{-}{Cl}$
(ii) ____________	HCl	$(C_2H_5)_3\overset{+}{N}H\overset{-}{Cl}$

103. Determine the product(s) of the following reaction.

$$C_6H_5NH_2 + CH_3I\text{ (excess)} \xrightarrow{Na_2CO_3}$$

____

104. Aniline reacts with benzoyl chloride as follows

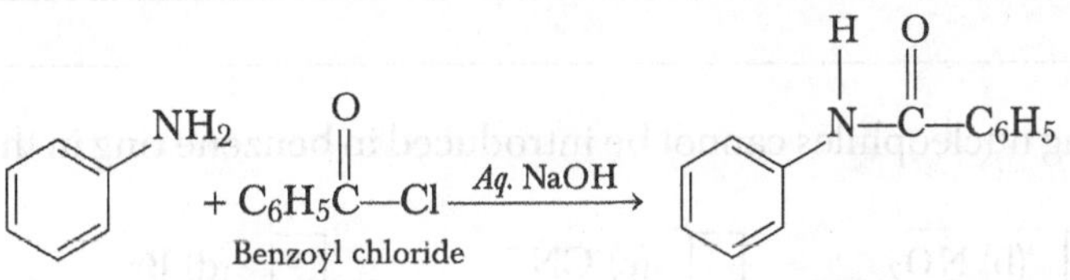

The name of a product formed is ____________.

105. Which of the given isomers of C_3H_9N will not liberate N_2 gas on treatment with nitrous acid?

I. $CH_3CH_2CH_2NH_2$

II. $CH_3-\underset{NH_2}{\underset{|}{CH}}-CH_3$

III. $CH_3-NH-C_2H_5$

IV. $CH_3-\underset{CH_3}{\underset{|}{N}}-CH_3$

Select the correct option.

(a) Only I ☐ (b) Only IV ☐ (c) I and II ☐ (d) III and IV ☐

TOPIC 7

Methods of Preparation, Physical and Chemical Properties of Diazonium Salts

NCERT Pg 274-276

106. General formula for diazonium salts is

(a) $R\overset{+}{N}_2 X^-$ ☐ (b) $R_2\overset{+}{N}_2 X^-$ ☐

(c) $R\overset{+}{N}_3 X^-$ ☐ (d) $R\overset{+}{N} X_2^-$ ☐

107. Name the given diazonium compounds.

(i) $C_6H_5\overset{+}{N}_2Cl^-$ __________ (ii) $C_6H_5\overset{+}{N}_2HSO_4^-$ __________

108. Primary aliphatic amine form highly unstable alkyl diazonium salts.

True ☐ False ☐

109. Draw resonating structures of arene diazonium ion.

____

110. Write diazotisation reaction.

____

111. How many of the following amines will undergo diazotisation?

Ethanamine, tert-butylamine, aniline, N-methylaniline, m-chloroaniline

(a) 2 ☐ (b) 3 ☐ (c) 4 ☐ (d) 5 ☐

112. Choose the correct property/properties of benzene diazonium chloride.

Colourless, Amorphous solid, Crystalline solids, Soluble in ether, Soluble in water

____

113. Which of the following nucleophiles cannot be introduced in benzene ring in the presence of Cu(I) ion?

(a) Cl^- ☐ (b) $N\bar{O}_2$ ☐ (c) CN^- ☐ (d) Br^- ☐

114. Sandmeyer reaction can be correctly represented as

I. $Ar\overset{+}{N}_2\overset{-}{X} \xrightarrow{CuCN/KCN} ArCN + N_2$

II. $Ar\overset{+}{N}_2\overset{-}{X} \xrightarrow{Cu/HBr} ArBr + N_2 + CuX$

(a) Only I ☐ (b) Only II ☐

(c) Both I and II ☐ (d) Neither I more II ☐

115. Predict the product(s) of the following reaction.

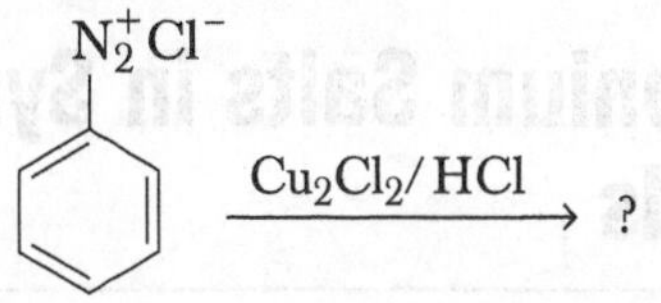

116. Determine the missing compounds in following reactions.

(i) $Ar\overset{+}{N}_2Cl^- + ? \longrightarrow ArI + ? + N_2$ ____________________

(ii) $Ar\overset{+}{N}_2Cl^- + ? \longrightarrow ? \xrightarrow{\Delta} Ar-F + BF_3 + N_2$ ____________________

117. Pick the correct reagent from the given choices for the following reaction.

$$Ar\overset{+}{N}_2\,Cl^- \longrightarrow ArH$$

H_3PO_2/H_2O, H_2O, $Cu(OH)_2/H_2O$, $NaNO_2/HCl$

118. Determine *X*, *Y* and *Z* in the following reactions.

(i) $Ar\overset{+}{N}_2Cl^- + H_2O \longrightarrow X + N_2 + HCl$

(ii)

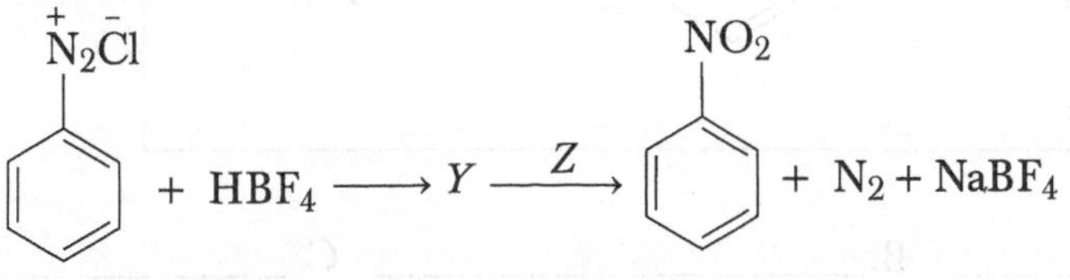

X = ____________ *Y* = ____________ *Z* = ____________

***119.** Which of the following compounds will not undergo azo coupling reaction with benzene diazonium chloride? **[NCERT Exemplar]**

(a) Aniline ☐

(b) Phenol ☐

(c) Anisole ☐

(d) Nitrobenzene ☐

TOPIC 8

Importance of Diazonium Salts in Synthesis of Aromatic Compounds

NCERT Pg 276-277

120. Match the following Column I with Column II.

Column I (Reactions)	Column II (Reagents)
A. 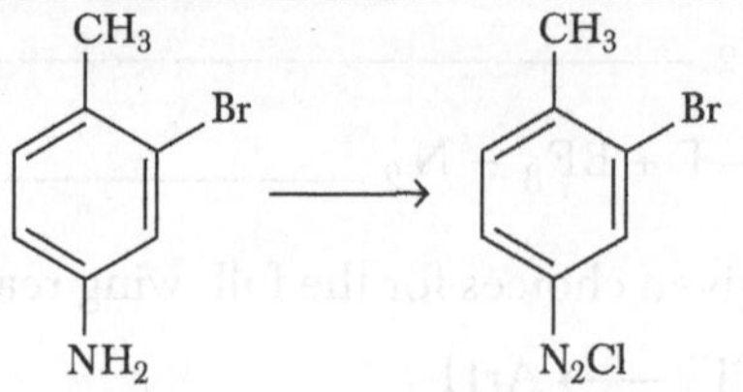	1. H_2O/H_3PO_2
B. 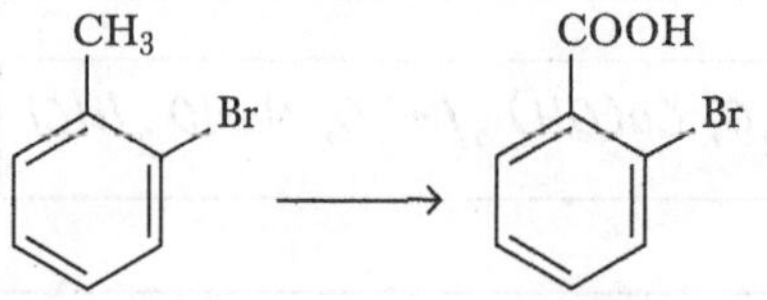	2. $NaNO_2$ / HCl 273-278 K
C. 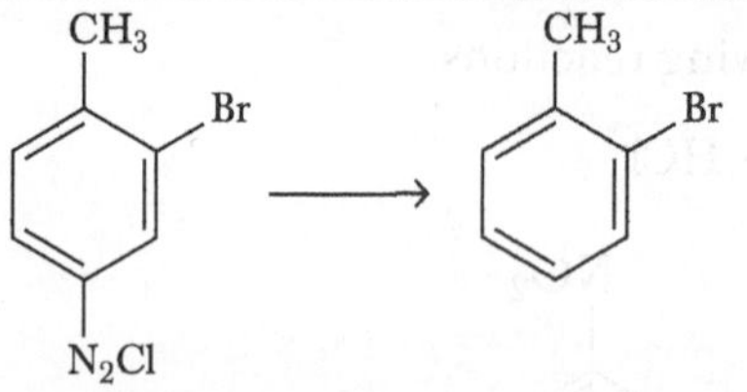	3. $KMnO_4/\bar{O}H$

A. ____________ B. ____________ C. ____________

121. Identify the reagents for the following conversion.

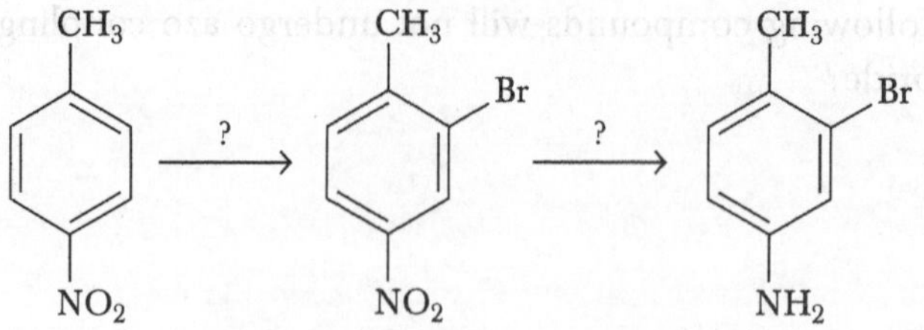

____

122. 3-methyl aniline on reaction with $NaNO_2/HBF_4$ at 273-278 K gives *A*. *A* on further heating with $NaNO_2$/Cu gives *B*. Write the structures of *A* and *B*.

A = ____________ *B* = ____________

123. Write product(s) for the following reaction.

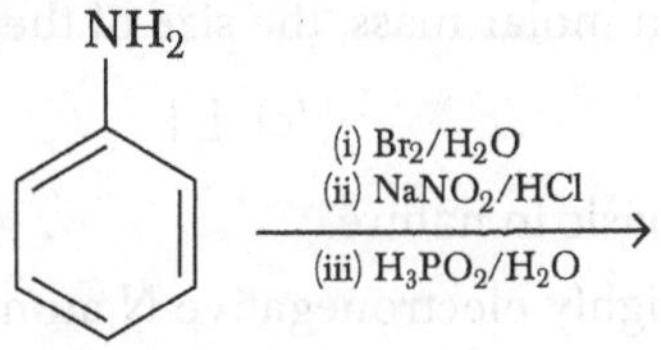

____

***124.** Diazonium chloride salt reacts with aniline as shown below :

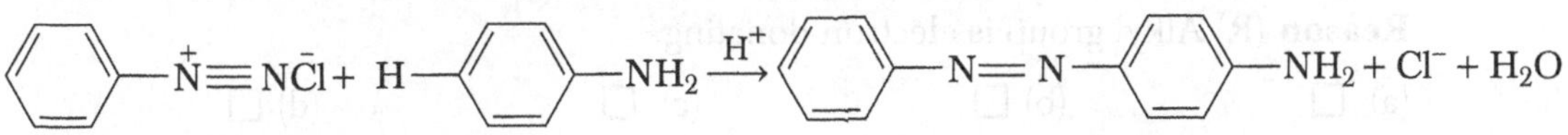

The colour of the dye produced is

(a) orange ☐ (b) red ☐ (c) yellow ☐ (d) blue ☐

125. __________ are very good intermediates for the introduction of —F, —Cl, —CN, —OH, groups into the aromatic ring.

Assertion-Reason Questions

Given below are two statements, one is labelled as Assertion (A) and other is labelled as Reason (R). Select the most appropriate answer from the options given below.

(a) Both A and R are true and R is correct the explanation of A.

(b) Both A and R are true but R is not the correct explanation of A.

(c) A is true but R is false.

(d) A is false but R is true.

1. **Assertion** (A) The bond angle C — N — H in amines is 108° unlike tetrahedral bond angle which is 109.5°.

Reason (R) Lone pair of electrons in fourth orbital of nitrogen is responsible for decrease of bond angle.

(a) ☐ (b) ☐ (c) ☐ (d) ☐

2. **Assertion** (A) The correct IUPAC name for the compound $H_2N—CH_2—CH_2—NH_2$ is ethane-1, 2-diamine.

Reason (R) According to IUPAC system, amines are named as alkanamines derived by replacement of 'e' of alkane by the word amine.

(a) ☐ (b) ☐ (c) ☐ (d) ☐

3. **Assertion** (A) Reduction of nitroalkanes to amines using iron scrap requires small amount of hydrochloric acid for initiation of reaction.

Reason (R) $FeCl_2$ gets hydrolysed to release hydrochloric acid during the reaction.

(a) ☐ (b) ☐ (c) ☐ (d) ☐

4. **Assertion** (A) Solubility of amines in water increase with increase in molar mass.
Reason (R) With increase in molar mass, the size of the hydrophobic alkyl part, increases.
(a) ☐ (b) ☐ (c) ☐ (d) ☐

5. **Assertion** (A) Amines are basic in nature.
Reason (R) Amines have highly electronegative N atom.
(a) ☐ (b) ☐ (c) ☐ (d) ☐

6. **Assertion** (A) In aqueous medium, tertiary amines are more basic than secondary amines.
Reason (R) Alkyl group is electron donating.
(a) ☐ (b) ☐ (c) ☐ (d) ☐

7. **Assertion** (A) In aqueous phase, ammonium cations get stabilised due to electron releasing (+*I*) effect of alkyl group and destabilised due to solvation with water molecules.
Reason (R) Greater the size of ion, lesser will be the solvation.
(a) ☐ (b) ☐ (c) ☐ (d) ☐

8. **Assertion** (A) Nitration of aniline at lower temperatures and in strongly acidic conditions yields *m*-nitroaniline as major product.
Reason (R) In acidic medium, NH_2 group is converted into $-\overset{+}{N}H_3$ group which is *meta* directing.
(a) ☐ (b) ☐ (c) ☐ (d) ☐

9. **Assertion** (A) Nitration of aniline can be conveniently done by protecting the amino group by acetylation.
Reason (R) Acetylation makes the NH_2 group less reactive hence making the benzene less electron rich.
(a) ☐ (b) ☐ (c) ☐ (d) ☐

10. **Assertion** (A) Pent-1-amine is more soluble in water than pentan-1-ol.
Reason (R) Alcohols are more polar than amines and form stronger intermolecular hydrogen bonds.
(a) ☐ (b) ☐ (c) ☐ (d) ☐

Case-Based Questions

1. Amines are bases because the nitrogen atom in the —NH_2 group has a lone pair of electrons that it can share with electron-deficient compounds. Aliphatic amines, which have alkyl groups attached to the nitrogen, are stronger bases than ammonia (NH_3) due to the electron-donating effect of these alkyl groups. More alkyl groups typically mean stronger basicity, so we would expect tertiary amines (3°) to be the strongest, followed by secondary (2°), and then primary (1°). However, the actual order is 2° > 1° > 3°. This is because bulky alkyl groups in tertiary amines crowd the nitrogen atom, making it harder for a proton to approach and bond with it. Aromatic amines are weaker bases than both ammonia and aliphatic amines. The presence of electron-donating groups (like —CH_3 or —OCH_3) on the aromatic ring increases basicity, while electron-withdrawing groups (like —NO_2, —CN, or halogens) decrease it. This effect is more pronounced when these groups are in the *para* position compared to the *meta* position.

(i) Which one of the following is the strongest base in aqueous solution?

(a) Propyl amine ☐ (b) Triethyl amine ☐
(c) Aniline ☐ (d) Diethyl amine ☐

(ii) Which order of basicity is correct?

(a) Aniline > *m*-toluidine > *o*-toluidine ☐ (b) Aniline > *o*-toluidine > *m*-toluidine ☐
(c) *o*-toluidine > aniline > *m*-toluidine ☐ (d) *o*-toluidine < aniline < *m*-toluidine ☐

(iii) What is the decreasing order of basicity of following amines in aqueous medium?

(a) $NH_3 > C_6H_5NH_2 > (C_2H_5)_2NH > (C_2H_5)_3N$ ☐
(b) $(C_2H_5)_3N > (C_2H_5)_2NH > C_6H_5NH_2 > NH_3$ ☐
(c) $(C_2H_5)_2NH > (C_2H_5)_3N > NH_3 > C_6H_5NH_2$ ☐
(d) $(C_2H_5)_2NH > C_6H_5NH_2 > (C_2H_5)_3N > NH_3$ ☐

(iv) Choose the incorrect statement.

(a) Methylamine is slightly acidic. ☐
(b) Methylamine is more basic than ammonia. ☐
(c) Aniline is a weaker base than ammonia. ☐
(d) Hydrazine is stronger base than ammonia ☐

2. Aromatic amines, like aniline, stand apart from their aliphatic counterparts due to the nitrogen atom's involvement in the aromatic ring's resonance. This delocalization of the nitrogen's lone pair electrons into the ring weakens its basicity compared to alkylamines. The presence of electron-donating groups (EDG) like —OCH_3 on the ring can partially counteract this effect boosting basicity. Conversely, electron-withdrawing groups (EWG) like —NO_2 further diminish the amine's basicity by intensifying the electron withdrawal. This substituent effect is location-dependent. with groups in the *para* position (opposite the amine) exerting a more significant influence than those in the *meta* position.

(i) Which factor is primarily responsible for the weaker basicity of aromatic amines compared to aliphatic amines?

(a) Inductive effect ☐ (b) Resonance ☐
(c) Steric hindrance ☐ (d) Hydrogen bonding ☐

(ii) Which of the following statement is incorrect regarding the effect of substituents on the basicity of aromatic amines?

(a) Electron-donating groups increase basicity. ☐
(b) Electron-withdrawing groups decrease basicity. ☐
(c) The effect is stronger in the *meta* position than in the *para* position. ☐
(d) The substituent effect is due to its influence on the resonance of the aromatic ring. ☐

(iii) In the reaction of aniline with nitrous acid (HNO_2) at low temperatures, the major product formed is

(a) benzene ☐ (b) phenol ☐
(c) benzene diazonium chloride ☐ (d) nitrobenzene ☐

(iv) The reaction of aniline with acetic anhydride $(CH_3CO)_2O$ yields.

(a) Acetanilide ☐ (b) Benzanilide ☐
(c) N-methylaniline ☐ (d) N-phenylacetamide ☐

COMPETITION EDGE UP

1. *Find out the major product formed from the following reaction. [Me: —CH_3]*
[NCERT (New) Pg. 262, JEE Main 2024]

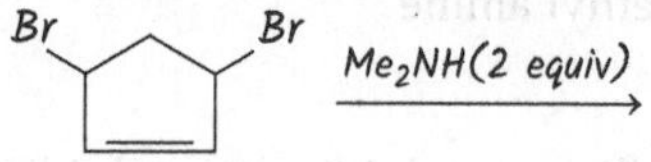

(a) 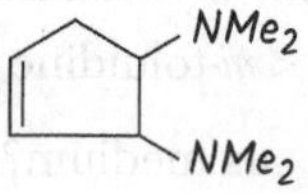

☐

(b) 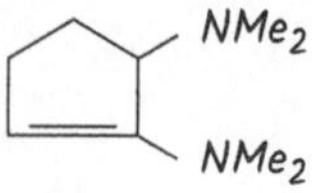

☐

(c) 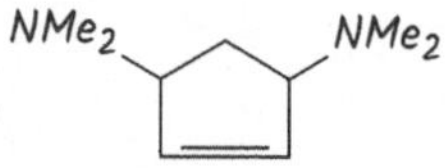

☐

(d) 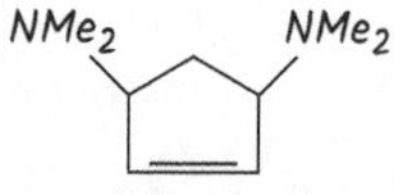

☐

2. *Identify B formed in the reaction.*
[NCERT (New) Pg. 262, JEE Main 2024]

$$Cl(CH_2)_4Cl \xrightarrow{\text{Excess } NH_3} A \xrightarrow{NaOH} B + H_2O + NaCl$$

(a) 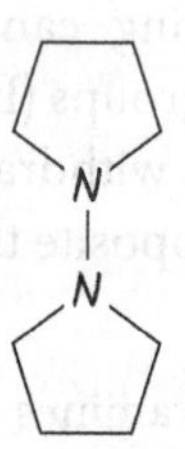

☐

(b) 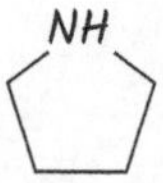

☐

(c) $H_2N—(CH_2)_4—NH_2$ ☐

(d) $Cl\overset{+}{N}H_3(CH_2)_4\overset{+}{N}H_3Cl^-$ ☐

3. *Correct order of basic strength of*
[NCERT (New) Pg. 266, JEE Main 2024]

pyrrole 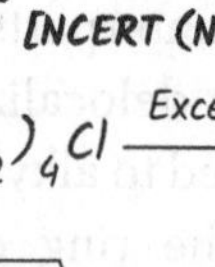, *pyridine* 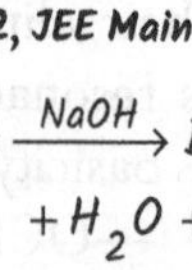

and piperidine 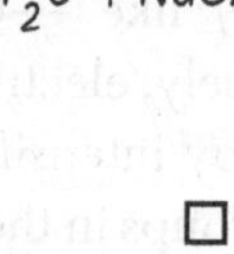 *is*

(a) *pyridine > piperidine > pyrrole* ☐
(b) *piperidine > pyridine > pyrrole* ☐
(c) *pyrrole > piperidine > pyridine* ☐
(d) *pyrrole > pyridine > piperidine* ☐

4. *Given below are two statements.*
[NCERT (New) Pg. 269 & 270, JEE Main 2024]

Statement I *The NH_2 group in aniline is ortho and para-directing and a powerful activating group.*

Statement II *Aniline does not undergo Friedel-Craft's reaction (alkylation and acylation).*

In the light of the above statements, choose the most appropriate answer from the options given below.

(a) *Both Statement I and Statement II are correct.* ☐
(b) *Statement I is correct but Statement II is incorrect.* ☐
(c) *Statement I is incorrect but Statement II is correct.* ☐
(d) *Both Statement I and Statement II are incorrect.* ☐

5. *Given below are two statements :*
[NCERT (New) Pg. 271, JEE Main 2024]

Statement I *All the following compounds react with p-toluene sulphonyl chloride.*

$C_6H_5NH_2$, $(C_6H_5)_2NH$, $(C_6H_5)_3N$

Statement II *Their products in the above reaction are soluble is aqueous NaOH.*

In the light of the above statements, choose the correct answer from the options given below:

(a) *Statement I is true but statement II is false.* ☐
(b) *Both statement I and statement II are true* ☐
(c) *Both statement I and statement II are false.* ☐
(d) *Statement I is false but statement II is true.* ☐

6. *Given below are two statements.*
[NCERT (New) Pg. 260, JEE Main 2024]

Statement I *Aminobenzene and aniline are same organic compounds.*

Statement II *Aminobenzene and aniline are different organic compounds.*

In the light of the above statements, choose the most appropriate answer from the options given below.

(a) Statement I is incorrect but Statement II is correct. ☐

(b) Both Statement I and Statement II are correct. ☐

(c) Both Statement I and Statement II are incorrect. ☐

(d) Statement I is correct but Statement II is incorrect. ☐

7. The product A formed in the following reaction is

[NCERT (New) Pg. 271, JEE Main 2024]

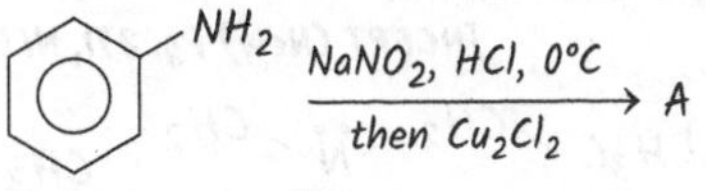

(a) 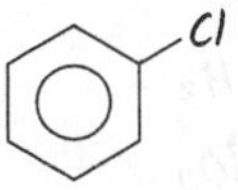 ☐ (b) 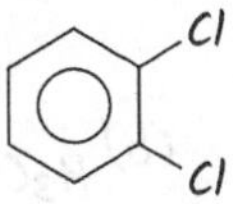 ☐

(c) 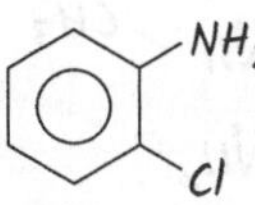 ☐ (d) 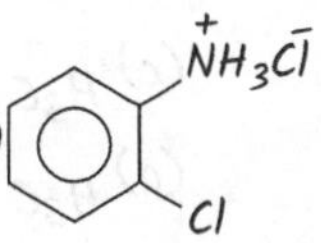 ☐

8. The arenium ion which is not involved in the bromination of aniline is ....

[NCERT (New) Pg. 272, JEE Main 2024]

(a) 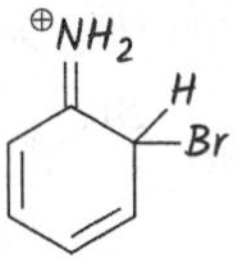 ☐ (b) 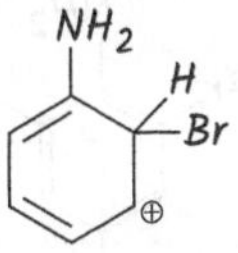 ☐

(c) 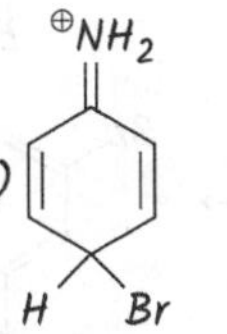 ☐ (d) 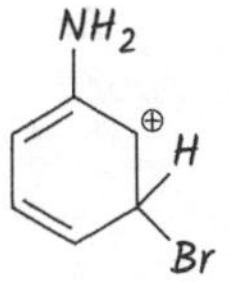 ☐

9. Identify the product (A) in the following reaction.

[NCERT (New) Pg. 271, JEE Main 2024]

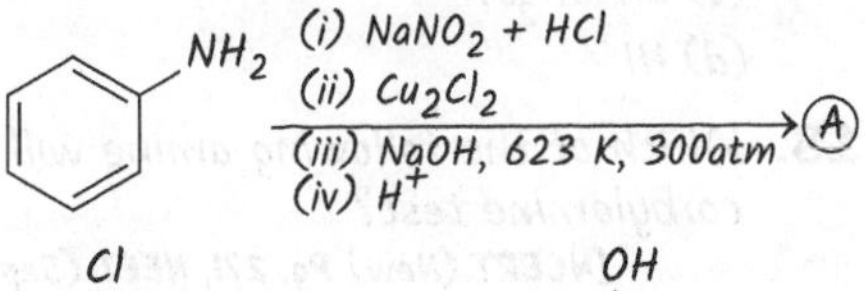

(a) 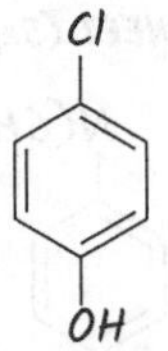 ☐ (b) 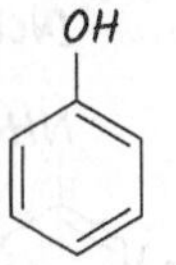 ☐

(c) 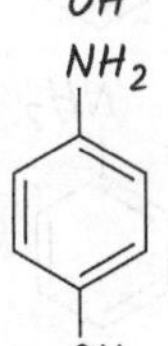 ☐ (d) 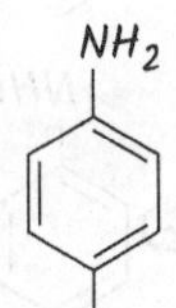 ☐

10. The azo-dye (Y) formed in the following reactions is:

Sulphanilic acid $+ NaNO_2 + CH_3COOH \longrightarrow X$

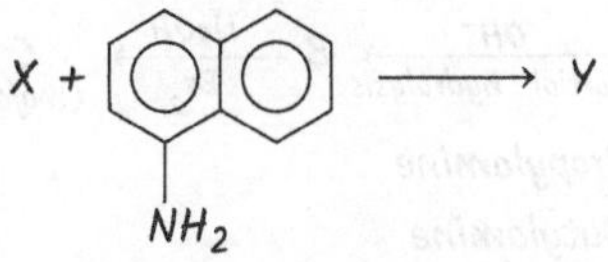

[NCERT (New) Pg. 276, JEE Main 2024]

(a) 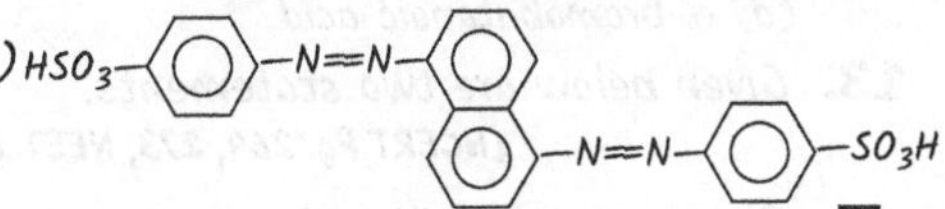 ☐

(b) 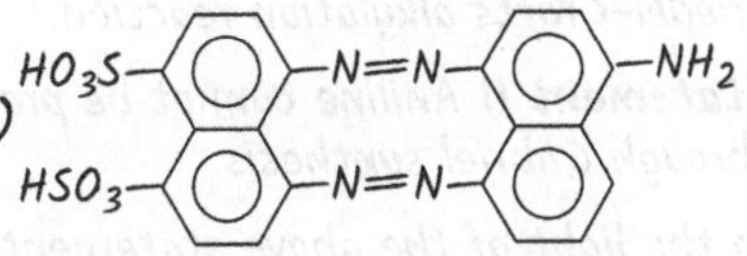 ☐

(c) 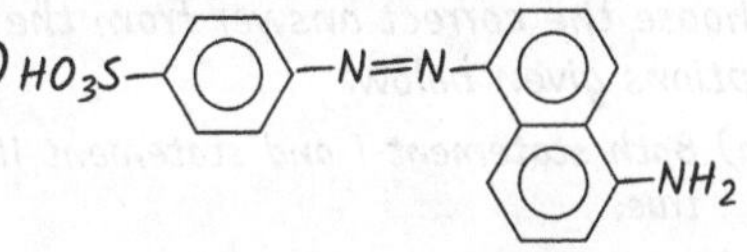 ☐

(d) 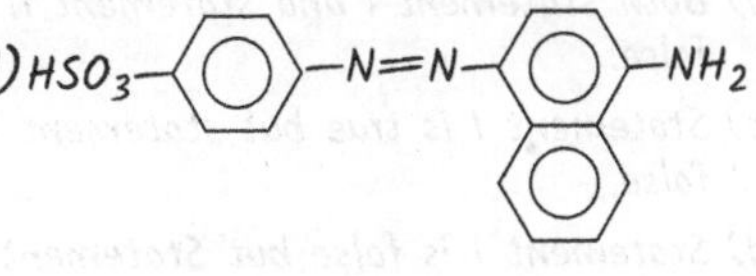 ☐

11. The products A and B formed in the following reaction scheme are respectively

[NCERT (New) Pg. 273, JEE Main 2024]

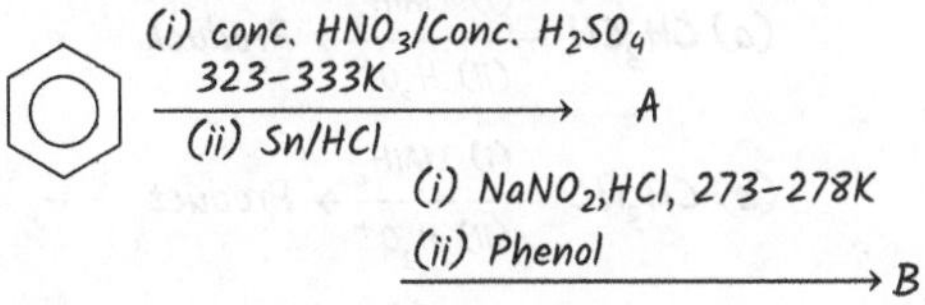

(a) 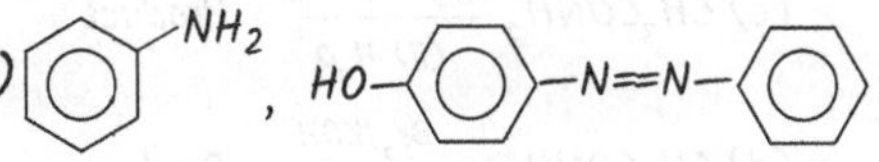 ☐

(b) 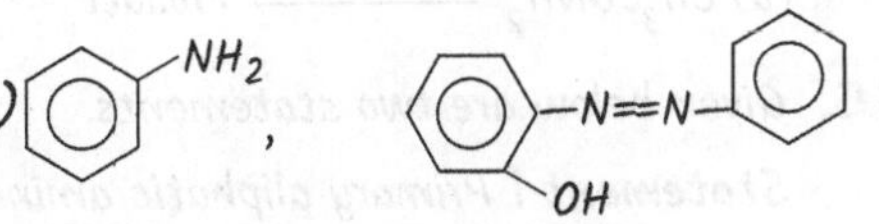 ☐

(c) 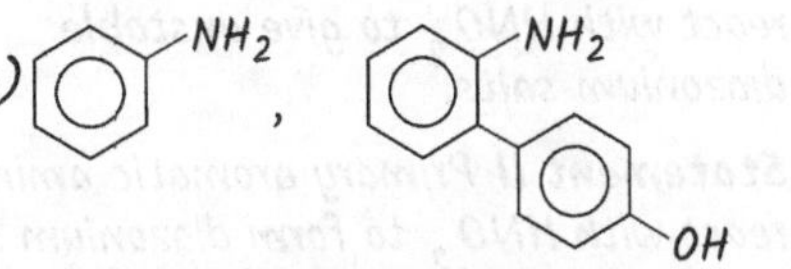 ☐

(d) 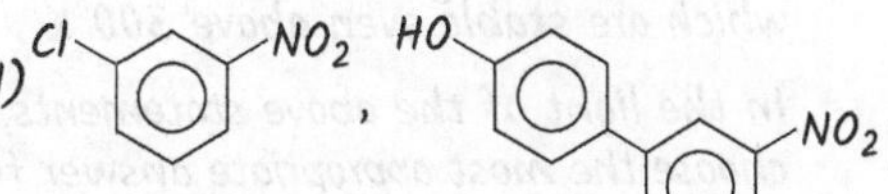 ☐

12. *Identify the major product C formed in the following reaction sequence:*
[NCERT (New) Pg. 273, NEET 2024]

$$CH_3—CH_2—CH_2—I \xrightarrow{NaCN} A \xrightarrow[\text{Partial hydrolysis}]{OH^-} B \xrightarrow[Br_2]{NaOH} \underset{(major)}{C}$$

(a) Propylamine ☐
(b) Butylamine ☐
(c) Butanamide ☐
(d) α-bromobutanoic acid ☐

13. *Given below are two statements.*
[NCERT Pg. 264, 273, NEET 2024]

Statement I Aniline does not undergo Friedel-Crafts alkylation reaction.

Statement II Aniline cannot be prepared through Gabriel synthesis.

In the light of the above statements, choose the correct answer from the options given below:

(a) Both statement I and statement II are true. ☐
(b) Both statement I and statement II are false. ☐
(c) Statement I is true but statement II is false. ☐
(d) Statement I is false but Statement II is true. ☐

14. *Which of the following reactions will not give primary amine as the product?*
[NCERT (New) Pg. 271, NEET 2023]

(a) $CH_3CN \xrightarrow[(ii)\ H_3O^+]{(i)\ LiAlH_4}$ Product ☐

(b) $CH_3NC \xrightarrow[(ii)\ H_3O^+]{(i)\ LiAlH_4}$ Product ☐

(c) $CH_3CONH_2 \xrightarrow[(ii)\ H_3O^+]{(i)\ LiAlH_4}$ Product ☐

(d) $CH_3CONH_2 \xrightarrow{Br_2/KOH}$ Product ☐

15. *Given below are two statements.*

Statement I Primary aliphatic amines react with HNO_2 to give unstable diazonium salts.

Statement II Primary aromatic amines react with HNO_2 to form diazonium salts which are stable even above 300 K.

In the light of the above statements, choose the most appropriate answer from the options given below.
[NCERT (New) Pg. 274, NEET 2022]

(a) Both statement I and statement II are incorrect. ☐
(b) Statement I is correct but statement II is incorrect. ☐
(c) Statement I is incorrect but statement II is correct. ☐
(d) Both statement I and statement II are correct. ☐

16. *Identify the compound that will react with Hinsberg's reagent to give a solid which dissolve in alkali.*
[NCERT (New) Pg. 271, NEET 2021]

(a) $H_3C—CH_2—\ddot{N}(CH_3)—CH_2—CH_3$ ☐

(b) $H_3C—CH_2—\ddot{N}O_2$ ☐

(c) $H_3C—CH_2—\ddot{N}H—CH_3$ ☐

(d) $H_3C—CH_2—\ddot{N}H_2$ ☐

17. *The reagent 'R' in the given sequence of chemical reaction is*
[NCERT (New) Pg. 276, NEET 2021]

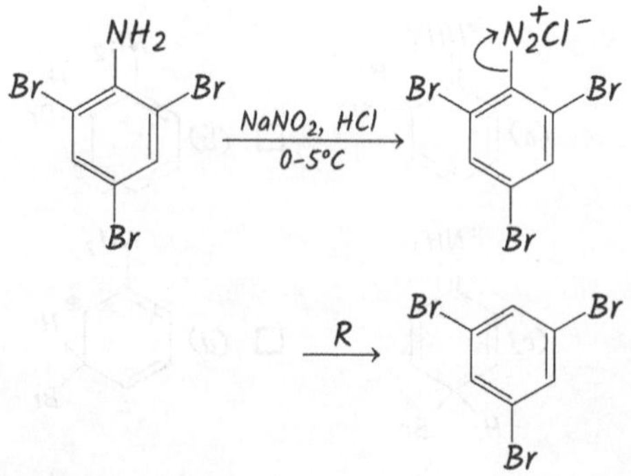

(a) CuCN/KCN ☐
(b) H_2O ☐
(c) CH_3CH_2OH ☐
(d) HI ☐

18. *Which of the following amine will give the carbylamine test?*
[NCERT (New) Pg. 271, NEET (Sep.) 2020]

(a) 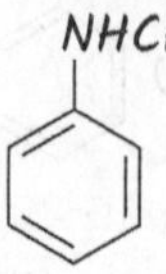

☐

(b) 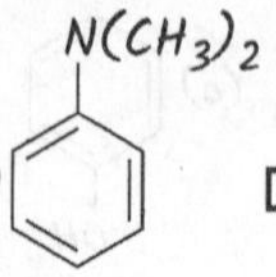

☐

(c) 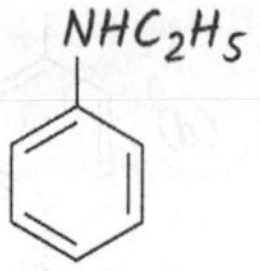

☐

(d) 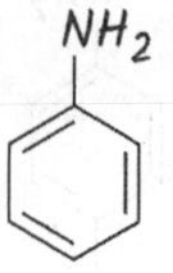

☐

Chapter 10

Biomolecules

Scan and take Chapter Test

TOPIC 1
Introduction & Carbohydrates

NCERT Pg 281-290

1. Name any three complex biomolecules present in living organisms.

(i) ________ (ii) ________ (iii) ________

2. Initially the general formula of carbohydrate was considered as ________.

3. Carbohydrates are optically active polyhydroxy aldehydes or ketones.

True ☐ False ☐

4. Classify the following into monosaccharides, oligosaccharides and polysaccharides.

Glucose, Fructose, Sucrose, Starch, Cellulose, Maltose, Glycogen

____

5. Which of the following polysaccharide is found most abundantly in nature?

(a) Fructose ☐ (b) Cellulose ☐ (c) Glucose ☐ (d) Lactose ☐

____

6. Polysaccharides are not sweet in taste, hence they are also called as non-sugars.

True ☐ False ☐

7. Complete the following reaction,

$$\text{Sucrose} \xrightarrow{\text{Hydrolysis}} \underline{\quad A \quad} + \underline{\quad B \quad}$$

A = ________ B = ________

8. Complete the following analogy.

Plants : Starch : : Animals : X

X = ________

Concepts of all questions bearing * are important for JEE/NEET/CUET.

9. Consider the following statements.

I. Carbohydrates which reduce Fehling's solution and Tollen's reagent are referred as reducing sugars.

II. Glucose is a ketohexose carbohydrate.

Which of the above statement(s) is/are correct?

(a) Only I ☐ (b) Only II ☐

(c) Both I and II ☐ (d) Neither I nor II ☐

10. On hydrolysis of starch by boiling it with dilute H_2SO_4, X is obtained. X is the most abundant organic compound on earth. Identify X

X = ______________________

11. Write the product formed when glucose reacts with

(i) hydrogen iodide at elevated temperatures ______________

(ii) hydroxylamine ______________

(iii) HCN ______________

12. Which of the following reactions indicates the presence of five —OH groups in glucose?

(a) 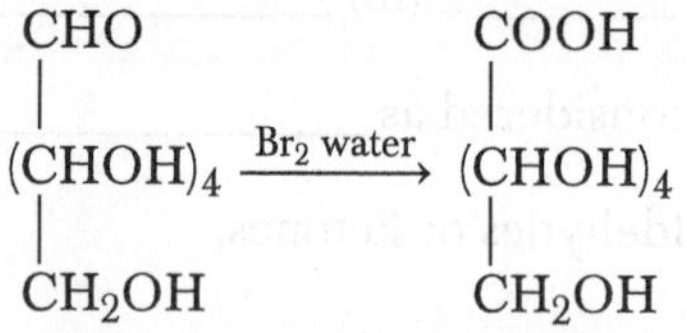 ☐

(b) 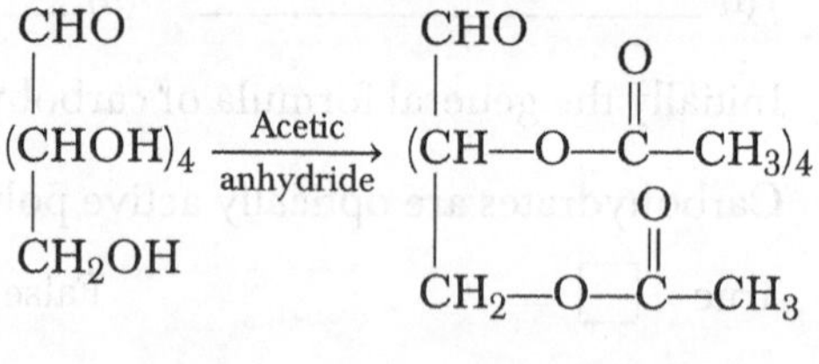 ☐

(c) 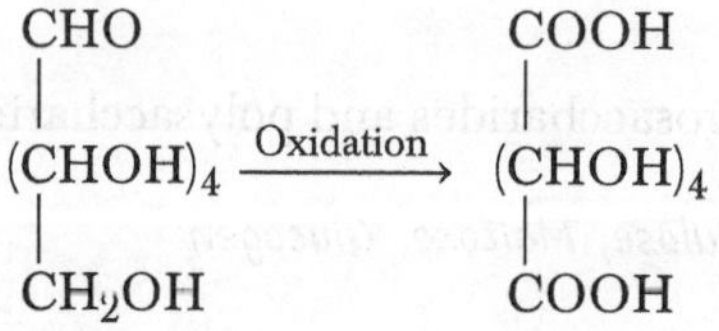 ☐

(d) All of these ☐

***13.** Match the names of the following compounds in Column I with their respective structures in Column II.

Column I (Names)		Column II (Structures)
A. Glucose	1.	$COOH-(CHOH)_4-COOH$
B. Saccharic acid	2.	$CHO-(CHOH)_4-CH_2OH$
C. Gluconic acid	3.	$COOH-(CHOH)_4-CH_2OH$

A. ______________ B. ______________ C. ______________

14. Pick the non-reducing sugar from the following disaccharides.

(a) 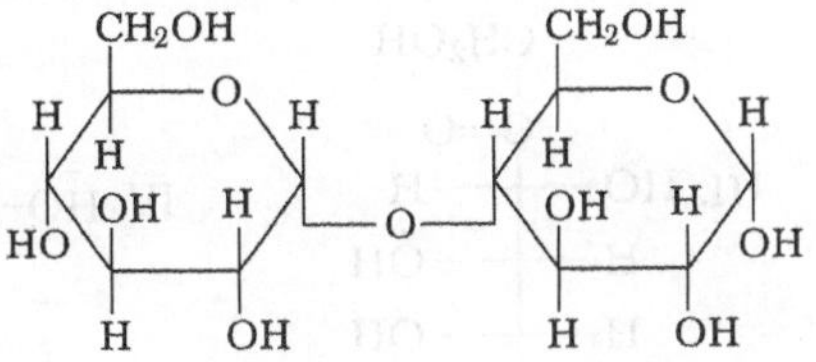

(b) 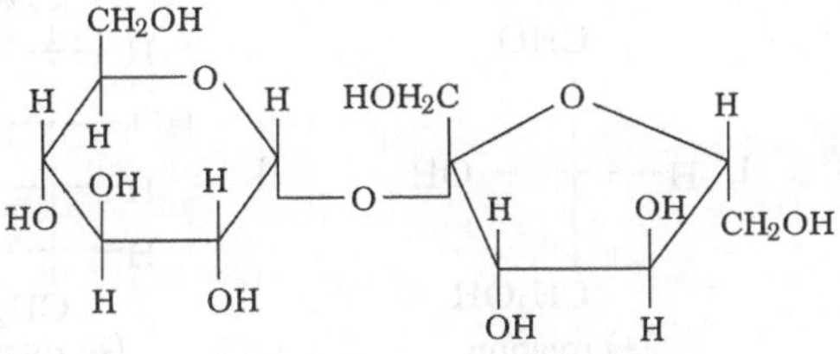

(c) 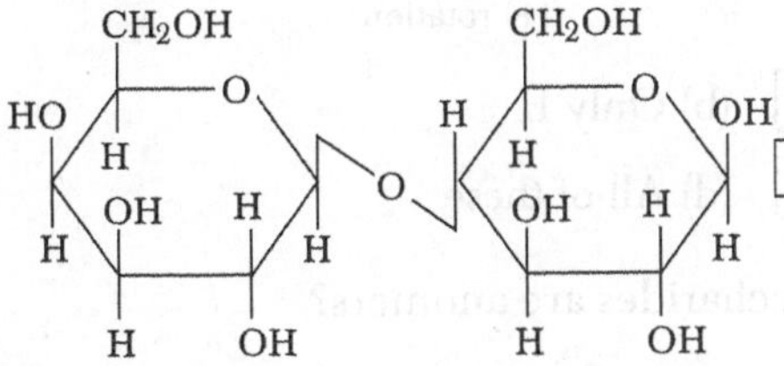

(d) 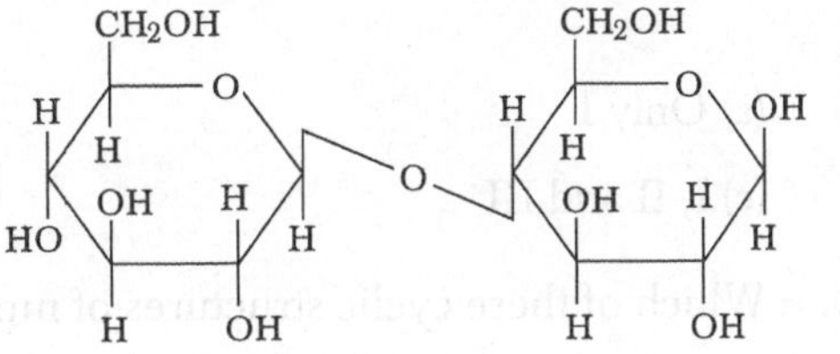

15. On oxidation with nitric acid, glucose yield saccharic acid which indicates the presence of secondary alcoholic (—OH) group in glucose.

True ☐ False ☐

16. Glucose is correctly named as D-(+)-glucose, where 'D' represents ___*X*___, whereas (+) represents ___*Y*___ nature of molecule.

X = ______________________

Y = ______________________

17. From the following monosaccharides the number of aldoses is

Glucose, Fructose, Galactose, Ribose, Deoxyribose

(a) 2 ☐ (b) 3 ☐

(c) 4 ☐ (d) 1 ☐

18. Consider the following statements.

I. The α-form of glucose is obtained by crystallisation from concentrated solution of glucose at 303 K.

II. The β-form of glucose is obtained by crystallisation from hot and saturated aqueous solution of glucose at 371 K.

Which of the following statements is/are correct?

(a) Only I ☐ (b) Only II ☐

(c) Both I and II ☐ (d) Neither I nor II ☐

19. Select the compound(s) which have D-configuration.

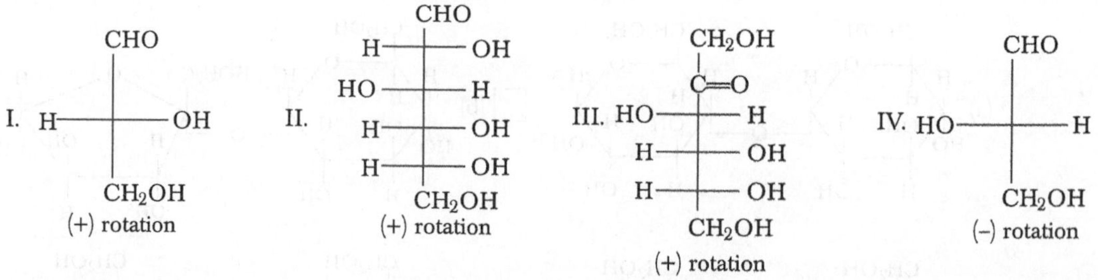

(a) Only I

(b) Only II

(c) I, II and III

(d) All of these

20. Which of these cyclic structures of monosaccharides are anomers?

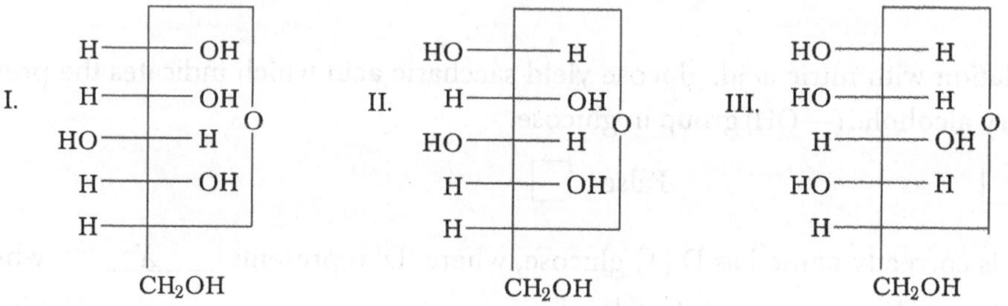

(a) I and II

(b) II and III

(c) I and III

(d) III is anomer of I and II

***21.** Which one of the following reactions is not explained by the open chain structure of glucose ?

(a) Formation of penta-acetate of glucose with acetic anhydride.

(b) Formation of addition product with 2,4-DNP reagent.

(c) Silver mirror formation with Tollen's reagent.

(d) Existence of alpha and beta forms of glucose.

22. Which of the following statement(s) is/are not correct regarding fructose?

I. It is a laevorotatory compound.

II. It contains ketonic functional group at carbon number 2.

III. It is obtained by hydrolysis of glucose.

Mark (✓) and (×) under correct and incorrect with respect to given statements.

	Correct	Incorrect
I.	________	________
II.	________	________
III.	________	________

23. Complete the following analogy.

Pyranose structure : Pyran : : X: Furan

X = ____

24. State whether True or False.

Furan is a five membered cyclic compound with one oxygen and four carbon atoms.

True ☐ False ☐

25. Choose the correct structure of β-D-(–)-fructofuranose.

(a) 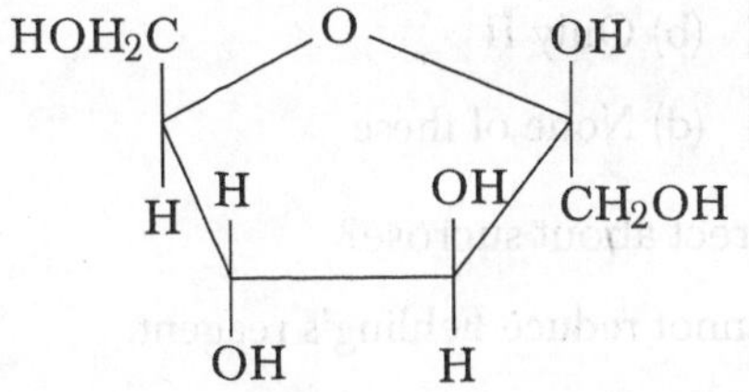 ☐

(b) 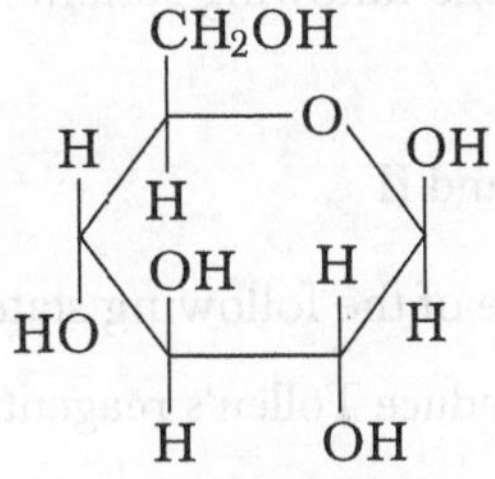 ☐

(c) 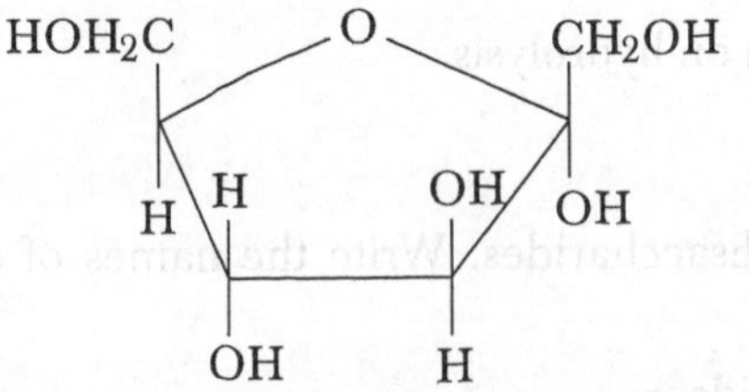 ☐

(d) 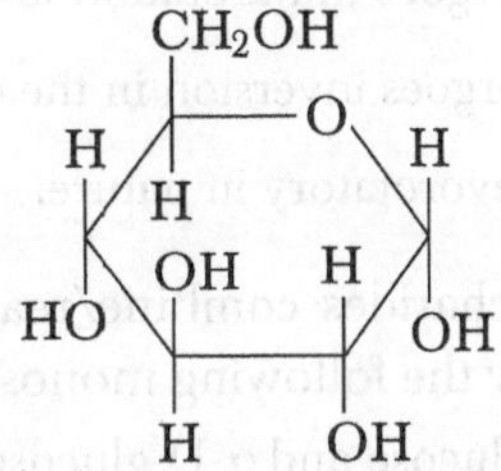 ☐

26. Mention the linkage between two monosaccharide units through oxygen atom to form a disaccharide.

____

27. Pick the odd one out from the following in context of non-reducing sugar.

Sucrose, Maltose, Lactose, Cellobiose

____

28. Identify the products *X* and *Y*.

$$C_{12}H_{22}O_{11} + H_2O \longrightarrow X + Y$$

X = ______________ *Y* = ______________

29. Complete the following statement.

In sucrose, the two monosaccharide units are held together by ___*A*___ linkage between C_1 of ___*B*___ and C_2 of ___*C*___.

A = ______________ *B* = ______________ *C* = ______________

30. Consider the following statements.

I. Sucrose is dextrorotatory and after hydrolysis, it gives dextrorotatory glucose and dextrorotatory fructose.

II. Hydrolysis of sucrose results to change in the sign of rotation therefore it is also known as invert sugar.

Which of the following statement(s) is/are correct regarding sucrose ?

(a) Only I ☐ (b) Only II ☐

(c) Both I and II ☐ (d) None of these ☐

31. Which one of the following statement is correct about sucrose?

(a) It can reduce Tollen's reagent, however cannot reduce Fehling's reagent. ☐

(b) It undergoes mutarotation like glucose and fructose. ☐

(c) It undergoes inversion in the configuration on hydrolysis. ☐

(d) It is laevorotatory in nature. ☐

32. Monosaccharides combine/react to form disaccharides. Write the names of disaccharides formed by the following monosaccharides

(i) α-D-glucose and α-D-glucose; Disaccharide = ________________

(ii) β-D-galactose and β-D-glucose; Disaccharide = ________________

***33.** Consider the following structure.

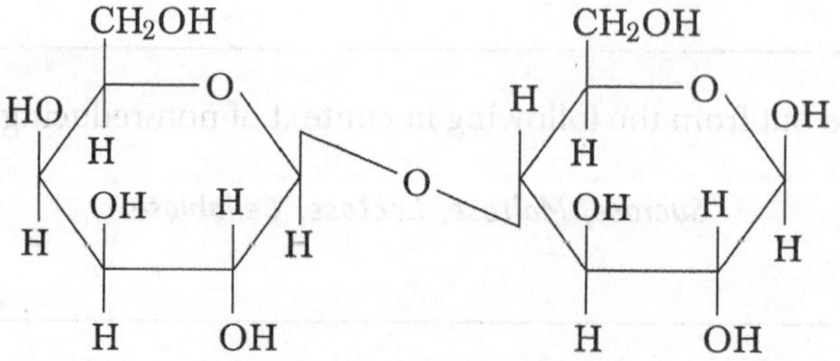

X *Y*

Lactose (milk sugar) is composed of *X* and *Y*. Identify *X* and *Y*.

X = ________________ *Y* = ________________

34. Which of the following is the monomer unit of starch ?

(a) β-glucose ☐ (b) α-glucose ☐

(c) β-galactose ☐ (d) α-fructose ☐

35. Starch consist of two components *A* and *B*, where *A* is water soluble component, while *B* is water insoluble component and it constitutes about 80-85% of starch.
Identify *A* and *B*.

A. ________________ *B*. ________________

36. ________________ (Amylose/Amylopectin) is a long branched polymer of α-D-glucose units.

37. Write the names of the following.

(i) Polysaccharide which is predominant constituent of the cell wall of a plant cell. _____

(ii) Carbohydrate which is stored in animal body. ____________

38. Cellulose is a polysaccharide composed of

(a) β-D-galactose unit and β-D-glucose unit ☐

(b) β-D-glucose units which are joined together by glycosidic linkage between C_1 of one glucose unit and C_4 of next glucose unit. ☐

(c) β-D-glucose units which are joined together by glycosidic linkage between C_2 of one glucose unit and C_3 of next glucose unit. ☐

(d) Both (a) and (c) ☐

39. Fill in the blanks with the appropriate choice.

(i) ____________ is also known as animal starch. (Glycogen/Cellulose)

(ii) Glycogen is present in ____________ of animals. (muscles/kidneys)

40. Identify '*X*' from the given statement.

When body needs energy or when body is not getting glucose, then compound (*X*) breaks down to release glucose into the bloodstream.

X = ____________

41. Enlist any three uses of carbohydrates in industries.

(i) ____________

(ii) ____________

(iii) ____________

42. Mention the two aldopentoses which are present in nucleic acids.

(i) ____________ (ii) ____________

43. Out of glycogen and cellulose, which one is

(i) found in yeast and fungi ____________

(ii) found in cell wall of plant cells ____________

TOPIC 2

Proteins

NCERT Pg 290-295

44. Biomolecule present in milk, cheese, pulses, peanuts etc., are ____________ (carbohydrates/proteins).

45. On hydrolysis of proteins, the type of amino acids obtained are

(a) β-amino acids ☐ (b) α-amino acids ☐

(c) γ-amino acids ☐ (d) All of these ☐

46. Consider the following statements.

I. Depending on relative number of amino and carboxyl groups, amino acids are classified as acidic, basic or neutral.

II. Amino acids which can be synthesised in the body are called essential amino acids.

Which of the above statement(s) is/are incorrect ?

(a) Only I ☐ (b) Only II ☐

(c) Both I and II ☐ (c) Neither I nor II ☐

---

47. Separate essential and non-essential amino acids from the following.

Glycine, Valine, Leucine, Glutamine, Tyrosine, Lysine, Tryptophan, Serine, Cysteine

---

48. The behaviour shown by amino acids in Zwitter ionic form is

(a) Acidic ☐ (b) Basic ☐

(c) Neutral ☐ (d) Amphoteric ☐

49. Pick the odd one out from the following with respect to optical activity.

Tyrosine, Lysine, Glycine, Valine, Serine

---

50. Consider the following reaction between two molecules of different amino acids.

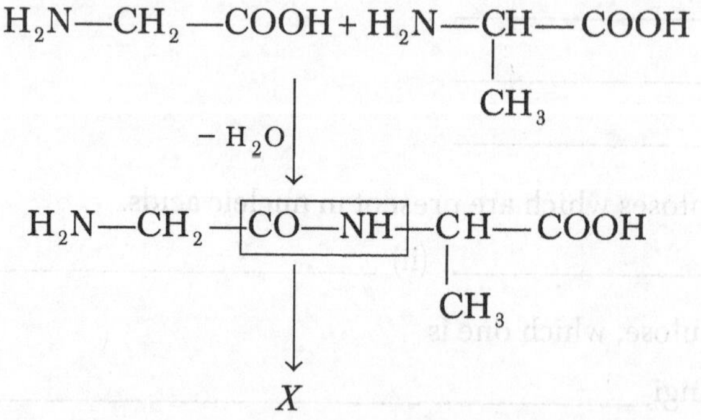

(i) Here, *X* linkage is known as ________________.

(ii) The product formed is ________ (tripeptide/dipeptide).

51. Give the name of two amino acids which combines to form glycylalanine.

(i) ________________ (ii) ________________

52. Number of amino acids from the following which are acidic in nature,

Glycine, Aspartate, Glutamate, Valine, Isoleucine

(a) 1 ☐ (b) 2 ☐

(c) 3 ☐ (d) 4 ☐

53. Check whether the given statement is correct or incorrect.
Insulin contains 21 amino acids.

True ☐ False ☐

54. Classify the following into acidic, basic and neutral amino acids.

Arginine, Aspartic acid, Glycine, Glutaric acid

____

55. Tick the correct one.

(i) Keratin – Fibrous proteins ☐ Globular proteins ☐

(ii) Albumin – Fibrous proteins ☐ Globular proteins ☐

56. Give any two examples of fibrous proteins present in our body.

(i) ______________ (ii) ______________

57. Proteins are found to have two different types of secondary structures, i.e. α-helix and β-pleated sheet structure, α-helix structure of protein is stabilised by

(a) van der Waals' forces ☐ (b) Peptide bonds ☐

(c) Dipole-dipole interaction ☐ (d) Hydrogen bonds ☐

____

58. Match the Column I (type of proteins) with Column II (types of bonding present).

Column I (Protein)		Column II (Bonding)	
A.	Fibrous	1.	Intermolecular H-bond
B.	α-helix	2.	Hydrogen and disulphide
C.	β-pleated	3.	Intramolecular hydrogen bond

A. ______________ B. ______________ C. ______________

59. Enlist the factors (forces) which stabilise the 2° and 3° structures of proteins.

(i) ______________ (ii) ______________

(iii) ______________ (iv) ______________

60. Each polypeptide in a protein has amino acids linked with each other in a specific sequence. This sequence of amino acids is said to be the ______________.

(a) primary structure of protein ☐ (b) secondary structure of protein ☐

(c) tertiary structure of protein ☐ (d) quaternary structure of protein ☐

61. During denaturation, secondary and tertiary structures are destroyed but primary structure remain intact.

True ☐ False ☐

62. Choose the factor which is not responsible for denaturation of proteins.

Change in pH, Temperature change, Organic solvents, Mass of protein.

____

***63.** Which of the following statements about denaturation are correct?

I. In denaturation, globules unfold in protein and helix get uncoiled. As the result the protein loses its biological activity.

II. Denaturation affects primary structure which gets distorted.

III. Denaturation leads to conversion of double strand of DNA into single strand.

IV. Coagulation of egg white on boiling and curdling of milk are examples of denaturation of proteins.

Mark (✓) and (✗) under correct and incorrect with respect to given statements.

	Correct	Incorrect
I.	________	________
II.	________	________
III.	________	________
IV.	________	________

64. Which of the following statement is correct?

(a) Fibrous proteins are generally soluble in water. ☐

(b) Albumin is an example of fibrous proteins. ☐

(c) In fibrous proteins, the structure is stabilised by hydrogen bonds and disulphide bonds. ☐

(d) pH does not affect the primary structure of protein. ☐

TOPIC 3
Enzymes

NCERT Pg 295

65. The conversion of maltose into glucose is possible by enzyme ________________.

***66.** Which of the following statement regarding enzymes is incorrect?

(a) Enzymes are usually globular proteins. ☐

(b) Enzymes are biocatalyst. ☐

(c) Enzymes are very specific for a particular reaction and particular substrate. ☐

(d) Enzymes increases magnitude of activation energy. ☐

67. Activation energy for acid hydrolysis of sucrose is 2.15 kJ mol^{-1} in the absence of enzyme.

True ☐ False ☐

***68.** Choose the appropriate word from the following to complete the sentences.

Activation energy, Sucrose, Glucose, Biocatalyst, Chemical energy, Antioxidants

Enzymes are ___A___ which reduces the magnitude of ___B___. ___C___ helps in acid hydrolysis of sucrose while maltase catalyses hydrolysis of maltose into ___D___.

A = ____________ B = ____________

C = ____________ D = ____________

TOPIC 4

Vitamins

NCERT Pg 295-297

69. Name the following.

(i) Vitamin which is an acid ____________

(ii) Vitamin which can be synthesised in human body. ____________

70. Pick the odd one out on the basis of fat solubility.

Vitamin-D, Vitamin-A, Vitamin-E, Vitamin-K, Vitamin-C

____

71. Complete the following analogy.

Ascorbic acid : Vitamin C : : Pyridoxine : X

X = ____________

***72.** Match the vitamins given in Column I with deficiency diseases given in Column II.

	Column I (Vitamins)		Column II (Diseases)
A.	Vitamin-A	1.	Scurvy
B.	Vitamin-B_{12}	2.	Xerophthalmia
C.	Vitamin-C	3.	Muscular weakness
D.	Vitamin-E	4.	Pernicious anaemia

A. ____________ B. ____________

C. ____________ D. ____________

73. Which of the following statement is incorrect?

(a) Deficiency of riboflavin causes cheilosis. ☐

(b) Deficiency of vitamin-B_6 present in egg yolk can cause convulsion. ☐

(c) Rickets and osteomalacia are disease caused by deficiency of vitamin-K. ☐

(d) Deficiency of vitamin-A can cause night blindness. ☐

74. Which of the following vitamin helps in blood clotting?

(a) Vitamin-A ☐ (b) Vitamin-C ☐

(c) Vitamin-D ☐ (d) Vitamin-K ☐

75. Which of the following acids is a vitamin?

(a) Aspartic acid ☐ (b) Ascorbic acid ☐

(c) Adipic acid ☐ (d) Saccharic acid ☐

76. Number of vitamins from the following which are fat-soluble are

Retinol, Tocopherol, Ascorbic acid, Phylloquinone, Biotin, Cobalamin, Calciferol

(a) 2 ☐ (b) 3 ☐ (c) 4 ☐ (d) 5 ☐

TOPIC 5

Nucleic Acids

NCERT Pg 297-300

77. Particles (threads) in nucleus of the cell, responsible for heredity are called _A_ which are made up of proteins and _B_. Write *A* and *B*

A = ____________________ *B* = ____________________

78. Consider the following statements.

I. The complete hydrolysis of DNA yields β-D-2-deoxyribose sugar, phosphoric acid and sulphur contains heterocylic compound called bases.

II. RNA contains four bases adenine, guanine, cytosine and uracil.

Which of the following statement(s) is/are correct?

(a) Only I ☐ (b) Only II ☐

(c) Both I and II ☐ (d) Neither I nor II ☐

79. Tick the correct structure of pentose sugar present in DNA.

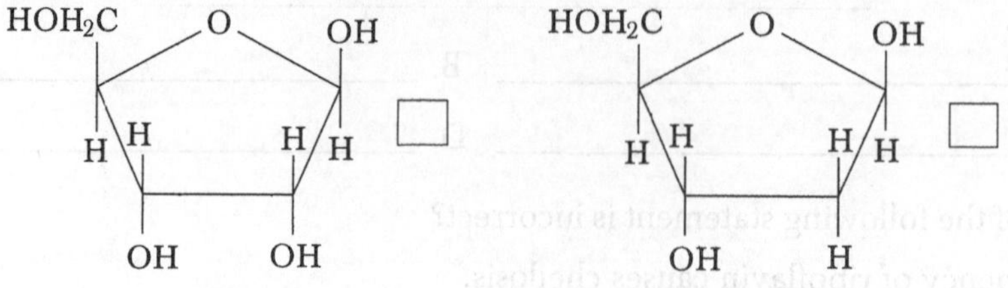

(*A*) (*B*)

80. Nucleic acids are the polymers of ________.

(a) nucleosides ☐ (b) nucleotides ☐

(c) bases ☐ (d) sugars ☐

81. Name the linkage through which nucleotides are joined together with 5′ and 3′ carbon atoms of pentose sugars.

____

82. When nucleoside is linked to phosphoric acid at 3′-position of sugar moeity, it results in nucleotide.

True ☐ False ☐

83. Consider the following structure and answer the questions in one or two words

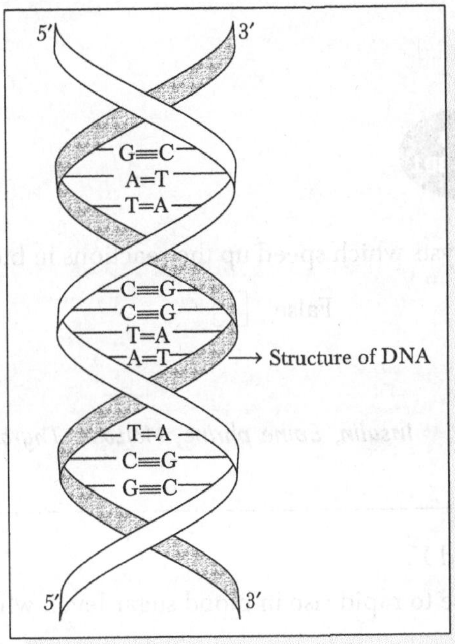

(i) Who gave double helix structure of DNA? ______________

(ii) The bond which holds two nucleic acid chains together is ______________.

84. Identify X and complete the following analogy.

Adenine : Thymine : : Cytosine : X.

X = ______________

85. Number of nitrogenous bases from the following which are purines.

Adenine, Guanine, Cytosine, Thymine, Uracil

(a) 2 ☐ (b) 3 ☐

(c) 4 ☐ (d) 1 ☐

____

86. Enlist any four uses of DNA fingerprinting.

(i) ______________ (ii) ______________

(iii) ______________ (iv) ______________

87. Select the correct one for the given choices with respect to RNA and DNA.

(i) Capable of self duplication. (RNA/DNA) ____________

(ii) Protein synthesis. (RNA/DNA) ____________

(iii) Message for synthesis of a particular protein. (RNA/DNA). ____________

88. Write the products formed when a nucleotide from the DNA containing thymine is hydrolysed.

____

TOPIC 6 Hormones

NCERT Pg 300-301

89. Hormones are biocatalysts which speed up the reactions in bio-system.

True ☐ False ☐

90. Pick the odd one out.

Insulin, Epine phrine, Maltose, Thyroxine

____

91. Identify hormone *X* and *Y*.

X is released in response to rapid rise in blood sugar level, whereas *Y* is released to increase the blood sugar level.

X = ____________ *Y* – ____________

92. Which hormone is an iodinated derivative of amino acid tyrosine?

(a) Thyroxine ☐ (b) Epinephrine ☐

(c) Glycogen ☐ (d) Insulin ☐

93. Match the following hormones with the respective diseases.

Column I (Hormone)	Column II (Disease)
A. Insulin	1. Addison's disease
B. Thyroxine (low level)	2. Diabetes
C. Corticoids	3. Hyperthyroidism
D. Thyroxine (high level)	4. Goitre

A. ____________ B. ____________

C. ____________ D. ____________

94. Which of the following is a peptide hormone?

(a) Glucagon ☐ (b) Testosterone ☐

(c) Thyroxine ☐ (d) Adrenaline ☐

95. Name the hormone.

(i) Responsible for development of secondary male characteristics. ______

(ii) Responsible for carbohydrate metabolism. ______

96. Which hormone is responsible for preparing uterus for implantation of fertilized egg?

(a) Estradiol ☐ (b) Glucocorticoids ☐

(c) Thyroxine ☐ (d) Progesterone ☐

Assertion-Reason Questions

Given below are two statements, one is labelled as Assertion (A) and other is labelled as Reason (R). Select the most appropriate answer from the options given below.

(a) Both A and R are true and R is correct the explanation of A.
(b) Both A and R are true but R is not the correct explanation of A.
(c) A is true but R is false.
(d) A is false but R is true.

1. **Assertion** (A) Pentaacetate of glucose does not react with hydroxylamine.
Reason (R) Glucose on reaction with $NaHSO_3$, does not form hydrogen sulphite addition product.

(a) ☐ (b) ☐ (c) ☐ (d) ☐

2. **Assertion** (A) Melting points and solubility in water of amino acids are generally higher than that of corresponding halo acids.
Reason (R) Dipolar behaviour due to proton acceptor and proton donor moiety results in strong electrostatic interaction.

(a) ☐ (b) ☐ (c) ☐ (d) ☐

3. **Assertion** (A) Cellulose is a polysaccharide that provides structural support to plants.
Reason (R) Cellulose is composed of β-D-glucose units linked by glycosidic bonds.

(a) ☐ (b) ☐ (c) ☐ (d) ☐

4. **Assertion** (A) Amino acids are amphoteric in nature.
Reason (R) Amino acids can act as both acids and bases due to the presence of both carboxyl and amino groups.

(a) ☐ (b) ☐ (c) ☐ (d) ☐

5. **Assertion** (A) Water present in the egg disappears after boiling the egg.
Reason (R) Protein present inside the egg get denatured and coagulate which absorb all water present.

(a) ☐ (b) ☐ (c) ☐ (d) ☐

6. **Assertion** (A) Denaturation of proteins involves the disruption of their secondary and tertiary structures.

Reason (R) Denaturation leads to the loss of biological activity of proteins.

(a) ☐ (b) ☐ (c) ☐ (d) ☐

7. **Assertion** (A) Vitamins are essential micronutrients required in small amounts for various physiological functions.

Reason (R) Vitamins cannot be synthesized by the human body and must be obtained from the diet.

(a) ☐ (b) ☐ (c) ☐ (d) ☐

8. **Assertion** (A) Vitamin-D can be stored in our body.

Reason (R) Vitamin-D is fat soluble vitamin. **[NCERT Exemplar]**

(a) ☐ (b) ☐ (c) ☐ (d) ☐

9. **Assertion** (A) RNA has double strand helix structure.

Reason (R) When RNA is hydrolysed, there is no relationship among the quantities of different bases obtained.

(a) ☐ (b) ☐ (c) ☐ (d) ☐

10. **Assertion** (A) Enzymes are highly specific in their action.

Reason (R) The active site of an enzyme has a unique shape and structure that is complementary to its substrate.

(a) ☐ (b) ☐ (c) ☐ (d) ☐

Case Based Questions

1. Carbohydrates are essential biomolecules that serve as our primary energy source. They come in various forms, ranging from simple sugars like glucose and fructose to complex polysaccharides like starch and cellulose. The sweetness of different sugars varies, with fructose being the sweetest and lactose the least sweet among common sugars. The human body processes these carbohydrates through a series of enzymatic reactions, ultimately converting them into glucose, which is used for energy production.

(i) Which of the following is the sweetest natural sugar?

(a) Glucose ☐ (b) Sucrose ☐

(c) Fructose ☐ (d) Lactose ☐

(ii) Which polysaccharide serves as the primary energy storage molecule in plants?

(a) Cellulose ☐ (b) Glycogen ☐

(c) Starch ☐ (d) Chitin ☐

(iii) Which of the following enzymes is involved in the breakdown of starch?

(a) Amylase ☐ (b) Lactase ☐

(c) Sucrase ☐ (d) Maltase ☐

(iv) Which of the following carbohydrates is a non-reducing sugar?

(a) Maltose ☐ (b) Lactose ☐

(c) Sucrose ☐ (d) Glucose ☐

2. Proteins are complex biomolecules composed of amino acids linked together by peptide bonds. They play crucial roles in various biological processes, serving as enzymes, hormones, antibodies, and structural components. The sequence of amino acids in a protein determines its unique three-dimensional structure and function. Proteins can be denatured by factors like heat, pH changes, and chemicals, leading to the loss of their biological activity.

(i) Which of the following is the bond that links amino acids in a protein?

(a) Glycosidic bond ☐ (b) Ester bond ☐

(c) Peptide bond ☐ (d) Hydrogen bond ☐

(ii) Which level of protein structure is characterized by the formation of alpha-helices and beta-sheets?

(a) Primary ☐ (b) Secondary ☐

(c) Tertiary ☐ (d) Quaternary ☐

(iii) Which of the following is a fibrous protein?

(a) Insulin ☐ (b) Haemoglobin ☐

(c) Collagen ☐ (d) Amylase ☐

(iv) Which of the following factors can denature proteins?

(a) High temperature ☐ (b) Extreme pH ☐

(c) Heavy metals ☐ (d) All of these ☐

COMPETITION EDGE UP

1. Which of the following is the correct structure of L-glucose? [NCERT (New) Pg 283, JEE Main 2024]

(a)
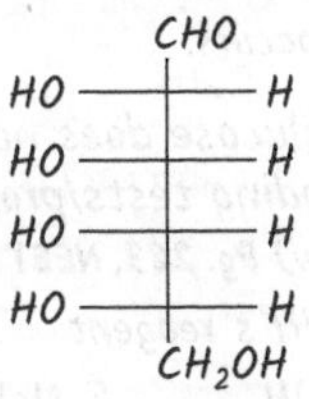
☐

(b)
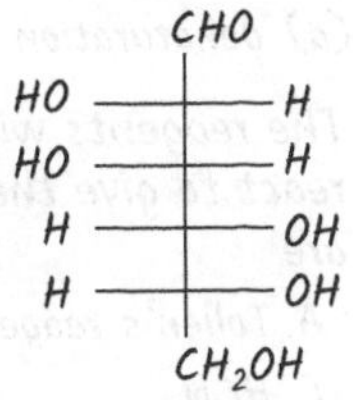
☐

(c)
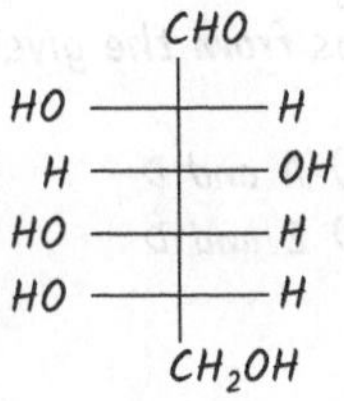
☐

(d)
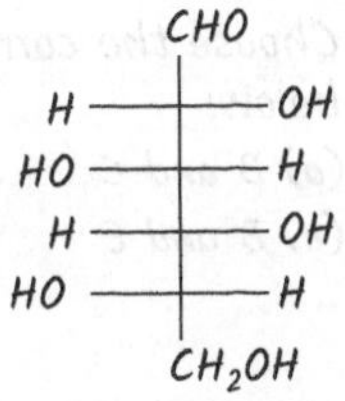
☐

2. The incorrect statement about glucose is [NCERT (New) Pg 283, JEE Main 2024]

(a) Glucose is an aldohexose. ☐

(b) Glucose is one of the monomer unit in sucrose. ☐

(c) Glucose is soluble in water because of having aldehyde functional group. ☐

(d) Glucose remains in multiple isomeric form in its aqueous solution. ☐

3. Sugar which does not give reddish brown precipitate with Fehling's reagent, is [NCERT (New) Pg 287, JEE Main 2024]

(a) maltose ☐

(b) lactose ☐

(c) glucose ☐

(d) sucrose ☐

4.

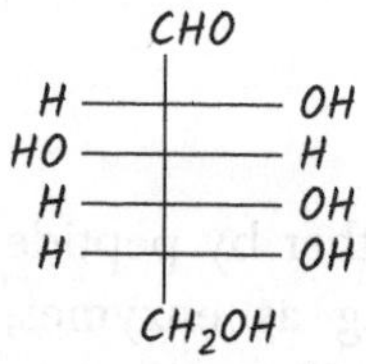

The incorrect statement regarding the given structure is **[NCERT (New) Pg 283, JEE Main 2024]**

(a) will coexist in equilibrium with 2 other cyclic structure ☐

(b) has 4 asymmetric carbon atom ☐

(c) despite the presence of —CHO does not give Schiff's test ☐

(d) can be oxidised to a dicarboxylic acid with Br_2 water ☐

5. Match List I with List II.

[NCERT (New) Pg 286, JEE Main 2024]

	List I		List II
A.	α- Glucose and α- Galactose	I.	Functional isomers
B.	α- Glucose and β- Glucose	II.	Homologous
C.	α- Glucose and α- Fructose	III.	Anomers
D.	α- Glucose and α- Ribose	IV.	Epimers

Choose the correct answer from the options given below:

(a) A- III, B- IV, C- II, D- I ☐

(b) A- III, B- IV, C- I, D- II ☐

(c) A- IV, B- III, C- II, D- I ☐

(d) A- IV, B-III, C- I, D- II ☐

6. Match List-I with List-II.

[NCERT (New) Pg 283, JEE Main 2024]

	List-I		List-II
A.	Glucose/ $NaHCO_3/\Delta$	I.	Gluconic acid
B.	Glucose/HNO_3	II.	No reaction
C.	Glucose HI/Δ	III.	n-hexane
D.	Glucose/bromine water	IV.	Saccharic acid

Choose the correct answer from the options given below.

	A	B	C	D	
(a)	II	IV	III	I	☐
(b)	IV	I	III	II	☐
(c)	III	II	I	VI	☐
(d)	I	IV	III	II	☐

7. The incorrect statements regarding enzymes are **[NCERT (New) Pg 295, JEE Main 2024]**

A. Enzymes are biocatalysts.

B. Enzymes are non-specific and can catalyse different kinds of reactions.

C. Most enzymes are globular proteins.

D. Enzyme-oxidase catalyses the hydrolysis of maltose into glucose.

Choose the correct answer from the options given below

(a) B and D ☐

(b) B and C ☐

(c) A, B and C ☐

(d) B, C and D ☐

8. Type of amino acids obtained by hydrolysis of proteins is **[NCERT (New) Pg 294, JEE Main 2024]**

(a) γ ☐ (b) α ☐

(c) β ☐ (d) δ ☐

9. Coagulation of egg, on heating is because of **[NCERT (New) Pg 294, JEE Main 2024]**

(a) biological property of protein remains unchanged ☐

(b) the secondary structure of protein remains unchanged ☐

(c) breaking of the peptide linkage in the primary structure of protein occurs ☐

(d) denaturation of protein occurs. ☐

10. The reagents with which glucose does not react to give the corresponding tests/products are **[NCERT (New) Pg. 283, NEET 2024]**

A. Tollen's reagent B. Schiff's reagent

C. HCN D. NH_2OH E. $NaHSO_3$

Choose the correct options from the given below:

(a) B and C ☐ (b) A and D ☐

(c) B and E ☐ (d) E and D ☐

11. Given below are two statements.

Statement I A unit formed by the attachment of a base to 1'-position of sugar is known as nucleoside.

Statement II When nucleoside is linked to phosphorus acid at 5'-position of sugar moiety, we get nucleotide.

In the light of the above statements, choose the correct answer from the options given below **[NCERT (New) Pg 298, NEET 2023]**

(a) Both Statement I and Statement II are false. ☐
(b) Statement I is true but Statement II is false. ☐
(c) Statement I is false but Statement II is true. ☐
(d) Both Statement I and Statement II are true. ☐

12. The incorrect statement regarding enzymes is **[NCERT (New) Pg 295, NEET 2021]**

(a) Like chemical catalysts enzymes reduce the activation energy of bio processes. ☐
(b) Enzymes are polysaccharides. ☐
(c) Enzymes are very specific for a particular reaction and substrate. ☐
(d) Enzymes are biocatalysts. ☐

13. The RBC deficiency is deficiency disease of **[NCERT (New) Pg. 296, NEET 2021]**

(a) Vitamin B_2 ☐ (b) Vitamin B_{12} ☐
(c) Vitamin B_6 ☐ (d) Vitamin B_1 ☐

14. Sucrose on hydrolysis gives **[NCERT (New) Pg. 287, NEET 2020]**

(a) β-D-glucose + α-D-fructose ☐
(b) α-D-glucose + β-D-glucose ☐
(c) α-D-glucose + β-D-fructose ☐
(d) α-D-fructose + β-D-fructose ☐

15. The reaction of concentrated sulphuric acid with carbohydrates ($C_{12}H_{22}O_{11}$) is an example of **[NCERT (New) Pg. 283, NEET (Oct.) 2020]**

(a) dehydration ☐
(b) oxidation ☐
(c) reduction ☐
(d) sulphonation ☐

16. Deficiency of which vitamin causes osteomalacia? **[NCERT (New) Pg. 296, NEET (Oct.) 2020]**

(a) Vitamin A ☐
(b) Vitamin D ☐
(c) Vitamin K ☐
(d) Vitamin E ☐

17. Which of the following statements is not true about glucose? **[NCERT (New) Pg. 283, NEET (Oct.) 2020]**

(a) It is an aldohexose. ☐
(b) It contains five hydroxyl groups. ☐
(c) It is a reducing sugar. ☐
(d) It is an aldopentose. ☐

NCERT
REVISION WORK BOOK

Competition Connect

p-Block Elements

Scan and take Chapter Test

TOPIC 1

Introduction & Group 13 Elements : The Boron Family

NCERT Pg 315-320

1. The number of groups of elements in *p*-block is ______.

2. The general electronic configuration of *p*-block elements is

(a) $ns^2 np^{1-6}$ ☐ (b) ns^{1-2} ☐

(c) $(n-1)d^{1-10} ns^{1-2}$ ☐ (d) $(n-2)f^{1-14} (n-1) d^{1-10} ns^{1-2}$ ☐

3. The first member of each of the groups of *p*-block elements differs in many respects from the other members of their respective groups.

True ☐ False ☐

4. Mention the general oxidation states of

(i) group 16 ______ (ii) group 18 ______

***5.** Consider the following statements,

I. The non-metallic character of the elements decreases down the group.

II. The heaviest element in each *p*-block group is the most non-metallic element.

III. The compounds formed by highly reactive non-metals with highly reactive metals are generally ionic.

Mark (✓) and (✗) under the correct and incorrect with respect to given statements.

	Correct	Incorrect
I.	______	______
II.	______	______
III.	______	______

6. The vacant orbital used by the third period elements of *p*-block in order to expand their covalency above four is ______.

Concepts of all questions bearing * are important for JEE/NEET/CUET.

7. Aluminium can expand its covalency and form ions like ________ ($[AlF_7]^{4-}$ / $[AlF_6]^{3-}$).

8. Mention the types of π-bonds formed in the compounds of heavier elements of *p*-block.

____

9. The ground state electronic configuration of boron is ________________.

10. Boron occurs mainly as orthoboric acid, borax and kernite.

True ☐ False ☐

11. The relative abundance of ^{10}B and ^{11}B isotopes in nature is ______ and ______ respectively.

12. Match the following columns.

Column I (Element)	Column II (Abundance in Earth crust)
A. Oxygen	1. Less than 0.0001% by mass
B. Silicon	2. Most abundant metal
C. Boron	3. 45.5% by mass
D. Aluminium	4. 27.7% by mass

A. ________________ B. ________________

C. ________________ D. ________________

***13.** Which of the following is the correct order of atomic radii in group 13 elements ?

(a) B < Ga < Al < Tl < In ☐ (b) B < Al < Ga < In < Tl ☐

(c) B < Al < In < Ga < Tl ☐ (d) B < Ga < Al < In < Tl ☐

***14.** The order of ionisation enthalpies of group 13 elements is

(a) $\Delta_i H_1 < \Delta_i H_2 < \Delta_i H_3$ ☐ (b) $\Delta_i H_1 > \Delta_i H_2 > \Delta_i H_3$ ☐

(c) $\Delta_i H_1 < \Delta_i H_2 > \Delta_i H_3$ ☐ (d) $\Delta_i H_1 > \Delta_i H_2 < \Delta_i H_3$ ☐

15. Boron is extremely hard and has unusually high melting point because of its

(a) small size ☐ (b) high ionisation enthalpy ☐

(c) low electronegativity ☐ (d) very strong crystalline lattice ☐

16. Which amongst of these correctly depicts the physical properties of boron?

I. Extremely hard solid. II. Has low density.

III. Melting point greater than 2450 K. IV. Low electrical conductivity.

V. Shows allotropy.

(a) I and II ☐ (b) III, IV and V ☐

(c) I, II, III, IV and V ☐ (d) I, II and III ☐

17. The relative stability of +1 oxidation state of group 13 elements follows the order.

(a) Al < Ga < Tl < In ☐ (b) Al < Ga < In < Tl ☐

(c) Tl < In < Ge < Al ☐ (d) Ga < Al < In < Tl ☐

***18.** Which of the following is a Lewis acid ? **[NCERT Exemplar]**

(a) $AlCl_3$ ☐ (b) $MgCl_2$ ☐

(c) $CaCl_2$ ☐ (d) $BaCl_2$ ☐

19. Draw a structure of $BCl_3 \cdot NH_3$. ____________.

20. Write the value of x, y and z in the given structure of dimer $AlCl_3$.

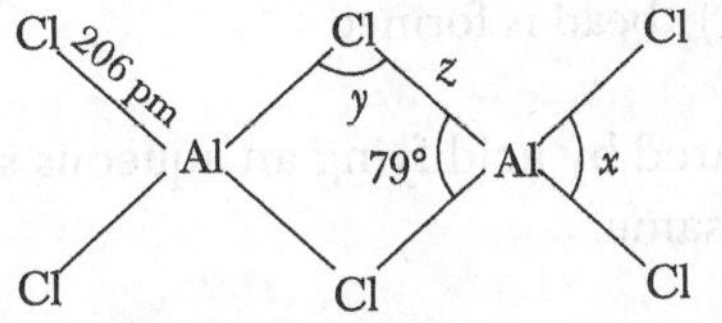

$x =$ ____________ $y =$ ____________ $z =$ ____________

21. Using the following information choose the right one from the brackets.
Standard electrode potential values, $E°$ for Al^{3+}/Al is −1.66 V and that of Tl^{3+}/Tl is +1.26 V.

(i) More stable in solution (Tl^+/Tl^{3+}) ____________.

(ii) More electropositive (Al/Tl) ____________.

***22.** Which of the following oxides is acidic in nature ? **[NCERT Exemplar]**

(a) B_2O_3 ☐ (b) Al_2O_3 ☐ (c) Ga_2O_3 ☐ (d) In_2O_3 ☐

23. Aluminium reacts with concentrated nitric acid and liberates dihydrogen.

True ☐ False ☐

24. Complete the following reaction,

$$2Al(s) + 2NaOH(aq) + 6H_2O(l) \longrightarrow \_\_\_\_\_\_ + 3H_2(g)$$

TOPIC 2

Important Trends and Anomalous Properties of Boron and Some Important Compounds of Boron

NCERT Pg 320-322

25. Boron is unable to form BF_6^{3-} ion because of the ____________.

26. The correct formula of borax is

(a) $Na_2[B_4O_5(OH)_4]\cdot 7H_2O$ ☐ (b) $Na_2[B_4O_5(OH)_6]\cdot 8H_2O$ ☐

(c) $Na_2[B_4O_5(OH)_4]\cdot 8H_2O$ ☐ (d) $Na_2[B_4O_5(OH)_3]\cdot 8H_2O$ ☐

27. Write the balanced chemical equation for the reaction that takes place, when borax dissolves in water.

____

28. Borax bead test can be used to identify ________ (transition metal ions/alkali metal ions) in the laboratory.

29. When borax is heated in a Bunsen burner flame with CoO on a loop of platinum wire,

(a) Blue coloured $Co(BO_2)_2$ bead is formed ☐

(b) Yellow coloured $Co(BO_2)_2$ bead is formed ☐

(c) Blue coloured $Co(BO_2)_2$ bead is formed ☐

(d) Green coloured $Co(BO_2)_2$ bead is formed ☐

30. Boric acid is usually prepared by acidifying an aqueous solution of borax. Write a balanced chemical equation for the same.

____

31. Boric acid is a weak monobasic acid.

True ☐ False ☐

32. Heating orthoboric acid above 370 K leads to partial removal of water to yield ________.

33. Which of the following is a principle oxide of boron?

(a) B_2O ☐ (b) B_2O_3 ☐

(c) HBO_2 ☐ (d) B_2O_6 ☐

34. Show with the help of equations, how boric oxide can be obtained from orthoboric acid?

____

35. Boric acid is considered as a weak acid because

I. it is not able to release H^+ ions on its own.

II. it receives OH^- ions from water.

Which one of the given statement(s) is/are correct ?

(a) Only I ☐ (b) Only II ☐

(c) Both I and II ☐ (d) Neither I nor II ☐

36. Write the balanced equation for

(i) the laboratory preparation of diborane. ________

(ii) the preparation of diborane on an industrial scale. ________

37. Compound X is a colourless, highly toxic gas with a boiling point of 180 K. It catches fire spontaneously upon exposure to air. It burns in oxygen releasing an enormous amount of energy. What is X?

____

38. Boranes are readily hydrolysed by water to give boric acid.

True ☐ False ☐

***39.** Consider the figures of diborane given below and answer the following.

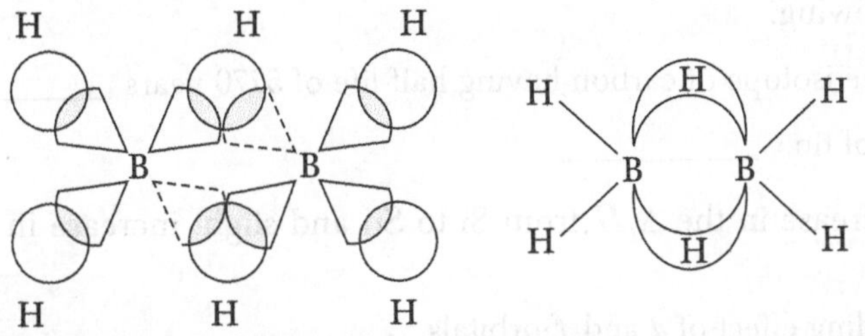

(i) In diborane, each B-atom uses ____________ (sp / sp^3) hybrid orbitals for bonding.

(ii) The terminal B—H bonds are normal ____________ bonds but the two bridge bonds are ____________ bonds. (Use : 2-centre-2-electron and 3-centre-2-electron).

40. Write a balanced equation for the preparation of metal borohydrides.

____

41. Name the compounds of boron which are used as reducing agents in organic synthesis.

____

42. Mention any two uses of borax.

(i) ______________________________

(ii) ______________________________

TOPIC 3

Uses of Boron and Aluminium and Their Compounds

NCERT Pg 322

43. Aluminium cannot form alloys with

(a) Cu ☐ (b) Zn ☐

(c) Li ☐ (d) Si ☐

44. The domestic use of aluminium is reduced considerably because of its ____________ (corrosive/toxic) nature.

TOPIC 4

Group 14 Elements : The Carbon Family

NCERT Pg 322-325

45. Enlist three isotopes of naturally occurring carbon atom.

(i) ______________

(ii) ______________

(iii) ______________

46. Name the following.

(i) Radioactive isotope of carbon having half-life of 5770 years ________.

(ii) Chief ore of tin ________.

47. The small decrease in the $\Delta_i H$ from Si to Sn and slight increase in $\Delta_i H$ from Sn to Pb is because of

I. poor shielding effect of *d* and *f*-orbitals.

II. increase in size of the atom.

Which of the following reason is/are correct ?

(a) Only I ☐ (b) Only II ☐

(c) Both I and II ☐ (d) Neither I nor II ☐

48. The elements of group 14 are slightly more electronegative than those of group 13.

True ☐ False ☐

***49.** Classify the following elements into metals, non-metals and metalloids.

C, Si, Pb, Ge, Sn

____

50. Which of the following species is not stable?

(a) $[GeCl_6]^{2-}$ ☐ (b) $[Sn(OH)_6]^{2-}$ ☐ (c) $[SiCl_6]^{2-}$ ☐ (d) $[SiF_6]^{2-}$ ☐

51. The hybridisation of central atom in the following compounds is

(i) SiF_6^{2-} = ______________ (ii) $[GeCl_6]^{2-}$ = ______________

***52.** The elements of group 14 that forms acidic oxides are ______________.

53. Which amongst the following reacts with water (steam)?

(a) Carbon ☐ (b) Germanium ☐

(c) Tin ☐ (d) Lead ☐

54. Select the odd one which is not hydrolysed easily by water.

CCl_4, $PbCl_4$, $SiCl_4$, $GeCl_4$

____

TOPIC 5

Important Trends and Anomalous Behaviour of Carbon & Allotropes of Carbon

NCERT Pg 325-327

55. Heavier elements do not form $p\pi$-$p\pi$ bonds because

(a) their atomic orbitals are too large ☐

(b) their atomic orbitals are too small ☐

(c) their atomic orbitals are too large and diffuse to have effective overlapping ☐

(d) Both (a) and (b) ☐

56. The correct order of catenation among group 14 elements is

(a) C > Ge > Si > Sn ☐ (b) C > Si > Ge = Sn ☐

(c) Si > Ge > C > Sn ☐ (d) Si > C = Ge > Sn ☐

57. Arrange the following bonds in increasing order of their bond enthalpy.

C—C, Ge—Ge, Si—Si, Sn—Sn

____

***58.** In diamond and graphite, each carbon atom undergoes ____________ and ____________ hybridisation respectively.

***59.** State whether True or False.

(i) Diamond is covalent, yet it has low melting point.

True ☐ False ☐

(ii) Graphite is used as a dry lubricant in machines.

True ☐ False ☐

***60.** Which amongst the following statements is true about fullerenes?

(a) All carbon atoms in fullerene undergo sp^2-hybridisation. ☐

(b) Each carbon atom forms three sigma bonds with three other carbon atoms. ☐

(c) One electron at each carbon is delocalised in molecular orbitals, which in turn give aromatic character to molecule. ☐

(d) All of the above ☐

***61.** C_{60}, an allotrope of carbon contains

(a) 16 hexagons and 16 pentagons ☐

(b) 20 hexagons and 12 pentagons ☐

(c) 12 hexagons and 20 pentagons ☐

(d) 18 hexagons and 14 pentagons ☐

62. Which allotrope of carbon is thermodynamically most stable? (*Tick the correct one.*)

Graphite ☐ Diamond ☐ Fullerene ☐

TOPIC 6

Some Important Compounds of Carbon and Silicon

NCERT Pg 327-330

63. The mixture of CO and H_2 gas is known as water gas.

True ☐ False ☐

64. Write the chemical equation involved in the formation of producer gas.

____

65. Name the characteristic of CO which enables it to be used in the extraction of many metal oxides from their ores.

____

***66.** CO is a highly poisonous gas because

(a) it leads to coagulation of blood ☐

(b) it is carcinogenic ☐

(c) it forms highly stable complex with haemoglobin ☐

(d) it binds less strongly with haemoglobin than oxygen ☐

67. ____________ helps to maintain the pH of blood between 7.26 - 7.42.

68. Increase in the CO_2 content in the atmosphere leads to increase in __________ (greenhouse effect/acid rain).

69. In CO_2 molecule, carbon atom undergoes _______ hybridisation.

(a) sp ☐ (b) sp^2 ☐ (c) sp^3 ☐ (d) sp^3d ☐

70. Give the resonating structures of CO_2.

____

71. Write the reaction of SiO_2

(i) with NaOH ____________________

(ii) with HF ____________________

72. Name the compound of silicon which has made it possible to develop extremely accurate clocks, modern radio, television broadcasting and mobile radio communications.

____

73. Choose the appropriate one

(i) Kieselghur is ____________ (an amorphous form/a crystalline form) of silica.

(ii) Kieselghur is used in ____________ (filtration/synthesis) plants.

74. ____________ are used as the starting material for the manufacture of silicones.

75. The repeating unit in silicones is

(a) $RSiO$ ☐ (b) R_2SiO ☐ (c) R_3SiO ☐ (d) R_4SiO ☐

76. Complete the following reaction,

$$2CH_3Cl + Si \xrightarrow[570\ K]{Cu\ powder} \underline{\quad A \quad} \xrightarrow[-2HCl]{+2H_2O} \underline{\quad B \quad}$$

77. Which amongst the following properties are true about silicones?

(a) They are water repelling in nature. ☐

(b) They have high thermal stability. ☐

(c) They are resistant to oxidation and chemicals. ☐

(d) All of the above ☐

78. Feldspar is an example of silicate mineral.

True ☐ False ☐

79. The basic structural unit of silicates is ____________.

80. Name two important man-made silicates.

(i) ____________ (ii) ____________

81. Consider the following statements.

I. Aluminosilicates are formed when aluminium atoms replace few silicon atoms in silicon dioxide.

II. Zeolites are used as a catalyst in petrochemical industries.

Which one of the following statement is/are correct ?

(a) Only I ☐

(b) Only II ☐

(c) Both I and II ☐

(d) Neither I nor II ☐

82. Complete the following analogy.
A zeolite which is used to convert alcohol directly into gasoline : *A* :: A chemical substance which is used as ion exchanger in softening hard water : *B*.

A = ____________ *B* = ____________

83. Match the following columns.

Column I (Substances)	Column II (Uses)
A. Silicones	1. Mild antiseptic
B. Graphite	2. Flux
C. Carbon black	3. Crucible
D. Borax	4. Filler in automobile tyres
E. Orthoboric acid	5. Surgical and cosmetic plants

A. ____________ B. ____________

C. ____________ D. ____________

E. ____________

TOPIC 7

Group 15 Elements

NCERT Pg 165-168

84. Write the name of any two metalloids belonging to group 15 elements.

____

85. Nitrogen in the earth crust occurs as Chile saltpetre and Indian saltpetre.

True ☐ False ☐

86. Choose the elements from the given pairs which are present

I. in bones as well as in living cells.

II. in proteins of plants and animals.

(a) As and Sb ☐ (b) P and N ☐

(c) N and Bi ☐ (d) Sb and N ☐

87. Write the complete electronic configuration of moscovium.

____

***88.** Organise the following elements in increasing order of ionic radii.

N, P, As, Sb, Bi

____

89. The correct order of melting points for group 15 element is

(a) N < P < As > Sb > Bi ☐ (b) N < P < As < Sb < Bi ☐

(c) N > P > As > Sb > Bi ☐ (d) N > P > As < Sb < Bi ☐

***90.** Answer the following.

(i) Common oxidation states of *p*-block element are – 5, – 3, + 3 and + 5.

True ☐ False ☐

(ii) Stability of + 5 oxidation state ____________ (increases/decreases) and + 3 state ____________ (increases/decreases) as we go down in group 15 due to inert pair effect.

91. Consider the given reaction and answer the following,

$$3HNO_2 \longrightarrow HNO_3 + H_2O + 2NO$$

(i) Oxidation state of nitrogen increases from + 3 to ______ and decreases from + 3 to ______.

(ii) Write the type of reaction shown above ____________________.

92. Element restricted to maximum covalency of 4 is ____________ (nitrogen/phosphorus).

***93.** Enlist the properties of nitrogen due to which it differs from rest of members.

(i) ____________ (ii) ____________

(iii) ____________ (iv) ____________

94. Consider the following statements.

I. Bond enthalpy of N≡N is very high.

II. Due to high interelectronic repulsion of non-bonding electrons N—N bond is weaker than P—P bond.

Which of the following statement(s) is/are correct?

(a) Only I ☐ (b) Only II ☐

(c) Both I and II ☐ (d) None of these ☐

95. Which of the following element can be involved in *dπ*-*dπ* bonding?

(a) Carbon ☐ (b) Phosphorus ☐

(c) Nitrogen ☐ (d) Both (b) and (c) ☐

96. Arrange the following hydrides.

NH_3, PH_3, AsH_3, SbH_3, BiH_3

(i) In increasing order of stability of hydrides. ____________________

(ii) In decreasing order of reducing character of hydrides. ____________________

***97.** Which one is the strongest reducing agent?

(a) NH_3 ☐ (b) BiH_3 ☐

(c) AsH_3 ☐ (d) PH_3 ☐

98. Due to presence of hydrogen bonding, ____________ (NH_3 /PH_3) has higher boiling point.

***99.** Mention the nature of oxides of the following.

Oxides		**Nature** (Acidic/basic/amphoteric)
(i) Oxides of N and P	—	________
(ii) Oxides of As and Sb	—	________
(iii) Oxides of Bi	—	________

100. Pentahalides of group 15 elements are more covalent than their trihalide because

(a) ion with least charge has large polarising power. ☐

(b) ion with high charge has more polarising power. ☐

(c) covalent character doesn't depend on polarising power. ☐

(d) All of the above ☐

101. Though nitrogen exhibits + 5 oxidation state still it does not form pentahalide as

(a) Its maximum covalency is 4. ☐

(b) It doesn't have *d*-orbitals to expand its covalency. ☐

(c) Both (a) and (b) ☐

(d) None of the above ☐

TOPIC 8
Dinitrogen
NCERT Pg 169-170

102. On heating ammonium dichromate and barium azide separately, we get **[NCERT Exemplar]**

(a) N_2 in both cases. ☐

(b) N_2 with ammonium dichromate and NO with barium azide. ☐

(c) N_2O with ammonium dichromate and N_2 with barium azide. ☐

(d) Both (b) and (c) ☐

103. Nitrogen is relatively inactive element because its ________ (electronegativity/ dissociation energy) is very high.

104. Which of the following is not the correct usage of dinitrogen?

(a) To preserve biological materials. ☐ (b) In cryosurgery ☐

(c) As refrigerant ☐ (d) For welding purpose ☐

105. Complete the following reaction,

$$2NaN_3 \xrightarrow{\Delta} A + B$$

A = ________ B = ________

TOPIC 9

Ammonia & Oxides of Nitrogen

NCERT Pg 170-173

106. $NH_2CONH_2 + 2H_2O \longrightarrow CO_2 + H_2O + X$

In the above reaction, product X is ______________.

107. Choose the correct word given in the bracket with respect to Haber's process.

(i) Temperature required (high/low) ______________.

(ii) Catalyst used (iron oxide/platinised asbestos) ______________.

(iii) Pressure required (low/high)______________.

(iv) To increase rate of attainment of equilibrium compound used (Li_2O /K_2O)

______________.

108. On adding NH_4OH in two salt solutions X and Y, white ppt. and brown ppt. are obtained respectively. Name the compounds X and Y.

X= ______________ Y = ______________

109. Match the following columns.

Column I (Reaction)	Column II (Property)
A. $Cu^{2+} + 4NH_3$	1. Used as fertilizer
B. $AgCl + 2NH_3$	2. Deep blue color compound
C. NH_4NO_3	3. Colourless

A. ______________ B. ______________ C.______________

110. Answer the given questions with respect to the following oxides of nitrogen.

N_2O, NO, N_2O_3, NO_2, N_2O_4, N_2O_5

(i) Which oxide exhibits maximum oxidation state? ______________.

(ii) Out of the above given oxides, which are neutral in nature? ______________.

***111.** On heating lead nitrate, a brown gas (X) is released which is acidic in nature. Identify X.

(a) NO_2 ☐ (b) N_2O_4 ☐ (c) N_2O ☐ (d) N_2O_3 ☐

112. The nitrogen oxide that does not contain N—N bond is

(a) N_2O ☐ (b) N_2O_4 ☐ (c) N_2O_3 ☐ (d) N_2O_5 ☐

113. Which oxide of nitrogen is not a common pollutant introduced into the atmosphere both due to natural and human activity?

(a) N_2O_5 ☐ (b) NO_2 ☐ (c) N_2O ☐ (d) NO ☐

114. Amongst the following, the total number of species that does not form pentahalides is

N, P, As, Sb, Bi

(a) 1 ☐ (b) 2 ☐ (c) 3 ☐ (d) 4 ☐

115. Answer the following.

(i) The oxidation state of nitrogen in N_2O_3 is ____________ .

(ii) NO_2 dimerise to form stable N_2O_4 molecule.

True ☐ False ☐

TOPIC 10

Nitric Acid

NCERT Pg 173-175

116. Identify *P*, *Q*, *R* in the following reactions involved in preparation of nitric acid by Ostwald process.

(i) $P(g) + 5O_2(g) \xrightarrow{\text{Pt/Rh}} 4Q(g) + 6H_2O(g)$

(ii) $2Q(g) + O_2(g) \rightleftharpoons 2R(g)$

(iii) $3R(g) + H_2O(l) \longrightarrow 2HNO_3(aq) + Q(g)$

P = ____________ *Q* = ____________ *R* = ____________

117. In the preparation of HNO_3, we get NO gas by catalytic oxidation of ammonia. The moles of NO produced by oxidation of two moles of NH_3 will be **[NCERT Exemplar]**

(a) 2 ☐ (b) 3 ☐ (c) 4 ☐ (d) 6 ☐

118. Fill the missing products in the given reaction.

(i) $3Cu + 8HNO_3$ (dil.) $\longrightarrow$ ______ + ______ + $4H_2O$

(ii) $Zn + 4HNO_3$ (conc.) $\longrightarrow$ ______ + ______ + $2H_2O$

119. A brown ring is formed in the ring test for nitrate ion. It is due to the formation of **[NCERT Exemplar]**

(a) Fe_3O_4 ☐ (b) $[Fe(H_2O)_5(NO)]^{2+}$ ☐

(c) $[Fe(H_2O)_2(NO)]^{2+}$ ☐ (d) $[Fe(H_2O)_5]^{2+}$ ☐

120. Which reagent is predominantly used in pickling of stainless steel?

(a) Iodic acid ☐

(b) Phosphoric acid ☐

(c) Nitric acid ☐

(d) Sulphuric acid ☐

TOPIC 11

Phosphorus : Allotropic Forms & Phosphine

NCERT Pg 175-177

121. An allotrope (X) of phosphorus is poisonous, soluble in carbon disulphide and glows in dark. Identify X.

X = ____________________

122. Consider the following,

$$X \xrightarrow[\text{Inert atmosphere}]{573\text{ K}} \text{Red phosphorus} \xrightarrow[\text{Sealed tube}]{803\text{ K}} A$$

$$\text{Red phosphorus} \xrightarrow[\text{High pressure}]{473\text{ K}} B$$

Identify X, A and B

X = __________ A = __________ B = __________

123. White phosphorus is heated with concentrated NaOH solution in an inert atmosphere of CO_2 to produce.

(a) PH_4OH ☐ (b) PH_3 ☐

(c) NaH_2PO_2 ☐ (d) Both (b) and (c) ☐

124. Phosphine become inflammable in the presence of P_2H_4 or P_4 vapours.

True ☐ False ☐

125. In the following reactions,

$$PH_3 + HI \longrightarrow PH_4I$$

$$PH_3 + HBr \longrightarrow PH_4Br$$

PH_3 behaves as

(a) acid ☐ (b) neutral ☐

(c) base ☐ (d) None of these ☐

126. A cloud of smoke created to conceal military operation called smoke screen contains two compounds. Name these two compounds.

(i) __________ (ii) __________

127. Colourless oily liquid 'A' hydrolysis in the presence of moisture to give fumes of 'B'. Write A and B.

A = __________ B = __________

TOPIC 12

Phosphorus Halides

NCERT Pg 177-178

128. What is the hybridisation of phosphorus in PCl_3?

(a) sp^3d ☐ (b) sp^3d^2 ☐ (c) sp^3 ☐ (d) sp^2 ☐

129. Amongst the following, the total number of species that can react with PCl_5 to give $POCl_3$ is

O_2, CO_2, SO_2, H_2O, H_2SO_4, P_4O_{10}

(a) 3 ☐ (b) 4 ☐ (c) 5 ☐ (d) 6 ☐

130. On thermal decomposition, PCl_5 gives P_4 and Cl_2.

True ☐ False ☐

131. Fill the missing products in the given reactions.

(i) $CH_3COOH + PCl_5 \longrightarrow$ ________ + ________ + HCl

(ii) $C_2H_5OH + PCl_5 \longrightarrow$ ________ + $POCl_3$ + ________

132. Provide hybridisation of PCl_5 in

(i) Liquid state ________

(ii) Solid state ________

133. For structure of PCl_5,

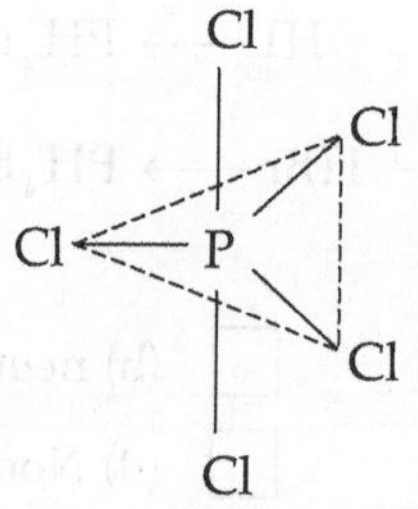

Answer the following questions.

(i) Number of equatorial bonds ________.

(ii) Which bonds are longer, axial or equatorial? ________

***134.** The oxidation state of pyrophosphorus and hypophosphoric acids are respectively.

(a) + 3 and + 3 ☐ (b) + 4 and + 5 ☐

(c) + 3 and + 4 ☐ (d) + 1 and + 4 ☐

TOPIC 13

Oxoacids of Phosphorus

NCERT Pg 178-180

135. Consider the following compounds/ species.

(i) Hypophosphorus
(ii) Orthophosphorus
(iii) Pyrophosphorus
(iv) Hypophosphoric
(v) Orthophosphoric
(vi) Pyrophosphoric
(vii) Metaphosphoric

The number of compounds/species in which phosphorus has +5 oxidation state.

(a) 2 ☐ (b) 3 ☐ (c) 4 ☐ (d) 6 ☐

136. Name the oxoacid of phosphorus which have four P—OH, two P=O and one P—O—P bonds.

____

137. The pair that contains two P—H bonds in each of the oxoacids is

(a) $H_4P_2O_5$ and $H_4P_2O_6$ ☐ (b) H_3PO_3 and H_3PO_2 ☐

(c) $H_4P_2O_5$ and H_3PO_3 ☐ (d) H_3PO_2 and $H_4P_2O_5$ ☐

138. Consider the following statements.

I. Hypophosphoric acid contain one P—P bond.
II. When white P_4 reacts with alkali, it forms hypophosphoric acid.

Which of the following statement(s) is/are correct?

(a) Only I ☐ (b) Only II ☐ (c) Both I and II ☐ (d) None of these ☐

139. Complete the following table regarding oxoacids of phosphorus.

Oxoacids (Formula)	Basicity
H_3PO_3	(i) ________
(ii) ________	Tribasic

140. When H_3PO_3 is heated, it disproportionates into two products. The oxidation states of these two products are

(a) + 4 and + 3 ☐ (b) + 5 and + 4 ☐

(c) + 5 and – 3 ☐ (d) + 3 and + 3 ☐

141. All elements of group 15 show allotropy except

(a) nitrogen ☐ (b) arsenic ☐

(c) antimony ☐ (d) bismuth ☐

TOPIC 14

Group-16 Elements

NCERT Pg 180-183

142. Name the non-metal which is common in gypsum, epsom salt and barytes.

____

143. Give the chemical formula of the following compounds.

(i) Copper pyrite ________________.

(ii) Zinc blende ________________.

(iii) Galena ________________.

144. Oxygen has less negative electron gain enthalpy than sulphur due to its compact nature.

True ☐ False ☐

145. Consider the following statements.

I. There is large difference in melting and boiling point between oxygen and sulphur.

II. Oxygen exists as polyatomic molecule, while sulphur exists as diatomic molecule.

Which of the following statement(s) is/are not correct?

(a) Only I ☐ (b) Only II ☐

(c) Both I and II ☐ (d) Neither I nor II ☐

***146.** Write the name of the effect due to which stability of + 6 oxidation state decreases and stability of + 4 oxidation state increases down the group.

____

147. Anomalous behaviour of oxygen in comparison to rest of its members is due to

(i) ________________

(ii) ________________

(iii) ________________

(iv) high ionisation energy

***148.** Rearrange the given hydrides of group 16 elements in increasing order of their acidic character.

H_2O, H_2Te, H_2S, H_2Se

____

149. Answer the following questions in one word.

(i) Due to which property thermal stability of group 16 hydrides decreases from H_2O to H_2Po.

____

(ii) Hydride of which element of group 16 does not posses reducing property.

____

150. Tick the oxidising agent from the given options.

SO_2 ☐ TeO_2 ☐

151. Select the incorrect pair of compound with respect to its physical state.

(a) SF_4-gas ☐ (b) SeF_4-gas ☐

(c) TeF_4-solid ☐ (d) All are correct pair. ☐

152. Mention the hybridisation and geometry of fluorides of group 16 elements.

____

153. Organise them in increasing order of their thermal stability.

$H_2S, H_2O, H_2Po, H_2Se, H_2Te$

____

154. H_2O is liquid, while H_2S is a gas due to

(a) covalent bonding ☐ (b) molecular attraction ☐

(c) H-bonding ☐ (d) Both (b) and (c) ☐

TOPIC 15

Dioxygen

NCERT Pg 184

155. Complete the reaction given below.

$$2KClO_3 \xrightarrow[MnO_2]{Heat} \_\_\_\_\_\_ + \_\_\_\_\_\_$$

156. Name the catalyst used for decomposition of H_2O_2 into water and oxygen.

____

157. Electrolysis of water produces

(i) at cathode ____________. (ii) at anode ____________.

158. Complete the following statements with appropriate words.

Dioxygen is obtained from air by first removing ________ (CO/CO_2) and water vapour and remaining gases are ________ (evaporated/liquified) and fractionally distilled to give dioxygen and ________ (dihydrogen/dinitrogen).

159. O_2 is unique in being paramagnetic inspite of having even number of electrons.

True ☐ False ☐

160. Name the catalyst used in oxidation of sulphur dioxide.

____

161. Choose the incorrect use of oxygen from the following.

(a) It is used in oxyacetylene welding. ☐

(b) Used in combustion of fuels to provide tremendous thrust in rockets. ☐

(c) Used as a solvent to dissolve number of organic and inorganic chemical. ☐

(d) Used in high altitude and mountaineering. ☐

162. Which of the following does not react with oxygen directly?

(a) Zn ☐ (b) Fe ☐ (c) Ti ☐ (d) Pt ☐

163. Complete the following reactions.

(i) $C_2H_4 + 3O_2 \longrightarrow$ ________. (ii) $4Al + 3O_2 \longrightarrow$ ________.

TOPIC 16

Simple Oxides & Ozone

NCERT Pg 185-186

164. Metal oxides with higher oxidation state have basic nature.

True ☐ False ☐

***165.** Amongst the following, the total number of species which are not basic oxides is

Na_2O, BaO, SO_2, Cl_2O_7, N_2O_5

(a) 2 ☐ (b) 3 ☐ (c) 4 ☐ (d) 5 ☐

166. Identify X and Y in the following reaction.

$$X(s) + 6HCl(aq) + 9H_2O(l) \longrightarrow 2[Al(H_2O)_6]^{3+}(aq) + 6Cl^-(aq)$$

$$X(s) + 6NaOH(aq) + 3H_2O(l) \longrightarrow 2Y(aq)$$

X = ________ Y = ________

***167.** Write an example for following type of oxides of p-block elements.

(i) Amphoteric ________ (ii) Neutral ________

168. Silent electrical discharge is used in the formation of ozone from oxygen as it is an ________ (exothermic/endothermic) process.

169. For decomposition of ozone into oxygen, which of the following is correct?

(a) ΔH is negative. ☐ (b) ΔS is positive. ☐

(c) Large negative Gibbs energy. ☐ (d) All of the above ☐

170. Complete the following reaction.

$$PbS(s) + O_3 \longrightarrow$$ ________

171. Complete the following statement with appropriate words.

Ozone can be estimated ____________ (quantitatively/qualitatively) with the help of potassium iodide. Ozone reacts with KI buffered with borate buffer, ________ (oxygen/iodine) is liberated which can be titrated against solution of ____________ ($Na_2S_2O_3/Na_2SO_4$).

172. Which of the following reason is responsible for ozone layer depletion?

(a) Nitrogen oxide emitted by supersonic get aeroplanes. ☐
(b) Use of freon in aerosol spray. ☐
(c) Use of freon in refrigerants. ☐
(d) All of the above ☐

TOPIC 17

Sulphur-Allotropic Form & Sulphur Dioxide

NCERT Pg 187-188

173. Name the two important allotropes of sulphur.

(i) ____________ (ii) ____________

174. Choose the incorrect solvent with respect to rhombic sulphur.

Benzene, Water, Alcohol, Ether

____

175. At what temperature, both α-sulphur and β-sulphur are stable?

____

176. Write the structural form of

(i) S_8 = ____________ (ii) S_6 = ____________

177. In which form, sulphur shows paramagnetic behaviour.

(a) Rhombic ☐ (b) Monoclinic ☐ (c) In vapour state ☐ (d) All of these ☐

178. Sulphur dioxide can be prepared by

(a) treating a sulphite with dilute sulphuric acid. ☐
(b) produced as the byproduct on roasting of sulphide ores. ☐
(c) burning sulphur in air or oxygen. ☐
(d) All of the above ☐

179. Compound X reacts with chlorine in the presence of Y (catalyst) to give Z.
Z is oxidised to sulphur trioxide by oxygen in presence of vanadium oxide catalyst.
Write the X, Y and Z.

X = ____________ Y = ____________ Z = ____________

180. When sulphur dioxide is passed through an aqueous solution of Fe (III) salt

(a) ferric ion gets converted to ferrous ion. ☐

(b) ferrous ion gets converted to ferric ion. ☐

(c) No change in oxidation number of Fe atom. ☐

(d) Both (a) and(b) ☐

---

181. When SO_2 is passed through an acidified potassium permanganate solution, it decolourises the solution.

True ☐ False ☐

182. Sulphur dioxide (SO_2) has ____________ (bent/tetrahedral) structure in which both S—O bonds are ______ (equal/unequal).

TOPIC 18

Oxoacids of Sulphur & Sulphuric Acid

NCERT Pg 189-191

***183.** Select the peroxoacids of sulphur from the following.

H_2SO_5, $H_2S_2O_7$, $H_2S_2O_6$, $H_2S_2O_8$

____

184. In which pair of ions both the species contain S—S bonds ?

(a) $S_2O_7^{2-}$, $S_2O_3^{2-}$ ☐ (b) $S_4O_6^{2-}$, $S_2O_3^{2-}$ ☐

(c) $S_2O_7^{2-}$, $S_2O_8^{2-}$ ☐ (d) $S_4O_6^{2-}$, $S_2O_7^{2-}$ ☐

185. In which of the following structures, lone pair on sulphur is present?

(a) H_2SO_4 ☐ (b) $H_2S_2O_7$ ☐ (c) H_2SO_3 ☐ (d) $H_2S_2O_8$ ☐

186. Catalyst used in manufacturing of sulphuric acid by contact process is

(a) Mo ☐ (b) V_2O_5 ☐ (c) Fe ☐ (d) Platinum ☐

187. Choose the following favourable condition for contact process.

(i) Temperature (High/Low) __________ (ii) Pressure (High/Low) __________

188. Enlist the factors which are responsible for chemical reactions of sulphuric acid.

(i) ______________________________

(ii) ______________________________

(iii) ______________________________

(iv) ______________________________

189. Which of the following is not correct for sulphuric acid?

(a) Conc. H_2SO_4 is a strong dehydrating agent. ☐

(b) Sulphuric acid forms two series of salts, i.e. normal sulphates and acid sulphates. ☐

(c) Both metal and non-metal are oxidised by conc. H_2SO_4. ☐

(d) Sulphuric acid removes water from inorganic compounds. ☐

190. Hot concentrated H_2SO_4 acts as moderately strong oxidising agent. It oxidises both metals and non-metals. Which of the following element is oxidised by H_2SO_4 into two gaseous products?

(a) Cu ☐ (b) S ☐ (c) C ☐ (d) Zn ☐

191. Write four uses of sulphuric acid.

(i) ____________ (ii) ____________

(iii) ____________ (iv) ____________

192. Complete the following reactions.

(i) $CaF_2 + H_2SO_4 \longrightarrow$ ________ + ________

(ii) $SO_3 + H_2O \longrightarrow$ ________

193. In which of the following reactions, conc. H_2SO_4 is used as an oxidising reagent?

(a) $CaF_2 + H_2SO_4 \longrightarrow CaSO_4 + 2HF$ ☐

(b) $Cu + 2H_2SO_4 \longrightarrow CuSO_4 + SO_2 + 2H_2O$ ☐

(c) $NaCl + H_2SO_4 \longrightarrow NaHSO_4 + HCl$ ☐

(d) None of the above ☐

194. H_2SO_4 in water, has $k_{a_2} << k_{a_1}$.

True ☐ False ☐

TOPIC 19

Group-17 Elements

NCERT Pg 192-196

195. Fluorine is not present in

(a) cryolite ☐ (b) fluoroapatite ☐

(c) fluorspar ☐ (d) chile saltpetre ☐

196. "Sea weeds contains upto 0.2% of sodium iodate".

True ☐ False ☐

197. Halogens have smallest atomic radii in their respective periods due to ______ (maximum/minimum) effective nuclear charge.

198. Negative electron gain enthalpy of fluorine is less than that of chlorine.

True ☐ False ☐

199. Which of the following is not correct regarding halogens with respect to periods?

(a) Ionisation energy – High value ☐

(b) Electron gain enthalpy – Maximum negative ☐

(c) Electronegativity – Least value ☐

(d) Atomic radii – Largest ☐

200. Fill the appropriate words in the following table containing halogen and its characteristic colour.

Halogen	Colour
Fluorine	(i) ______
(ii) ______	Greenish yellow
Bromine	(iii) ______
(iv) ______	Violet colour

201. Fluorine is a stronger oxidising agent than chlorine due to

I. low enthalpy of dissociation of F—F bond.

II. low ionisation energy.

III. high hydration enthalpy of F^-.

Choose the correct option.

(a) Only I ☐

(b) II and III ☐

(c) I and III ☐

(d) Only II ☐

202. Provide the oxidation states shown by halogens (except fluorine).

______

203. Standard electrode potential of halogens are dependent on the parameters.

(a) Dissociation enthalpy ☐

(b) Electron gain enthalpy ☐

(c) Hydration enthalpy ☐

(d) All of the above ☐

204. Identify A, B and C.

Fluorine oxidises water to $\underline{A}$, whereas Cl_2 and Br_2 reacts with water to form corresponding $\underline{B}$ and $\underline{C}$ acids.

A = ________ B = ________ C = ________

205. Enlist four factors due to which fluorine shows anomalous behaviour.

(i) ________.

(ii) ________.

(iii) ________.

(iv) ________.

206. Identify the incorrect information regarding fluorine.

(a) Most of the reaction of fluorine are exothermic. ☐

(b) It forms only one oxoacid due to its high electronegativity. ☐

(c) Hydrogen fluoride is a gas due to strong hydrogen bonding. ☐

(d) Fluorine has maximum affinity for hydrogen to form hydrogen halide. ☐

207. Rearrange the given hydrogen halides according to their stability.

H—Br, H—F, H—I, H—Cl

____

208. Which of the following halogen acid have highest bond dissociation enthalpy?

(a) HF ☐ (b) HCl ☐

(c) HBr ☐ (d) HI ☐

209. Fluorine forms two compounds with oxygen, i.e. X and Y, which are strong fluorinating agents. Name the compounds X and Y.

X = ________ Y = ________

210. Match the uses given in Column II with the compounds given in Column I.

	Column I (Compounds)	Column II (Uses)
A.	ClO_2	1. Remove plutonium from spent nuclear fuel.
B.	O_2F_2	2. Estimation of CO.
C.	I_2O_5	3. Bleaching agent for paper and textiles

A. ________ B. ________ C. ________

211. Which one of the following are correctly arranged on the basis of the property indicated?

(a) $I_2 < Br_2 < F_2 < Cl_2$ (increasing bond dissociation enthalpy) ☐

(b) $H_2O < H_2S < H_2Te < H_2Se$ (increasing acidic strength) ☐

(c) $NH_3 < N_2O < NH_2OH < N_2O_5$ (increasing oxidation state) ☐

(d) $BiH_3 < SbH_3 < AsH_3 < PH_3 < NH_3$ (increasing bond angle) ☐

TOPIC 20

Chlorine

NCERT Pg 197-198

212. A student treated sodium chloride with concentrated sulphuric acid in a test tube in the presence of MnO_2. He observed greenish yellow gas is releasing pungent odour. Name the gas.

___

213. Name the catalyst used in Deacon's process to produce chlorine gas.

___

214. If chlorine gas is passed through (hot and concentrated) NaOH solution, two changes are observed in the oxidation number of chlorine during the reaction. These change in oxidation number are from 0 to ________ and ________.

(a) + 3 and + 5 ☐ (b) + 3 and − 1 ☐

(c) 0 and + 1 ☐ (d) − 1 and + 5 ☐

215. Consider the following reactions,

$$\underset{\text{(Cold and dilute)}}{2NaOH} + Cl_2 \longrightarrow A + B + H_2O$$

$$\underset{\text{(Hot and conc.)}}{6NaOH} + 3Cl_2 \longrightarrow 5C + D + 3H_2O$$

Here, *A*, *B*, *C* and *D* refer to

	A	*B*	*C*	*D*	
(a)	NaCl	$NaClO_3$	NaOCl	5NaCl	☐
(b)	5NaCl	$NaClO_3$	NaOCl	NaCl	☐
(c)	NaCl	NaOCl	NaCl	$NaClO_3$	☐
(d)	5NaCl	NaOCl	NaCl	$NaClO_3$	☐

216. Write the composition of bleaching powder.

___

217. Chlorine water on standing loses its yellow colour due to the formation of

(a) Cl and HOCl ☐ (b) HCl and HOCl ☐

(c) HOCl and $HOCl_2$ ☐ (d) HCl and $HOCl_2$ ☐

218. Oxidising and bleaching properties of chlorine is due to ________ (nascent oxygen/oxygen molecule).

219. Complete the following sentences.

Bleaching powder oxidises

(i) Ferrous to ________________ (ii) ________________ to sulphate.

(iii) ________________ to sulphur trioxide (iv) Iodine to ________________.

220. Choose the correct use of bleaching powder from the doublets given below

(a) in extraction of – (gold/sodium) ________________.

(b) in water – (softening/sterilising) ________________.

(c) in manufacturing of – (glass/dyes) ________________.

(d) in bleaching of – (paper/polythene) ________________.

221. Two poisonous gases prepared from chlorine gas are

(a) laughing gas and methane gas ________________.

(b) phosgene and mustard gas ________________.

(c) carbon dioxide and hydrogen gas ________________.

(d) nitrogen dioxide and H_2 gas ________________.

TOPIC 21

Hydrogen Chloride

NCERT Pg 198-199

222. Hydrogen chloride as an acid is much stronger than hydrogen fluoride under the same conditions.

True ☐ False ☐

223. A compound X has high value of dissociation constant. When it reacts with ammonia, it gives white fumes of Y. Identify X and Y.

X = ________________ Y = ________________

224. One day Anu went to a jewellery shop and asked the goldsmith to polish the old gold jewellery. Next day when they brought the jewellery they found that there was a slight loss in its weight as

(a) jeweller stolen gold from jewellery. ☐

(b) jeweller cleans it with aqua regia which dissolves gold. ☐

(c) gold is very reactive metal, it reacts with oxygen to form oxide. ☐

(d) All of the above ☐

225. Name the acid which is used in extracting glue from bones and purifying bone black.

____

226. When HCl reacts with finely powdered iron, it forms ferrous chloride not ferric chloride.

True ☐ False ☐

TOPIC 22

Oxoacids of Halogens and Interhalogens Compounds

NCERT Pg 199-202

227. The halogen which forms only one oxoacid is

(a) F
(b) Cl
(c) Br
(d) I

228. The formulae of hypochlorous acid and perchloric acid are respectively

(a) $HOCl$ and $HClO_4$
(b) $HOCl$ and $HClO_3$
(c) $HClO_2$ and $HClO_3$
(d) $HClO_2$ and $HClO_4$

229. Draw the structure of $HClO_3$.

230. Write the number of double bond and single bond present in perchloric acid.

231. Consider the following statements.

I. In interhalogen compounds, as the ratio between radii of X and X' increases, number of atoms per molecule also increases.

II. Iodine fluoride should have maximum number of atoms as ratio of radii between I and F should be maximum.

Which of the following statement(s) is/are correct?

(a) Only I
(b) Only II
(c) Both I and II
(d) Neither I nor II

232. Write the interhalogen product formed when

(a) $Cl_2 + F_2 \xrightarrow{473\text{ K}}$ ______

(b) $\underset{\text{(Equally volume)}}{Cl_2 + 3F_2} \xrightarrow{473\text{ K}}$ ______

(c) $\underset{\text{(Equimolar)}}{I_2 + Cl_2} \longrightarrow$ ______

(d) $I_2 + \underset{\text{(Excess)}}{3Cl_2} \longrightarrow$ ______

233. Match the structure in Column II with the interhalogen compounds given in Column I.

Column I (Compound)		Column II (Structure)
A.	BrF_3	1. Square pyramidal
B.	IF_7	2. Bent T-shaped
C.	ClF_5	3. Pentagonal bipyramidal

A. ________ B. ________ C. ________

234. In the structure of ClF_3, the number of lone pair of electrons on central atom 'Cl' is

(a) four ☐ (b) two ☐ (c) one ☐ (d) three ☐

235. Which of the following compound is used for production of UF_6?

(a) ClF_3 ☐ (b) IF_7 ☐ (c) BrF_3 ☐ (d) Both (a) and (c) ☐

236. ICl is more reactive than I_2 because

(a) $X—X'$ bond in interhalogens is weaker than $X—X$ bond in halogen. ☐

(b) Bond strength of $X—X'$ and $X—X$ is same. ☐

(c) $X—X'$ bond are stronger than $X—X$ bond in halogen. ☐

(d) Both (a) and (b) ☐

TOPIC 23

Group 18 Elements

NCERT Pg 202-205

237. Main commercial source of helium is ________.

238. Mention the decay products of $^{226}_{88}Ra$.

____

239. (i) Noble gases exhibit very high ionisation energy and very small positive value of electron gain enthalpy.

True ☐ False ☐

(ii) Due to weak dispersion forces, noble gases have very ________ (high/low) melting and boiling point.

240. Consider the following statements.

I. Helium diffuses through most commonly used material like rubber, glass etc.

II. Helium used in diving apparatus because of high solubility in blood.

Which of the following statement(s) is/are correct?

(a) Only I ☐ (b) Only II ☐ (c) Both I and II ☐ (d) Neither I nor II ☐

241. In the preparation of compound of Xe, Bartlett had taken $O_2^+PtF_6^-$ as a base compound. This is because

(a) both O_2 and Xe have almost same size. ☐

(b) both O_2 and Xe have almost same electron gain enthalpy. ☐

(c) both O_2 and Xe have almost same first ionisation energy. ☐

(d) both O_2 and Xe are gases. ☐

242. When Xe reacts with fluorine in 1 : 5 ratio at 873 K, it forms

(a) XeF_2 ☐ (b) XeF_4 ☐ (c) XeF_6 ☐ (d) $XeOF_4$ ☐

243. Identify *A* and *B* in the following reaction of xenon.

(i) $\underset{\text{(Excess)}}{Xe(g)} + F_2(g) \xrightarrow{673\text{ K, 1 bar}} A$

(ii) $A + B \longrightarrow [XeF]^+[PF_6]^-$

A = __________ *B* = __________

244. Complete the following reaction

(i) $XeF_4 + SbF_5 \longrightarrow$ __________

(ii) $XeF_4 + O_2F_2 \xrightarrow{143\text{ K}}$ __________

245. Write the stoichiometric coefficient with compound formula for all blank spaces in the given reaction in accordance to balance the reaction.

$$6XeF_4 + 12\,H_2O \longrightarrow 4Xe + \_\_\_\_ + \_\_\_\_ + 3O_2$$

246. On partial hydrolysis, XeF_6 gives

(a) $XeO_3 + 4HF$ ☐ (b) $XeO_2F + HF$ ☐

(c) $XeOF_4 + H_2$ ☐ (d) $XeO_2F_2 + 4HF$ ☐

247. Match the compounds given in Column I with hybridisation and shape given in Column II.

Column I (Compounds)	Column II (Hybridisation-shape)
A. XeF_4	1. sp^3d^3-distorted octahedral
B. XeO_3	2. sp^3d^2-square planar
C. $XeOF_4$	3. sp^3-pyramidal
D. XeF_6	4. sp^3d^2-square pyramidal

A. __________ B. __________

C. __________ D. __________

248. Among the given molecules, choose the molecules which have same number of lone pair on Xe.

I. XeO_3, II. XeF_6, III. $XeOF_4$

(a) I and II ☐ (b) I and III ☐

(c) II and III ☐ (d) I, II and III ☐

249. Which of the following reaction in an example of redox reaction?

(a) $XeF_4 + O_2F_2 \longrightarrow XeF_6 + O_2$ ☐

(b) $2XeF_2 + O_2 \longrightarrow 2XeOF_2$ ☐

(c) $XeF_6 + H_2O \longrightarrow XeOF_4 + 2HF$ ☐

(d) $XeF_6 + 2H_2O \longrightarrow XeO_2F_2 + 2HF$ ☐

250. Answer the following questions.

(i) Which noble gas is used in magnetic resonance imaging systems ? __________

(ii) Name a noble gas which is used for filling electric bulbs. __________

251. Argon is used in discharge tubes and fluorescent bulbs.

True ☐ False ☐

Assertion-Reason Questions

Given below are two statements, one is labelled as Assertion (A) and other is labelled as Reason (R). Select the most appropriate answer from the options given below.

(a) Both A and R are true and R is the correct explanation of A.
(b) Both A and R are true but R is not the correct explanation of A.
(c) A is true but R is false.
(d) A is false but R is true.

1. **Assertion** (A) The chemical behaviour of the first member of a group of elements in the *p*-block is different from the subsequent members of the group.

Reason (R) This is because of the small size and high electronegativity of the first member of the group.

(a) ☐ (b) ☐ (c) ☐ (d) ☐

2. **Assertion** (A) Boron does not form +3 ions and forms only covalent compounds.

Reason (R) Due to the small size of boron, the sum of the first three ionisation enthalpies is very high.

(a) ☐ (b) ☐ (c) ☐ (d) ☐

3. **Assertion** (A) White fumes appear around the bottle of anhydrous aluminium chloride.
Reason (R) Moist HCl appears white in colour.
(a) ☐ (b) ☐ (c) ☐ (d) ☐

4. **Assertion** (A) Borazine is called inorganic benzene.
Reason (R) Borazine has ring structure with alternate BH and NH groups with π-bonds.
(a) ☐ (b) ☐ (c) ☐ (d) ☐

5. **Assertion** (A) $[SiF_6]^{2-}$ is known whereas $[SiCl_6]^{2-}$ is not known.
Reason (R) The interaction between lone pair of chloride ion and Si^{4+} is very weak due to high inter-electronic rupulsions.
(a) ☐ (b) ☐ (c) ☐ (d) ☐

6. **Assertion** (A) SiO_2 reacts with both HF and NaOH, but not with dihydrogen.
Reason (R) Silica is highly reactive in its normal form.
(a) ☐ (b) ☐ (c) ☐ (d) ☐

7. **Assertion** (A) First ionisation enthalpy of group 15 elements is much smaller than that of group 14 elements.
Reason (R) Group 15 elements have extra stable half-filled *p*-orbital electronic configuration.
(a) ☐ (b) ☐ (c) ☐ (d) ☐

8. **Assertion** (A) HNO_3 makes iron passive.
Reason (R) HNO_3 forms a protective layer of ferric nitrate on the surface of iron.
(a) ☐ (b) ☐ (c) ☐ (d) ☐

9. **Assertion** (A) Bond angle in PH_4^+ is higher than that in PH_3.
Reason (R) Due to absence of lone pair in PH_4^+, there is no lone pair-bond pair repulsion.
(a) ☐ (b) ☐ (c) ☐ (d) ☐

10. **Assertion** (A) H_3PO_2 reduces $AgNO_3$ to metallic silver.
Reason (R) In H_3PO_2, P—H bonds are not ionisable.
(a) ☐ (b) ☐ (c) ☐ (d) ☐

11. **Assertion** (A) Elements of group 16 generally show lower value of first ionisation enthalpy as compared to elements of corresponding periods of group 15.
Reason (R) Due to extra stable half-filled *p*-orbitals in group 15, ionisation energy is high.
(a) ☐ (b) ☐ (c) ☐ (d) ☐

12. **Assertion** (A) Ozone (O_3) acts as a powerful oxidising agent.
Reason (R) Ozone oxidises lead sulphide to lead sulphate and iodide ions to iodine.
(a) ☐ (b) ☐ (c) ☐ (d) ☐

13. **Assertion** (A) H_2SO_4 is strong acid.
Reason (R) H_2SO_4 has greater value of dissociation constant.
(a) ☐ (b) ☐ (c) ☐ (d) ☐

14. **Assertion** (A) All halogens are coloured.
Reason (R) Due to absorption of radiation in visible region, electrons excited to higher energy level thus imparting colour.
(a) ☐ (b) ☐ (c) ☐ (d) ☐

15. **Assertion** (A) $SnCl_4$ is more covalent than $SnCl_2$.
Reason (R) Halides in higher oxidation state will be more ionic than the one in lower oxidation state.
(a) ☐ (b) ☐ (c) ☐ (d) ☐

16. **Assertion** (A) Noble gases are chemically unreactive.
Reason (R) Valence shell orbitals of noble gases are completely filled.
(a) ☐ (b) ☐ (c) ☐ (d) ☐

Case-Based Questions

1. Interhalogen compounds are formed when halogen group elements react with each other. These are the compounds which consist of two or more different elements of group 17. A halogen with large size and low electronegativity reacts with an element of group17 with small size and high electronegativity. As the ratio of radius of larger and smaller halogen increases, the number of atoms in a molecule also increases.

(i) The stability of interhalogen compounds follows the order.
(a) $IF_3 > BrF_3 > ClF_3$ ☐ (b) $ClF_3 > BrF_3 > IF_3$ ☐
(c) $BrF_3 > IF_3 > ClF_3$ ☐ (d) $ClF_3 > IF_3 > BrF_3$ ☐

(ii) Identify the correct match from the following.
(a) $[ICl_2]^-$-Bent ☐ (b) IF_7-Pentagonal bipyramidal ☐
(c) ClF_3-Trigonal planar ☐ (d) $[BrF_4]^-$-Square pyramidal ☐

(iii) In XA_5, the central atoms has (both X and A are halogens)
(a) 5 bp and no lp ☐ (b) 5 bp and 1 lp ☐
(c) 6 bp and no lp ☐ (d) 4 bp and 1 lp ☐

(iv) In the known interhalogen compounds, the maximum number of atoms are
(a) 4 ☐ (b) 5 ☐
(c) 8 ☐ (d) 7 ☐

2. Chlorine is a greenish yellow gas with pungent and suffocating odour. With dry slaked lime, it gives bleaching powder. Bleaching powder is a mixture of calcium hypochlorite and basic calcium chloride [$Ca(OCl)_2 \cdot CaCl_2 \cdot Ca(OH)_2 \cdot 2H_2O$]. The amount of chlorine obtained from a sample of bleaching powder by the treatment with excess of dilute acids or CO_2 is called available chlorine. Chlorine is a powerful bleaching agent. Bleaching effect of chlorine is permanent.

(i) Chlorine gas reacts with which of the following to form bleaching powder.

(a) $Ca(OH)_2$ ☐ (b) $CaCl_2$ ☐

(c) $CaSO_4$ ☐ (d) dry CaO ☐

(ii) Chlorine reacts with cold and dilute alkali to form

(a) chloride ☐ (b) hypochlorite ☐

(c) chlorate ☐ (d) Both (a) and (b) ☐

(iii) Which of the following is produced on the reaction of bleaching powder with a few drops of conc. HCl?

(a) Hypochlorous acid ☐ (b) Oxygen ☐

(c) Chlorine ☐ (d) Calcium oxide ☐

(iv) Chlorine is used as a bleaching agent. The bleaching action is due to

(a) oxidation ☐ (b) chlorination ☐

(c) hydrogenation ☐ (d) reduction ☐

COMPETITION EDGE UP

1. The correct order of the first ionisation enthalpy is
[NCERT (Old) Pg. 317, JEE Main 2024]
(a) B > Al > Ga ☐ (b) Ga > Al > B ☐
(c) Al > Ga > Tl ☐ (d) Tl > Ga > Al ☐

2. The number of ions from the following that are expected to behave as oxidising agent is
Sn^{4+}, Sn^{2+}, Pb^{2+}, Tl^{3+}, Pb^{4+}, Tl^{+}
[NCERT (Old) Pg. 324, JEE Main 2024]
(a) 1 ☐ (b) 3 ☐
(c) 4 ☐ (d) 2 ☐

3. Given below are two statements.
[NCERT (Old) Pg. 324 & 325, JEE Main 2024]
Statement I SiO_2 and GeO_2 are acidic while SnO and PbO are amphoteric in nature.
Statement II Allotropic forms of carbon are due to property of catenation and pπ - dπ bond formation.
In the light of the above statements, choose the most appropriate answer from the options given below
(a) Both Statement I and Statement II are false ☐
(b) Statement I is true but Statement II is false ☐
(c) Statement I is false but Statement II is true ☐
(d) Both Statement I and Statement II are true ☐

4. Consider the oxides of group 14 elements.
SiO_2, GeO_2, SnO_2, PbO_2, CO and GeO.
The amphoteric oxides are
[NCERT (Old) Pg. 324, JEE Main 2024]
(a) SnO_2, CO ☐ (b) SnO_2, PbO_2 ☐
(c) SiO_2, GeO_2 ☐ (d) GeO, GeO_2 ☐

5. Given below are two statements.
Statement I The electronegativity of group 14 elements from Si to Pb, gradually decreases.
Statement II Group 14 contains non-metallic, metallic, as well as metalloid elements.
[NCERT (Old) Pg. 323, JEE Main 2024]
In the light of the above statements, choose the most appropriate from the options given below.
(a) Statement I is false but Statement II is true. ☐
(b) Both Statement I and Statement II are false. ☐
(c) Statement I is true but Statement II is false. ☐
(d) Both Statement I and Statement II are true. ☐

6. The strongest reducing agent among the following is
[NCERT (Old) Pg. 168, JEE Main 2024]
(a) NH_3 ☐ (b) PH_3 ☐
(c) BiH_3 ☐ (d) SbH_3 ☐

7. Anomalous behaviour of oxygen is due to its [NCERT (Old) Pg. 182, JEE Main 2024]
(a) large size and high electronegativity ☐
(b) small size and low electronegativity ☐
(c) small size and high electronegativity ☐
(d) large size and low electronegativity ☐

8. Among group 16 elements, which one does not show −2 oxidation state?
[NCERT (Old) Pg. 181, NEET 2024]
(a) O ☐ (b) Se ☐
(c) Te ☐ (d) Po ☐

9. Which of the following material is not a semiconductor?
[NCERT (Old) Pg. 324, JEE Main 2023]
(a) Silicon ☐
(b) Graphite ☐
(c) Germanium ☐
(d) Copper oxide ☐

10. Taking stability as the factor, which one of the following represents correct relationship?
[NCERT (Old) Pg. 318, JEE Main 2023]
(a) TlI_3 > TlI ☐ (b) AlCl > $AlCl_3$ ☐
(c) TlI > TlI_3 ☐ (d) $TlCl_3$ > TlCl ☐

11. Among the given options which of the following molecules/ions acts as a Lewis acid? [NCERT (Old) Pg. 319, NEET 2023]
(a) H_2O ☐ (b) BF_3 ☐
(c) OH^- ☐ (d) NH_3 ☐

12. Match List-I with List-II.

List-I	List-II
A. Coke	I. Carbon atoms are sp^3-hybridised.
B. Diamond	II. Used as a dry lubricant.
C. Fullerene	III. Used as a reducing agent.
D. Graphite	IV. Cage like molecules.

Choose the correct answer from the options given below :
[NCERT (Old) Pg. 325, 326, 327, NEET 2023]

(a) A-IV, B-I, C-II, D-III ☐
(b) A-III, B-I, C-IV, D-II ☐
(c) A-III, B-IV, C-I, D-II ☐
(d) A-II, B-IV, C-I, D-III ☐

13. Match List-I with List-II.

List-I (Oxoacids of sulphur)	List-II (Bonds)
A. Peroxodisulphuric acid	I. Two S—OH, four S=O, one S—O—S
B. Sulphuric acid	II. Two S—OH, one S=O
C. Pyrosulphuric acid	III. Two S—OH, Four S=O, one S—O—O—S
D. Sulphurous acid	IV. Two S—OH, two S=O

Choose the correct answer from the options given below. **[NCERT (Old) Pg. 189, NEET 2023]**

(a) A-III, B-IV, C-I, D-II ☐
(b) A-I, B-III, C-IV, D-II ☐
(c) A-III, B-IV, C-II, D-I ☐
(d) A-I, B-III, C-II, D-IV ☐

14. Which of the following statement is not correct about diborane?
[NCERT (Old) Pg. 321, NEET 2022]

(a) The four terminal B — H bonds are 2-centre-2 electron bonds. ☐
(b) The four terminal hydrogen atoms and the two boron atoms lie in one plane. ☐
(c) Both the boron atoms are sp^2-hybridised. ☐
(d) There are two 3-centre-2-electron bonds. ☐

15. Choose the correct statement.
[NCERT (Old) Pg. 325, 326, NEET 2022]

(a) Diamond is covalent and graphite is ionic. ☐
(b) Diamond is sp^3-hybridised and graphite is sp^2-hybridised. ☐
(c) Both diamond and graphite are used as dry lubricants. ☐
(d) Diamond and graphite have two dimensional network. ☐

16. Given below are two statements one is labelled as Assertion (A) and the other is labelled as Reason (R).

Assertion (A) ICl is more reactive than I_2.

Reason (R) I—Cl bond is weaker than I—I bond.

In the light of the above statements, choose the most appropriate answer from the options given below.
[NCERT (Old) Pg. 200, NEET 2022]

(a) Both A and R are correct but R is not the correct explanation of A. ☐
(b) A is correct but R is not correct. ☐
(c) A is not correct but R is correct. ☐
(d) Both A and R are correct and R is the correct explanation of A. ☐

17. Which of the following oxide is amphoteric in nature? **[NCERT (Old) Pg. 324, NEET (Oct.) 2020]**

(a) SnO_2 ☐ (b) SiO_2 ☐
(c) GeO_2 ☐ (d) CO_2 ☐

18. Identify the correct statements from the following

1. $CO_2(g)$ is used as refrigerant for ice-cream and frozen food.
2. The structure of C_{60} contains twelve six carbon rings and twenty five carbon rings.
3. ZSM-5, a type of zeolite, is used to convert alcohols into gasoline.
4. CO is colourless and odourless gas.

[BCERT (Old) Pg. 327, NEET (Sep.) 2020]

(a) (1) and (3) only ☐
(b) (2) and (3) only ☐
(c) (3) and (4) only ☐
(d) (1), (2) and (3) only ☐

19. Which of the following is not correct about carbon-monoxide?
[NCERT (Old) Pg. 327, NEET 2020]

(a) It reduces oxygen carrying ability of blood. ☐
(b) The carboxyhaemoglobin (haemoglobin bound to CO) is less stable than oxyhaemoglobin. ☐
(c) It is produced due to incomplete combustion. ☐
(d) It forms carboxyhaemoglobin. ☐

Hints & Solutions

Chapter-1
Solutions

1. Composition

2. Copper

3. A → (2), B → (3), C → (1)

4. (c)

5. False; Intravenous injections are always dissolved in water containing salts at particular ionic concentrations that matches with blood plasma concentrations.

6. Homogeneous

7. A = Composition, B = Properties

8. (i) Solvent (ii) Solvent (iii) Solutes

9. (i) Copper dissolved in gold
(ii) Amalgam of mercury with sodium

10. (c) Ethanol dissolved in water is an example of liquid-liquid solution. Mixture of O_2 and N_2 gas and camphor in nitrogen gas are the example of gas-gas solution.

11. X = Qualitative, Y = Quantitative

12. Solute

13. (b) **Correct statement I** : 10% of glucose means 10 g of glucose is dissolved in 90 g of water.

14. (i) Parts per million (ppm)
(ii) Mass by volume percentage
(iii) Mole fraction

15. (i) A → (3), B → (1), C → (2)
(ii) A = Bleaching solution
B = Antifreeze

16. (i) $\chi_A = \dfrac{n_A}{n_A + n_B}$ (ii) $\chi_B = \dfrac{n_B}{n_A + n_B}$
(iii) $\chi_A + \chi_B = 1$

17. One, $\chi_A + \chi_B + \chi_C \ldots\ldots = 1$

18. (b) **Hint** : Molar mass of $C_2H_6O_2$
$= 62 \text{ g mol}^{-1}$

$$\chi_{\text{glycol}} = \frac{\text{Moles of } C_2H_6O_2}{\text{Moles of } C_2H_6O_2 + \text{Moles of } H_2O}$$

19. (i) 0.25 M (ii) 0.278 M
Hint : Molarity
$$= \frac{\text{Moles of solute}}{\text{Volume of solution (in L)}}$$

20. True;
Hint : 1m KCl
$$= \frac{\text{Moles of KCl}}{\text{Mass of solvent (in kg)}}$$

21. (c) **Hint** : Molar mass of $C_2H_4O_2$
$= 60 \text{ g mol}^{-1}$

Molality of $C_2H_4O_2$
$$= \frac{\text{Moles of } C_2H_4O_2}{\text{Mass of benzene (in kg)}}$$

22. 15.28, 84.72
Hint : Mass % of benzene
$$= \frac{\text{Mass of benzene in the solution}}{\text{Total mass of the solution}} \times 100$$
Mass % of CCl_4
$$= \frac{\text{Mass of } CCl_4 \text{ in the solution}}{\text{Total mass of the solution}} \times 100$$

23. (i) 0.024 M
Hint : Molarity
$$= \frac{\text{Moles of solute}}{\text{Volume of solution (in L)}}$$
(ii) 0.03 M
Hint : $M_1V_1 = M_2V_2$

24. (a) **Hint** : Use Molality
$$= \frac{\text{Moles of solute}}{\text{Mass of solvent (in kg)}}$$

25. (i) 1.51 m
(ii) 1.45 M
(iii) 0.0263
Hint : 20% (m/m) 100 g solution has 20 g of KI and 80 g solvent.
(i) Molality
$$= \frac{\text{Moles of KI} \times 1000}{\text{Mass of solvent (in g)}}$$
(ii) Molarity
$$= \frac{\text{Moles of KI} \times 1000}{\text{Volume of solution (in mL)}}$$
$$\left[\text{Volume} = \frac{\text{Mass}}{\text{Density}}\right]$$
(iii) Mole fraction of KI
$$= \frac{\text{Moles of KI}}{\text{Total number of moles present in solution}}$$

26. (d) Mass %, ppm, mole fraction and molality are independent of temperature whereas molarity is a function of temperature.

27. (i) Nature of solute
(iii) Nature of solvent
(iv) Pressure

28. (c) **Correct pair** : Anthracene is insoluble in water but soluble in organic solvents.

29. Intermolecular interactions

30. (i) Crystallisation
(ii) Dynamic equilibrium

31. (c)

32. Saturated

33. (b)

34.

	Correct	Incorrect
I.	✓	×
II.	×	✓
III.	✓	×

Correct statement II :
Pressure does not have any significant effect on solubility of solid in liquid.

35. (i) (b)
(ii) Solubility increases with increase in pressure.
(iii) Henry's law
According to Henry's law, solubility of a gas in liquid is directly proportional to the pressure of a gas.

36. (c)

37. Gas B,
Higher the value of Henry's law constant, lower is the solubility of gas in water.

38. Order of solubility is
$O_2 > H_2 > He$

39. (i) Less (ii) Decreases

40. (b) **Hint** :
$p_{(\text{Nitrogen})} = K_H \cdot \chi_{(\text{Nitrogen})}$
$\chi_{(\text{Nitrogen})}$
$$= \frac{\text{No. of moles of } N_2 \text{ in solution}}{\text{Total no. of moles in solution}}$$
$$= \frac{n}{n + 55.5} = \frac{n}{55.5} \quad [\because n << 55.5]$$

41. (d) **42.** Low

43. (c) **Hint** : From molality, extract no. of moles and then calculate mole fraction.

∴ Pressure of H_2S

$$= \frac{\text{Pressure at STP}}{\text{Mole fraction of } H_2S}$$

44. (a) **Hint** : $p = K_H \cdot \chi$

Calculate mole fraction (χ) and extract no. of moles of carbon dioxide.

Then, mass of CO_2 dissolved $= n_{CO_2} \times 44$

45. (b)

46. (i) I → Partial pressure of component 1.

II → Partial pressure of component 2.

III → Total pressure

(ii) p_1° (iii) p_2°

(iv) linearly

47. A → (3), B → (1), C → (2)

48. (i) (a) $\chi_{CHCl_3} = 0.18$

(b) $\chi_{CH_2Cl_2} = 0.82$

(ii) Vapour pressure

= 347.9 mm Hg

49. Decrease in vapour pressure of solvent depends on the quantity of non-volatile solute present in solution.

50. (i) Vapour pressure of pure solvent.

(ii) Raoult's law; $p \propto \chi$

51. (c) **Hint** : No heat is released or absorbed during mixing of two pure components to form an ideal solution.

Volume change of mixing does not change in an idea solution.

52. (i) *A—A* (ii) *B—B* (iii) *A—B*

53. (a) Phenol and aniline, chloroform and acetone shows negative deviation from Raoult's law.

54. (i) Positive deviation

(ii) Negative deviation

(iii) Negative deviation

(iv) Near to ideal solution

55. Negative deviation Negative deviation from Raoult's law arises when the vapour pressure of a mixture is lower than expected from Raoult's law.

56. Negative deviation

57. A → (3), B → (4), C → (1), D → (2)

58. 68, 32

59. (a)

60. (a)

61. (a)

Hint : Use, $\frac{p_A^\circ - p_A}{p_A^\circ} = \frac{w_B \times M_A}{M_B \times w_A}$

62. (b)

63. Molal elevation constant or ebullioscopic constant.

Unit of K_b = K kg mol^{-1}

64. (c) **Hint** : $\Delta T_b = K_b \times m$

65. (b) **Hint** : $M_2 = \frac{K_b \times w_2 \times 1000}{\Delta T_b \times w_1}$

66. *A* = Liquid solvent

B = Solution

C = Frozen solvent

67. (b) **Hint** : $\Delta T_f = \frac{K_f \times w_2 \times 1000}{M_2 \times w_1}$

Depression in freezing point is inversely proportional to molar mass of solute.

68. (c) **Hint** : Molality of solution

$$= \frac{\text{Moles of ethylene glycol}}{\text{Mass of water (in kg)}}$$

and $\Delta T_f = K_f \times m$

69. 256 g mol^{-1}

Hint : Molar mass of solute

$$= \frac{K_f \times w_B \times 1000}{\Delta T_f \times w_A}$$

70. Diluted, concentrated

71. (a)

72. (c) **Hint** : $M_B = \frac{w_B RT}{\pi V}$

73. (i) Osmotic pressure

(ii) Depression in freezing point

(iii) Elevation in boiling point

(iv) Osmotic pressure

74. (i) True (ii) True

75. (i) Cellulose acetate

(ii) Reverse osmosis

76. *B* to *A*,

If a pressure higher than the osmotic pressure is applied on the solution, the solvent will flow from the solution into the pure solvent through semipermeable membrane.

77. (i) 23.4 mm of Hg

(ii) 0.0173

Hint : Raoult's law,

$$\frac{p_A^\circ - p_A}{p_A^\circ} = \frac{n_B}{n_A + n_B}$$

78. (a) **Hint** : $\Delta T_f = K_f m$

79. (a) **Hint** : $M_B = \frac{K_b \times W_B \times 1000}{w_A \times \Delta T_b}$

80. (a) The species which have van't Hoff factor equal to S is $Al_2(SO_4)_3$ only.

81. (a) **Hint** : $\pi = \frac{n}{V} RT$

where, $n = \frac{1}{185000}$ mol

82. A → (2), B → (4), C → (3), D → (1)

83. *A* = Hydrogen

B = Decrease

C = Abnormal molar mass

84. $i = \frac{\text{Normal molar mass}}{\text{Abnormal molar mass}}$

85. (b) NaCl, $i = 2$

KCl, $i = 2$

$MgSO_4$, $i = 2$

K_2SO_4, $i = 3$

$CaCl_2$, $i = 3$

86. (b)

87. (d) **Hint** : $\pi_{XY} = 4\pi_{BaCl_2}$

$iCRT = 4 \times iCRT$

For *XY*, $i = 2$ and for $BaCl_2$, $i = 3$

88. (b) **Hint** : i = Observed freezing point/calculated freezing point

and $K_a = \frac{[CH_3COO^-][H^+]}{[CH_3COOH]}$

Assertion-Reason

1. (b) A homogeneous mixture consists of a single phase which has properties that may differ from those of the individual components.

2. (a)

3. (a)

4. (a)

5. (b)

6. (c) **Correct Reason** : Molarity is not a colligative property. It is only a concentration term.

7. (b)

8. (c) When a volatile solute is added to volatile solvent depression in boiling point is observed.

9. (a) Both A and R are correct and R is the correct explanation of A.

10. (c) Sodium ion (Na^+) and potassium ion (K^+) are responsible for maintaining proper osmotic pressure balance inside and outside of the cells of organisms.

Case-Based

1. (i) (d) II represents negative deviations and III represents positive deviations.

(ii) (a) Acetone and aniline mixture represents negative deviation from Raoult's law hence for this mixture, ΔH_{mix} and ΔV_{mix} is negative.

(iii) (b) For positive deviations, $p_A > p_A^\circ \chi_A$ and $p_B > p_B^\circ \chi_B$.

(iv) (b) Water and nitric acid mixture shows negative deviations from Raoult's law, hence

$p_A < p_A^\circ \chi_A$ and $p_B < p_B^\circ \chi_B$.

2. (i) (a) Vapour pressure of water $(p_A^\circ) = 17.5$ mm of Hg

Lowering of vapour pressure $(p_A^\circ - p_A) = 0.061$

Relative lowering of vapour pressure

$$= \frac{p_A^\circ - p_A}{p_A^\circ}$$

$$= \frac{0.061}{17.5} = 0.00348$$

(ii) (c) Vapour pressure of solution = Vapour pressure of solvent – Lowering in vapour pressure = 17.5 – 0.061

= 17.439 mm of Hg

(iii) (a) $\frac{p_A^\circ - p_A}{p_A^\circ} = \chi_B = 0.00348$

Hence, mole fraction of sugar = 0.00348

(iv) (c) $M_B = \frac{w_B M_A}{w_A \left[\frac{p_A^\circ - p_A}{p_A^\circ}\right]}$

$$= \frac{5 \times 18}{108 \times 0.00348} = 239.96 \text{ g}$$

Competition Edge Up

1. (b) Given,

Mass of NaCl = 5.85 g

Volume of water = 500 mL = 0.5 L

Using, Molarity

$$= \frac{\text{No. of moles of NaCl}}{\text{Volume of solution (in L)}}$$

$$M = \frac{\frac{5.85}{58.5}}{0.5}$$

$\Rightarrow M = 0.2\text{ M}$

2. (d) Concentration terms such as mass percentage, mole fraction and molality are independent of temperature.

However, molarity is a function of temperature. Since, it depends on the total volume of the solution.

Molarity

$$= \frac{\text{Mole of solute}}{\text{Volume of solution (in L)}}$$

3. (b) The A—B interactions in negative deviation solutions are stronger than the A—A and B—B interactions in the two liquids.

Due to greater interactions, A and B types of molecules have a lower tendency to escape from solutions than pure liquids.

As a result based on Raoult's law, each component of solution has a partial pressure lower than expected.

4. (a) Among the given options $(CH_3)_2CO + CS_2$, i.e. shows positive deviation from Raoult's law. Since, acetone-CS_2 attractions are and weaker than acetone-acetone attractions and $CS_2 - CS_2$ attractions.

5. (d) As dilution increases concentration of solution decreases and degree of dissociation increases, resulting in increase of van't Hoff factor.

So, the correct order will be

$i_A < i_B < i_C$.

Hence, option (d) is correct.

6. (5) $\Delta T_b = 0.52°C$

$\Delta T_b = i \times K_b \times m$

$0.52 = i \times 0.52 \times \frac{10}{200 \times 0.1}$

$i = 2$ ...(i)

$\alpha = \frac{i-1}{n-1}$

$AB_2 \rightarrow A^{2+} + 2B^-$

$n = 3$

$\alpha = \frac{2-1}{3-1}$

$\alpha = \frac{1}{2} = 0.5 = 5 \times 10^{-1}$

Hence, degree of ionisation is 5×10^{-1}.

7. (b) The relation between solubility and Henry's law constant is

Solubility $\propto \frac{1}{K_H}$

If K_H decreases, then solubility increases.

$\therefore$ Order of solubility of gases in water D > C > A.

8. (a) Osmotic pressure is given by

$\pi = CRT$

Plot is of between osmotic pressure and concentration. i.e. π *vs* C.

On comparing with $y = mx + C$

Slope $m = RT$

$25.73 = 0.083 \times T$

$T = 310\text{ K} = 37°C$

9. (c) (A) is true while (R) is false. This is because at normal temperature and pressure helium is practically insoluble in oxygen. However under extreme conditions very small amount of helium dissolve in oxygen.

10. (a) We know that,

Molality

$$= \frac{\text{Number of moles of solute}}{\text{Weight of the solvent (g)}} \times 1000$$

Given that molality = 1

Moles of solute = 0.5

$$1 = \frac{0.5}{\text{Weight of the solvent (g)}} \times 1000$$

Weight of the solvent (g) = 500 g of solvent.

Hence, option (a) is correct.

11. (c) According to Dalton's law of partial pressure,

Partial pressure of gas = mole fraction of gas in gaseous mixture × total pressure of gaseous mixture.

So, $p_1 = \chi_1 p$; $p_2 = \chi_2 p$; $p_3 = \chi_3 p$

Then, the total pressure is

$$p = p_1 + p_2 + p_3.$$

Hence, statement (c) is incorrect.

12. (a) van't Hoff factor for glucose, urea and sucrose is one as all are non-ionic.

Mass of glucose = 10 g

Molar mass of glucose = 180 g mol^{-1}

Number of moles of glucose

$$= \frac{10}{180} = \frac{1}{18} \text{ mol}$$

$$= 0.056 \text{ mol}$$

Mass of urea = 10 g

Molar mass of urea = 60 g mol^{-1}

Number of moles of urea

$$= \frac{10}{60} = \frac{1}{6} \text{ mol} = 0.167 \text{ mol}$$

Mass of sucrose = 10 g

Molar mass of sucrose = 342 g mol^{-1}

Number of moles of sucrose

$$= \frac{10}{342} = 0.029 \text{ mol}$$

Osmotic pressure is a colligative property which depends on the amount of solute present in the solution.

As the amount of urea is more than that of glucose and sucrose.

Amount of solute :
Urea > Glucose > Sucrose

∴ Osmotic pressure,

$$p_2 > p_1 > p_3$$

13. (b) From Dalton's law of partial pressure of gases.

We know,

$$p_i = \chi_i \times p$$

where,

p_i = partial pressure of ith component

χ_i = mole-fraction of ith component

p = total pressure = 27 bar

$$(\text{partial pressure})_{N_2} = (\text{mole-fraction})_{N_2} \times p$$

$$= \frac{n_{N_2}}{n_{N_2} + n_{Ar}} \times p$$

$$= \frac{\frac{7}{28}}{\frac{7}{28} + \frac{8}{40}} \times 27 \text{ bar} = 15 \text{ bar}$$

∴ Partial pressure of N_2 in the mixture is 15 bar.

14. (b) Let us study the nature of binary solutions made of two volatile liquids:

(a) **(Benzene + Toluene)** Ideal solution, obeys Raoult's law.

(b) **(Acetone + Chloroform)** Non-ideal solution, shows negative deviation from Raoult's law.

(c) **(Chloroethane + Bromoethane)** Ideal solution, obeys Raoult's law.

(d) **(Ethanol + Acetone)** Non-ideal solution, shows positive deviation from Raoult's law.

15. (c) Isotonic solutions have same osmotic pressure (π) at a given temperature.

$$\pi = CRT$$

When, two solutions have same molar concentration (C) their osmotic pressure will be equal.

Chapter-2

Electrochemistry

1. (d) **2.** True **3.** (d)

4. (i) Chemical, electrical

(ii) Copper to zinc electrode

(iii) Zinc to copper electrode

5. (i) Current flows from Cu to Zn electrode.

(ii) No flow of current.

(iii) Current flows from Zn to Cu electrode.

6. False; In galvanic cell, Gibb's energy of the spontaneous redox reaction is converted into electrical work.

7. (i) $Cu^{2+} + 2e^- \longrightarrow Cu(s)$

(Reduction half-reaction)

(ii) $Zn(s) \longrightarrow Zn^{2+} + 2e^-$

(Oxidation half-reaction)

8. (b) **9.** (c)

10. (i) Cell potential, volts

(ii) Cell emf

(iii) $E^\circ_{cell} = E^\circ_{cathode} - E^\circ_{anode}$

11. (i) $2Ag^+(aq) + 2e^- \longrightarrow 2Ag(s)$

(ii) $Cu(s) \longrightarrow Cu^{2+}(aq) + 2e^-$

12.

	Correct	Incorrect
I.	✓	×
II.	✓	×
III.	×	✓

Correct statement III :

$$E^\circ_{cell} = E^\circ_{right} - E^\circ_{left}$$

13. (a)

14. (i) One bar (ii) One molar

15. (i) Cu^{2+} (ii) Cu (iii) Cu

16. (b)

17. (b) Pb, Cr, Zn and Li are stronger reducing agent than H^+/H_2 couple.

18. + 0.34

Hint : $E^\circ_{cell} = E^\circ_{right} - E^\circ_{left}$

19. A→(3), B→ (2), C→ (4), D→ (1)

20. (i) Au^{3+} (ii) Br^-

21. Any three of the following

(i) pH of solution

(ii) Solubility product

(iii) Equilibrium constant

(iv) Potentiometric titration

(v) Other thermodynamic properties

22. False; A negative E° means that the redox couple is a stronger reducing agent than the H^+ / H_2 couple.

23. (d)

24. (c)

25. (i) Decrease (ii) Increase

26. (i) $E_{cell} = E^\circ_{cell} \dfrac{0.0591}{n} \log \dfrac{[Mg^{2+}]}{[Zn^{2+}]}$

Or

$$E_{cell} = E^\circ_{cell} - \frac{0.0591}{n} \log \frac{0.001}{0.0001}$$

(ii) $E_{cell} = E^\circ_{cell} - \dfrac{0.0591}{n} \log \dfrac{[Pb^{2+}]}{[H^+]^2}$

Or

$$E_{cell} = E^\circ_{cell} - \frac{0.0591}{n} \log \frac{0.001}{1}$$

27. (i) $Mg(s) \mid Mg^{2+}(aq)(0.130\ M) \parallel Ag^+(aq)(0.0001\ M) \mid Ag(s)$

(ii) 2.96 V

Hint :

$$E_{cell} = E^\circ_{cell} - \frac{2.303\,RT}{2F} \ln \frac{[Mg^{2+}]}{[Ag^+]^2}$$

28. (i) $Al(s) \mid Al^{3+}(aq)(0.01\ M) \parallel Cd^{2+}(aq)(0.1\ M) \mid Cd(s)$

(ii) 1.269 V

Hint :

$$E_{cell} = E^\circ_{cell} - \frac{0.059}{n} \log \frac{[Al^{3+}]}{[Cd^{2+}]}$$

29. Remains same, zero

30. $E^\circ_{cell} = \dfrac{2.303\,RT}{nF} \log K_C$

31. (b) **Hint** : $E^\circ_{cell} = \dfrac{0.059}{2} \log K_C$

32. True

33. (d) **Hint** : $\Delta_r G^\circ = -nFE^\circ_{cell}$

34. − 0.591 V

Hint :

$$E_{cell} = E^\circ_{cell} - \frac{0.0591}{n} \log \frac{[H_2]}{[H^+]}$$

35. (c) **Hint** :

$$E_{cell} = E^\circ_{cell} - \frac{0.0591}{n} \log \frac{[Ni^{2+}]}{[Ag^+]^2}$$

36. (a) **Hint** : Use : $\Delta G = -nE^\circ_{cell}F$

37. (d) **Hint** : $K = e^{nFE^\circ/RT}$

38. (d) **Hint** : Use $E^\circ_{cell} = E^\circ_{red} - E^\circ_{ox}$

39. (a) Among the given species Graphite and alloys are conductors.

40. A → (3), B → (2), C → (1)

41.

	Correct	Incorrect
I.	×	✓
II.	✓	×
III.	✓	×

Correct statement I : On increasing length of wire to double resistance of wire will be two times.

42. (i) Resistance (ii) Resistivity (iii) Sm^{-1}

43. Silver > Sodium > Iron > Graphite

44. 0.01 M KCl

45. **Insulators**–Glass, Teflon

Semiconductors–CuO, Silicon, Germanium.

46. Magnitude of their conductivity

47. False; The number of ceramic materials and mixed oxides show superconductivity at high temperature (150 K).

48. (d)

49. (i) Nature of electrolyte

(ii) Size of ion produced and their solvation.

(iii) Nature of solvent and viscosity.

(iv) Concentration of electrolyte.

(v) Temperature

50. *A*–decreases, *B*–increases

51. (a)

52. Cell constant, $G^* = \dfrac{l}{A}$

53. **Correct statements** :

I. The cell constant depends upon the distance between electrodes and their area of cross-section.

III. Change in temperature does not affect the value of cell constant.

54. A→ (2), B→(1), C→(4), D→(3)

55. (c)

56. (i) 0.248 $S\ m^{-1}$

(ii) $124 \times 10^{-4}\ S\ m^2\ mol^{-1}$

Hint : Cell constant = conductivity × resistance.

Molar conductivity $(\Lambda_m) = \dfrac{\kappa}{C}$

57. (i) 87.135 Ω cm

(ii) 0.01148 $S\ cm^{-1}$

(iii) 229.6 $S\ cm^2\ mol^{-1}$

Hint : Use, $\rho = \dfrac{RA}{l}$; $\kappa = \dfrac{1}{\rho}$

$$\Lambda_m = \frac{\kappa \times 1000}{C}$$

58. (a)

59. (i) (1)

(ii) Limiting molar conductivity

(iii) Type of electrolyte

60. $CaCl_2$, CaF_2, $MgCl_2$ have same value.

61. (i) (a)

(ii) $\Lambda^\circ_m = 150.0\ S\ cm^2\ mol^{-1}$

$A = 87.46\ S\ cm^2\ mol^{-1}$

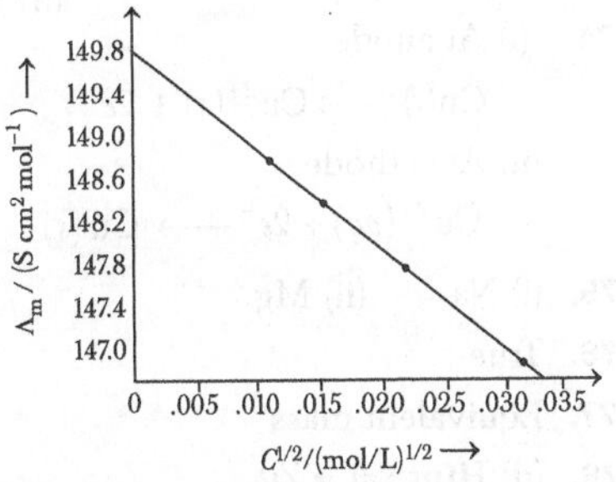

62. (i) True

(ii) False; Kohlrausch law shows that at infinite dilution concentration of ions decreases.

63. (i) H^+ (ii) Ca^{2+} (iii) Br^-

64. (a)

65. (i) Λ_m° for any electrolyte.
(ii) Determining dissociation constant for weak electrolytes.

66. (b)

67. (b) **Hint :**
$\Lambda_m^\circ(CaCl_2) = \lambda^\circ_{Ca^{2+}} + 2\lambda^\circ_{Cl^-}$
$\Lambda_m^\circ(MgSO_4) = \lambda^\circ_{Mg^{2+}} + \lambda^\circ_{SO_4^{2-}}$

68. 390.5 S cm^{2}mol^{-1}
Hint : $\Lambda_m^\circ(HAc) = \lambda^\circ_{H^+} + \lambda^\circ_{Ac^-}$
$= \lambda^\circ_{H^+} + \lambda^\circ_{Cl^-} + \lambda^\circ_{Ac^-} + \lambda^\circ_{Na^+} - \lambda^\circ_{Cl^-} - \lambda^\circ_{Na^+}$
$= \Lambda^\circ_{m(HCl)} + \Lambda^\circ_{m(NaAc)} - \Lambda^\circ_{m(NaCl)}$

69. (b) **Hint** : $\Lambda_m = \dfrac{K}{C}$; $\alpha = \dfrac{\Lambda_m}{\Lambda_m^\circ}$
and $K = \dfrac{C\alpha^2}{1-\alpha}$

70. (b)

71. **Hint** : $\Lambda^\circ_{m\,(HCl)} + \Lambda^\circ_{m\,(NaOH)} - \Lambda^\circ_{m\,(NaCl)}$

72. (a) **Hint :**
$\Lambda^\circ_{m\,(HCOOH)} = \lambda^\circ_{m\,(H^+)} + \lambda^\circ_{m(HCOO^-)}$
$\alpha = \dfrac{\Lambda_{m\,(HCOOH)}}{\Lambda^\circ_{m\,(HCOOH)}}, K = \dfrac{C\alpha^2}{(1-\alpha)}$

73. (d) **Hint :**
$\Lambda^\circ_{m\,(H_2SO_4)} = 2\lambda^\circ_{m\,(H^+)} + \lambda^\circ_{(SO_4^{2-})}$
$\Lambda^\circ_{m\,(K_2SO_4)} = 2\lambda^\circ_{(K^+)} + \lambda^\circ_{(SO_4^{2-})}$
$\Lambda^\circ_{m\,(CH_3COO^-K^+)} = \lambda^\circ_{(CH_3COO^-)} + \lambda^\circ_{(K^+)}$
and $\Lambda^\circ_{m\,(CH_3COOH)} = \lambda^\circ_{(CH_3COO^-)} + \lambda^\circ_{(H^+)}$

74. (i) At anode,
$Cu(s) \longrightarrow Cu^{2+}(s) + 2e^-$
(ii) At cathode,
$Cu^{2+}(aq) + 2e^- \longrightarrow Cu(s)$

75. (i) Na (ii) Mg

76. True

77. Equivalent mass

78. (d) **Hint** : $m = Zit$

79. (c) **Correct pair** :
Electricity/Current (in amp) $= \dfrac{\text{Charge}}{\text{Time}}$

80. (i) 3F (ii) 2F
Hint : 1 mole of electron has a charge of 1 Faraday.
(i) $Al^{3+} + 3e^- \longrightarrow Al$;
The reduction will require 3 Faraday.
(ii) The reduction of Cu^{2+} to Cu requires 2 Faraday.

81. (b) **Hint :**
Charge = Current × Time
We require 2F or 2 × 96500 C to deposit 1 mol or 63 g of Cu.
∴ Mass of Cu deposited
$= \dfrac{\text{Molar mass of Cu} \times \text{Charge}}{2\,F \text{ or } 2\times 96500 \text{ mol}^{-1}}$

82. (i) Nature of material being electrolysed.
(ii) Type of electrodes being used.

83. True; Such type of electrode work as a source or sink of electrons only.

84. (i) Reaction *A* (ii) Reaction *B*

85. (i) At cathode,
$Ag^+(aq) + \bar{e} \longrightarrow Ag(s)$
At anode,
$Ag(s) + NO_3^- \longrightarrow AgNO_3(aq) + \bar{e}$
(ii) At cathode,
$4Ag^+ + 4\bar{e} \longrightarrow 4Ag(s)$
At anode,
$4(OH)^- \longrightarrow O_2(g) + H_2O$

86. (c) **Hint** : $Q = I \times t$
We know that, 96487 C
$= 6.023 \times 10^{23}$ electrons

87. (b) **Hint** : In reduction, 6 electrons are involved means reduction requires 6 F.

88. 96487 C
Hint : $4FeO + O_2 \longrightarrow 2Fe_2O_3$
$Fe^{2+} \longrightarrow Fe^{3+} + e^-$

89. Chemical, electrical

90. False; Primary battery can not be revised again.

91. Used in (i) transistor (ii) clocks

92. (d) Electrolyte used in dry cell is a paste of ammonium chloride.

93. (i) At anode,
$Zn(s) \longrightarrow Zn^{2+}(aq) + 2e^-$
(ii) At cathode,
$MnO_2 + NH_4^+ + e^- \longrightarrow MnO(OH) + NH_3$
(iii) $NH_4Cl + ZnCl_2$
(iv) + 4 to + 3

94. (b) **Correct statement II** :
NaOH or KOH is used as an electrolyte in mercury cell.

95. (i) Mercury cell
(ii) $Zn(Hg) + 2OH^- \longrightarrow ZnO(s) + H_2O + 2e^-$
(iii) $HgO + H_2O + 2e^- \longrightarrow Hg(l) + 2OH^-$
(iv) Reducing agent = Zn
Oxidising agent = HgO

96. 1.5 V, 1.35 V

97. (d) **Correct statement** : It is a secondary cell.

98. $PbSO_4$ and $PbSO_4 + 2H_2O$

99. (b) On charging the battery, the reaction is reversed and $PbSO_4$ on anode and cathode is converted into Pb and PbO_2, respectively.

100. (i) Secondary lead storage battery.
(ii) 38% H_2SO_4

101. (a)

102. False; Ni - Cd cell is more expensive than lead storage cell.

103. $a = Ni(OH)_3$, $b = CdO$

104. (a) Mercury cell,
Anode :
$Zn(Hg) + 2\bar{O}H \longrightarrow ZnO(s) + H_2O + 2e^-$
Cathode :
$HgO + H_2O + 2e^- \longrightarrow Hg(l) + 2\bar{O}H$

105. A → (3), B → (1), C → (2)

106. (b) **Correct statement I** :
Thermal plants contribute to air pollution.

107. (i) Methane (ii) Methanol

108. (i) Fuel cell
(ii) (a) electrical power
(b) producing water
(iii) (a) Pt, (b) Pd
(iv) $2H_2(g) + O_2(g) \longrightarrow 2H_2O\,(l)$

109. A →(4), B →(3), C →(1), D →(2)

110. (i) Rusting of iron
(ii) Tarnishing of silver
(iii) Corrosion of copper

111. (a)

112. (d)

Assertion-Reason

1. (c) **Correct Reason** : At anode, oxidation takes place and at cathode, reduction takes place.
2. (b)
3. (c) The position of Zn is higher than Cu in electrochemical series.
4. (a) **5.** (a) **6.** (a)
7. (c) The process has lower value of electrode potential.
8. (a) **9.** (a) **10.** (b)

Case-Based

1. (i) (c) The half-cell having the higher reduction potential will undergo reduction process.

(ii) (d) Electrode potential of Mn^{3+} is higher than O_2.

(iii) (a) Half reactions :

$$I_2 + 2e^- \longrightarrow 2I^-$$

$$2Cl^- \longrightarrow Cl_2 + 2e^-$$

Reduction, $E° = 0.54$ V

Oxidation, $E° = -1.36$ V

emf $= -0.82$ V

(iv) (c) $Fe^{3+} + Mn^{2+} \longrightarrow Mn^{3+} + Fe^{2+}$

Two half reactions :

$$Fe^{3+} + e^- \longrightarrow Fe^{2+}$$

$$Mn^{2+} \longrightarrow Mn^{3+} + e^-$$

Reduction, $E° = 0.77$ V

Oxidation, $E° = -1.50$ V

emf $= -0.73$ V

Since, emf is negative, the reaction does not occur, i.e. Fe^{3+} does not oxidise Mn^{2+}.

2. (i) (b) $0.059 = \dfrac{+0.059}{2} \log \dfrac{0.001}{[M^{2+}]}$

$$\log \frac{0.001}{[M^{2+}]} = 2 \text{ or } [M^{2+}] = 10^{-5}$$

Let solubility of salt be S mol/litre

Thus, $\underset{S}{MX_2} \longrightarrow \underset{S}{M^{2+}} + \underset{2S}{2X^-}$

$$\therefore K_{sp} = 4S^3$$
$$= 4 \times (10^{-5})^3 = 4 \times 10^{-15}$$

(ii) (d) $\Delta G = -nFE$

$$= -2 \times 96500 \times 0.059$$
$$= -11387 \text{ J mol}^{-1}$$
$$= -11.4 \text{ kJ mol}^{-1}$$

(iii) (a) $E°_{cell} = \dfrac{0.059}{1} \log K_C$

$$E°_{cell} = E°_{Fe^{2+}/Fe^{3+}} + E°_{Ce^{4+}/Ce^{3+}}$$
$$= -0.68 + 1.44 = 0.76 \text{ V}$$

$$\log_{10} K_c = \frac{0.76}{0.059} = 12.88$$

$$K_c = 7.6 \times 10^{12}$$

(iv) (a) emf $= E_{cathode} - E_{anode}$

Competition Edge Up

1. (c) An electrochemical cell can be converted into an electrolytic cell by applying an external potential greater than $E°_{cell}$.
   The entire cell reaction will be reversed. The oxidised species will be reduced and the reduced species will be oxidised.
2. (d) $M \mid M^{+2} \parallel X \mid X^{2-}$
   The cell potential is given by
   $$E°_{cell} = -E°_{M/M^{+2}} + E°_{X/X^{-2}}$$
   $$= -0.46 + 0.34 = -0.12 \text{ V}$$
   As $E°_{cell}$ is negative, so anode becomes cathode and cathode becomes anode.
   Spontaneous reaction will be
   $$M^{+2} + X^{2-} \rightarrow M + X$$
   Hence, option (d) is correct.
3. (a) Among the given options only nature of electrode does not affect electrolytic conductance of a solution.
4. (a) The electrolytes A and B are weak and strong electrolyte respectively.
5. (a) Amount of substance deposited is given by Faraday's law,
   $$W = Zit$$
   $$W = ZQ \qquad [Q = it]$$
   $$Q = \frac{W}{Z}$$
   $W = QZ$ when $Q = 1$ then $W = Z$
   where, Z is electrochemical equivalent
   Hence, option (a) is correct.
6. (a) Given,
   Ionic conductivities,
   $\lambda_{C^{2+}} = 57 \text{ Scm}^2/\text{mol}$
   $\lambda_{A^{2-}} = 73 \text{ Scm}^2/\text{mol}$
   Molar conductivity of solution is given by
   $$\Lambda_{solution} = \lambda_{C^{2+}} + \lambda_{A^{2-}}$$
   $$= 57 + 73 = 130 \text{ S cm}^2/\text{mol}$$
   Hence, option (a) is correct.
7. (c) Units of molar conductivity $= \text{Scm}^2\text{mol}^{-1}$.
   Unit of (concentration)$^{1/2}$ $= \text{mol}^{1/2}\text{L}^{-1/2}$
   Units for slope
   $$= \frac{\text{Unit of molar conductivity}}{\text{Unit of (concentration)}^{1/2}}$$
   $$= \text{Scm}^2\text{mol}^{-3/2}\text{L}^{1/2}$$
8. (a) The correct match is
   A-II, B-IV, C-I, D-III
   A. $2H_2O \longrightarrow O_2 + 4H^+ + 4e^-$
   2 mol H_2O require 4F charge
   1 mol H_2O will require 2F charge.
   B. $8H^+ + MnO_4^- + 5e^- \longrightarrow Mn^{2+} + 4H_2O$
   1 mol of MnO_4^- will require 5F charge
   C. $CaCl_2 + 2e^- \longrightarrow Ca + 2Cl^-$
   1 mol of Ca will require 2F charge.
   1.5 mol of Ca will require 3F charge.
9. (b) Given, current (i) = 9.6487 A = 96487 C
   $t = 100$ s
   $$w = \frac{E(it)}{96487}$$
   $$\Rightarrow w = \frac{\frac{63}{2} \times 9.6487 \times 100}{96487}$$
   $w = 0.315$ g of Cu
10. (b) Given, conductivity (κ) $= 0.0210\ \Omega^{-1}\text{cm}^{-1}$

Resistance $= 60\ \Omega$

Cell constant = ?

We know that,

$$\kappa = \frac{1}{R} \times \frac{l}{a}$$

$$\text{Cell constant} = \frac{l}{a} = \kappa \times R$$

$$= 0.0210 \times 60$$

$$= 1.26\ \text{cm}^{-1}$$

11. (d)

Reduction

$$MnO_4^- + 8H^+ + 5e^- \longrightarrow Mn^{2+} + 4H_2O$$

$$E_{Mn^{2+}/MnO_4^-} = -1.510\ V$$

$$1/2O_2 + 2H^+ + 2e^- \longrightarrow 2H_2O$$

Reduction

$$E^\circ_{O_2/H_2O} = 1.223\ V$$

Reaction at cathode (reduction)

$$2MnO_4^- + 16H^+ + 10e^- \longrightarrow$$

$$2Mn^{2+} + 8H_2O;\ E^\circ_{RP} = 1.510\ V$$

Reaction at anode (oxidation)

$$5H_2O \longrightarrow \frac{5}{2}O_2 + 10H^+ + 10e^-$$

$$E^\circ_{OP} = -1.223\ V$$

The overall reaction is

$$2MnO_4^- + 6H^+ \longrightarrow 2Mn^{2+} + \frac{5}{2}O_2 + 3H_2O$$

$$E^\circ = E^\circ_{MnO_4^-/Mn^{2+}} - E^\circ_{O_2/H_2O}$$

$$E^\circ = 1.510 - 1.223$$

$$= 0.287\ V$$

Here, since the value of E° is positive, the reaction is spontaneous.

Hence, MnO_4^- will liberate O_2.

12. (b) Given, $E^\circ_{cell} = 1.05\ V$

$$\frac{2.303\ RT}{F} = 0.059$$

$$[Ni^{2+}] = 0.001\ M = 10^{-3}\ M$$

$$[Ag^+] = 0.001\ M = 10^{-3}\ M$$

Using Nernst equation,

$$E_{cell} = E^\circ_{cell} - \frac{0.059}{n}\log\frac{[Ni^{+2}]^1}{[Ag^+]^2}$$

$$= 1.05 - \frac{0.059}{2}\log\frac{(10^{-3})}{(10^{-3})^2}$$

$$= 1.05 - \frac{0.059}{2}\log 10^3$$

$$= 1.05 - \frac{0.059}{2} \times 3$$

$$= 1.05 - 0.0885;\ E_{cell} = 0.9615$$

13. (c) $\lambda_{CH_3COOH} = 20\ S\ cm^2\ mol^{-1}$

Concentration of CH_3COOH, $C = 0.007\ M$

$$\lambda^\circ_{H^+} = 350\ S\ cm^2\ mol^{-1}$$

$$\lambda^\circ_{CH_3COO^-} = 50\ S\ cm^2\ mol^{-1}$$

According to Kohlrausch's law,

$$\lambda^\circ_{CH_3COOH} = \lambda^\circ_{H^+} + \lambda^\circ_{CH_3COO^-}$$

$$\lambda^\circ_{CH_3COOH} = 350 + 50$$

$$= 400\ S\ cm^2\ mol^{-1}$$

Degree of dissociation,

$$\alpha = \frac{\lambda_{CH_3COOH}}{\lambda^\circ_{CH_3COOH}}$$

$$\alpha = \frac{20}{400} = \frac{1}{20} = 0.05 = 5 \times 10^{-2}$$

$$CH_3COOH \rightleftharpoons CH_3COO^- + H^+$$

$t = 0$ $\quad C \quad - \quad -$

$t = t_{eq}$ $\quad C - C\alpha \quad C\alpha \quad C\alpha$

Equilibrium constant,

$$k = \frac{C^2\alpha^2}{C(1-\alpha)} = \frac{C\alpha^2}{1-\alpha}$$

As $\alpha << 1; 1 - \alpha \approx 1$

$$k = C\alpha^2$$

$$= 0.007 \times (0.05)^2$$

$$= 0.007 \times 25 \times 10^{-4}$$

$$= 1.75 \times 10^{-5}\ mol\ L^{-1}$$

14. (b) Molar conductance of NaCl,

$$\lambda^\circ_{NaCl} = 126.45\ S\ cm^2\ mol^{-1}$$

Molar conductance of HCl,

$$\lambda^\circ_{HCl} = 426.16\ S\ cm^2\ mol^{-1}$$

Molar conductance of $CH_3CO\overset{-}{O}\overset{+}{N}a$,

$$\lambda^\circ_{CH_3COONa} = 91.0\ S\ cm^2\ mol^{-1}$$

According to Kohlrausch's law;

$$\lambda^\circ_{HCl} = \lambda^\circ_{H^+} + \lambda^\circ_{Cl^-} \quad \ldots(i)$$

$$\lambda^\circ_{NaCl} = \lambda^\circ_{Na^+} + \lambda^\circ_{Cl^-} \quad \ldots(ii)$$

$$\lambda^\circ_{CH_3COONa^+} = \lambda^\circ_{Na^+} + \lambda^\circ_{CH_3COO^-} \quad \ldots(iii)$$

$$\lambda^\circ_{CH_3COOH} = (\lambda^\circ_{CH_3COO^-} + \lambda^\circ_{H^+})$$

$$\lambda^\circ_{CH_3COONa} = (\lambda^\circ_{CH_3COO^-} + \lambda^\circ_{Na^+}) + (\lambda^\circ_{H^+} + \lambda^\circ_{Cl^-}) - (\lambda^\circ_{Na^+} + \lambda^\circ_{Cl^-})$$

$$\lambda^\circ_{CH_3COOH} = \lambda^\circ_{CH_3COONa^+} + \lambda^\circ_{HCl} - \lambda^\circ_{NaCl}$$

$$\lambda^\circ_{CH_3COOH} = 91.0 + 426.16 - 126.45$$

$$\lambda^\circ_{CH_3COOH} = 390.71\ S\ cm^2\ mol^{-1}$$

15. (b) The reaction that takes place in a fuel cell is

$$\overset{0}{2H_2}(g) + \overset{0}{O_2}(g) \longrightarrow 2\overset{+1\ -2}{H_2O}(l)$$

[at anode] [at cathode] — Reactants (R); Product (P)

[Heat energy gets converted into electrical energy]

Hence, option (b) is the correct.

16. (c) Let us consider the segment of EMF series (standard reduction potential) of the given reduction half-cell reactions :

Reduction half reaction	E/V at 298K
(a) $Mg^{2+} + 2e^- \longrightarrow Mg$	− 2.36
(b) $Fe^{2+} + 2e^- \longrightarrow Fe$	− 0.44
(c) $Au^{3+} + 3e^- \longrightarrow Au$	+ 1.40
(d) $K^+ + e^- \longrightarrow K$	− 2.93

Hence, option (c) is correct.

Chapter-3

Chemical Kinetics

1. (d)

2. Reaction rate, mechanism

3. A = Thermodynamics

B = Chemical kinetics

4. (d)

5. (i) $-\frac{\Delta[R]}{\Delta t}$ (ii) $+\frac{\Delta[P]}{\Delta t}$

6. Change in concentration of reactants or products per unit time.

7. True **8.** (b)

9. $A - r_{inst} = \frac{-d[R]}{dt} = -\text{slope}$

$B - r_{inst} = \frac{-d[P]}{dt} = \text{slope}$

10. True

11. (i) $5.12 \times 10^{-5}\ mol\ L^{-1}\ s^{-1}$

(ii) (a) 1.90 (b) 0.0905

(c) 100 (d) 0.0741

12. False; The instantaneous rate is used to predict the rate of reaction at particular instant.

13. (d) **Hint** : Initial rate of conversion of $P = \frac{[\Delta P]}{\Delta t}$

14. (c)

15. (b)

16. (a) **Hint** : Average rate $= \frac{-\Delta[R]}{\Delta t} = \frac{\Delta[P]}{\Delta t}$

17. True

18. (a) **Hint** : Rate $= -\frac{d[R]}{dt} = \frac{d[P]}{dt}$

19. Temperature, catalyst, pressure and concentration of reactants.

20. False; Exponents x and y are not necessarily equal to the stoichiometric coefficients a and b.

21. (i) Four times (ii) Doubled

22. (c)

23. (c) **Correct statement :** Order of a reaction may be zero, whole number or fraction number.

24. III < II < I

$$\text{Rate} = k[A]^x[B]^y$$
$$\text{Order} = x + y$$

25. (i) First order reaction
(ii) mol L^{-1} s^{-1}
(iii) Second order reaction

26. (c) For second order reaction, units of $k = \text{mol}^{-1}\text{L s}^{-1}$
For zero order reaction, units of $k = \text{mol L}^{-1}\text{ s}^{-1}$

27. (i) Unimolecular
(ii) Bimolecular
(iii) Trimolecular
(iv) Bimolecular

28.

	Correct	Incorrect
I.	✓	×
II.	×	✓
III.	×	✓

Correct statements :
II. Molecularity is applicable for unimolecular reaction.
III. Slowest step controls rate of overall reaction as determining step.

29. (c) Order of a reaction may be zero, whole number or fraction number.

30. Zero order

31. (a) **Correct statement II** : Sum of power of the concentration of reactants in rate law expression is called order of the reaction.

32. (b) Rate $= k[NH_3]^0$ for given reaction.

33. Zero order reaction

34. (b) **35.** First order

36. First,
$$C_2H_4(g) + H_2(g) \longrightarrow C_2H_6(g);$$
$$\text{Rate} = k[C_2H_4]^1$$

37. (c) NH_4, NO_2, NO and O_3 undergoes unimolecular decomposition reaction.

38. (a) **Correct statement II** : Radioactive decay of unstable nuclei takes place by first order kinetics.

39. (b) NH_3 undergoes zero order, N_2O_5, N_2O, H_2O undergo 1st order while NO_2 undergo second order reaction.

40. (c)

41. (d) All of the given species are examples of pseudo first order reaction is under photochemical reactions.

42. (d) **Hint** : Rate $= k[P][Q_2]$ and $[P] = \{k_{eq}[P_2]\}^{1/2}$

43. (c) **Hint** : $k = \frac{2.303}{(t_2 - t_1)} \log \frac{[R]_1}{[R]_2}$

44. (c) **Hint** : $k = \frac{2.303}{t} \log \frac{p_i}{p_A}$

45. (c) **Correct pair** : First order reaction $= t_{1/2} = \frac{0.693}{k}$

46. 1.26×10^{13} s
Hint : $t_{1/2} = \frac{0.693}{k}$

47. (a) **Hint** : $k = \frac{2.303}{t} \log \frac{p_0}{p_0 - x}$

48. (b)

49. (i) $[R] = [R]_0 e^{-kt}$
or $kt = \ln \{[R]_0/[R]\}$
(ii) time^{-1} or s^{-1}
(iii) 0
(iv) $[R]_0/2k$

50. (b)

51. False; The reactions which are not actually of first order but behave so due to altered conditions are called pseudo first order reaction.

52. Pseudo first order

53. (i) Rate $= k[C_{12}H_{22}O_{11}]$
(ii) Pseudo first order reaction

54. (c) **Hint** : $k = \frac{2.303}{t} \log \frac{C_0}{C}$

55. (c) **Hint** : $k = \frac{2.303}{t} \log \frac{C_1}{C_2}$

56. 1.925×10^{-4} s^{-1}

57. False; Most of the reactions are accelerated by increase in temperature.

58. (b)

59. False; Potassium permanganate gets decolourised faster at a higher temperature.

60. (i) A (ii) Fraction of molecules

61. (i) A (ii) C

62. Released

63. Nature of reactants and products

64. (a) **65.** True

66. A : Most probable kinetic energy

67. Increases

68. (i) (b) (ii) broadens, right

69. (b) **Correct statement II** : On increasing temperature by 10°C, rate of reaction gets doubled.

70. (i) $-E_a / R$
(ii) $\log \frac{k_2}{k_1} = \frac{E_a}{2.303\,R}\left[\frac{1}{T_1} - \frac{1}{T_2}\right]$

71. (c) **Hint** :
$$\log \frac{k_2}{k_1} = \frac{E_a}{2.303\,R}\left[\frac{T_2 - T_1}{T_1 T_2}\right]$$

72. 6.36×10^{-3} s^{-1}
Hint : $\log k_2 - \log k_1 = \frac{E_a}{2.303\,R}\left[\frac{T_2 - T_1}{T_1 T_2}\right]$

73. To increase its rate

74. Inhibitor

75. False; Catalyst form temporary bonds with reactant resulting in an intermediate complex to yield product.

76. (b) **Correct statement** : It decreases the activation energy between reactants and products.

77. E_a ; Catalyst affects the activation energy by lowering the reaction pathway.

78. (b) **Correct statement** : It does not alter ΔG of the reaction.

79. (d) **Correct statements** :

I. In the presence of a catalyst heat does not evolved.

II. It only catalyses spontaneous reactions fast and effectively.

80. Collision frequency

81. (d) **82.** True

83. (b) **84.** (b)

85. (a) **86.** 1.47×10^{-19}

87. (b) **Hint** : $\log\frac{k_2}{k_1}=\frac{E_a}{2.303\,R}\left[\frac{T_2-T_1}{T_1T_2}\right]$

Assertion-Reason

1. (a)

2. (d) **Correct Assertion** : Order and molecularity are same for most of the reactions but not for all.

3. (c) **Correct Reason** : For complex reactions molecularity has no meaning.

4. (b) **Correct Reason** Order is determined experimentally hence can be zero or fractional.

5. (c) $t_{1/2}=\frac{0.693}{k}$

6. (b)

7. (b) **Correct Reason** : For zero order reaction, rate is independent of concentration.

8. (c) **Correct Reason** : Reactant molecules undergo chemical change respective of their orientation during collision.

9. (a)

10. (d) **Correct Assertion** : Only effective collision of reactant molecules lead to product formation.

Case-Based

1. (i) (c) $2NO(g)+Cl_2(g)\longrightarrow 2NOCl(g)$

Molecularity = 3

(ii) (d) As the order w.r.t NO is 2 and order w.r.t Cl_2 is 1, hence the overall order is 3.

(iii) (c) Substituting the values of experiment 1 in rate law expression.

$$0.60\text{ M min}^{-1}=K\,(0.15\text{ M})^2\,(0.15\text{ M})^1$$

$$\text{or } k=\frac{0.60\text{ M min}^{-1}}{0.0225\times0.15\text{ M}^3}=177.77\text{ M}^{-2}\text{ min}^{-1}$$

(iv) (d) $r=177.77\text{ M}^{-2}\text{ min}^{-1}\times(0.25\text{ M})^2\,(0.25\text{ M})=2.77\text{ M min}^{-1}$

2. (i) (a) Unit of rate constant for a reaction of nth order $=(\text{conc.})^{1-n}\text{ time}^{-1}$

(ii) (d) $\underset{\text{Initial conc.}}{12\text{M}}\xrightarrow{t_{(1/2)}}6\text{M}\xrightarrow{t_{(1/2)}}3\text{M}$

$t_{1/2}=10$ min

$$k=\frac{0.693}{10}=0.0693\text{ min}^{-1}$$

As $t_{1/2}$ is 10 min, after 20 minutes the concentration will be 3M.

Hence, rate = 0.0693×3 M min^{-1}

(iii) (b) $t_{1/2}=23$ min

$$t_{1/2}=\frac{0.693}{k}\Rightarrow k=\frac{0.693}{3}\text{ min}^{-1}$$

For 90% completion,

$$t=\frac{2.303}{k}\log\left(\frac{a}{a-x}\right)$$

$$=\frac{2.303\times23}{0.693}\log\left(\frac{100}{100-90}\right)$$

= 76.4 min

(iv) (a) $t_{\frac{1}{2}}=\frac{0.693}{k}$

$$\Rightarrow k=\frac{0.693}{60}=0.01155\text{ min}^{-1}$$

$$k=\frac{2.303}{t}\log\left(\frac{a}{a-x}\right)$$

$$0.01155\text{ min}^{-1}=\frac{2.303}{240\text{ min}}\log\left(\frac{100}{a-x}\right)$$

$(a-x)=6.25\%$

Competition Edge Up

1. (8) Given $r=k\,[A]^2\,[B]$

If concentration is doubled

$r'=k\,[2A]^2\,[2B]^1$

$r'=8r\Rightarrow x=8$

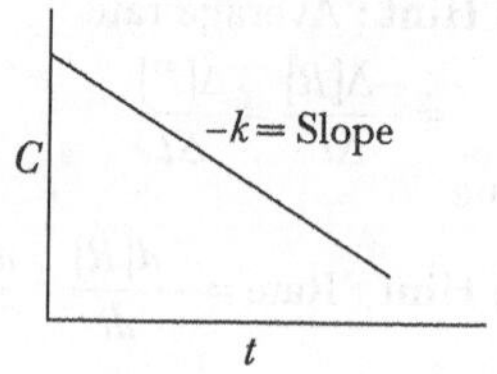

Zero order $y=0$

So $x+y=8$

2. (17) For reaction,

$2N_2O_5(g)\longrightarrow4NO_2(g)+O_2(g)$

Rate of reaction (*ROR*)

$$=-\frac{1}{2}\frac{\Delta[N_2O_5]}{\Delta t}$$

$$=\frac{1}{4}\frac{\Delta[NO_2]}{\Delta t}=\frac{\Delta[O_2]}{\Delta t}$$

$$ROR=-\frac{1}{2}\frac{\Delta[N_2O_5]}{\Delta t}$$

$$=-\frac{1}{2}\frac{(2.75-3)}{30}\text{ mol L}^{-1}\text{min}^{-1}$$

$$ROR=-\frac{1}{2}\frac{(-0.25)}{30}$$

$$=\frac{1}{240}\text{ mol L}^{-1}\text{ min}^{-1}$$

Rate of formation of NO_2

$$=\frac{\Delta[NO_2]}{\Delta t}$$

$=4\times ROR$

$$=\frac{4}{240}$$

$=16.66\times10^{-3}$ mol L^{-1} min^{-1}

$\approx17\times10^{-3}$ mol L^{-1} min^{-1}

3. (b)

	$A(g)$ $\longrightarrow$	$B(g)$ +	$C(g)$
At $t=0$	p	0	0
At $t=0$	p_i-x	x	x

$p_t=p_i-x+x+x$

$p_t=p_i+x$

$$k=\frac{2.303}{t}\log\frac{p_i}{(2p_i-p_t)}$$

4. Reaction rate,

$$R=\frac{1}{\text{Time required}}\ln\left[\frac{\text{Initial conc.}}{\text{Final conc.}}\right]$$

Acc. to question,

$$R = \frac{1}{t_{99.9\%}} \ln\left[\frac{100}{0.1}\right]$$

$$t_{99.9\%} = t_{90\%} \frac{\ln [10^3]}{\ln [10]}$$

$$t_{99.9\%} = 3 \times t_{90\%}$$

5. (399) Rate of reaction, $r = k[A]$

Order of reaction = 1

$$k = \frac{2.303}{t} \log\left(\frac{a}{a-x}\right)$$

$$t = 399 \text{ min}$$

6. (24) Rate of 1st order reaction,

$$R = k[A]_0 e^{-kt}$$

$$t_{\frac{1}{2}} = \frac{600 \times \log 2}{\log 4 - \log 3}$$

$$= 24 \text{ min}$$

7. (b) Given,

Rate $(r) = k[A]^2 [B]$ ...(i)

$r_1 = k[3A]^2 [B]$ ...(ii)

Dividing Eqs. (i) by (ii) we get

$$\frac{r}{r_1} = \frac{k\ [A]^2\ [B]}{k\ [3A]^2\ [B]}$$

$$\frac{r}{r_1} = \frac{1}{9} \Rightarrow r_1 = 9r$$

The initial rate would increase by a factor of nine.

8. (d) Formula for calculating activation energy is given by

$$\log_{10}\left(\frac{k_2}{k_1}\right) = \frac{E_a}{2.303\,R}\left[\frac{1}{T_1} - \frac{1}{T_2}\right]$$

Here, k_1 is rate constant at T_1

k_2 is rate constant at T_2.

Hence, rate constant at two different temperatures should be known to calculate the activation energy of any chemical reaction.

9. (d) According to Arrhenius equation,

$$k = A.e^{-E_a/RT}$$

$$\ln k = \ln A - \frac{E_a}{RT}$$

$$\ln k = \frac{-E_a}{R}\left(\frac{1}{T}\right) + \ln A$$

Compare it with $y = mx + c$

$\ln k \to y$ and $1/T \to x$

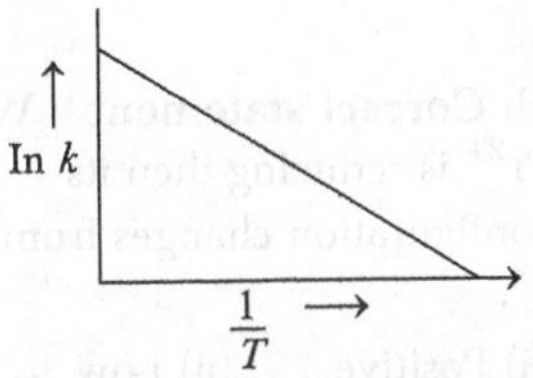

Hence, option (d) match the correct graph.

10. (a) Given, rate is quadruples, i.e.

$r_2 = 4r_1$

We know,

$$\frac{r_2}{r_1} = 4 = \frac{k_2}{k_1}$$

Now,

$$\log_{10}\left(\frac{k_2}{k_1}\right) = \frac{E_a}{2.303R}\left[\frac{1}{T_1} - \frac{1}{T_2}\right]$$

[where, $T_1 = 27°\text{C} = 300\text{K}$,

$T_2 = 57°\text{C} = 330\text{K}$]

$$\log_{10}(4) = \frac{E_a \times 1000}{2.303 \times 8.314}\left(\frac{1}{300} - \frac{1}{330}\right)$$

$$E_a = 38.04 \text{ kJ/mol}$$

11. (a) Given, Initial concentration $[A_0] = 0.1$ M

Conc. after 5 min $[A_t] = 0.001$ M

$t = 5$ minutes

Using rate constant formula for 1st order reaction

$$k = \frac{2.303}{t} \log\left(\frac{A_0}{A_t}\right)$$

$$= \frac{2.303}{5} \log\left(\frac{0.1}{0.001}\right)$$

$$k = \frac{2.303 \times 2}{5} = 0.9212 \text{ min}^{-1}$$

Hence, the rate constant for the reaction is $k = 0.9212 \text{ min}^{-1}$.

12. (b) The enthalpy of reaction is negative, -4.2 kJ mol^{-1}. So, the reaction is an exothermic reaction.

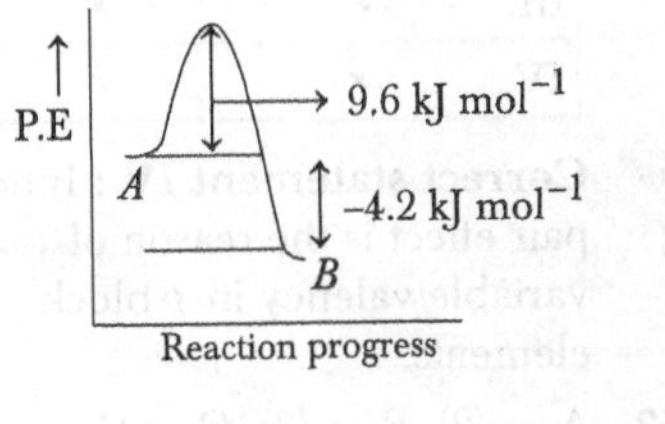

13. (a) Arrhenius equation,

$$k = Ae^{\frac{-E_a}{RT}}$$

$$E_a = 41.5 \text{ kJ/mol}$$

14. (c) An increase in the concentration of the reactants of a reaction leads to change in collision frequency. It is defined as the number of collisions per second per unit volume of reaction mixture.

15. (*b*) For a first order reaction,

Rate constant $(k) = 4.606 \times 10^{-3} \text{ s}^{-1}$

Initial amount $(a_0) = 2$g

Final amount $(a) = 0.2$ g

So, time required,

$$t = \frac{2.303}{k} \log \frac{a_0}{a}$$

$$= \frac{2.303}{4.606 \times 10^{-3}} \times \log \frac{2}{0.2} = 500 \text{ s}$$

16. (*a*) For a zero order reaction,

$$t = \frac{1}{k}(a_0 - a)$$

$$\Rightarrow t_{50} = \frac{1}{k} \times \frac{a_0}{2} \quad [\because \text{at } t_{50},\ a = a_0/2]$$

$$\Rightarrow k = \frac{a_0}{2 \times t_{50}} = \frac{0.02 \text{ M}}{2 \times 100 \text{ s}}$$

$$= 1 \times 10^{-4} \text{ Ms}^{-1}$$

$$= 1 \times 10^{-4} \text{ mol L}^{-1} \text{ s}^{-1}$$

Chapter-4

d- and f-Block Elements

1. (c)

2. Lanthanoids, actinoids

3. (i) True

(ii) False; According to IUPAC, transition metals are those metals which have incomplete *d*-subshell.

4. (i) Gold, silver, platinum

(ii) Iron, titanium and copper

5. (b) Cu(I) is more stable than Cu(II) because of fully-filled electronic configuration.

6. 4*s* to 3*d*, small

7. (ii) $(n-1)d^{10}ns^2$

8. Any four of the following

(i) Catalytic property

(ii) Paramagnetic behaviour

(iii) Formation of coloured ions
(iv) Complex formation
(v) Variable oxidation states

9. (b) Rh has 8 and Pt has 9 electrons in outermost *d*-orbital.

10. (i) $[Kr]4d^{10}5s^1$
(ii) $[Kr]4d^9$

11. Malleability, high thermal conductivity, lustre.

12.

ccp	bcc	hcp
Ni	Cr	Tc
Cu	Mo	Zn

13. (i) Mn has d^5 configuration, i.e. half-filled orbital, thus more stable hence, lesser possibility of metallic bonding.
(ii) Metal-metal bonding in compounds of 3*d*-transition metal is less than 4*d* and 5*d* series compounds.
(iii) Tungsten.

14. (c) **Correct pair** : The transition metals are very hard and have low volatility.

15. (a) Absence of unpaired *d*-electrons and larger size of Zn atoms, make the crystal lattice of Zn less closely packed.

16. (b) **17.** (b)

18. Lanthanoid contraction

19. (b) **Correct statement II** : Second ionisation enthalpy of Zn is also higher that of Cr.

20. Cr > Mn > V > Ti

21. (d) Due to stable configuration, i.e. $3d^5$ (Mn^{2+}).

22. (d) **23.** (a) (i), (b) (i)

24. Manganese **25.** (b)

26.

	Correct	Incorrect
I.	×	✓
II.	✓	×
III.	✓	×
IV.	×	✓

27. False; Given statement is true for *d*-block elements, however for *p*-block elements, the higher oxidation states are favoured by heavier members.

28. (c)

29. (d) **Correct statement** : When Cr^{2+} is reducing then its configuration changes from d^4 to d^3.

30. (i) Positive (ii) Low
(iii) High

31. (i) $TiCl_4$ (ii) VF_5 (iii) CrF_6

32. (a) **33.** (i) Cu (ii) Ni

34. (d)

35. $VO_2^+ < Cr_2O_7^{2-} < MnO_4^-$

As the oxidation state increases, the oxidising power increases.

36. A → (2), B → (3), C → (1)

37. (c)

38. A → (2), B → (3), C → (1)

39. Cr^{2+}, – 0.41 V

40. (i) Spin angular momentum
(ii) Orbital angular momentum

41. (i) Unpaired electrons, spin only
(ii) $\mu = \sqrt{n(n+2)}$

42. $Sc^{3+} < Ti^{3+} < Ti^{2+} < Co^{3+} < Fe^{2+} < Mn^{2+}$

43. (b) M^{2+} $(Z = 27)$:

$1s^2 2s^2 2p^6 3s^2 3p^6 3d^7$

No. of unpaired electrons = 3

44. Co^{2+} and Cr^{3+}

45. (a) V^{2+} and Co^{2+} have magnetic moment 3.87.

46. True

47. (i) Colourless (ii) Fe^{3+}
(iii) Ti^{3+} (iv) Blue
(v) Pink

48. $[Fe(CN)_6]^{3-}$, $[Fe(CN)_6]^{4-}$

49. (b)

50. (d)

51.

	Correct	Incorrect
I.	✓	×
II.	✓	×
III.	✓	×
IV.	×	✓

Correct statement IV : Inert pair effect is the reason of variable valency in *p*-block elements.

52. A → (2), B → (3), C → (1)

53. (d) Interstitial compounds are chemically inert.

54. Any two of the following
(i) $VH_{0.56}$, (ii) $TiH_{1.7}$ (iii) TiC, (iv) Mn_4N (v) Fe_3H

55. Homogeneous, hard, melting point

56. (c) **Correct pair** : Brass is an alloy of copper and zinc.

57. (d)

58. $x = +6, y = +7, z = +4$

59. False; As oxidation number of a metal increases, ionic character decreases.

60. V_2O_5, Cr_2O_3

61. (b)

62. $A = FeCr_2O_4$
$B = Na_2CrO_4$
$C = Na_2Cr_2O_7 \cdot 2H_2O$,

Reactions involved in the question are

$$4FeCr_2O_4 + 8Na_2CO_3 + 7O_2 \longrightarrow 8Na_2CrO_4 + 2Fe_2O_3 + 8CO_2$$

$$2Na_2CrO_4 + 2H^+ \longrightarrow Na_2Cr_2O_7 + 2Na^+ + H_2O$$

63. $Na_2Cr_2O_7 + 2KCl \longrightarrow K_2Cr_2O_7 + 2NaCl$

64. (i) $Na_2Cr_2O_7$ (ii) $K_2Cr_2O_7$

65. (c)

66. False; Acidified $K_2Cr_2O_7$ oxidises Fe^{2+} to Fe^{3+}.

67. (i) Tetrahedral
(ii) 126°

68. (c) $2CuSO_4 + KI \longrightarrow 2CuI + I_2 + 2K_2SO_4$

$$H_2O_2 + 2KI \longrightarrow 2KOH + I_2$$

$$Cl_2 + 2KI \longrightarrow 2KCl + I_2$$

$$O_3 + H_2O + 2KI \longrightarrow 2KOH + O_2 + I_2$$

$$FeCl_3 + 2KI \longrightarrow 2KCl + FeCl_2 + I_2$$

$$HNO_3 + KI \longrightarrow KNO_3 + I_2 + NO$$

69. $X = MnO_2$
$Y = K_2MnO_4$
$Z = MnO_4^-$

70. (d) Acidified potassium dichromate will oxidise iodide to iodine, sulphide to sulphur, tin(II) to tin(IV) and iron(II) salts to iron(III).

71. (a) **Correct statement II** : Green manganate ion is paramagnetic, while purple permanganate ion is diamagnetic in nature.

72. (i) $MnO_2 + KOH + KIO_3$
(ii) $I_2 + H_2O + Mn^{2+}$

73. (a) **74.** $KClO_4$

75. (a) Overall reaction

$$5C_2O_4^{2-} + 2MnO_4^- + 16H^+ \longrightarrow 10CO_2 + 2Mn^{2+} + 8H_2O$$

$\therefore$ 5 moles of oxalic acid are oxidised by 3 moles of $KMnO_4$ in acidic medium.

76. (i) $5NO_2^- + 2MnO_4^- + 6H^+ \longrightarrow 2Mn^{2+} + 5NO_3^- + 3H_2O$

(ii) $8MnO_4^- + 3S_2O_3^{2-} + H_2O \longrightarrow 8MnO_2 + 6SO_4^{2-} + 2OH^-$

77. False; Manganous salt is oxidised to MnO_2 in the presence of zinc sulphate or zinc oxide.

78. (b)

79. $KMnO_4$

80. (d)

81. (i) Wide range of oxidation states
(ii) Radioactive nature

82. (c)

83. (b) **Correct statement II** : Yb^{3+} has f^{13} configuration.

84. (a)

85. (i) True
(ii) False; E°_{value} of Ce^{4+}/Ce^{3+} is + 1.74 V which suggest that it can oxidise water.

86.

	Correct	Incorrect
I.	✓	×
II.	✓	×
III.	×	✓

Correct statement III : Tb (IV) has half-filled f-orbitals and it is an oxidant.

87. A→ (2), B → (4), C → (1), D → (3)

88. (i) Colourless-(b)
(ii) Paramagnetic-(a), (c)

89. 600, 1200

90. (i) LnX_3 (ii) $Ln(OH)_3$, H_2
(iii) Ln_2O_3

91. (a)

92. (i) Petroleum cracking
(ii) Bullets
(iii) Television screen

93. True

94. (c) Tm is a lanthanoid.

95. $[Rn] 5f^{1\text{-}14} 6d^{0\text{-}1} 7s^2$

96. (b) **97.** (b)

98. Pa : $5f^2 6d^1 7s^2$; U : $5f^3 6d^1 7s^2$
Np : $5f^4 6d^1 7s^2$

99. (i) Np (ii) Pu

100. (i) True (ii) True

101. (c) Np and Pu shows maximum oxidation state of +7.

102. (d) $Ln(OH)_3 + H_2, Ln_2O_3, H_2$

103. A → (4), B → (3), C → (1), D → (2)

104. (a) True (b) False
Silver UK coins are made up of copper (Cu) and Nickel (Ni) alloy.

Assertion-Reason

1. (a)

2. (b) **Correct Reason** : Osmium shows +8 oxidation state due to its ability to expand its octet by using its all electrons.

3. (a) **4.** (a)

5. (b) **Correct Reason** : Catalytic action of Fe^{3+} is due to its ability to adopt multiple oxidation states and form complexes.

6. (b) Due to charge transfer spectrum from ligand to metal the colour developed is intense as compared to d-d transition.

$CrO_4^{2-} \Rightarrow x + 4(-2) = -2$
$x = +6$

7. (a)

8. (c) **Correct Reason** : Oxidation state of Mn changes from +7 to +2 during reaction.

9. (a)

10. (d) **Correct Assertion** : Actinoids form relatively more stable complexes than lanthanoids.

Case-Based

1. (i) (a)
(ii) (a) Lesser and negative reduction potential indicates that Cr^{2+} is a reducing agent. Higher and positive reduction potential indicates that Mn^{3+} is a stronger oxidising agent.
(iii) (a) The electrode which has more reduction potential is a good oxidising agent and has least reducing power.
(iv) (a) The stability of $Cu^{2+}(aq)$ rather than $Cu^+(aq)$ is due to the much more negative $\Delta_{hyd}H^\circ$ of $Cu^{2+}(aq)$ than Cu^+, which more than compensates for the 2nd ionisation enthalpy of Cu.

2. (i) (a) X = Tb→ $4f^9 6s^2$
$= Tb^{3+} \rightarrow 4f^8$
$Y = Er \rightarrow 4f^{12} 6s^2$
$= Er^{3+} \rightarrow 4f^{11}$
$Z = Yb \rightarrow 4f^{14} 6s^2$
$= Yb^{3+} \rightarrow 4f^{13}$
(ii) (a) (iii) (c) (iv) (a)

Competition Edge Up

1. (d) The metal which shows highest and maximum number of oxidation state is Mn.
Oxidation number (Highest) = + 7

2. (b) Given, atomic number of Es = 99
So, its electronic configuration
$= [Rn] 5f^{11} 6d^0 7s^2$

3. (d) Lanthanoids = Eu, Er, Tb, Yr and Lu
Actinoides = Cm
Hence, Cm does not belongs to lanthanoid.

4. (b) Atomic number for Nd = 60
Electronic configuration is
$1s^2 2s^2 2p^6 3s^2 3p^6 3d^{10} 4s^2 4p^6 4d^{10} 4f^4 5s^2 5p^6 6s^2$.

5. (a) Spin only magnetic moment is given by,
$\mu_s = \sqrt{n(n+2)}$
where, n = number of unpaired electrons

A. $Ti^{3+} \longrightarrow 3d^1, n=1$
$\mu_s = \sqrt{1(1+2)} = \sqrt{3}$
B. $Cr^{2+} \longrightarrow 3d^4, n=4$
$\mu_s = \sqrt{4(4+1)} = \sqrt{20}$
C. $Mn^{2+} \longrightarrow 3d^5, n=5$
$\mu_s = \sqrt{5(5+1)} = \sqrt{30}$
D. $Fe^{2+} \longrightarrow 3d^6, n=4$
$\mu_s = \sqrt{4(4+1)} = \sqrt{20}$
E. $Sc^{3+} \longrightarrow 3d^0, \mu_s = 0$
Hence, B and D have same value of magnetic moment.

6. (c) $E° = +ve$ for Mn^{3+}/Mn^{2+}
$Mn = 25 \longrightarrow 3d^5 4s^2$
$Mn^{2+} \longrightarrow 3d^5$
$Mn^{3+} \longrightarrow 3d^4$
Mn^{2+} has half-filled ($3d^5$) stable configuration.
Thus, Mn^{3+} has very high tendency to gain an electron due to this it has high +ve value of electrode potential ($E°$) while in other case, they does not gain electron easily.
Hence, the reason is change of d^4 to d^5-configuration.

7. (a) $Ce^{4+} = [Xe]\,4f^0\,5d^0$
$Yb^{2+} = [Xe]4f^{14}5d^0$
Both ions does not contain any unpaired electrons.
Hence, they are diamagnetic.

8. (b) In aqueous solution, copper (I) undergoes disproportionation reaction.
$2Cu^+(aq) \longrightarrow Cu^{2+} + Cu(s)$
The highest stability of Cu^{2+} ion in aqueous solution is due to negative enthalpy of hydration.

9. (a) The atomic number of Pt is 78. Its exceptional electronic configuration can be written as $[Xe]\,4f^{14}5d^9 6s^1$.
According to Aufbau's principle of filling electrons, the electronic configuration of Pt should be $[Xe]4f^{14}5d^8 6s^2$. But as the number of electrons increases, interelectronic repulsion also increases. In higher atomic number elements energy difference between shells decreases. Hence, $6s$ and $5d$ come closer due to which electronic transition from $6s$ to $5d$ is easily done. Therefore, we have the electronic configuration as $[Xe]\,4f^{14}5d^9 6s^1$.

10. (a) The electronic configuration of Gadolinium is
$Gd = [Xe]4f^7 5d^1 6s^2$.
$Gd^{3+} = [Xe]4f^7$
After removal of 3rd electron, it will attain half-filled electronic configuration. Due to which $4f$ will have high exchange energy. So, Gd has low value of third ionisation energy. Hence, option (a) is correct.

11. (b) The shielding effect of $5f$-orbitals in actinoids is poor than the shielding effect of $4f$-orbitals. So, the effective nuclear charge on valence electrons is more in actinoids.
Hence, actinoid contraction is greater than lanthanoid contraction.
∴ Statement (a) is correct.
Trivalent lanthanoid ions are coloured in the solid state due to presence of f-electrons.
∴ Statement (b) is incorrect.
Lanthanoids are inner transition metals.
So, they are good conductors of heat and electricity.
∴ Statement (c) is correct.
The surface area increases when actinoids are finely divided which results in exposure of more reactant molecules to react.
Hence, rate increases and so, actinoids are highly reactive metals when finely divided.
∴ Statement (d) is correct.

12. (c)
$Zr(Z=40) \rightarrow 1s^2, 2s^2\,2p^6 3s^2\,3p^6\,3d^{10}, 4s^2 4p^6 4d^2, 5s^2$
$Hf(Z=72) \rightarrow 1s^2, 2s^2 2p^6, 3s^2 3p^6 3d^{10}, 4s^2 4p^6 4d^{10}, 5s^2 5p^6 4f^{14} 5d^2, 6s^2$
Hf is a post lanthanoid element. Due to presence of $4f$-orbitals which have poor shielding effect, the effective nuclear charge on valence shell electrons is more which result in the decrease of the size of Hf. This effect is known as lanthanoid contraction.

13. (b) A-III, B-IV, C-I, D-II.
(A) Mn shown six oxidation states in its compounds, *viz*, + 2, + 3, + 4, + 5, + 6 and + 7 ⇒ (III)
(B) Zn is a pseudo transition element like Cd and Hg of group12 (d^{10}-configuration) ⇒ (IV)
(C) Sc does not exhibit variable oxidation states. Only + 3 state is shown by to Sc in its compounds ⇒ (I)
(D) Cu^+ disproportionation in aqueous solution as,
$2Cu^+ \longrightarrow Cu^0 + Cu^{2+} \Rightarrow$ (II)

14. (a) Electronic configuration of Cr^{2+} ion is
Cr^{2+} : $[Ar]3d^4$ or [Ar] | 1 | 1 | 1 | 1 | |
$(22e^-)$ $3d^4$
It has four ($n = 4$) unpaired electrons.
∴ Spin only magnetic moment
$(\mu) = \sqrt{n(n+2)}$ BM
$= \sqrt{4\,(4+2)}$ BM $= 4.90$ BM

15. (c) Statements in options (a), (b) and (d) are correct.
Statement in option (c) is incorrect, because oxidation states of Cr in CrO_4^{2-} (chromate) and $Cr_2O_7^{2-}$ (dichromate) are same and it is +6.
i.e. $\overset{x}{Cr}O_4^{2-} \Rightarrow x + 4(-2) = -2$
$\Rightarrow \quad x = +6$
$\overset{y}{Cr_2}O_7^{2-} \Rightarrow 2y + 7(-2) = -2$
$\Rightarrow \quad y = +6$

Chapter-5

Coordination Compounds

1. (c)

2. (i) Chlorophyll (ii) Vitamin B_{12}

3. False; Haemoglobin is the coordination compound of iron and chlorophyll is the coordination compound of magnesium.

4. Any three of the following
(i) Electroplating
(ii) Textile dying
(iii) Medicinal chemistry
(iv) Metallurgical processes
(v) Industrial catalysts
(vi) Analytical reagents

5. (i) 3 (ii) 2 (iii) 2,
The primary valency can be calculated from the number of negative ions which are equivalent to the charge on the metal ion.

6. (i) $[Co(NH_3)_6]^{3+} 3Cl^-$
(ii) Green, (iii) 1 : 1 electrolyte
(iv) $[CoCl(NH_3)_5]^{2+} 2Cl^-$

7. False; Two compounds having identical empirical formula but different properties are called isomers.

8. Ionisable, negative

9. (c)

10. (i) Coordination entity or complex
(ii) Counter ion

11. (a) The species that does not have octahedral geometry is $[Ni(CO)_4]$ and $[PtCl_4]^{2-}$.

12. (i) 4 (ii) 6 (iii) 6 (iv) 6 (v) 4
The secondary valency is the number of ions of molecules that form coordinate bond with the metal ion.

13. (b)

14. (a) **Correct statement II** :
Complex ions like $[Fe(CN_6)]^{4-}$ does not dissociate into Fe^{2+} and CN^- ions.

15. (c) $CoCl_3 \cdot 3NH_3$ is not a double salt. It is a coordination compound, while rests are double salts.

16. Lewis acids

17. (i) Cl^- (ii) H_2O
(iii) $H_2NCH_2CH_2NH_2$
(iv) Proteins

18. A→(1), B→(3), C→(2), D→(4)

19. (d) **20.** (b)

21. (i) Nitrito-N
(ii) Nitrito-O

22. (b) The coordination number of the central atom/ion is determined only by the number of sigma bonds formed by the ligand with the central atom.

23. (i) Octahedral (ii) Square planar
(iii) $[Ni(CO)_4]$

24. A→(3), B→(2), C→(4), D→(1)

25. (b) Homoleptic – 1, 3, 5
Heteroleptic – 2 and 4

26. (b) **Correct statement I** :
While writing the formula, the placement of a ligand does not depend on its charge.

27. (i) 6 (ii) + 3

28. (i) $[Co(NH_3)_4(H_2O)Cl]Cl_2$
(ii) $K_2[Zn(OH)_4]$
(iii) $K_3[Al(C_2O_4)_3]$
(iv) $[CoCl_2(en)_2]^+$

29. (i) Diamminechloridonitrito-N-platinum (II).
(ii) Potassium- trioxalatochromate (III)
(iii) Dichlorido*bis* (ethane-1, 2-diamine) cobalt (III) chloride
(iv) Pentaammine carbonatocobalt (III) chloride

30. (b) **Correct pair** :
Potassiumtetracyanonickelate (II) – $K_2[Ni(CN)_4]$

31. (i) +4 (ii) $Fe_4[Fe(CN)_6]_3$
(iii) Hexaamminecobalt (III) chloride.
(iv) Pentaamminechloridocobalt (III) chloride

32. A→(4), B→(1), C→(2), D→(3)

33. *A* - Structural isomerism
B - Geometrical isomerism
C - Coordination isomerism
D - Ionisation isomerism

34. *X* = chemical formula,
Y = spatial arrangement

35. (b)

36. Heteroleptic, different

37. (b) and (d) are *cis*-isomer

38. (d) All the complexes given show *cis-trans* isomerism.

39. (a) *Facial* and *meridional* isomers are present in an octahedral complex having two different types of monodentate ligands.

40. True

41. (a) **Correct statement I** : $[MA_2B_2]$ type tetrahedral complexes do not show geometrical isomerism.

42. (b)

43.

(i) 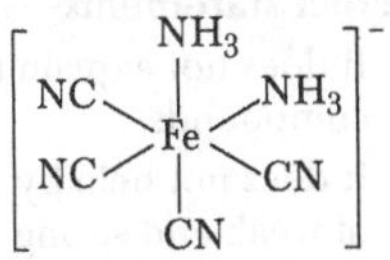

cis

(ii) 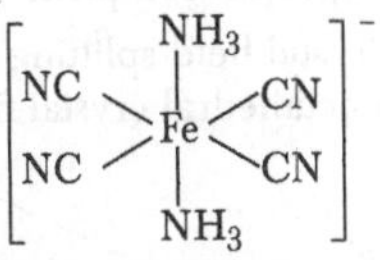

trans

44. (a) **45.** (b)

46. (i) Red-through oxygen (—ONO)
(ii) Yellow-through nitrogen(—NO_2)

47. (c)

48. $[Pt(NH_3)_4][CuCl_4]$

49. $[Co(NH_3)_5(SO_4)]Br$ and $[Co(NH_3)_5Br] SO_4$

50. False; Solvate isomerism is also known as hydrate isomerism when water is solvent.

51. (b)

52. (i) Both (ii) Optical
(iii) Geometrical

53. True

54. (i) Octahedral (ii) 4 (iii) *dsp*^{2}

55. (a) **Correct statement II** :
Coordination compounds with coordination number 5 exhibit trigonal bipyramidal geometry.

56. $Sc^{3+} < Ti^{3+} < Ti^{2+} < V^{2+}$
Magnetic moment $(\mu) = \sqrt{n(n+2)}$;
where, n = unpaired electrons.

57. (d)

58. (b) $[Mn(CN)_6]^{3-}$ has d^2sp^3 $[BrF_2]^-$ has sp^3d-hybridisation, while rest has sp^3d^2-hybridisation.

59. (c)

60. False; $[Mn(CN)_6]^{3-}$ has magnetic moment of 2 unpaired electrons while $[MnCl_6]^{3-}$ has magnetic moment of 4 unpaired electrons.

61. (i) Four (ii) Five

62. (d) $[MnBr_4]^{2-}$ has sp^3-hybridisation

63.

	Correct	Incorrect
I.	✓	×
II.	×	✓
III.	×	✓
IV.	✓	×

Correct statements :

II. It does not explain the colour of compounds.

III. It does not help by giving idea of weak and strong ligands.

64. (i) High spin complex.

(ii) Crystal field splitting diagram in octahedral crystal field.

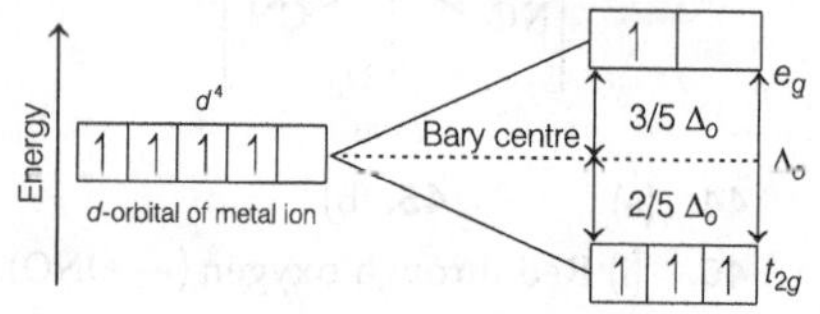

65. (d)

66. False; Three t_{2g} will decrease by $(2/5)\Delta_0$.

67. $SCN^- < Cl^- < F^- < C_2O_4^{2-} < [EDTA]^{4-} <$ en

68. Weak, high

69. $[Cu(H_2O)_4]^{2+} > [Co(NH_3)_6]^{3+} > [Co(CN)_6]^{3-}$

70. (c) **Hint** : $E = \dfrac{hc}{\lambda}$

In VIBGYOR

$\lambda\uparrow, E\downarrow$

71. (i) Violet (ii) Yellow

(iii) $[Co(NH_3)_6]^{3+}$

72. False; Colour of coordination compounds is due to *d-d* transition of electrons.

73. Colourless, blue

74. X - $[Ni(H_2O)_4(en)]^{2+}$

Y- $[Ni(H_2O)_2(en)_2]^{2+}$

Z - $[Ni(en)_3]^{2+}$

75. False; Ruby is aluminium oxide containing about 0.5 -1% Cr^{3+} ions.

76. $[NiCl_4]^{2-}$

77. $[Fe(H_2O)_6]^{3+}$, Greater the number of unpaired electrons, more is the paramagnetic behaviour.

78. (c)

79. No unpaired electron

80. (i) CN^- (ii) $[Mn(H_2O)_6]^{2+}$

81. (b) Pentacarbonyliron (0) has trigonal bipyramidal geometry.

82. (i)

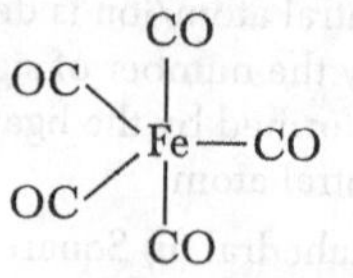

$[Fe(CO)_5]$

(ii)

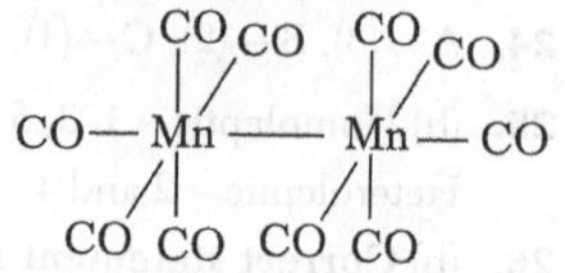

$[Mn_2(CO_{10})]$

83. (d)

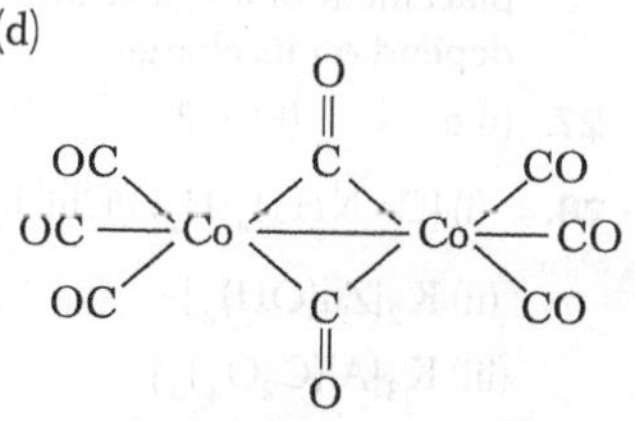

$[Co_2(CO)_8]$

84. (a) When C in the CO ligand donate its lone pair to an empty orbital of metal atom, first bond formed is sigma.

85. (c) π-bond is formed by donation of electron pair of filled *d*-orbital of metal into vacant antibonding π^* orbital of carbon monoxide.

86. (a) In $Al(OEt)_3$, the ligand is bonded to Al through O-atom. Hence, it does not have a M—C bond.

87. (b) Statement (b) is incorrect its correct form is the metal-carbon bond in metal carbonyl possess both σ and π character.

88. (c)

89. Na_2EDTA

90. X = D-penicillamine,

Y = Desferrioxamine-B

91. (i) Treatment of lead poisoning

(ii) Titration of hard water

92. True

93. (i) Analytical chemistry

(ii) Metallurgy

(iii) Medicinal chemistry

94. (b) **Correct statement II** : Articles can be electroplated with silver and gold from $[Ag(CN)_2]^-$ and $[Au(CN)_2]^-$ solution.

95. A → (4), B → (1), C → (2), D → (3)

96. $[Ag(S_2O_3)_2]^{3-}$

Assertion-Reason

1. (a)

2. (d) Chelate are more stable than corresponding coordination compounds.

3. (a)

4. (a) Linkage isomerism arises in coordination compounds containing ambidentate ligand because ambidentate ligand has two different donor atoms.

e.g., SCN, NO_2 etc.

5. (c) **Correct Reason** : Geometrical isomerism arises in heteroleptic complexes due to different possible geometric arrangement of the ligands.

6. (c) **Correct Reason** : Complex of coordination number 4 can show geometrical isomerism if two ligands are same. e.g. MA_2BC,

7. (c) **Correct Reason** : Large splitting of *d*-orbitals occurs due to strong field ligands.

8. (d) $[Fe(CN)_6]^{3-}$ ion shows magnetic moment corresponding to one unpaired electron.

9. (b) **10.** (a)

Case-Based

1. (i) (b) (ii) (d) (iii) (d)

(iv) (b) Ligand NO_2^- is ambidentate ligand as it can donate electrons through either nitrogen (NO_2) or oxygen (ONO).

2. (i) (c) It has 5 unpaired electrons.

(ii) (c) As H_2O is a weak ligand so, it should be $t_{2g}^3 eg^2$

(iii) (a) Magnetic moments of (A), (B), (C) and (D) are respectively. $\sqrt{4\,(4+2)}$, $0, \sqrt{5\,(5+2)}, \sqrt{1\,(1+2)}$

(iv) (c)

Competition Edge Up

1. (b) The correct IUPAC name of $[PtBr_2(PMe_3)_2]$ is dibromo *bis*-(trimethylphosphine) platinum (II).

2. (c) Compound = K_2MnO_4

Oxidation state of Mn,

$0 = 2\times1 + x - 4\times2$

$x = +6$

Therefore, IUPAC name
= Potassium tetraoxidomanganate (VI)

3. (d) The coordination environment of Ca^{2+} ion in its complex with $EDTA^{4-}$ is octahedral.
As $EDTA^{4-}$ is hexadentate ligand.

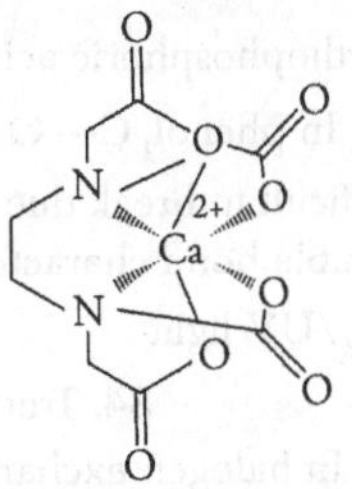

4. (b) The correct match is
A-III, B-I, C-IV, D-II

- $K_2[Ni(CN)_4]$ is dsp^2 hybridised as Ni is present in + 2 oxidation state and CN^- is a strong field ligand.
- $[Ni(CO)_4]$ is sp^3 hybridised as Ni is present in zero oxidation state.
- $[Co(NH_3)_6]Cl_3$, Co is d^2sp^3 hybridised as NH_3 acts as strong field ligand for Co^{3+}.
- $Na_3[CoF_6]$ is sp^3d^2 hybridised act as strong field ligand.

5. (d) For the given complex $[Fe(NH_3)_x(CN)_y]^-$ if it has no electron in its e_g orbital then, it will become
$[Fe^{III}(NH_3)_2(CN)_4]^-$ so,
$x = 2, y = 4$
Hence, $x + y = 6$.

6. (b) According to spectrochemical series the correct sequence of ligands in the order of decreasing field strength is
$CO > H_2O > F^- > S^{2-}$.

7. (a) In complex $[Co(NH_3)_6]^{3+}$, Co is present in +3 oxidation state. So, configuration of Co^{3+} in presence of strong field ligand (i.e. NH_3) is $3d^6(t_{2g}^6e_g^0)$.

Its hybridisation is d^2sp^3 and is an inner orbital complex, i.e. (spin paired complex).

In $[CoF_6]^{3-}$, Co is present in +3 oxidation state. So, configuration of Co^{3+} in presence of weak field ligand (i.e. F^-) is $3d^6(t_{2g}^4e_g^2)$.

Its hybridisation is sp^3d^2 and is an outer orbital complex *i.e.* (spin free complex).

8. (a) Both statement I and statement II are true.

9. (d) Among the given option potassium trioxalatoaluminate (III) is an example of homoleptic complex while all other are examples of heteroleptic complex.

Complexes in which a metal is bound to only one kind of donor groups are known as **homoleptic complexes**. Complexes in which a metal is bonded to more than one kind of donor groups are known as heteroleptic complexes.

10. (c) The complex $[Ag(H_2O)_2][Ag(CN)_2]$ has coordination number 2 and oxidation state is Ag^+ in both cationic and anionic parts.
Hence, its IUPAC name is diaquasilver (I) dicyanidoargentate (I).

11. (a) Ethylene diaminetetraacetate (EDTA) ion.

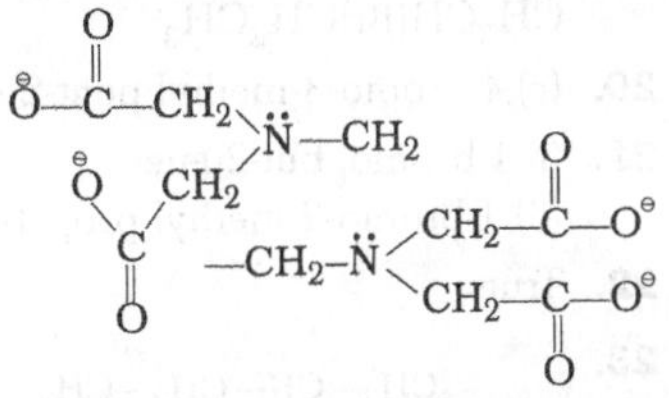

EDTA is a hexadentate ligand with four 'O' and two 'N' donor atoms.

12. (d)

A. $[Fe(CN)_6]^{3-}$

Oxidation number of
$Fe = x + 6(-1) = -3$
$x - 6 = -3$
$\Rightarrow \quad x = +3$

Electronic configuration of
$Fe^{3+} \rightarrow [Ar]\ 3d^5\ 4s^0$

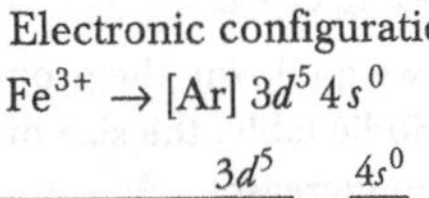

CN^- is a strong field ligand so, pairing of electrons occurs.

$[Fe(CN)_6]^{3-}$ = 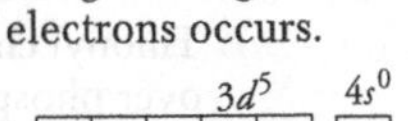

Number of unpaired electrons = 1

$\mu_s = \sqrt{n(n+1)} = \sqrt{1(1+2)} = \sqrt{3}$
= 1.73 BM

B. $[Fe(H_2O)_6]^{3+}$ Oxidation state of Fe is +3.

Water is weak field ligand, so pairing of electron do not take place.

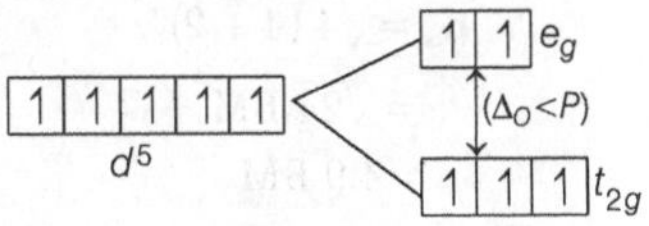

Number of unpaired electrons = 5.

$\mu_s = \sqrt{n(n+2)} = \sqrt{5 \times (5+2)}$
$= \sqrt{5 \times 7} = \sqrt{35} = 5.92$ BM

C. $[Fe(CN)_6]^{4-}$ Oxidation state of Fe is +2.

Electronic configuration of
$Fe^{2+} = [Ar]\ 3d^6\ 4s^0$

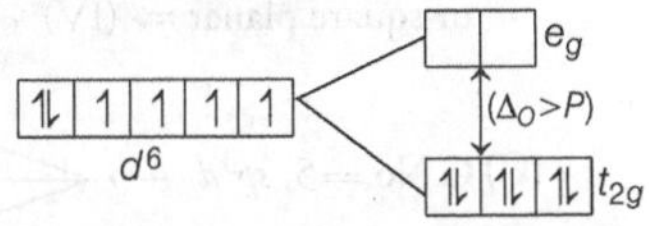

Number of unpaired electrons = 0

$\mu_s = \sqrt{0(0+1)} = 0$ BM

D. $[Fe(H_2O)_6]^{2+}$ Oxidation state of Fe is + 2($3d^6$).

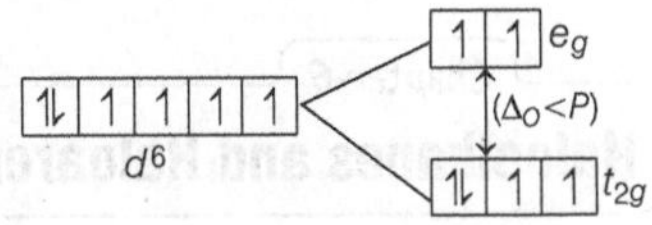

Number of unpaired electrons = 4

$\mu_s = \sqrt{4(4+2)}$
$= \sqrt{4 \times 6}$
$= \sqrt{24} = 4.90$ BM

Hence, correct match is
A → 4, → B → 1, C → 2, D → 3.

13. (d) Increasing field strength of ligands to form coordination compounds, we have to follow the spectrochemical series.

$I^- < Br^- < SCN^- < Cl^- < S^{2-} < F^- < OH^- < C_2O_4^{2-} < H_2O < NCS^- < EDTA^{4-} < NH_3 <$ en $< CN^- < CO$

So, the order given in option (d) is correct.

$SCN^- < F^- < C_2O_4^{2-} < CN^-$

14. (a) Electronic configuration of Cr^{2+} is $[Ar]\ 3d^4$.

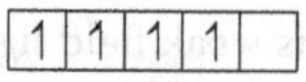

$\mu_s = \sqrt{n(n+2)}$

$\therefore\ \mu_s = \sqrt{4(4+2)}$

$= \sqrt{24}$ BM

= 4.9 BM

Thus, option (a) is correct.

15. (b)

(A) C.No. = 4, $sp^3 \longrightarrow$ 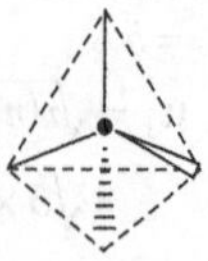

or tetrahedral ⇒ (III)

(B) C.No. = 4, $dsp^2 \longrightarrow$ 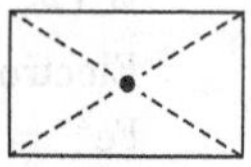

or square planar ⇒ (IV)

(C) C.No. = 5, $sp^3d \longrightarrow$ 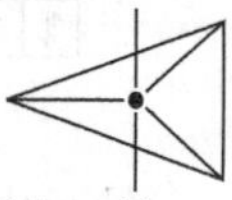

or trigonal bipyramidal ⇒ (I)

(D) C.No. = 6, $d^2sp^3 \longrightarrow$ 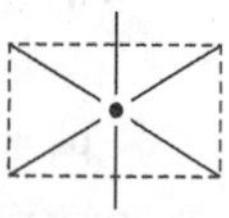

or octahedral ⇒ (II)

Hence, option (b) is correct.

Chapter-6
Haloalkanes and Haloarenes

1. sp^3, sp^2 **2.** (b)

3. Thyroxine

4. A → (2), B → (3), C → (1)

5. Secondary haloalkane;
In rest haloalkanes number of halogen atoms are 1, 2 and 3.

6. $C_nH_{2n+1}X$

7. Carbon **8.** (a)

9. 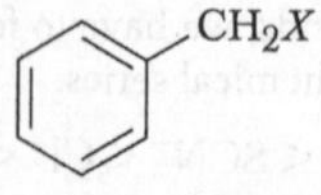

10. False; Vinylic halide are compounds in which halogen atom is bonded to sp^2-hybridised carbon atom of carbon-carbon double bond.

11. 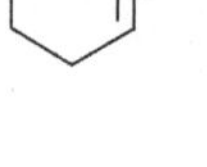

(Vinylic halide)

Vinylic halide is the compound in which the halogen atom is bonded to sp^2-hybridised C-atom of C=C.

12. Aryl halide

13. (b) Aryl halides are the compounds in which the halogen atom is directly bonded to sp^2-hybridised carbon atom of an aromatic ring.

14. (d) (5)

15. (i) 1-chloro-2-methylpropane
(ii) 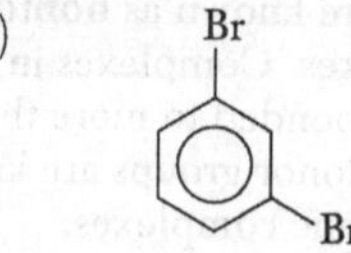

(iii) *sym*-tribromobenzene

16. (b) **Correct statement II** : Dihalogen compounds having both halogen compounds present on same carbon atom are called *gem* or *geminal* dihalides.

17. *gem*, *vic*

18. A → (4), B → (3), C → (2), D → (1)

19. $(CH_3)_2CHBr$ and $CH_3CH(Br)CH_2CH_3$

20. (c) 4-bromo-3-methyl pent-2-ene

21. (i) 1-bromo, but-2-ene
(ii) 1-bromo-2-methyl prop-1-ene

22. True

23. 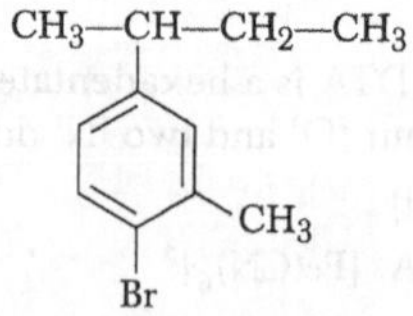

24. (b)

25. $CH_3I < CH_3Br < CH_3Cl < CH_3F$;
C—X bond length increases from C—F to C—I.
As we go down the group in periodic table, the size of halogen atom increases.

26. Alcohols

27. (d) **Correct statements** :
I. Thionyl chloride is preferred over phosphorus chloride for the preparation of alkyl chloride from alcohols.
II. Although phosphorus chlorides give pure alkyl halides but thionyl chloride is preferred because other two products are escapable gases.

28. (i) $X = ZnCl_2$
(ii) $Y = H_3PO_3$

29. (i) $R—OH + SOCl_2 \longrightarrow R—Cl + SO_2 + HCl$
(ii) $R—OH + NaBr + H_2SO_4 \longrightarrow R—Br + NaHSO_4 + H_2O$

30. Orthophosphoric acid

31. (b) In phenol, C—O bond is difficult to break due to partial double bond character.

32. Cl_2 /UV light

33. (d) **34.** True

35. (a) In halogen exchange reaction, one halogen atom is replaced by other halogen atom.

36. (b)

37. Melting point

38. Oxidising agent

39. (a) **40.** (b)

41. Iodobenzene and dinitrogen

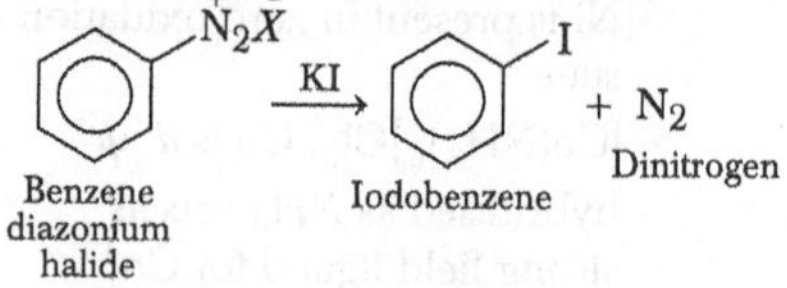

42. Markovnikov's rule

43. (i) ethene (ii) *vic*-dibromide
(iii) unsaturated

44. (i) 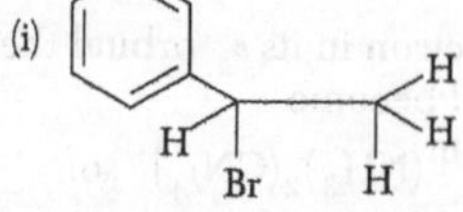

(ii) 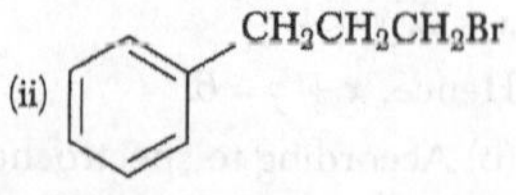

45. CoF_2, Hg_2F_2

46. False; HI is used during the reaction of alcohol with KI to produce I_2 gas.

47. A → (3), B → (1), C → (2)

48. (i) 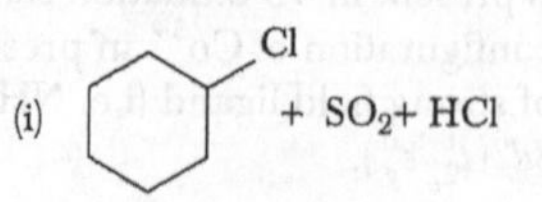

(ii) 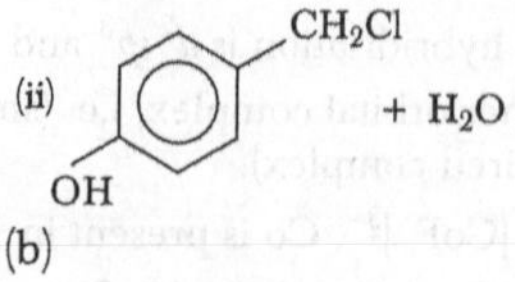

49. (b)

50. (i) 1-iodo-1-methylcyclohexane
(ii) 3-bromocyclohexene and hydrogen bromide

51. (i) Colourless (ii) Sweet

52. Hexyl chloride; Hexyl chloride is a clear liquid.

53. Dipole-dipole interactions

54. (a)

55. (d) **56.** (c)

57. $n\text{-}C_3H_7Cl < CHCl_3 < n\text{-}C_3H_7Br$;

The density increases with increase in number of carbon atoms, halogen atoms and atomic mass of the halogen atoms.

58. (b) **Correct statement** :
II. Solubility of haloalkanes in organic solvent is high.
III. Boiling point of isomeric haloalkane decreases with increase in branching.

59. (i) Chloromethane < Bromomethane < Dibromomethane < Bromoform
(ii) Isopropyl chloride < 1-chloropropane < 1-chlorobutane

60. Nucleophilic substitution reaction

61. (b)

62. OH^-; The ambident nucleophiles are those nucleophiles which can attack through two different sites.

63. (b)

64. (i) Second order
(ii) Concentration of both reactants.

65. (d) **Correct statement** : Carbon atom is bonded to five atoms during the transition state.

66.

	Correct	Incorrect
I.	✓	×
II.	×	✓
III.	✓	×

Correct statement II :
Its rate depends on concentration of both the reactants.

67. False; Order of reactivity for S_N2 reaction is
Tertiary halide < secondary halide < primary halide
Rate of S_N2 reaction depends upon the steric hinderance (crowding) of alkyl halide.

68. Methyl halide > ethyl halide > isopropyl halide > *tert*-butyl halide.

69. (a)

70. (*A*) only

71. (i) S_N1 (ii) S_N1

72. (b)

73. (i) 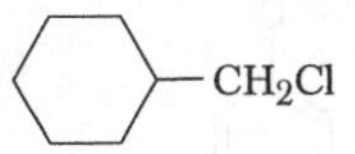

(ii) 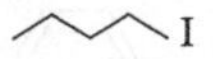

74. (d) $S_N2 = 3° < 2° < 1°$
$S_N1 = 3° > 2° > 1°$

75. Clockwise, dextrorotatory

76. (a)

77. (d) The compounds having chiral carbon shows enantiomers.
Butan-2-ol, 2-hydroxypropanoic acid, 2-chlorobutane, 2-bromo-2-chlorobutane.

78. (b)

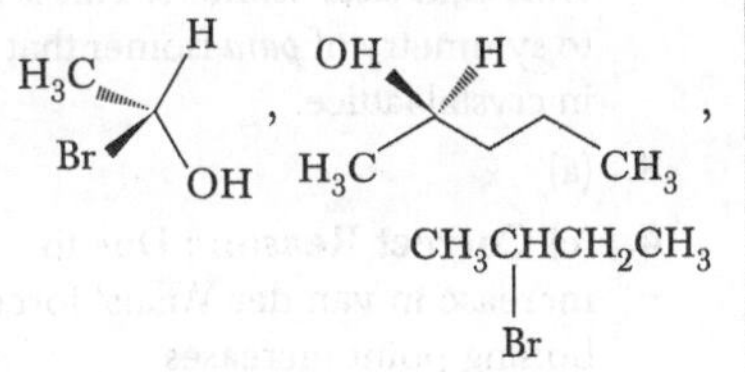

79. (i) (b) (ii) (a)

80. (i) Enantiomers
(ii) Racemic mixture

81. Incorrect; Enantiomers possess unidentical chemical and physical properties.

82.

(i) 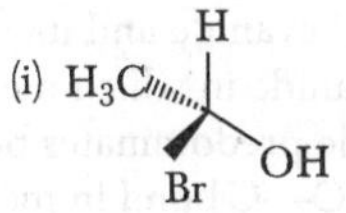

(ii) 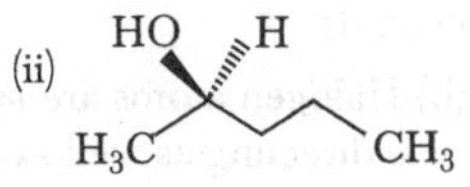

(iii) $CH_3\underset{\large Br}{CH}CH_2CH_3$

83. (i) $A \rightarrow$ Retention
(ii) $B \rightarrow$ Inversion of configuration
(iii) $A + B \rightarrow$ Racemisation

84. (c)

85. (d) II contains no asymmetric C-atom, while III contains Br on primary C-atom.

86. $A =$ 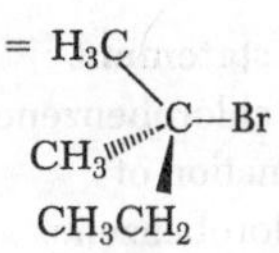

$B = CH_3CH_2—\underset{\large Br}{CH}—CH_3$

87. (b)

88. (b) **Hint** :

$X =$ 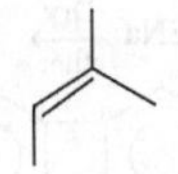 (Saytzeff product)

89. $H_3C—CH_2—CH{=}CH—CH_3$

90. (i) Nature of alkyl halide
(ii) Strength and size of nucleophile
(iii) Reaction conditions

91. (i) Elimination (ii) Substitution

92. (a) **93.** (d)

94.

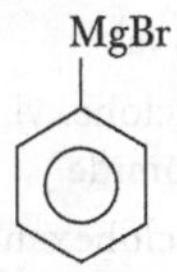

95. (d)

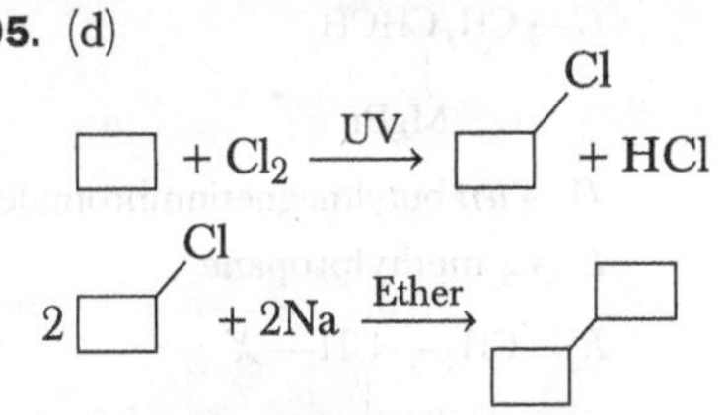

96. False; Haloarenes do not show nucleophilic addition reaction.

97.

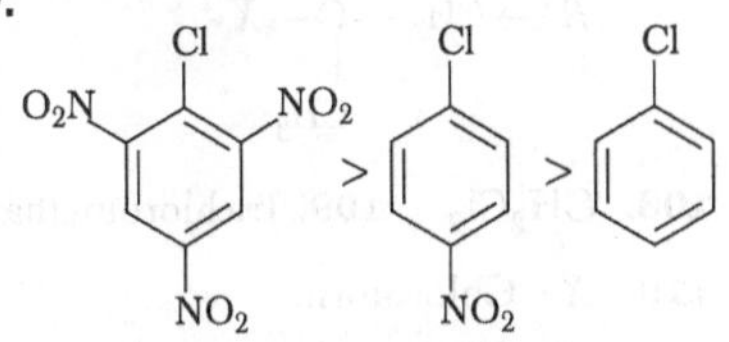

Electron withdrawing groups increase and electron donating groups decrease the reactivity of aryl halides towards nucleophilic substitution.

98.

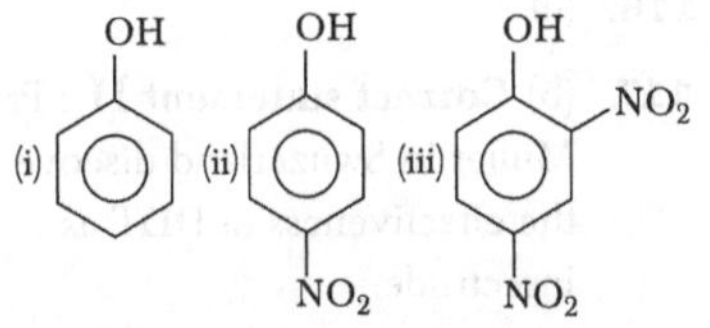

99. (b)

100. (b) **Correct statement** : Nitration of chlorobenzene leads to formation of *o*/*p*-nitrochlorobenzene.

101. (c)

102. (d)

103. A →(3), B →(4), C →(2), D →(1)

104.

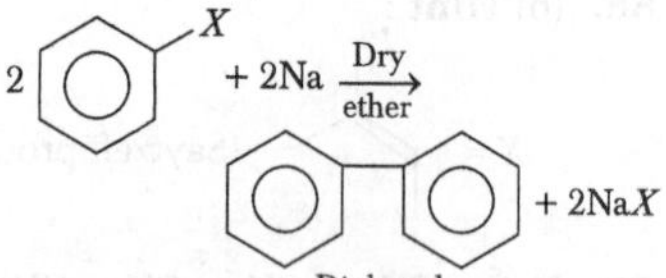

Diphenyl

105. (i) $CH_3CH_2CH_2CH_2Br$

(ii) $CH_3CH_2\underset{Br}{CH}CH_3$

(iii) $CH_3\underset{CH_3}{CH}CH_2CH_2Br$

106. (i) (a) (ii) (a)

107. $A \rightarrow$ Cyclohexylmagnesium bromide

$B \rightarrow$ Cyclohexane

$C \rightarrow CH_3\underset{MgBr}{CH}CH_3$

$D \rightarrow$ *tert*-butylmagnesiumbromide

$E \rightarrow$ 2-methylpropane

$R \rightarrow CH_3-\underset{CH_3}{CH}-X$

$R' \rightarrow CH_3-\underset{CH_3}{\overset{CH_3}{C}}-X$

108. CH_2Cl_2 **109.** Trichloromethane

110. X= Chloroform

Y= Phosgene

111. (a) **112.** (c)

113. X= Dichloromethane

114. Diarrhoea

115. False; Freon-12 is CCl_2F_2

116. (c)

117. (b) **Correct statement II** : Paul Muller in Switzerland discovered the effectiveness of DDT as insectiside.

118. (b)

119. A →(2), B →(3), C →(4), D →(1)

120. Dichlorodiphenyltrichloroethane

IUPAC name

2,2-*bis* (4-chlorophenyl-1,1, 1-trichloroethane)

Structure

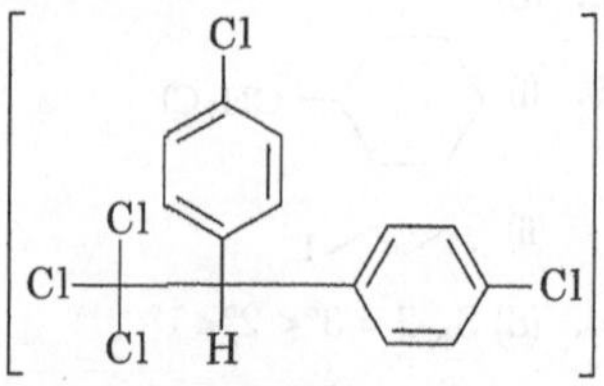

DDT

Assertion-Reason

1. (c) Allyl halides are the compounds in which the halogen atom is bonded to an sp^3-hybridised carbon atom next to carbon-carbon double bond.

2. (d) The *para*-isomers are high melting point as compared to their *ortho*- and *meta*- isomers. This is due to symmetry of *para*-isomer that fit in crystal lattice.

3. (a)

4. (c) **Correct Reason** : Due to increase in van der Waals' force, boiling point increases.

5. (d) Aryl halides are less reactive towards nucleophilic substitution reactions as C—Xbond acquires a partial double bond character due to resonance.

6. (d) KCN reacts with methyl chloride to give the mixture of methyl cyanide and methyl iso-cyanide in which methyl cyanide predominates because of stable C—C bond in methyl cyanide.

7. (b) Halogen atoms are *ortho* and *para* directing as well as ring deactivators.

8. (c) **Correct Reason** : This reaction proceeds through S_N2 mechanism in which no carbocation is formed.

9. (a)

10. (c) Oxidising agent oxidises HI to I_2.

Case-Based

1. (i) (c) Allylic chlorides are most reactive.

(ii) (c) 2° alkyl halides undergo hydrolysis by S_N1 or S_N2 mechanism.

(iii) (a) Smaller the size of the nucleophile (i.e. CH_3O^-) more reactive it is.

(iv) (d) Steric hindrance due to bulky alkyl groups prevents the attack of the nucleophile in S_N2 mechanism.

2. (i) (a) $\underset{(A)}{CH_3-\underset{CH_3}{\overset{CH_3}{C}}-CH_2-Cl} \xrightarrow{Ether/Na}$

1-chloro-2, 2-dimethyl propane

$CH_3-\underset{CH_3}{\overset{CH_3}{C}}-CH_2-CH_2-\underset{CH_3}{\overset{CH_3}{C}}-CH_3$

2, ,2, 5, 5-tetramethylhexane

(ii) (c) $\underset{(A)}{CH_3-\underset{CH_3}{\overset{CH_3}{C}}-CH_2Cl} \xrightarrow{Alc.\ KCN}$

$\underset{(C)}{CH_3-\underset{CH_3}{\overset{CH_3}{C}}-CH_2CN} \xrightarrow{Na/C_2H_5OH}$

$CH_3-\underset{CH_3}{\overset{CH_3}{C}}-CH_2CH_2NH_2$

(iii) (a)

(iv) (b) $\underset{(A)}{CH_3-\underset{CH_3}{\overset{CH_3}{C}}-CH_2Cl}$

$\xrightarrow{Zn-Cu/C_2H_5OH} \underset{(B)}{CH_3-\underset{CH_3}{\overset{CH_3}{C}}-CH_3}$

Competition Edge Up

1. (d) For the structure,

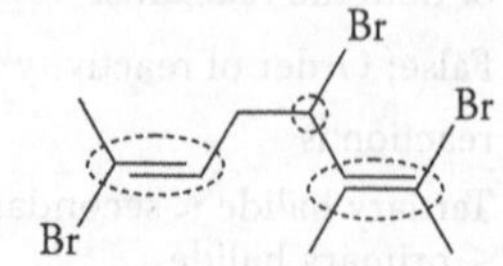

Total 3 stereocentres are there

So, total stereoisomers possible are $2^3 = 8$.

2. (d) The complete reaction is as follows

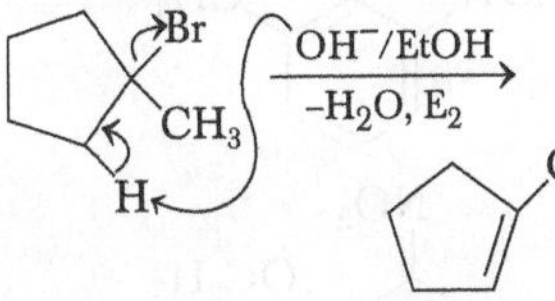

(Major)

Hence, option (d) is correct.

3. (a) The structure of 2, 3-dibromo-1-phenylpentane is

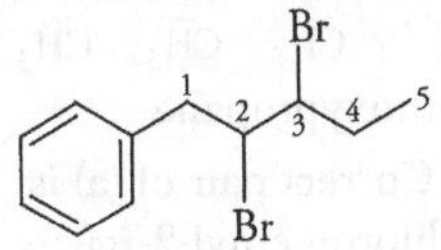

4. (c) Vinyl carbon is sp^2-hybridised aliphatic carbon.

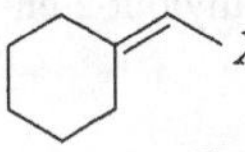 *X* is vinyl halide.

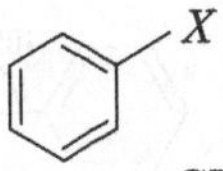 is aryl halide.

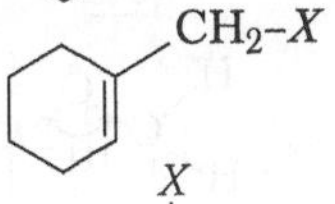

and 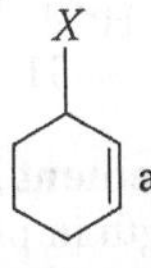 are allyl halide.

> **Concept Enhancer** Vinylic halides are the compounds in which the halogen atom is bonded to a sp^2 hybridised carbon atom of C=C. In such compounds, if lone pair is present, then the lone pair if always in conjugation with π-bond.

5. (d) Alkyl halide is converted into alkyl isocyanide by reaction with AgCN.

$$\underset{\text{Alkyl halide}}{R{-}X} + AgCN \xrightarrow[\text{reaction}]{\text{Substitution}} \underset{\text{Alkyl isocyanide}}{R{-}NC} + AgX$$

6. (b) Rate of S_N2 reaction depends on steric hindrance, less the steric hindrance more will be rate of reaction 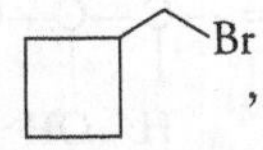, it will undergoes S_N2 reaction fastest.

Rate of S_N2 reaction is

$Me{-}X > 1°{-}X > 2°{-}X > 3°{-}X$

7. (b) The complete reaction takes place as follows

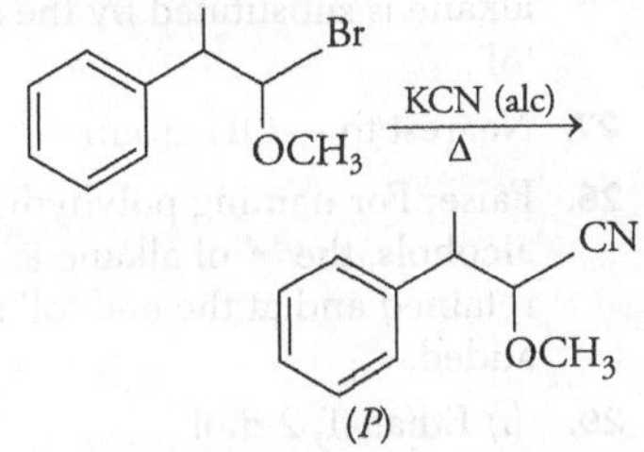

Nucleophilic substitution reaction will occur.

8. (d) The reaction involves are,

$$3R{-}OH + PCl_3 \longrightarrow 3RCl + H_3PO_3(A)$$

$$R{-}OH + PCl_5 \longrightarrow R{-}Cl + HCl + POCl_3(B)$$

Hence, products *A* and *B* are

$A = H_3PO_3$; $B = POCl_3$

9. (d) Reactivity toward $S_N1 \propto$ stability of carbocation, and stability of carbocation depends on number of α-hydrogen.

Hence, (d) is correct option.

10. (b) The given compound is an example of allylic halides. As in this the halogen is bonded to the sp^3-hybridised carbon atom next to the carbon-carbon double bond, which is called as allylic halides.

Benzylic halides In these halides, the halogen atom is bonded to the sp^3-hybridised carbon atom next to an aromatic ring.

Vinylic halide In these halides, the halogen atom is bonded to the sp^2-hybridised carbon of one of the carbon atoms of a double bond.

Aryl halide In these halides, the halogen atom is bonded to the sp^2-hybridised carbon atom of an aromatic ring.

11. (c) Enantiomers are non-superimposable mirror images of each other. They have identical physical properties i.e. melting point, boiling point, refractive index etc. and differ only with respect to the rotation of plane polarised light. If one of the enantiomer is dextrorotatory, then the other will be laevorotatory.

12. (d) To synthesise chlorobenzene, benzene reacts with Cl_2 in the presence of $FeCl_3$.

The reaction takes place as follows

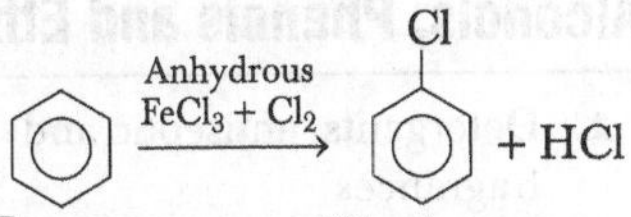

Benzene Chlorobenzene

13. (c) As the size of halide increases, bond length increases and bond enthalpy decreases.

Thus, the correct order of bond enthalpy is

$CH_3{-}F > CH_3{-}Cl > CH_3{-}Br > CH_3{-}I$

14. (a) Saytzeff's rule states that more substituted alkene is formed as major product in a dehydrohalogenation reaction.

In dehydrohalogenation of 2-bromopentane, pent-2-ene is formed as major product being more substituted alkene.

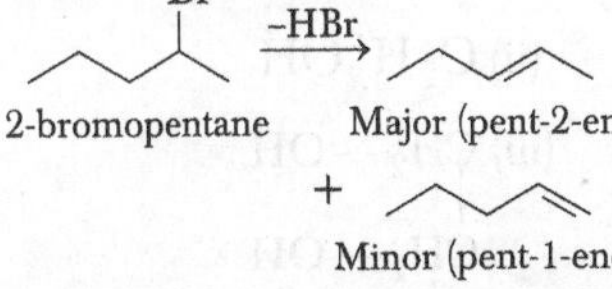

2-bromopentane Major (pent-2-ene) + Minor (pent-1-ene)

15. (c) An S_N1 reaction proceeds through formation of a stable carbocation as an intermediate. Here,

(a) $CH_2{=}CH{-}CH_2Cl \xrightarrow{-Cl^-} CH_2{=}CH{-}\overset{\oplus}{C}H_2$

Allyl-1°-carbocation (stable)

(b) $(CH_3)_3CCl \xrightarrow{-Cl^-} CH_3{-}\overset{\oplus}{C}(CH_3){-}CH_3$

tert-butyl carbocation (stable)

(c) 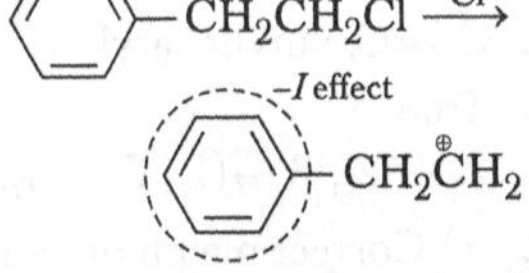

1°-carbocation (less stable due to −*I* effect of the phenyl group)

(d) 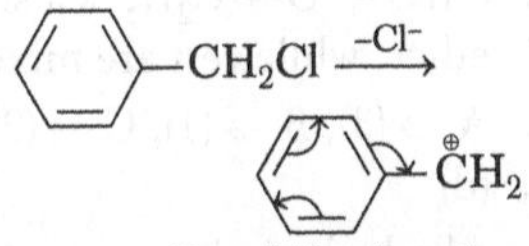

Benzyl-1°-carbocation (stable)

So, option (c) will not undergo S_N1 reaction with OH^-.

Chapter-7

Alcohols, Phenols and Ethers

1. Detergents, antiseptic and fragrances
2. (a)
3. Ethanol
4. True
5. (a) **Correct statement II** : In the given statement formula of phenol is wrong.
   The correct formula is C_6H_5OH.
6. Alkoxy, aryloxy
7. $CH_3—O—CH_3$
8. (c)
9. (i) CH_2OH
   $CHOH$
   CH_2OH
   (ii) C_2H_5OH
   (iii) $CH_2—OH$
   $CH_2—OH$
10. (b) Primary, secondary and tertiary monohydric alcohol contains —OH group attached to sp^3-hybridised carbon.
11. (a)
12. sp^3-hybridised, double
13. $(CH_3)_2CH—OH$
14. False; In benzylic alcohols, the —OH group is attached to a sp^3-hybridised carbon atom next to an aromatic ring.
15. (c)
16. True
17. C = C, vinylic, aryl
18. True
19. A →(2), B →(1), C →(4), D →(3)
20. (c) Correct match of (c) is $C_{sp^3}—OH$.
21. $C_2H_5—O—C_2H_5$ is a simple ether, while rest are mixed.
22. A → (3), B → (1), C → (2)
23. (d)
24. Alkyl, alcohol
25. CH_3OH
26. (a) **Correct statement II** : In IUPAC name of alcohol '*e*' of alkane is substituted by the suffix 'ol'.
27. Nearest to —OH group
28. False; For naming polyhydric alcohols, the '*e*' of alkane is retained and at the end 'ol' is added.
29. (i) Ethan-1, 2-diol
    (ii) Propan-1, 2, 3-triol
30. (i) *n*-propyl alcohol
    (ii) Propan-1-ol
    (iii) $CH_3—CH(OH)—CH_3$
    (iv) Propan-2-ol
    (v) $CH_3—CH(OH)—CH_2CH_3$
    (vi) *sec* - butyl alcohol
31. (i) $HO—CH_2—CH_2—OH$
    (ii) (iii)
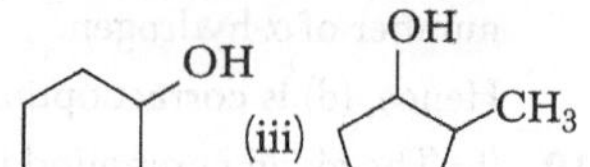

32. A →(2), B →(4), C →(1), D →(3)
33.
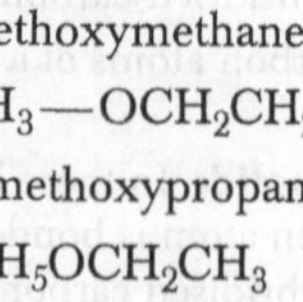

Common name Resorcinol
34. (c)
35. (i) Dimethyl ether
    (ii) Methoxymethane
    (iii) $CH_3—OCH_2CH_2CH_3$
    (iv) 1-methoxypropane
    (v) $C_6H_5OCH_2CH_3$
    (vi) Ethyl phenyl ether (phenetole)
36. A →(3), B →(1), C →(2)
37.
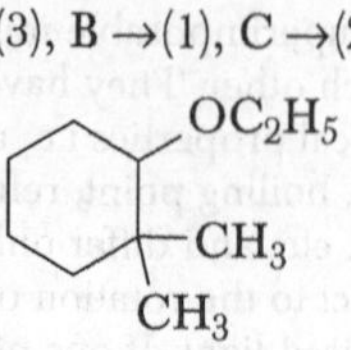

38. (a)
39. Hydrogen, —*O**R* or —OAr
40. True
41. (i)
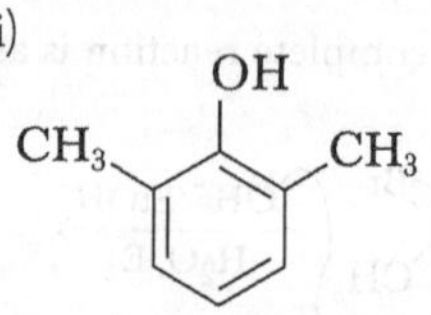

    (ii)
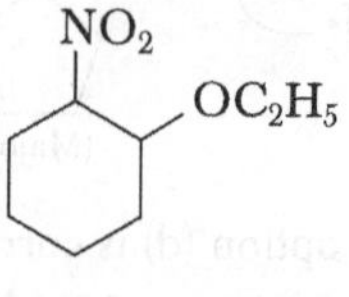

    (iii) $CH_3—CH(Cl)—CH(CH_3)—CH(CH_3)—CH_2OH$
42. 2-ethoxypropane
43. (a) Correct pair of (a) is 3-chloromethyl-2-*iso*-propylpentan-1-ol
44. (i) 3, 3-dimethylpentan-2-ol
    (ii) 2-bromo-3-methylbut-2-en-1-ol
45. (c)
46.
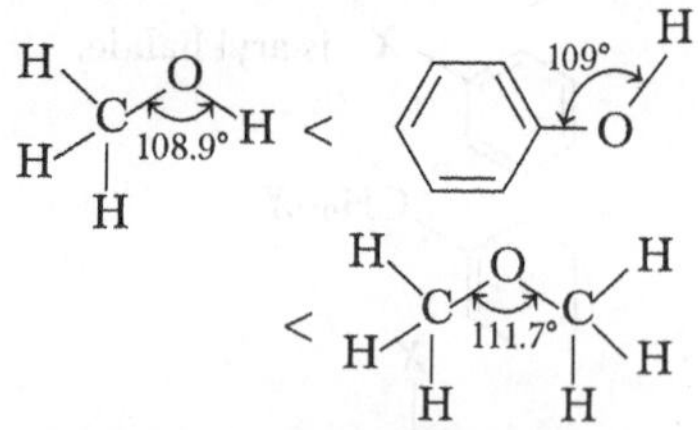

47. (b) **Correct statement I** : The C—O bond length in phenol is less than that in methanol.
48. (a)
49. (i) Greater (ii) Alcohols
50. False; Alkenes on reaction with water in acidic medium forms **alcohols**.
51. Markownikoff's rule
52. $CH_3—CH(OH)—CH_3$
    The given reaction follows Markownikoff's rule.
53. $A = H_3O^+$, $B =$
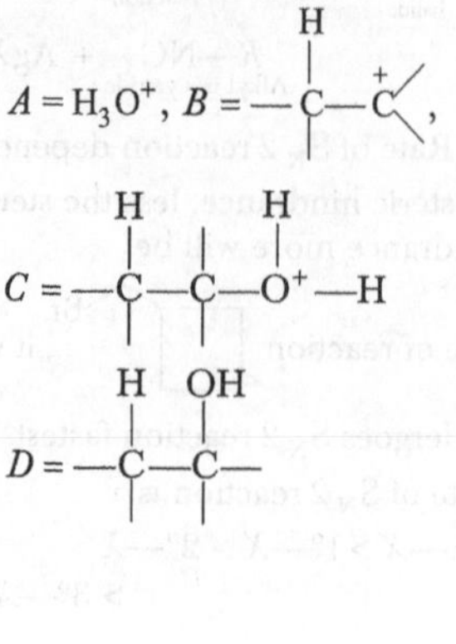

54. $X = CH_3—CH(H)—CH_2(BH_2)$

$Y = (CH_3CH_2CH_2)_3B$

$Z = 3CH_3—CH_2—CH_2—OH$

55. (c)

56. (i) Pd (ii) $NaBH_4$

57. (b)

58. (i) RCH_2OH

(ii) $RCH_2OH + R'OH$

59. (a) **Correct reaction** :

$CH_3—CH=CH_2 + H_2O \xrightarrow{H^+} CH_3—CH(OH)—CH_3$

60. Carbolic **61.** (d)

62. $A = NaOH$, $B =$ 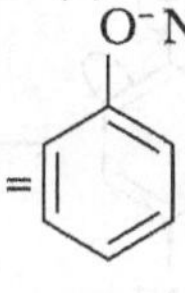

63. $A =$ 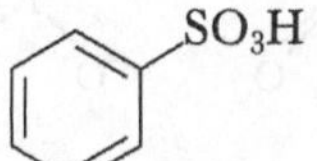

$B =$ 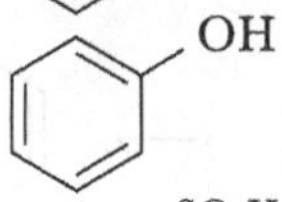

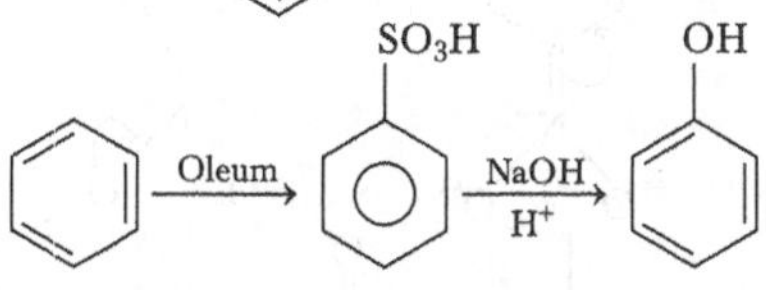

64. (b)

65. Grignard reagent A :

$CH_3—CH(CH_3)—MgBr$

Grignard reagent B : 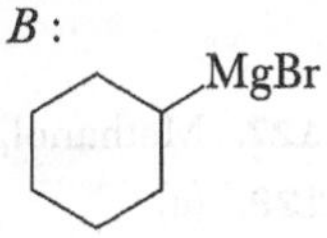

66. (i) $CH_3CH=CH_2$

(ii) 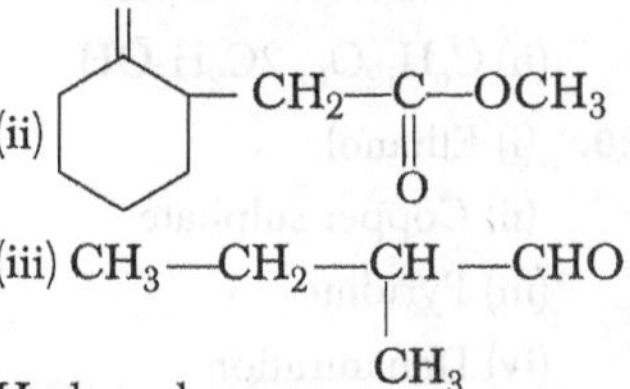

(iii) $CH_3—CH_2—CH(CH_3)—CHO$

67. Hydroxyl group

68. (d)

69. False; With increase in branching in carbon chain, the van der Waals' forces of attraction decreases.

70. (c)

71. (i) Pentan-1-ol > butan-1-ol > butan-2-ol > ethanol > methanol

(ii) Pentan-1-ol > pentanal > ethoxyethane > *n*-butane

Boiling point increases with increase in molecular mass of compounds and intermolecular interactions.

72. (a) Oxygen of alcohol

(b) Proton

Compound with electron pair acts as nucleophile whereas positively charged compounds acts as electrophile.

73. (i) $2\left(CH_3—C(CH_3)_2—O\right)_3Al + 3H_2$

(ii) 2 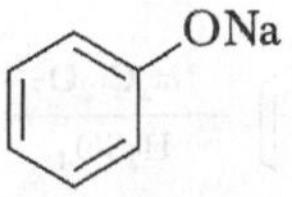 $+ H_2$

74. (c)

75. Bronsted acids; Bronsted acids can donate a proton to a stronger base.

76. Increases, decrease

77. $R_3C—OH < R_2CH—OH < R—CH_2OH$

Acidic character of alcohols depends on the polarity of O—H bond.

78. No; Alcohols are weaker acid than water.

79. (i) H—O—H (ii) $R—O^-$

(iii) R—O—H (iv) $\bar{O}H$

80. (c)

81. Lone pair of electrons present on oxygen.

82. Phenoxide, decrease

83. Cresol

84. Ethanol < *p*-cresol < *m*-cresol < Phenol < *m*-nitrophenol < *o*-nitrophenol.

In substituted phenols, presence of electron withdrawing group enhances the acidity.

85. (d)

86. (i) R'—COOH (ii) H^+

(iii) $R—O—C(=O)—R' + R'COOH$

87. Aspirin

88. (i) 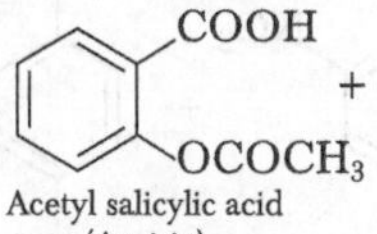 $+ CH_3COOH$ (Acetic acid)

Acetyl salicylic acid (Aspirin)

(ii) Acetylation

89. (c)

90. $R—OH + HX \longrightarrow \underset{(A)}{R—X} + \underset{(B)}{H_2O}$

91. (b)

92. A→(2), B→(3), C→(1)

93. Alkyl

94. (b) Only HCl, PCl_5, PCl_3, $ZnCl_2$ can carry out the given transformation.

95. (d)

96. (i) $CH_2=CH_2 + H_2O$

(ii) $CH_3CH=CH_2 + H_2O$

(iii) $CH_3—C(=CH_2)—CH_3 + H_2O$

97. Primary < Secondary < Tertiary

98. Tertiary

99. (a)

100. Dehydrogenation

101. (b)

102. (c) When ethanol will react with CrO_3, or PCC or PDC, it will be converted into aldehyde.

$KMnO_4$ and $K_2Cr_2O_7$ will convert ethanol into aldehyde but further into carboxylic acid.

DIBAL-H is a reducing agent while O_3 will have no effect on alcohols.

103. CrO_3

104. (i) PCC (ii) CrO_3 (iii) Cu

105. (b) **Correct reaction** :

$CH_3—C(CH_3)_2—OH \xrightarrow[573\,K]{Cu} CH_3—C(CH_3)=CH_2$

106. False; A methanol poisoned patient is treated by giving intravenous infusions of diluted ethanol.

107. In phenols 1 lone pair of oxygen is in conjugation with benzene ring. Thus, increasing the electron density on benzene nucleus.

108.

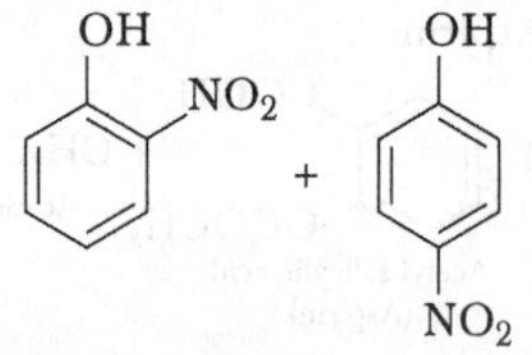

109. Steam distillation

110. *o*-nitrophenol

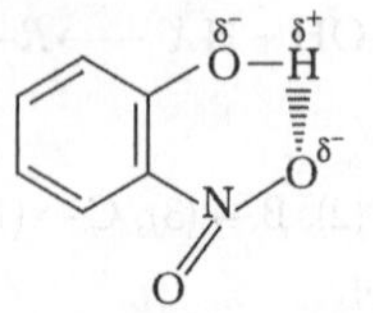

111. False; *p*-nitrophenol is less volatile than *o*-nitrophenol and shows more association of molecules.

112. (b)

113. **Route *A***

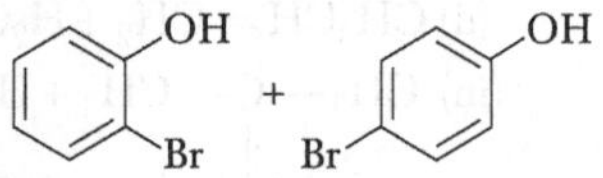

Route *B*

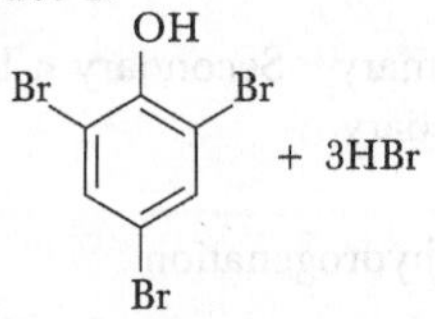

114. Lewis acid, activating, —OH

115. (*A*)

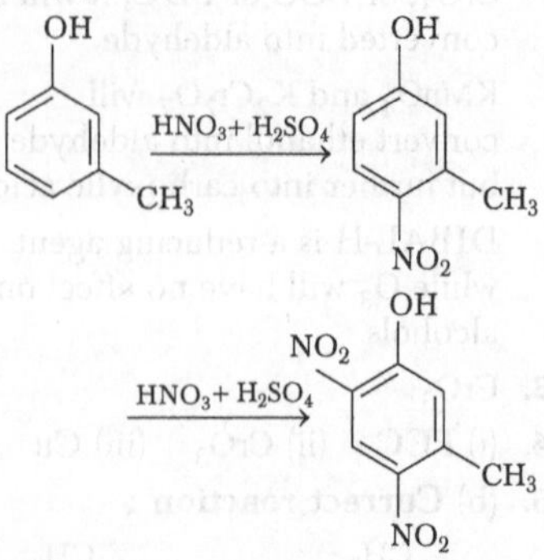

116.

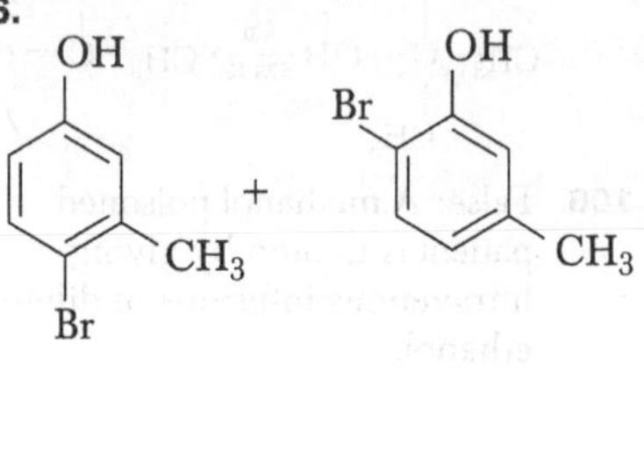

117.

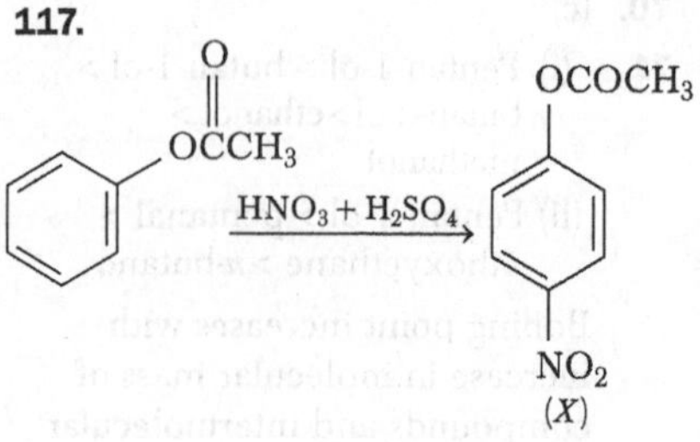

118.

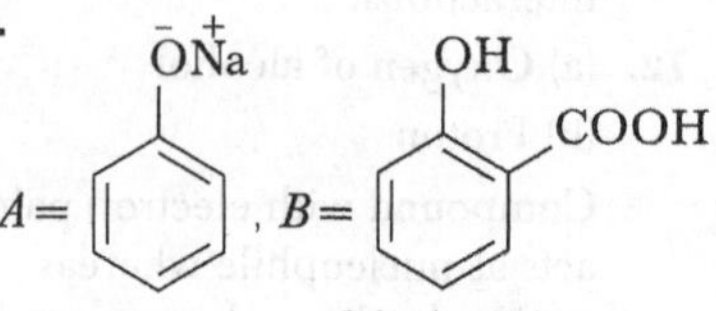

Salicylic acid

119. Reagent A : $CHCl_3$ + *aq.* NaOH

Reagent B : NaOH

Reagent C : H^+

120. (b) **Correct reaction II :**

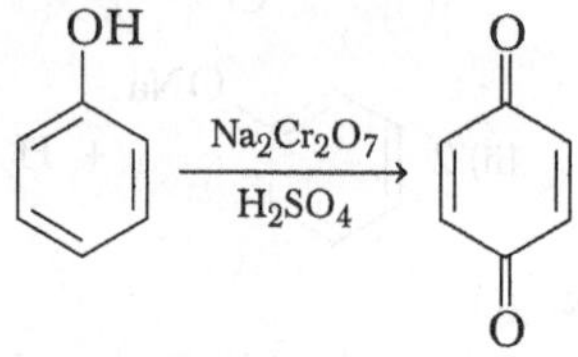

121. (i) No reaction at room temperature

(ii) $CH_3-\underset{Cl}{\overset{CH_3}{C}}-CH_2CH_3$

122. (b) Only ethanol and *iso*-propanol will show iodoform test. Alcohols having alpha methyl-group only give positive iodoform test.

123. (i) $CH_3-\underset{OH}{\overset{CH_3}{C}}-CH_2CH_3 + HBr \xrightarrow{\Delta}$

2-methylbutan-2-ol

$CH_3-\underset{Br}{\overset{CH_3}{C}}-CH_2CH_3 + H_2O$

2-bromo-2-methyl butane

(ii) $CH_3CH_2CH_2CH_2OH$

Butan-1-ol

$+ SOCl_2 \xrightarrow{\Delta}$

$CH_3CH_2CH_2CH_2Cl + HCl$

1-chlorobutane

124.

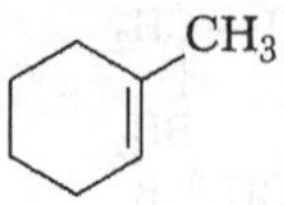

125. *p*-nitrophenol

126.

(i)

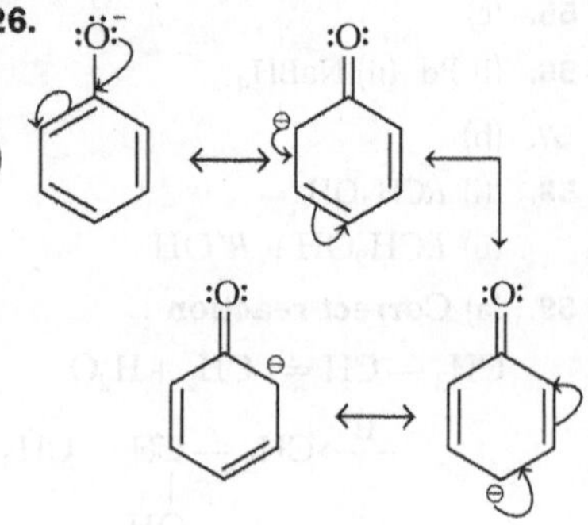

(ii)

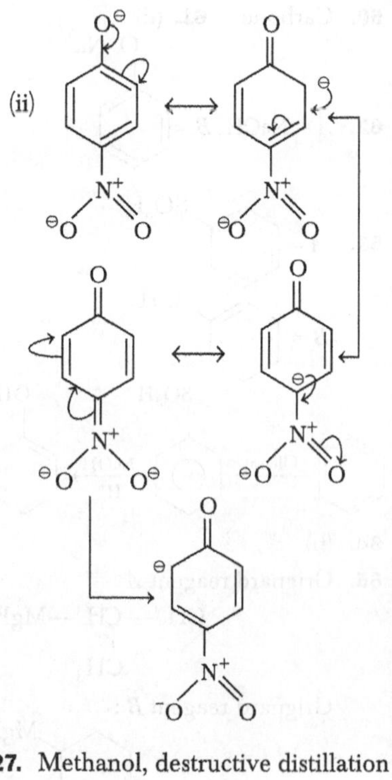

127. Methanol, destructive distillation

128. (a)

129. (i) $C_6H_{12}O_6 + C_6H_{12}O_6$

Glucose Fructose

(ii) $C_6H_{12}O_6$, $2C_2H_5OH$

130. (i) Ethanol

(ii) Copper sulphate

(iii) Pyridine

(iv) Denaturation

131. (i) $CH_2 = CH_2$

(ii) $C_2H_5OC_2H_5$

132. (a)

133. (b) **Correct statement I** : Williamson's synthesis involves S_N2 attack of alkoxide ion on primary alkyl halide.

134. (ii)

135.

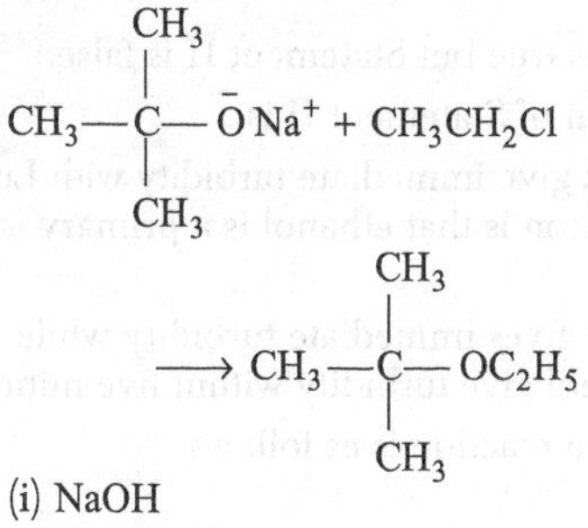

136. (i) NaOH

(ii) 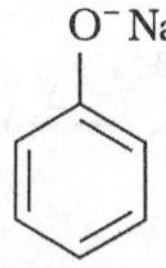 (iii) R—X

137. Butan-1-ol > n-pentane > Ethoxyethane

138. (c)

139. $A = R—X$; $B = R—OH$
$X = R—X$; $Y = H_2O$

140. $HCl < HBr < HI$

141. No;

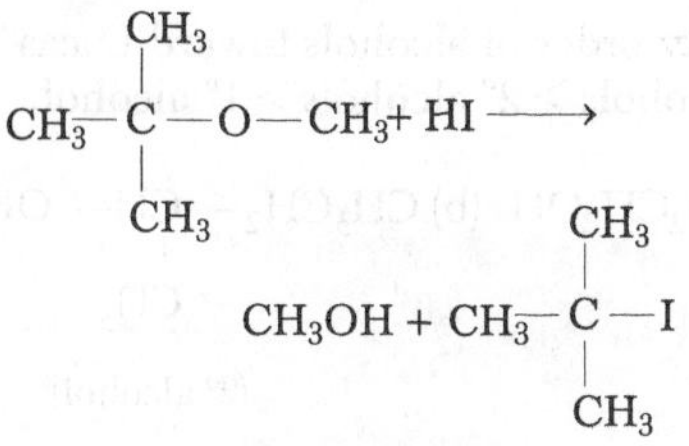

142. (i)

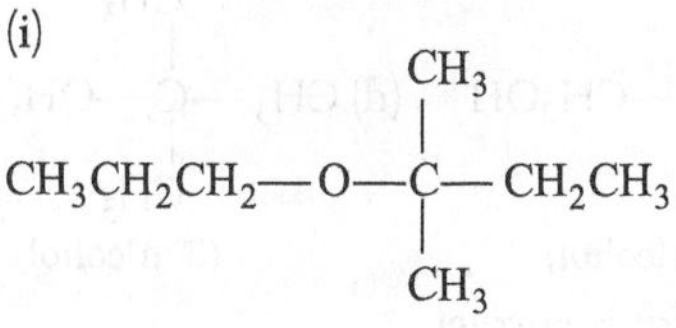

(ii)

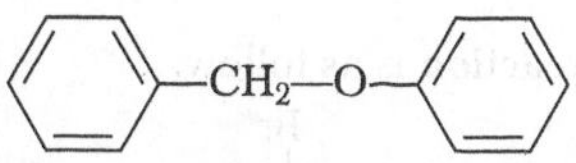

143.

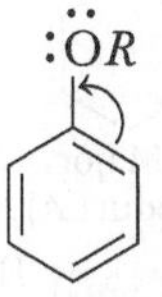

Shows wrong direction of arrows and the structure without changes.

144.

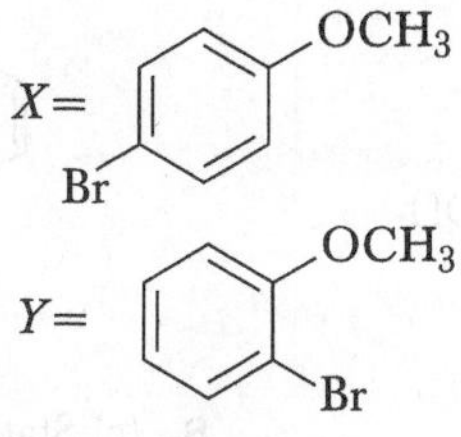

145. (i)

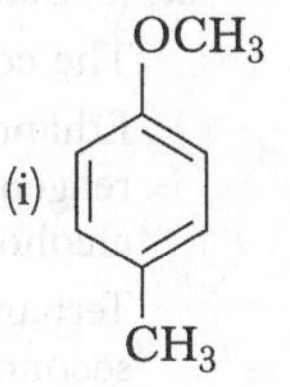

(ii)

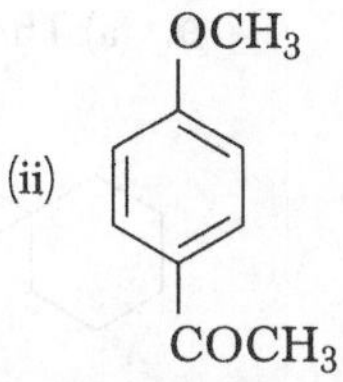

146. (i) HNO_3,

(ii)

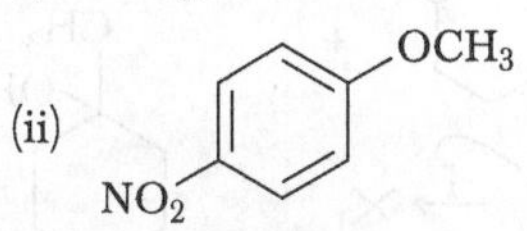

147. Williamson's synthesis

148.

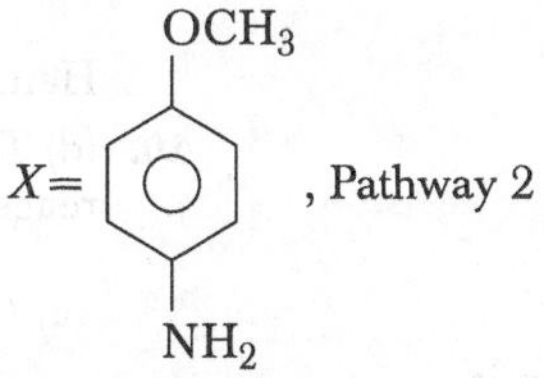

1-methoxy-4-nitrobenzene

149. A → (2), B → (3), C → (1)

Assertion-Reason

1. (c) **Correct Reason** : If the alkyl or aryl groups attached to the oxygen atom are same, it is simple ether.
If two groups are different, it is mixed ether.

2. (a)

3. (a)

4. (c) A is true but R is false.
Correct R is : Iodide ion combines with smaller group to avoid steric hindrance.

5. (a)

6. (a)

7. (a)

8. (a)

9. (a)

10. (b) There is no hydrogen bond between the molecules of ether, hence their boiling points are lower.

Case-Based

1. (i) (c) Phenols are more acidic than aliphatic alcohols due to resonance and stable anion.
(ii) (c) Phenol will give green color with $FeCl_3$ while aliphatic alcohols show no change.
(iii) (c) Mineral acids can effectively cleave C—O bond in ethyl methyl ether.
(iv) (b) Ethers have lower boiling points than alcohols. As branching in alkyl chains in alcohols increase, boiling points decrease. Hence (b) is the correct option.

2. (i) (b) Ethers do not have H atoms attached to O atoms hence cannot form H bonding.
(ii) (a) Symmetrical ethers cleave symmetrically hence will give ethyl iodide and ethyl alcohol.
(iii) (d) Diethyl ether is more prone to oxidation by O_2 as it has CH_2 group next to O-atom.
(iv) (d) Ethers are often used as solvents because they are relatively unreactive towards many chemicals.

Competition Edge Up

1. (b) The complete sequence of the given reaction is as follows

$$CH_3—CH{=}CH_2 \xrightarrow{H_2O,\ H^+} \underset{\text{(Markownikoff product)}\ (A)}{CH_3—CH(OH)—CH_3}$$

$$CH_3—CH{=}CH_2 \xrightarrow{(BH_3)_2} (CH_3CH_2CH_2)_3B$$

$$\xrightarrow{H_2O,\ H_2O_2,\ OH^-} \underset{\text{(Hydroboration-oxidation reaction)}\ (B)}{CH_3CH_2CH_2OH}$$

2. (c) The complete reaction is as follow,

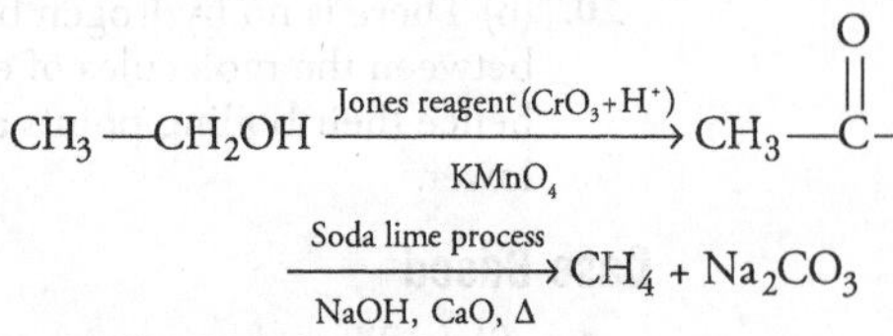

The major product is methane.
Hence, option (c) is correct.

3. (c)

4. (c) The complete reaction is as follows,

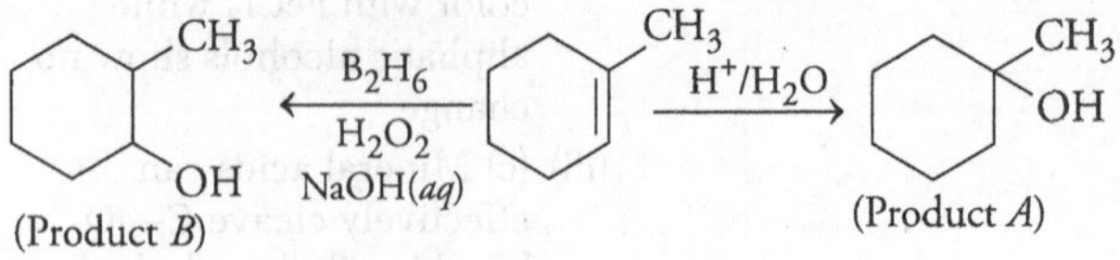

(Product *B*) (Product *A*)

Hence, option (c) is correct.

5. (b) The complete reaction is as follows.

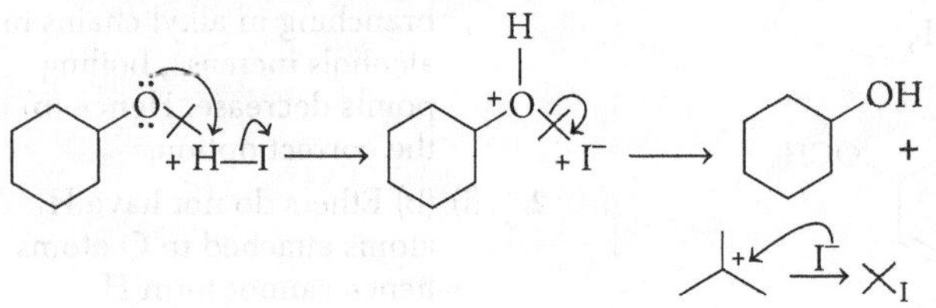

Thus, the major product formed in the reaction is

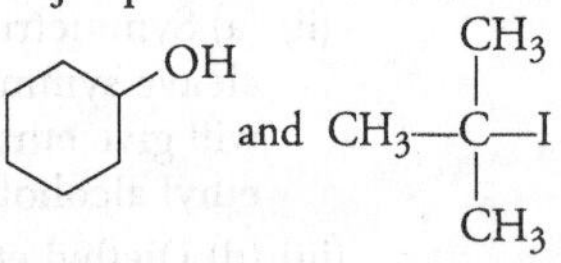

Hence, option (b) is correct.

6. (c) The complete Reimer-Tiemann reaction is

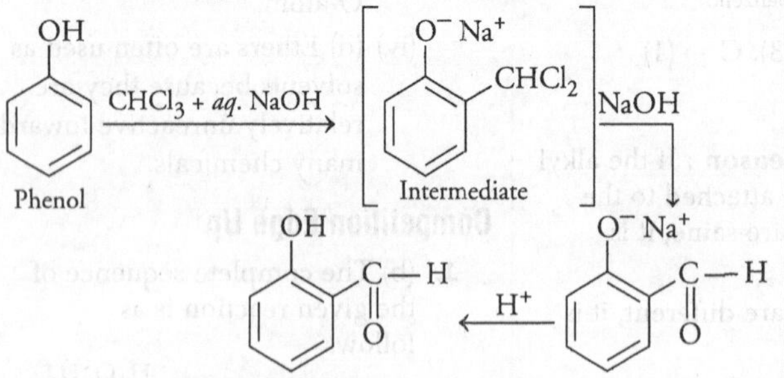

Hence, option (c) is correct.

7. (c) The complete reaction is as follows

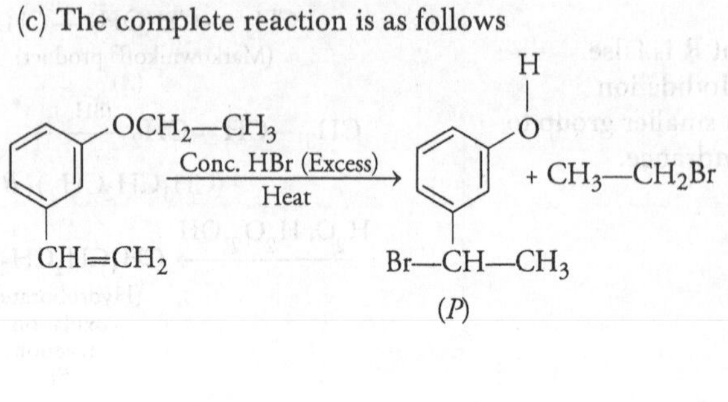

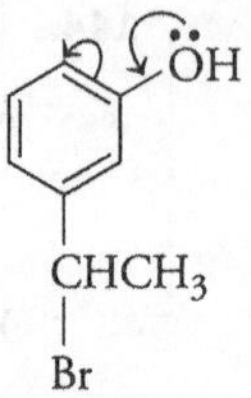

does not react further with HBr due to double bond character between C—O bond.

8. (c) Statement I is true but Statement II is false.
The correct form of Statement II is :
Ethanol will not give immediate turbidity with Lucas reagent. The reason is that ethanol is a primary alcohol.
Tertiary alcohol gives immediate turbidity while secondary alcohol give turbidity within five minutes.

9. (a) The complete reaction is as follows,

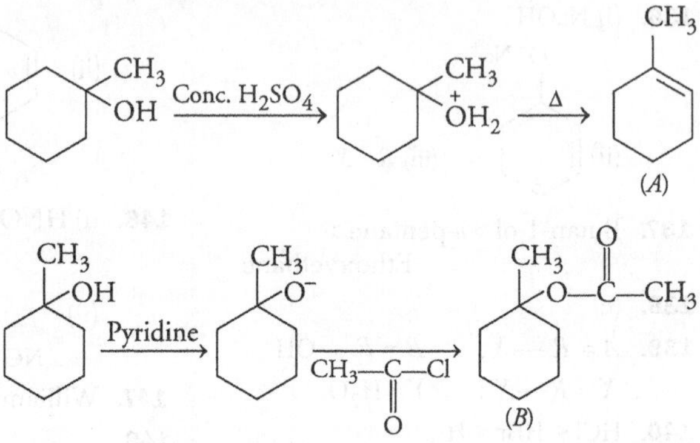

Hence, option (a) is correct.

10. (d) The reactivity order of alcohols toward Lucas' reagent is 3° alcohols > 2° alcohols > 1° alcohol.

(a) $CH_3CH_2CH_2CH_2OH$ (1° alcohol)

(b) $CH_3CH_2—CH(CH_3)—OH$ (2° alcohol)

(c) $CH_3—CH(CH_3)—CH_2OH$ (1° alcohol)

(d) $CH_3—C(CH_3)_2—OH$ (3° alcohol)

Hence, option (d) is correct.

11. (a) The complete reaction is as follow,

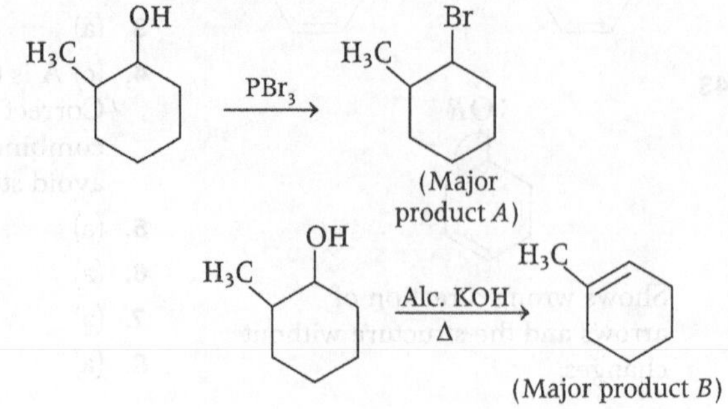

12. (d)

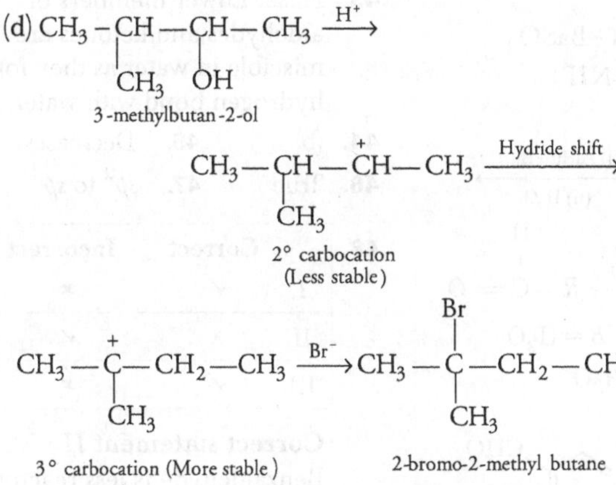

13. (a) Among the given alcohols,

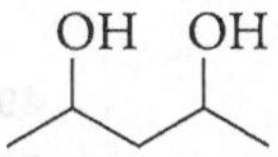

will be most readily dehydrated under acidic conditions to give

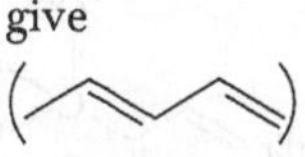

1, 3-butadiene as a product, in which double bonds are present in conjugation.

> **Concept Enhancer** 2° and 3° alcohols give dehydration reaction under acidic condition due to high stability of these carbocation than primary alcohol

14. (b) 1°, 2°, 3° alcohols can be distinguished by using Lucas reagents (conc. HCl + anhy. $ZnCl_2$) on the basis of the time taken for turbidity to appear,

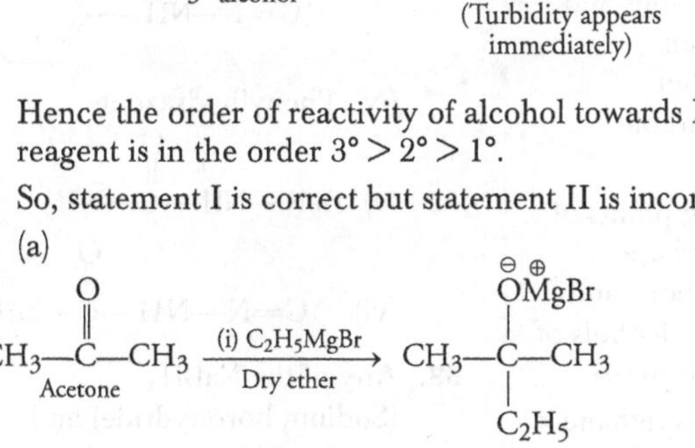

Hence the order of reactivity of alcohol towards Lucas reagent is in the order 3° > 2° > 1°.

So, statement I is correct but statement II is incorrect.

15. (a)

16. (c) The given equation is represented as

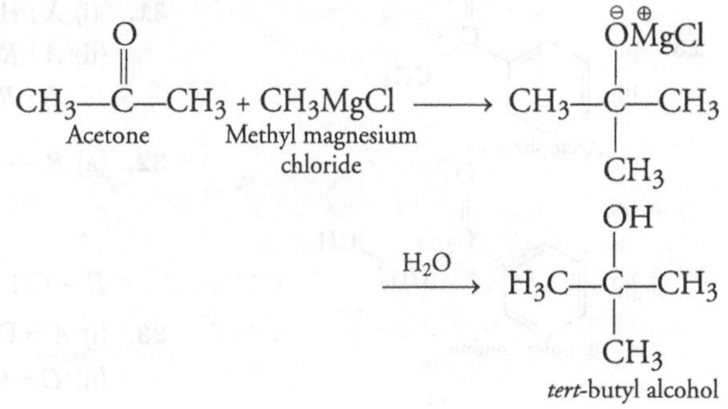

17. (a)

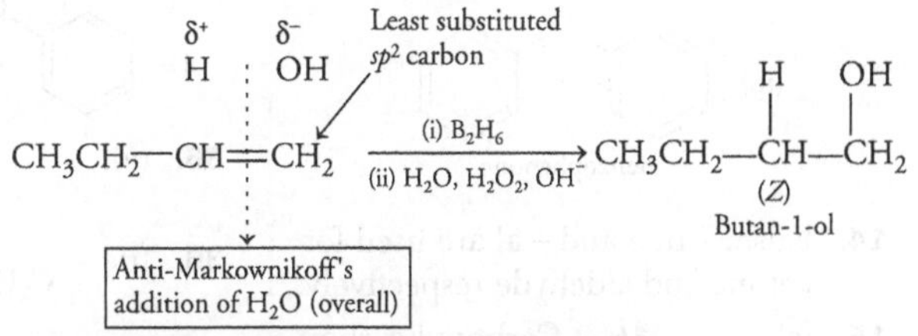

It is hydroboration-oxidation (HBO) reaction of an alkene which undergoes hydration to give an alcohol.

18. (d)

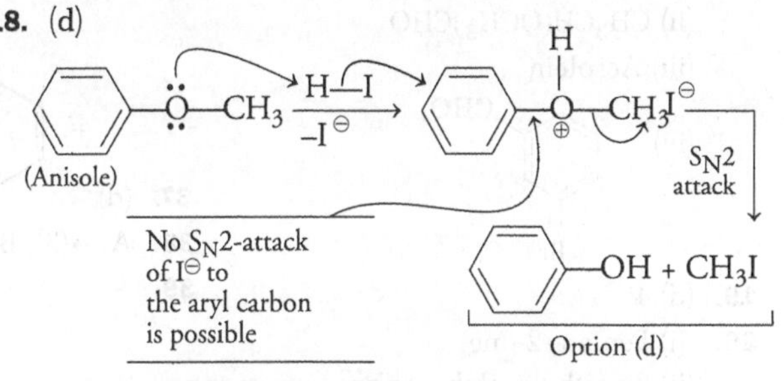

So, even with excess of HI, anisole will give phenol and methyl iodide (as in option-d)

Chapter-8

Aldehydes, Ketones and Carboxylic Acids

1. Double

2. False; In aldehyde, carbonyl group is bonded with a carbon and a hydrogen atom whereas in ketone it is bonded with two carbon atoms.

3. A →(2), B →(3), C →(1), D →(4)

4.

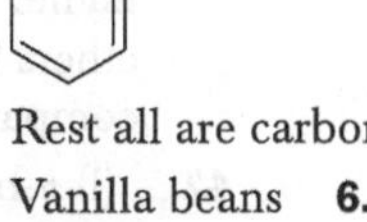

Rest all are carbonyl compounds.

5. Vanilla beans **6.** (c)

7. Acetone

8. Carboxylic acids

9. β-bromobutyraldehyde

10. (c) **11.** (b) **12.** Acyl

13. (i)
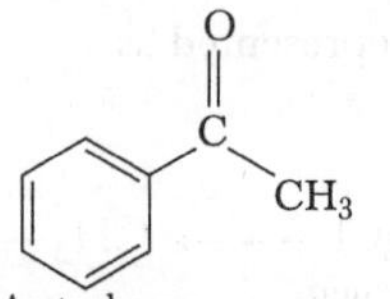
Acetophenone

(ii)
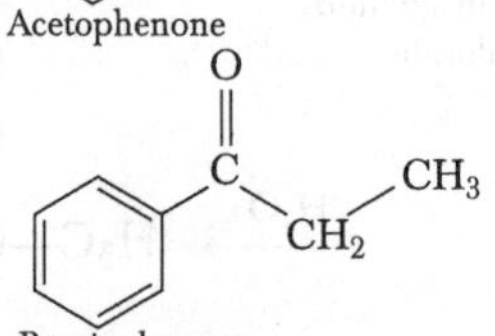
Propiophenone

(iii)
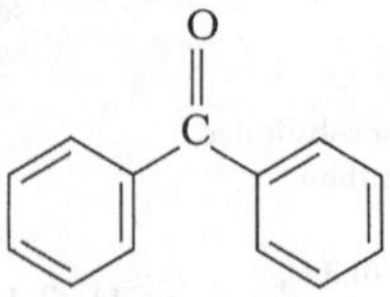
Benzophenone

14. False; – one and – al are used for ketone and aldehyde respectively.

15. (c) **16.** Carbonyl carbon

17. (a)

18. (i) 2-methylpropanal
(ii) $CH_3CH(OCH_3)CHO$
(iii) Acrolein
(iv)
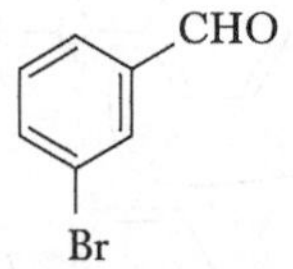

19. (d) 4

20. (i) Pentan -2-one
(ii) 2-methylcyclohexanone
(iii) 4-methylpent-3-en-2-one

21. (b)
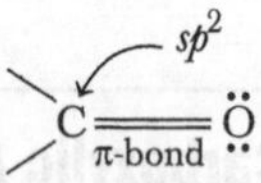

Presence of π-bond between C-atom and O-atom suggests that carbonyl carbon atom is sp^2-hybridised.

22. Same, π-electron

23. (c)

24. (b) The carbonyl carbon is electrophilic, which is Lewis acid and carbonyl oxygen, is nucleophilic which is Lewis base centre.

25. A →(2), B →(3), C →(1)

26. (b) **27.** (a)

28. (i) Dehydrogenation
(ii) False; Ag or Cu are used as metal catalysts in this method.

29. Ketone

30. (b)

31. (i) $X: H_2$, $Y: Pd - BaSO_4$
(ii) $A: R—CH=NH$
$B: RCHO$

32. (a) $R—C \equiv N \xrightarrow[\text{(ii) } H_2O]{\text{(i) } AlH(i-Bu)_2}$

$R—CH=N \xrightarrow{H_2O} R—\overset{H}{\overset{|}{C}}=O$

33. (i) $A =$ DIBAL-H, $B = H_2O$
(ii) $C = CS_2$, $D = H_3O^+$

34.
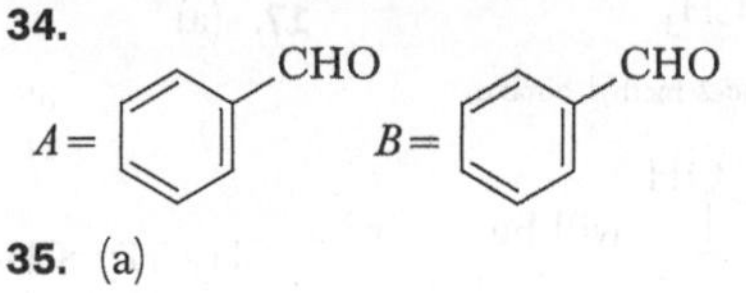

35. (a)

36. (i)
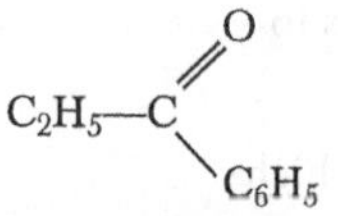
Propiophenone
(1-phenylpropanone)

(ii)
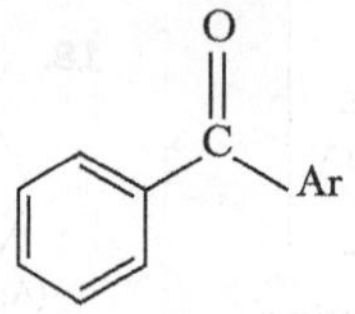

37. (d)

38. A →(3), B →(4), C →(1), D →(2)

39.
(i) $X=$
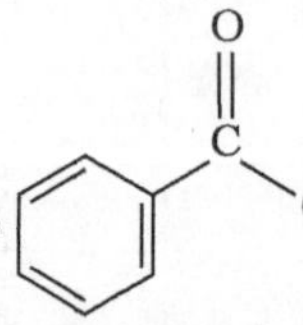
$+ HCl$

(ii) $Y = Hg^{2+}/H_2SO_4, H_2O$ (hydration)

40. (b) **Correct statement I** : Boiling point of aldehydes and ketones are higher than hydrocarbons and other compounds of comparable masses.

41. Alcohols; The boiling points of aldehydes and ketones are higher than hydrocarbons and ethers but lower than alcohols of comparable molecular masses.

42. (i) *n*-butane < Methoxyethane < Propanal < Acetone < Propan-1-ol
(ii) $CH_3CH_2CH_2CH_3 <$
$H_5C_2—O—C_2H_5 <$
$CH_3CH_2CH_2CHO <$
$CH_3CH_2CH_2CH_2OH$

43. False; Lower members of aldehydes and ketones are miscible in water as they forms hydrogen bond with water.

44. (b) **45.** Decreases

46. True **47.** sp^2 to sp^3

48.

	Correct	Incorrect
I.	✓	×
II.	×	✓
III.	✓	×

Correct statement II : Benzaldehyde is less reactive than propanal.

49. A →(3), B →(1), C →(2)

50. (b)
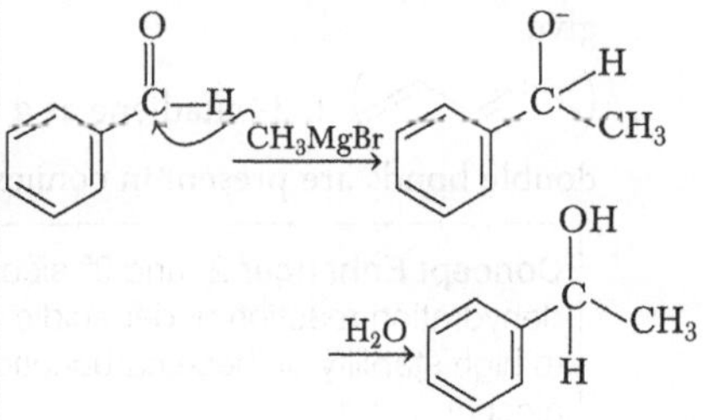

51. (i)
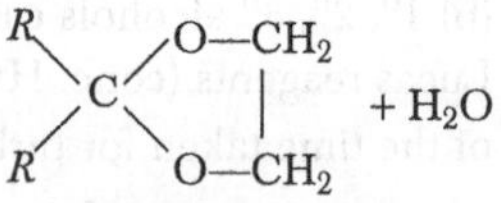
Ethylene glycol ketal

(ii) $R_2C=N—R + H_2O$
A component of Schiff's base

52. (i) $H_2N—OH$
(ii) Oxime
(iii)

(iv) Phenylhydrazone
(v) $H_2N—NH—\overset{O}{\overset{||}{C}}—NH_2$
(vi) $>C=N—NH—\overset{O}{\overset{||}{C}}—NH_2$

53. Any of the $NaBH_4$ (Sodium borohydride) and $LiAlH_4$ (Lithium aluminium hydride)

54. (b) It is hydrogenation reaction, where hydrogen atoms are added to carbon containing double bond.

55. (i) $>C{=}O \xrightarrow[HCl]{Zn\text{-}Hg} >CH_2 + H_2O$

(ii) $>C{=}O \xrightarrow[-H_2O]{NH_2NH_2} >C{=}N{-}NH_2 \xrightarrow[\Delta \text{ (ethyne glycol)}]{KOH} >CH_2 + N_2$

56. (b) $[Ag(NH_3)_2]NO_3$ is also called Tollen's reagent.

57. Ammoniacal silver nitrate, silver metal

58. (a) **Correct statement II :** In Fehling's test, Cu_2O is responsible for red-brown ppt.

59. Aromatic aldehydes

60. Iodoform test

$$CH_3CH_2CH_2{-}\overset{O}{\overset{\|}{C}}{-}CH_3 \xrightarrow{NaOI} CHI_3$$

Pentan-2-one; CHI_3 Yellow ppt.

$$CH_3CH_2\overset{O}{\overset{\|}{C}}{-}CH_2CH_3 \longrightarrow \text{No yellow ppt.}$$

Pentan-3-one

61. CH_3CO or $CH_3CH(OH)$

62. (d) 7

63. A: 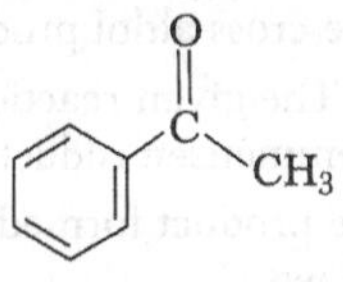

C_8H_8O

B: 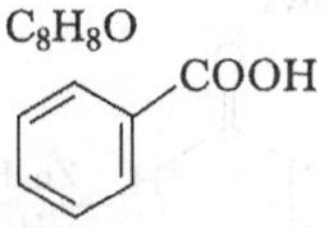

$C_7H_6O_2$

64. (a)

65. *A.* NaOH *B.* Heat

C. $CH_3{-}CH{=}CH{-}CHO$

D. $CH_3{-}CH{=}\overset{CH_3}{\overset{|}{C}}{-}CHO$

E. $CH_3{-}CH_2{-}CH{=}CH{-}CHO$

66. α-hydrogen atom, concentrated alkali

67. (c) All carboxylic acids and phenols are soluble in aqueous NaOH. So, four compounds are soluble in aqueous NaOH.

68. (c)

69.

(i) 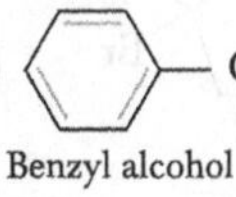 CH_2OH +

Benzyl alcohol

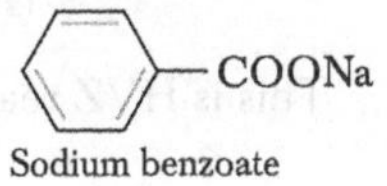 COONa

Sodium benzoate

(ii) 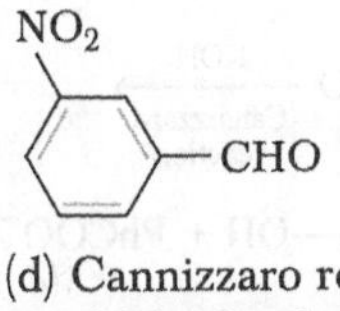

70. (d) Cannizzaro reaction is shown by aldehydes that don't have alpha hydrogen.

71. Ethanal > Propanal > Propanone > Butanone

The arrangement is based on steric effect and electronic effect.

72. (i) $HO{-}NH_2$ (ii) H^+

(iii) 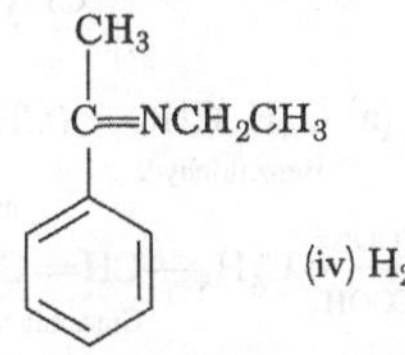 (iv) H_2O

73. Formaldehyde [formalin (40%) solution]

74. (d)

75. -ic acid, Latin or Greek

76. Propanoic acid; Propanoic acid is IUPAC name of CH_3CH_2COOH. While formic acid, acetic acid and butyric acid are common names of some carboxylic acids.

77. Formic acid

78. False; In this case the C-atom of carboxyl group is not considered for numbering and alkyl chain is numbered.

79. (i) Isobutyric acid , 2- methyl propanoic acid

(ii) $HOOC{-}COOH$, Ethanedioic acid

(iii) $HOOC{-}CH_2{-}CH{-}(COOH){-}CH_2{-}COOH$, No common name

80. (b)

81. Carbonyl carbon; Because of the possible resonance structure of carboxyl group.

82. A →(2), B →(3), C →(1)

83. (i) $R{-}CN \xrightarrow[H_2O]{2 \text{ moles } H^+ \text{ or } \bar{O}H} RCOOH$

Alkyl cyanide; Carboxylic acid

(ii) 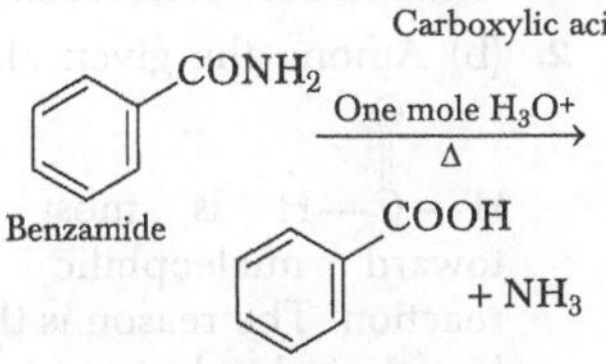

Benzamide; Benzoic acid

84. (i) *R*COOH (ii) *R*COOH

(iii) $2C_6H_5COOH$

85. True

86. (i) *X*= 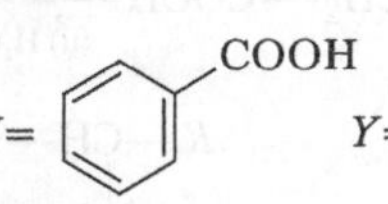

Benzoic acid

$Y = C_2H_5OH$ Ethanol

(ii) $Z = C_6H_5CH_2CN$

87.

	Correct	Incorrect
I.	✓	×
II.	×	✓
III.	✓	×

Correct statement II : On heating cyclohexane with $KMnO_4{-}H_2SO_4$, it forms adipic acid.

88. (i) Ethanol < Ethanoic acid < Benzoic acid

Boiling point increases with increase in molar mass.

(ii) Picric acid < Salicylic acid < Benzoic acid < Phenol.

Weaker is the acid, higher is the pK_a value.

89. Carbonates, hydrogen carbonates

90. (a) **Correct statement II :** Larger the value of pK_a, weaker is the acid.

91. (b)

92. (i) Mineral acid > Carboxylic acid > Phenol > Ethanol.

(ii) $CHCl_2COOH > NC{-}CH_2COOH > BrCH_2COOH > HCOOH > C_6H_5COOH > C_2H_5COOH$

93. (a) **94.** (c)

95. (i) 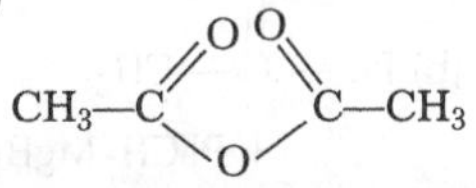

Ethanoic anhydride

(ii) $RCOCl + POCl_3 + HCl$

(iii) CH_3CONH_2 (Acetamide)

96. *X*= 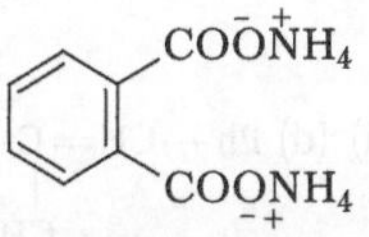

Y= 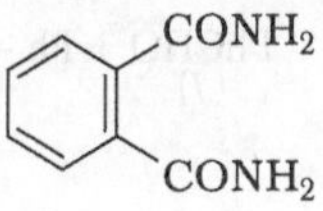

97. $R—CH_2—COOH \xrightarrow[\text{(ii) } H_2O]{\text{(i) } X_2, \text{ Red P}} R—\underset{X}{\underset{|}{CH}}—COOH$ $(X = Cl, Br)$

98. A →(2), B →(3), C →(4), D →(1)

99. True

100. (a)

101. Sodium benzoate

102. Higher fatty acids

Assertion-Reason

1. (b)

2. (c) **Correct Reason** : The polarity of carbon-oxygen double bond of carbonyl compounds is due to higher electronegativity of oxygen relative to carbon.

3. (a)

4. (d) The correct order is $CH_3CH_2CH_2CH_2CH_3 < H_5C_2OC_2H_5 < CH_3CH_2CH_2CHO < CH_3CH_2CH_2CH_2OH$

5. (d) **Correct Assertion** : Ketones are less reactive than aldehydes in nucleophilic addition reactions.

6. (a) **7.** (a) **8.** (a)

9. (b) Aldehydes which do not contain α-hydrogen undergo Cannizzaro reaction.

10. (c) **Correct Reason** : As the chain length of hydrocarbon increases, hydrophobic interactions increases.

Case-Based

1. (i) (b) $Ph—\overset{O}{\overset{||}{C}}—CH_3 + PhCH_2MgBr \longrightarrow Ph—\overset{OH}{\overset{|}{\underset{CH_2—Ph}{\underset{|}{C}}}}—CH_3$ (H)

(ii) (d) $Ph—CH=\underset{CH_3}{\underset{|}{C}}—Ph \xrightarrow{\text{Ozonolysis}} \underset{(J)}{PhCHO} + Ph—\underset{CH_3}{\underset{|}{C}}=O$ (K)

$\underset{(J)}{Ph—CHO} \xrightarrow[\text{Cannizzaro reaction}]{KOH} Ph—CH_2—OH + \underset{(L)}{PhCOO^-K^+}$

(iii) (a) $PhCH_2—\overset{OH}{\overset{|}{\underset{CH_3}{\underset{|}{C}}}}—Ph \longrightarrow Ph—CH=\underset{CH_3}{\underset{|}{C}}—Ph$ (H) (I)

(iv) (a) $\underset{\text{Benzaldehyde}}{C_6H_5CHO} + \underset{\text{Acetic anhydride}}{(CH_3CO)_2O} \xrightarrow[CH_3COOH]{CH_3COONa} \underset{\text{Cinnamic acid}}{C_6H_5—CH=CH—COOH}$

2. (i) (a) It is an example of cross Cannizzaro reaction.

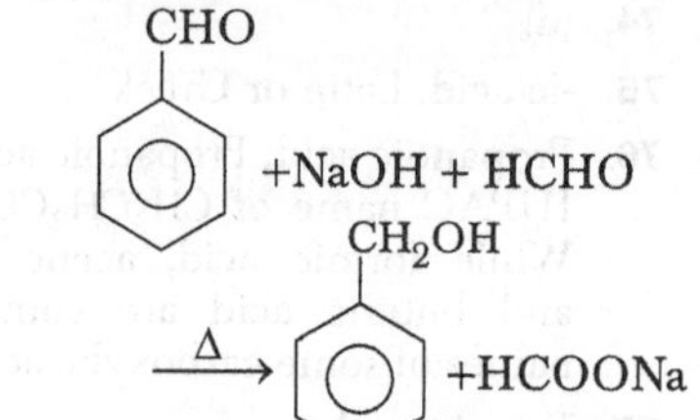

(ii) (c)

(iii) (a) The Cannizzaro product of given reaction yields 2, 2, 2-trichloroethanol.

(iv) (a) C—C bond is not formed in Cannizzaro reaction while other reactions result in the formation of C—C bond.

Competition Edge Up

1. (a) The given reaction proceeds as follows

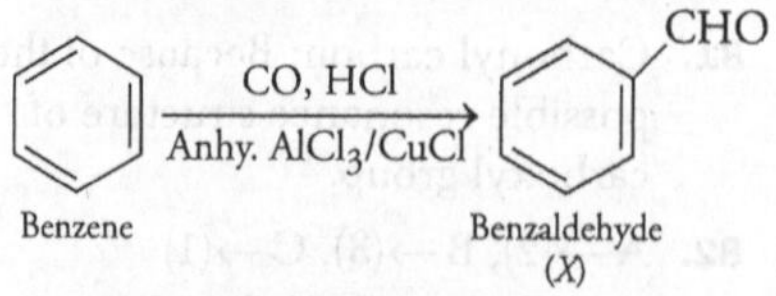

This reaction is called as Gattermann-Koch reaction.

2. (b) Among the given aldehydes, $H—\overset{O}{\overset{||}{C}}—H$ is most reactive toward nucleophilic addition reaction. The reason is that it has low steric hindrance at carbonyl carbon and high partial positive charge at carbonyl carbon.

3. (b) The given reaction is : Gattermann-Koch reaction.

In this reaction, benzene is treated with carbon monoxide in the acidic medium in presence of anhydrous aluminium chloride to give benzaldehyde.

The complete reaction is as follow,

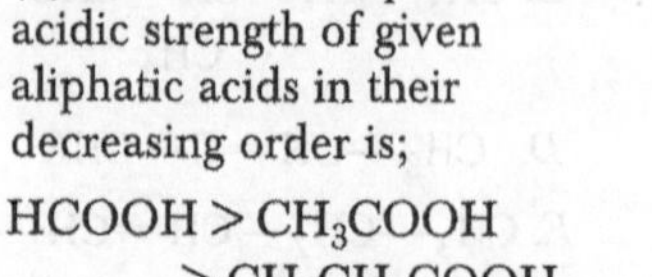

4. (c) Structure of 4-methyl pent-2-enal

$\overset{5}{C}H_3—\underset{CH_3}{\underset{|}{\overset{4}{C}H}}—\overset{3}{C}H=\underset{2}{C}H—\underset{1}{\overset{O}{\overset{||}{C}}}—H$

Hence, option (c) is correct.

5. (d) Statement I is correct but Statement II is incorrect.

The correct form of Statement II is reaction between benzaldehyde and ethanal will give cross-aldol product.

6. (b) The given reaction is a Clemmensen reduction.

The product formed is as follows

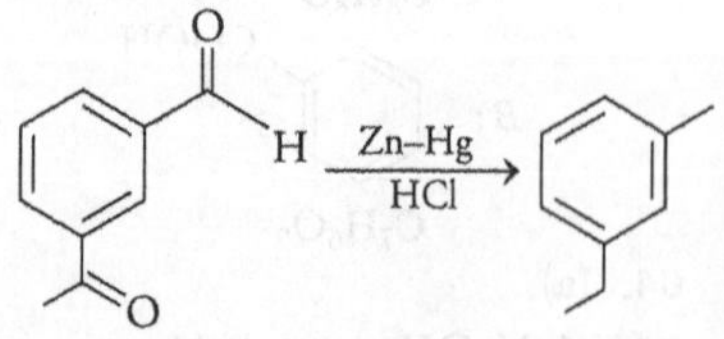

7. (b) The correct sequence of acidic strength of given aliphatic acids in their decreasing order is;

$HCOOH > CH_3COOH > CH_3CH_2COOH > CH_3CH_2CH_2COOH$

8. (d) The complete reaction is as follows,

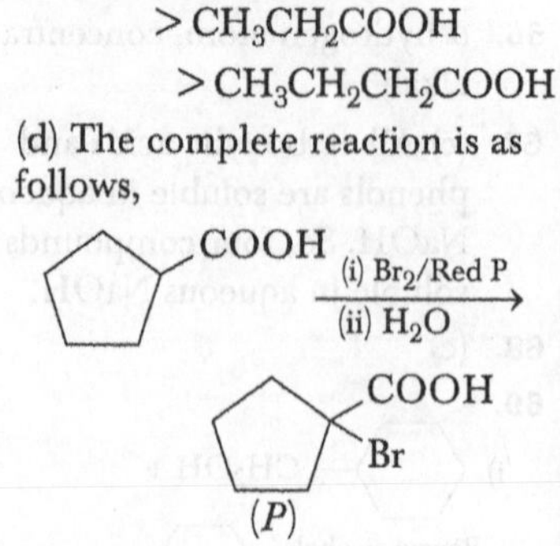

This is HVZ reaction.

9. (b) The complete reaction is as follows,

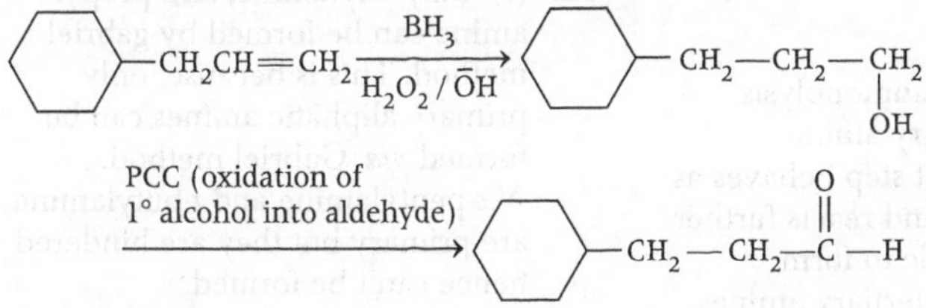

10. (b)

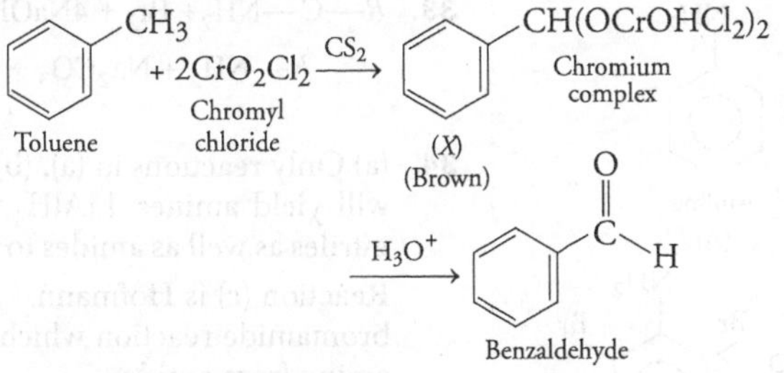

This is called Etard reaction.

11. (c) Dilute NaOH is the reagent for aldol condensation. Dilute NaOH process enolate ion from acetophenone which attacks benzaldehyde to give aldol.

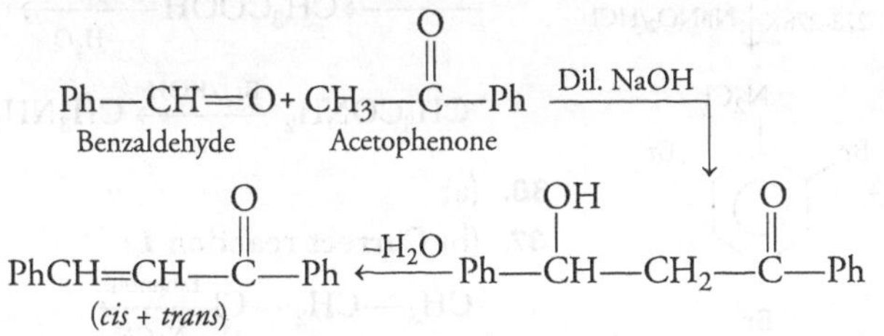

It is cross aldol condensation or Claisen-Schmidt reaction or Claisen reaction.

12. (c)

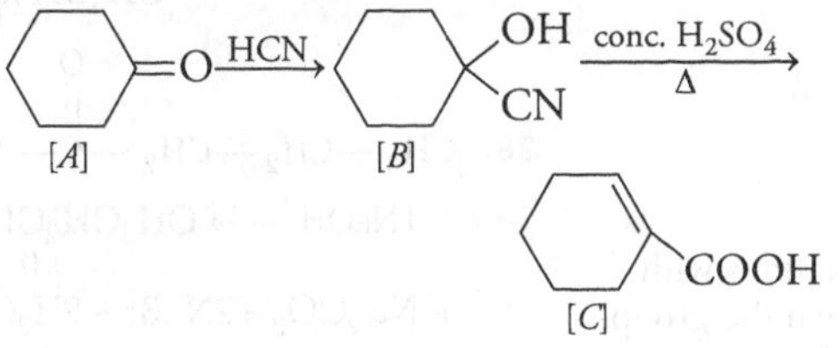

13. (d) The final reaction is as follows

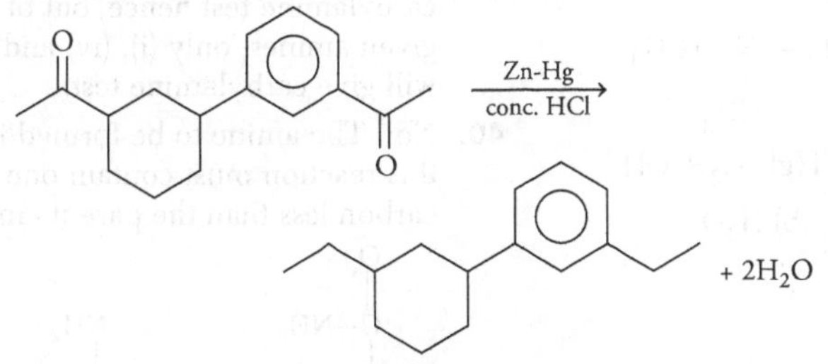

This reaction is an example of Clemmensen reduction reaction.

14. (a) When acetone reacts with 2-pentanone in presence of dilute NaOH followed by heating then the products will be formed according to cross aldol condensation.

Self aldol

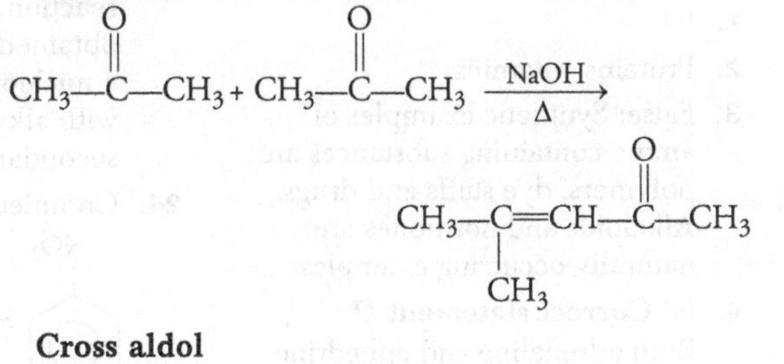

Cross aldol

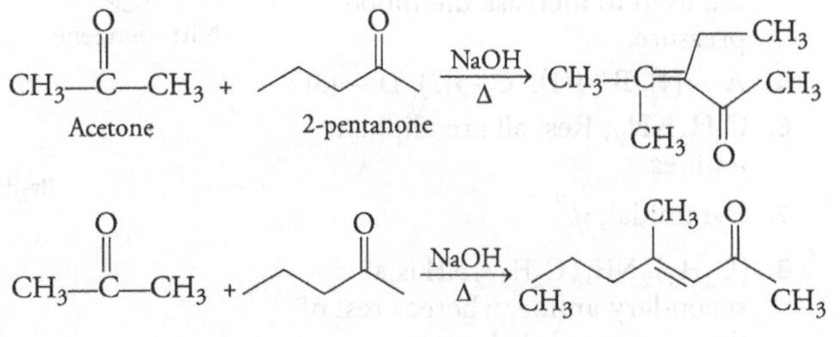

So, among the given options compound (a), *i.e.*

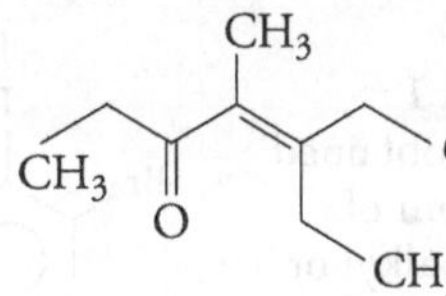

will not form.

15. (c) The correct match is option (c), i.e. (A)-(iv), (B)-(iii), (C)-(ii), (D)-(i)

Products formed	Reaction of carbonyl compound with
Cyanohydrin	HCN
Acetal	Alcohol
Schiff's base	RNH_2
Oxime	NH_2OH

The reactions involved are as follows

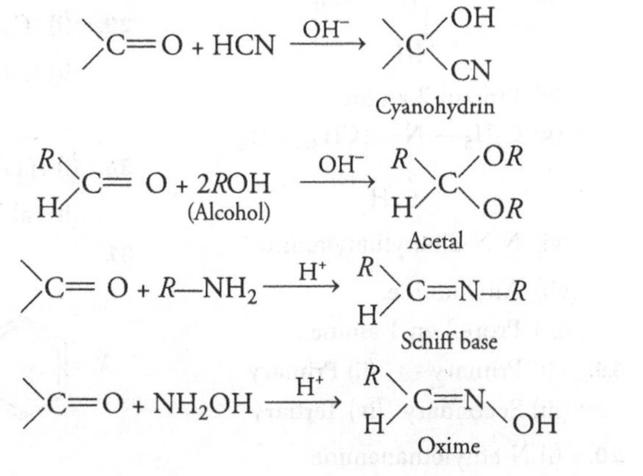

Chapter-9
Amines

1. (c)
2. Proteins, vitamins
3. False; Synthetic examples of amine containing substances are polymers, dye stuffs and drugs. Alkaloids and hormones are naturally occurring examples.
4. (a) **Correct statement II** : Both adrenaline and ephedrine are used to increase the blood pressure.
5. A →(4), B →(1), C →(2), D →(3)
6. $C_6H_5NH_2$; Rest all are aliphatic amines
7. Pyramidal, sp^3
8. $(C_2H_5)_2NH$; $(C_2H_5)_2NH$ is a secondary amine, whereas rest of the compounds belong to primary amines.
9. (b)
10. (b) **Correct statement I** : Secondary amines are obtained by replacing one H-atom of primary amine by one alkyl or aryl group.
11. (c)
12. Methylamine
13. di, tri, alkyl
14. True
15. Aniline
16. *e*, amine
17. A→(3), B→(1), C→(2)
18. (i) *n*-propylamine
 (ii) Propan-1- amine
 (iii) $CH_3—CH(NH_2)—CH_3$,
 (iv) Propan-2-amine
 (v) $C_2H_5—N(C_2H_5)—(CH_2)_3CH_3$
 (vi) N-N-diethylbutylamine
 (vii) Allyl amine,
 (viii) Prop-2-en-1-amine
19. (i) Primary (ii) Primary
 (iii) Secondary (iv) Tertiary
20. (i) N-ethylethanamine
 (ii) N- methylpropan-2-amine
21. Ammonia, nucleophilic
22. (b)
23. False; During ammonolysis reaction, primary amine obtained in first step behaves as a nucleophile and reacts further with alkyl halide to form secondary and tertiary amines.
24. Complete reaction is as follows

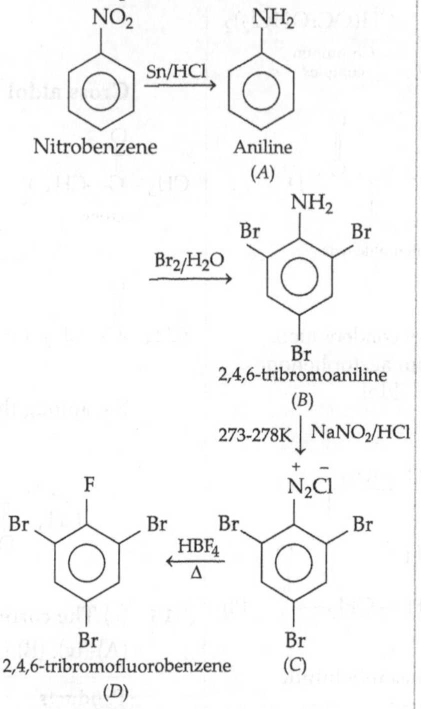

25. (i) R_2NH, (ii) RX
26. $R—\overset{+}{N}H_2 + H_2O + NaX^-$
27. Mixture
28. $RCl < RBr < RI$
 Reactivity of alkyl halides with amines increases down the group.
29. (i) $(C_2H_5)_3\overset{+}{N}Cl^-$
 (ii) $C_6H_5—CH_2—N(CH_3)—CH_3$
30. (i) H_2 / Ni, Na(Hg) /C_2H_5OH
 (ii) (a) $LiAlH_4$, (b) H_2O
31.

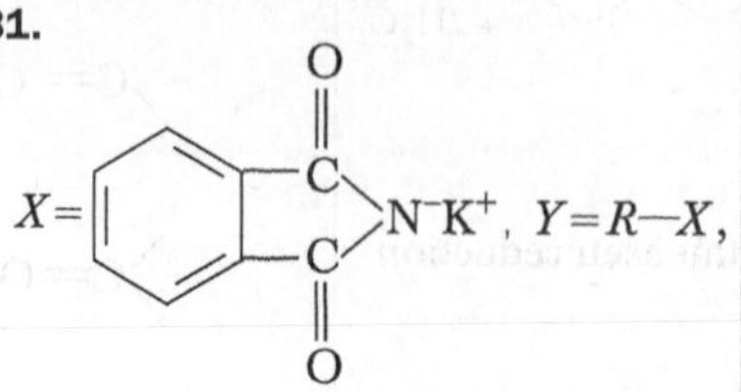

$Z = R—NH_2$

32. (c) Only allylamine, and propyl amine can be formed by gabriel method. This is because, only primary aliphatic amines can be formed *via* Gabriel method. *Neo*-pentylamine and *t*-butylamine are primary but they are hindered hence can't be formed.
33. $R—\overset{O}{\overset{\|}{C}}—NH_2 + Br_2 + 4NaOH \longrightarrow$
 $R—NH_2 + Na_2CO_3 + 2NaBr + 2H_2O$
34. (a) Only reactions in (a), (b) and (c) will yield amines. $LiAlH_4$ reduces nitriles as well as amides to amine. Reaction (c) is Hofmann bromamide reaction which yields amine from amide.
35. Chloroethane to methanamine
 $$\underset{\text{Chloroethane}}{CH_3CH_2Cl} \xrightarrow{Aq.\ NaOH} \underset{\text{Ethanol}}{CH_3CH_2OH} \xrightarrow{KMnO_4} CH_3COOH \xrightarrow[-H_2O]{NH_3\ /Heat}$$
 $$CH_3CONH_2 \xrightarrow{Br_2\ /KOH} CH_3NH_2$$
36. (a)
37. (b) **Correct reaction I** :
 $$CH_3—CH_2—Cl \xrightarrow[NaCN]{Ethanolic} CH_3CH_2C{\equiv}N \xrightarrow{Reduction} CH_3CH_2CH_2NH_2$$
38. $CH_3—CH_2—CH_2—\overset{O}{\overset{\|}{C}}—NH_2 + Br_2 + 4NaOH \longrightarrow \underset{(A)}{CH_3CH_2CH_2NH_2} + Na_2CO_3 + 2NaBr + 2H_2O$
39. (a) Only primary amines give carbylamine test hence, out of the given amines, only (i), (iv) and (v) will give carbylamine test.
40. No; The amine to be formed in this reaction must contain one carbon less than the parent amide.

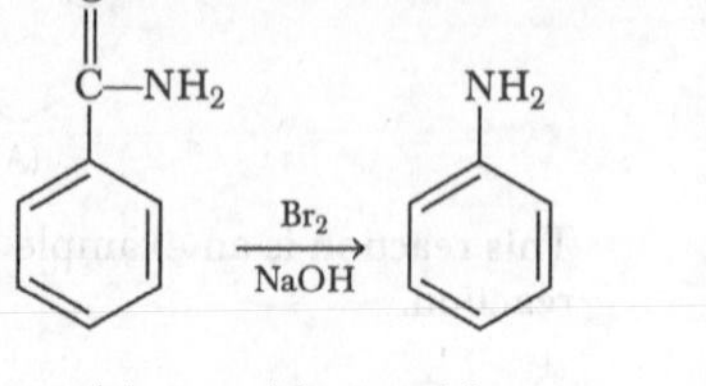

41. A →(3), B →(1), C →(2)

42. Fishy

43. (b) **Correct form** : Primary amines with 4 carbon atoms exists in liquid state.

44. False; Aniline and aryl amines are initially colourless and become coloured due to atmospheric oxidation.

45. (a)

46. $C_6H_5NH_2 < (C_2H_5)_2NH < C_2H_5NH_2$

Solubility of amines decreases with increase in molar mass.

47. (b) **48.** Insoluble

49. (b) **Correct statement I** : Alcohols are more polar than amines.

50. Primary amines; Lesser the number of substituted hydrogen more the number of alkyl groups in amines, less will be the hydrogen bonding.

51. No

52. Tertiary < Secondary < Primary; Stronger the hydrogen bonding, higher will be the boiling point.

53. n-C_4H_9OH

54. (i) Difference in electronegativity between N and H.

(ii) Presence of lone pair of electron over nitrogen.

55. True

56. (b) Nucleophiles are electron rich species with the ability to donate the lone pair.

57. Basic

58. $R—NH_2 + HX \rightleftharpoons R—\overset{+}{N}H_3X^-$ (salt)

59. $A = \overset{-}{O}H$, $B = H_2O$, $C = \overset{-}{X}$

60. Ether

61. (a) Species which are capable of donating electron pairs are known as Lewis bases.

62. Lower

63. $+I$-effect of alkyl group

64. Aromatic amines

65. (a)

66. (d) Amines are basic not acidic so the correct statement are

I. Basic character of an amine depends upon the ease of formation of the cation by accepting a proton from the acid.

II. More stable the cation is relative to amine, more basic is amine.

67. (a)

68. Stronger

69. NH_3 < Primary amine < Secondary amine < Tertiary amine

70. (c)

71. False; More bulkier group on amines, more will be the steric hindrance to H-bonding.

72. (i) Inductive effect

(ii) Solvation effect

(iii) Steric hindrance

73. $NH_3 < C_2H_5NH_2 < (C_2H_5)_3N < (C_2H_5)_2NH$;

In aqueous phase, solution effect is also taken in consideration along with stability of cation.

74. (c) **75.** High

76. (b) Correct representation

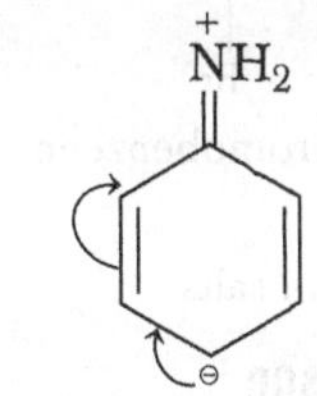

77. True

78. (a) Electron releasing groups increase basic strength, whereas electron withdrawing groups decrease when it attached to aniline.

79. (b)

80. $C_2H_5—\underset{H}{\underset{|}{N}}—\overset{}{\underset{O}{\underset{\|}{C}}}—CH_3 + HCl$

81. (i) $CH_3—\underset{O}{\underset{\|}{C}}—Cl$

(ii) $C_6H_5—\underset{H}{\underset{|}{\ddot{N}}}—H$, CH_3COOH

82. Benzoylation

83. $R—NH_2 + CHCl_3 + 3KOH \xrightarrow{\Delta} R—NC + 3KCl + 3H_2O$

84. False; Isocyanides or carbylamines are foul smelling substances.

85. (c)

86. Nitrogen, amino acid and proteins

87. (c) $\underset{\text{Methylamine}}{CH_3—NH_2} + HNO_2 \xrightarrow{NaNO_2+HCl} CH_3—\overset{+}{N_2}\overset{-}{Cl} \xrightarrow[-HCl]{H_2O} CH_3OH + N_2\uparrow$

88. (i) $NaNO_2 + HCl$

(ii) H_2O

89. $C_6H_5—\overset{+}{N_2}Cl^- + NaCl + 2H_2O$

90. **Name** Benzene sulphonyl chloride

Formula $(C_6H_5SO_2Cl)$

91. $A = C_2H_5—\overset{H}{\overset{|}{N}}—H$, B : HCl

92. (b) **Correct statement** : Hydrogen attached to nitrogen in sulphonamide is strongly acidic.

93.

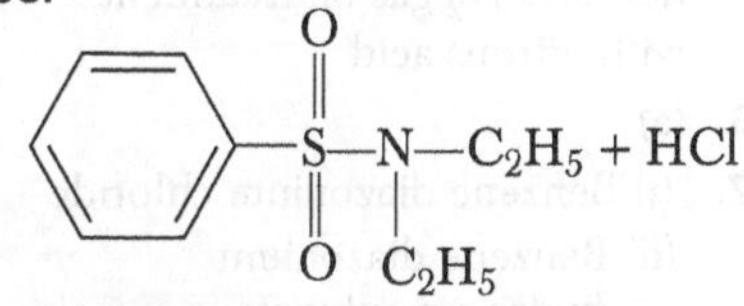

94. Insoluble

95. A. Br_2/H_2O

B. Br_2/CH_3COOH

96.

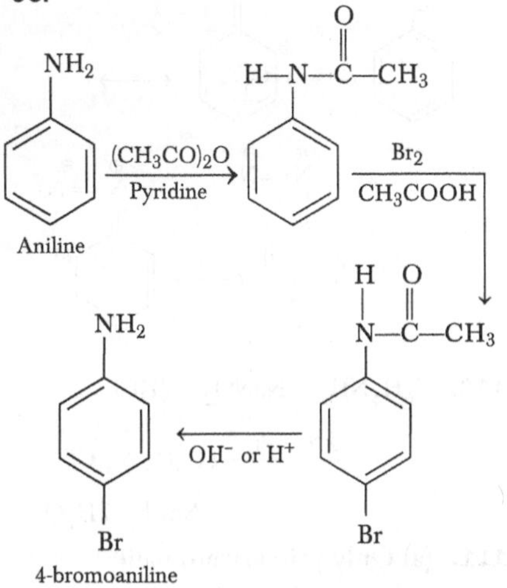

97.

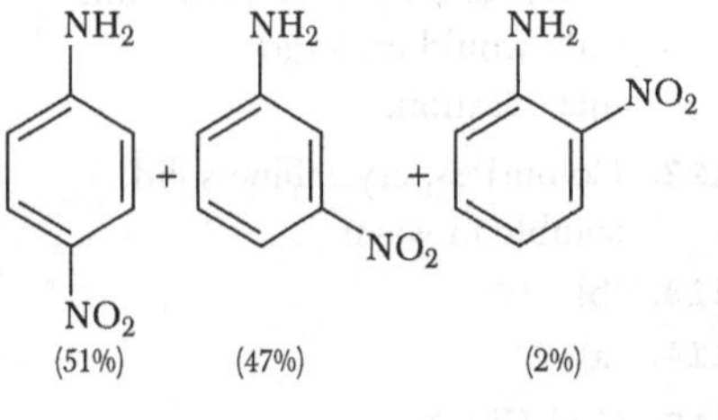

98. 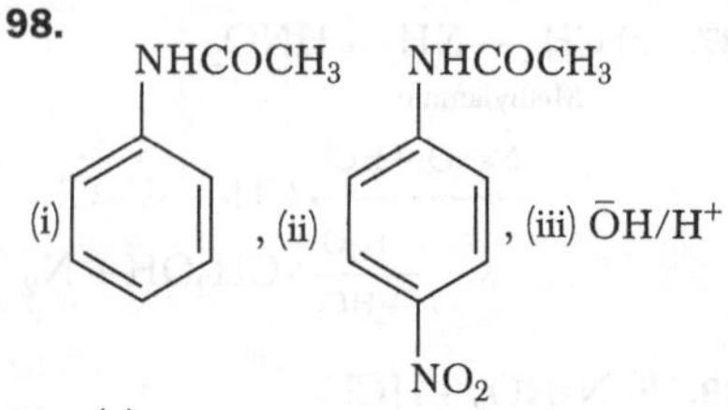

99. (a)

100. Aniline

101. $C_6H_5NH_2 < C_6H_5CH_2NH_2 < (CH_3)_3N < CH_3NH_2 < (CH_3)_2NH$

102. (i) HCl (ii) $(C_2H_5)_3N$

103. $[C_6H_5\overset{+}{N}(CH_3)_3]_2CO_3^{2-} + 2NaI$

104. N- phenylbenzamide (Benzanilide)

105. (d) Only primary amines liberates N_2 gas on treatment with nitrous acid.

106. (a)

107. (i) Benzene diazonium chloride
(ii) Benzene diazonium hydrogen sulphate

108. True

109.

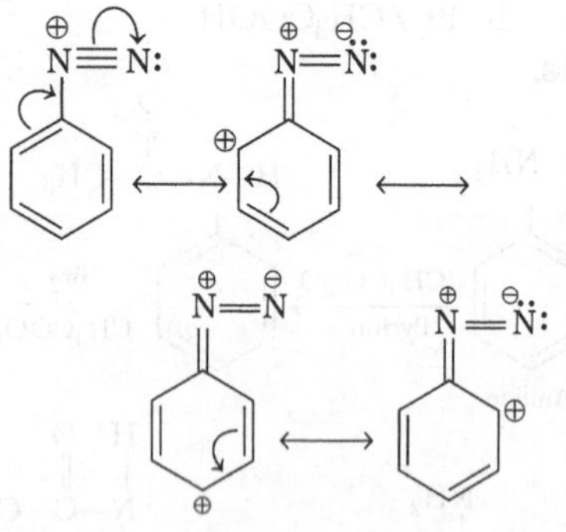

110. $C_6H_5NH_2 + NaNO_2 + 2HCl \xrightarrow{273\text{-}278K} C_6H_5\overset{+}{N_2}Cl^- + NaCl + 2H_2O$

111. (a) Only primary aromatic amines undergo diazotisation.

Hence aniline, *m*-chloroaniline only would undergo diazotisation.

112. Colourless, crystalline solid, soluble in water

113. (b)

114. (a)

115. $C_6H_5Cl + N_2$

116. (i) KI, KCl
(ii) HBF_4, $Ar—\overset{+}{N_2}BF_4^-$

117. H_3PO_2 / H_2O

118. (i) $X = ArOH$

(ii) $Y=$ 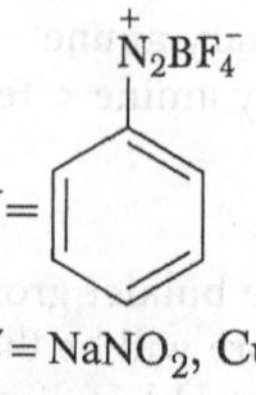

$Z = NaNO_2$, Cu , Δ

119. (d)

120. A →(2), B →(3), C → (1)

121. Br_2, Sn/HCl

122. 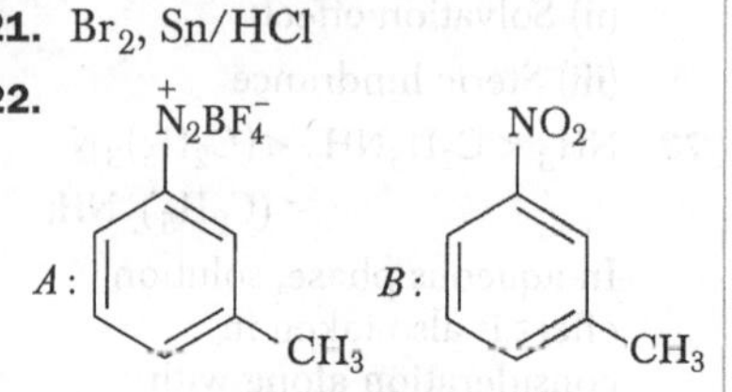

123. 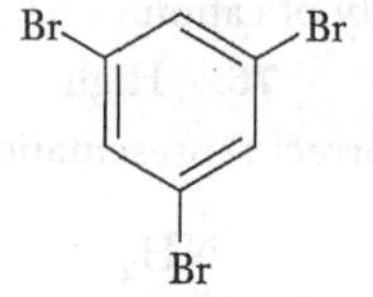

1,3,5 -tribromobenzene

124. (c)

125. Diazonium salts

Assertion-Reason

1. (a) **2.** (a)

3. (a)

4. (d) **Correct Assertion** : Solubility of amines in water decrease with increase in molar mass.

5. (b) Both A and R are correct, but R is not the correct explanation of the A. Correct explanation is N has lone pair of electrons which are donated.

6. (a)

7. (d) **Correct Assertion** : In aqueous phase ammonium cations gets stabilised due to both electron releasing effect of alkyl group and solvation with water molecules.

8. (a)

9. (b) The NH_2 group of aniline is acetylated before nitration to control the nitration reaction and the formation of oxidation products and nitro derivatives.

10. (d) **Correct Assertion** : Alcohols are more soluble in water than amines.

Case-Based

1. (i) (d) In aqueous solutions, 2° amines are more basic as 3° amines are more crowded hence lone pair is sterically hindered.

(ii) (d) Due to ortho effect, ortho substituted anilines are weaker bases. Hence, correct order is (d).

(iii) (c) As anilines are weaker bases than aliphatic bases, hence correct choice is (c).

(iv) (d) All other statements except (d) are correct. Hydrazine is a weaker base than ammonia due to presence of electronegative N atom next to NH_2 group.

2. (i) (b) Due to resonance, lone pair of N is delocalised hence is not available for donation to electron deficient species. This is why aromatic amines are weaker bases.

(ii) (c) Incorrect statement is (c) as the effect is more dominant in *para* position than in *meta* position.

(iii) (c) In reaction of aniline with HNO_2, diazonium salt is formed.

$$\underset{\text{Aniline}}{C_6H_5NH_2} + HNO_2 \xrightarrow{2HCl} \underset{\text{Benzene diazonium salts}}{C_6H_5—N_2^+Cl^-} + NaCl + 2H_2O$$

(iv) (a) On reaction of acetic anhydride with aniline, acetanilide is formed.

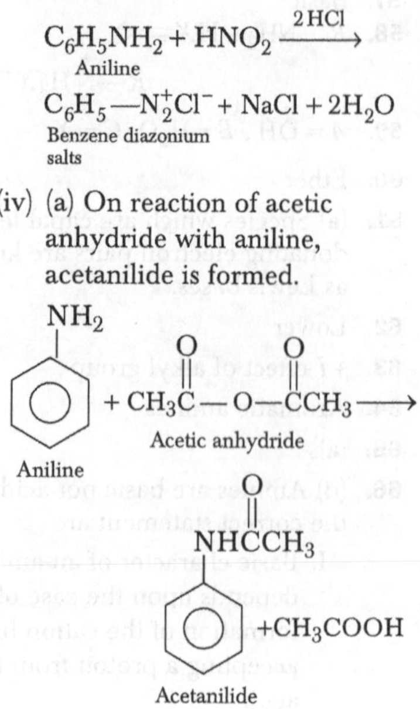

Competition Edge Up

1. (a) The complete reaction, takes place as follows

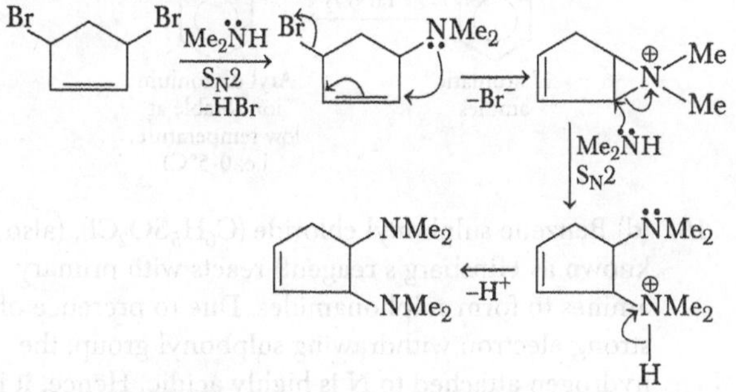

2. (c) The complete reaction is as follows

$$Cl(CH_2)_4Cl \xrightarrow{\text{Excess } NH_3} \underset{(A)}{Cl^-NH_3^+—(CH_2)_4—NH_3^+Cl^-}$$

$$\xrightarrow{NaOH} \underset{(B)}{H_2N—(CH_2)_4—NH_2} + 2NaCl + 2H_2O$$

3. (b) Among the given compounds

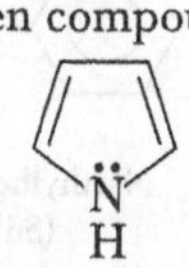

is weakest as in this the lone pair is completely delocalised *via* cyclic resonance to show aromaticity. While among pyridine and piperidine due to $+I$ effect of substituents piperidine is more basic. Hence, the correct order of basic strength is

Piperidine > Pyridine > Pyrrole

4. (a) Both statement I and statement II are correct. The NH_2 group in aniline is *ortho* and *para* directing and a powerful activating group as NH_2 has strong $+M$ effect.

Thus, aniline does not undergo Friedel-Craft's reaction because it will form complex with $AlCl_3$ that will deactivate the benzene ring.

Hence, option (a) is correct.

5. (c) Both statement I and statement II are false. The reason is that, 1° and 2° amines only reacts with *p*-toluene sulphonyl chloride and product of 1° amine only is soluble in aqueous NaOH.

6. (d) Statement I is correct but Statement II is incorrect. Correct form of Statement II is

Aniline is also known as amino benzene. It is a liquid organic compound formed by bond formation between benzene and ammonia. Chemical formula $= C_6H_5NH_2$

Hence, option (d) is correct.

7. (a) The complete reaction takes place as follows,

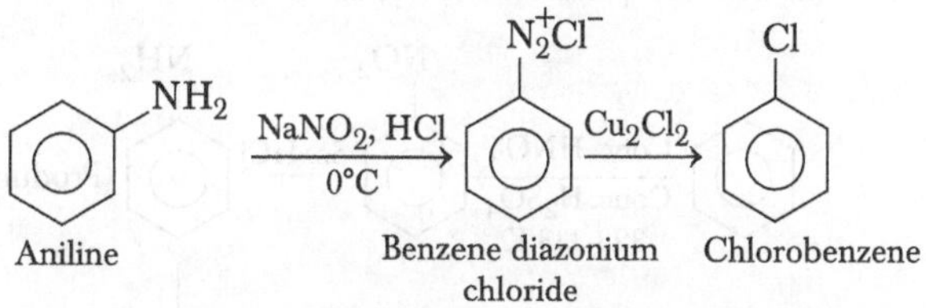

8. (d) As $—\ddot{N}H_2$ group is o/p-directing, hence arenium ion will be formed by attack at metal position i.e.

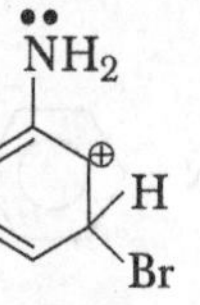

Hence, option (d) is correct.

9. (b) The complete reaction is as follows:

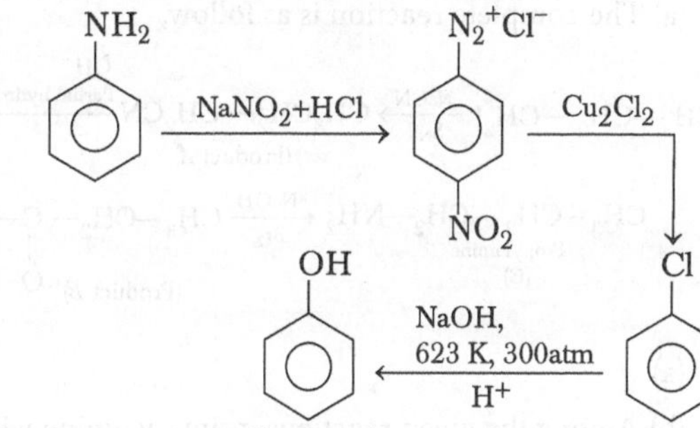

10. (d) The complete reaction is as follow,

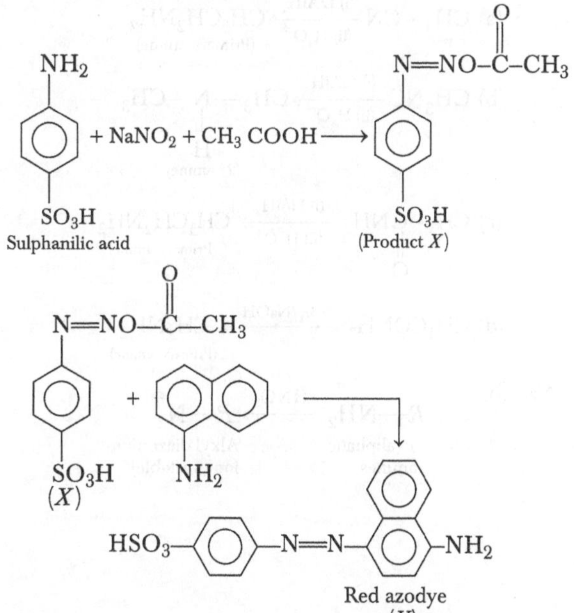

11. (a) The complete reaction is as follows:

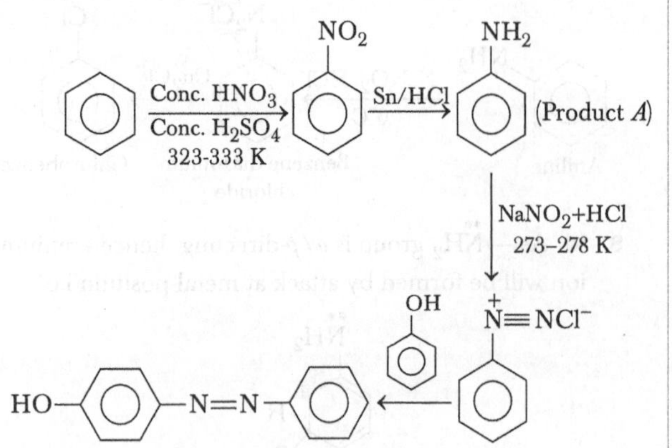

(Product B)

Hence, option (a) is correct.

12. (a) The complete reaction is as follow,

$$CH_3-CH_2-CH_2I \xrightarrow[S_N2]{NaCN} CH_3CH_2-CH_2CN \xrightarrow{OH^-\text{ Partial hydrolysis}}$$

(Product A)

$$CH_3-CH_2-CH_2-NH_2 \xleftarrow[Br_2]{NaOH} CH_3-CH_2-\underset{\underset{O}{\|}}{C}-NH_2$$

Propylamine (C) (Product B)

13. (a)

14. (b) Among the given reactions, primary amine will not form in case of (b) reaction.

(a) $CH_3-CN \xrightarrow[\text{(ii) } H_3O^+]{\text{(i) } LiAlH_4} CH_3CH_2NH_2$ (Primary amine)

(b) $CH_3NC \xrightarrow[\text{(ii) } H_3O^+]{\text{(i) } LiAlH_4} CH_3-\underset{\underset{H}{|}}{N}-CH_3$ (2° amine)

(c) $CH_3-\underset{\underset{O}{\|}}{C}NH_2 \xrightarrow[\text{(ii) } H_3O^+]{\text{(i) } LiAlH_4} CH_3CH_2NH_2$ (Primary amine)

(d) $CH_3CONH_2 \xrightarrow{Br_2/NaOH} CH_3NH_2$ (Primary amine)

15. (b) $R-NH_2 \xrightarrow{HNO_2} R-\overset{\oplus}{N_2}$

1° aliphatic amines — Alkyl diazonium ion (unstable)

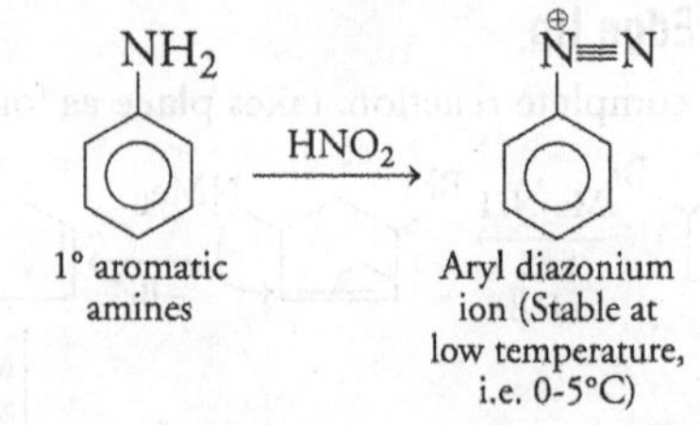

16. (d) Benzene sulphonyl chloride ($C_6H_5SO_2Cl$), (also known as Hinsberg's reagent) reacts with primary amines to form sulphonamides. Due to presence of strong electron withdrawing sulphonyl group, the hydrogen attached to N is highly acidic. Hence, it is soluble in alkali.

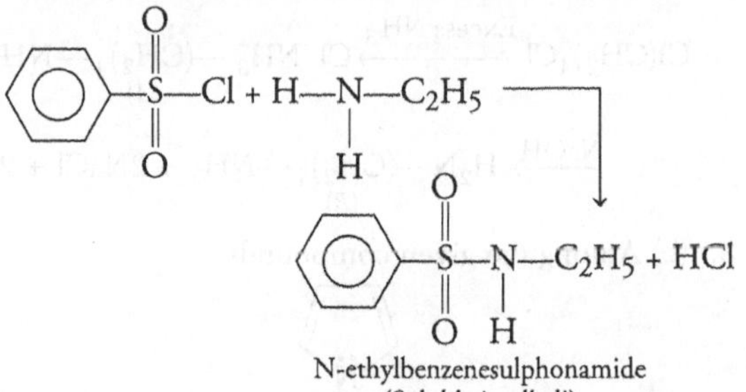

N-ethylbenzenesulphonamide (Soluble in alkali)

17. (c) The given chemical reaction is represented as

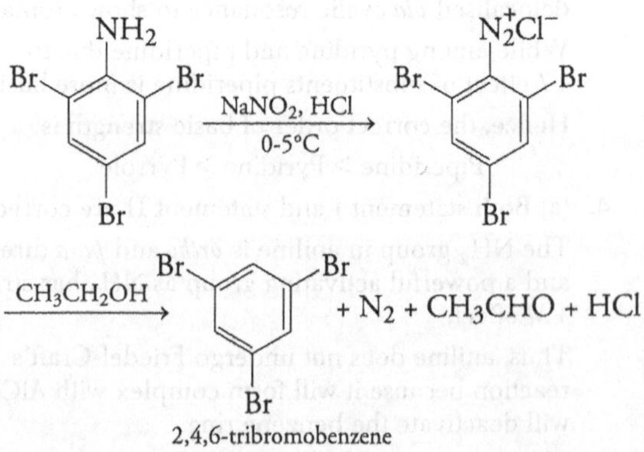

2,4,6-tribromobenzene

18. (d) Carbylamine test is responded by primary or 1°-amine (aliphatic or aromatic) only.

$$R-NH_2 \xrightarrow[KOH/\Delta]{CHCl_3} R-NC + KCl + H_2O$$

$$Ar-NH_2 \xrightarrow[KOH/\Delta]{CHCl_3} Ar-NC + KCl + H_2O$$

Carbylamine

Thus, aniline responds to carbylamine test.

Chapter-10

Biomolecules

1. Any three of the following
(i) Carbohydrates
(ii) Proteins
(iii) Nucleic acids
(iv) Lipids

2. $C_x(H_2O)_y$

3. True

4. Monosaccharides : glucose, fructose.
Oligosaccharides : sucrose, maltose.
Polysaccharides : starch, cellulose, glycogen.

5. (b)

6. True

7. Glucose + Fructose
(*A*) (*B*)

8. *X*= glycogen

9. (a) **Correct statement II** : Glucose is aldohexose carbohydrate.

10. $\underset{\text{Starch or cellulose}}{(C_6H_{10}O_5)_n} + nH_2O \xrightarrow[\text{393 K; 2-3 atm}]{H^+} \underset{\text{Glucose }(X)}{nC_6H_{12}O_6}$

11. (i) $\underset{\text{(Glucose)}}{CHO-(CHOH)_4-CH_2OH} \xrightarrow{HI,\ \Delta} \underset{(n\text{-hexane})}{CH_3-CH_2-CH_2-CH_2-CH_2-CH_3}$

(ii) $\underset{\text{(Glucose)}}{CHO-(CHOH)_4-CH_2OH} \xrightarrow{NH_2OH} \underset{\text{(Glucose oxime)}}{CH{=}N-OH-(CHOH)_4-CH_2OH}$

(iii) $\underset{\text{(Glucose)}}{CHO-(CHOH)_4-CH_2OH} \xrightarrow{HCN} \underset{\text{(Glucose cyanohydrin)}}{CH(CN)(OH)-(CHOH)_4-CH_2OH}$

12. (b)

13. A→ (2), B→ (1), C→ (3)

14. (b) Structure given in option (b) represents sucrose in which α-D-glucose and β-D-fructose are attached to each other by C_1-C_2 glycosidic linkage and there is no free aldehyde or ketone adjacent to >CHOH group.

15. False; **True statement** : On oxidation with nitric acid, glucose yield saccharic acid, which indicates the presence of a primary alcoholic (—OH) group in glucose.

16. *X*= Configuration
Y= Dextrorotatory

17. (c) Except fructose all are aldose sugar while fructose is a ketose.

18. (c)

19. (c) I, II and III structures have —OH group on the lowest asymmetric carbon on the right side.

20. (a)

21. (d) α- and β- form of glucose are six membered cyclic structure. Their structure are as follows

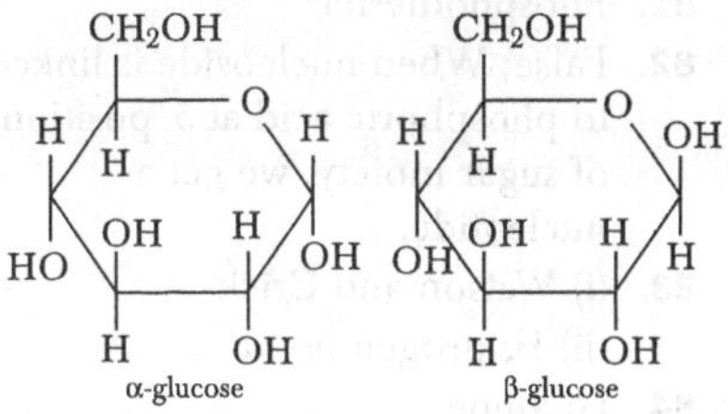

22.

	Correct	Incorrect
I.	✓	×
II.	✓	×
III.	×	✓

Correct statement III : It is a monosaccharide isomer of glucose.

23. *X* = Furanose structure

24. True **25.** (a)

26. Glycosidic linkage

27. Sucrose is a non-reducing sugar, rest all are reducing sugars.

28. $X = C_6H_{12}O_6$ (Glucose)
$Y = C_6H_{12}O_6$ (Fructose)

29. *A* = Glycosidic
B = α-glucose
C = β-fructose

30. (b) **Correct statement I** : Sucrose is dextrorotatory and after hydrolysis, gives dextrorotatory glucose and laevorotatory fructose.

31. (c)

32. (i) Maltose
(ii) Lactose

33. *X* = β-D-galactose
Y = β-D-glucose

34. (b)

35. *A* = Amylose
B = Amylopectin

36. Amylopectin

37. (i) Cellulose (ii) Glycogen

38. (b)

39. (i) Glycogen (ii) Muscles

40. Glycogen

41. Any three of the following
- Carbohydrates are essential for life in both plants and animals. They form a major portion of our food.
- Honey has been used for a long time as an instant source of energy by **'Vaids'** in ayurvedic system of medicine.
- Carbohydrates are used as storage molecules as starch in plants and **glycogen** in animals. Cell wall of bacteria and plants is made up of cellulose.
- We build furniture, etc. from cellulose in the form of wood and clothes ourselves **with cellulose** in the form of cotton fibre.
- They provide raw materials for many important **industries like textiles**, paper, lacquers and breweries.

42. (i) D-ribose
(ii) 2-deoxy-D-ribose

43. (i) Glycogen
(ii) Cellulose

44. Proteins

45. (b)

46. (a) **Correct statement II** : Amino acids which can be synthesised in our body are non-essential amino acids.

47. **Essential**–Valine, leucine, lysine, tryptophan
Non-essential–Glycine, glutamine, tyrosine, serine, cysteine

48. (d)

49. Glycine; Except glycine, all other naturally occuring α-amino acids are optically active as the α -C atom is asymmetric.

50. (i) Peptide linkage
(ii) Dipeptide
51. (i) Glycine (ii) Alanine
52. (b) Only aspartate or aspartic acid and glutamate or glutamic acid have acidic chains hence behave as acids.
53. False; **True statement** : Insulin contains 51 amino acids.
54. **Acidic** – Aspartic acid, glutaric acid
Basic – Arginine
Neutral – Glycine
55. (i) Fibrous proteins
(ii) Globular proteins
56. (i) Keratin, (ii) Myosin
57. (d)
58. A→(2), B→(3), C→(1)
59. (i) Hydrogen bond
(ii) Disulphide linkage
(iii) van der Waals' forces
(iv) Electrostatic force of attraction
60. (a)
61. True
62. Mass of protein
63.

	Correct	Incorrect
I.	✓	×
II.	×	✓
III.	✓	×
IV.	✓	×

Correct statement II : Denaturation does not affect the primary structure.
64. (d)
65. Maltase
66. (d) **Correct statement** : Enzymes reduce the magnitude of activation energy.
67. False; Activation energy for acid hydrolysis of sucrose is 6.22 kJ mol^{-1}
68. A = Biocatalyst
B = Activation energy
C = Sucrose
D = Glucose
69. (i) Ascorbic acid (Vitamin-C)
(ii) Vitamin-B_3
70. **Vitamin-C** Fat soluble vitamins are insoluble in water. However, vitamin C is soluble in water.
71. Vitamin-B_6
72. A→(2), B→(4), C→(1), D→(3)
73. (c) **Correct statement** : Rickets and osteomalaria are caused by deficiency of vitamin-D.
74. (d)
75. (b)
76. (c) Total vitamins which are fat soluble are 4 which are Retinol and Tocopherol, Phylloquinone and Calciferol. Other vitamins are water soluble.
77. A = chromosomes
B = nucleic acids
78. (b) **Correct statement I** : The complete hydrolysis of DNA yields deoxyribose sugar, phosphoric acid and nitrogen containing heterocylic compounds are called bases.
79. (B) **80.** (b)
81. Phosphodiester
82. False; When nucleoside is linked to phosphoric acid at 5′ position of sugar moiety, we get a nucleotide.
83. (i) Watson and Crick
(ii) Hydrogen bond
84. Guanine
85. (a) Only adenine and guanine are purines which are used in making of building blocks of DNA and RNA.
86. (i) Identification of criminals
(ii) Identify racial group
(iii) Identify dead body
(iv) Determine paternity
87. (i) DNA (ii) RNA
(iii) DNA
88. β-D-2-deoxyribose and phosphoric acid.
89. False; Enzymes are biocatalyst which speed up reaction in biosystem.
90. Maltose; Rest all are proteins.
91. X = Insulin Y = Glucagon
92. (a)
93. A→(2), B→(4), C→(1), D→(3)
94. (a)
95. (i) Testosterone
(ii) Glucocorticoids
96. (d)

Assertion-Reason

1. (b) **Correct Explanation :** In pentaacetate of glucose aldehyde group is absent.
2. (a)
3. (a)
4. (a)
5. (a)
6. (d) A is incorrect but R is correct. Correct A is Denaturation of proteins involves the disruption of their secondary, tertiary and quaternary structures.
7. (c) A is correct but R is incorrect. Correct R is except vitamin D and B_3 none other vitamins can be produced by our body and should be taken from food.
8. (a)
9. (d) **Correct Assertion** : RNA is single stranded molecule.
10. (a)

Case-Based

1. (i) (c) Fructose is the sweetest natural sugar.
(ii) (c) Starch is a polysaccharide which acts as a energy storage unit in plants.
(iii) (a) Amylase is an enzyme which acts on starch in foods and breaks it down into small carbohydrate molecules.
(iv) (c)Sucrose is a non-reducing sugar.
2. (i) (c) Peptide bonds are formed between the carboxyl group of one amino acid and the amino group of another.
(ii) (b) Secondary structure refers to the local folding patterns of the polypeptide chain, including alpha-helices and beta-sheets.
(iii) (c) Collagen is a fibrous protein that provides structural support in connective tissues.
(iv) (d) All the listed factors can disrupt the delicate balance of forces that maintain a protein's structure, leading to denaturation.

Competition Edge Up

1. (c) The correct structure of L-glucose is given in option (c).

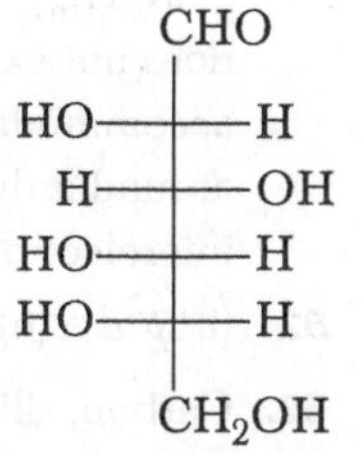

2. (c) The incorrect statement about glucose is given in option (c). It is because glucose readily dissolves in water, as it has lots of polar hydroxyl groups which can form hydrogen bond with water and not because of aldehyde functional group.
3. (d) Sucrose do not contain hemiacetal group. Hence, it does not give test with Fehling solution. All other given solutions give positive test with Fehling solution. Hence, option (d) is correct.
4. (d) Statement given in option (d) is incorrect, its correct form is glucose on reaction with Br_2 oxidised to give gluconic acid.
5. (d) The correct match is A-IV, B-III, C-I, D-II.
   - α-glucose and α-galactose differs in configuration of one asymmetric carbon. Thus they are epimers.
   - α and β-glucose differs at anomeric carbon. Thus, they are anomers.
   - α-glucose and α-fructose have different functional groups. Thus, they are functional isomers.
   - α-glucose and α-ribose are homologous.
6. (a) The correct match is A-II, B-IV, C-III, D-I.
   - $\text{Glucose} \xrightarrow[\Delta]{NaHCO_3} \text{No reaction}$
   - $CHO-(CHOH)_4-CH_2OH \xrightarrow[\Delta]{HNO_3} COOH-(CHOH)_4-COOH$ (Saccharic acid)
   - $CHO-(CHOH)_4-CH_2OH$ (Glucose) $\xrightarrow{HI, \Delta} (CH_3CH_2CH_2CH_2CH_2CH_3)$ (n-hexane)
   - $CHO-(CHOH)_4-CH_2OH$ (Glucose) $\xrightarrow{Br_2 \text{ water}} COOH-(CHOH)_4-CH_2OH$ (Gluconic acid)
7. (a) Statements given is A and C are correct, while B and D are incorrect. It is because
   Enzymes are biocatalysts and are very specific for a particular reaction and for a particular substrate. Almost all enzymes are globular proteins. Enzyme maltase hydrolyses maltose into glucose.
   $$\text{Maltose} \xrightarrow{\text{Maltase}} \text{Glucose}$$
8. (b) Proteins are natural polymers composed of α-amino acids which are connected by peptide linkage. Hence, proteins upon acidic hydrolysis produces α-amino acids.
9. (d) Denaturation of proteins is a condition when the unique three-dimensional structure of a protein is exposed to changes.
   Coagulation of egg gives primary structure of protein, which changes on heating and is known as denaturation of protein.
   Hence, option (d) is correct.
10. (c) Glucose does not react with Schiff's reagent and $NaHSO_3$.
    $\text{Glucose} + \text{Tollen's reagent} \longrightarrow \text{silver mirror}$
    $\text{Glucose} + HCN \longrightarrow \text{cyanohydrin formation}$
    $\text{Glucose} + NH_2OH \longrightarrow \text{oxime formation}$
11. (b) Statement I is correct while statement II is incorrect. The correct form of statement II is – When nucleoside is linked to phosphoric acid at 5′- position of sugar moiety, we get nucleotide.
12. (b) The incorrect statement about enzymes is option (b) because enzymes are protein in nature and comprised of amino acids that are linked together in one or more polypeptide chains. Rest all other given options are correct.
13. (b) When body is affected by anaemia, it does not have enough RBC's which is result of deficiency of vitamin B_{12}. Vitamin B_{12} is important for production of RBC's.
14. (c) Sucrose is composed of α-D-glucose and β-D-fructose. They are held together by a glycosidic linkage between C-1 of glucose and C-2 of fructose respectively.
    $$\text{Sucrose} \xrightarrow{\text{Hydrolysis}} \alpha\text{-D-glucose} + \beta\text{-D-fructose}$$
15. (a) Conc. H_2SO_4 removes water, i.e. dehydrates carbohydrates into carbon (black residue) or charred sugar.
    $$C_{12}H_{22}O_{11} \text{ or } C_{12}(H_2O)_{11} \xrightarrow[-11\,H_2O]{\text{Conc.}H_2SO_4} \underset{\text{(Black)}}{12C}$$
16. (b) Deficiency of
    Vitamin A causes–Xerophthalmia
    Vitamin D causes–Osteomalacia and rickets
    Vitamin E causes–Fragility of RBCs
    Vitamin K causes–Increase in blood clotting time.
17. (d) Glucose is an aldohexose (made of six carbon atoms) and it is a reducing sugar. Containing five –OH groups.
    Hence, option (d) is incorrect statement.
    $$\underbrace{HO-CH_2}_{\text{One } 1°\text{- OH group}}-\underbrace{(CHOH)_4}_{\text{Four } 2°\text{- OH group}}-\underbrace{CH{=}O}_{\text{Aldehyde group}}$$

p-Block Elements

1. 6 (groups 13-18)

2. (a) **3.** True

4. (i) + 6, +4, +2, − 2
(ii) + 8, + 6, + 4, + 2

5.

	Correct	Incorrect
I.	✓	×
II.	×	✓
III.	✓	×

Correct statement II :

The heaviest element in each *p*-block group is the most metallic element.

6. 3*d* **7.** $[AlF_6]^{3-}$

8. $d\pi$-$p\pi$ or $d\pi$-$d\pi$ **9.** $1s^2 2s^2 2p^1$

10. True

11. 19% and 81%

12. A→(3), B→(4), C→(1), D→(2)

13. (d) On moving down the group, atomic radius increases as an extra shell of electrons is added.

14. (a) **15.** (d)

16. (c)

17. (b) The relative stability of +1 oxidation state progressively increases for heavier elements.

18. (a) Lewis acids are those which accept a pair of electrons to achieve stable electronic configuration.
$AlCl_3$ has vacant orbital to accept electron pair.

19.

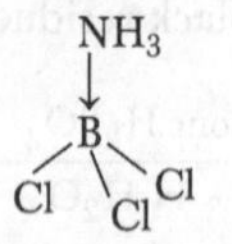

(Tetrahedral)

20. $x = 118°$, $y = 101°$, $z = 221$ pm

21. (i) Tl^+ (ii) Al
Tl^{3+} is not only unstable in solution but is a powerful oxidising agent also.
Aluminium being able to form + 3 ions easily is more electropositive than Tl.

22. (a) Acidic nature of group 13 elements decreases down the group.

23. False; Aluminium dissolves in dilute HCl to liberate dihydrogen.

24. $2Na^+[Al(OH)_4]^-(aq)$

25. Non-availability of *d*-orbitals.

26. (c)

27. On dissolution in water, borax gives an alkaline solution as

$$Na_2B_4O_7 + 7H_2O \longrightarrow 2NaOH + \underset{\text{Orthoboric acid}}{4H_3BO_3}$$

28. Transition metal ions

29. (a)

30. $Na_2B_4O_7 + 2HCl + 5H_2O \longrightarrow 2NaCl + 4B(OH)_3$

31. True

32. Metaboric acid, (HBO_2)

33. (b)

34. $H_3BO_3 \xrightarrow[\text{Above 370 K}]{\Delta} HBO_2 \xrightarrow{\Delta} B_2O_3$

35. (c)

36. (i) $2NaBH_4 + I_2 \longrightarrow B_2H_6 + 2NaI + H_2$
(ii) $2BF_3 + 6NaH \xrightarrow{450\text{ K}} B_2H_6 + 6NaF$

37. Diborane

38. True

39. (i) sp^3
(ii) 2-centre-2-electron, 3-centre-2-electron

40. $2MH + B_2H_6 \longrightarrow 2M^+[BH_4]^-$ (M = Li or Na)

41. $LiBH_4$ and $NaBH_4$

42. (i) Manufacture of heat resistant glass.
(ii) Flux for soldering metals and constituent of medicinal soaps.

43. (c)

44. Toxic

45. (i) ^{12}C (ii) ^{13}C (iii) ^{14}C

46. (i) ^{14}C
(ii) Cassiterite (SnO_2)

47. (c)

48. True

49. Non-metals – C and Si
Metalloid – Ge
Metals – Sn and Pb
Metallic character increases down the group.

50. (c) $[SiF_6]^{2-}$, $[GeCl_6]^{2-}$ and $[Sn(OH)_6]^{2-}$ exist but $[SiCl_6]^{2-}$ does not exist because Si cannot accommodate 6 chlorine atoms around it due to high interelectronic repulsions.

51. (i) sp^3d^2 (ii) sp^3d^2

52. Carbon, silicon and germanium

53. (c)
$Sn + 2H_2O \xrightarrow{\Delta} SnO_2 + 2H_2$

54. CCl_4; Except CCl_4, other tetrachlorides are easily hydrolysed by water because the central atom can accommodate the lone pair of electrons from oxygen atom of water molecule in their *d*-orbital.

55. (c)

56. (b) Catenation tendency decreases down the group.

57. C—C > Si—Si > Ge—Ge > Sn—Sn

58. sp^3, sp^2

59. (i) False; Diamond has high melting point, as it is a hardest substance on the earth.
(ii) True

60. (d) **61.** (b)

62. Graphite

63. True

64. $2C(s) + O_2(g) + 4N_2(g) \xrightarrow{1273\text{ K}} \underbrace{2CO(g) + 4N_2(g)}_{\text{Producer gas}}$

65. Reducing nature

66. (c)

67. H_2CO_3 / HCO_3^- (Buffer system)

68. Greenhouse effect

69. (a) *sp*

70. $:\ddot{O}^{-}—C\equiv O^{+}: \longleftrightarrow :\ddot{O}=C=\ddot{O}: \longleftrightarrow :O^{+}\equiv C—\ddot{O}^{-}:$

71. (i) $SiO_2 + 2NaOH \longrightarrow Na_2SiO_3 + H_2O$
(ii) $SiO_2 + 4HF \longrightarrow SiF_4 + 2H_2O$

72. Quartz

73. (i) An amorphous form
(ii) Filtration

74. Alkyl or aryl substituted silicon chlorides, $R_nSiCl_{(4-n)}$

75. (b)

76. $A = (CH_3)_2SiCl_2$
$B = (CH_3)_2Si(OH)_2$

77. (d) **78.** True **79.** SiO_4^{4-}

80. (i) Glass (ii) Cement

81. (c)

82. $A =$ ZSM-5
$B =$ Hydrated zeolite

83. A→(5), B→(3), C→(4), D→(2), E→(1)

84. Arsenic and antimony

85. True

86. (b)

87. $[Rn]\,5f^{14}\,6d^{10},\,7s^2\,7p^3$

88. Sb < Bi < N < P < As
Ionic radii increases down the group. However, the difference here is because of the fact that N, P and As form E^{3-} ion, while Sb and Bi form E^{3+} ion.

89. (a)

90. (i) False; Common oxidation state of group 15 elements are −3, + 3 and +5.
(ii) Decreases, increases

91. (i) + 5, + 2
(ii) Disproportionation reaction

92. Nitrogen

93. (i) Small size
(ii) High electronegativity
(iii) High first ionisation enthalpy
(iv) Non-availability of *d*-orbitals

94. (c)

95. (b)

96. (i) $BiH_3 < SbH_3 < AsH_3 < PH_3 < NH_3$
The thermal stability decreases as the size of the central atom increases down the group.
(ii) $BiH_3 > SbH_3 > AsH_3 > PH_3 > NH_3$
Reducing character is inversely proportional to thermal stability.

97. (b)

98. NH_3

99. (i) Acidic (ii) Amphoteric
(iii) Basic

100. (b)

101. (c)

102. (a) $\underset{\text{Ammonium dichromate}}{(NH_4)_2Cr_2O_7} \xrightarrow{\Delta} \underset{\text{Nitrogen}}{N_2} + \underset{\text{Water}}{4H_2O} + \underset{\text{Chromium oxide}}{Cr_2O_3}$

$\underset{\text{Barium azide}}{Ba(N_3)_2} \longrightarrow \underset{\text{Barium}}{Ba} + \underset{\text{Nitrogen}}{3N_2}$

103. Dissociation energy

104. (d)

105. $2NaN_3 \longrightarrow \underset{(A)}{2Na} + \underset{(B)}{3N_2}$

106. NH_3

107. (i) High (ii) Iron oxide
(iii) High (iv) K_2O

108. $X = ZnSO_4$
The ppt. obtained are
$\underset{\text{White}}{Zn(OH)_2(s)}$ and $\underset{\text{(Brown)}}{F_2O_3 \cdot xH_2O}$
$Y = FeCl_3$

109. A→(2), B→(3), C→(1)

110. (i) N_2O_5
$N_2O_5 : +5;\ N_2O_4 : +4$
$NO_2 : +4;\ N_2O_3 : +3$
$NO : +2;\ N_2O : +1$
(ii) N_2O, NO

111. (a)

112. (d)

113. (a)

114. (a) Only nitrogen cannot form pentahalide

115. (i) + 3 (ii) True

116. $P = NH_3;\ Q = NO;\ R = NO_2$

117. (a) $2NH_3(g) + \frac{5}{2}O_2(g) \longrightarrow 2NO(g) + 3H_2O$

118. (i) $3Cu + 8HNO_3(\text{dil.}) \longrightarrow \underline{3Cu(NO_3)_2} + \underline{2NO} + 4H_2O$
(ii) $Zn + 4HNO_3(\text{conc.}) \longrightarrow \underline{Zn(NO_3)_2} + \underline{2NO_2} + 2H_2O$

119. (b) **120.** (c)

121. White phosphorus

122. $X =$ White phosphorus
$A = \alpha$-black phosphorus
$B = \beta$-black phosphorus

123. (d) $P_4 + 3NaOH + 3H_2O \longrightarrow PH_3 + 3NaH_2PO_2$

124. True **125.** (c)

126. (i) CaC_2 (Calcium carbide)
(ii) Calcium phosphide

127. $A = PCl_3$ $B = HCl$

128. (c)

129. (b)

130. False;
$PCl_5 \xrightarrow{\text{Heat}} PCl_3 + Cl_2$

131. (i) $CH_3COCl + POCl_3$
(ii) $C_2H_5Cl + HCl$

132. (i) sp^3d (ii) sp^3

133. (i) 3 (ii) axial

134. (c)

135. (b) Orthophosphoric
Pyrophosphoric,
Metaphosphoric

136. Pyrophosphoric acid

137. (d)

138. (a) **Correct statement II** :
Red P_4 reacts with alkali to form hypophosphoric acid.

139. (i) Dibasic (ii) H_3PO_4

140. (c) $4H_3\overset{+3}{P}O_3 \xrightarrow{\text{Heat}} 3H_3\overset{+5}{P}O_4 + \overset{-3}{P}H_3$

141. (a) Due to small size of nitrogen and its high electronegativity, N does not show allotropy.

142. Sulphur

143. (i) $CuFeS_2$ (ii) ZnS (iii) PbS

144. True

145. (b) **Correct statement II** :
Oxygen exists as diatomic molecule (O_2), whereas sulphur exists as polyatomic molecule (S_8).

146. Inert pair effect

147. (i) Small size
(ii) High electronegativity
(iii) Non-availability of *d*-orbitals

148. $H_2O < H_2S < H_2Se < H_2Te$
The increase in acidic character can be explained in terms of decrease in bond enthalpy for the dissociation of H—*E* (*E* = O, S, Se, Te, Po) bond down the group.

149. (i) Dissociation enthalpy
(ii) Oxygen

150. TeO_2

151. (b) **Correct pair** : SeF_4-Liquid

152. sp^3d, Triagonal bipyramidal

153. $H_2Po < H_2Te < H_2Se < H_2S < H_2O$
Due to decrease in dissociation enthalpy of H—*E* bond down the group, the thermal stability of hydrides also decreases from H_2O to H_2Po.

154. (c)

155. $2KCl + 3O_2$

156. Finely divided metals and MnO_2

157. (i) H_2 (ii) O_2

158. CO_2, Liquified, dinitrogen

159. True **160.** V_2O_5

161. (c) **162.** (d)

163. (i) $2CO_2 + 2H_2O$
(ii) $2Al_2O_3$

164. False; Metal oxides in higher oxidation state have acidic nature.

165. (b) Acidic oxides– SO_2, Cl_2O_7, N_2O_5
Basic oxides –Na_2O, BaO

166. $X = Al_2O_3$
$Y = Na_3[Al(OH)_6]$

167. (i) Al_2O_3 (ii) CO

168. Endothermic

169. (d)

170. $PbS(s) + 4O_3(g) \longrightarrow PbSO_4(s) + 4O_2$

171. Quantitatively, Iodine, $Na_2S_2O_3$

172. (d)

173. (i) Rhombic sulphur
(ii) Monoclinic sulphur

174. Water; Rhombic sulphur cannot be dissolved in water because of its high density.

175. 369 K

176. (i)

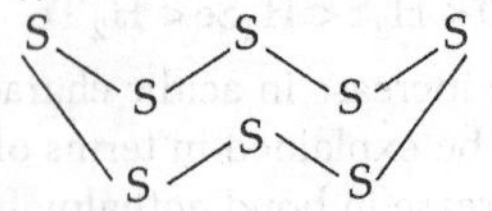

(S_8 form)

(ii)

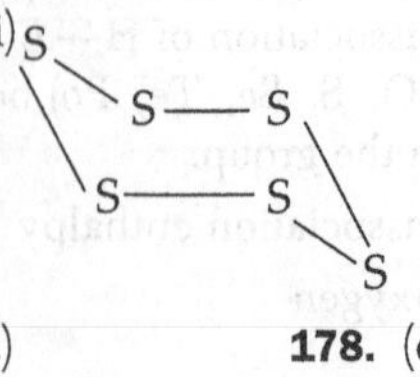

(S_6 form)

177. (c) **178.** (d)

179. $X = SO_2$ $Y =$ Charcoal
$Z = SO_2Cl_2$

180. (a) **181.** True

182. Bent, equal

183. $H_2S_2O_8$, H_2SO_5

184. (b)

185. (c)

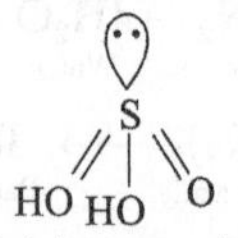

Sulphurous acid (H_2SO_3)

186. (b)

187. (i) Low
(ii) High

188. (i) Low volatility
(ii) Strong acidic character
(iii) Ability to act as oxidising agent
(iv) Strong affinity for water

189. (d) **Correct statement** : Sulphuric acid removes water from organic compounds.

190. (c) SO_2 and CO_2

191. Any four of the following.
(e.g. ammonium sulphate superphosphate). Other uses are in (i) petroleum refining, (ii) manufacture of pigments, paints and dyestuff intermediates, (iii) detergent industry, (iv) metallurgical applications (e.g. cleansing metals before enameling, electroplating and galvanising, (v) storage batteries, (vi) in the manufacture of nitrocellulose products, (vii) as a laboratory reagent.

192. (i) $CaSO_4 + 2HF$ (ii) H_2SO_4

193. (b) **194.** True **195.** (d)

196. False; Sea weeds contains upto 0.5% of iodine.

197. Maximum

198. True

199. (d) **Correct pair** : Atomic radii–Smallest

200. (i) Yellow (ii) Cl_2
(iii) Red (iv) I_2

201. (c)

202. –1, +1, +3, +5 and +7

203. (d)

204. $A =$ Oxygen
$B =$ Hydrohalic acid
$C =$ Hypohalous acid

205. (i) High electronegativity
(ii) Low F—F bond dissociation energy
(iii) Small size
(iv) Non-availability of *d*-orbital

206. (c) **Correct statement** : Hydrogen fluoride is a liquid due to strong hydrogen bonding.

207. H—F > H—Cl > H—Br > H—I

208. (a)

209. $X = O_2F_2$ $Y = OF_2$

210. A → (3), B → (1), C → (2)

211. (d) Correct orders ;
(a) $Cl_2 > Br_2 > F_2 > I_2$ (increasing bond dissociation enthalpy)
(b) $H_2O < H_2S < H_2Se < H_2Te$ (increasing acidic strength)
(c) $NH_3 < NH_2OH < N_2O < N_2O_5$ (increasing oxidation state)

212. Cl_2 **213.** $CuCl_2$

214. (d) **215.** (c)

216. $Ca(OCl)_2 \cdot CaCl_2 \cdot Ca(OH)_2 \cdot 2H_2O$

217. (b)

218. Nascent oxygen

219. (i) Ferric
(ii) Sulphite
(iii) Sulphur dioxide
(iv) Iodate

220. (a) Gold (b) Sterilising
(c) Dyes (d) Paper

221. (b)

222. True

223. $X =$ HCl $Y = NH_4Cl$

224. (b) **225.** HCl

226. True

227. (a) HOF (Hypofluorous acid) is only one oxoacid of fluorine.

228. (a)

229.

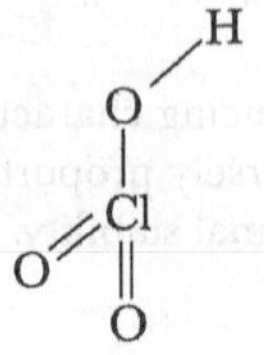

Chloric acid ($HClO_3$)

230. Double bonds-3
Single bonds-2

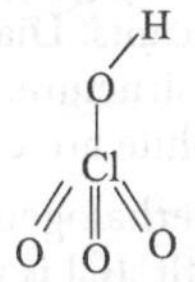

(Perchloric acid)

231. (c)

232. (a) ClF (b) ClF_3 (c) ICl (d) ICl_3

233. A→ (2), B→ (3), C→ (1)

234. (b)

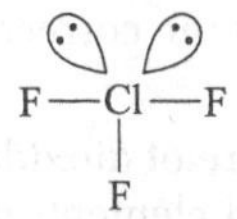

(ClF_3)

235. (d)

236. (a)

237. Natural gas

238. $^{222}_{86}Rn + ^{4}_{2}He$

239. (i) False; Noble gases exhibit very high ionisation energy and very high positive value of electron gain enthalpy.
(ii) Low

240. (a) **Correct statement II** : Helium used in diving apparatus because of low solubility in blood.

241. (c)

242. (b)

243. $A = XeF_2$; $B = PF_5$

244. (i) $XeF_4 + SbF_5 \longrightarrow [XeF_3]^+ [SbF_6]^-$
(ii) $XeF_4 + O_2F_2 \longrightarrow XeF_6 + O_2$

245. $2XeO_3$ + 24HF

246. (d)

247. A→(2), B→ (3), C→ (4), D →(1)

248. (d)

249. (a)

250. (i) Helium (ii) Argon

251. False; Neon is used in discharge tubes and fluorescent bulbs.

Assertion-Reason

1. (a) **2.** (a)
3. (a) **4.** (a)
5. (a)

6. (c) **Correct Reason** : Silica is almost non-reactive in its normal form.

7. (d) **Correct Assertion** : First ionisation enthalpy of group 15 elements is much greater than that of group 14 elements.

8. (a)

9. (a)

10. (b) **Correct Reason** : H_3PO_2 is a good reducing agent as, it contains two P—H bond. These bonds helps in reduction and does not play any role in acidic behaviour.

11. (a)

12. (b) Ozone on decomposition, form oxygen and nascent oxygen, which is very reactive. Hence, it acts as a powerful oxidising agent.

13. (b) Correct form of Reason is, H_2SO_4 is a strong acid due to its high degree of dissociation in water.

14. (a)

15. (c) **Correct Reason** : Halides in higher oxidation state will be more covalent than one in lower oxidation state.

16. (a)

Case-Based

1. (i) (a) Thermal stability decreases as the size difference or the electronegativity difference between the two halogen atom decreases.
(ii) (b)$[ICl_2]^-$-linear, ClF_3-T-shaped, $[BrF_4]^-$-square planar
(iii) (b) It has square pyramidal shape and has 5 *b.p.* and 1 *l.p.*
(iv) (c) In IF_7, iodine is the least electronegative halogen, so its highest oxidation number (+7) is more stable than those of the lighter member of the group.

2. (i) (a) $Ca(OH)_2 + Cl_2 \longrightarrow CaOCl_2 + H_2O$
(ii) (d) In cold, chlorine reacts with dilute alkalies to form chlorides and hypochlorites
(iii) (c) $CaOCl_2 + 2HCl \longrightarrow CaCl_2 + H_2O + Cl_2$
(iv) (a) The bleaching action is due to the formation of nascent oxygen.

Competition Edge Up

1. (d) The values of 1st ionisaion enthalpy of Tl, Ga and Al are 589 kJ/mol, 579 kJ/mol and 577 kJ/mol respectively. Thus, the correct order of first ionisation enthalpy is

$$Tl > Ga > Al$$

2. (d) The number of ions from the following which are expected to behave as oxidising agent are two, namely Tl^{3+} and Pb^{4+}. Due to inert pair effect; Tl^{3+} and Pb^{4+} can behave as oxidising agent.

3. (b) Statement I is true but Statement II is false.
The correct form of Statement II is :
Due to property of catenation and $p\pi - p\pi$ bond formation carbon shows allotropic forms.

4. (b) Among the given options only SnO_2, PbO_2 are amphoteric oxides while SiO_2, GeO_2 and GeO are acidic oxide and CO is a neutral oxide.

5. (a) Statement I is false, but Statement II is true. The correct form of Statement I is : The electronegativity value of group 14 elements from Si to Pb are almost same. Hence, option (a) is correct.

6. (c) The reducing character of hydrides of group 15 elements increases from top to bottom because the strength of *M*—H (where, *M* = N, As, Sb or Bi) bond decreases down the group due to increase in the size of central atom.
Hence, among the given options, BiH_3 will be strongest reducing agent.

7. (c) Anomalous behaviour of oxygen is due to its small size and high electronegativity.

8. (d) Among the given elements, only Po does not show −2 oxidation state due to its highly metallic nature.

9. (b) In semiconductor energy band gap falls between conductor and insulator (around 1 eV).

Silicon, germanium and copper oxide falls into semiconductor category, while graphite is a conductor.

10. (c) Among the given relation $TlI > TlI_3$ is correct. As in group 13 element +1 oxidation state becomes more and more stable as we go down the group, i.e. Al < Ga < In < Tl. This is because of the presence of intervening *d* and *f*-orbitals which do not shield the nucleus efficiently.

Consequently effective nuclear charge increases, that hold the *ns* electron tightly, so that they do not participate in bonding (inert pair effect). Thus, in Tl +1 oxidation state is more predominent whereas the +3 is strongly oxidising nature.

11. (b) Among the given option BF_3 molecule acts as a Lewis acid. As it is an electron deficient molecule and have the tendency to accept the electron pair.

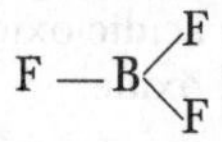

BF_3 has six electrons around B that means its octet is not complete.

12. (b) The correct match is A–III, B–I, C–IV, D–II.

13. (a) The correct match is A–III, B–IV, C–I, D–II.

Structure of given oxoacids of sulphur are as follows

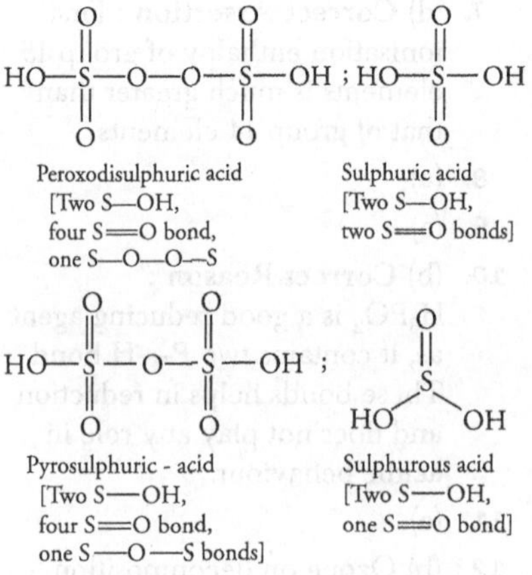

14. (c) The incorrect statement about diborane is option (c) because boron has sp^3-hybridisation and it is non-planar.

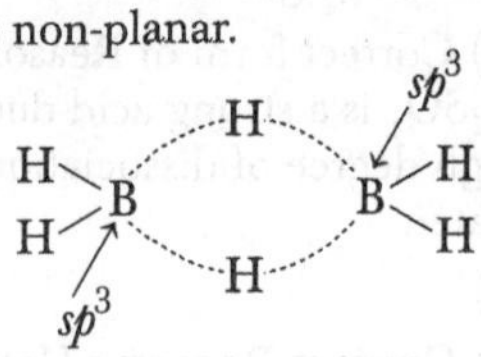

15. (b) The correct statement is option (b). It is because in diamond, each carbon is bonded with four other carbon atoms. So, hybridisation of carbon atom is sp^3. In graphite each carbon atom is bonded with three other carbon atoms.

So, hybridisation of carbon atom in graphite is sp^2.

Hence, diamond is sp^3-hybridised and graphite is sp^2-hybridised. Rest all other options are incorrect. It is because only graphite is used as dry lubricants. Diamond has 3-D network structure. Both diamond and graphite are covalent.

16. (d) In interhalogen compound of group 17th, ICl is more reactive than I_2 due to polar bonds. Also, $X—X'$ bond is weaker than $X—X$ bond except F_2. So, I—Cl bond is weaker than I—I bond.

Hence, both A and R are correct and R is the correct explanation of A.

17. (a) Nature of dioxides (MO_2) of group 14 elements can be represented as,

CO_2 SiO_2 GeO_2 (Acidic oxides) SnO_2 PbO_2 (Amphoteric oxides)

Hence, option (a) is correct.

18. (c) 3 and 4 are correct statements, whereas 1 and 2 are incorrect. The correct form of 1 and 2 are

1. Dry ice or $CO_2(s)$ [not $CO_2(g)$] is used as refrigerant for ice-cream and frozen food.
2. C_{60} contains 20 hexagones (not 12) and 12 pentagones (not 20).
3. ZSM-5, a type of zeolite, is used to convert alcohols directly into gasoline. It is true.
4. CO is a colourless and odourless gas. It is true.

19. (b) Carboxyhaemoglobin is about 300 times more stable than oxyhaemoglobin.